The Chicago Board of Trade
Battery in the Civil War

The Chicago Board of Trade Battery in the Civil War

Dennis W. Belcher

McFarland & Company, Inc., Publishers
Jefferson, North Carolina

LIBRARY OF CONGRESS CATALOGUING-IN-PUBLICATION DATA

Names: Belcher, Dennis W., 1950– author.
Title: The Chicago Board of Trade Battery in the Civil War / Dennis W. Belcher.
Description: Jefferson, North Carolina : McFarland & Company, Inc., Publishers, 2022 |
Includes bibliographical references and index.
Identifiers: LCCN 2022006462 | ISBN 9781476683911 (paperback : acid free paper) ∞
ISBN 9781476645629 (ebook)
Subjects: LCSH: United States. Army. Chicago Board of Trade Light Artillery
Battery (1862-1865)—History. | United States—History—Civil War, 1861-1865—Campaigns.
| United States—History—Civil War, 1861-1865—Regimental histories. | BISAC: HISTORY /
Military / United States | HISTORY / United States / Civil War Period (1850-1877)
Classification: LCC E505.8 .C45 2022 | DDC 973.7/473—dc23/eng/20220225
LC record available at https://lccn.loc.gov/2022006462

BRITISH LIBRARY CATALOGUING DATA ARE AVAILABLE

ISBN (print) 978-1-4766-8391-1
ISBN (ebook) 978-1-4766-4562-9

On the cover: William B.T. Trego's *Battery of Light Artillery en Route*,
1882, oil on canvas 30⅛ × 64⅛ in. (76.5 × 162.9 cm.)
(courtesy of the Pennsylvania Academy of the Fine Arts,
Philadelphia; gift of Fairman Rogers)

Printed in the United States of America

McFarland & Company, Inc., Publishers
Box 611, Jefferson, North Carolina 28640
www.mcfarlandpub.com

This book is dedicated to George Skoch who has been
with me through this whole process, producing topnotch maps
for eight books. George is so knowledgeable about the Civil War
and so skilled at creating maps that I have heavily relied on him
to produce one of the most valuable parts of any history, the maps.

Table of Contents

Acknowledgments

Lesley Martin, Research Librarian, Chicago History Museum; Katie Levi, Rights & Reproductions Coordinator, Chicago History Museum; Lisa Schoblasky, Special Collections Services Librarian, Newberry Library; Brooke Guthrie, Research Services Librarian, Rubenstein Library, Duke University; Kathy Bean, Historian, Grayslake, Illinois; Danielle Ireland, Archive Technician, National Archives and Records Administration; Jim Ladd, Archivist, Illinois State Archives; Fred Burwell, Archivist, Beloit College; Kevin Abing, Ph.D., Archivist, Milwaukee County Historical Society; Jim Lewis, Chief of Interpretation, Education and Cultural Resource Management, National Parks Service; Gordon L. Jones, Ph.D., Senior Military Historian and Curator, Atlanta History Center; Jennifer Blomqvist, Archivist & Volunteer Coordinator, DeKalb History Center; Charlie Crawford, president, Georgia Battlefields Association; Kellee E. Warren, Assistant Professor and Special Collections Librarian, University of Illinois–Chicago; Craig Swain for his information about ordnance reports; Nick Anderson, Special Collections Librarian, University of Illinois–Chicago; Andy Papen, Civil War historian, proofread this manuscript from beginning to end and this is a second time for him. This is difficult, laborious, and often dull but I am very grateful for his diligence and for his always helpful suggestions.

Our Honored Dead

We look upon these forms, which no devotion of countrymen,
no care of woman's tenderness could save from death, and our hearts are
sad when we think that such a price had to be paid even for National
honor or National existence, but the offering has been made, the price
has been paid in blood and tears and death, and now let all fitting
honor be given to these forms. Let loving kindness tend and patriotic
justice guard the places of their rest. Let public munificence erect
enduring tablets which shall bear their names, record their valor
and perpetuate their fame. And in all the future, let our children and
our children's children be taught the lessons of their martyrdom.
After war peace!

—Dr. O.H. Tiffany (an address in 1866
to honor the Chicago artillery units.)

Preface

A full history of the Chicago Board of Trade Battery is long overdue. This history is a continuation of the series on the cavalry forces in the heartland during the Civil War. For those familiar with the cavalry in the west, particularly the Battle of Stones River or the Battle of Chickamauga, this is a familiar battery with significant accomplishments. The battery was involved in 11 major battles, 26 minor battles and 42 skirmishes in the heartland in the Civil War. The part that the Chicago Board of Trade organization played in the life of this battery adds more interest to this unit. While a well-known battery, there was a large gap in the supporting material that often accompanies unit histories. In particular, the National Archives generally has very complete unit records, extending from morning reports, rosters, orders, and correspondence. This was not the case with this battery and the missing material would have been extremely helpful in tracking its history. Fortunately, a historical sketch of the unit was written by a committee of surviving members of the unit in 1902 titled *Historical Sketch of the Chicago Board of Trade Battery,* and in the introductory section there is a single sentence which explains much about the limited history. "Unfortunately in the burning of Chicago and in a subsequent fire, all of the Chicago Board of Trade Battery records and mementos, except such as are in the possession of the United States Government or of individual members of the Battery, were destroyed, hence, the value of the existing records herein compiled and which are not dependent for accuracy upon the memory of surviving members of the organization alone."

Upon digging deeper into the supporting material for the history of the battery, it was disappointing to discover that no battery books or other specific material directly relating to the battery were held at the National Archives. This made writing the history of the battery more difficult; however, based on the make-up of the battery, several very important resources were discovered. Two of the most valuable turned out to be the Chicago History Museum and the Illinois State Archives, both of which held important records. As in many Civil War era records, the spelling of names is often incorrect and variable due to a variety of reasons. As a result, the names of the soldiers in this unit will be inconsistent and incorrect in some cases. Every effort has been made to make these as accurate as possible. Importantly, several "voices" of the battery had been preserved and this made the compilation of materials and records much more successful. Some of the more important accounts came from the following individuals:

1. Benjamin Nourse
2. Sylvanus Stevens
3. A.B. Lake
4. Calvin Durand
5. Silas Stevens
6. John Fleming

7. John Toomey
8. Lewis B. Hand
9. Frederick A. Lord
10. Trumbull Griffin

11. George Robinson
12. James Stokes
13. John A. Nourse
14. Tobias Miller

Of this group, Silas Stevens, Benjamin Nourse, John Nourse and John Fleming left the most complete records of the events of the battery. The Nourse brothers left a diary and journal of the daily events of the battery from the beginning to the end of the war and they were instrumental in the completion of the *Historical Sketch of the Chicago Board of Trade Battery*, the definitive record of the battery to this point, but the historical aspect of this work was only 17 pages in length. John Nourse also left a series of letters during his time in the battery. Not to be outdone, John Fleming left a complete record of the battery through a series of eighty letters. In addition, Tobias Miller, a graduate of Knox College, left a series of letters and a diary which proved invaluable in the understanding of actions of the battery. The remainder of the men on the list left valuable pieces of the history of the battery detailing significant events in their own words.

The history of the Board of Trade Battery encompasses some of the most compelling action of the Civil War. The first major action took place at the Battle of Stones River, and as General William Rosecrans rallied his troops, the battery was positioned in the center of the Union line and while "seeing the elephant," held its ground as men were falling by the guns. Lines of Confederate infantry rushed the guns and men fired away until the enemy reached only a few yards away, but the center held. A few days later, the battery joined fifty other Union guns and stopped one of the most dramatic attacks in the western theater of the Civil War when Breckinridge's charge was stopped. The Battle of Stones River began nearly three years of prominence for artillerists of this battery. Following the success at Stones River, Lieutenant Trumbull Griffin joined Colonel Robert Minty's brigade at the battle at Reed's Bridge in successfully resisting an overwhelming attack by Confederate infantry on September 18 along the banks of the Chickamauga Creek. Again, the battery made signification contributions to the success of the Union troops in an action similar to Buford's defense at Gettysburg. A second significant action took place in the Battle of Chickamauga at the little-known battle at Glass Mill where the Board of Trade battery faced an overwhelming enemy attack. Other important actions took place at the Battle of Farmington, the Battle of Dallas, the Battle at Noonday Creek, the Battle of Atlanta, Kilpatrick's Raid, the Battle of Nashville, and the Battle of Selma. In writing the history of the Board of Trade Battery, it was important to include the other events occurring outside the battery which directly affected the action of the battery. This context provided a more complete understanding of battery's movements.

This battery was made up of men from various walks of life, but the original members of the battery were all from Chicago and had a connection with the Chicago Board of Trade. The overwhelming numbers of the original enlistees, who would become the "battery boys," were clerks, and these men proved to be industrious, energetic, and intelligent individuals. The controversial first captain of the battery, James H. Stokes, would be a prime example of a multi-dimensional commander with good as well as difficult traits. There would be ambitious men and men who only wanted to serve their country to the best of their ability. Among the men who would receive permanent recognition were Trumbull Dorrance Griffin, Henry Bennett, and George Irving Robinson, three of the most notable officers of the battery. One important part of the history of the battery was the official casualty rate. In most Civil War units, disease was the greatest killer, not battles. In the Chicago Board of Trade Battery, this was not the case. Only nine men died as a result of disease compared to an equal number dying as a result of their wounds in battle. This was a testament to the support received from Chicago and this offers a valuable lesson about the support those at home could provide the men in the field. The Chicago Board of Trade operated a war committee throughout the conflict and at one point over one hundred and fifty individuals worked to be sure the men in the field did not suffer unduly. The battery records also mention numerous visits from people from Chicago bringing daily necessities. The Chicago Board of Trade also sent medical personnel to the battery after some of the hardest fighting.

It is interesting to note that the battery had a variety of names during the war: Stokes' Independent Battery; the Chicago Board of Trade Light Artillery Battery; Chicago Board of Trade Independent Battery Light Artillery; Chicago Board of Trade Battery, Horse Artillery; and finally, Illinois Light Artillery, Board of Trade Battery. The history of the Chicago Board of Trade Battery would involve some of the most important fighting in the heartland (Kentucky, Tennessee, Georgia and Alabama) in the Civil War. By the very nature of field artillery, there would be no dramatic charges or storming the barricades, but the men of this battery saw a lot of action and their story is compelling. From the first battle to the last, the battery left its mark on the battlefields in the most important battles in the west.

When the war was over, this battery was arguably the most prominent artillery unit in this region of the Civil War. These were men who answered the call of their country and gave their all to preserve the United States. These men faced death many times and yet stuck to their task while heaping honor and glory on those who served in this battery. This is their story.

CHAPTER ONE

The Organization of the Battery and Movement to Kentucky

Every thing is war! war!! war!!!—Private Benjamin Nourse

In the summer of 1862, the war was not going well for the Northern forces. Most recently, the Seven Days' Battles in the Peninsula Campaign resulted in another defeat for the Northern armies. Lincoln, becoming increasingly aware that the war would be a long, hard-fought affair, communicated with the governors in the Northern states and, bolstered by their support, concluded another 300,000 men were needed to enter the war. On July 1, 1862, Lincoln made this decision and called on Illinois to furnish 26,148 additional men for the war effort. Illinois had already provided many troops and this call for more soldiers resulted in a slow recruitment. Governor Richard Yates responded by issuing a vigorous call to the citizens to meet the new quota, but Illinois could muster only two regiments of infantry in the month of July. Yates dejectedly, but optimistically, wrote to Lincoln that "[i]n any event, Illinois will respond to your call." On August 4, Lincoln called another 300,000 for service in the Northern armies through the Militia Act, and for both the July and August calls, Illinois needed over 52,000 men to enlist. Despite the early sluggish enlistment, the state successfully furnished the required number of recruits and actually exceeded the number by greater than 2,000 men. From July to December 1862, Illinois mustered into service 52 infantry regiments and four artillery batteries, and only New York furnished more recruits.[1]

During the July 1862 call for new recruits, the board of directors of the Chicago Board of Trade decided to put their not-insignificant influence into the recruiting efforts. On July 16, 10 directors signed a letter and sent it to their president, C.T. Wheeler: "We, the undersigned members, request you to call at an early day a general meeting of the Board to pledge ourselves to use our influence and money to recruit a battery to be known as the Board of Trade Battery." Directors George Steel, William Sturges, K. Akin, M.C. Stearns, I.Y. Munn, G.L. Scott, T.J. Bronson, C.H. Walker, Jr., E.G. Wolcott, and Flint & Thompson all signed the letter. Wheeler vigorously endorsed the sentiment at a meeting held on July 21 in the offices of the Chicago Board of Trade. Second Vice-President John L. Hancock presided over the meeting held at the corner of Water and Wells streets and the organization whole-heartedly supported resolutions introduced by C.H. Walker to fund the organization of military units. Over $5,000 was pledged with additional monetary subscriptions assigned to the members. The first formal move to form an artillery battery came when a muster roll was presented to the organization titled the "Chicago Board of Trade Battery." Immediately, nine members signed the roll: Sylvanus H. Stevens, Silas C. Stevens, James W. Bloom, Calvin Durand, Valentine Steel, Henry B. Chandler, Albert F. Baxter, Henry J. Baxter, and John A. Howard. With the Board of Trade seeking to support the organization of artillery and infantry regiments, the adjutant general for the State of Illinois declared: "Thus was established a precedent of commercial leadership with the material result of placing in the field the Chicago Board of Trade Battery; the 72nd, 88th and 113th infantry regiments, Illinois Volunteers, and $50,000 war funds on deposit." The *Chicago Tribune* was quick to report the decision of the evening's meeting, explaining that only about one-fifth of the Board of Trade was present but they subscribed over $5,000, in addition to over $10,000 previously committed to the war effort. The editors wrote: "All honor to the Board of Trade. Other associations in the city would do well to 'go and do likewise.'" Certainly, each man had his own reason for enlisting but the patriotic sentiment of Chicago called the men to defend their country which was threatened to be torn apart. The *Chicago Tribune* would declare that the time had come to "crush the copperhead of slavery."[2]

The fervor for the war effort resulted in a call for enlistees, including the Young Men's Christian Association (YMCA) in conjunction with the Board of Trade. Five companies were pledged from that organization. An important individual for the future of the Board of Trade Battery was George Irving Robinson who provided a company of enlistees and even offered a second company from the YMCA. The men of the battery came from varied backgrounds and many were used to a high standard of living, but these men hurried to the defense of their nation. All of the men, or their families, were part of the Chicago Board of Trade and considered the "flower" of the business world in the city. In all, the Board of Trade Battery and three infantry regiments (72nd, 88th and 113th Illinois) were supported by the Chicago Board of Trade.[3]

The Chicago Board of Trade was a business organization founded on April 3, 1848, by 83 merchants at 101 South Water Street. In a time when railroads were rare in the Midwest,

Incorporated in 1837, Chicago was rapidly becoming the major business center in the Midwest. The Chicago Board of Trade called for the organization of an artillery battery in July 1862 (image depicts the Board of Trade in session, ca. 1900, Library of Congress).

the port status of Chicago made it a center of commerce. The organization's purpose was the facilitation of commerce in the city. It began by hiring inspectors for the fish and grain industry and it made grading of the products more uniform. Initially, the Board of Trade encouraged the improvement of the port of Chicago and the transportation of commerce on the Great Lakes, but its efforts in measuring, inspecting, storing, transporting and transferring grain made this a very important organization. Over the subsequent years, the Board of Trade became best known as a futures trading and financial entity in the city serving national commerce and extending its efforts internationally. By 1862, the Chicago Board of Trade totaled 924 members and was a formidable financial, staunchly pro–Union organization. Thus far in the war, the Board had been very active in supporting both the patriotic and business aspects of the war, including, dealing with the devaluation of Southern securities, supporting a continuation of Canadian and British treaties, supporting the issuance of Union bonds, reproving Southern leaders and supporting oaths of allegiance.[4]

Acting swiftly after the meeting and pledging support for the formation of the battery, the next night the business leaders in Chicago started organizing the battery and at this meeting 63 men added their names to the roll. The *Chicago Tribune* reported the enlistment results and predicted that the battery would be fully recruited by that evening. Sure enough, by the next day (July 23), the roll was full with 180 names with others waiting. The same evening, the Board of Trade sent a one-line message directly to Abraham Lincoln: "The Board of Trade of this city have within the last forty eight hours raised $5,000 bounty money, and have recruited a full company of Artillery." The members of the Board of Trade also pledged that their employees would be returned to their positions within the business upon the completion of the enlistment period. In addition, if within the employer's power, the enlistee would receive half wages while part of the battery. Many in the business area of downtown Chicago hurried to enlist. Six clerks of Shay's Dry Goods enlisted together, prompting the *Chicago Tribune* to write "Well Done for the Dry Goods Clerks." The enlistment fervor was so great that when a single member of the Board of Trade exclaimed, "Humbug," he was picked up by the other members and hurled into the street.[5]

Patriotic fever seized the city. "Every thing is war! war!! war!!! That is all people seem to talk about or to think of...," wrote new battery recruit Benjamin Nourse. War fever gripped Illinois as the push for recruits increased. After filling the ranks of the battery, the Chicago Board of Trade War Committee moved on to sponsor and fill the ranks of infantry regiments, too. Colonel John L. Hancock was instrumental in the actions of the Board of Trade in support of the war effort. Hancock, a Chicago resident since 1854 and a prominent meat packer in the city, was elected as chairman of the war committee and worked tirelessly in equipping and organizing the Board of Trade battery and infantry regiments. Once mustered, the battery marched down the streets of Chicago to Camp Douglas, but stopped at Hancock's residence where they received lemonade, sandwiches, and a bouquet of flowers. In a humorous note, a band escorted the members of the battery and provided music for the march. While the parade advanced a cow escaped its pen, and, enraged, it attacked one of the musicians, tossing him into the air. Nourse humorously noted that this marked the first attack on the battery, but the men had prevailed. On Saturday July 26, a massive war rally was held near the courthouse in Chicago and all the businesses and shops closed in support. The bells began to ring in the city at 2:00 p.m. and bands began to play. A procession began at the offices of the Board of Trade and marched to the courthouse. Four different speakers' stands had been erected to allow

The Tribune.

MONDAY, JULY 28, 1862.

THE GREAT WAR RALLY.

The immense mass meetings of the people on Saturday to respond to the President's call for more men, and to give expression to the sentiment of Chicago upon the present national crisis, furnish abundant sources of congratulation to every loyal man. This vast uprising of the people—the second time within a week—will give a material impetus to recruiting, will encourage the good work in every part of the State and of the west, will gladden and inspire our sons and brothers in the field to new and more glorious efforts, and will give to the President and his Cabinet the assurance that the great popular heart of the West beats responsive to those national edicts which mark a new and glorious page in the volume of our country's history.

The city of Chicago rallied in support of the Union cause (*Chicago Tribune*).

speeches to be heard by crowds in each location and 35 prominent men gave speeches throughout the afternoon and into the night. Of note, Captain James H. Stokes was present as one of the judges for a demonstration of the Coffee Mill gun, an early type of manual machine gun. Stokes would soon play a significant role in the organization of the Board of Trade Battery. In the meantime, the press used the successes of the Board of Trade to pressure other commercial units to follow this example. Later in July, the *Chicago Tribune* called on the railroads to form either batteries or infantry regiments made up of men from that industry.[6]

The Organization of the Battery

Of the original men of the battery, all enlisted between July 21–23 and all the men came from Chicago. The men, mustered into service on July 31, began active duty on August 1, 1862. Of the 180 names on the roll, 155 were selected to be mustered into service and this was done without a medical examination. Elections for officers were held on August 1 and James H. Stokes was elected captain of the battery. George I. Robinson and Albert F. Baxter were elected first lieutenants and Henry Bennett and Turnbull Griffin were elected second lieutenants.[7]

In addition, eight sergeants and twelve corporals completed the ranks of the non-commissioned officers. From August 1 until August 15 the new battery went through a process of assigning tasks and equipping the unit. On August 7–8, the soldiers received their signing bounties—$60 each from the Chicago Board of Trade and $27 of a $100 bounty promised by the U.S. government. Great excitement greeted the soldiers of the battery on August 11 when six James six-pounder (6.6 lb. cannons, designated as 10-pounders in some records) rifled bronze guns arrived along with horses and harnesses. The battery also received a forge, a blacksmith shop and one battery wagon complete with carpentry and saddlery tools. The battery began drilling in earnest and on August 22, the drill included the use of horses for the first time. This was the time for amateur soldiers to learn the art of their new trade.[8]

The age of the typical enlistee in the Civil War ranged between 18 and 45 years old, but it is important to remember that age was self-reported. So, some members of the battery could possibly have been either under or over the reported ages. A good example of this was the 17-year-old John A. Nourse, who described how he overcame the issue of enlisting while being under age. On July 22, the recruiting officer refused to accept his enlistment unless he had his father's permission. So, Nourse agreed, then, wrote the permission slip himself and signed his father's name. He returned with this document and he was entered onto the rolls of the battery. Remarkably, Nourse entered service in the battery despite his young age and small physique, even though there were several others on the waiting list. One of those on the waiting list offered Nourse a thousand dollars if he would withdraw his name and allow the other to enlist in his stead. Nourse, feeling the patriotic sentiment in the community, refused the offer and remained on the rolls. When Nourse returned home that night he told his parents, who had forbidden John's request to enlist a few months earlier.

John A. Nourse enlisted and chronicled the events of the battery through diaries and letters (Chicago History Museum, ICHi-176912).

John's father still opposed the enlistment. However, John's mother decided the issue. She reasoned that since John's older brother Benjamin had enlisted, John should be allowed to enlist also so that the two brothers could take care of one another.[9]

Many in the battery had been office workers, clerks, or salesmen and were unaccustomed to horses. Sergeant Calvin "Cam" Durand, only 22 years old but who had grown up on a farm, watched with humor as the new recruits interacted with the horses for the first time. Durand smiled as those serving as postillions, battery men who rode the horses of a team, handled their new role in an awkward manner; however, these were industrious young men who quickly adapted to their hooved companions. A member of the battery, Daniel Richardson—a 31-year-old clerk, claimed to have drawn the first blood in the war. He was on his way to church when he met an acquaintance who opposed the war and told Richardson that he was a fool to enlist, even hurrahing for Jeff Davis. Richardson promptly "thrashed" the man, who was much larger than Richardson. Richardson brushed himself off and continued on his way to church.[10]

Indeed, there was much to be learned as the battery was formed. From the original enlistees there seemed to be a serious lack of experience with horses, but the enlistees were a homogenous lot of men drawn from all sorts of active business endeavors in Chicago. Most were clerks at the time they joined the battery, but others came from a variety of other occupations:

Clerks/Bookkeepers	71	Merchants/Grocers/Butchers	10
Carpenters/Painters	13	Mechanics/Steamfitters	3
Printers	11	Coopers	3
Tobacconists	3	Boatmen/Seamen	4
Railroad workers	7	Metalworkers	4
Lumbermen/merchants	3	Blacksmiths	3
Leather/Fabric Workers	6	Other	4
Professionals (dentists, druggists, engineers, architects, designers, barbers)[11]	10		

The pre-war occupations of the enlistees caused some concerns because many of the men were unaccustomed to physical labor. Private Tobias Miller wrote a letter on August 14 explaining the new challenges for some of the men: "The hard labor of camp begins to tell on many of our tender handed companions. We have so many who have never labored a day in their lives." Tobias Charles Miller came from a very prominent family in Chicago. His father John Miller participated in the early history of Chicago and is credited with the development of the articles of incorporation of the city in 1833. Tobias was a native of Chicago but was an active explorer of the West beginning at the age of sixteen. He participated in four expeditions across the Great Plains. He graduated from Knox College before enlisting in the Board of Trade Battery where his letters would provide important insight into the workings of the battery.[12]

Of the original members of the battery, only a small percentage were native Illinois residents, only about seven percent of the total enlistees. About a third of the enlistees were from New York and about 18 percent of the enlistees were from foreign countries

(England 7, Ireland 7, Canada 5, Germany 2, Sweden 2, Denmark 1, Norway 1, Prussia 1, and Scotland 1). Most the men arrived in Chicago during a period of rapid growth looking for business opportunities. The city was only incorporated in 1837 with a population of a mere 350 residents. The population increased to about 30,000 residents in 1850 and surged to over 100,000 in 1860.

Place of Origin—Board of Trade Battery Enlistees

New York	51	Massachusetts	13
Ohio	12	Illinois	11
Michigan	9	Pennsylvania	9
Vermont	6	Maine	4
New Hampshire	3	Rhode Island	3
New Jersey	3	Alabama	1
Mississippi	1	Connecticut	1
Maryland	1	Foreign	27[13]

Despite John Nourse's situation, only 25 of the enlistees were less than 20 years old. About 15 were in their 30s, four in their 40s and one man enlisted at the age of 50. The oldest member was 50 years old, Private David McMunn, and he was appointed artificer, a skilled craftsman who cared for the guns and other equipment. Because of McMunn's skills, a professional saddler and experienced soldier, he was allowed to enlist despite his age. Six artificers were appointed at the organization of the battery along with two buglers. The Illinois adjutant general recorded the official enlistment date as August 1 and all were mustered into service on July 31, 1862. Elections of officers occurred immediately after the battery was organized.[14]

Chicago Board of Trade Battery

Commissioned Officers and Sergeants [15]	
James H. Stokes	Captain
George I. Robinson	1st Lt.
Albert Baxter	1st Lt.
Trumbull Griffin	2nd Lt.
Henry Bennett	2nd Lt.
Sylvanus H. Stevens	1st Sergeant
Myron S. Sanford	Quartermaster Sergeant
Frederick Deane	1st Sergeant
Lewis Hand	2nd Sergeant
William Randolph	3rd Sergeant
Abbott L. Adams	4th Sergeant
George Bowers	5th Sergeant
Menzo Salisbury	6th Sergeant

Though still young, 4th Sergeant Abbott Adams, only 20 years old, had experience with artillery, having served for three months in Battery A, Illinois Light Artillery. Adams, a native of New Hampshire, had been a student and clerk prior to his enlistment. The battery needed experienced men and Adams offered that. Another experienced sergeant was Lewis B. Hand. Hand moved to Chicago from Utica, New York, in 1856. Upon his arrival, he worked for a few years as a clerk in the companies of Potter, Palmer and others. Near the beginning of the war, he enlisted in the Ellsworth Zouaves, a precision drill team. When the conflict began, he was contracted by the government to drill troops in the eastern theater. He returned to Chicago and enlisted in the Board of Trade Battery. He had no direct training with artillery, but he was familiar with drill and troop training.[16]

Captain James H. Stokes, the first commander of the Chicago Board of Trade Battery (MOLLUS Mass Civil War Collection, United States Army Heritage and Education Center, Carlisle, PA).

The general plan for the battery specified that the captain had overall command of the battery, which was considered a company. Then, the battery was subdivided into three two-gun sections, often referred to the left-, right- and center-section, or by number: first, second or third. Each section fell under the direct authority of a lieutenant and the sections were supported by six caissons. Then in each individual gun platoon, a sergeant had supervisory responsibility for each gun along with a corporal. The other corporals had responsibility for the caissons and other carriages. The lieutenant commanding the section decided the manner in which ammunition was handled from the caisson to the gun. The men, cannoneers, who loaded, fired, and cleaned the gun carried no firearms. The other privates in the gun platoon had responsibilities for security, as horse handlers, and as ammunition carriers. Generally, seven to 11 men served as cannoneers for each gun, but overall, more than 150 men and 110 horses or mules were needed to operate a Union six-gun light artillery battery.[17]

Of paramount importance to the battery were the horses or mules. The animals quickly moved the battery where it was needed, but required a great amount of care and training. A horse could carry a load of 250–300 pounds 20 miles a day but they required rations of about 14 pounds of hay and 12 pounds of oats, barley or corn per day. The forage became difficult to obtain when in droughty or winter conditions and when in close proximity to the enemy. In addition, the leather harnesses needed constant attention and repair.[18]

The Officers

Captain James Hughes Stokes was by no means a young officer, nor was he inexperienced. Stokes, born in Maryland in 1815, attended the U.S. Military Academy at West Point from 1831 to 1835. Upon graduation (17th in a class of 56), Second Lieutenant Stokes was assigned to the 4th U.S. Artillery in New York and subsequently, passed through a series of promotions until he was promoted captain and Assistant Quartermaster in 1839. He served primarily in New York during this period but he also served in Florida in the Seminole War. He had active participation in the Battle of Okeechobee, December 25, 1837. He also had duty with the transfer of the Cherokee Nation in the late 1830s and afterward, returned to his quartermaster duty. In 1840, he again returned to Florida for action in 1840–1841. He served in his quartermaster capacity until 1843 when he resigned and went to work in the manufacturing and railroad industry. He ran the Clyde Glass Factory, New York, from 1843-1853. Next, he served as Treasurer and Secretary of the New York and Boston Railroad Company, 1856-1858. In 1858 he moved to Illinois and served as auditor and local treasurer of Illinois Central Railroad Company.[19]

It is interesting to note that in the descriptive roll for the battery Stokes is recorded being 45 years old and if his obituary is correct, he was closer to 47 or 48 years old. The descriptive roll also recorded Stokes' occupation to be that of an insurance agent.[20]

Stokes made an immediate contribution as the Civil War began. While Illinois strongly supported the Union, the neighboring state of Missouri remained conflicted regarding its allegiance to the Union. After Ft. Sumter, Abraham Lincoln called for 75,000 three-month volunteers and Missouri was asked to furnish 4,000 of these men which Governor Claiborne Fox flatly refused to provide. Para-military organizations had been assembled prior to the Ft. Sumter incident, particularly in the St. Louis area where pro–Southern Minute Men and pro–Northern Home Guards were being trained in response to the deteriorating state and national situation. Governor Jackson's refusal to furnish the recruits requested by Lincoln offered an opportunity for the pro–Union Home Guards to be mustered into service. The commander of the Union military forces in St. Louis was Captain Nathaniel Lyon, a hard line, pro–Union military officer. As Lyon mustered the Home Guards into service, the importance of protecting and controlling the St. Louis arsenal was clear. Stokes was credited with moving the arms from the St. Louis arsenal to Springfield, Illinois, where they were secure from the threat of Confederate capture and were used to arm the Illinois volunteers. Afterwards, he served as a state commissioner to purchase arms for Illinois military forces. As the new battery was being formed, the West Point trained, commercially active Stokes seemed an excellent candidate to command the new battery. The elections on August 1 confirmed his position as commander of the battery. By those who knew Stokes at West Point, he was noted for his "marked soldierly qualities and manly personal bearing, of resolute will, tempered by kindly and gentlemanly disposition and manners."[21]

First Lieutenant George I. Robinson

George Robinson was a clerk in Durand Brothers & Powers grocers in Chicago. Robinson was tall, with black hair and hazel eyes, and proved to be one of the most effective and notable officers of the battery. He worked quietly and efficiently with the men to make this a premier battery and he was always present when needed. Robinson drilled with the Ellsworth Zouaves, as had Lewis B. Hand, and he became part of the Wide Awakes, a uniformed Republican marching organization supporting Lincoln during the

1860 presidential election. He enlisted with two of his friends, Calvin "Cam" Durand and Thomas Watson. Cam Durand recalled that he proposed Robinson for the position of first lieutenant and he was elected to that rank. Robinson (born in 1840) was a native of Narraganset or Wakefield, Rhode Island, where he lived until he was 16 years old. Then, he moved to Chicago and began working for the Durand Brothers in 1858.[22]

First Lieutenant Albert F. Baxter

Albert Francis Baxter, the son of a tailor, was born on August 22, 1838, in Massachusetts. Albert was a clerk before the war and his older brother, Henry, also joined the battery. The Baxter brothers were among the first to sign up for enlistment and Albert's zeal rewarded him with an election to the rank of lieutenant when the battery was organized. The 23-year-old Albert, six feet tall, was described as having black hair and dark eyes.[23]

First Lieutenant George I. Robinson, a brave, trustworthy and higher regarded officer of the battery (courtesy Milwaukee County Historical Society).

Second Lieutenant Trumbull Griffin

Trumbull Dorrance Griffin was born in Clinton, New York, on October 11, 1835, on an estate which had been owned by George Washington. Griffin's grandfather purchased the property in New York in 1790. His ancestors settled in Massachusetts and Connecticut prior to 1700. Griffin, a printer by trade before the war, moved to Michigan in 1847 and became a printer's apprentice at the *Detroit Advertiser* in the spring of 1848. He worked at various locations in Michigan in the printing business. He also traveled west to Omaha and in 1857 he worked in Council Bluffs. He moved to Chicago in 1858, working for various daily papers until his enlistment. Griffin, nicknamed "Trum" by the men, was similar to George Robinson in many ways in his command style. In 1860, he lived in a rooming house, which included a fellow comrade in the battery, Andrew Baskerville. Along with Baskerville and Menzo Salisbury, the three young men enlisted together. Robinson would prove to be an exemplary officer and held a steady hand on the guns in even the most challenging situations.[24]

Second Lieutenant Henry Bennett

Henry Bennett was one of two sons of William and Rachel Bennett. He was born in Chicago on June 15, 1841. He was educated in public schools in Chicago and when he was

15 years old, he began an apprenticeship as a carpenter, where he earned $.50 per day. After the apprenticeship, Bennett continued to work as a carpenter. At the beginning of the war, he enlisted in the 90-day Battery A, Chicago Light Artillery. He served most of this enlistment at Cairo, Illinois, where he saw light action. He became ill with chills and fever by the end of his time with the battery. Due to his illness, he could not re-enlist and he returned to Chicago to recuperate. When the Board of Trade Battery was organized, the quiet and thoughtful Bennett enlisted and his previous experience earned him a rank of second lieutenant when elections were held.[25]

The Battery Moves South

Once the guns, horses and equipment arrived, the members of the battery began training at the old armory on Franklin and Monroe Street under the tutelage of Stokes, but the training in Chicago would be short. The Confederate States of America launched a grand offensive in the summer and autumn of 1862 with the purpose of moving the war northward. This offensive included the movement of two Confederate armies into Kentucky from Tennessee—Major General E. Kirby Smith's Army of Kentucky and Major General Braxton Bragg's Army of the Mississippi. Smith marched from Knoxville on August 13 and Bragg began his movement on August 28. Facing the two Confederate armies, Major General Don Carlos Buell's Army of the Ohio, supported by whatever forces he could move into Kentucky, prepared to meet the enemy. By September 7, Buell's army, which originally had Chattanooga as its objective, hastily hurried northward from Tennessee to stop the Southern advance. The cities of Louisville and Cincinnati appeared to be at risk from the Confederate armies. Two impressive victories during the early part of the campaign came with Bragg's capture of Union-held Munfordville (September 14–17) and Smith's overwhelming victory at Richmond, Kentucky (August 29–30).[26]

The Federal forces hurried to protect the two large cities threatened by the advancing enemy troops. Although with only a few weeks training, on September 9 the Chicago Board of Trade Battery began its movement to Louisville to provide additional defense for the city. The battery moved by train from Chicago via Michigan City, through Lafayette, Indiana, and then to Jeffersonville, just opposite the Ohio River from Louisville. Support by the Northern citizens was seen in Lafayette when the train stopped at 10 p.m., and the soldiers received a "splendid supper" from the local citizens, explained Private Benjamin Nourse. Nourse wrote in his journal, "this has been the happiest day of my life." The battery passed through Louisville and men saw only a few white people, mostly Black women. The next day the battery moved six miles east of Louisville on the Shelbyville Pike and went into camp. Along the way, the men of the battery met some Southern-supporting citizens for the first time. Private John Fleming didn't mind these people but the tensions increased when they verbalized their position on the war to the soldiers in blue. Fleming wrote that these people "have got to keep their mouths closely shut!" Pushing further into Kentucky, the battery, being unfamiliar with the necessity of moving with minimal baggage, discovered they had brought enough to have the appearance of a group on "a long pleasure trip," observed Sergeant Calvin Durand.[27]

The battery remained in the same general vicinity over the next few days and found time to improve its organization. Calvin Durand, who had originally been appointed ordnance sergeant, was appointed assistant quartermaster and Smith Randolph replaced him as ordnance sergeant. Calvin Durand, Jr., born May 7, 1840, was originally from Clintonville,

New York. Durand was the youngest of four brothers and one sister. He worked on the family farm, hauled iron ore, and had experience teaching while in New York. Relatively new to Chicago, Durand clerked in a grocery business, Durand Brothers and Powers, owned by his brothers. Durand seemed perfectly selected for his new role as quartermaster. Though not noted in the roster, Durand replaced Myron Sanford. Early on, Captain Stokes decided Sanford "did not fit the bill." Of note, Benjamin Nourse recorded in his diary, "Sanford got drunk." Other accounts recorded that Sanford went to Louisville and returned inebriated. One account detailed that when Sanford arrived at camp from his trip to Louisville to get bread, Captain Stokes was waiting for him. Sanford mumbled, "I, I, I, go- go- got the bread." Stokes immediately had him arrested. The next day he was reduced in ranks and the quartermaster job fell to Durand. (Sanford would remain with the battery until 1863 when he received a commission in the Massachusetts heavy artillery with the rank of lieutenant.) The presence and impact of Stokes, the West Point trained officer, cannot be overlooked. Stokes brought confidence, experience, and discipline to the battery. Private Tobias Miller wrote, "Our captain is placing us under the strictest of West Point rules."[28]

Meanwhile, the horses, wagons, and canteens arrived in camp on September 14. Durand found he had a new challenge with his new duties as quartermaster sergeant. He had the responsibility of dealing with six supply wagons, an ambulance, and thirty-six mules all overseen by six men with little experience. "[Y]ou can imagine the time we had taking six of our boys who knew nothing about mules, going down to the corral, catching the animals, getting harness onto them, and finally hitching six to a wagon." Then, each of the soldiers had to ride the rear most mule, as postillions, with only one harness line. They found they had to lock the rear wheels of the wagons to control the mules until they gained increased experience with the animals. In addition to dealing with the animals, the men in the new battery had to learn how to prepare their own rations. For example, their first attempt at preparing bacon, by boiling it, resulted in a fatty glob in their haversacks. They also found they had too much baggage and this was quickly discarded. The new uniforms, some of which had been tailor-made, proved unsuitable, especially those with paper collars. Meeting experienced artillerymen along the road soon set the men right and the uniforms were adapted to more practical fashions.[29]

The battery moved to Louisville on September 15 and passed in review before some of the commanding generals. This was done as a show of force and to calm the citizens in Louisville, who feared the approaching Confederate army. The weather was very hot and droughty, and the conditions persisted throughout the Perryville Campaign. The heavy uniforms, the hot weather, and light limestone pavement caused as many as 50 soldiers to suffer heat stroke during the review. Afterwards, the battery returned to camp. The next morning four guns (Guns number 2, 3, 4 and 5) were exchanged for four six-pounder smooth bore field guns. The battery began its organization with six six-pounder James Rifles with a 3.8-inch diameter rifled bore, but by September four of these guns were replaced with 1840–41 (1844) version six-pounder, smooth-bore, field guns with a 3.67-inch diameter barrel. All six guns were bronze in construction and had a range of 320–1525 yards with a muzzle velocity of over 1400 feet/second. Presumably, the replacement of the guns resulted from bronze-rifled tubes wearing out fairly quickly. Stokes told the men that they received these new splendid guns "based on our reputation," wrote John Fleming. Both guns and caissons had two wheeled portions—the carriage and the limber. Each was mounted on two wheels and joined by a lunette (an iron ring at the end of the trail of the gun carriage) and a pintle. The lunette was dropped over the pintle and held in place with a pintle hook. This allowed for quick attachment and detachment of the gun carriage to the limber. The carriage referred to the two-wheeled structure on which the gun rested, or was carried. The stock trail, unhitched from the limber, rested on the ground and was designed to allow for the proper recoil of the gun. The gun carriages were attached to limbers, a two-wheeled carriage topped with an ammunition chest. Caissons were carriages with two ammunition chests attached to a limber and there was generally one caisson, which also carried a spare wheel, for each field piece. In addition, each battery had a battery wagon, also connected to a limber, which was a long-bodied cart with a rounded canvas top. The battery wagon carried a forage rack, tools, spare parts, extra harness, and other maintenance materials. The final carriage was the traveling forge which served as a blacksmith shop on wheels and contained the tools and materials needed by blacksmiths, artificers, and farriers to shoe horses and repair guns, wagons and carriages.[30]

The battery trained and practiced on the new and old guns over the next two weeks. Stokes continually built up the morale of the men in the battery. The reviews went well and he stressed the new cannons were a direct result of

CALVIN DURAND, JR.
YEAR 1862

The picture was taken just after he enlisted in the Chicago Board of Trade Battery

Twenty-two-year-old New York native Calvin Durand, Jr., served as quartermaster sergeant (*Genealogy of the Durand, Whalley, Barnes and Yale Families* (1912), p. 114).

the quality of the battery. Stokes addressed the men on September 14, telling them what an excellent job they were doing during the drill. John Fleming said he "praised us up to the handle." In an interesting note, Sergeant Sylvanus Stevens' wife accompanied him from Chicago and into Kentucky. She lived in the tent with him, but Fleming noted that she had had a rough first month despite the fact that she had her own horse. The men liked Stevens and they helped his wife as much as they could in camp. Stevens' younger brother, Silas C. Stevens, served as a private and would leave a detailed memoir of the actions of the battery in the war. Fleming, though, concluded that camp was no place for a woman and he thought that she had come to the same opinion. (Fleming would become one of the most prolific chroniclers of the events of the battery, penning over eighty letters. Fleming was born in Eutaw, Greene County, Alabama, in 1845 and his family subsequently moved to Chicago. His father died of cholera while Fleming was young. Fleming, 18 years old when he enlisted, had been working as a clerk.)[31]

A few days after receiving the new guns, the battery was loaded onto a train and prepared to move south, but the arrival of Buell's army from Nashville delayed this

The Board of Trade Battery received six six-pounder James Rifles (National Park Service, Stones River National Battlefield).

movement. So, the battery stayed near Louisville and continued to train in the art of war. Finally, on October 1, the battery began its march toward Bragg's army which advanced into central Kentucky. Edmund Kirby Smith's Confederate Army of Kentucky moved in a parallel path to Bragg, capturing Richmond and Lexington along the way. Frankfort became the only Northern state capital to be captured in the Civil War, and to make things worse for the Federals, the Confederates inaugurated a new governor, Richard Hawes. Union troops from Louisville, Sill's and Dumont's divisions, converged on the state capital on October 7, including the Chicago Board of Trade Battery but the Confederate troops withdrew from the city. While some Union troops descended on Frankfort, others clashed about 60 miles south with Bragg's Army of the Mississippi at the Battle of Perryville on October 8. The battle was a chaotic and bloody affair after which Bragg chose to withdraw from Kentucky, giving the Union forces a strategic victory.[32]

The Chicago Board of Trade Battery, being an independent battery, soon found itself attached to Brigadier General Ebenezer Dumont's 12th Division, Army of the Ohio, during its first active service. Dumont's division was also an independent division. A second division under the command of Joshua Sill moved with Dumont toward Frankfort while much of the rest of Buell's army concentrated at Perryville.[33]

Twelfth Division

Brig. Gen. Ebenezer Dumont

Thirty-Eighth Brigade, Col. Marshal W. Chapin

Thirty-Ninth Brigade, Col. George T. Limberg

Fortieth Brigade, Brig. Gen. Robert S. Granger
Ward's Brigade, Brig. Gen. William Ward

Artillery
Chicago Board of Trade Battery, Capt. James H. Stokes
13th Indiana Battery, Capt. Benjamin S. Nicklin
18th Indiana Battery, Capt. Eli Lilly[34]

As the battery moved toward the converging armies in central Kentucky, the men found their first real opportunity at foraging. About a mile from Shelbyville, some of the men ran into a young lady who remarked what a difference a week made, because only a week ago, the area was occupied with Southern soldiers. Often, the men sought food for themselves and their horses from local farmers. Such was the case with Private John Fleming who extracted his breakfast from an "old secesh" whose "chickens suffered slightly." Fleming greatly respected Captain Stokes, although this sentiment would not be shared by all the members of the battery. On October 7, Fleming wrote in a letter to his mother: "One thing is extremely evident that our captain is a man bound to see his men taken care of." The soldiers were under strict rules regarding plundering the citizens and Fleming explained that Stokes said, "His company was made up of men who could help themselves without being caught." While Stokes' attitude showed some flexibility, Fleming noted the difference between lifting a few chickens and more severe misconduct. Only that morning, Fleming observed an infantry regiment "completely ransack a house," acting shamefully, because they had heard the owner was a Southern sympathizer who had fled. In addition to the foraging activities, many of the men were sick, which was not uncommon during the early parts of the war when the men were still learning how to maintain proper hygiene and accustom themselves to sleeping outdoors. One of the men to fall ill was Sergeant George Bowers, who had resigned his rank in late September and moved to a hospital in Louisville. It took two months for him to recuperate and he was able to return to duty in December. On a positive note, the battery had just gained a battery physician, Dr. Frederick A. Lord, from Chicago. The battery also named Daniel D. Jacobs hospital steward.[35]

Dr. Lord did not have an easy process in joining the battery. His reputation as a physician interested in homeopathy tainted the examination board regarding his qualifications. Granted, Lord would later be very involved with this type of medicine, but at the time of the examination, he was a physician using common practices of his profession. Lord went to Springfield to discuss his appointment as medical officer of the battery with letters of support from the officers but the examining board suspected him of "heterodoxy in my therapeutic views." At that point, he gave up any hope of joining the service but when the crisis of Bragg's invasion of Kentucky developed, he was summoned to Louisville, not as an enlistee, but under contract with the government. This was an unusual situation because batteries typically did not have medical staff assigned, but the efforts of Stokes resulted in Dr. Lord's appointment.[36]

The First Fight—Lawrenceburg, Kentucky

Immediately after the Battle of Perryville, Bragg withdrew northward to Harrodsburg before deciding to withdraw from the state. Twenty-five miles north, the Board of

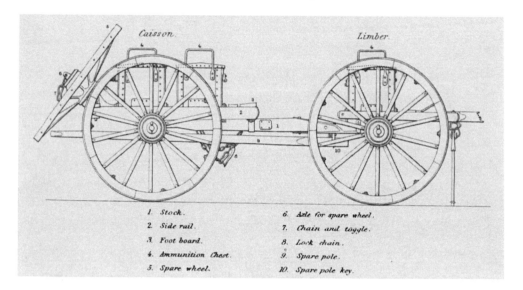

A caisson and limber (*Instruction for Field Artillery*, by William French et. al., 1864, Plate 13).

Trade Battery fired its first shots in anger on October 11, 1862, near Lawrenceburg, Kentucky. After arriving at Frankfort and finding the enemy gone, Brigadier General Robert S. Granger took his brigade along with the Board of Trade Battery to fill the gap between Major General Alexander McCook's corps near Harrodsburg and the forces at Frankfort. The battery and infantry brigade marched southward from Frankfort through Lawrenceburg and found a body of Confederate cavalry at the town, near the site of Brigadier General Joshua Sill's skirmish a few days before. Sill had subsequently moved southwest to Willisburg while Dumont pushed the enemy south from Frankfort toward Versailles. The Confederate cavalry had the duty of screening for Smith's and Bragg's armies and the clashes often resulted between Northern troops and Southern horsemen.[37]

Running into the Confederate cavalry, the Board of Trade Battery fired its first real shots of the war. Benjamin Nourse recorded: "The rear guard of Bragg's army is in front of us—and we over took them at Lawrenceville and the first fireing of our battery was from the 6th piece—we ran up into a wheat field and quickly getting into position we opened with shell on a squad of cavalry at 1600 yards tearing up a barn and the trees to pieces and killing several rebels (the darkies say 6) but they were carried off by their comrades." John Fleming, assigned to gun number 6, explained that a section of guns number 2 and number 6 were involved in the skirmish and that the battery was supported by a strong contingent of Federal cavalry. Only gun number 6 fired on the enemy and Stokes personally oversaw the firing. Stokes rode to the gun, dismounted, with his pipe firmly in his mouth, calmly sighted the gun, and gave the order—"Fire!" The shell fell right in the midst of the enemy who mounted and hurried away. Fleming thought the shells killed one and wounded four in the fight. The next day gun number 2 got into action when it accompanied a cavalry mission pursuing the retreating enemy, resulting in a fight which drove the Confederates from a wooded area, and assisted in the capture of over 100 prisoners and a six-pounder field gun.[38]

The grand Confederate offensive proved unsuccessful as Bragg's armies marched out of Kentucky. In addition, the Confederates were defeated at Iuka and Corinth, and this made Bragg feel he was in a vulnerable position because the "whole country in our rear was left open to the enemy's victorious forces." In addition, a large number of Federal reinforcements were moving southward from Cincinnati. Bragg chastised the Kentuckians for their failure to "rise in mass to assert their independence." George Knox Miller, an officer in the 8th Confederate Cavalry, gave a little more balanced observation of the situation in Kentucky: "[U]pon the whole the Kentuckians were not enthusiastic, if so at all it was those who espoused the cause of Abraham [Lincoln]. They [pro–Confederate Kentuckians] wanted some assurance that we were going to hold the state before they would compromise themselves.... But what a pity we could not hold the 'dark & bloody ground'—it is inestimable value to us—so rich, so plethoric with the necessaries of life—what we now need above all things."[39]

While the Federal position was secured at Lawrenceburg, the first real pursuit of Bragg's and Smith's armies began the same day outside of Danville. The forces clashed west of the town and the Confederates fell back east of Danville and during the night of October 12, Bragg sent orders to start moving back to Tennessee by way of Cumberland Gap. The next morning, Bragg appointed Colonel Joseph Wheeler chief of cavalry; Wheeler was ordered to organize all the mounted troops and to provide rearguard action as the Confederate army withdrew. Once Bragg started his withdrawal the Federal army followed in pursuit in a tentative manner. Buell, while an industrious and efficient officer, alienated many powerful military and political figures because of his rigid and inflexible personality. Buell considered his pursuit of Bragg, but he delayed because he believed a Confederate attack on his flank would result in disaster for his Army of the Ohio. Buell wrote, "My studies have taught me that battles are only to be fought for some important object; that success must be rendered reasonably certain if possible—the more certain the better; that if the result is reasonably uncertain, battle is only to be sought when very serious disadvantage must result from a failure to fight, or when the advantages of a possible victory far outweigh the consequences of probable defeat." Buell's cautious pursuit, poor performance at Perryville, and own ability to alienate important political figures, would result in his removal from command.[40]

Once Bragg moved past Crab Orchard, Buell decided to end the pursuit. There was only one poor route to pursue Bragg, and the pursuit would go through rugged, hilly terrain along a narrow road. After marching a short distance, the lack of forage was already felt, but the decision to halt the pursuit did not sit well with those in Washington. Buell's conduct, committing only a fraction of his troops at Perryville, resulted in anger in Washington and the field. Buell's decision to stop the pursuit into East Tennessee and his focus on Nashville resulted in exasperation by his commanders, because Henry Halleck, General-in-Chief of all Union forces, wanted Buell's army in East Tennessee and not in Middle Tennessee. Halleck directly told Buell that the capture of East Tennessee should be the main objective of the Union army in Kentucky and Tennessee. Halleck concluded his message to Buell telling him that the President declared that Buell's army had to "enter East Tennessee this fall."[41]

The Northern governors, also unhappy with the outcome of the Battle of Perryville, applied pressure on those in the War Department in Washington. Finally, Buell simply failed to grasp the need to follow Halleck's orders. Washington had finally had enough of Buell's command. On October 24, Major General William S. Rosecrans received his orders to take command of the Department of the Cumberland and command of army operations which were currently under authority of Buell. Meanwhile, Buell was ordered to face a court of inquiry in November regarding the appropriateness of his actions during the Perryville Campaign.[42]

While most historians grant the Union forces a strategic victory at the Battle of Perryville, the victory showed little dominance of the Army of the Ohio. On the Southern

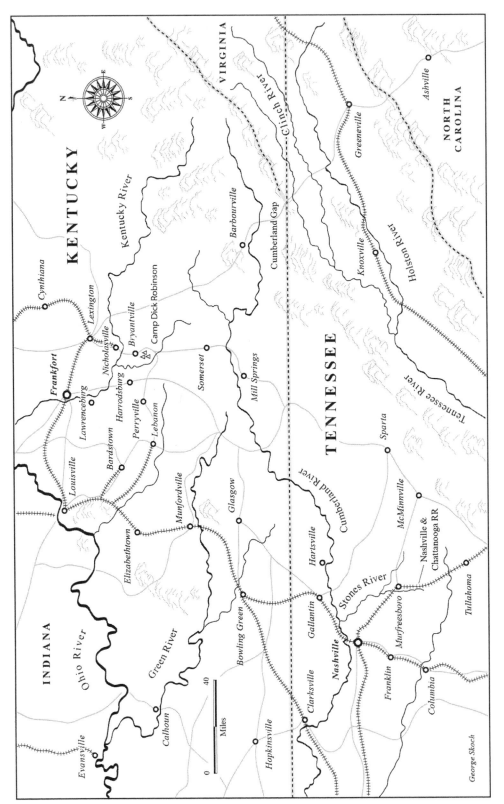

Central Kentucky and central Tennessee, October 1862.

side of the line, the campaign yielded mixed results for Bragg's forces although he claimed positive results—booty to supply his army and the liberation of North Alabama and Middle Tennessee for the Confederacy by drawing the Union forces northward. However, the campaign resulted in an inglorious exit from Kentucky, the exhaustion of both Southern armies, a serious rift between Smith and Bragg, and alienation and distrust of Bragg by some of his top commanders. After reaching Tennessee, Bragg decided his army would subsist from the bounty of the countryside in central Tennessee after reclaiming Cumberland Gap as a result of the Kentucky Campaign. The opposing armies would converge again just south of Nashville.[43]

The Chicago Board of Trade Battery joined in the initial pursuit of Bragg's and Smith's armies. After the skirmish at Lawrenceburg, the battery moved southward, reached Crab Orchard (about fifteen miles southeast of Danville), stopped and returned to Perryville, arriving on October 23. Along the way, oldest member of the battery David McMunn's health gave out and he was sent to the hospital and would soon be discharged due to the illness. (McMunn had been in the fight at Fort Donelson and had lost some fingers in that battle. Now, he was so sick that rumors abounded in the battery that McMunn was dying.) Next the battery received orders to march to Bowling Green as the Confederate forces began concentrating south of Nashville. In a rare October snowstorm, the men awoke on October 26 to a four-inch snowfall. In groups, 20 men slept warmly and dry under a large tarpaulin and experienced no significant discomfort. The battery reached Munfordville later in the day, and reached Bowling Green on October 30 where they pitched their tents for the first time since leaving Louisville on September 20. The battery remained in Bowling Green awaiting orders. In the meantime, the Union army moved southward across a broad front and continued its advance to Nashville. The battery, being independent and somewhat loosely attached to Dumont, remained without direction. In the meantime, Dumont was concentrating on a political career. He would be elected to Congress in 1862 and would resign in early 1863.[44]

While the situation in the Federal army left much to be desired, the situation among the top Confederate generals was no better. The withdrawal caused the relationship between Bragg and the commander of the Army of Kentucky to further deteriorate. E. Kirby Smith, who commanded his own army, had voluntarily agreed to serve under Bragg, but now felt Bragg disproportionally favored his Army of the Mississippi over the Army of Kentucky during the withdrawal. During the retreat to Tennessee and while Bragg's column was approaching Mt. Vernon, Kirby Smith's army lagged some 20 to 30 miles to the rear. Smith was correct in his changing feelings about Bragg and Bragg admitted to Leonidas Polk on October 16 that his withdrawal put Smith's army at risk of being cut off and surrounded. Smith's tardiness resulted because Bragg had "imposed" his trains on Smith "by which he is retarded" and allowed the Army of the Mississippi to move quickly at the detriment to the other Southern column. The grueling trek resulted in men marching all night and Smith's army being "very much scattered along the road." A member of the 34th Alabama Infantry, John Crittenden, wrote to his wife: "Then commenced our suffering for some thing to eat. We were allowed only one meal a day. That was two small biscuits and a plenty of meat to eat with it." As both Confederate armies returned to Tennessee, Smith drew a sigh of relief and dispatched his infantry to various locations to recuperate and to prepare for further action against the Union forces. Smith recorded: "My men have suffered on this march everything excepting actual starvation. There must be not less than 10,000 of them scattered through the country trying to find something upon which to live."[45]

By October 23 Kirby Smith put his foot down after receiving an order from Bragg

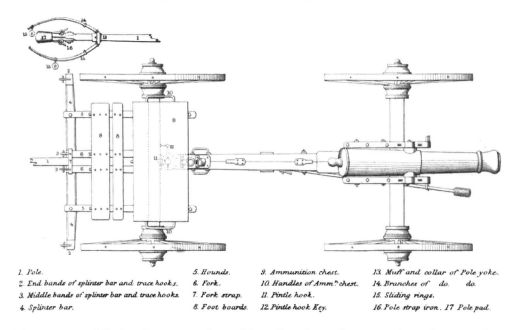

1. Pole.
2. End bands of splinter bar and trace hooks.
3. Middle bands of splinter bar and trace hooks.
4. Splinter bar.
5. Hounds.
6. Fork.
7. Fork strap.
8. Foot boards.
9. Ammunition chest.
10. Handles of Amm.ⁿ chest.
11. Pintle hook.
12. Pintle hook Key.
13. Muff and collar of Pole yoke.
14. Branches of do.   do.
15. Sliding rings.
16. Pole strap iron. 17 Pole pad.

The cannon and limber (*Instruction for Field Artillery*, by William French et. al., 1864, Plate 11).

to move to Middle Tennessee. Though wearied of working with Bragg, he acknowledged the order in which Bragg wanted the bulk of his army in Middle Tennessee, leaving only 3,000 men to guard Cumberland Gap. Smith responded: "The condition of my command now is such as to render any immediate operations with it impossible." Bragg argued that the advance into Kentucky resulted in a stronger and better supplied army and he claimed the retrograde back to Tennessee did not signify a defeat, but rather a victorious expedition by his army. Not all of Bragg's subordinates agreed with his handling of the campaign and Bragg and some of his top commanders waged a war of letters about how the Perryville Campaign was handled. Bragg, West Point class of 1837, assumed command of the Army of the Mississippi in June 1862 and while he had many good qualities, he would remain unpopular as long as he commanded the Confederate army. Historian Peter Cozzens wrote: "Bragg seemed to repel men with disarming ease."[46]

Despite Bragg's exclamations of success during the recent campaign, he also acknowledged the recent campaign took a great toll on the Army of the Mississippi, but he moved his army into Middle Tennessee. He reluctantly admitted, "The Army of the Mississippi is much shattered." In the final result, Bragg's army had just marched 1,000 miles and then returned to Tennessee with no positive results except "Bragg's prestige was a little more tarnished," wrote historian Stanley Horn.[47]

As Confederate troops began to arrive, the increased activity at Murfreesboro did not go unnoticed by Brigadier General James Negley who commanded Union troops in Nashville. By mid–October, Negley wrote: "Our defenses are in best possible condition. Continue to improve them…. Command in good health and spirits." Negley observed the concentration of the enemy at La Vergne, just north of Murfreesboro, and later the Union reconnaissance revealed three artillery batteries, 5,000 cavalry, and 3,000 infantry in the town. Negley expected to face as many as 20,000 Confederates by the end of the week. The two armies were converging just south of Nashville.[48]

On to Tennessee and the
Battle of Stones River

We went down like grass before a scythe—Captain W.P. O'Connor, CSA

Rosecrans Assumes Command of the Army of the Cumberland

On October 24, Major General William S. Rosecrans received formal orders granting him command of the Department of the Cumberland. The orders directed Rosecrans to travel to Buell's headquarters and formally relieve him of command, but the transition of command from Buell to Rosecrans was handled poorly. Buell found out he had been superseded through the newspapers before Rosecrans reached his headquarters, making the process awkward at best. Then, Halleck assigned Rosecrans' strategic objectives: (1) drive the enemy from Kentucky and Middle Tennessee and (2) take and hold East Tennessee. Halleck acknowledged there were two ways of reaching East Tennessee. Perhaps, Halleck suggested, the most expedient was just to push Bragg's retreating army directly into East Tennessee, but Halleck also gave Rosecrans the option of securing Nashville before moving eastward. He further urged Rosecrans to move quickly and if needed, Rosecrans should support Grant, or vice versa, depending on the actions of the Confederates. Halleck concluded with a serious warning: "I need not urge upon you the necessity of giving active employment to your forces. Neither the country nor the Government will much longer put up with the inactivity of some of our armies and generals." But Rosecrans felt he needed to ensure that his army was well supplied before he made any drastic advances. One final complication of the transition came from Major General George Thomas. Thomas served as second-in-command to Buell, and he was not at all happy with Rosecrans' assignment to command the Department of the Cumberland. Though the decision was difficult for Thomas, he accepted Halleck's explanations, remained a corps commander and would continue to be proven as one of the best commanders in the west.[1]

Rosecrans did not waste any time in accomplishing Halleck's first objective and continued the march to Nashville; his army moved south across a 70 mile front stretching from Columbia to Bowling Green, clearing Kentucky of any remaining concentrations of Confederates along the way. The advance was desperately needed in the eyes of General James Negley, commanding the Federal forces at Nashville. Alexander McCook's corps led the movement to Nashville and he received intelligence that Bragg's army was racing toward Middle Tennessee hoping to arrive there before Rosecrans.[2]

Nashville was vitally important to both opposing forces. It was the geographic center of the state and it was a major hub of transportation in Tennessee. The city was located on the Cumberland River and was the rail center for central Tennessee. The Federals saw the route to East Tennessee through Chattanooga and the railroad was the key to capturing the eastern part of the state. Rosecrans knew as long as the Confederates controlled east Tennessee, communications, supplies and cooperation between the Confederate troops in the Mid–South and Virginia were "rapid and direct." In addition, no further southward movement into the Confederate territory was practical with strong Confederate forces occupying eastern Tennessee, which threatened the rear of the Union army. In capturing Chattanooga, East Tennessee would be open to a well-supplied Union army which utilized the Nashville and Chattanooga Railroad; then, the route into Georgia would be within reach.[3]

Camp Life at Bowling Green

The attachment of the Board of Trade Battery to Dumont's infantry division was to be short-lived. As the men adjusted to the new life in camp at Bowling Green, military discipline was again imposed and the battery was reviewed by Stokes on November 3; two days later Rosecrans arrived and also reviewed the battery. The arrival of the new commanding general made a positive impression and Rosecrans told the men they should not remain with this "infantry command any longer than he could make a place for us at the front," according to Private Benjamin Nourse. This was just the news the men wanted to hear. The movement to Nashville would still be a few weeks away and in the meantime, guns number five and six fired their charges which had remained in place (resisting all efforts to clear the tubes) since the fight at Lawrenceburg on October 11. A couple of days later the battery received two visitors from Chicago who arrived by train bearing the national colors and battery standard. The company standard was yellow silk with B.T.B. embroidered on the flag.[4]

The first few months on the march had taken a toll on the new enlistees and on November 14, six men were discharged due to disability:

G. A. Cooper	W. A. Crocker	A. N. Downer
F. W. Gregory	I. A. Pease	S. T. Phillips

It is important to remember that many of the men were clerks, business men, and office workers in Chicago and the efforts of sleeping on the ground and the constant march revealed physical limitations that they may have never experienced in civilian life. Discharges due to active campaigning were common and would continue in the battery throughout the war. For those who remained with the battery, the loneliness of life on the march also crept into their thoughts. John Nourse lamented sleeping in tents in November while so many at home slept in their own beds. He wrote in his journal "Never mind—who cares for the soldier—None—No one."[5]

There were various reasons why men joined the army in the Civil War. Certainly, the issue of slavery was key in the precipitation of the conflict. For the individual, the personal reasons were often quite different. Calvin Durand eloquently wrote in a letter his reasons for joining the war: "1 really wish myself that this wicked Rebellion might soon be crushed and put down so that I could return to my kind friends again, but as much as I dislike the service, I hate Rebellion worse and desire to use the little strength I have in crushing it and it cannot be crushed any too soon for me. I believe that, although the end can be seen only through a heavy mist, that the veil will soon be lifted and that the people of this country are destined to be happier, freer and more peaceful than ever before, because it will have freedom for its foundation.... God is afflicting us sorely, but I believe only to refine us and make us purer and better as a people."[6]

Anger Between the Troops and Stokes

By mid–November a fracture in the positive relationship between the men and Captain Stokes erupted into a tense situation. Stokes, an older, West Point–trained officer, found himself at cross purposes with the men of the battery in regard to the new battery flags. On November 15, the battery had field drill which was a common practice, but resentment resulted when all the men were ordered to go and wash in the river. Benjamin Nourse recorded in his journal that the purpose of this was "to prevent Mr. Weeks and Mr. Pense from presenting the colors to the company in a formal manner." These men from Chicago arrived with the new battery flags and the difficulty apparently arose because of the name of the unit. Certainly, the name of the battery was very fluid throughout the war. Formally, the name varied from The Chicago Board of Trade Light Artillery Battery or Chicago Board of Trade Independent Battery, Light Artillery. More importantly, many early records show the battery named "Stokes' Battery" which Stokes preferred, and desired. Weeks arrived at camp with the colors and standard, causing the problem. Private John Fleming described that Stokes "utterly refused" to accept the new flags with the name as the Board of Trade Battery while the men in the camp were "crazy to have them." Weeks told Stokes that he was presenting the flags to the men even without his consent. Stokes responded by marching all the men out of camp two miles to wash so that Weeks' plan was foiled. However, Stokes' action incensed the men who considered themselves intelligent enough to stay clean and as a result the men just sat sullenly on the banks of the river. Fleming described the angry men as a "mutinous band we were threatening to throw the first man in who dared to wash himself." The men marched back to camp in a dark mood. The animosity continued the next day when some of the men of the battery left camp without permission because Stokes had arranged for a local minister to perform religious services. The men balked, declaring they left "to prevent a rebel clergyman from preaching to them," according to Nourse. Stokes, nonplussed by the action of his men, responded by tripling the guards around the camp. (In an interesting footnote to this incident, the flags were finally unveiled after the Battle of Stones River, but the reason given at that time suggested the decision rested on Buell's shoulders, who had refused to allow artillery batteries to show their own flags. This twist begs the question of whether Stokes was just following orders or whether he selfishly wanted the battery named after himself as some of the men supposed. If Stokes was following Buell's orders, he did not indicate this as a reason to the men. Either way, tension between the commanding officer and the men of the battery increased after this incident.)[7]

The next morning (November 17) Stokes, realizing that he needed to deal with the situation, called the battery together and addressed the men. He strove to keep command and he wanted to move past these problems. Benjamin Nourse recorded the address: "The capt. being very angry this a.m. and somewhat afraid of mutiny in the camp—compelled us to hitch up and marched us out on the turnpike five miles and back—but he got quite cooled off by the time of our return to camp—and he then tried (in every poor way) to show he defied us—riding up in front of us before we dismounted he told how he would cut down the first man who showed any signs of mutiny—aye, cut him down as he would cut the head off a dead goose—poor Stokes—then he more quietly said—we will begin anew—from this date—I think none will be hurt. The rations have been very short and poor—but one the sergeants going to the capt. tonight he quickly had them corrected." While the immediate situation was defused, the relationship between the men and Stokes remained strained. The battery would be shown alternately as Stokes' Battery and Chicago Board of Trade Battery in official reports through late 1863 when Stokes was promoted and left the battery. Reportedly, Stokes had been offered a rank of colonel in one of the Board of Trade infantry regiments, but decided to remain with the battery. Perhaps, he felt his efforts in training the men had earned him the recognition of Stokes' Battery.[8]

The deteriorating situation with Stokes was also reflected in John Nourse's letter to his father regarding the resignation of Lieutenant Albert Baxter, a well-liked officer, on November 18. Nourse reported that some of the men had been discharged due to disability, and Baxter had been very sick. Nourse explained that in addition to Baxter's illness, the "cap[tain] has abused him" and the combination of factors resulted in Baxter's resignation. But, not all the members of the battery felt the way Nourse did. A few days later, Private Tobias Miller wrote a letter saying the officers treated the men kindly and the experience as a soldier was pleasant. Only a few weeks before, John Fleming of gun number 6 wrote to his mother: "Our captain is just a splendid man and he is also a pious man." Stokes discussed prayer meetings with the men and told them that he prayed three times a day—morning, noon and night. Stokes, an Episcopalian, led an entire service for the men and for General Gordon Granger, who commanded the Army of Kentucky, and his staff. Fleming was well pleased with not only Stokes, he also felt Sergeant Sylvanus Stevens and lieutenants Robinson and Bennett were excellent officers. However, he described Lieutenant Albert Baxter as "not worth a gross of pins" because he was completely worn out. A surgeon's disability certificate accompanied Baxter's resignation. After these incidents, the men would never quite see Stokes in the same manner as before.[9]

Private Benjamin F. Nourse, an important author of diaries documenting his time in the battery (Chicago History Museum, ICHi-176913).

The stay in Bowling Green resulted in more training for the battery, but it left the men without a clear plan of where they would go next. The camp was near Granger's headquarters and he often invited the men to come and sing in the evening for him and his staff. While in camp, Henry Baxter, the brother of Lieutenant Alfred Baxter, was discharged due to disability (consumption) on November 3 having been "worn out and wasted by disease," wrote John Fleming. Illness was prevalent and Tobias Miller wrote that there were between 2,000 and 3,000 men sick in Bowling Green. "More than half of these are laying in churches, on the floor, but with a scanty supply of straw under them.... No wonder the dead wagon is ever moving through the streets, and that daily fourteen pass to their long home." John Nourse wrote to family and asked the question: "What is the opinion about the end of the war?" Nourse wisely wrote that it looked like they would see the entire three years of their enlistment completed before they could return home. The battery remained in Bowling Green for the rest of the month and worked on the guns and carriages, drilled, and were reviewed constantly. But there was time for enjoyment too. At Thanksgiving, the men received a hearty dinner and E.B. Stevens arrived from Chicago with a load of packages from the families at home. The battery was roused into action on November 29 when a nervous sentry fired at a noise in the night, which turned out to be a stray farm animal, and the whole battery prepared for an attack which never came. While hitching the horses in preparation to move, Private Robert Barry mistakenly put the bridle under the horse's tail rather than on its head and Private John Kennedy tried to get into the blacksmith forge for safety. Both actions brought a great deal of humor to the rest of the men.[10]

December—The March South

As the new month arrived, the battery remained firmly ensconced at Bowling Green but this was not to last long. On December 2, the battery received the transfer of a harness maker, 29-year-old James Campbell, from the 102nd Ohio Infantry. Then, the battery received orders to march to Nashville. (Corporal John Toomey recalled that the orders came as a result of Stokes wiring Rosecrans directly for permission to move on to Nashville.) The next morning, those men who had revolvers were ordered up a hill to an old fort to discharge their weapons which had not been discharged since September 20. The gunfire resulted in the arrival of an officer of the provost guard who wanted to arrest all those firing their weapons, but the intervention by Sergeant Sylvanus Stevens prevented the arrests. The provost marshal grumbled, "Them battery fellows wouldn't arrest worth a D[amn]!" The remainder of the battery repacked the caissons and limbers and prepared to start early the next morning.[11]

First Sergeant Sylvanus Harlow Stevens was born on October 26, 1827, in Livermore, Maine. The family subsequently moved to Dover, Maine, and then relocated to Adams County, Illinois. Stevens attended public school in Quincy and worked in the office of his uncle. In 1848 he worked as a clerk in the sheriff's office and became a deputy in 1849, serving until 1850. In 1852, he became a grain buyer for a Quincy business. Stevens and his wife moved to Chicago in 1856 where he formed a grain commission business, called Stevens Brothers, with his brother, Enoch. The brothers became part of the Chicago Board of Trade and in 1860, he became Chief Grain Inspector for the organization. He was instrumental in the organization of the battery and was one of the first to enlist.[12]

The men were rousted out at 4:30 a.m. on December 4 and prepared for a three-day march to Nashville. Four guns limbered and moved out of camp while a single two-gun section and supporting personnel remained in camp until a relief battery arrived to take their place. The two sections marched without escort which was a risky endeavor because unescorted guns provided an excellent target for the enemy still in the countryside. The other section remained in Bowling Green overnight and the next morning began its move to Nashville, but had a cavalry escort for about 15 miles. This section traveled 27 miles that day, ending up at Mitchellville, Tennessee, where the men found an abandoned barn to sleep in that night. The night was extremely cold and Benjamin Nourse recorded in his journal: "[W]e crawled up on the rafters and slept or tried to sleep on several boards—We almost froze—and our boots were on

Lieutenant Sylvanus S. Stevens, well-liked by Captain Stokes, but an ambitious officer (*The Descendants of Samuel Stevens*, 1968, p. 116).

our feet all night—which was well as had they been off we never could put them back on—This is the worst we have seen yet but I suppose it is as mole hill to a mountain in comparison with what we shall have to suffer before our three years run." The two parts of the battery never united on the march to Nashville, although they tried. Lieutenant George Robinson, commanding the trailing section, telegraphed ahead to Stokes, but Stokes never received the message because the two columns traveled on different roads. By December 7, the battery united in Nashville, no longer part of Dumont's division. Instead it was officially designated as part of the Pioneer Brigade commanded by Colonel James St. Clair Morton, although this practically did not take place until the last couple of days of December.[13]

Soon after the arrival in Nashville more personnel changes were made: "At dress parade we were astonished and made happy. Yes, too full for utterance by the orders read by Capt. Stokes, i.e., orderly [sergeant] Stevens made 1st Lieut.—Corp. Lester reduced in ranks—Sergt. Hand promoted to orderly Sergt.—Corpl. Jacobs to Sergt. Gale & Howard to corporals," wrote John Nourse. After dress parade and into the next day, the men prepared their tents for the cold weather. The promotion of Stevens to 1st lieutenant was pleasantly received by some of the men in the battery, but the promotion from sergeant to first lieutenant over the existing second lieutenants did not go without objection. Trumbull D. Griffin appealed to the Illinois adjutant general, Allen Fuller, about the move. Fuller graciously wrote an apologetic letter to Griffin with the reasons for the promotion, which were made at the recommendation of Stokes, explaining that Stevens was one of the originators of the battery. Fuller assured Griffin that there was nothing adverse towards him in this promotion and he spoke highly of Griffin's performance. How Griffin took this letter is not known, except that he continued to perform his duty well despite the fact that he believed Stevens received his promotion as a result of influential friends in Chicago and through the lobbying efforts of Stevens' wife in Springfield. Griffin appeared to be correct about the efforts back home because Mrs. Stevens sent a letter to Fuller thanking him for the promotion of her husband. These efforts revealed Stevens' ambitious nature, a lesson his comrades would not forget.[14]

December 14—The Second Skirmish

Over the next few days, men of the battery continued drilling and working on the various items of equipment, including oiling and repairing harnesses in preparation for action. New horses arrived on December 9–10 and Gun number 3 assembled an impressive team of all black horses. The battery changed camps a few times and on December 12 moved seven miles south through Nashville on Franklin Pike. The 15th U.S. Infantry camped near the battery, calming some nerves and providing some security for the battery. Despite officially being transferred to the Pioneer Brigade, many in the battery remained unsure of their next assignment and rumors suggested they would be assigned to Rosecrans' headquarters. The battery passed Rosecrans reviewing James Negley's division during its travels and the men remarked that the ranks of Union soldiers provided a splendid sight.[15]

Skirmishing between the opposing armies occurred throughout December, with notable actions at Hartsville, where Morgan defeated the Union forces, a Union cavalry victory at Franklin, and various clashes while the forces were on foraging missions. The battery remained inactive on December 13, but the next day at 10:30 a.m., newly promoted Lieutenant Sylvanus Stevens led a squad of men with three wagons on a foraging mission south on Franklin Pike. Stevens' detachment was just one of several parties foraging in the area. Stevens spoke with a lieutenant of another party and discovered a source of forage two miles ahead and that yet another party commanded by Colonel Joseph Scott escorted by a formidable force, 19th Illinois, 69th Ohio, and a section of the 4th Kentucky Battery, had already moved past the plantation where the forage was located. As Stevens' party arrived at a plantation, he posted Sergeant Calvin Durand as a lookout on a hill overlooking the detail. As the forage was loaded into the wagons, 20 Southern cavalrymen, armed with carbines and revolvers, attacked and surrounded the small Federal force.[16]

Calvin Durand, Quartermaster Sergeant, recalled that the Union men were armed with Springfield muskets. They had to pass through three gates to get to the corn cribs. Durand remained mounted on his horse as lookout on a hill behind the house when he heard the whiz of the first ball go past his ear. The gunfire from Confederate cavalry alerted the men with the wagons, who quickly headed for the main road. Durand spurred his horse and rode to open the gates. Everything worked well as the wagons rushed through the first two gates, but as they reached the third and last gate, one of the wagon's hubs struck the gatepost and blocked the road. The men tried to fight off the attacking cavalry but were overwhelmed. Durand and Stevens had revolvers which were quickly emptied. Stevens ordered Durand to ride to Scott's column and bring help. In the meantime, Stevens was making his escape by jumping off his horse, climbing a stone wall, and hurrying away. By this time, Durand returned with a group of 19th Illinois Infantry and saw the Confederates ride into the woods with their prisoners and a single captured wagon. A wounded private, John Carroll, was found in the house of the plantation and was moved by ambulance to the hospital while the infantry escorted the other two wagons back to the Union lines. Stevens' after-action report described; "[T]he sergeant and myself held the party at the gate with our pistols while the teams were escaping. Five privates and 1 corporal were taken prisoners; 1 private wounded in the back. This man we brought away. Five horses were captured and 2 killed. The guard under Colonel Scott with train had passed without my knowledge, leaving my party about a half mile in the rear." Stevens, Durand and two wagons along with teamsters made an escape. One final note, the Federals arrested a civilian who allegedly assisted the enemy in the attack and Negley promised to have his trial the next day.[17]

The Board of Trade Battery Casualties—December 14, 1862

John Carroll	wounded while trying to climb the wall
Homer Baker	captured
John H. Buckingham	captured
Francis Richmond	captured
John Sleman	captured
Thomas Tinsley	captured
Thomas N. Williams	captured

Private John J. Carroll exclaimed, "Let me give them just one shot" just before he was wounded (Chicago History Museum, ICHi-176921).

The battery had just received its first blooding.[18]

Sylvanus Stevens explained that as he was trying to extract his small command, he noticed that John Carroll was not with them. He turned and saw that Carroll had his musket resting on a gate, taking aim at the approaching enemy. Stevens yelled for him to withdraw but Carroll ignored the order. Stevens rode closer to him and yelled, "Johnny fall back or you will be captured sure." He replied, "Let me give them just one shot." As the riders approached, Carroll's musket fired, but only dust rose between the riders. Then, Carroll ran for the rear, only to be shot in the shoulder, near his spine, while climbing the next fence. He would survive, with the ball remaining in his shoulder, but would be discharged in November 1863.[19]

Washington Urges Rosecrans to Attack

Meanwhile at army headquarters, Rosecrans dealt with several issues. One of the most immediate was the impatience of those in Washington. As the case with many Union officers, those in Washington urged a quick and aggressive movement against the enemy. In the first few days of December Henry Halleck exchanged communications regarding Rosecrans' failure to advance against Bragg's position south of Nashville. On December 4, Halleck told Rosecrans that the President was growing impatient with Rosecrans' delay in moving forward. Those in Washington worried that the winter weather would make any campaigning impossible and six months would be lost. Halleck wrote: "You give Bragg time to supply himself by plundering the very country your army should have occupied.... Twice have I been asked to designate someone else to command your army. If you remain one more week at Nashville, I cannot prevent your removal." The threat in Halleck's message was clear to Rosecrans, who had commanded the Army of Cumberland for about a month, but Rosecrans was not ready to move and told Halleck so. Rosecrans replied: "In front, because of greater obstacles, enemies in greater force, and fighting with better chances of escaping pursuit, if overthrown in battle. In rear, because of insufficiency and uncertainty of supplies, both of subsistence and ammunition, and no security of any kind to fall back upon in case of disaster.... Many of our soldiers are to this day barefoot, without blankets, without tents, without good arms, and cavalry without horses. Our true objective now is the enemy's force. If the Government which ordered me here confides in my judgment, it may rely on my continuing to do what I have been trying to—that is, my whole duty. If my superiors have lost confidence in me, they had better at once put someone in my place and let the future test the propriety of the change. I have but one word to add, which is, that I need no other stimulus to make me do my duty than the knowledge of what it is. To threats of removal or the like I must be permitted to say that I am insensible."[20]

Halleck explained that Lincoln felt only Tennessee could be seen as a Confederate success over the past year, and this Confederate progress could be used as an argument to draw England into the war on the side of the South. Washington saw the action, or rather inaction, on the part of Rosecrans as having "an importance beyond mere military success." Halleck mollified Rosecrans by explaining that those in Washington wanted nothing but success for Rosecrans, and he reminded him that Washington had little doubt that Buell would have eventually defeated Bragg, only he was too slow in achieving this objective. While the communications flowed between Tennessee and Washington, Rosecrans continued moving his forces to Nashville. Alexander McCook and Thomas Crittenden formed the front lines of the Army of the Cumberland at Nashville and Thomas's trailing center wing continued to march southward. Rosecrans still awaited trailing infantry, ammunition and artillery. He felt his rations and proper arms for the soldiers were still deficient.[21]

The Board of Trade Battery was officially shown as part of the Pioneer Brigade from November 1862, but the battery acted independently until December 28 when it was actually attached to the Pioneer Brigade. From December 14 until December 25, the men performed routine camp activities—drill, cleaning, foraging, and inspections. On December 21, the battery seemed to fall under the direct command of James Negley who held the unit at his headquarters. Negley commanded a division in Thomas' infantry corps, named the center wing. Also, during this time news about Burnside's defeat at

Fredericksburg reached the men north of Murfreesboro. In light of this defeat, the Union forces needed a victory in Tennessee. One unfortunate event occurred during this period. John Nourse explained that Private William N. Bagley "went to the caisson to get something, he very carelessly took a musket off the limber and holding it by the muzzle set it down and in so doing struck the hammer against the coupling of the carriage discharging the musket and sending the ball through his wrist." This proved to be a fatal wound due to the medical conditions of the time and Bagley died in Cincinnati in February 1863. Meanwhile, the battery remained active south of Nashville. In one case, after being sent in support of the foraging expeditions, the enemy was gone upon the battery's arrival. Benjamin Nourse wrote in his journal an ominous line on December 24: "It seems as though the battery was destined never to see an armed reb." Nourse just violated the old adage "be careful what you wish for."[22]

On the same day as Nourse's journal entry, Rosecrans began moving his wings into position for an advance on the Confederate army at Murfreesboro. Delays prevented the advance until December 26, but initial moves revealed a strong Confederate cavalry force, John Wharton's, at Franklin and Triune, and the majority of Joseph Wheeler's cavalry near Stewarts Creek. The initial movements on December 24 found that the Confederate defenders withdrew rather than contest the advance. However, Negley reported skirmishes with the Southern mounted forces: "Rebel cavalry quite numerous and impudent." On December 26, Rosecrans' army of 43,000 began its advance in earnest against Bragg's army of 37,000.[23]

Chicago Board of Trade Battery—Strength*[24]

Present for Duty	Officers	Men	Total
Chicago Battery, Capt. J.H. Stokes	5	128	133

*(aggregate both present and absent—147)

Murfreesboro, located about thirty miles southeast of Nashville, is situated in a large, fertile plain that extends from Nashville to the Cumberland Mountains. The nature of the plain and rolling hills made the area an important center of agriculture. The west fork of Stones River, a tributary of the Cumberland River, ran just west and north of the town and provided little difficulty for infantry seeking to cross. At the fords, the water was very shallow, and only heavy rainfall made the stream an obstacle. The area north and west of Murfreesboro was scattered with cultivated fields, limestone outcrops, cedar breaks, and woods in the slightly rolling, almost flat, terrain. The Nashville & Chattanooga Railroad ran through Murfreesboro and provided an important transportation link between Nashville and points east.[25]

The skies on December 26 were dark and ominous as the Union army began its advance and the rain fell "in torrents during the entire morning." Rosecrans determined Leonidas Polk's and E. Kirby Smith's (now only a single division) forces held the line at Murfreesboro, and William Hardee's troops were concentrated to the west between Triune and Eagleville, on the Shelbyville and Nolensville Pike with an advance guard at Nolensville. His strategy was to press Hardee with Alexander McCook's corps moving in the center of Rosecrans' army with three divisions, while Thomas advanced on his right (west) with Negley's and Rousseau's divisions. Crittenden's three divisions moved directly toward Murfreesboro on the left flank. McCook planned to attack Hardee at Triune and if Bragg moved to support Hardee, then Thomas would join the Union attack. If McCook successfully defeated Hardee, or if Hardee retreated, and Bragg held his line north of Murfreesboro then Crittenden would attack, supported by Thomas and then McCook, while holding Hardee in place, would swing the remainder of his wing into Polk's rear. If Hardee moved to join Bragg and Polk at Murfreesboro, then Rosecrans would concentrate his army to oppose Bragg's entire force.[26]

McCook's infantry ran into Wharton's Confederate cavalry after marching two miles and the Southern cavalrymen resisted the Federal advance throughout the day. On the left (east) flank, Crittenden began his march toward La Vergne on the morning of December 26. Three regiments of cavalry in Robert Minty's cavalry brigade succeeded in reaching the front of Crittenden's wing and screened the Union advance. There was reason to suspect this would be the most difficult movement of the day. Crittenden's wing moved directly toward the concentration of Bragg's army at Murfreesboro by the most direct route. Wheeler's cavalry was based at Stewarts Creek, a few miles south of La Vergne. Also, Brigadier General George Maney's brigade of Tennessee infantry held a position north of Stewarts Creek. As the day developed, General Leonidas Polk concluded that Crittenden was moving in force and he also heard the noise of battle along McCook's advance to the west. Polk ordered Maney and Wheeler to delay the Union forces while Bragg determined what reaction he would make. Wheeler alerted Bragg to the Union movements and sent orders to his cavalry commanders, Brigadier General John Pegram and Brigadier General Wharton, to prepare for a general Union advance.[27]

By the end of the first day of the advance toward Murfreesboro, Wheeler had fallen back about three miles, Crittenden's corps moved just north of La Vergne, and McCook pushed beyond Nolensville. The stiff resistance by the Southern cavalry had accomplished its objective—the prevention of a rapid penetration of the Confederate line granting time for the infantry to prepare a defense. Bragg was still unsure of Rosecrans' intent. If Rosecrans wanted to develop the Confederate position, this could just be a bluff and Rosecrans could easily return to Nashville during the night. However, the extent of the advance had gained the attention of the Southern commanders and the next day would be critical in determining Rosecrans' plan.

On the Union side of the line, the day proceeded pretty much as expected. Crittenden had reached La Vergne. Thomas Wood, commanding the Left Wing First Division, described the terrain: "The country occupied by these bodies of hostile troops affords ground peculiarly favorable for a small force to retard the advance of a larger one. Large cultivated fields occur at intervals on either side of the turnpike road, but the country between the cultivated tracts is densely wooded, and much of the woodland interspersed with thick groves of cedar. The face of the country is undulating, presenting a succession of swells and subsidences." On the evening of December 26, Rosecrans directed McCook to continue his advance the next day to Triune and attack Hardee's infantry. This was the key to Rosecrans' plan and Hardee's response would determine Rosecrans' next action. Thomas' two divisions also moved ahead. Rousseau still held the Union right flank and Negley's division pushed ahead toward Nolensville in support of McCook. On the Union left flank, the bridge over Stewarts Creek, if it could be captured intact, would allow Crittenden's march toward Murfreesboro to go faster. As Rosecrans left McCook's headquarters, McCook said, "Good night, General … with the blessing of God, General, I will whip my friend Hardee tomorrow!"[28]

The Board of Trade Battery

For the Chicago Board of Trade Battery, marching orders for the advance on Murfreesboro arrived on the evening of December 24, but the order was rescinded. On Christmas Day, the men again did mundane tasks and received updated orders that evening to begin marching the next day. In a humorous account, Benjamin Nourse described his experiences of trying to cook and wash for the first time: "Nothing unusual in the camp to day except that I cooked a pan of baked beans. My second attempt to cook any thing to eat…. This mess I first boiled our beans, then put them in a thin iron pan, covered with a piece of tin, dug a hole in the hot sand and sank the pan, covering the top with hot coals, when they came out they were good—In the afternoon I boiled my clothes and crowded too many in the sheet iron kettle and when they came out where ever the cloth touched the iron the blue was yellow and to cap all—I did not rinse them but hung them up to dry full of strong soap suds—(you may imagine their condition when I next put them on)…. I wonder where I shall be next Christmas."[29]

The weather had been pleasant but when the advance began on December 26, so did the rain. The Board of Trade Battery began its advance as part of Negley's division of Thomas's wing at about 9 o'clock. At this point, the men of the battery considered themselves an independent, non-brigaded unit attached to Negley's headquarters. By the time the movement began most of the troops in the vicinity had already moved south as part of the general movement toward Bragg's troops. The battery began marching southward on Franklin Pike, moved east to reach Murfreesboro Pike, and then moved a few miles south. The pike was clogged with troops of Crittenden's wing; the battery halted and allowed the infantry and supply trains to pass. The movement that day was a frustrating process and Benjamin Nourse recorded: "We moved a short distance & halt, another short move, and halt. Move again and halt, ½ a mile, ¼ of a mile, a rod at a time, very tedious, I assure you." While waiting in the afternoon, Rosecrans, his staff, and his headquarters escort, the 4th U.S. Cavalry, rode past providing a grand display for the men of the battery. At the front, Crittenden's infantry and Minty's cavalry brigade sparred with the Confederates throughout the day. The slow advance continued until 11 p.m. when the battery pulled off the road to camp for the night. The rain made conditions so bad that the artillerymen could find little comfort. Nourse recorded: "yes—we camp, or rather stand ourselves on end in the mud for if we laid ourselves down, we never should get up. We unhitched and unharnessed, throwing the harness up on the limbers and wheels— then it took two hours to bring rails enough to make a platform to build a fire up out of the mud—said mud being actually up to the tops of our boots—it held up raining long enough to boil our coffee but just, as we got it down came the rain again—I wish you at home could see us, as we stood stuck fast in the mud with a cup of hot coffee in one hand (just as we would raise the cup, a drop of rain would strike it sending the liquid into the face to bring a blister), a wet cracker in the other." The men found little rest with the muddy, wet conditions and the supply trains and trailing soldiers marched past throughout the night. At the end of the day, the battery had moved 11 miles in 12 hours.[30]

At Murfreesboro, Bragg and his top-ranking officers were still unsure whether the action during the day was just a feint or whether it marked a general advance, but those troopers facing Crittenden's soldiers had no doubt what was happening. George Knox Miller, 8th Confederate Cavalry, was convinced it was a serious situation. "It took no ghost to us that Rosencranz had begun his long expected advance from Nashville, and what confirmed it, we could distinctly hear heavy cannonading all day to our left on the Nolensville pike, showing that he was advancing with a heavy column on each road." Miller's men withdrew after determining the size of the Union force. At Confederate headquarters, Bragg met with his commanders and decided to pull Hardee closer to Murfreesboro. He asked Wheeler how long he could delay Rosecrans' advance and Wheeler responded two to four days, depending on the source. Wheeler's plan brought good news to Bragg. It gave him time to determine the Union actions the following day and also time to concentrate his army to face a determined advance, if it really was one. So, Wheeler's cavalry moved to absorb the blows while punishing the Union soldiers who slowly moved south. William Hardee, like Rosecrans, had ridden to the front to determine the opposing force he faced. In light of the large Union force, Pat Cleburne's infantry, facing McCook south of Nolensville, was ordered to move to Murfreesboro. Although Cleburne would not receive his orders to move until early the next morning, S.A.M. Wood's infantry and John Wharton's cavalry were ordered to delay the Union advance at Triune. Isaac Barton Ulmer, 3rd Confederate Cavalry, wrote a letter during the evening: "Firing has been very severe on both the Murfreesboro and Nolensville Pikes all day. The Yankees may have commenced their forward movement. Tomorrow I suppose will decide."[31]

The Advance on Murfreesboro—December 27–28, 1862

The next day, Rosecrans continued his advance across a broad front. The mud, knee deep in places, made marching difficult. The Board of Trade Battery hitched up at 8:00 a.m., but did not move until mid-afternoon. The men stood by their horses anticipating the orders to move out at any time until "we looked like so many drowned rats." The orders never came and at 4:00 p.m. the carriages and guns were unhitched, but the horses remained harnessed. Fortunately, the rain ceased and the men pitched their tents and had a good night's sleep.[32]

In contrast, the rest of Rosecrans' army had a busy day. Cleburne's division, McCook's target, hastily began a march of its own toward Murfreesboro under orders from Hardee, who was convinced after his late-night reconnaissance that a general Federal advance was taking place. S.A.M. Wood and John Wharton skirmished throughout the day. Crittenden's wing pushed forward and the Union general felt he needed support on his right flank. As McCook and Thomas began their movements during the day, Crittenden remained idle awaiting support to arrive on his flank while his immediate objective was to get his wing over Stewarts Creek, which promised to be a cold, wet process. Crittenden sent a brigade east on Jefferson Pike to attempt to capture a bridge over the creek, which his scouts reported was defended by a relatively small number of cavalry. Negley's division of Thomas' wing was still moving from the west to cover Crittenden's right flank, but McCook was still fifteen miles away. As Crittenden waited, cannon fire was heard from the west. McCook was moving.[33]

In the meantime, Crittenden sent Thomas Wood's infantry ahead hoping to secure the bridge over Stewarts Creek along the Murfreesboro Pike. Wood determined the terrain in front of his division to be unsuitable for cavalry, so, he dispatched the cavalry to the rear and advanced with his infantry. Milo Hascall's infantry brigade took the lead, flanked by Wagner's and Harker's brigades on either side of the road. Hascall's attack pushed the defenders out of La Vergne, Wood's first objective, and then moved to secure a crossing over Stewarts Creek, Wood's second objective. In a steady, drenching rain, Wood's division rushed ahead with such vigor that the defenders "could not materially

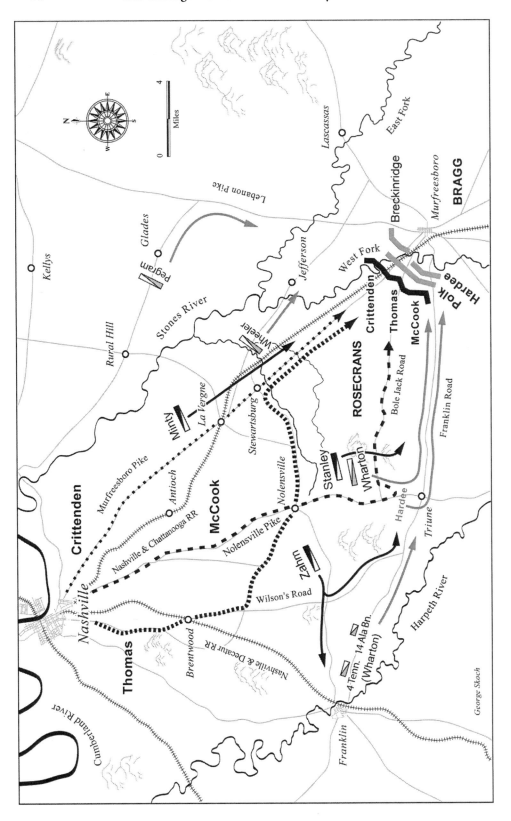

The march on Murfreesboro, December 26–30, 1862.

retard the advance." Wood repulsed a counter attack and claimed the bridge. In a similar clash, the 4th Michigan Cavalry secured a bridge on Jefferson Pike to the east.[34]

During the evening of December 27, the rain finally stopped and the weather turned cold. At 6:00 p.m., James Negley's division reached the right of Crittenden's wing after a long day marching over muddy roads. The remainder of Thomas's wing remained near Nolensville during the evening, but Thomas planned to march to join Crittenden the next day, taking up position as the center wing of Rosecrans' army. The Federal cavalry, in cooperation with Thomas, maintained a close eye on the Confederate cavalry at Franklin and patrolled Wilson Pike. On the Southern side of Stones River, Bragg determined the Union advance proved to be real and began to pull his army together at Murfreesboro. Bragg sent orders to Wheeler to attack the rear of Rosecrans' army, destroying his supply trains in the process. So, the decision had been made and the fight would take place at Murfreesboro.[35]

The morning of December 28 found Crittenden's wing firmly in control of the crossings on Stewarts Creek. Benjamin Nourse wrote in his journal: "Things look well this morning especially the weather. It has cleared off pleasant." In addition to the bridge captured at Jefferson the day before, fords, although poor ones, and two other bridges nearby were available for use by the Federal infantry, if needed. Importantly, William Hazen's infantry found there were no enemy troops south of his position along Jefferson Pike. To the west, Alexander McCook also awoke and found the enemy in front of his wing was gone. Despite the removal of the enemy, McCook still faced poor conditions in which to march. David Stanley had his cavalry up early, screening the front of McCook's infantry. McCook concluded, through the efforts of August Willich's infantry and Robert Klein's 3rd Indiana Cavalry, Hardee's route of retreat was not south, but east to Murfreesboro.[36]

Rosecrans accomplished what he desired during the first days of his advance. He wanted to know if Bragg would retreat southward, or concentrate his army and contest Rosecrans. It was the latter, and Bragg appeared to choose Murfreesboro as the location to fight. In addition, Federal scouts determined that more Southern units had been ordered up to Murfreesboro. Rosecrans concluded: "Everything indicates a determination to fight us." McCook turned east, pushing all resistance aside on his way to Murfreesboro starting early on December 28, despite Rosecrans' inclination not to move his army on the Sabbath. The wings were still too disconnected to suit McCook and he decided to march on Sunday, closing up on Thomas's right flank. McCook knew his march threatened Bragg's flank and expected stiff resistance during the day.[37]

The men of the Chicago Board of Trade Battery dried their blankets in a rather uneventful day. Importantly, the battery joined the Pioneer Brigade for the first time. They cleaned their equipment and horses and awaited new orders. About 1:00 p.m., Rosecrans and staff rode past the battery which signaled time to start marching again. "[W]e immediately struck tents and moved out on the road one mile and halted—moved again and turned into camp on the right of the road one mile south of La Vergne, a good camp, ground high and dry."[38]

Pioneer Brigade

Captain James St. C. Morton

1st Battalion, Capt. Lyman Bridges

2nd Battalion, Capt. Calvin Hood

3rd Battalion, Capt. Robert Clements

Illinois Light Artillery, Stokes' Battery, Capt. James H. Stokes[39]

Meanwhile, Thomas also continued his march toward Murfreesboro on Sunday. At noon on December 28, Lieutenant Colonel Julius Gareché, Rosecrans chief of staff, wrote to hurry Thomas forward. Gareché emphasized that Bragg showed "a stubborn determination on the part of the enemy to fight this side of Murfreesborough ... close in upon them as rapidly as possible ... you must lose no time." Gareché, a West Point graduate, class of 1841, was Rosecrans' very efficient chief of staff. Bragg did not exhibit any reluctance of moving his troops on Sunday as his troops were ordered to move to their assigned positions. At 9:00 p.m. on December 27, Bragg sent orders directing Wheeler, Wharton and Pegram (Confederate cavalry brigade commanders) to "fall back before the enemy tomorrow. The move of the enemy is evidently on this place." He ordered Hardee's corps into position on the right of Murfreesboro with his left on the Nashville Pike. Breckinridge's division formed the first battle line and Cleburne's division fell 800–1,000 yards behind him. Leonidas Polk's corps formed on the left of Hardee with Jones Withers' division in the forward position, while Benjamin Cheatham occupied the second battle line. McCown's division served as the reserve. Bragg ordered all the troops to be in position to meet the Federals at 9:00 a.m. the next morning. At 10:00 a.m., Bragg had time to prepare and confidently wrote: "Enemy stationary, 10 miles in our front. My troops all ready and confident."[40]

The Advance on Murfreesboro—December 29–30, 1862

Captain James St. Clair Morton commanded the Pioneer Brigade and the battery at the Battle of Stones River (John Fitch, *Annals of the Army of the Cumberland*, 1864).

The Board of Trade Battery was up early and at 7:00 a.m. moved about three miles southward "to the front" and halted at 3:00 p.m. The men kept a close eye on their new commanding officer, Captain James St. Clair Morton, who was in charge of the Pioneer Brigade. Morton, a West Point graduate, class of 1851, had served as an engineer in the regular army since his graduation until he gained command of the Pioneer Brigade in early November. Morton positioned the battery along the Murfreesboro Road near Stewart's Creek. He placed Lieutenant Sylvanus Stevens with one section to the right of the road and the other four guns were placed on the left of the road. Then, he ordered each of his battalions to begin constructing bridges. Even though Crittenden had successfully captured bridges over the creek, the commanding generals felt the primary bridge over the creek would be unable to handle the flow of men if a retreat was necessary.

The Pioneer Brigade tore down a large barn and began their construction duties at 4:00 p.m., planning to work throughout the night. In the meantime, the artillerymen provided security at the road. With the Federal army pushing south the area was fairly secure, leaving an opportunity for some of the men to begin foraging. The men were unaccustomed to night foraging and soon found success at a plantation owned by a member of the Confederate army, now some seven miles south at Murfreesboro. The men found fodder for the animals and food for themselves, including, "ham, eggs, butter, bread, meal and milk … and after dark six of us went off into a pasture and caught and killed six sheep, large, fat ones, brought them into camp and we shall have fresh mutton for a week if this cool weather continues." This food would be important in the days to come.[41]

Crittenden's wing started its advance at 10:00 a.m., expecting to find stiff resistance after a series of enemy troop movements and signals had been observed during the night. Instead, Crittenden found only Wheeler's cavalry resisting the movement. Negley's division joined the right flank of Crittenden's wing about 3:00 p.m., finally linking Crittenden with Thomas' wing. An hour later, Crittenden's march was over. Three-quarters of a mile north of Murfreesboro, Crittenden observed Bragg's infantry in plain view in battle line and had no option but to halt. In response, Crittenden's troops formed a double battle line and then refused his vulnerable left flank. Thomas ordered Rousseau's division to Jefferson to bolster that flank. McCook's wing remained separated, but it marched down Wilkinson Pike and at the end of the day it would be only three miles away from Murfreesboro. Meanwhile, Bragg waited and watched the dispositions of the various Union forces and concluded to draw Rosecrans into a fight on his chosen ground. Bragg pulled his infantry closer to Murfreesboro while his cavalry slackened its resistance, allowing Rosecrans to develop his line. Bragg's only real questions were where Rosecrans would place his strength and when he would attack. The next day these questions would be answered.[42]

McCook's wing pushed forward on December 30 and approached Bragg's army, but the Southern resistance stiffened as McCook reached Hardee's main line of infantry on the western flank. In the late afternoon, Stanley's cavalry probed the Confederate line accompanied by Colonel Philemon Baldwin's infantry brigade from Brigadier General Richard Johnson's division. As the combined Union line advanced, the Southern defenders fell into a battle line and prepared to resist the attack. Again, a heated skirmish lasted for about thirty minutes but Stanley and Johnson decided to withdraw.[43]

The Board of Trade Battery also moved forward and took a position on the eastern side of Crittenden's line but the advance did not go smoothly. An orderly arrived and guided the battery to its assigned campground, but the man led the battery about a quarter mile past the Union lines. A vulnerable unescorted battery provided an excellent target for the enemy. The men were alarmed as they looked ahead and clearly saw lines of Confederate soldiers. The battery immediately reversed its direction and safely made it back through the Federal lines, camping in a large bend of Stones River about three miles north of Murfreesboro near McFadden's and Hoover's Fords. Once in proper position, the men began throwing up log breastworks around the guns. As they worked, the sounds of skirmishing echoed across the fields throughout the day. As the day ended, the men used pine boughs for their beds and sang songs until taps was sounded. The men slept near their guns.[44]

December 30 would prove to be an important day because the two armies had finally reached as far as they could go without initiating a battle. Both opposing commanding generals decided to attack early the next morning. Rosecrans met with his generals on the evening of December 30 and laid out a plan for battle the next morning. McCook's wing would hold its position, securing the western flank while Thomas' corps and Palmer's division of Crittenden's wing were ordered to begin skirmishing and occupy the center of Bragg's army. Crittenden would move Van Cleve's division, followed by Wood's, across the river and attack Breckinridge's division on the eastern flank. Once these two Union divisions dislodged Breckinridge, Rosecrans explained that batteries would be placed on the heights on the Union left which "would see the enemy's works in reverse, would dislodge them, and enable Palmer's division to press them back, and drive them westward across the river or through the woods, while Thomas, sustaining the movement on the center, would advance on the right of Palmer, crushing their right, and Crittenden's corps, advancing, would take Murfreesborough, and then, moving westward on the Franklin road, get in their flank and rear and drive them into the country toward Salem, with the prospect of cutting off their retreat and probably destroying their army." Importantly, the planned main thrust of the Union attack was directly in front of the Board of Trade Battery. If Rosecrans' plan worked as he had hoped, the battery would have plenty of action the next day. The battery, securely behind breastworks, directed the muzzles of the six guns in the direction of Breckinridge's division.[45]

Two parallel battle lines faced each other over a three-mile-long line running roughly northeast to southwest. The east flank extended past Stones River to Lebanon Pike and the western line extended south of Franklin Pike. Willich's brigade of McCook's corps was refused and positioned roughly perpendicular to the main battle line. McCook's troops occupied a wooded, slight ridge with open ground in front. About 400 yards away lay Hardee's troops positioned in a wooded area behind rough breastworks. The center was located along Nashville Pike and Breckinridge's large division covered the Confederate eastern flank. While the Union army settled in for the night, the report that General Joseph Wheeler had caused havoc to Union supply trains by moving along the rear of the Union army resulted in more action on the part of the Federal cavalry, which went in search of the Confederate raiders. Overall, Rosecrans had built a reasonable plan, if the situation remained static for another eight hours. Rosecrans felt his plan gave a vastly superior force on the eastern end of the line which would turn Bragg's flank. All that was needed was for McCook to hold his position for three hours as the battle unfolded.[46]

On the Confederate side of the field, Bragg's army also prepared for the battle, but not all in the Confederate army were pleased with Bragg's selection of position for the battle. William Hardee acknowledged that the open terrain allowed for the advantageous use of artillery, but wrote the field "offered no peculiar advantage for defence." Bragg felt because his 37,000 men faced 60,000 Union soldiers, certainly a strong defensive position was needed. Key to Bragg's decision to fight at this location was the fact that Murfreesboro was his supply center and that part of Middle Tennessee provided the food and support for his army. By defending Murfreesboro, the Confederate army also controlled most of the roads in the area which converged on the town. The Southern defense was developed along Stones River. Breckinridge's division was placed in an advantageous position to provide artillery support to Polk's flank, and Breckinridge had placed a concentration of Confederate artillery on Wayne's Hill, a few hundred yards in advance of the Confederate line on the eastern flank. Breckinridge had one brigade entrenched there and the remainder of his division was a half mile to the rear. But the decision had been made and the ground chosen. They would fight where they were.[47]

Bragg identified the weakest part of the Union line to be McCook's wing for his attack. Rosecrans was also concerned about McCook and the success of Rosecrans' plan called for McCook to hold or slowly withdraw under a determined Confederate attack. In return, Bragg planned to capitalize on this weakness by making his attack on McCook an "unequal contest." That evening, it appeared to the Southern general that McCook's line was attempting to extend past the Confederate left flank. Because of this, Bragg finalized his plan of attack and shifted his forces. On the same morning the Union attack was planned, Bragg planned to attack McCook's flank with Hardee's Corps, led by McCown's division and followed by Cleburne's division. Bragg planned: "These dispositions completed, Lieutenant-General Hardee was ordered to assail the enemy at daylight on Wednesday, the 31st, the attack to be taken up by Lieutenant-General Polk's command in succession to the right flank, the move to be made by a constant wheel to the right, on Polk's right flank as a pivot, the object being to force the enemy back on Stone's River, and, if practicable, by the aid of the cavalry, cut him off from his base of operations and supplies by the Nashville pike. The lines were now bivouacked at a distance in places of not more than 500 yards, the camp-fires of the two being within distinct view."[48]

The Battle of Stones River—December 31, 1862

As Bragg contemplated his situation, Leonidas Polk suggested the plan that would be implemented by the Army of Tennessee—with Cleburne and McCown in position and overlapping McCook's wing, the attack would be made on the western flank. Hardee would strike the vulnerable end of McCook's line of infantry and then wheel to the right and while pushing forward, Wharton's cavalry would swing to the rear of the Union army, and Polk would attack the center of Rosecrans' line. While the plan seemed simple enough in concept, the broken terrain interspersed with cedar thickets, woods, and rocks concerned the Southern officers. After the meeting, Hardee positioned his infantry throughout the night for early attack on December 31. Under the cover of darkness, Hardee placed McCown's division facing Jefferson C. Davis's and Richard Johnson's Union divisions, about 500 yards away with Pat Cleburne's division behind McCown.[49]

While the Confederate infantry quietly moved into position, Rosecrans prepared his own troops for Crittenden's attack scheduled for 8:00 the next morning. The previous evening Rosecrans met with Alexander McCook to ensure he understood the necessity of holding his position for three hours during the initial attack and gave him authority to adjust his lines if he felt he needed to. In the early morning hours, Brigadier General Joshua Sill rode to his commanding officer Phil Sheridan's tent at 2:00 a.m. and explained he heard troops moving along the Union right flank. Sheridan rode to investigate and confirmed the sounds and both generals rode to McCook's tent with the news. McCook "dismissed their concerns on the grounds that Crittenden's early morning attack would put a swift end to any Confederate designs against the Union right." As dawn approached, Major General John P. McCown and Major General Patrick Cleburne reported to Hardee's headquarters for their final orders. The Union line was about 500–800 yards ahead of the newly arranged Southern line and the final order was given to begin the attack at 6:00 a.m. The two generals rode back to their commands and the long lines of gray infantry slowly began to march forward. John Wharton began his cavalry movement along the west flank of the Southern infantry at the same time.[50]

The Battle of Stones River had begun.

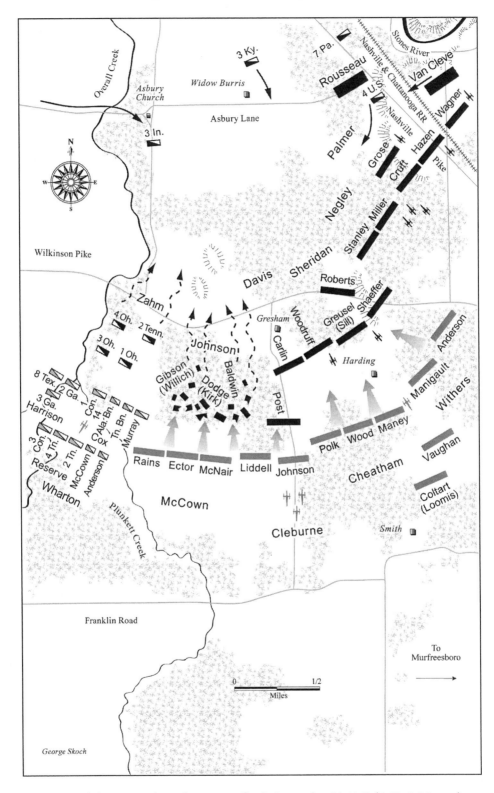

The Confederate attack on the western flank, December 31, 1862 (6:00–9:00 a.m.).

The Attack Begins (6:22–9:00 a.m.)

While the Army of the Cumberland also prepared to attack, Bragg won the race and Hardee's infantry moved swiftly and effectively. Brigadier General August Willich, First Brigade of Richard Johnson's division, held the far right of the Union infantry line. Willich positioned his infantry along the east-west Franklin Road with Gresham Lane running perpendicular through his command. Next in line, and to the east, was Brigadier General Edward Kirk's Second Brigade, and Colonel Philemon Baldwin's Third Brigade held its position as the reserve, about a half mile to the rear on the edge of a wooded area, facing south across a large cornfield behind Johnson's other two brigades. To the east of Johnson's division was Jefferson C. Davis's division—P. Sidney Post's, William Carlin's and William Woodruff's brigades, from west to east. Johnson's and Davis' divisions, were positioned to receive the full force of Bragg's attack that morning. Phil Sheridan's division held the next position in line to the east of Davis. Negley's, Palmer's and Wood's divisions extended from Sheridan to Stones River to the east.[51]

The noise the Union sentries heard in the early morning hours came as McCown and Cleburne moved their divisions forward. Now, they attacked with the full might of their infantry first on Willich's and Kirk's brigades and then planned to pivot to the right after gaining the flank and rear of McCook's corps. McCown led the attack with James Rains', Mathew D. Ector's, and Evander McNair's brigades (brigades which the Chicago Board of Trade Battery would face later in the day) from west to east. Cleburne followed with Lucius E. Polk's, St. John R. Liddell's, and Bushrod Johnson's brigades. The Confederate lines emerged from the fog and the trees, and quietly made a steady advance on McCook's brigades. At 200 yards distance, the Union artillery opened up on McCown's advancing Confederates; McCown ordered his men to double-quick march and slammed into Willich's troops as they hastily prepared for the attack. The Southern cavalry was concealed in a large wooded area in preparation for the attack and as the infantry surged forward, Wharton's cavalry brigade swept along the western flank of Hardee's infantry.[52]

The early morning attack swept away the forward Federal infantry. At 7:30 a.m. St. John Liddell's and Evander McNair's Confederate infantry brigades reached Philemon Baldwin's Union reserve brigade which had been positioned in the rear of Richard Johnson's other troops. At the same time, Bushrod Johnson's brigade converged on P. Sidney Post's troops, the next brigade still in McCook's original line established the evening before. After a thirty-minute bloody fight, both Union brigades collapsed adding to the confused mass of blue-coated soldiers running for safety. The cavalry and infantry moved along the flanks of the regiments which gave way. Mathew Askew, 1st Ohio Infantry, observed Confederate infantry "marching up 4 regements deep in front of us and the Texes Raingers on our flank, bad for all the roring of musketry and artilery it beat all. I bellive it was about 8 oclock in the morning, the calvery run over me. I was knocked down and taken prisnar." Alexis Cope, 15th Ohio, wrote that he was enjoying a hot cup of coffee when "blowing our coffee cool enough to drink, suddenly came the sharp zt, zt of bullets." The bullets startled the men into action and they observed the enemy advancing along their flank and even reaching their rear. Then the soldiers broke for the rear to evade capture.[53]

To the east of Johnson's division, Hardee directed his infantry toward Jefferson C. Davis's division, in particular, P. Sidney Post's brigade of Indiana and Illinois infantry which began the morning facing the southeast. Post's soldiers heard the battle begin before they saw any enemies, and his right flank extended into a "dense and almost impenetrable thicket of cedars" as it connected with Kirk's infantry. Then, the lines of gray rushed Post's position and Pinney's 5th Wisconsin Artillery exploded in a barrage with solid shot and shifted to canister as the Confederates got nearer. The infantry and artillery fired into the attacking line which wavered, rallied and again advanced. The battled raged for thirty minutes when Post saw the enemy in his rear and realized he could not hold the position without being captured. The 5th Wisconsin Artillery had paid a terrible price for its efforts so far. Captain Pinney was mortally wounded, eighteen of the battery horses were shot, and one gun had to be abandoned as Post ordered the battery to withdraw. Post's infantry and artillery fell back as the Confederate line overwhelmed his brigade, capturing large numbers of prisoners.[54]

Captain William Henry Harder, 23rd Tennessee Infantry, in Bushrod Johnson's brigade recorded: "There was no halt. Yet our center moved steadily under the terrible fire from two batteries and the infantry in front. The 23rd found herself under scarcely any fire as the near approach to the low ridge covered it front. I charged my company first to the right and poured a steady, and incessant fire on the stone fence ... and the nearest battery, which was silenced, our fire covered the right flank of the Federal center sweeping the whole line.... We ... advanced rapidly to find the federal[s] that faced us in full retreat, scarcely firing a shot at us." John Routt, 44th Tennessee Infantry, described the battle: "[M]en engaged in deadly conflict and heard sharp cracking of small arms and the dreadful booming of cannon and the loud bursting of shells and the rattling of fragments as they went tearing and whizzing through the air and timber."[55]

As the Confederates successfully crushed the Union western flank, the entire Confederate army joined the fight. Polk advanced his corps in the center and Withers' and Cheatham's Confederates attacked Sheridan's division about 7:30 a.m. The enemy forced Sheridan slowly northward until his left flank connected with Negley's right in a rough area of cedars and rocky outcroppings. Sheridan and Negley, showing great resolve, held the enemy at this location, and Lovell Rousseau moved his division from his reserve position to support Sheridan's and Negley's flanks, strengthening the Federal line. The two opposing lines fought savagely for an hour, resulting in the name "Slaughter Pen" for the area of the most heated fighting. Rousseau's units on the right of Sheridan were battered as they tried to hold the flank which had collapsed, but it was forced rearward and Hardee, making his pivot to the east, drove toward Nashville Pike. Samuel Beatty's brigade provided stout resistance along that flank for a time but it was also forced back. With the continued collapse of the right flank, Sheridan and Negley had to withdraw rearward or be encircled. At 11:00 the withdrawing Federal units rallied along the Nashville Pike. Rosecrans worked desperately to reposition his forces and his presence enabled many of the routed troops to reorganize along the pike. The next critical fight promised to be a bloody affair and the Union troops dug in, but both Hardee's and Polk's corps jointly focused on driving the soldiers in blue from the field. Rosecrans needed to bolster his line and importantly, the Confederate attack was driving into the center of his new line along the Nashville Pike. He scrambled to strengthen this line. At mid-morning, the Pioneer Brigade, which had been ordered to support the center, reached its position in the maelstrom and held a critical position between the railroad and Nashville Pike. If the enemy could continue the morning's successes, then all would be lost for Rosecrans.

The Battery to the Center at the Railroad (6:00–10:00 a.m.)

"Long to be remembered, this day," wrote Benjamin Nourse in his diary.

On the eastern flank and near McFadden's Ford, the men of the battery were up early and with the muzzles of the guns pointing southeast, the battery was in proper position to support the planned Union attack on Breckinridge's Division. At 7:00 a.m. the tenacious, bespectacled Brigadier General Horatio Van Cleve received his orders and advanced his 3,800 man-division across Stones River in preparation for the attack. However, the critical unfolding situation with the Federal right flank halted Van Cleve's plans. After McCook's wing was attacked, it was apparent Rosecrans' planned attack on the east was no longer feasible and to save his army he needed to support his center and right flank with units intended for the attack. Van Cleve was ordered to re-cross Stones River to support the collapsing western flank of the Federal army. The Pioneer Brigade also hurried to join the fight.[56]

At daylight the Pioneer Brigade worked at improving the fords across Stones River. Captain Calvin Hood's battalion was peppered with fire from John Pegram's Confederate cavalry brigade but the pioneers continued their work on the fords. Benjamin Nourse recorded, "The day opened by cannon ball and musket shot falling into my breakfast mess before I had finished my meal—which was boiled salt pork and hard crackers—our team had been harnessed and hitched well before we ate—and, we were ordered to mount, a shell came over the trees into camp." Like many on the eastern flank, the men of the Board of Trade Battery expected fighting on their flank but the developing situation, the increasing roar of cannons and muskets to the west, brought the unhappy news. The Confederate infantry was following up the collapse of McCook's corps and the Confederates continued their success by attacking the center. As the enemy got closer, James Stokes received his orders at 8:00 a.m. to move west and to prepare to fight. Between 9 and 10:00, the battery mounted and moved onto clear, high ground near the Nashville & Chattanooga Railroad separating the tracks and the pike. The infantry at the tracks assisted the battery by making a bridge over a ditch near the rails so the guns could be positioned. While being placed in good position to fire, Benjamin Nourse soon found the artillerymen made excellent targets in this open ground. "We sat in full view of several regiments of rebels, and four batterys—while sitting there on my horse, a shell went over my head and struck in the ground under a mule but doing no damage—soon a shell passed between us and the passing driver. I thought that was coming close enough, but they soon came thick and fast." Nourse began mentally tracking the near misses but, just as quickly, discarded that idea because there were so many near misses coming his way. In a letter to his brother, Private Jackson Howard, the 25-year-old pre-war clerk from Chicago, wrote: "[T]he enemy commenced shelling us with the intention of driving us back; but they found we were not so easily driven."[57]

The idea that this was their first fight never entered the minds of many of the men at the guns, and the hours of training under Stokes over the past few months took over. Private Silas Stevens, manning his gun, was struck by the strangeness of this new situation and mentally asked, "Why are they shooting at me?" The men set about their jobs as a line of Confederate infantry advanced in the distance and the battery boys loaded the guns as fast as they could. At the order "Load!," a cannoneer stepped to the side of the gun, pressed his left thumb (in a thumb-stall) on the vent; a cannoneer "searched the piece" for any material left from the last charge; the tube was sponged, a round was loaded in the

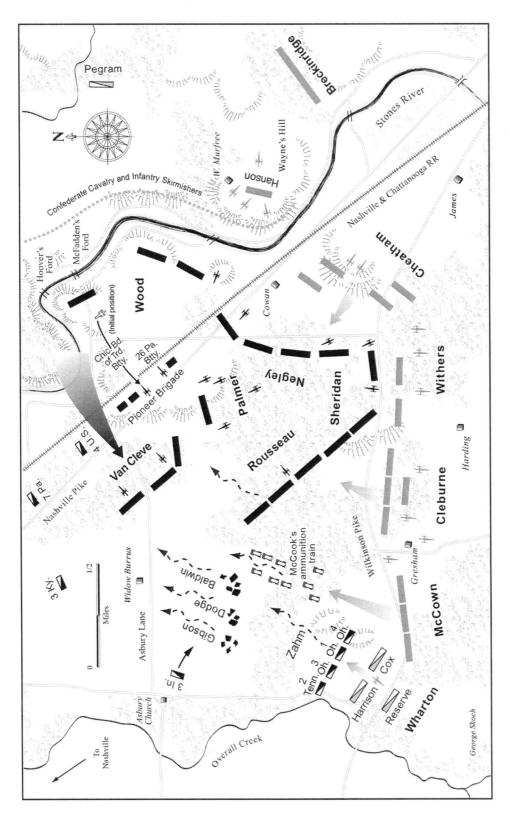

The Chicago Board of Trade Battery moves from McFadden's Ford to the center, December 31, 1862 (6:00–10:00 a.m.).

muzzle, the round was rammed into the gun; the gun was sighted; another round was carried from the limber; the command "Ready" was given; the cartridge bag was punctured with the vent pick; the primer was inserted into the vent; and the lanyard was attached to the friction primer. Then, the gunner yelled "Fire!" The lanyard was yanked, the cannon fired, and recoiled 5–6 feet after firing. Good artillerymen could fire about two shots per minute. This was done over and over again. Upon the first firing of the guns, the horses began neighing and rearing, expressing in their own way the tension of the situation. The postillions attempted to calm the horses and more men had to be assigned to steady the beasts. Then, Rosecrans arrived and personally directed the battery to reposition about 1,000 yards west of Nashville Pike on the brow of a low hill. At this location, the battery would remain through the next day. The gunners immediately loaded and sent a bar-

Private Silas Stevens left a detailed account of the actions of the battery in letters to his brother (*The Descendants of Samuel Stevens,* 1968, p. 170).

rage into the lines of McCown's infantry, driving the enemy into the woods. Rosecrans returned to the battery's new position at 10:30 a.m. and told Stokes that "if he could hold that place for one hour, he would save the day." Due to the repeated recoil of the gun, which made a deeper and deeper trench, the axel of one of the Board of Trade Battery guns broke early in the fighting. It had to be taken off the field for repair.[58]

Repositioned West of Murfreesboro Pike

The men of the Pioneer Brigade observed the chaos and the routed Union troops surging to the rear. Sergeant Henry Freeman of the Pioneer Brigade described upon arriving at the new location: "[T]he woods were suddenly filled with stragglers, riderless horses, and ambulances driven with frantic speed…. Not until then did we begin to comprehend the full extent of the disaster." Rosecrans and his staff were present on the field pulling these units back into fighting regiments. Once Rosecrans observed McCook's rout, he sent Van Cleve's division to the right of Rousseau's division, and north of the Pioneer Brigade which was now positioned on the knoll west of Murfreesboro Pike, about 400 yards to the rear of Palmer's Division, facing southwest. Once McCook's wing retreated, this left Sheridan's, Negley's, and Palmer's divisions from west to east (anchored on Murfreesboro Pike and Stones River). Sheridan held his position through four attacks until he was pushed back and Negley's right flank subsequently yielded to the intense fighting. Rousseau's division was thrown into the battle to stem the progress of the Confederate troops. As these troops were pushed toward Murfreesboro Pike, Rosecrans rallied the troops and the Board of Trade Battery fired into the long lines of gray clad soldiers.[59]

Upon the arrival at the new location, Rosecrans rallied the 21st Ohio, 1st Kentucky, and 78th Pennsylvania, which had fallen back. The battery opened fire at once. Rosecrans was correct in his assessment of the importance of the Board of Trade Battery and the Pioneer Brigade. The men of Pioneer Brigade, although expert construction workers, were also trained fighting infantrymen. To the left of this position, Negley's, Sheridan's and Rousseau's intense infantry struggled to hold their position and the Confederate cavalry and infantry penetrated far north on the western flank where Colonel Samuel Beatty, Colonel James Fyffe, and Colonel Charles Harker were fighting Cleburne's

Rosecrans rallied his troops after the early collapse and directed the Board of Trade Battery into position (*Frank Leslie's Illustrated Newspaper*, February 28, 1863).

division. A gap formed between the fight on the left and the right of the Pioneer Brigade and McCown's Division (Ector's, Vance's and Harper's brigades) threatened to cut the Union line in two.[60]

To the left of the Pioneer Brigade's position, James E. Rains' Confederate brigade (later commanded by Robert Vance) battled the Federals in a dense cedar break. Rains, who was killed in the fight, pushed the Union line steadily back toward Nashville Pike until his men cleared the cedars. Four hundred yards ahead lay the pike, but a fresh brigade of Union infantry, Grose's brigade and two companies of Parsons' U.S. Artillery accompanied by six guns of Guenther's U.S. Artillery awaited. Just like the Board of Trade Battery, the men at this location knew if the Confederate attack proved successful, all was lost. The fresh Federal troops stopped Rains who could make no further progress. Benjamin Scribner's brigade, which had served as a reserve a little in the rear of the Board of Trade Battery (at the first location near the railroad), also arrived to provide infantry support, placing the 38th Indiana just south of the Board of Trade Battery. Of note, the 26th Pennsylvania Light Artillery was also on the field nearby and complemented the fire of the Board of Trade Battery. To the north of Rains was Robert Harper's brigade of McCown's Division and to the north of Harper was Mathew Ector's brigade. Ector's brigade marched directly

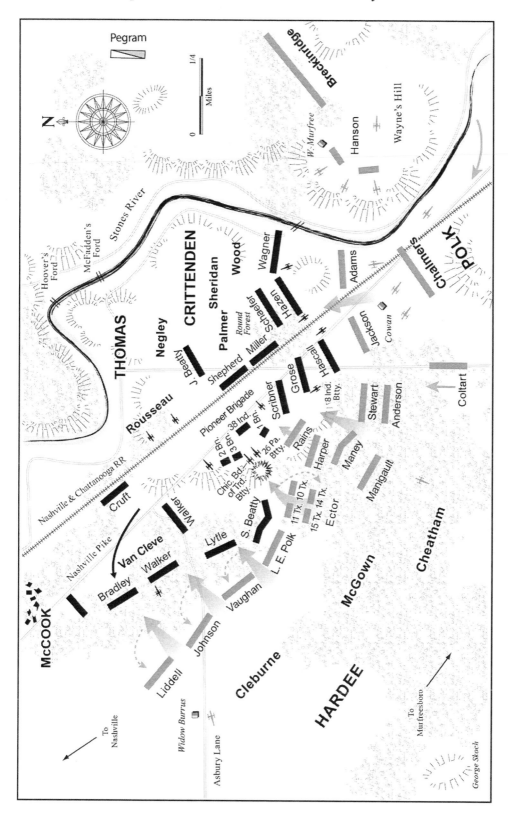

The battle for the center. The Board of Trade Battery, supported by the Pioneer Brigade, moves west of the Murfreesboro-Nashville Pike, December 31, 1862 (10:00 a.m.—dark).

toward the Pioneer Brigade positioned around the Board of Trade Battery, described as the new point of danger by W.D. Bickham, author and journalist. Garesché arrived at Morton's position and admonished, "Support the battery, Morton." Morton placed the First Battalion of Pioneers to the left of the battery in a thicket and the Third Battalion went to the right. The Second Battalion moved into position to the right of the Third Battalion. The three battalions of the pioneers held their position on the flanks of the battery and were determined to maintain the line. Morton, riding among his command, looked and saw one of the many groups of Union infantrymen which had been routed during the morning. This group had just been rallied by the help of Rosecrans himself, but next, Stokes saw an ominous sight as lines of gray coated soldiers emerged from the cedars—McCown's division, as "numberless as the leaves themselves" in front of the battery. The enemy lines moved silently through the woods as the battery prepared to fire on Ector's Texas Brigade, while Colonel Robert Harper's Arkansas Brigade moved into position to attack the newly formed Union troops, pushing ever eastward. Ector placed his brigade with the 15th Texas Cavalry, 14th Texas Cavalry, 11th Texas Cavalry, and 10th Texas Cavalry from left to right. The Texans moved out of the woods and saw a rocky ridge and cedar brake in front of Nashville Pike. Morton also saw Ector's lines emerge from the trees about 250 yards away and rode to Stokes and told him to open fire.[61]

From the Confederate side of the field, Mathew Ector had experienced hard fighting since the early hours of the morning but things had pretty much gone his way. Now, in conjunction with Harper, the two brigades marched toward the Pioneer Brigade with the Board of Trade Battery in place. To the right of Harper was Rains' brigade. These brigades were immediately in a desperate struggle; Robert Harper's brigade advancing to Ector's right fell under the same battery and infantry fire. Ector met a hail of musket and artillery fire, and sent couriers to Harper asking for assistance. Ector explained: "I hastened to the left of my command. My men had driven back one line of their infantry upon the second line; still behind them was a third line. I have since learned that a short distance behind these was General Rosecrans' headquarters." The shower of shells and musket fire resulted in a rain of lead and cedar branches falling on Ector's men. This halted Ector's advance and caused his men to seek shelter behind some rocks. At 60 yards away from the Federal line, they began returning a deadly musket fire on the Federal infantry and artillery.[62]

A member of the 84th Illinois, part of Grose's Brigade of Crittenden's Wing, explained that the Confederates were hitting the regiment in the front and also enfilading the regiment in the flank. The Illinois infantrymen, while still trying to hold their position, then came under fire from the enemy artillery on the east side of the river. Soon, the enemy infantry began to edge around the rear of the regiment which mandated a withdrawal. The regiment found a more favorable position on a slight ridge under the protection of Mendenhall's and the Board of Trade's guns "throwing shells, grape and canister over our right and Mendenhall's battery over our left, sweeping trees and enemy at each discharge…. The Board of Trade battery saved us very much, as we were falling back, and deserves great credit for the pertinacity with which they held their position."[63]

As Rousseau's division had been driven back, the 15th U.S. Infantry received orders to move into position to support the Board of Trade Battery and with them came a two-gun section of the 5th U.S. Artillery, which was placed south of the Board of Trade and the 26th Pennsylvania batteries. Infantryman Frank Reed described the chaos as the Regulars re-formed in the center near the batteries to halt the Confederate attack. "Here, which was to the right and rear of the place where we had been engaged, I found that the enemy had almost succeeded in taking the above named artillery [Board of Trade Battery], for his dead and wounded lay within two or three rods of it. About the same time a desperate attempt was made by the enemy to take a Battery which had position on our left, but were repulsed with terrible slaughter…. The enemy again formed his line of battle, which could be seen for half a mile across an open field … and attempted once more to take the Battery. The [dismounted] cavalry rushed boldly forward, but before they had reached halt at the distance required, they were met by such a shower of grape and canister that it was almost certain death to proceed further." John Carroll, cannoneer of the 5th U.S. Artillery, described the effect of the line of artillery: "Loomis' Michigan Battery, the Chicago Board of Trade Battery, and our battery were in a line on this hill. The rebels cheered at their success so far and followed our men out of the wood into the open field, headed by their flag, determined no doubt to capture the battery and chase us off from the field. Now was the time for the artillery—fate relied on them here—and such a roar of cannon never was heard before; three batteries, making eighteen guns, pouring in cannister and shell at short range upon them, soon checked them, and made them hunt their holes and flee in all directions but towards us. After we had ceased firing not a rebel was to be seen, with the exception of a squad of 8 or 10 who rose from their hiding places with a white handkerchief, and hollering, 'don't fire'; they were our prisoners. This was the hardest contest of the day…."[64]

The Union guns fired, sending shells, exploding amid McCown's lines. With each discharge, gaps formed in the Confederate lines steadily advancing and the Confederate soldiers adjusted, filling in the gaps. The Texans returned the fire with their muskets. The Board of Trade's Jackson Howard described the heated battle: "The balls were whizzing, and shells were bursting on every side of us, and we were almost blinded from the dirt flying from the bursting of the shells." John Nourse heard a ball whiz past his head, striking the horse behind him as the musket fire began. William Wiley, killed in the afternoon battle, had written his brother before the battle: "I have not found the soldier's life harder than I expected, I cannot do too much for our country." When he was hit, those around him heard him say before he died on the field, "My God! I am wounded." The 26th

The Union artillery played a critical role in establishing the new defensive line (from a sketch by A.E. Mathews depicting Rousseau's division, Library of Congress).

Pennsylvania Battery, just to the left of the Board of Trade guns, fired away and still the Confederate line advanced. The Texans passed through about 100 yards of open ground under a hail of shot, shell and infantry fire. The James Rifles of the battery initially fired Schenkl shells on the advancing enemy and one of the ammunition carriers got too close to the gun when it fired. He was blown down the hill in front of the gun by the discharge, but dazed and burned, he returned to his position. At last, the enemy came within range of cannister and the batteries fired with fearsome effect. The front line wavered but the second line urged them forward. The line advanced until the men sought shelter behind a rail fence where it halted and fired into the waiting Federals, but the position was untenable. Then, the command "Charge!" was ordered by the Confederate officers. The Texans charged another hundred yards in a valiant effort to take the guns but the attack ground to a halt. The entire Confederate line wavered, stalled, and then with a loud cheer the Second Pioneer Battalion charged, supported by the 79th Indiana Infantry, which had rallied to the right of the Pioneer Brigade, on Ector's men. As Ector's attack stalled, the Union artillery continued to hammer away on the enemy position. Nourse described: "As the rebs came up the hill we just poured the articles of war into them—the ground was piled up with dead and wounded rebels after they returned to the woods." Cannoneer John Toomey recalled that the order to fire yielded a "terrible effect as the enemy fell within 30 yards of our guns." The battery fired into the first wave for about 30 minutes "turning the rebel lines—breaking them all to fragments." Toomey was so exhausted that, despite men falling around him, he kept at his task of loading and sponging the cannon, unaware of his position on the battlefield or even caring "anything about the bullets whistling over my head." Stokes recorded that he remained under fire of three Confederate batteries during this time. Private Tobias Miller manned one of the Board of Trade guns and he explained that when the attack came, a barrage from the Confederate cannons landed among the battery. Miller watched as the first Confederate round killed three men in the battery and wounded two others. Jackson Howard explained that he was stunned: "I was struck, while sighting my gun, by a piece of shell right in the centre of my forehead, exactly between the eyes. This sent me whirling for a while, but I soon recovered." The men stuck by their guns and Miller wrote "here the fire became terific … some of the guns discharge six shots in a minute, but succeeded in nocking out one of the rebel batteries all to pieces and driving the other two, badly damaged, from the field." The battery doctor found the experience unnerving. Dr. F.A. Lord, the physician from Chicago, "was so badly scared that he will soon turn up in Chicago," wrote John Fleming.[65]

At 60 yards away from the Federal line, the Texans returned a deadly musket fire on the Federal infantry and artillery. Ector's right two regiments (10th Texas Cavalry and 11th Texas Cavalry) fell under the same fire as the 14th and 15th Texas, and withdrew before the two regiments on the left. Ector wrote: "Believing it to be impossible to bring my entire brigade to bear with full force, and that an attempt to do it would be attended with great sacrifice of life, I ordered them to fall back. The enemy did not, so far as I was able to discover, follow us." Once back into the woods, Ector had the opportunity to re-form his command and remained in a defensive position. On the right of Ector was Harper, commanding the brigade due to Evander McNair's illness. Harper had been marching northward and McCown ordered him to march northeasterly to the waiting Union line. Harper entered a cedar thicket with Ector on his flank and found that he was in the middle of a heated fight. Here, Harper received Ector's request for assistance. Harper wrote: "No time was now to be lost, as the enemy had evidently made this their last stand-point, and had opened upon us with artillery and musketry. Almost simultaneously with General Ector's request, I received an order from the major-general commanding to charge the batteries. The order was immediately repeated to the command, and, flushed with success and buoyant with hope, they rushed forward to accomplish more brilliant results." The order to attack directed Vance (now in command of Rains' brigade) to attack the Federal troops to the right of the Pioneer Brigade—Scribner's, Shepherd's, and John Beatty's brigades. Harper's attack was closely coordinated with Rains and this left Ector to deal with the Pioneer Brigade alone. Stokes gave a great compliment regarding the bravery of the enemy attacks: "[N]ever did men fight better than the rebels on this occasion, our shot would cut clear through them, yet they moved on to within a pistol shot."[66]

Captain Lyman Bridges, 1st Battalion Pioneer Corps, described the attack: "General McCown's division, came down, upon the double-quick, with their standards flying, in splendid order. They were allowed to come within 300 yards, when the musketry of the entire brigade and the battery opened with grape and canister a most deadly fire, which he returned as earnestly. The column reeled and fell back in disorder, their colors struck down and barely rescued…. The number of killed and wounded left on the field tells how severe was his loss. Many of his wounded reached our lines during the day and night, all declaring that the 12 o'clock charge was an expensive one for them." Calvin Hood, commanding the 2nd Battalion on the extreme right of the Brigade, recorded; "The troops in front of us there gave way, and regiment after regiment came through our lines entirely broken up. We here received orders from Captain Morton to fix bayonets and allow no stragglers to pass our lines, and to hold fire and give the enemy the cold steel. The retreating troops passed on our right, except the Seventy-ninth Indiana, whose commander rallied them on my right and rear. The Eleventh and Fourteenth Texas came on at a charge, and tried to flank our right, when my battalion changed positions by the right flank and fronted toward them." During the attack, General Van Cleve arrived and told Hood that he needed to fall back, but the pioneer battalion commander replied that he would hold his position at all costs. Hood told his men to lie down until the enemy got closer and then, the pioneers unleashed a murderous volley. With bayonets fixed, Hood's battalion, accompanied by the 79th Indiana, charged, driving the enemy back to the woods. Morton found Rosecrans after the repulse of Ector and calmly asked, "We're doing it about right now, General, ain't we?" No doubt, Rosecrans just smiled. In the afternoon, Samuel Beatty's Brigade arrived to support the Board of Trade Battery, and Mendenhall's 4th U.S. Artillery Battery unlimbered on the left of the brigade.[67]

The most severe fighting at this location occurred between noon and 2:00 p.m. At that time, the firing ceased and remained quiet until about 4:00 p.m. when another Confederate attack began. During the interlude, Stokes ordered the men of the battery to lie down beside the guns due to their exposed position and to prevent being picked off by enemy infantrymen. At 4:00 the Confederates made one final attack in an attempt to break the Federal lines, but the men of the Board of Trade Battery misread the attack. Morton split the battery, taking two sections to the left of the First Battalion of Pioneers. The remaining section dealt with an attack from the right. Most accounts by the men of the battery suggested the attack from the right unfolded as an opportunistic attack as the wounded were being removed from the field. According to Stokes, the Confederate brigade fired on, or under the cover of, ambulances picking up the wounded. Benjamin Nourse explained that as the attack unfolded "the ambulances came in on the double quick and we received them as warmly as in the morning—but they had no courage to fight up to the very guns and a few quick rounds of grape told the same tale as in the forenoon—they broke and ran, then virtually closing the work of the day." The wounded enemy soldiers said the final barrage "entirely annihilated" their brigade, according to Stokes.[68]

Meanwhile, the other two sections realigned to the left of the First Battalion and faced southwest. Captain Lyman Bridges, commanding the Pioneer Brigade's first battalion, recorded the last attack of the day: "advancing a brigade upon my left flank through a skirt of wood, attempting a surprise. My pickets being fired upon by the enemy, who took advantage of a train of ambulances being in the vicinity, firing upon ambulances and pickets indiscriminately, I ordered this battalion to change front and commence firing. Lieutenant Stevens, of Stokes' battery, opened fire upon him simultaneously with grape and canister. Our new line fortunately rested upon the crest of the hill. Each volley by us thinned his ranks. He advanced, perhaps 40 paces, discharging repeated volleys of musketry, but his repulse was complete, and they fell back to the wood, 1,000 yards in the rear, cursing their fate. Dozens of their wounded men, found within our lines of skirmishers, all corroborated each other in stating that a brigade was repulsed in attempting to take our position. He left 60 of his men upon the field." Again, the enemy reached to within 60 yards of the battery by the time the attack was stopped.[69]

An interesting post-war account from a Southern soldier, Captain W.P. O'Connor, described the surprise his regiment received from the Board of Trade Battery on the first day of the battle. O'Connor recalled that his regiment emerged from some trees and a saw a group of men standing, holding the right side of their overcoats away from their bodies with their right hands. One of the men was wearing a gray overcoat. This display confused the approaching Confederates and O'Connor asked, "Who are those men?" The reply came, "Why, these are Yankees." At that point, the Union men in front dropped their overcoat lapels, revealing the Board of Trade Battery which opened fire. O'Connor exclaimed, "An instant they opened on us with cannister and we went down like grass before a scythe."[70]

The last attack was made as Breckinridge's forces made one last try to break the Union lines, and the fighting ended for the day. At this point Rosecrans had formed a strong defensive line which extended from Hazen's brigade along Murfreesboro Pike. Rousseau's division filled the area between Hazen (now supported by Hascall's brigade) and the Pioneer Brigade. Negley's division was positioned as a reserve and Van Cleve's division was to the right of the Pioneer Brigade with McCook refusing the right flank. Stanley's cavalry was along Overall Creek further to the right.

The night was cold as the men of the battery tried to recover from the day's action, the first real day of battle for the battery, which had performed so well. Benjamin Nourse recorded: "Clear cold night—I watched the old year standing and stomping my feet to keep from freezing—We have no fires—for fear the rebs will see us. Have had nothing all day except crackers in our haversacks. At 10 oc. by the light of the moon we dug a grave and laid to rest poor boys gone where there is no fighting—hard to put them into the ground—Andrew Finney & Wm. H. Wiley were instantly killed at gun #3 by a shell. J.A. Stagg of #2 was killed by round shot, Sergt. A.K. Adams wounded by a shell on the ankle bone. J.W. Blume burnt by powder. J.C. Camberg shot through the calf of leg. Corpl. A.H. Carver shot through the bowels—dead—W. H. O'Dell stunned by the concussion of a shell. Lieut. T.D. Griffith [Griffin] shot through the body. The wounded were sent to the rear—the night was more bitter cold and we have no over coats, by carelessness all overcoats were in the wagons and we hear they are on their way to Nashville if not captured—If I live to be 100 years old, I never will forget this day or night—this watching out the old year, may it be the last to be spent in so unfavorable a manner." The battery had fired 1,400–1,500 rounds during the first day of the battle.[71]

Overnight, the artificers went to work on the gun with the broken axle. The gun had been taken off the field and out of range of the enemy, but later returned to the field. The old gun carriage was replaced by an abandoned carriage from the field. In the meantime, the caissons were re-filled from the supply wagons and the men prepared for more fighting the next day. Dr. Frederick Lord was very busy during the first day of the battle and afterwards. He described, "I was constantly on the field, or in the field-hospital, myself, & did duty not only as surgeon & nurse, but also as purveyor & cook for the men, who were not allowed to

The men of the battery dug a grave that night and buried their dead (*Frank Leslie's Illustrated Famous Leaders and Battle Scenes of the Civil War*, 1896, p. 352).

leave their guns for a moment for four days & nights, subsisted mainly on what myself & one negro servant (the rest all ran away) could prepare & carry to them in our own hands. Had it not been for a stray cow we captured & butchered in the woods, we should have all suffered the pangs of hunger in addition to other distresses, for on the second day our supplies were cut off, or either destroyed, or driven back to Nashville by the rebel cavalry in our rear."[72]

January 1

No one knew what to expect the next morning. Would the two armies begin the fight in earnest again at daybreak? Morton held his brigade in readiness and was greeted with an exchange of fire from some Confederates probing along the left flank of the Pioneer Brigade. The skirmishers of the 22nd Illinois reported a strong line of Confederate infantry advancing toward Morton's position in a dense early morning fog. The Confederate infantry probed to find a weakness in the Union lines, but Morton only realigned the front of the brigade. After the day before, those on the front lines were nervous about another attack. As the Confederates emerged from the tree-line, Morton ordered his pioneers along with Stokes' to open fire, driving the enemy back into the woods. The enemy got no closer than 500 yards of the Union line. Benjamin Nourse noted, "As soon as it was light enough to distinguish objects we were all action for we did not know what an hour might bring forth. The rebels gave us no time for surmises, as they came charging up the slope hoping to take our guns—we were not found sleeping, and they received a hot welcome. More than they wished for and soon they were driven off the field and into the woods— at 9 oc. we changed fronts to the south, and the fighting lasted about one hour. The rest of the day passed without much more fighting in our front. We lay on the ground or stood behind the guns or trees, any where to keep sheltered from the sharpshooters who fired very accurately killing two horses and wounding three at long range." The Confederate fire into the battery was so accurate that the bridle reins Nourse held was shot in half.[73]

John Toomey, part of the gun number 1 crew, suddenly felt a sharp pain in his side which knocked him to the ground. Toomey heard the lieutenant says "another man gone." The pain was so intense Toomey knew he had been shot through the body and he was hurriedly moved to the hospital. While waiting to be attended, the pain diminished and he felt brave enough to look at the wound when the ball fell into his hand. Fortunately, he had been hit with a spent ball resulting in only a painful bruise. He applied some salve to the wound and quickly returned to the battery which was being withdrawn from the front line. For Private Toomey, his eventful day wasn't over. As the battery moved to the eastern flank later that evening, Toomey rode on an ammunition chest when the wheel struck a stump, throwing him into the air. "I did not think I would ever get down to earth alive," but he landed on his feet and yelled to the postilion to stop. Then, he mounted the gun and rode on the gun until he reached camp.[74]

This ended the day for the battery and the Pioneer Brigade, when they were relieved after being on the line for two days. Stokes summarized: "About 10 p.m. it was ordered to the rear to rest, having been thirty-six hours to the front. In this engagement the battery, with a strength of 98, all told, lost 3 privates killed; 1 officer, 3 non-commissioned officers, and 5 privates wounded, being 12 killed and wounded, or about one-eighth." John Nourse wrote in his journal: "[W]ent to the rear where we got some supper and had a few hours sleep … we had no blankets."[75]

At the end of the first day of January, Wheeler returned from a raid in the rear of the Federal forces with good news for the commanding general of the Army of Tennessee. It appeared that Rosecrans was ready to withdraw, but Wheeler's claims of success and description of the rear of the Federal army gave Bragg the wrong impression. Bragg wrote: "No doubt this induced the enemy to send large escorts of artillery, infantry, and cavalry with later trains, and thus the impression was made on our ablest cavalry commanders that a retrograde movement was going on." This faulty intelligence from Wheeler helped Bragg form the decision to firmly hold his position and gave him the impression that only a little more pressure would cause Rosecrans to rapidly withdraw. The stage was set for another bloody battle on January 2, because contrary to Wheeler's report, Rosecrans had decided to stay and fight.[76]

Another important voice of the battery was pre-war carpenter John D. Toomey (Chicago History Museum, ICHi-176924).

January 2—Misdirected Fire from the Board of Trade Battery

After receiving a temporary respite overnight, early on January 2 the Pioneer Brigade went back to work as a construction force building easy crossings ("bridges") over the railroad tracks, but the Confederates saw the brigade as an easy target and opened an artillery fire on the men. Benjamin Nourse and his comrades were up at 4:00 and breakfasted on mutton, from the prior foraging expeditions. The battery was still in position near the front line of Union infantry. Then, "[T]he rebels opened on us with several batteries, killing almost at first fire, three of the brigades what supported us. One of the batteries was the famous Washington Light Artillery of New Orleans—we had a sharp duel for one hour. Then we withdrew to the rear—fireing, having ceased by mutual consent." During the artillery duel, a round shot rolled so slowly through the battery that an infantryman put out his foot to stop it. "He had no further use for that foot," wrote John Nourse. Another shot struck in the vicinity of the battery and rebounded, killing an infantryman in the rear.[77]

Earlier that morning, the Confederates masked 22 guns of Carnes', Stanford's and Smith's Confederate batteries, northwest of the Cowan's house, a house just west of Murfreesboro Pike opposite Hascall's Federal infantry division. Ten additional guns of Robertson's and Scott's batteries fired from between the railroad and the river. The batteries were supported by three brigades of Confederate infantry. A Confederate force pushed into Round Forest and drove the Federal skirmishers back to the main line, but a strong counter-attack drove the Confederates to the rear. The mass of Confederate guns opened fire on the Federal infantry and sent them hurrying back to the main line. After dealing with the blue-coated infantry and clearing the forest, the Confederate guns focused on the artillery of Hascall's division. The 8th Indiana Artillery received the major portion of the Confederate cannonade which drove this battery to the rear, resulting in two pieces being left on the field, which were later retrieved by infantrymen. After driving the 8th Indiana off the field, Scott's Battery shifted to Battery B, 1st Ohio; at the same time, Carnes', Stanford's and Smith's guns fired on the 6th Ohio, 26th Pennsylvania, and the Board of Trade batteries. The 6th Ohio received the greatest concentration of fire at this point. These Union batteries held their positions, counter-fired, and the Confederate cannonading stopped soon thereafter.[78]

The Board of Trade Battery was placed in line facing southwest early on January 2, but was shifted early in the morning to a position a little closer to Murfreesboro Pike, facing south in the rear of Harker's Brigade. The Confederate artillery began a barrage all along the Federal line starting on the eastern flank. Captain John Mendenhall, 4th U.S. Artillery and Crittenden's chief of artillery, explained that Bragg opened fire on the Federal left flank, doing little damage, but soon shifted to fire on the Union troops along the railroad and Murfreesboro Pike. The Federal guns answered and soon the firing stopped. In an unfortunate event, Mendenhall recorded: "When the enemy had nearly ceased firing, the Board of Trade Battery (Captain Stokes) opened with canister upon Captain Bradley's battery and Colonel Harker's brigade, wounding several men and horses." General Milo Hascall, commanding the First Division after Thomas Wood had been wounded, explained that the 6th Ohio Battery (Bradley's) had longer range guns and they were effective in counter-firing on the enemy guns during the Confederate cannonade, but the Board of Trade Battery in the rear opened fire and forced Bradley to withdraw his guns. Harker's infantry was able to maintain its position in line. Hascall was enraged by the action and demanded an investigation into the incident referring to gross carelessness on the part of the battery. Five men and five horses were wounded in the action and the evidence was damning. The battery fired on the 6th Ohio at a distance of 300 yards while the enemy was some 2,000 yards away from the battery. While the initial reports condemned the firing, Charles Harker, commanding the infantry brigade, hastened to note that as soon as Stokes became aware of what was occurring, he stopped firing. In historian Edwin Bearss' analysis of this event, he placed the blame for the firing on the Board of Trade gun officers, who were impatient for Stokes to give the order to return fire. "And before Stokes could put a stop to this promiscuous firing the damage had been done," wrote Bearss. It was later revealed that the Board of Trade Battery received erroneous information that the position of the 6th Ohio had been overrun by the enemy and battery was just attempting to halt the attack. A mistake, nonetheless.[79]

This event was not documented in the Chicago Board of Trade Battery records or in Morton's report. There was one account in the recollections of Silas Stevens written after the turn of the century. It is necessary to pause and note that Private Stevens' reminiscences should be taken with caution, especially when someone's reputation could be damaged. Stevens' accounts are filled with rich detail missing from many other accounts and provides a valuable resource. As might be expected, Stevens did not always provide unbiased accounts of events. A notable example of this would be his account of the broken axle on the guns during the first day's fighting. In his account, he alone was responsible for securing the gun and returning to the lines at dark so that it could be repaired and put back into the battery. Stevens, in that situation, asked Stokes for permission to return the gun and Stevens described Stokes as dazed and unable to comprehend the need to return the gun to the line. In regard to firing on the 6th Ohio Battery, Stevens placed the blame of this cannonade on Stokes' shoulders and wrote "the Captain in his excited condition, without orders fired into, and wounded several of our men belonging to a battery.... It was my opinion then ... and now that the Captain imbibed too much of the contents of the canteen, he carried as his side, and also, I am confirmed in my judgment when I met him in the woods down in front ... in regard to my instructions about bringing up the gun from the rear, that he was also at that time considerably under the influence of brandy." There are no other accounts of Stokes being inebriated.[80]

In a somewhat confusing but significant event, the battery gained an additional cannon during the Battle of Stones River. Without details of the timing, the post war history of the unit revealed that on the morning of January 2, six members of the battery spotted an abandoned six-pounder cannon between the two opposing lines, made a dash, captured the cannon and rolled it back to battery under enemy fire. Benjamin Nourse noted that the gun was "one that the rebs had taken from our Ohio battery." This gun would be retained by the battery, making it the only seven-gun battery in the Army of the Cumberland which Rosecrans allowed due to the performance of the battery during the battle.[81]

Breckinridge's Charge

While the Confederate cavalry attacked wagon trains near La Vergne the day before, Rosecrans ordered Samuel Beatty, in command of Van Cleve's division supported by William Grose's brigade of John Palmer's division, to move to the east side of Stones River. This Federal line of infantry threw up some rough defenses and faced Breckinridge's division. During the night, Grose's brigade returned to the west side of the river, but returned early the next morning to support Beatty, accompanied by the 3rd Wisconsin Artillery. This movement presented a significant problem for Bragg. The placement of artillery on the east side of the river made the Confederate infantry around the Round Forest vulnerable to shelling from Beatty's position. Bragg could not allow the Union troops to remain in position on the east side of Stones River and, at the same time, if Bragg could retain the high ground at this location, he could continue to shell Rosecrans' army utilizing the concentration of artillery on Wayne's Hill.[82]

Before noon, Crittenden sent Brigadier General John Palmer's division to join Beatty as Breckinridge's activity increased and more Confederate infantry and artillery moved into position. Around noon, Negley's division was also placed on a ridge overlooking McFadden's Ford, bolstering the Union left flank. Along with Negley came six guns replacing the six guns of the 7th Indiana Battery which had moved to the east side of the river. More batteries arrived at the area just west of McFadden's Ford, including Parsons' eight guns of Battery H and M of the 4th U.S. Artillery and also Battery F, 1st Ohio Artillery. In the late afternoon, six guns of Battery B, 1st Ohio Artillery, were also dispatched to the east flank. At 2:00 on January 2, Bragg summoned Breckinridge and then ordered him to lead an attack on Beatty's troops. Breckinridge returned to his headquarters and informed his brigade commanders who all opposed the order. One brigade commander reportedly even considered going to army headquarters and shooting Bragg. Breckinridge began his attack at 4:00 p.m. on Van Cleve's/Beatty's and Palmer's divisions on the east side of Stones River. Breckinridge's large division sent the Union troops retreating back across Stones River. M.B. Butler of the 44th Indiana in Van Cleve's Division recalled that "legions of Rebels" formed and Confederate artillery was wheeled into position to support the attack. The Confederate lines moved forward like an "irresistible tidal wave," wrote Butler. Then, Rosecrans ordered Negley's division to support Van Cleve against this furious attack. Van Cleve's division was driven into the river and just when things seemed lost, Negley's infantry came running into place and opened fire on the charging enemy. The Union infantry faced 4,500 Confederates charging ahead, supported by artillery, and now Negley looked for help. The Confederate attack was one of the grandest in the Civil War and they swept down as an overwhelming force on Beatty's division. The attack forced the Federal infantry, except for Fyffe's and Grose's brigade, to the west side of Stones River. Benjamin Nourse recorded, "Again, in reserve at 4 oc. The rebels advanced their right driving our troops before them like scattered sheep—just at this time Gen. Negley rode over the hill & asked 'whose command is this?' The reply 'Capt. Morton's Pioneers' 'For God's sake Captain save my left!'" Morton acted quickly and sent his brigade running to Negley's aid. He placed the 3rd Battalion in the second line behind Davis' division, the 1st Battalion extended to the river and finally the 2nd Battalion extended the line closer to the river left of the 3rd. Nourse continued: "Away we went like the wind over the rise of ground that hid them from view and as the flying troops were in the way. It was several minutes (which seemed like hours) before we got into action."[83]

The Confederates continued forward, ultimately driving Grose and Fyffe across the river, too. When Breckinridge began his attack, Rosecrans rode to Morton and ordered the Pioneer Brigade to hurry to support the infantry on the left flank. The Chicago Board of Trade Battery moved by trot and then by gallop, to the bend in Stones River and into position with a large open field in front. Pressing through the routed soldiers, the Pioneer Brigade placed its left flank on the river and the battery formed on the military crest of the ridge a short distance to the left of the 2nd Kentucky Battery. An old abandoned house was in front and slightly right of the battery's position. The 8th Indiana Artillery arrived shortly thereafter. Fifty-seven Union artillery pieces went to work, including the 26th Pennsylvania and 6th Ohio batteries, almost a mile away. Forty-five of the guns were massed on the west side of McFadden's Ford. The Board of Trade Battery received fire from the Confederate guns, as long lines of Confederate infantry drove the Union infantry to the rear. The artillery sergeants, who were now experienced veterans after the last two days' fighting, calmly and quickly gave the orders which prepared and loaded the guns. The battery began with shot and shell. Captain Stokes ordered the gunners to open fire with shells with 5-second fuses. Shifting to counter-battery fire, the Board of Trade Battery targeted Wright's Tennessee Battery. The guns fired so rapidly the sergeants worried about the heat of the barrel and ordered water to be poured onto the guns to cool them. Nourse explained, "We opened lively and soon stopped the Butternuts who in turn fled faster than our men had done before." At least for the Board of Trade Battery, the enemy guns had no impact on the battery and the enemy shells passed overhead. M.B. Butler, 44th Indiana, noted that the compact and concentrated mass of the enemy made the effects of the artillery firing canister worse, doing terrific damage to the lines of Confederate soldiers. The Confederates fired on the Federal guns, trying to stop the destruction coming from the mouths of the guns. A grand artillery duel resulted between some of the batteries. Twenty-two Confederate guns fired on twenty-four Union guns which counter-fired.[84]

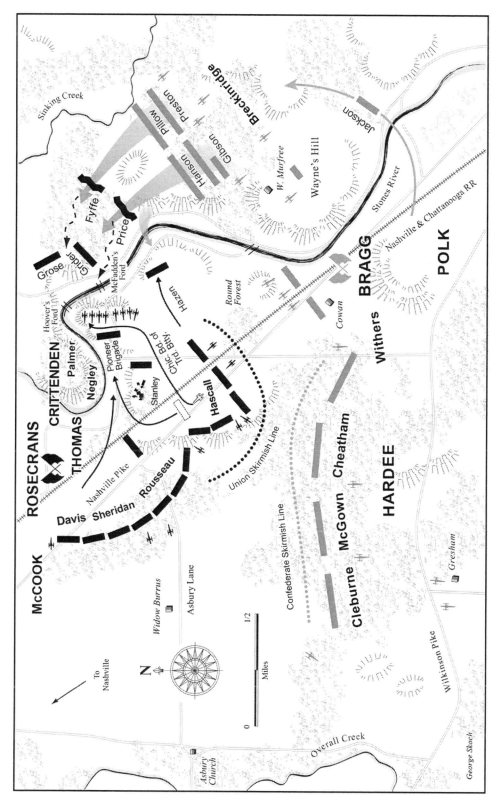

Breckinridge's Charge, January 2, 1863. The Board of Trade Battery begins the day along Nashville Pike and moves to a line of artillery during the attack.

Union Artillery in the Repulse of Breckinridge's Attack January 2, 1863[85]

Unit	No. Guns	Unit	No. Guns
Chicago Board of Trade Battery	6	8th Indiana Light Artillery	6
6th Ohio Light Artillery	6	Batt. B. 1st Ohio Light Artillery	3
Batt. F, 1st Ohio Light Artillery	4	7th Indiana Light Artillery	6
Batt. H and M, 4th U.S. Light Artillery	8	3rd Wisconsin Light Artillery	6
26th Pennsylvania Light Artillery	6	2nd Kentucky Light Artillery	1
Batt. G., 1st Ohio Light Artillery	2	Batt. M, 1st Ohio Light Artillery	3

The arrival of the Union artillery reinforcements began with the 8th Indiana Battery. Then, the Board of Trade Battery arrived followed by Battery B, 1st Ohio. The 3rd Wisconsin, repositioning from the east side of the river, joined the cannonading. Negley's infantry initially fell into position on the west side of the river. Negley ordered his men to lie down on the military crest which made them poor targets for the Confederates and then, Negley's and Charles Cruft's men opened fire on the Confederate infantry. With new infantry units, the massing of over 50 artillery pieces, and the excellent location of the batteries resulted in the destruction of Breckinridge's attack. The "murderous fire" of the Union cannons decimated the Confederate attack resulting in the loss of more than 1,800 Confederate soldiers, killed or wounded, in an hour's time. As the attack ground to a halt under the hail of artillery and musket fire, the Federals which had been so handily pushed across the river, rose and plunged into Stones River in a counterattack. Stokes ordered the battery limbered and dashed across the river where the water reached only to the edges of the ammunition boxes, leaving the powder dry. The Pioneer Brigade and battery halted and unlimbered in the location where a Confederate battery had been located before the Confederate attack. The battery remained secure in this position without receiving any fire from the enemy, but it was in the midst of men wounded in the recent attack. The wounded asked for water and "groans of the dying were piteous," recalled Silas Stevens. After dark, the artillery was ordered back to the west side of the river and as they rode to the rear, they heard the wounded imploring not to be run over by the battery.[86]

Stokes' after action report: "The battery opened a destructive fire of shell on the rebel battery, so destructive to our troops, completely silencing and destroying it, so that several of its pieces were captured by our advancing infantry. The battery that night occupied the ground of this rebel battery. The commanding general, who witnessed the bearing of this gallant little band, will do justice to its discipline and bravery. All were brave; all nobly did their duty to their country." During Breckinridge's withdrawal, Stokes described his artillery charge being made by the battery when he advanced to a second position placing the guns "almost within the enemy's lines. And doing wonderful execution."[87]

Benjamin Nourse described: "We followed them across the ford to one mile of Murfreesboro, then, darkness shut down its quiet cover over the sights of horror—Genl. Negley rode over to us, saying 'I cannot bestow too many thanks upon the Board of Trade

Battery, as it has won this day'…. The ground was littered with every thing that could belong to a soldier—and the dead rebels lay so thick on the ground that we could not draw the guns across the field until the bodies had been removed, allowing us a path—at midnight, it commenced to rain, cold, and the poor wounded men suffered terribly. Along towards morning we were relieved and moved back to the rear."[88]

Overnight the men of the battery, simply exhausted after the fighting over the past three days just lay down and went to sleep. Nourse explained: "Last night, we were drowned out—So tired we lay down just where we happened to be and daylight found us in a hole and water half up our sides—We have not been engaged today, but lay in the mud near the ford. Misery indeed." Despite the poor conditions, the battle was over, and the battery had indeed performed well, firing 1,450 rounds in the battle. Some of the battery felt Stokes was a difficult commander, but there can be little doubt that he had prepared an efficient and effective battery, one which could not have performed better in its first major battle. Negley praised Stokes for his command of the battery during the battle and referred to the "evidence of his marked ability and bravery as an officer and patriot." The men of the Board of Trade Battery had seen the "Elephant" and proved themselves worthy of their uniforms. John Fleming wrote: "In all of the fight our officers behaved nobly and very frequently Genl. Rosecrans rode along the front cheering forward the men."[89]

Stokes did not gloat at the end of the battle and merely said that circumstances forced his men to "play unfortunate part in the late battle. Each man did his duty … we mourn the loss of our companions." Piecing together the accounts of the battle plus some official documents, eleven names can be identified as casualties:

Sgt. Abbott Adams	wounded by a shell on the ankle bone
J.W. Blume	burnt by powder
J.C. Camberg	shot through the calf of leg
Corpl. A.H. Carver	shot through the bowels, mortally wounded, died
W.H. O'Dell	concussion from explosion of a shell
Andrew Finney	killed instantly by enemy artillery fire at gun number 3
Lt. Trumbull Griffin	shot through the body, seriously wounded
Jackson Howard	struck in forehead by shell fragment
J.A. Stagg	killed by enemy artillery fire at gun number 2
John Toomey	minor wound, spent ball to the body
Wm. H. Wiley	killed instantly by enemy artillery fire at gun number 3

John Camberg's (a native Norwegian and a pre-war newspaperman) wound kept him hospitalized for ten weeks. Griffin was stuck with a ball that nearly severed the belt of his sword and initially the surgeons thought that it was unlikely that he would return to duty. They were wrong. Lieutenant Griffin returned on June 21 almost two months after Sergeant Abbott Adams who returned to duty on April 26, 1863.[90]

Not mentioned in the casualty list, was Stokes himself, who was struck in the head by part of a bursting shell, but Stokes never left the field. Tobias Miller was also not listed in the casualty list, but he was also struck with a bursting shell and remained on the field. In addition, one man was listed as missing/captured during the battle. The artillerists were also subject to long-term deafness after so much explosive noise and in the case of

Private Loyal A. Stevens, this condition persisted permanently. The official casualties for the battery were 13. Rosecrans, who was positioned in the center of the battery for part of the battle, observed first-hand the part played by the Board of Trade Battery. Rosecrans' use of his artillery during the battles on December 31 and January 2 saved his army, but more battles awaited. Prophetically, Tobias Miller foresaw the next steps in the campaign against the Army of Tennessee, "One more battle at Chattanooga and the west will be free." But that battle was many months ahead. John A. Nourse wrote a letter to his mother after the battle: "Before the fight I was anxious to have one, but I have had enough now." Nourse explained that after the battle, the Pioneer Brigade was glad to have the battery. Before the battle, people had called the bat-

Sergeant Abbott Adams was wounded by a shell and would be away from the battery for several months (Chicago History Museum, ICHi-176920).

tery the "$100Men," the "Chicken Roost Battery," and the "Ban[d]box Battery." After the battle, the pioneers threatened to fight anyone who disparaged the battery. Meanwhile, the newspapers reveled in the victory at Murfreesboro and several highlighted the action of the battery. The Evansville *Daily Journal* wrote: "The Chicago Board of Trade Battery, Capt. Stokes, shed luster upon the name of every man connected with it."[91]

Lieutenant Sylvanus Stevens sent a message at the end of the battle on January 3 stating: "Murfreesboro is ours. Terrific fighting on Friday. No casualties on the battery, it has won a glorious distinction."[92]

Battery Losses and Changes July 31–December 31, 1862*

Pvt. Henry J. Baxter	Discharged	November 3, 1862	Disability
Pvt. George A. Cooper	Discharged	November 13, 1862	Disability
Pvt. William Crocker	Discharged	November 13, 1862	Disability
Pvt. Andrew Downer	Discharged	November 13, 1862	Disability
Pvt. John J. Everts	Discharged	November 4, 1862	Disability
Pvt. David H. McMunn	Discharged	November 26, 1862	Disability
Pvt. Samuel T. Phillips	Discharged	November 31, 1862	Disability
Pvt. Ira A. Pease	Discharged	November 26, 1862	Disability
Lt. Albert F. Baxter	Resigned	November 18, 1862	Disability
Sgt. Sylvanus H. Stevens	Promoted to 1st Lt.	November 18, 1862	
Pvt. Andrew B. Finney	Killed-in-Action	December 31, 1862	

Pvt. John S. Stagg	Killed-in-Action	December 31, 1862	
Pvt. William H. Wiley	Killed-in Action	December 31, 1862	
Sergt. Abbott Adams	Wounded	December 31, 1862	
Pvt. William N. Bagley	Wounded	December 23, 1862	
Pvt. James W. Bloom	Wounded	December 31, 1862	
Pvt. John C. Camburg	Wounded	December 31, 1862	
Pvt. John J. Carroll	Wounded	December 14, 1862	
Corpl. Augustus H. Carver	Wounded (mortally)	December 31, 1862	
Pvt. William H. O'Dell	Wounded	December 31, 1862	
Lieut. Trumbull D. Griffin	Wounded	December 31, 1862	
Pvt. Jackson D. Howard	Wounded	December 31, 1862	
Pvt. John D. Toomey	Wounded	December 31, 1862	
Pvt. Homer Baker	Captured	December 14, 1862	
Pvt. John H. Buckingham	Captured	December 14, 1862	
Pvt. Francis R. Richmond	Captured	December 14, 1862	
Pvt. John B. Sleman	Captured	December 14, 1862	
Pvt. Thomas Tinsley	Captured	December 14, 1862	
Pvt. Thomas N. Williams	Captured	December 14, 1862	

*While not recorded as wounded in battery records, Stokes and Miller were also wounded during the battle. This would bring the total to 13 wounded during the Battle of Stones River as shown in Stokes' after-action report.

CHAPTER THREE

Horse Artillery and
the Tullahoma Campaign

*We are engaged in what promises to be a long
and bloody war....*—Private Tobias Miller

After the Battle of Stones River

The Board of Trade Battery's financial, commissary and medical support from Chicago went into action after the recent battle. This was evident by the numerous visits of people from Chicago, usually bringing letters and supplies to camp. In a new effort, the Board of Trade War Committee in Chicago organized and sent a contingent of representatives and nurses to Murfreesboro to aid those who were wounded after the recent battle. The medical personnel dispatched to Murfreesboro remained there until March when most of the wounded had recovered or been transferred elsewhere. The War Committee not only supported the battery but also the infantry regiments organized through the effort of the Chicago Board of Trade. Those in Chicago sent clothes, food, and a large amount of sanitary and medical supplies through the Sanitary Commission. After the Battle of Stones River, the *Chicago Tribune* reported that 150 women of the Ladies War Fund committee prepared supplies for the regiments and battery still in the field. Stokes wrote a letter of thanks to those in Chicago for their support and reported that with the arrival of supplies and medical personnel the battery gave "three hearty cheers."[1]

After the Battle of Stones River until mid-May, the battery remained assigned on a practical level to the Pioneer Brigade. The battery remained in the Murfreesboro area with little to do except to drill in anticipation of the next campaign. The official records show the battery assigned to the 2nd Brigade, 2nd Cavalry Division, Army of the Cumberland in March 1863. In reality, this did not occur until mid–May when the battery became part of the cavalry as a horse artillery battery, the only battery with this designation in the Army of the Cumberland. At this point in the war in the west, only the 1st Missouri Horse Artillery had this designation.[2]

Certainly, January was a month of rest, re-supply and recuperation for many in the battery. On January 4, the battery moved back to the area near McFadden's Ford where it had camped on the evening of December 30. The men unharnessed the horses for the first time in a week and commented that the "poor brutes were sore and tired." The men were equally tired and found time to wash and change clothes. A couple of days later the battery moved to Murfreesboro and was subsequently repositioned about a half mile outside of the town, again providing security for the workmen of the Pioneer Brigade who would be involved in the construction of Fortress Rosecrans. The battery retained the abandoned gun they had acquired during the recent fighting, becoming the only seven-gun battery in the Army of the Cumberland. Private William Shipley led a squad of men to Murfreesboro and returned with a captured limber, marked Augusta Arsenal Ga. 1862, for the new gun. Afterward, the battery reported its complement of guns as: four six-pounder field guns, two James rifles (3.80"), and one six-pounder rifle (3.67").[3]

The recent battle and the conditions under which the men lived resulted in illnesses of several in the battery. Already the attrition so common in the Civil War had taken its toll to such an extent that Stokes sent an appeal for 12 men to replace those that had been lost so far. Two men, Jacob Grosch (25 years old, artificer-blacksmith) and Frederick Favor (48-year-old "horse doctor"), were so ill they had to be discharged. August Carver, a printer before the war, was wounded on the first day of the Battle of Stones River and died on January 30 while in the hospital at Nashville. In addition, 22-year-old Andrew Baskerville also died in January. Baskerville, a clerk at J.B. Shay's Dry Goods before the war, contracted typhoid fever and died on his way to the hospital in Louisville. In addition, two of the battery, Corporal James Hildreth and Private Charles Johnston, were detached to look for horses and had apparently been captured, because they returned a couple of days later with hand-written paroles at which Stokes looked with some disbelief. These two walked away from the battery a few days later, but ultimately returned in March. (Hildreth, a pre-war clerk, six feet tall with light hair and blue eyes, would be reduced in rank to private over this event, but would be re-appointed corporal later in August.) The battery had frequent visitors from Chicago and the battery boys received an unwelcome one. The man, referred to as a "blow hard" who never brought any positive news, had a very cold welcome. Captain Stokes told some of the men that he needed to be kicked out of camp, but they let him "go in peace." On a positive note, the men captured during the December 14 foraging expedition were paroled and were currently in a camp for parolees in Annapolis, Maryland. In an attempt to keep up morale, Captain Stokes continued to offer Episcopal Church services for the men when a regular minister was not present. In a humorous response, Private John Fleming, a Presbyterian, wrote to his mother of that service: "I am getting pretty sick of." One last significant event occurred late in January when Rosecrans allowed the battery to unfurl their flags and fly them. This put an end to an issue that seethed within the battery since last fall when Stokes refused to allow the flags to be used, much to the displeasure of the men. Now in January, the issue was put to rest after Stokes wrote to Rosecrans requesting permission to use the flags. "But the gallant conduct of this well drilled Battery in the late fight at Murfreesboro, so won the admiration of Gen. Rosecrans, that he has conferred upon it the well-merited privilege of hereafter carrying the colors presented by its numerous friends at home," reported the *Chicago Tribune*. Stokes, who liked to talk with his meerschaum pipe in his hand, remarked that Buell had ordered batteries not to use individual flags as the reason he had disallowed their use.[4]

While the Board of Trade Battery dealt with issues within the battery, larger more complicated issues faced the Army of the Cumberland and its commanding general. Rosecrans did not gain a decisive victory at the Battle of Stones River, but in the end, his army claimed Murfreesboro. Bragg retreated southward about 30 miles and began preparing defenses along the Highland Rim south of the Duck River. With Bragg's southward

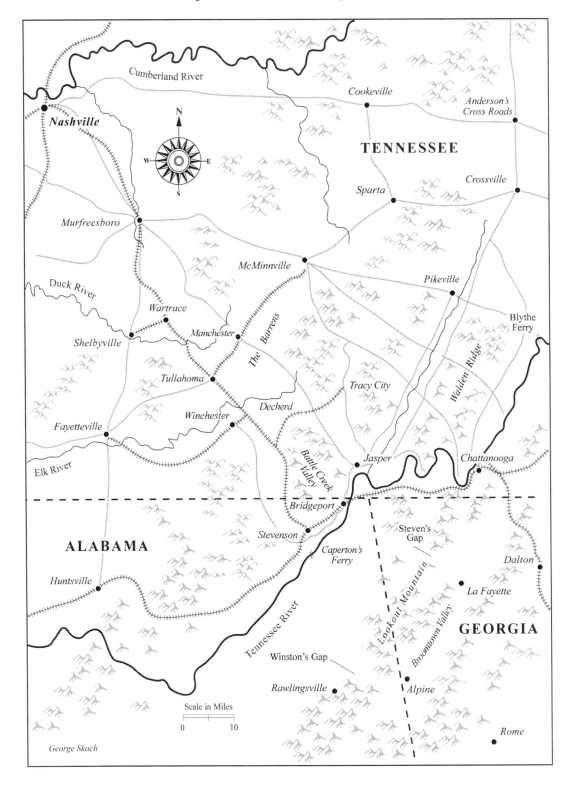

Middle Tennessee, northern Alabama and northern Georgia, Summer 1863.

march, Washington heaped accolades on Rosecrans and his army. This much-needed victory was exactly what those in Washington needed in light of the defeat at Fredericksburg, the stalemate along the Mississippi River, and the recent raid by Major General Earl Van Dorn on the Union supply depot at Holly Springs, Mississippi. Rosecrans focused his efforts on fortifying the area around Murfreesboro, including constructing the largest fort to be built during the Civil War, Fortress Rosecrans.[5]

At least for that time, the Army of the Cumberland was the darling of the Union Army. This pleasant situation did not last long. Almost immediately, pressure mounted for Rosecrans to continue with his offensive. Secretary of War Edwin Stanton wrote on January 7, "[T]his opens Eastern Tennessee; and if General Rosecrans takes possession of it, 200,000 rebel troops cannot drive him out." Those in Washington saw the victory at Murfreesboro as the first step in gaining control of East Tennessee, an objective which had been clearly communicated to Rosecrans when he assumed command of the Army of the Cumberland. However, Rosecrans had no intention of resuming the offensive at this time. He wanted to be sure the railroad was secured and then he set about reorganizing the personnel in the Army of the Cumberland. In addition, Rosecrans needed supplies because his army only had rations until January 15. After the battle, he sent a variety of requests ranging from tents to kettles in an effort to fully supply his army. Rosecrans had no plans of moving away from his base of supplies, particularly as he was perilously low on provisions, and in light of the Confederate cavalry's ability to cut the Federal supply line.[6]

After withdrawing from Murfreesboro, Bragg established his headquarters at Tullahoma, while Polk's Corps settled in at Shelbyville and Hardee moved into winter quarters near Tullahoma. While the Union and Confederate infantry remained relatively stationary, the cavalry of both armies worked hard during the first six months of 1863, a time often referred to as the "interlude" in this Tennessee Campaign. After the battle, Bragg established a defensive line of cavalry across a 75-mile front stretching from Spring Hill and extending to McMinnville in the east.[7]

Stanley and Rosecrans Rebuild the Cavalry Division

During the Stones River Campaign, Rosecrans' newly appointed chief of cavalry, Brigadier General David Stanley, provided immediate benefits to the army. Stanley's fledging cavalry division had just fought Joseph Wheeler's division to a standstill. After the battle, both Stanley and Rosecrans saw the need to gain parity with Confederate cavalry forces as the path to victory.

Relative Strength of Union and Confederate Cavalry[8]

Date (1863)	Present for Duty–Union	Present for Duty–Confederate
January 31	4,549	8,707
February 28	5,040	9,101
April 30	4,961	15,125
May 20	-	15,096

Rosecrans and Stanley were correct in their assessment of the Union cavalry and requested more horses, regiments, equipment, and artillery batteries from the War

Department to support this growing part of the Army of the Cumberland. To reflect the increased emphasis on the cavalry and based on his performance during the Battle of Stones River, Stanley was promoted to the rank of major general in early 1863. Stanley, a native Ohioan, was a West Point trained professional soldier who served in the cavalry before the war. Stanley graduated in 1852 and, before the war, served on the western frontier with a variety of men who would become comrades, as well as enemies. Stanley began the war as a captain in the 4th U.S. Cavalry and received a promotion to the rank of brigadier general in the volunteer forces in November 1861. Then, he commanded infantry divisions during the New Madrid-Island No. 10 Campaign, the Battle of Iuka, and the Battle of Corinth where he demonstrated his fighting ability and command skills. Rosecrans, greatly impressed with Stanley, appointed him chief of cavalry when he assumed command of the Army of the Cumberland.[9]

While this discussion of the efforts to enhance the cavalry division seems somewhat removed from the Board of Trade Battery and its attachment to the Pioneer Brigade, the cavalry corps would soon become very important to the battery, because Stanley needed artillery support. Based on Stokes' ability to train good artillerymen, Rosecrans' high regard for the battery during the recent battle, and its independent designation, the battery was selected by Stanley to join the new cavalry corps. The attachment to the Second Cavalry Division would officially be backdated to March 1863, but practically this did not occur until May 1863. The same was true for the appointment of Brigadier General John Turchin, a Chicagoan, who would command the Second Division.[10]

February to May—Board of Trade Battery

The battery had no significant action during February and remained near Murfreesboro throughout the month. Based on the correspondence of the members of the battery, discipline intensified which probably resulted from Rosecrans' emphasis on re-building the army and Stokes' training at the U.S. Military Academy. Private Benjamin Nourse wrote in his diary on February 2, "New order of things—if our horse gets loose in the night the party to whom he belongs shall get up and tie said horse and stand the remaining duty of the guard who discovered said horse loose. Orr was the first victim relieving Robt. Worrell." The next day he continued: "two minutes to haul on your boots and get into ranks at morning roll call. Conklin & Ford among the victims for discipline today." The increased emphasis on discipline continued throughout the month and on February 18, it was Robert Worrell's turn to "walk the battery with a knap sack because a horse broke the halter in the night. This caps the climax of petty tyranny and shows how mean and detestable our first lieut. can be if he chooses." The last remark was notable because the Nourse brothers had been happy when Sylvanus Stevens had been promoted to 1st lieutenant. Stevens demonstrated remarkable ambition moving from private to sergeant on to 1st lieutenant, but Stevens was not finished yet. In January, he was seeking the rank of major and his father was campaigning with the Illinois Adjutant General, just as his wife had done when he received his last promotion. Meanwhile, back in Chicago, those supporting the war effort clashed verbally with the Copperheads, Northerners opposed to the war. The Copperheads printed sheets seeking support for their cause, but the *Chicago Tribune* struck back using the Board of Trade Battery as its foil: "Every discharge of the Board of Trade Battery, at the bloody battle of Stones River, sent scores of vipers to their long home, and thus intensified the venom of the traitor sheet in this city."[11]

Despite the increased discipline, camp life went on. Soon the men received the disturbing news that Private William Bagley, accidentally wounded before the Battle of Stones River, died in a hospital in Cincinnati. Bagley was a 28-year-old pre-war sailor. At Murfreesboro, the Sanitary Commission personnel were on-site helping with the care of some of the wounded and ill, hoping to keep others from Bagley's fate. February was a rainy, cool, and overall gloomy month for many of the men and conversations inevitably led to discussions about the previous battle, Lincoln's Emancipation Proclamation and the length of the war. Benjamin Nourse recorded in his diary, "I am alone in our squad in saying that we shall see our time out in the service. I got hooted at, but we shall see if we live." Otherwise, the men went through daily drills and training exercises.[12]

With March, spring arrived at Murfreesboro with trees blossoming and the weather starting to warm, but mud, 10 inches deep, was a constant companion for the first part of the month. Refugees poured into the Federal lines and the civilians gave stories of rough treatment by the Confederate army, conscripting on-the-spot every male between 15 and 65. Training, inspections and drilling were still the main duties in camp and these had been done for the last two months without the field guns which had been stored in an artillery park since January 6. With the improving weather, the guns were returned to battery. With the increased drills, the unhappiness between some of the men and the commanding officers increased throughout the month. Nourse wrote "'Manual of piece' in the p.m. under Lieut. Stevens. Every day shows more and more clearly that he is a military fool." (In an annotation in his diary, Nourse by mid–June would write that Stevens was improving.) On March 15, another unfortunate incident occurred, this time over the attendance of soldiers at Sunday services. "Today we had service read by Capt. S. In the p.m. went down to the hospital to see our boys—only two absent from service—[Robert] Worrell & [Philip] Auten—a corpl. Guard could not find W.A. (whose excuse was sickness) but he came out by the corpls. order from his tent before the command and received all the abuse & insults that only such a low, mean mind of Jim Stokes is capable of thinking and delivering." Silas Stevens, in his post-war recollections, continued his allegations that Stokes drank to excess. Stevens concluded: "In this way I have accounted for his moods and absences, in other words he was drunk."[13]

Silas Stevens, the younger brother of First Lieutenant Sylvanus Stevens, recalled an unpleasant punishment inflicted on Private Seth Ford, a 21-year-old pre-war printer. Ford mischievously climbed a tree on the edge of the camp without anyone noticing, even the camp guard, and sat atop a high branch. He called down to the guard proudly about this accomplishment. Captain Stokes became aware of Ford's position, approached the tree, and words were exchanged between the two. Then, Ford was ordered down from the tree and arrested. He was taken to the guardhouse and then sentenced to extra guard and to "carry the rail." Stevens explained the punishment: "A good stout, long rail is obtained, and placed across the offenders shoulders, and fastened securely to his person; the arms are then outstretched and the hands are strongly tied with cords beneath the rail. The victim of the Captains displeasure is then, in this position with arms stretched on either side of his body, bound to the rail, made to walk his beat, in front of the guns, the regular guard duty, two hours. Then at the end of four hours, off, the treatment is renewed two hours more, or, as long as the Captains orders continue, if the offender does not completely succumb, or die before that time." This severe punishment fell like a pall on the men of the battery. The innocent act of climbing a tree turned into torture and men looked on in "horror and disgust." Afterward, the mood of the camp shifted to a process of mechanically performing duties and the whole atmosphere changed. Stevens and the men knew they had to serve under "one man's tyranny and brutally" and Stevens began looking for ways of "quitting this servile service."[14]

On a more positive note, more visitors and packages arrived from Chicago. Also, 20 new horses arrived for the battery and the men expected 30 more. In the continued efforts to improve discipline, the men of the battery were called onto the parade ground and the "50 Articles of war" were read to them. One private wrote that they were bored in the process but it "didn't hurt much" to hear them read. In a solemn service, the three bodies of those of the battery killed at the Battle of Stones River were taken to the train and returned to Chicago for burial, fulfilling the promise Nourse described the ceremony: "Capt. S. wore his dress coat and for the first time—this a.m. we cleaned up and looked our best—at one oclock we left camp in the following order—two first guns—in advance—three caissons with the coffins—flagged—third gun, caisson etc.—with due ceremony we put them on the cars—gone to their last resting place."[15]

On March 2, Private Lawson M. Andrews was part of a foraging party on the Lebanon Pike and was taken prisoner, but it was surmised that he had deserted. The men of the battery would not know the truth until Andrews was seen in Chicago in 1867. Despite Andrews' explanation some of the men doubted its veracity. The incident provided enough interest for the correspondent of the *Chicago Tribune* to write his opinion of the affair:

> *Writing of foraging, gives opportunity for the story of private, L.M. Andrews, of the Board of Trade Battery. On Sunday, the battery sent out an expedition, of which, private A. formed a part. The expedition came back on Monday, but alas! Private A. came not, leaving his messmates the sad conclusion that he had been foully dealt with—shot or "gobbled" by voracious "butternuts." When the matter came to discussion, however, it appeared that private A. had, on the morning preceding the march, made a systematic disposition of his company affairs. To one messmate he had given his spoon, to another his fork, to another his knife, etc., etc.; his debts had been paid, and, in short, every arrangement of that one designing to take a short leave absence would make, had been made by private A. This is all there is of the story of private L.M. Andrews. He may be dead, he may not be—the probability is that he still lives, and is not "gobbled." The young man may come to grief.*

Meanwhile, Lieutenant George Robinson left Tennessee and returned to Chicago on a fifteen-day recruiting trip. He returned on March 22 with eight new men, along with James Hildreth and Charles W. Johnston. Benjamin Nourse described Hildreth as "the runaway." Because there was no verification of Hildreth's and Johnston's capture or parole, there was some skepticism among the men. To make matters worse these men left the battery on their own accord. Robinson left Chicago with 11 men but three of the recruits deserted in Indianapolis. While in Chicago, Robinson married Miss Jane Adams Porter in Aurora, Illinois.[16]

New Recruits Board of Trade Battery—March 1863[17]

Charles Baldwin	Charles Kinger	Christian Smith
George Crane	Alexander Lewis	Charles S. Williams*
Robert Johnston/	Silas Peckham	George Mason*
Johnson	Albert Pontius	Charles Evans*

*Deserted.

Robinson's effort with recruiting was very important to the future of the battery. He was aided through the efforts of the *Chicago Tribune* which posted advertisements calling for 20 men to join the battery with the promise of a $60 bounty for enlistment. Among the new enlistees was Silas Peckham, a farmer and teacher who had moved to Chicago in March from New York and joined the battery in March. The newspaper urged, "Young men of Chicago, avoid the disgrace and dishonor of being conscripted." The first priority was to fill the ranks of those wounded, killed or discharged, but Stokes had grander plans. He wanted to increase the size of the battery from a six-gun to either an eight- or twelve-gun battery. When Robinson returned with only eight men, those plans were scrapped.[18]

While the Board of Trade Battery seemed comfortable on the outskirts of Murfreesboro and very inwardly focused, other units were actively battling the enemy, most notably the cavalry forces of both opposing armies. Colonel Robert Minty's cavalry brigade, supported by General Jefferson C. Davis' infantry division, clashed with the enemy at Franklin in February. In addition, the Confederate cavalry under the command of Nathan Bedford Forrest and Joseph Wheeler were repulsed in an attack on Federal forces at Dover. Fights on Manchester Pike and Bradyville rounded out the action in February with the Union forces performing well. March began with an early fight at Thompson's Station which went in favor of the Confederate forces. Minty had success at Rover and Vaught's Hill, and the Confederates gained another victory at Brentwood on March 25. Nine expeditions, nine reconnaissance actions, and 50 skirmishes occurred in the first six months of 1863 as the two armies remained stationary in Middle Tennessee.[19]

April proved to be equally unexciting for men stationed near Murfreesboro. Of note, Private Samuel Lord, an 1861 graduate of the University of Michigan, was court martialed and sentenced to guard duty on alternate days and fined $6 for impudence toward Lieutenant Bennett. In one significant event, Private Charles Maple was captured while on his way to Nashville. A mail agent managed to escape and told authorities that Maple, part of a small detachment, and the other men were robbed of their money and clothes before being taken away. Equally unpleasant was the work on "stump day" when the men appeared not to have enough to do. The men of the battery and the Pioneer Brigade were tasked to pull out stumps on and near the parade ground. Benjamin Nourse, expressing his continual unhappiness with Captain Stokes, wrote: "[T]he work as useless and mean as Stokes can make it and the boys not all saints, you may imagine we had some tall swearing. At it all day." Otherwise, the battery moved northward of Murfreesboro to La Vergne on April 21 and then just south of Nashville on April 26. Perhaps the Board of Trade Battery might have had higher morale if they had an opportunity to engage the enemy, but camp life proved monotonous. The men watched passively as the construction of the defenses around Murfreesboro continued. The news of the war also lowered the morale of the men. Private Tobias Miller wrote to his brother on April 20: "[T]he spirits of the men are now zero.... The Vicksburg, Fredericksburg, Charleston disasters must have greatly encouraged the south and given an impression of power throughout Europe."[20]

Rumors circulated in April that Stokes would leave his position as captain of the battery and the ambitious Sylvanus Stevens began jockeying to take over command. This prompted a long letter from Lieutenant George Robinson to the Illinois Adjutant General, Allen Fuller, on April 7. Robinson and others in the battery were familiar with the methods Stevens had used in Illinois to gain promotions in the past and he detected that Stevens was using the same process to obtain the promotion to captain. Robinson reminded Fuller that he was the next senior officer in the battery after Stokes and therefore it was natural to expect that he would succeed Stokes. Robinson acknowledged that Stevens was instrumental in the early organization of the battery and used his influence to get Stokes appointed to command. In return, Stokes tried to get Stevens elected as lieutenant, but the battery did not elect him. After that time, Stokes appointed Stevens as sergeant and gave Fuller his recommendation, which helped Stevens' to become appointment as lieutenant. Robinson explained that Stevens' and Stokes' prejudice and jealously towards him was "plainly visible." As a result, Robinson suffered through "disagreeable and persecuting acts" at the hand of Stokes which he accepted with "grace" for the good of the service. He pointed out that through influence Stevens had been promoted to first lieutenant over two highly capable second lieutenants. Robinson urged that this record of promotions through influence rather than performance be considered and he told Fuller that he expected Stokes to recommend Stevens over him. He closed by mentioning his excellent performance on and off the battlefield; however, Robinson would have a long wait for Stokes' exit and his own promotion.[21]

"Jine the Cavalry"

The boredom of April changed in May when a tall general named David Stanley arrived at camp in the middle of the month. He came dressed in a blue uniform with yellow piping instead of the red of the artillery. Now, the Chicago Board of Trade Battery was no longer independent. It was part of the cavalry. On May 23, the *Chicago Tribune* printed the announcement by their war correspondent:

Chief of cavalry for the Army of the Cumberland was regular army officer General David Stanley (Library of Congress).

Stokes' Battery

An order issued yesterday, makes a new disposition of the famous Chicago Board of Trade Battery. It is detached from the Pioneer Brigade and assigned to the cavalry, a service, by the by, which will necessitate a separation of the command, as each section goes to a brigade. I do not understand the "whys and the wherefores" of the order, I only know that the regret is universal that so fine a company of artillerists is not to be preserved intact to the service. The boys are generally well pleased with the change, however, discovering in the roving life of the cavalry a chance for adventure and excitement.

The newspaper had better information than the men in the battery. John Nourse wrote home that the battery was still a single unit and would not be divided into sections. Nourse would later find the newspaper to be correct. Private Tobias Miller remarked that the battery had been unified for so long, this subdividing was like separating a family. The men believed that Stokes was the cause of the attachment to the cavalry. Miller voiced it: "[O]ur captain would sacrifice our best interests to aid him in his ambition." In a more balanced analysis, the inclusion of the Board of Trade Battery was just one more step in the process that Stanley and Rosecrans had pursued for seven months. The Federal cavalry was outmanned by the Confederates and the Union army scrambled to gain parity with their adversaries; though in the spring much had been accomplished. At the Battle of Stones River, Stanley had cobbled together enough regiments to form a fairly substantial division, and by mid–June he had gained a second division through his and Rosecrans' efforts.[22]

The Composition of The Cavalry Divisions

The Cavalry of the Army of the Cumberland—July 5, 1863[23]

Major General David S. Stanley
First Cavalry Division
Brigadier General Robert B. Mitchell

First Brigade—Colonel Archibald P. Campbell

4th Kentucky, Col. Wickliffe Cooper

6th Kentucky, Col. Louis D. Watkins

7th Kentucky, Col. John K. Faulkner

2nd Michigan, Maj. John C. Godley

9th Pennsylvania, Col. Thomas J. Jordan

1st Tennessee, Lt. Col. James P. Brownlow

1st Ohio Artillery, Battery D (one section),
Capt. Andrew J. Konkle

Second Brigade—Colonel Edward McCook

2nd Indiana, Lt. Col. Robert R. Stewart

4th Indiana, Lt. Col. John A. Platter

5th Kentucky, Lt. Col. William T. Hoblitzell

2nd Tennessee, Col. Daniel M. Ray

1st Wisconsin, Col. Oscar H. La Grange

Second Cavalry Division
Brigadier General John B. Turchin

First Brigade—Colonel Robert H.G. Minty

3rd Indiana [West Batt], Lt. Col. Robert Klein

5th Iowa, Lt. Col. Matthewson T. Patrick

4th Michigan, Maj. Frank W. Mix

7th Pennsylvania, Lt. Col. William B. Sipes

5th Tennessee, Col. William B. Stokes

4th United States, Capt. James B. McIntyre

1st Ohio Artillery, Battery D (one section)
Lieut. Nathaniel M. Newell

Second Brigade—Colonel Eli Long

2nd Kentucky, Col. Thomas P. Nicholas

1st Ohio, Col. Beroth B. Eggleston

3rd Ohio, Lt. Col. Charles B. Seidel

4th Ohio, Lt. Col. Oliver P. Robie

10th Ohio, Col. Charles C. Smith

Stokes' (Illinois–Chicago Board of Trade)
Battery, Capt. James H. Stokes

Unattached
39th Indiana Infantry (mounted), Col. Thomas J. Harrison

On paper, the Board of Trade Battery was attached to Colonel Eli Long's Second Cavalry Brigade in Brigadier General John Turchin's Second Cavalry Division. Stokes' battery would be called on to support four Ohio cavalry regiments and one from Kentucky. Stanley was well pleased with his brigade commanders and the new regiments, but he was singularly unhappy with the selection of the division commanders—Robert Mitchell and John Turchin. Stanley seemed to accept Mitchell but Turchin would not fit into Stanley's corps. Turchin lived in Chicago before the war and in some ways fit very well with the Board of Trade Battery, but Stanley had no misgivings that Turchin had to go. Turchin, a native Russian, was born Ivan Turchaninoff in 1822. Turchin had been involved in the "Rape of Athens" the previous year and had been subsequently cleared in a court martial for actions taken in the Alabama town. So disgusted by the actions being taken by Turchin, his commanding officer Major General Don Carlos Buell wrote that he wanted to relieve Turchin of command "in consequence of his utter failure to enforce discipline and render it efficient." Despite these concerns, on April 17 Turchin was given command of a division in the cavalry over Stanley's disapproval. More recently, Turchin's failure to support a cavalry attack near Middleton, Tennessee, put many at risk, including Stanley. Fortunately, brigade commanders Eli Long and Robert Minty ordered their commands forward and completed an attack which saved many in the cavalry division.

Once Stanley's rage subsided, he concluded that Turchin simply could not ride. Stanley described Turchin's leadership style which called to mind the actions in Athens, Alabama, the prior year. "A perfectly cold bloodied foreigner—he did not care a fig what became of me or of the few men who followed me. He did not care to be jostled in a rush of cavalry for anybody's sake.... Garfield who was everlastingly looking out for votes, had imposed Turchin on the cavalry without any inquiry as to his fitness...." Once the expedition was over, Stanley promptly marched to Rosecrans' headquarters and announced that Rosecrans would have to choose—Turchin or Stanley. Rosecrans retained Stanley and made plans to transfer Turchin back to the infantry, his original assignment. Turchin was just more suited

Colonel Robert Minty, First Cavalry Brigade commander, Army of the Cumberland (Joseph Vale, *Minty and the Cavalry*).

to infantry command than cavalry. While the Board of Trade Battery had command issues of its own, they seemed somewhat small when taken in light of the issues Stanley had with Turchin.[24]

Despite Stanley's unhappiness with Turchin, he could not have been more pleased with the two brigade commanders of the Second Cavalry Division. Colonel Robert H.G. Minty commanded the First Cavalry Brigade and was recognized as the premier Union cavalry brigade commander in the west during the Civil War. Minty had been serving as lieutenant colonel of the 3rd Michigan Cavalry before he gained command of the 4th Michigan Cavalry. Minty, born in County Mayo, Ireland, on December 4, 1831, was the son of an English soldier serving in Ireland. Following in his father's footsteps, Minty enlisted as an ensign in the British Army and served five years in the West Indies, Honduras, and the west coast of Africa. Minty's service in the Union Army began when he was commissioned major of the 2nd Michigan Cavalry in 1861. Stanley had great respect for Minty and his ability to command, both officers realizing the need to wield the saber when fighting in close quarters with enemy cavalry. Minty's brigade carried the nickname of the "Sabre Brigade" because of his insistence of the use of this weapon. Minty commanded five cavalry regiments, a cavalry battalion and Newell's two-gun section of 1st Ohio Artillery, Battery D.[25] While Minty would become the premier Union cavalry brigade commander in the west, Colonel Eli Long, also a professional cavalryman, would be a close second. Long, a Kentucky native, graduated from the Kentucky Military Institute in 1855 and served along with David Stanley in the 1st U.S. Cavalry before the war. Most recently Long held the rank of captain in the 4th U.S. Cavalry and participated in the Battle of Stones River. Long was wounded in that battle as his regiment began a series of counterattacks on the Confederate cavalry which changed the outcome of the cavalry battle. After he recuperated from his wound, Long was appointed colonel of the 4th Ohio Volunteer Cavalry. Upon assuming command of the regiment, he found a demoralized regiment with officers waiting to resign, but Long made an immediate positive impact on the regiment. He stabilized this good cavalry regiment and brought it back to its full fighting potential. In March, Long's leadership resulted in his promotion to brigade command. The pipe smoking colonel was noted of placing his favorite pipe in his teeth as he went into action with the enemy.[26]

Board of Trade Battery— May/June

The Board of Trade Battery would be assigned to the very capable Eli Long's

Regular army officer Colonel Eli Long commanded the Second Cavalry Brigade (MOLLUS Mass Civil War Collection, United States Army Heritage and Education Center, Military History Institute, Carlisle, PA).

brigade and would indeed be parceled for duty with other brigades as sections in most cases. Stanley would not strictly use the battery with Long's brigade, and would assign it where it was most needed because only two batteries were assigned to the entire corps. The Board of Trade Battery was assigned to the strongest cavalry division in cavalry corps, specifically because the brigades were commanded by Long and Minty. Many of the men of the battery welcomed the assignment to the cavalry. Lieutenant Henry Bennett wrote to his grandfather that he was "anxious to be led to battle so as to wind up this infernal rebellion, as long getting tired of laying still so long."[27]

Early in May, the battery replaced their large Sibley tents for the smaller pup tents which are so common today. The smaller tents were met with mixed opinions. For example, Benjamin Nourse noted that the new tents pleased the men more than the old ones, but not everyone agreed. Some of the men liked the smaller tents for dry weather, but not so for wet weather. The men of the Pioneer Brigade complained loudly about the smaller tents and when Rosecrans rode past the brigade he was greeted with signs "Pups for Sale," "Dog Hole # 1," and "Rat Terriers." The men good-heartedly waited out of sight in their tents and as Rosecrans rode past, first one, then all the doors of the tents were filled with soldiers bow-wowing and barking. Rosecrans paused, then burst out laughing, and continued on his way.[28]

Lieutenant Henry Bennett, a reliable and steady officer of the battery (*The Topeka State Journal*, May 31, 1909, p. 10).

Stanley, Turchin, and their staffs arrived in camp on May 18 and welcomed the battery to the cavalry. The men were informed that they would receive an additional gun and the total number of the battery would increase to 200, promises which were ultimately not fulfilled. Importantly, the men were informed that they were to become horse artillery or flying artillery and they would be the only unit with this designation in the Army of the Cumberland. All the other batteries in cavalry corps were still termed light artillery. Horse artillery was distinguished from light artillery primarily because all the members of the battery were mounted and armed with revolvers and sabers, while in light artillery many of the men rode on caissons and limbers. Speed and efficiency were of paramount importance for horse artillery. Because all the men now rode horses, the cannoneers had new responsibilities of caring for the animals. The officers ordered that all the horses be groomed regularly and when inspections occurred, the officers rubbed the coats of the animals with white handkerchiefs and if a spot or hair appeared, the men had to groom the animal again. On May 21 the battery joined Turchin's division on Lebanon Pike. By the end of the month, the men were practicing their riding skills, including jumping horses over hurdles. The new drills tested men and animals and one of Benjamin Nourse's horses failed. "One of my old horses was rode off by Saml. Lock, but failed to clear the pole and falling broke his knees." The process of requiring artillery horses to jump hurdles was short-lived when one of the men fell off a horse and dislocated his shoulder during the exercise. With the need to ride, all the men were equipped with spurs. In addition to riding, all the men were armed with Colt Navy revolvers in preparation for close quarters fighting, and they were ordered to carry their sidearms whenever outside of camp. Still, the men thought being part of the cavalry would have its advantages. No longer would they be asked to be involved with battles like that of Stones River, but they expected to more commonly participate in raids and reconnaissance.[29]

June began with the unpleasant news that Corporal Theodore E. Baker, the 28-year-old pre-war merchant, died of typhoid fever on June 1 in the hospital at Murfreesboro. Benjamin Nourse made a striking, and unexplained, comment in his diary: "His was a Christian death, his brother Daniel was with him and his remains went to Chicago this p.m. Poor man, he killed himself by over eating and it teaches me a lesson—never to be forgotten." Private John Fleming wrote that Baker was never sick before this short, but deadly, illness. Overall, the battery was in good health with only nine men on the sick list on May 20, despite the lack of fruit and vegetables. Private William Avery was transferred from the battery on May 18 to serve in the provost marshal's office in Washington. Still in camp, the men continued to work daily on their new assignment as horse artillery and they got their first chance to work with the cavalry on June 4. At least some part of the battery joined two of Minty's regiments,

the 4th Michigan and 4th U.S., riding down Manchester Pike and in driving the Confederate pickets back into their breastworks at Hoover's Gap. The entire expedition covered 26 miles and gave the artillerymen a chance to get used to long days in the saddle. Turchin joined in the expedition and the column returned at 9:00 that evening. While this appeared to be an unexciting event for some, it was vitally important to Stanley and Rosecrans. One of the principal routes to Tullahoma, Bragg's headquarters, and a concentration of Confederates was through Hoover's Gap. Rosecrans had been pushed by Washington, with good reason, to start his advance against Bragg. The numerous skirmishes and demonstrations, such as the one on June 4, helped Rosecrans decide where the enemy was concentrated and which route was the best to use in the upcoming campaign.[30]

General John Turchin, a Chicagoan, commanded the Second Cavalry Division until late July (MOLLUS Mass Civil War Collection, United States Army Heritage and Education Center, Military History Institute, Carlisle, PA).

Those who went to Hoover's Gap awoke the next morning tired and stiff. There would be little to do during the day except deal with some fresh horses. Stanley was provisioning his corps in preparation for the upcoming Tullahoma Campaign and provided 30 horses to the battery on June 4 and another 47 horses on June 6. A few days later new harnesses arrived. The new horses completed the mounting of all of the men in the battery. The next day Turchin appeared in camp and informed the men that they would be advancing in three days but gave no particulars. Due to the attrition of men, the battery gained four men each, detached from each of five cavalry regiments (4th Michigan, 4th U.S., 4th Ohio, 7th Pennsylvania, and 10th Ohio) and a squad of men from the 2nd Kentucky to work as artillerymen. The men were generally adapting well to their role as horse artillery, but there were notable exceptions. Benjamin Nourse described his experience on the new horses: "Cannoneers drilled with horses in the a.m. and p.m. I rode [James] Campbell's wild pony in the forenoon and [Stephen] Wilson['s] balkey colt in the afternoon—never came so near going off a horse before in all my life. He reared, jumped and threw himself round lively—but I rode him for three hours." However, the 23-year-old ex-printer Private Coleman Brown was so frustrated in dealing with his horse that he pulled his new revolver and shot the poor brute. The officers immediately arrested Brown, confiscated all his government property, and sent him to the provost marshal's office for court martial. (Brown was tried a few days later and fined $85 for shooting the horse, to be deducted from his pay at a rate of $6 per month until repaid.) Despite some of the problems, the battery was well-outfitted and had eight horses (two as reserves) for each of the guns. John Nourse would state in his letter home that six horses were assigned to the guns and eight horses pulled the caissons. This brought the number of horses for the battery to 262 and the total number of men to 157, but eight additional horses were expected to arrive along with two additional wagons, making a total of nine wagons.[31]

Private Homer Baker, Private Francis Richmond, Corporal Tom Tinsley and Private Tom Williams, captured outside of Nashville on December 14, arrived in camp on June 9–12, much the worse for their time away. Benjamin Nourse wrote in his diary, "They had a hard time." The remaining two men (John Sleman and J.H. Buckingham) also captured at the same time were expected to arrive in camp shortly. The next day the third section, guns number 6 and number 7 under the command of Lieutenant Sylvanus Stevens, moved to face the enemy near Hoover's Gap. The column again traveled south on Manchester Pike accompanying Lieutenant Colonel William Sipes with the 7th Pennsylvania Cavalry and the 3rd Indiana Cavalry. The expedition yielded little results. Benjamin Nourse wrote "…trotted out to Hoover's Gap, drove in the rebel outpost and pickets but could not draw them out." This action was taken in conjunction with the 2nd Kentucky Cavalry advancing on Wartrace Road. The Kentuckians found two squads of enemy cavalry of 60 men and dispersed them with a few shots. In this second expedition as in the first, the Board of Trade guns were not needed. The reconnaissance found two brigades of infantry at Liberty Gap, one of the three principal gaps leading to Tullahoma. The next day the battery received yet another upgrade when Dr. W. Richards arrived from Washington to serve as battery surgeon, replacing Dr. Frederick A. Lord who departed from the battery at the end of January 1863. Lord felt that the army would not move for months and because he would no longer be needed for such a long period, he decided to terminate his contract with the government. Richards was described as being English and wearing regular clothes, not a uniform. John Nourse wrote in a letter that Richards was the new doctor, but "I don't think he knows much about medicine."[32]

The men of the battery soon found that new changes came with the attachment to the cavalry. First of all, the men had to reduce their baggage to be able to move faster. Only a couple of shirts, two pairs of socks, a jacket, blanket and whatever they could carry on their back were allowed. Despite the reduction of baggage, overall, the battery was much better supplied. With the improved supplies and equipment, the training and drills with the cavalry were longer and more intense than before. Some of the drills lasted two hours, but the men were up to the challenge and received positive recognition for their efforts in the drills from Turchin. The men practiced dismounting the guns (taking the gun and carriage totally apart) and all the drills were then conducted at the trot. The rapid movements caused Stokes to remark that "a man would have to keep his skin buckled on after this," referring to the speed of movement by the battery. On June 16, the drills were paused long enough to march the men to the execution of William Minix, 9th Kentucky Infantry, for desertion. Minix, part of Van Cleve's division, was executed on the drill ground in front of a large concentration of soldiers. In regard to discipline in the battery, Private Charles Johnston, who returned to the battery with Robinson's recruits, was court martialed for desertion but he did not receive the punishment leveled on Minix. Johnston merely forfeited pay and allowances while he was absent.[33]

The men continued to deal with the issues of large animals in mid–June. A man unfamiliar with large animals had difficulty getting a mare to pull and the result was frustration on the part of the animal which broke a caisson pole. The next incident occurred with the stampede of 60 horses. The men routinely took horses to be watered and to graze in pastures when they were not being worked. On this occasion a dog created havoc, barking and snapping at the horses, causing them to stampede. The men mounted their horses and caught some that had run away; the remainder wandered into camp and the erstwhile dog was shooed away.[34]

Grumbling occurred again as the Episcopal Church service was ordered for the men on Sunday. This time the new surgeon led the service and not Stokes. Benjamin Nourse lamented: "Dr. read the Episcopal service—read it wrong too. When he should have kneeled, he stood & when he should have remained standing, he was on his knees— half the boys went to sleep and the other half were mad because they could not sleep. The extra swearing of this forenoon caused by standing out in the hot sun for this service." So much for improving one's outlook toward his fellow man. Nourse grumbled, "like the rest, the old Dr. is well under the thumb of Capt. S."[35]

The drills increased daily as Rosecrans prepared to begin the Tullahoma Campaign. The actions over the past six months revealed important information for Rosecrans. Historian Michael Bradley summarized that the successes in the cavalry actions on the eastern flank decided the route of the Union advance during the Tullahoma campaign. "Although the terrain was more challenging in the east, the success of Union cavalry probes revealed that the Confederate defenses were vulnerable in that sector and the potential rewards were much greater." The six-month interlude allowed Stanley to amass 22 regiments and two artillery batteries as his cavalry determined the route of the advance on the Confederate positions at Tullahoma. As the campaign began, the words of Private Tobias Miller echoed from a letter to his sister: "[W]ar is not a trade of kindness, and a nation situated as we are must not hesitate to use all its powers in vigorous action. We are engaged in what promises to be a long and bloody war...."[36]

The Tullahoma Campaign—June 24–July 3, 1863

Rosecrans wanted to avoid attacking Bragg's well-constructed defenses at Tullahoma and Shelbyville and he had to find a way around the defenses. Leonidas Polk's corps was

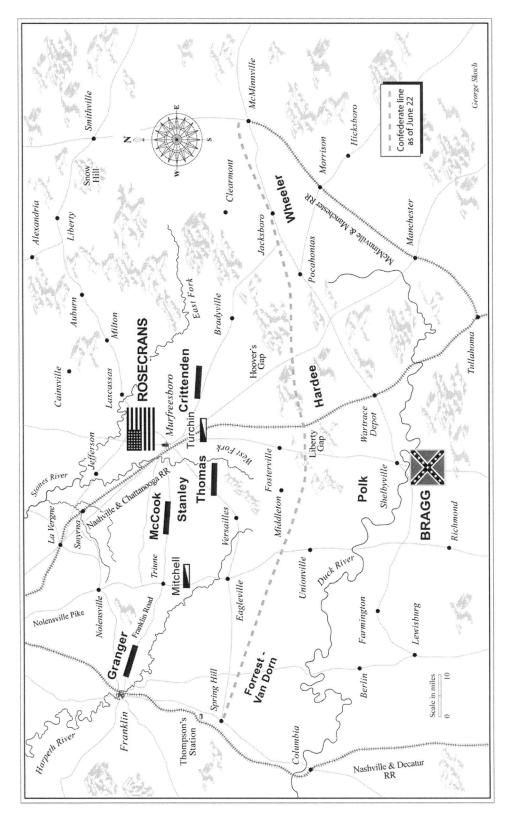

Union and Confederate positions, June 22, 1863.

located near Shelbyville, William Hardee was near Wartrace, and the Confederates also had the advantage of holding the highland passes along the three primary roads leading to Tullahoma. Rosecrans' strategic objective centered on capturing the bridges at Estill Springs and Pelham, turning Bragg's right flank in the process. He decided to confuse Bragg by advancing on the western flank with Stanley's and Granger's corps in a feint and then attack the Confederate eastern flank which the cavalry operations suggested was more vulnerable. This meant the concentration of Rosecrans' army would center on Manchester and then in a wheeling movement turn Bragg's right flank, placing him in the position of facing the Union infantry away from his entrenchments. Rosecrans' plan called for Thomas' Fourteenth Corps to move along the Manchester Pike and seize and hold Hoover's Gap. Rosecrans ordered Thomas and McCook to advance, each corps within supporting distance of

Illinois native and pre-war clerk William Burdell served as bugler for the battery and awakened the men to rich and lofty notes (Chicago History Museum, ICHi-176915).

the other. Meanwhile, Crittenden's Twenty-First Corps planned to advance and concentrate at Bradyville, forming the east flank of the Army of the Cumberland. Long's Second Brigade had orders to operate in conjunction with Crittenden. Stanley and the remainder of the cavalry advanced toward Versailles, west of the Shelbyville Road, and then moved southward to unite with Robert Mitchell's cavalry division, which had been placed under Gordon Granger's command.[37]

Relative Strength of Union and Confederate Cavalry in Middle Tennessee—1863[38]

Date	Present for Duty–Union	Present for Duty–Confederate
May 20	-	15,096
May 31	4,961	-
June 10	-	13,868
June 30	10,560	-

As the campaign began, Rosecrans hoped Bragg would send troops to an area Rosecrans did not plan to attack. The plan worked well as Stanley's main body of cavalry found and pushed back the Confederate cavalry at Eagleville, Rover, Middleton and Unionville. Rosecrans assigned Gordon Granger to the overall command of this part of the campaign. Just about all the Federal cavalry, except Long's brigade operating with Crittenden on the eastern flank, participated in this initial feint. On June 23, Granger ordered Robert Mitchell's First Cavalry Division along the Eagleville and Salem Roads pushing the enemy's cavalry and pickets in front of them. Granger also sent his infantry forward hoping to draw Confederate forces to the west. Mitchell's cavalry division had sharp fights as he pushed from Eagleville and Rover.[39]

As the campaign began, it began raining and rained until the end of the campaign, exhausting the soldiers and horses in the process. David Stanley recorded, "That day the rain set in … and which, converting the whole surface of the country into a quagmire, has rendered this one of the most arduous, laborious, and distressing campaigns upon man and beast I have ever witnessed." The feint worked well and the opening actions also confused Wheeler to "such an extent that for days he sent army headquarters erroneous, conflicting, and incomplete reports of enemy movements and intentions." One day before Rosecrans began his advance Wheeler moved his troopers toward Shelbyville away from the exact objective of the Union advance, leaving the critical Highland Rim gaps weakly defended as Rosecrans' main thrusts moved forward. Turchin's division, consisting of only Long's brigade, screened Crittenden's movement on the east which was almost totally unopposed. Despite Bragg having excellent terrain for his defenses, Rosecrans easily maneuvered past these obstacles.[40]

The Cavalry Battle at Shelbyville

The notable cavalry action in this campaign came when Stanley ordered Robert Minty to attack Wheeler's cavalry at Shelbyville. Thomas, McCook and Crittenden successfully moved through the treacherous gaps and marched toward Manchester. Realizing Rosecrans' success, the Confederate infantry began its retreat to Tullahoma on the morning of June 27. To Wheeler's credit, he resolutely planned to hold back the Union advance with just his cavalry as Polk and Hardee withdrew toward Tullahoma. Stanley rode at the head of about 5,000 cavalries—Mitchell's division plus Minty's brigade. He sent a rider to Minty asking him to move his brigade ahead and attack the gap, exclaiming the brigade in the lead was "so d[amne]d slow, he couldn't do anything with it." The slowness of the lead brigade was attributed to Mitchell's illness and delays in sending orders to the brigade commanders.[41]

Minty successfully cleared Guy's Gap and then continued at the gallop to Shelbyville where Brigadier General William "Will" Martin's Confederate cavalry, about 900 strong, defended the town in entrenchments. Stanley ordered Minty to attack with his entire brigade and ultimately drove the Confederates out of the town. Minty's men captured one piece of artillery near a railroad depot, followed by a second taken in a sharp fight in the town, and a third that was captured at the Skull Camp Bridge. The pursuit did not stop at the river and the Union cavalry chased their prey for another two miles before breaking off the pursuit. The engagement at Shelbyville carried great significance in terms of the strategic situation in the western theater of the Civil War. This engagement is generally recognized as a point where the dominance of Confederate cavalry over the Union cavalry in Tennessee ended.[42]

Meanwhile on the eastern flank, Turchin still suffered the displeasure of David Stanley. He operated with a single brigade, Long's, and saw little action. In the single event in which he could have made an important contribution, he was unsuccessful. Rosecrans needed to capture the bridges across the Elk River to ensure he could pursue Bragg even if he could not trap him. Under Stanley's orders, Turchin started for Hillsboro and Mitchell's division rode for Manchester. The next day, it was confirmed the route of the Confederate retreat was not through Pelham, but through Estill Springs. Upon this discovery,

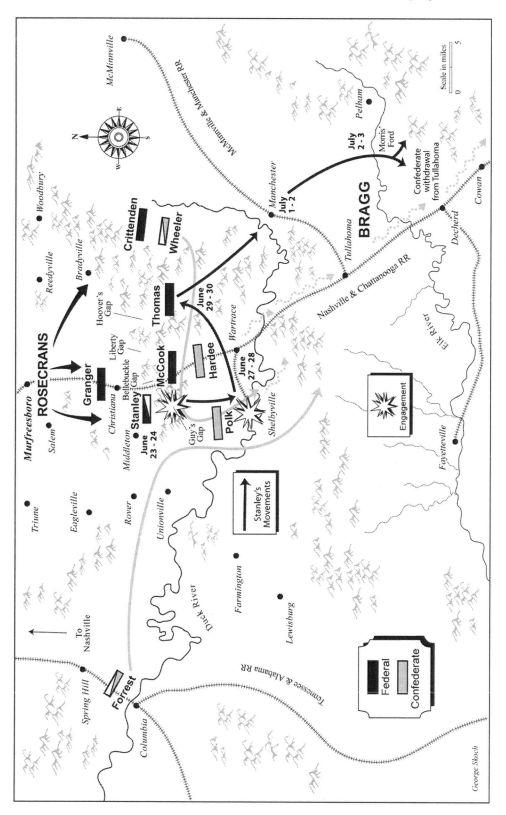

Union cavalry movements in the Tullahoma Campaign, June 24–July 3, 1863.

Stanley ordered Turchin to ride to Decherd but Turchin's advance was blocked at Morris' Ford on the Elk River by a Confederate rearguard. Turchin found the 51st Alabama Partisan Rangers and the 25th and 26th Tennessee (CSA) infantries on the opposite side of the river backed by Darden's Mississippi Battery in a strong position. Stanley dispatched Mitchell's cavalry to assist in the crossing, but Eli Long got his brigade across the river first and fought a determined rearguard action by Confederate cavalry as he advanced toward Decherd. Once Long crossed the ford, Turchin and Mitchell pressed their pursuit until nightfall and Stanley's cavalry claimed a Confederate colonel killed and a second mortally wounded, in addition to another 20 soldiers killed.[43]

Turchin was not successful with the cavalry. His reputation continued to suffer under the pen of T.F. Dornblaser, 7th Pennsylvania Cavalry, who noted Turchin decided to take a nap before attempting to push the Confederates from the ford at Elk River. "Here we halted for a few hours. Turchin took a nap in the shade of a tree. While he was napping, the writer saw the enemy on the south side of the river, placing a battery in position. The orderly felt it his duty to wake the general, and before a 'mad Dutchman' was done growling at the unnecessary interruption, the aforesaid battery opened fire, and dropped the shells in such close quarters as to cause the general and his staff to 'get up and dust.'" A member of the 3rd Ohio Cavalry also recorded Turchin's self-importance when his coffee pot was stolen on June 27, and the brigade waited as a member of Turchin's staff tried to find the culprit and the pot.[44]

Board of Trade Battery During the Tullahoma Campaign

The seven guns of the Board of Trade Battery (designated as Stokes' Battery, Horse Artillery in Stokes' report) began the Tullahoma Campaign with the men of the battery being called to duty at 2:00 a.m., with the march starting at 6 a.m. on June 24 from Murfreesboro. The battery marched south on Woodbury Pike about six miles and then Stokes sent a three-gun section (guns number 1, number 2, and number 7) under the command of Lieutenant Sylvanus Stevens to the concentration of the Federal cavalry pushing southward on the western flank. The remaining four guns, under Stokes' direct command, moved to Bradyville on the eastern flank. Stevens' section reported to Minty and moved another eight miles south on the Salem Road. One of Stevens' limbers broke an axle which had to be repaired but the other two guns continued forward. Any question of whether the battery would be used as separate sections or as a full battery was immediately determined. Both Stokes and Stevens ended the first day and encamped after little action. On June 25, Stevens advanced on the Shelbyville Road and halted in the vicinity of Granger's corps. On June 26, Stevens did not advance at all, remaining in camp as Granger's corps marched six miles south. The next day, Stevens was dispatched a mile to the rear to support Colonel Thomas Champion's 96th Illinois Infantry, which provided security for the baggage train near a bridge, and the section remained at this location for two days. But, on the night of June 27, the battery received word that Minty had attacked Shelbyville and Benjamin Nourse wrote in his diary, "Heavy cannonading about night & it is reported our cavalry are in Shelbyville." The next day Nourse wrote about Minty's fight: "[Y]esterday the cavalry went into the rebels driving them from their entrenchments, taking 3 guns and 800 cavalry. The charge was made by the third battalion of the 7th Penn. They lost 5 men & 2 lieuts. They sent back for us to come and support them, but the orderly did not find us." On June 29, Stevens joined Minty's main column at Shelbyville and accompanied Minty's brigade on June 30 through Shelbyville to Fairfield, a town of only four houses. Minty made an immediate positive impression on the men in Stevens' section. Private John Fleming wrote his father at the end of the campaign. "Our section is under Col. Minty ... a true Scotchman.... Command is one of the best in the service."[45]

On June 25, Stokes and four guns advanced along with Crittenden's corps on the eastern flank, passing through Major General John Palmer's Second Division. Stokes moved the two sections into position behind Palmer's artillery and stopped a mile south of Hollow Springs, about eight miles north of Manchester. The next day Stokes marched to the Duck River and halted. The following day (June 27) Stokes remained unengaged until 3 p.m. when he moved a few miles northwest toward Woodbury. On June 28 he arrived in Manchester and encamped a mile north of town and remained there until July 1.[46]

Stevens' section continued to be unengaged for the remainder of the campaign. On July 1, the section moved to just west of Manchester, then returned to Fairfield the next day. On July 3, the last day of the campaign, the section moved back to Manchester where two of the guns remained in camp while one gun moved to the Elk River, near Decherd Station. The traveling was very difficult in light of the terrain and the rains. Benjamin Nourse wrote: "We were over the worst road I ever saw. Sometimes on the side of a hill. Our caissons almost over and down the steepest hill, some at an angle of 45." On the eastern flank, it appeared that Stokes would also remain out of the action. On July 1, he left Manchester at 10 p.m. with one section (Robinson's), leaving the other at Manchester and arrived four miles southwest of Manchester at Hillsborough at 2 a.m. The next day, Robinson's section got into the fight. The guns started forward with Turchin and Eli Long's brigade. At 4:30, the section was a mile south of Hillsborough and moved initially to the town. Joining the rest of Long's brigade, it was ordered to march to Decherd Station via Morris' Ford in an active pursuit of the enemy. The Federal column reached the ford at 9 a.m. and met a line of enemy soldiers on the north side of the Elk River. Private Silas Stevens described the position where the road "wound around a large field of growing green corn and then the road turned to the right, and then fell away again, in a straight line toward the river: with trees on either side. Along the riverbank a heavy undergrowth of pine and cedars. On the opposite shore high bluffs intervened with a plateau somewhat back from the water's edge, and covered with trees, but open toward the approaches to the river." Long's troopers deployed, drove the enemy across the river and then Stokes ordered the section into position. The guns unlimbered about 30 yards from the crossing and then opened fire on the enemy on the opposite side of the stream with canister and shell. This drove the enemy away from the ford, pushing them up the hill which still gave them the advantage of firing down on anyone attempting to cross. Stokes felt pretty good until, much to his surprise, a four-gun enemy battery opened up on his section. Stokes exclaimed: "[T]hey were entirely concealed, with a battery of four guns, throwing shot and shell with great precision into my section, injuring none of my command, although the shells burst every time in our midst; but having taken the precaution to remove my horses, none were injured." The position of the guns near the river was not favorable because the enemy's guns were posted on the plateau some distance away. Stokes ordered "Limber up!" and directed George Robinson to move one of the guns to a hill just in the rear, near a house to get a better line of sight of the enemy battery. Robinson immediately began moving the gun, a six-pounder James Rifle, onto the hill, but the enemy guessed the nature of the movement and directed all four guns on Robinson. Fortunately, the ground was so wet as Robinson traversed a newly plowed field that the enemy balls simply plopped into the mud, burying the projectiles. The men urged the horses to pull the guns through the soggy ground and up the hill. Robinson quickly got the gun into action and his third shell stuck one of the enemy guns, disabling it. Robinson's position was so good and his firing so accurate, the enemy limbered and re-positioned in a less vulnerable location, but still covering the ford. In the meantime, Robinson continually fired and the citizens later reported several of the shells landed among enemy infantry troops supporting the battery. Turchin stopped his attempts to force the crossing at 10:30 because he learned there was another crossing in close proximity. He felt he was at risk of being encircled if he pushed across Morris' Ford. So, he decided to wait until Stanley arrived about four hours later. At 2:00 p.m., Turchin ordered Stokes to take both guns to a second hill further in the rear, but the order was never carried out because Stanley arrived with reinforcements. Stokes recorded, "An advance was then ordered, and the ford crossed, the artillery occupying its first position crossing the ford. The artillery remained on the north side—crossing the ford that night—having been joined by one gun, under Lieutenant Stevens." Turchin recognized Stokes and Robinson for their actions at Morris' Ford. "Capt. James H. Stokes, who directed his gun in person right at the ford, under the fire of sharpshooters posted not more than 75 yards from the gun; Lieutenant Robinson, of Stokes' battery, who at the third shot dismounted one of the enemy's guns."[47]

Lieutenant Sylvanus Stevens arrived and when asked how he managed to reach the battery in such muddy conditions, he merely replied, "Damnably!" Stokes continued on July 3 with all seven guns, crossing the Elk River at Morris' Ford and due to the high water, the ammunition had to be carried by cannoneers on horseback to keep it dry. He marched the battery 10 miles southeast of Tullahoma and encamped near Decherd Station on the Nashville & Chattanooga Railroad. The battery remained in place until July 6 when it moved five miles south of Winchester. In the entire campaign, Stokes reported his casualties: "No killed, no wounded, and no missing; no horses injured."[48]

In the final analysis, the Tullahoma Campaign was a remarkable feat of generalship on the part of Rosecrans. He maneuvered Bragg out of Middle Tennessee over a 10-day rain drenched campaign with only 570 casualties. The plan worked exactly as Rosecrans planned and by successfully attacking Bragg away from his prepared defenses,

Dragging the guns through the mud, a common sight in the Tullahoma Campaign (Alfred Waud sketch, Library of Congress).

the Southern general chose to withdraw to Chattanooga. In regard to the cavalry, the campaign was a major success for Stanley and his newly formed corps. The two cavalry divisions reported only 89 casualties in the campaign and many recognized that the Union cavalry in the west, for the first time in the war, had gained parity with their Confederate adversaries. Although the Board of Trade Battery had little to do, this was not unlike many units during this campaign. The only notable action by artillery in the cavalry portion of the campaign came at Shelbyville, when the 18th Ohio Battery fired on the Confederates preparing to defend the town. Stokes' command got into the exchange at Morris' Ford where Turchin continued to underperform as a cavalry commander.[49]

Battery Losses and Changes January 1–June 30, 1863

Pvt. William O. Avery	Discharged	May 18, 1863	
Pvt. Andrew Baskerville	Discharged	January 8, 1863	
Pvt. Frederick J. Favor	Discharged	January 16, 1863	
Pvt. Jacob Grosch	Discharged	January 16, 1863	
Corp. Charles Lesur	Discharged	April 5, 1863	Disability
Pvt. Charles H. Maple	Discharged	May 31, 1863	
Lawson M. Andrews	Deserted	March 3, 1863	
James Smith	Deserted	March 16, 1863	
Pvt. William N. Bagley	Died	February 8, 1863	Wounds
Pvt. Theodore E. Baker	Died	June 1, 1863	
Pvt. Augustus H. Carver	Died	January 30, 1863	Wounds
Pvt. Charles W. DeCosta	Died	February 2, 1863	

New Recruits	Enlistment Date	
James Burns	March 12, 1863	Deserted March 18, 1863
George Crane	March 17, 1863	
John Duffy	March 9, 1863	Deserted March 16, 1863
James F. Foster	March 10, 1863	Deserted March 16, 1863
Charles C. Kinger	March 12, 1863	
Alexander Lewis	March 7, 1863	
Silas C. Peckham	March 12, 1863	
Albert Pontius	March 12, 1863	
Christian Smith	March 14, 1863	
James Smith	March 9, 1863	

CHAPTER FOUR

March to Chickamauga Creek
(July 5–September 17, 1863)

[A]nother one of our battery, one who has always been a good soldier—
performing his duty faithfully, has gone from among us … reminding
us to live well … for we follow him shortly.—Private Tobias Miller

The Army of Tennessee marched toward Chattanooga after being physically and psychologically defeated in the Tullahoma Campaign. Morale was at an all-time low for the Confederate army. Bragg was a weary general in poor health and a man with many problems. If his health problems were not enough, he continued to be an unpopular general with his subordinates, an unpopularity which had continued to increase after the Perryville Campaign almost a year earlier. Polk and Hardee, Bragg's two most important infantry corps commanders, had long since wearied of his command, and in 1863 Bragg had added a list of other generals who mistrusted their commanding general. By mid–July, Lieutenant General Daniel Harvey Hill arrived in Chattanooga to assume command of William Hardee's infantry corps in the Army of Tennessee. Hill immediately became disturbed by the condition of his new army. The Confederate army had retreated to Chattanooga and without a fight forfeited almost all the territory west of the town to the Union army.[1]

Equally troubling on the Union side of the line, Rosecrans again settled his army around Middle Tennessee instead of actively pursuing Bragg. The Nashville & Chattanooga Railroad was a critical source of communications and supplies for his army and he needed to make it operational before he made any further advances. In addition, the roads the Army of Tennessee used in its retreat remained in terrible condition because of the excessive rains in July. While Rosecrans focused on the supply line from Nashville, Washington sent another series of demands to move, but Rosecrans remained in Middle Tennessee for six weeks as he prepared his army for another advance against Bragg. On July 24, Henry Halleck wrote to Rosecrans stating: "There is great disappointment felt here at the slowness of your advance. Unless you can move more rapidly, your whole campaign will prove a failure…." From Rosecrans' standpoint, he faced 30 miles of the Cumberland Mountains between Tullahoma and the Tennessee River. This was barren ground with little hope as a source of forage for his army or his animals. He needed to rely on the railroad for his supplies which amounted to 60 rail cars per day. Rosecrans wanted to repair the railroad to Bridgeport to support any advance made on the other side of the river by the Army of the Cumberland. He did not remain totally stationary and he sent some regiments to Bridgeport to repair the railroad. The risk of crossing the large Tennessee River, which could be heavily guarded by the enemy, also weighed on his mind.[2]

The Confederate initial line of defense, which Stanley's mounted forces faced, was Forrest's cavalry stretching northeast from Chattanooga, and Wheeler's cavalry extending southwest of Chattanooga. While repairing the railroad, Rosecrans positioned his army with Thomas' Fourteenth Corps at Decherd, and Alexander McCook's Twentieth Corps had headquarters at Winchester. Stanley moved his cavalry to Salem, Winchester and Fayetteville. Crittenden, whose Twenty-first Corps headquarters was at Manchester, had three divisions nearby, including one division at McMinnville.[3]

The Cavalry Corps and the Board of Trade Battery—July 1863

For the Union cavalry and artillery, the 10-day Tullahoma Campaign of continuous rainfall and the subsequent mud had taken a toll on horses and men. Stanley summarized the condition of his command: "The incessant rain and consequent condition of the roads rendered the operations of the cavalry difficult and exceedingly trying to men and horses." The day after the Tullahoma Campaign ended the men of the Board of Trade Battery rested and tried to clean the mud off their equipment and themselves. They had good moments and bad moments during the day. The good came as the army celebrated the Fourth of July by firing a cannon salute with part of the battery at Manchester while some of the battery was at Decherd. One bad moment came as the battery was placed on limited rations for the first time in the war due to an inability to move the supply train through the mud. Another bad moment came with a not-so-subtle message from the enemy. The enemy left a human skull, which reportedly had been from a Union soldier, dyed red and hanging at a house. To men of the Union army, this signified a black flag seen as an act of defiance. The black flag, opposite of a white flag of surrender, meant that the enemy would not give up, nor give or accept quarter. Though defeated in the Tullahoma Campaign, the enemy remained a formidable opponent and the black flag, in return, hardened the resolve of Federal soldiers.[4]

The next day the battery, united again, moved to Tullahoma over horrendous roads which were a muddy quagmire after the recent rain. The roads were so bad the men had to harness 12, 16, and at one point 28 horses to pull a carriage through the mud. To make matters worse, it rained again for two hours. John Nourse exclaimed, "Oh, I never saw such roads—I don't believe worse could exist." Reaching Tullahoma, the battery took a respite and began moving southward again the next day in the trail of Bragg's army, only to halt at the Elk River which was so swollen it was impassable. They remained there through July 7 after seeing that it would be some time before they could get across the river. The next day the battery moved six miles up-river to a bridge, built by the Pioneer Brigade. Another cannon salute was ordered that day to celebrate the fall of Vicksburg. The battery moved south, through Winchester, Stanley's headquarters, and moved about five miles south of the town to camp.[5]

With the cavalry corps camped near Winchester, the railroad transportation was soon back in service and the short rations gave way to normal conditions. After the recent campaign, Stanley worried about discipline for a variety of reasons, not only with the cavalry regiments, but throughout the Union army. He also tried to maintain the peace as much as possible with citizens, but in some cases he resorted to fear tactics. Stanley was a self-professed strict disciplinarian and was ever aware that lack of discipline could quickly turn into chaos and pillaging. On July 11, one of the cavalrymen detached to battery duty was found asleep at his post and was promptly arrested and sent back to his regiment. In addition, Stanley endorsed the verdict of a court martial of Corporal George W. Mercer, 1st Ohio Cavalry, who had been found guilty of setting fire to a cotton factory. Benjamin Nourse was part of the large number of men ordered to watch Mercer's punishment. "At 3 oc., we with the whole brigade were ordered out to witness the drumming out of camp of a corporal of the 1st Ohio Cavalry for burning a cotton press and fixtures at Salem after he had received the hospitalities of the owner. He was a hard looking man, head shaved and drummed out of camp—forfeit all pay and allowances with two years hard labor in prison at Alton, Illinois—I shall ever remember this scene—and that piece 'the rogues march.'" In another case, a member of the 4th Kentucky Cavalry had his head shaved and a sign placed on his back with the words "thief" after his court martial for horse theft. He received a two-year prison sentence for the crime. Discipline issues in the Union cavalry ranged the gambit of thievery, intoxication and being absent without leave.[6]

Huntsville Expedition—July 13–July 22, 1863

As Rosecrans tarried, he put his cavalry to work. On July 13 the cavalry rode to Huntsville, Alabama (about 40 miles south of Winchester) with both Turchin's and Mitchell's divisions on an expedition that lasted from July 13 through July 22, to secure Union possession of the territory north of the Tennessee River and to collect as much forage, horses and mules as could be found. Stanley's expedition proceeded south through New Market, then to Huntsville. As a show of force, the cavalry planned to occupy Huntsville, demonstrating to the citizens in Middle Tennessee and northern Alabama that the Federal forces had actually taken possession of the country. In addition, Rosecrans ordered Stanley to gather ex-slaves for the purpose of employing them as teamsters and laborers for the defenses at Nashville and Murfreesboro. The cavalry provost marshal decided the best way to accomplish its task was to converge on churches to collect the ex-slaves at the end of services. Stanley collected 600–1,000 ex-slaves during various cavalry patrols in the Huntsville area. These actions from the Southern point of view seemed to be achieving the desired effect. Local Huntsville resident Mary Jane Chadick wrote, "They are stealing all the Negroes and confining them in the Seminary building. Seventy have just passed by under a strong guard. All the good horses have been taken." Stanley promised the local civilians that he would keep the ex-slaves overnight and if any wanted to return to their old masters he would allow them to do so, but none did.[7]

Huntsville boasted a prosperous cotton and transportation industry prior to the war and it served as a resort town for some in Alabama. Stanley's cavalry remained in Huntsville for six days and he sent patrols scouting in all directions. The expedition included greater than 5,000 troopers and as a result the Confederate's cavalry remained in place on the south side of the river, content to watch the activities of Stanley's men. Several newspapers documented the expedition, including the *Abingdon Virginian*, which gave a balanced account in the form of a first-hand narrative. The citizens of Huntsville awoke in the morning to the sound of hoof beats and soon found the town full of "blue-coats." The cavalry entered the town during the early morning hours and quietly waited for the residents to begin their day. Stanley announced to the local authorities that he commanded the cavalry in possession of the town. The citizen explained of Stanley, "To all he was polite, considerate, and, as far as he could be, accommodating."[8]

The expedition to Huntsville was a great show of force for Stanley's cavalry and made an impressive showing for the citizens, but for the Board of Trade Battery this was a rather uneventful exercise, with some notable exceptions. Lieutenant Sylvanus Stevens, with a two-gun section (guns number 3 and number 5), remained at Winchester while the other five guns left Salem (serving as part of the rearguard). With one section attached to Minty's Brigade and the other to Long, they passed into Alabama on July 13, camping at New Market that evening. The next day the battery marched through a steady rain and reached 10 miles north of Huntsville before camping. The country the battery passed was overwhelmingly pro–Confederate and corn abounded in the fields. Benjamin Norse remarked that there was "[c]orn enough to supply the Confederacy a whole year." The battery reached Huntsville on July 15 and the two sections went into position on opposite sides of town. Then, the men aided in the process of collecting slaves and animals. On Sunday, July 20 the men collected a large number of slaves, as Stanley and his provost marshal had planned. "[C]amped at Belle Factory where we took several hundred negroes," wrote Nourse. At Huntsville, the news reached Stanley that General Nathaniel Banks had just captured Port Hudson and General William Sherman defeated General Joseph Johnston at Jackson, Mississippi. To celebrate the Union successes, he ordered the battery to move east of the courthouse and fire a salute. By July 21, the battery returned to Winchester, camping 10 miles south, and the column returned with several thousand ex-slaves, mules and horses.[9]

Brigadier General George Crook Replaces Turchin

After months of tension, John Turchin was relieved of duty with the cavalry on July 29. Upon his transfer back to the infantry, John Nourse wrote in his diary the men were told that Turchin requested the transfer because he disagreed with Stanley, whom Turchin thought was giving too many protection papers to local citizens. Private John Fleming wrote to his father, stating that Stanley and Turchin were opposites in regard to the pro–Confederate citizens. Fleming referred, probably in a derogatory manner, that Stanley was "extremely fond of guarding rebel property" while Turchin "treated the rebs [in this case the local citizens] in just the opposite manner." The presence of Turchin in the Huntsville expedition prompted the *Staunton Spectator* to recall Turchin's possession of another Southern town, Athens, the previous year. The editorial echoed the feelings of many Southerners regarding Turchin's role in the previous expedition and observed that Turchin had been court martialed for his role in the actions. It declared that Turchin allowed his troops unfettered liberties with the population in the town. According to the newspaper, Turchin reportedly told his men to proceed with their actions stating, "I shut my eyes for one hour." When his men replied that one hour was not enough time, he reportedly declared, "I shut my eyes for two hours."[10]

Brigadier General John Beatty's diary entry for July 31 recorded some important observations about the recent changes in the cavalry: "Met General Turchin for the first time since he was before our court-martial at Huntsville. He appeared to be considerably down in spirit…" because of the transfer. The historian of the 7th Pennsylvania Cavalry wrote of Turchin, "General Turchin, as a cavalry officer, was not a success.

He was personally brave, and had a good deal of dash in his mental make-up, but was physically out of place on horseback, the circumference of his body being equal to his height. His failure as a commander of cavalry was due, more than anything else, to the fact that he marched with too long a tail, orderlies and escort numbering nearly four hundred men…." George Crook, a West Point classmate of Stanley, assumed command of the Second Cavalry Division upon Turchin's removal. Crook served early in the war in western Virginia, at the Second Battle of Bull Run, and the Battle of Antietam. He and his division had been transferred west to IX Corps of the Department of the Ohio, and Crook commanded an infantry brigade in Fourteenth Corps during the Tullahoma Campaign. This was an important move and one which showed the good leadership skills of Stanley. He found Turchin unsuitable and returned him to a position where he would be more effective. Turchin would show his ability leading

General George Crook assumed command of the Second Cavalry Division in July (Library of Congress).

infantry at the upcoming Battle of Chickamauga. In the meantime, George Crook, who would gain fame in the west after the war, made an immediate and positive impact with the cavalry corps.[11]

Meanwhile in the north, John Carroll, who had been wounded in the December 14, 1862 foraging expedition, returned home to a heroes' welcome. Carroll, a printer who had previously lived in La Crosse, Wisconsin, went to his father's home to recuperate. Carroll was the only member of the expedition to be wounded and the local newspaper reported unfavorably that "he was left by his comrades to die in rebel hands…. He concluded to live." He still carried the Confederate ball in his shoulder and he would be discharged in November due to the severity of the wound. Other changes came to the Board of Trade Battery in July and early August, and the grumbling continued regarding Stokes' command. "The capt. is getting more arbitrary every day, more self-willed. The boys all pray that his resignation may be accepted," wrote Benjamin Nourse. The apparent unhappiness with Stokes continued with the men who seemed to be aware that Stokes, too, was seeking a change. The change would come but the men would have to wait a few months. In the meantime, Lieutenant Trumbull Dorrance Griffin, the 27-year-old New York native and pre-war printer, was about to be placed in a position that would require all his skills. This situation would take place on September 18 near the Chickamauga Creek. A remark in Nourse's diary set the course for Griffin's place in history. "This afternoon the 3rd & 5th pieces with Lieut. Griffin left us. The brigade of Col. Minty goes with them. Rumor says to McMinnville."[12]

Rumors abounded in the Union army in Tennessee, and those Federal troops in

Kentucky worried about another cavalry raid into the state. John Hunt Morgan, commanding a brigade in Wheeler's cavalry corps, had just completed a raid in July which drained much of the energy and reserves of the troops in the rear, although Morgan's raid was less than the Southern general had hoped. The new rumors predicted that Nathan Bedford Forrest would ride out of East Tennessee and into Kentucky. To counter this move, Stanley ordered Minty to move his brigade, now accompanied by Trumbull Griffin's section (guns number 3 and number 5), to Sparta, a pro–Southern town about 25 miles northeast of McMinnville, to counter any move made by Forrest. The rest of Stanley's cavalry remained relatively stationary at Winchester. Little occurred over the next two weeks except the men became increasingly familiar with the whiskey parlors in Winchester. On August 12, Crook arrived at the camp and visited with Stokes about the upcoming campaign and the condition of the battery. For the next five weeks, Griffin's section would be attached to Minty's brigade, operating on the left flank of the Army of the Cumberland. Stokes, with the two other sections (five guns) would be attached to the main concentration of Union cavalry operating on the right flank of the army with Long's brigade.[13]

The Battery Splits and Stanley Reorganizes the Cavalry

Major General Horatio Van Cleve's infantry division held a position in McMinnville, 27 miles southwest of the Tennessee town of Sparta. Forrest's move was just one additional action of many by the Confederate cavalry in July and early August. George Dibrell's (8th Tennessee Cavalry CSA) rather innocuous move to Sparta prompted an immediate response from Stanley and he dispatched his most capable brigade commander forward to address the situation. Minty's brigade, accompanied by Griffin's section, left Salem on August 1, arrived in McMinnville on August 3, and began to work in cooperation with Van Cleve's division. Van Cleve held the extreme eastern flank of Rosecrans' army and, ideally, once Burnside's Army of the Ohio began its advance on Knoxville, this division would operate in some manner to present a solid front. The Union commanders did not need Forrest slipping between Rosecrans and Burnside on a raid of his own.[14]

Dibrell's 8th Confederate Cavalry reached Sparta on July 29 and camped on Dibrell's own farm about two miles north of town. Over the next 10 days, Minty would make two expeditions to deal with Southerners. In both cases, Minty drove the enemy from their positions but did not decisively defeat them, and the Confederates melted into the countryside. In neither case did Griffin's guns accompany the column. Minty's actions at Sparta provided some much-needed offensive action for Rosecrans to satisfy his masters in Washington. Meanwhile on the other flank, Edward McCook, temporarily replacing Robert Mitchell who was on sick leave, commanded the First Cavalry division (Campbell's, La Grange's, and Watkins' brigades) on the southern flank. He was accompanied, a few miles to the north, by George Crook commanding the Second Cavalry Division with only one brigade of his command, Eli Long's. William Lowe's newly formed brigade operated as security in the rear.[15]

After the Tullahoma Campaign, Stanley formally shuffled the regiments of the two cavalry divisions to include an additional brigade in each division. His new organization included six brigades instead of four in the old organization. The Board of Trade Battery remained attached to the Second Cavalry Division.

Cavalry, Army of the Cumberland—August 31, 1863[16]
Major General David S. Stanley
Escort
4th Ohio Cavalry, Company D, Captain Philip H. Warner
First Division—Colonel Edward M. McCook

First Brigade	Second Brigade
Colonel Archibald P. Campbell	**Colonel Oscar H. La Grange**
2nd Michigan, Maj. John C. Godley	2nd Indiana, Maj. Joseph B. Presdee
9th Pennsylvania, Lt. Col. Roswell M. Russell	4th Indiana, Col. John A. Platter
1st Tennessee, Lt. Col. James P. Brownlow	2nd Tennessee, Col. Daniel M. Ray
1st Wisconsin, Lt. Col. Henry Pomeroy	

Third Brigade
Colonel Louis D. Watkins
4th Kentucky, Col. Wickliffe Cooper
5th Kentucky, Lt. Col. William T. Hoblitzell
6th Kentucky, Maj. Louis A. Gratz
7th Kentucky, Lt. Col. Thomas T. Vimont

Artillery
1st Ohio, Light, section Battery D (2nd Brigade), Lieutenant Nathaniel M. Newell

Second Division—Brigadier General George Crook

First Brigade	Second Brigade
Colonel Robert H.G. Minty	**Colonel Eli Long**
3rd Indiana (battalion), Lt. Col. Robert Klein	2nd Kentucky, Col. Thomas P. Nicholas
4th Michigan, Maj. Horace Gray	1st Ohio, Lt. Col. Valentine Cupp
7th Pennsylvania, Maj. James J. Seibert	3rd Ohio, Lt. Col. Charles B. Seidel
4th United States, Capt. James B. McIntyre	4th Ohio, Lt. Col. Oliver P. Robie

Third Brigade
Colonel William W. Lowe
5th Iowa, Maj. Alfred B. Brackett
10th Ohio, Lt. Col. William E. Haynes
5th Tennessee (1st Middle), Col. William B. Stokes

Artillery
Chicago (Illinois) Board of Trade Battery, Capt. James H. Stokes

In August Stanley faced a formidable cavalry force. This force included Wheeler's Corps stretching southwest from Chattanooga, minus John Hunt Morgan's cavalry brigade that had participated in the ill-fated raid into the north, and Forrest's division stretching northeast from Chattanooga. On a positive note, Bragg successfully integrated Simon Bolivar Buckner's troops from the Department of East Tennessee into his Army of Tennessee as a third corps in August. Along with infantry, Bragg gained more cavalry, which increased his cavalry by an additional division. The cavalry from the Department of East Tennessee included John Pegram's and John Scott's cavalry brigades. Forrest gained the new cavalry which allowed him to increase his division into a cavalry corps in early September. The addition of the new troops resulted in Brigadier General John Pegram maintaining division command under Forrest.[17]

Cavalry—Present for Duty, August 10, 1863[18]

Confederate Cavalry*		Union Cavalry	
Forrest's Division	3,842	Mitchell's Division[†]	5,540
Wheeler's Corps	7,143	Crook's Division	4,433
Pegram's Division[‡]	5,758	15th Pennsylvania[§]	427
Total	**16,743**		**10,400**

*Includes cavalry and artillery.
[†]Includes corps staff.
[‡]Part of the Department of East Tennessee.
[§]Detached to army headquarters (Wheeler's numbers include Morgan's detached brigade).

Rosecrans Begins the Advance on Chattanooga

In early August, Rosecrans told Halleck the disposition of his army—his reserve corps stretched from Nashville to Shelbyville. Thomas' Fourteenth Corps was in the vicinity of Decherd, Crittenden's Twenty-first Corps extended from McMinnville to Pelham and McCook's Twentieth Corps was located at Tullahoma and Winchester with a brigade at Bridgeport. The First Cavalry Division (Edward McCook's) was in position at Fayetteville and Salem, and Crook's division occupied Winchester with Minty's brigade at McMinnville. He explained that his command was scattered over a large geographic area and he needed time to concentrate his army for the advance on Chattanooga. Halleck had had enough of delays and responded to Rosecrans: "The orders for the advance of your army, and that its movements be reported daily, are peremptory." Rosecrans, obeying his direct orders from Washington, prepared to implement his plan to confuse Bragg about his line of march. Because Rosecrans still had to complete the task of crossing the Tennessee River, which could be easily defended, he planned to feint a crossing at or north of Chattanooga with Crittenden's Twenty-First Corps and Minty's cavalry brigade, when he really intended to cross near the town at Bridgeport. Rosecrans simply wrote to Washington: "Rebels expect us above Chattanooga."[19]

As the advance began, Edward McCook moved his division to Larkinsville, Alabama, on August 13 to scout and screen the southern flank of the Federal army. Long's brigade made a more direct advance over the Cumberland Mountains toward Stevenson. The remaining five guns of the Board of Trade Battery, attached to Crook's Division, would remain in close proximity to McCook's First Cavalry Division operating on the southern flank of the army. In preparation for the advance on Bragg's army, the battery was reduced to two-seven's rations on August 13 and the men drew rations for the next 10 days. The infantry began marching toward Stevenson and Bridgeport on August 16, but the Board of Trade Battery did not begin its movement until August 19, advancing only 10 miles to the foot of the Cumberland Mountains that lay between Winchester and

Stevenson. The next day (August 20), the trip up the mountain with guns, caissons and wagons was a day of horrors. Benjamin Nourse recorded in his diary:

> "Started at 6 of this morning to go over the mountains to Stevenson, Ala.—We were until noon going up the first side of the mountain. Our caissons went up by hand. The horses were taken off. After we got to the top, we had good sand road for five miles across the ridges up hill and down. One place we went down rock 8 ft. high. Horses all off but the wheel team. The cannoneers with a rope fastened to the rear of the carriages. One place the causeway was only 12 feet wide and the fall on each side was farther than the height of the tallest pine trees and as straight down as a plummers line. When we commenced to come down the horses were taken off except the wheel team and the wheels locked. Down we came over the rocks. I cannot tell or describe on paper the road. Nor can any one have an idea of the roughness who has not been over it. We (#7) broke 3 wheels and the battery wagon one. D.B. Richardson got his arm broken by the fall of horse throwing him over his head. The oldest inhabitant said that never had a wagon been over the mountain by this pass. They hardly believed their eyes when they saw all our cannons and wagons come down on the south side of this range."[20]

The workhorse of Union cavalry in the West, Colonel Edward McCook (Library of Congress).

In addition to Nourse, Tobias Miller wrote that the trek over the mountain was 10 miles long. Five miles up the "almost solid rock" mountain and five miles down the other side. Eli Long posted 25–30 cavalrymen at 100-yard intervals to assist the guns and wagons over the mountain. Miller explained that few human accidents occurred but horses and mules were killed and wagons disabled in the effort. He also mentioned Daniel B. Richardson's (the 32-year-old pre-war clerk) injury which occurred as the men moved the forge down the other side of the mountain. A chain broke and the blacksmith shop rolled down the hill, throwing horses to the ground, and in the process breaking Richardson's arm in two places. Private Silas Stevens also gave a detailed description of the crossing of the mountains covered with cedar, hemlock and fir trees. Stevens explained the route selected for the battery was an old abandoned trail over the mountain, straight up without any twists or turns on very rocky ground. Ten horses were hitched to gun number 1. Because the route was straight up the mountain, once the gun began moving it did not stop until it reached the top with no rest or chocking the wheels. Stevens explained that by "whip and spur, and constant urging" the guns moved up the mountain. Stevens' teams successfully pulled the guns up the hill but he acknowledged that some of the other guns and wheeled vehicles had to be unhitched and moved by hand. There was also little level ground at the top and once reaching the top, the descent began immediately. Once the gun reached the crest, the extra horses were unhitched and sent back down the hill to assist with the movement of caissons and wagons.[21]

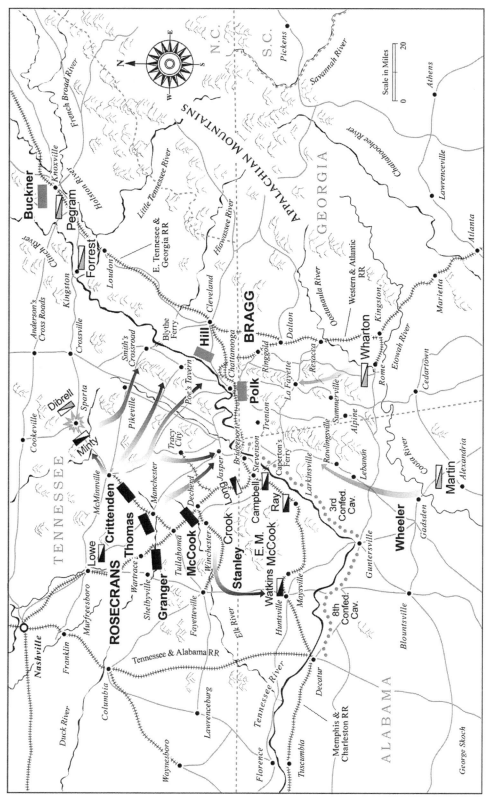

The advance on Chattanooga begins. The Chicago Board of Trade Battery is split between Minty's and Long's brigades, August 16–August 30, 1863.

George Skoch

Blacksmiths and artificers kept the battery operational. Note the traveling forge in the background ("Horseshoeing in the Army" from *Frank Leslie's Illustrated Famous Leaders and Battle Scenes of the Civil War*, 1896, p. 400).

The next day the battery remained stationary and awaited the arrival of the teams of horses. As it waited, "hordes of cavalry, and infantry troops passed by," wrote Stevens. The battery continued eastward, arriving in Stevenson on August 22. The men found Stevenson a dirty town on the river at the foot of the mountain with only a dozen houses. The battery moved northward to a creek just south of Bridgeport, settled into camp, and remained stationary for the next few days. The men could see the enemy pickets across the river and conversations began between the two opposing forces. The battery remained in place and because the men commonly swam in the river, three swam across and sat and talked with the enemy pickets. All remained quiet until August 28 when Long's cavalrymen cut a path to the river and the next day Long's brigade made an expedition to Trenton. Three days later Long returned after a rather uneventful trip over Sand Mountain. To the south, Edward McCook's division secured the southern flank; the trailing infantry troops filed into Huntsville and points east behind the cavalrymen.[22]

On the recent expedition, Long found traversing Sand Mountain no easy feat. Geologically, the impressive sandstone plateau was a continuation of Walden's Ridge from the north side of the Tennessee River. The mountain rose over 2,000 feet above the valley floor and a plateau, ranging from one to seven miles wide, crowned the elevation. Soldiers could look up the mountain and see men moving four miles away. When Long returned, he brought good news—there were no large concentrations of Confederate troops to delay Rosecrans' further movement eastward toward Chattanooga.[23]

Griffin's Section with Minty Moves to Smith's Crossroads

Little had been heard from Griffin's section at McMinnville, but Griffin wrote to Stokes that Private James Wallace died while in the hospital in McMinnville. He did not give any particular cause of death, but battery records indicated he had dysentery. The loss of a long-time member of the battery caused other men to pause. John Fleming reflected on Wallace's death and he wrote in a letter: "[A]nother one of our battery, one who has always been a good soldier—performing his duty faithfully, has gone from among us … reminding us to live well … for we follow him shortly."[24]

On August 17, Minty had another clash with Dibrell's cavalry at Sparta, this time resulting in higher casualties, but with essentially the same results. Minty drove Dibrell from his position but could not decisively defeat the Southern colonel. This was the last attempt to force Dibrell back into the main Confederate lines. With the Army of the Cumberland advancing on Chattanooga, Minty concluded that if Dibrell intended to cause havoc on the Federal rear then Gordon Granger's reserve corps or Lowe's cavalry brigade could deal with the threat. Again, Griffin's battery did not take an active role in this expedition and it was ordered to proceed forward along with Van Cleve's division.[25]

After remaining in the Sparta area overnight, Minty followed his orders to advance to Smith's Crossroads, Tennessee (near Blythe's Ferry and currently named Dayton, about 10 miles north of Poe's Tavern), to his position along Crittenden's flank. Minty rode forward with about 1,200 men, including Griffin's section. While there are no first-hand reports by members of the battery of the difficulty of getting the section over the mountains, Griffin struggled to get the guns to Smith's Crossroads. The journal of the 4th Michigan Cavalry recorded the task of getting the regiment over the elevations, and it was noted that the guns offered a particular challenge. T.F. Dornblaser, 7th Pennsylvania Cavalry, described the movement of Griffin's guns: "The artillery and wagon trains made slow progress. On that mountain side we saw more balky mules and horses in one day, than we ever expect to see again. Five horses in the battery teams would pull back while one would pull forward. In one case we saw all the team unhooked except the off-wheel horse: he was true as steel. A long rope was fastened to the tongue of the caisson; a regiment of infantry laid hold of the rope, and with the aid of the wheel horse they walked up the hill on a double-quick."[26]

Upon reaching eastern Tennessee many of the loyal pro–Union citizens celebrated the arrival of Minty's brigade and Griffin's section joined in the celebrations by firing salutes. Over the next three weeks, the interactions between Minty and Crittenden were contentious as Minty held a vulnerable position with only a partial brigade. Fortunately, Minty worked well with Horatio Van Cleve who interceded with Crittenden on Minty's behalf on several occasions. When Minty's cavalry arrived at Smith's Crossroads, his men found the other side of the river, at Blythe's Ferry, occupied with two firmly entrenched Mississippi infantry regiments of Brigadier General Mark Lowrey's brigade. The river was 700–800 yards wide at the ferry location. John McLain, 4th Michigan, recorded in his diary: "Our Company and Company B went in advance of the 7th Penn. to Washington, near ½ mile, the Tenn. River. No fighting except firing a few shots across the river.… Washington … 7 miles northeast of Smiths Crossroads. Not much of a place." Many of Crittenden's men had low rations, but Minty's brigade alone, unlike many of the other commands, had not been supplied when the march began because he had been battling Dibrell's cavalry. Minty's men had no supplies except what was carried on the horses.

Robert Burns explained, "We are again without tents, clothing baggage or wagons and have to go shirtless while one is being washed and dried … we are accustomed to sleep shelterless on the ground."[27]

From the arrival until August 24, Minty's brigade was a prime target for a Confederate attack if the enemy decided to take offensive action. Minty wrote: "My position here is, as I stated in my last, not good…. Forrest can take me in flank and rear, completely surrounding me." Despite these problems, this increased Confederate activity north of Chattanooga boded well for Rosecrans. Burnside's advance toward Knoxville and Crittenden's corps had the desired effects on the Confederate army. In regard to the cavalry at Smith's Crossroads, Van Cleve wrote, "Colonel Minty has every available man and horse with him, and urges sending him more." Minty still operated with only three regiments while the 3rd Indiana Cavalry remained detached from his command. On August 24, Crittenden wrote to Garfield; "I am all the time uneasy about Van Cleve's exposed left." Fortunately, Minty had little action as he held this important location.[28]

Crossing of the Tennessee River and Over Sand Mountain

On August 30, full divisions of Thomas' and McCook's corps crossed the river. The Federal cavalry moved across the Tennessee River securing the fords and the all-important infantry crossings went without a hitch. Also, Crittenden's corps, which had done a splendid job of occupying Bragg's attention, marched down Sequatchie Valley and began crossing at Shellmound, Jasper and Bridgeport. Only William Hazen's, George Wagner's, John Wilder's and Minty's commands would remain on the north side of the river to guard the crossings. Meanwhile to the south, Edward McCook began moving his division in preparation of a crossing near Bellefonte on August 30. All the units were on the move, and once the army crossed the river, all focus would be directed on the Confederate forces at Chattanooga with Rosecrans' broad sweeping movement by McCook and Stanley south of the town.[29]

The Army of the Cumberland marched ahead, and the Confederate commanders, though initially surprised, soon knew the extent of the movement. Wheeler made no direct move to block the Federal advance despite receiving this information from the 3rd Alabama Cavalry. The Union commanders had worried about a determined defense on the east side of the river and as historian Peter Cozzens observed: "Had the Confederates been on the opposite bank in force, few Yankees would have gotten across alive…." The crossing of the Tennessee River by the Army of the Cumberland

Private Fred Dupries, a native Canadian and a pre-war engineer (Chicago History Museum, ICHi-176927).

continued unabated but the weather was unpleasant. September arrived "dry, hot, dusty," wrote Marshall Thatcher, an officer in the 2nd Michigan Cavalry, and these conditions would generally continue throughout the campaign.[30]

The Chicago Board of Trade Battery also began to move into position to join in the crossing of the river near Bridgeport on September 2 over a pontoon bridge, but Sheridan was moving his division over the same bridge. The battery arrived at the crossing at 9:00 a.m. and had to wait until 4:00 p.m. before it could cross. Once across, the road was too poor to attempt to travel at night and the men camped after moving about five miles. Long's brigade had crossed the river early that morning and had traveled several miles in advance. The next day the battery caught up with Crook and remained with his headquarters for the rest of day. On September 4, the battery began moving up Sand Mountain on another poor trail and the ascent was difficult.[31]

The Union cavalry reached Winston's, the home of Colonel William O. Winston, on the evening of September 3. The Union horsemen were welcomed by Winston, a public figure in DeKalb County opposed to succession and loyal to the Union. Specifically, Edward McCook's division moved into position in Will's Valley near Allen's House, north of Rawlingsville, and Crook and Long remained near Stanley's headquarters at Winston's. The cavalry trains, including the Board of Trade Battery, still lagged behind due to the slow pace of getting wagons and guns over the mountains. Stanley, while happy with the ease of movement of his cavalry, knew that the Federal cavalry faced two enemy cavalry corps, Forrest's northeast of Chattanooga and Wheeler's directly east of his position.[32]

When the cavalry prepared for movement into Georgia, it traveled light—three days' rations in haversacks, no "led horses," no baggage and no dismounted troopers. The brigade commanders assigned the weakest regiment to escort the cavalry baggage train over Sand Mountain, a difficult enterprise. The 2nd Indiana Cavalry crossed the 18 mile path over the mountain on September 3 and Sergeant G.W. Baum wrote that the "land is poor you could not raise beens." Marshall Thatcher, 2nd Michigan Cavalry, observed that the mountain seemed more rock than sand and even the mule drivers had difficulty getting their teams over this imposing obstacle. Accidents occurred while moving over the mountains and troopers observed mules still hitched to wagons tumble over the mountainside. Certainly, topography and terrain became important parts of the campaign in the mountains near Chattanooga. The passage over the mountain was equally difficult for the artillery. Benjamin Nourse, whose section traversed the mountain, had a difficult time and while encouraging the horses up the mountain, his horse fell and landed on his leg. He made the remainder of the passage over the mountain in the rear of an ambulance.[33]

The Board of Trade Battery halted on top of the mountain and after a rest, Stokes decided to continue the movement to Winston's. However, the long procession of McCook's infantry marched steadily over the mountain in a single line and entering the line became a frustrating experience, resulting in the flaring of tempers. Nourse explained, "Our capt. was mad and broke through a baggage train. Then, we were put out by the col. commanding. At noon, he drew his saber on a major and had to beg pardon. Both incidents we broke the train—getting into line we kept there until a chance offered to get ahead. We came down the mountain and camped 12 miles from Lebanon, Ala." Despite the frustration of marching single file over the mountain, the view offered a breath-taking panorama of the Tennessee River to the west and the valley to the east. Private Silas Stevens remarked that the battery "coursing along the hard road on the top of Sand Mountain was more like a party of tourists than the participants of a body of United

States soldiery." The battery finally reached Stanley's and Crook's headquarters at Winston's and McCook's division camped a few miles south.[34]

Stanley's initial chore was locating Wheeler's cavalry and any concentrations of infantry on the southern flank. So far, Wheeler offered no resistance and would act defensively for most of the campaign. As Edward McCook began scouting the area, he soon discovered that Wheeler was not in Rawlingsville or Lebanon, nor was there any enemy infantry at Gadsden, which was good news for the Federal cavalry. The closest Confederate force was Wharton's division at Alpine on the east side of Lookout Mountain. Throughout the next phase of the Chickamauga Campaign (September 6–September 17), Stanley and Alexander McCook worked very closely together. They often moved units in conjunction, McCook supporting the cavalry which provided security along the flank; together the two Union forces intended to make a large wheeling movement from the west and south to cut Bragg's communications and supply lines to Rome and Atlanta.[35]

As Rosecrans might have expected, Bragg began to shift his forces to meet the new threat but he still took no offensive actions to delay the Union advance. Bragg had been blind to Rosecrans' crossing of the Tennessee River due in large part to Wheeler's failure to adequately monitor and communicate the Federal actions along the Tennessee River west of Chattanooga. Bragg's lack of offensive actions increased Rosecrans' confidence and belief that Bragg would not fight at Chattanooga. Because of the large territory, Wheeler assigned only small forces, ranging from three men to a maximum of forty men, to guard the major gaps over Lookout Mountain in front of McCook's Twentieth Corps and the cavalry.[36]

The Union Army Advances

Minty's brigade continued to watch Confederate activity on the northern flank of the army. On September 2, Minty's brigade worked for the first time in conjunction with troops of the Army of the Ohio. Minty's command, now about 1,100 men strong, collected 87 deserters over the last 10 days and led the advance of Burnside's troops into Kingston, capturing 12 prisoners while reporting one trooper mortally wounded during the skirmish which resulted. The action effectively drove the last Confederate cavalry across the Tennessee River. The Confederates had all moved to the eastern side of the Tennessee River and a change in the disposition of the enemy was detected at Blythe's Ferry. Minty dispatched Griffin's section to join the troops guarding the Ferry and wanted Griffin's guns to "feel them." The infantry troops exchanged fire but Griffin's guns remained quiet as the Confederate troops remained on the east side of the river.[37]

With the ease of movement in the campaign so far, Rosecrans issued new general orders on September 3 for all of his forces to push ahead. Stanley ordered Long's brigade and Edward McCook's entire division to advance to Valley Head and Rawlingsville on the extreme southern flank of the army. Then, Long's brigade was ordered to cooperate with Alexander McCook's advance and, with the remaining cavalry, Stanley was ordered to make an advance on Rome, about 70 miles south of Chattanooga and on the railroad connecting to Atlanta. As Rosecrans' orders clarified how the cavalry would be used, only Edward McCook's three brigades had the flexibility of independent action to conduct this raid. Long's brigade would remain in close proximity to Alexander McCook's corps.[38]

Opposite: **Union cavalry movements, September 2–8, 1863. The Chicago Board of Trade Battery is split between Minty's and Long's brigades.**

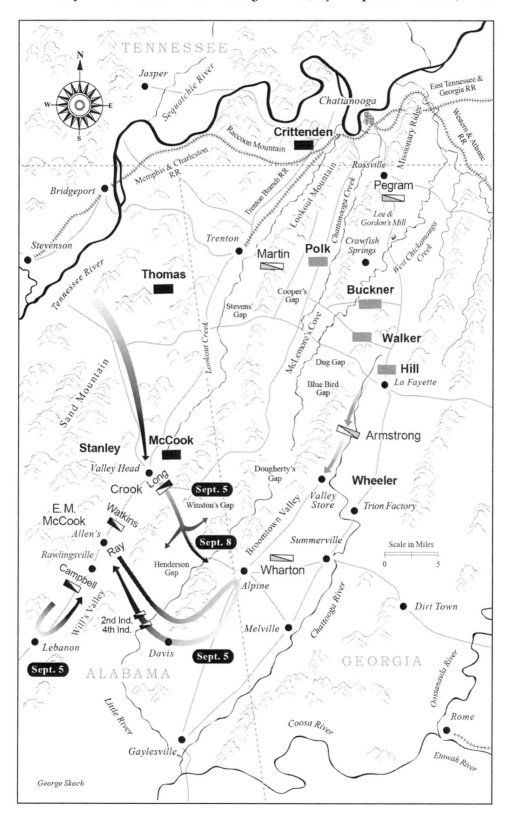

George Skoch

On September 4, Long's cavalry brigade moved into Broomtown Valley just east of Lookout Mountain. The cavalry commanders discovered the road forked with one route leading to Alpine and the other to Summerville, two towns that would receive much attention in the upcoming days. McCook and Stanley decided to send Long's brigade along a route which reached eight miles north of Alpine. McCook optimistically wrote: "I do not know what Stanley's instructions are, but he wrote me that he could carry them out as well on that side of Lookout Mountain. He has 5,800 sabers and can whip all before him." Stanley sent word to Garfield on the morning of September 4 that Long's brigade took possession of the gap over Lookout Mountain. The ascent of the mountain was not as difficult as the Cumberland Mountains or Sand Mountain, but the distance to the summit resulted in a long day for the artillerymen. Private Silas Stevens recalled that "considerable exertion" resulted in the guns reaching the summit well after the normal time of taps. In the meantime, Edward McCook had his cavalry in the saddle and found no enemy troops lingering along his southern flank.[39]

A battle of wills began on September 5 between the cavalry and army headquarters. Stanley's new orders required him to execute a raid on Rome, instead of "feeling" the enemy as previously ordered. Rosecrans and Garfield wanted Stanley to make a raid to disrupt the communication lines in the rear of Bragg's army. Stanley would resist these orders over the next few days until the commanding general insisted that they be carried out. Then, Stanley would direct McCook's cavalry division to carry out these orders. In the meantime, Stanley sent McCook to reconnoiter the area toward Rome and for Crook to move his cavalry into Broomtown Valley. George Crook sent two regiments, the 1st and 3rd Ohio, from Winston's on an expedition over Lookout Mountain on their way to Broomtown Valley. The civilians in the area told Crook that three companies of Wheeler's cavalry had just moved forward to attempt to block the road over the mountain. Crook found the first of Wheeler's vedettes three miles on top of Lookout Mountain and five miles from the valley floor. The Federals skirmished with the enemy before pushing the smaller force to the rear. Crook found the road leading to the valley blocked incompletely with felled trees, and the Union cavalry surprised the enemy which had not completed their task. The 1st Ohio Cavalry ran into the first enemy pickets at noon and the Ohioans raised their carbines: "bang! bang! and away we go at a sweeping gallop," wrote W.L. Curry. Because he needed to clear the obstructions, primarily pine trees and large boulders, Crook sent 100 men on foot to scout the valley, but the men found no enemy waiting at the base of the mountain, later returning to camp at Winston's.[40]

New Orders for the Cavalry on the Southern Flank

In an optimistic and professional summary of the events of September 8, Rosecrans wired Halleck: "Information tonight leads to the belief that the enemy has decided not to fight us at Chattanooga. Our reconnoitering today shows that he has withdrawn his pickets on Lookout Mountain, opposite and below us, and Winston's Gaps." Rosecrans explained that Alexander McCook and Stanley would advance further into Broomtown Valley the next day and Crittenden would march south through Chattanooga in pursuit of Bragg. Rosecrans' staff wrote to Thomas to send his most reliable men to confirm that Bragg was retreating and in which direction.[41]

However, Rosecrans raged at his cavalry in private. Stanley failed to make the raid on

Rome during the day as Rosecrans had expected and for which he even moved his infantry to assist in the movement. The exact cause for the failure to order the expedition remains a mystery and controversy. All the individual accounts from the troopers indicated the intention of making the raid on September 8. The delay, Stanley later explained, was caused because he needed to shoe his mounts. In addition, Stanley told Garfield that he believed he had an inadequate number of men to accomplish the task without Minty's brigade and he explained that delaying the raid by a single day allowed him to gain another 600 men. All evidence pointed to the fact that Stanley planned to delay the raid for a day to get his command fully prepared before initiating the raid on September 9. Despite Rosecrans' anger, Stanley's decision not to move on Rome was a good one. He faced enemy cavalry in terrain too easily defended by a relatively small force, either on his way to Rome or on his return.[42]

The Board of Trade Battery was not expected to be part of McCook's raid on Rome, but the events on the southern flank directly impacted the actions of the battery. On September 8, one section of the battery was sent to bolster the defenses on Lookout Mountain while the other section remained near Winston's. The section moving to Lookout Mountain was given 30 minutes to pack, harness, and be on its way which resulted in its arrival on top of the mountain where it camped for the night. In the process, the men observed the preparation of McCook's raid on Rome. Benjamin Nourse wrote in his diary, "Work tomorrow, I bet."[43]

During the day, Bragg evacuated Chattanooga, and James Garfield, Rosecrans' chief of staff, realized that Stanley's raid to Rome was no longer necessary. Instead, the Union generals needed to find Bragg's army. The next day, Edward McCook re-directed his division to scout further south and then move to Alpine to deal with Wharton's cavalry there, as reported by deserters. For the remainder of the cavalry corps, Garfield told Crook to move his cavalry quickly the next morning to the Chattanooga Road and then scout until he found the main Confederate column. The good news of Bragg's evacuation from Chattanooga caused Rosecrans to underestimate Bragg's will to fight and to continue to imagine the Confederates retreating to Rome or Atlanta, but Bragg had just shifted his strategy.[44]

On the morning of September 9, the Confederate forces marched toward La Fayette, but no farther. La Fayette was a small town and county seat of Walker County with a prewar population of 300–400. The town had two academies, a few churches, a hotel, a courthouse and 10 to 12 streets and cross streets. Both D.H. Hill and Joseph Wheeler received direct orders to proceed to La Fayette and Wheeler relayed orders to Forrest to bring his cavalry there also. Bragg could not allow his army to be cut off and isolated at Chattanooga, and his movement to La Fayette allowed him to neutralize Thomas' and McCook's forward movements which threatened his communication lines. At 8 a.m. on September 8, Forrest wrote to Wheeler and told him Bragg instructed him to delay the Union advance as much as possible. He told Wheeler, "If the enemy does not advance we must move on them." Granted, Forrest was still some few miles north of the proposed route of Stanley's ordered raid upon Rome, but the belief that a beleaguered, defeated army, vulnerable to a flank attack by a single Union cavalry division could not have been further from the truth.[45]

The Cavalry Fight at Alpine

Long's brigade camped on top of Lookout Mountain on September 8 and led the Union cavalry advance on Alpine the next morning, a location scouts determined to be defended by infantry, cavalry and artillery. As Long approached Henderson's Gap (the gap directly east of Valley Head), he drove enemy pickets to his front. Immediately he found the narrow gap obstructed with timbers felled across the road and boulders that had been rolled onto the road. In a post-war account of the action at Alpine, Lieutenant Colonel Elijah Watts of the 2nd Kentucky Cavalry explained that the regiment moved forward and found some recent campfires, still warm, which "showed plainly enough that we were fairly in presence of the enemy." After an hour of clearing the road, Long continued down into Broomtown Valley. The cavalrymen dismounted at the base of the mountain and allowed their horses to drink from a stream. Suddenly, gunfire erupted as scouts discovered a strong force of John Wharton's Confederate cavalry occupying a tree line. Near Alpine, Long approached the enemy across a large field and his Union cavalry returned the fire, resulting in a bloody fight. The arrival of Edward McCook's division decided the contest. McCook's line of march took his division from Allen's House near Rawlingsville, over Lookout Mountain and then descended at Davis. McCook attacked from the south while Long attacked from the west. McCook flanked the Confederate cavalry which was "forced to retire, fighting us, however, from the time we struck them in the valley until we drove them through Alpine, some retreating on the Rome road, but most of them on the road to Summerville," recorded Brigadier General Robert Mitchell. The path over Lookout Mountain was 14 miles long and McCook's cavalry initially found some pickets on the mountain. Upon hearing Long's battle, McCook's cavalry charged into a brigade of enemy cavalry, "driving them in every direction." After capturing Alpine, the Union soldiers found an unremarkable settlement of only three houses.[46]

Elijah Watts explained that the 2nd Kentucky Cavalry continued to lead Long's brigade and upon the explosion of gunfire, regimental commander Colonel Thomas Nicholas took 100 men dismounted forward at the run. These men found a strong force of enemy cavalry in line sending forward furious volleys in the approaching Union cavalry. The three Ohio regiments, 1st, 3rd, and 4th cavalries, hurried to the front, extending the line. Watts explained, "Orders arrived, and moving forward we met a stampede of Headquarters, servants and orderlies and other non-combatants, all of whom had (illegible) followed Col. Long down the mountain,—and hastily taking measures to have the led horses sent to one side to wait the call for them, one of the aides, Capt. Crane galloped up to where I was, calling out as he came to let go of the led horses. '[T]hey are charging!!,' he exclaimed … with all the others in the command hurried into the open, went into line— but immediately saw there was no fear of a charge by the enemy, for he had already been repulsed…. The situation was intensely dramatic, the scene inspiring. In our immediate front, to the right and left, were large grain fields covered with stubble only, undulating—slightly rolling, and three hundred yards away a slight incline; another hundred yards began a heavy timber it edges slightly irregular. Farther to the right, and the left were harvested cornfields, with a clear space beyond to the timber. On first observing the situation in our immediate front, a regiment of rebel cavalry was confused and broken, moving back to the woods. They had charged, been repulsed, and were retiring to shelter. The woods was alive with rebels. Halfway between us and the enemy, Lieutenant Hosmer and his gallant troop held a position on a light knoll, sustaining themselves as they always know how to do it, and Gen. Crook comdg. the Division and his escort behind

Opposite: **Union cavalry movements, September 9–11, 1863. The Chicago Board of Trade Battery is split between Minty's and Long's brigades.**

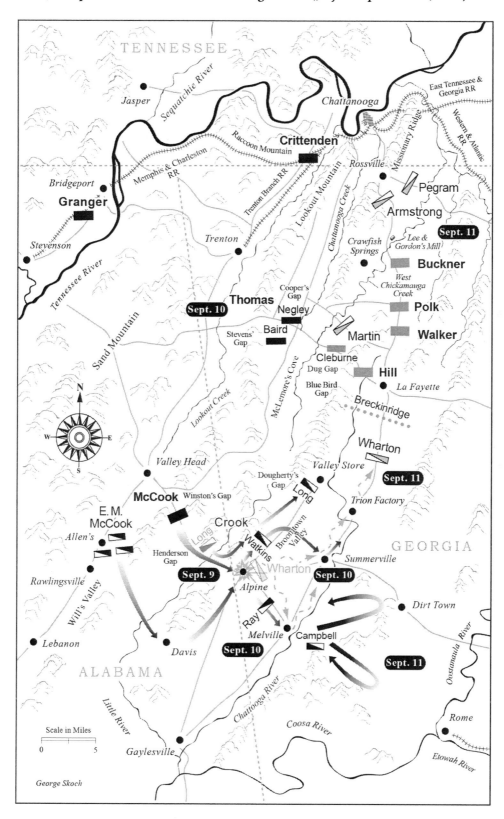

him, hastily making formations for a regular attack. The led horses were taken forward, and the regiment all remounted and together excepting Hosmer and his troop, still holding the position he won in the preliminary encounter. The Ohio regiments were placed in line of battle off to the right, rapidly taking their position behind a crest in point blank range of a heavy force of the enemy. Rising to the crest in excellent style, they opened fire effectually as shown by the disturbance among the rebels and slowly advancing toward them. In the meantime, the 2nd Kentucky was not idle. Joined by Col. Long, the regiment entered a field to the left, called in troop 'A,' and the command was given: 'Prepare to fight on foot!' Then a reformation and advance through the cornfield toward the timber, up to its very edge steady and without a halt, the resistance being only scattering shots, a rush and loud hurrah into the woods completed the work, the enemy men driven away and the field was won." Watts' account did not include the actions of McCook's cavalry on the opposite flank, but Watts found out later in the day the part that unit played. Crook told Watts that McCook attacked from the south striking Wharton's cavalry in the flank and rear while Long's brigade held the Confederate cavalry with a frontal attack.[47]

Board of Trade Battery—Battle at Alpine

One section of artillery accompanied Long's brigade at Alpine. The section traveled 12 miles to the base of the mountain after clearing the felled trees and rocks from the road. As the fight developed, the first Union cavalry forces drove the Confederate cavalry to the rear, but Wharton initiated a counter attack, striking the flank of the Federals. As the Union cavalrymen were being pushed to the rear, Benjamin Nourse recorded: "[W]e came into action on the double quick and opened on them sharply, checking them and by the few well directed shells started them from their corner of trees. Once broken there was no stop and our cavalry charged them. There was no stop until night closed down—We camped on the battle field. At 7 oc. #7 gun went out with Genl. Crook on a scout towards Rome—8 miles—found the rebels in force and came back at night and will wait for infantry. Part of Davis's division of infantry arrived today—the rebels will stand at Rome—Chattanooga is evacuated—around here every family left as we came in the valley, left everything so we fare well, good boys to all such as fear a Yankee." John Nourse wrote to his mother and recorded that 15 were killed and another 10 wounded.[48]

Among the Confederate regiments in the fighting at Alpine were the 8th Texas and 4th Georgia Cavalry regiments. Chaplain Robert F. Bunting wrote in a letter that the regiments tried to hold the line against Crook and McCook but they were just outnumbered and compelled to retreat. Crook sent a detachment of cavalry to follow up his victory but after following the enemy a few miles past Alpine toward Melville, the pursuers found a strong force of Wheeler's cavalry and stopped the pursuit. Prisoners told Stanley that Confederate infantry held Summerville and reinforcements were expected from Virginia. Among the prisoners was a courier with dispatches from Wheeler which indicated the Confederate army intended to concentrate at La Fayette. Upon the capture of Alpine, Stanley sent another scouting expedition toward Summerville to determine the strength of the enemy there.[49]

Over the next two days, Rosecrans would just miss an ambush at McLemore's Cove which could have held devastating effects for the Army of Cumberland. Bragg planned an attack on Negley's division at McLemore's Cove, but failed to get his force aligned to make a coordinated attack before Negley withdrew to safety. Meanwhile, Louis Watkins' brigade skirmished with the Confederate cavalry at Summerville during the day. Along a parallel road to the west, Long's brigade scouted in the direction of La Fayette and scooped up a few prisoners who confirmed Watkins' intelligence about the location and concentration of the Confederate cavalry. Finally, part of McCook's division scouted toward Rome in preparation for a reconnaissance in force the next day. Campbell's brigade rode to Melville without resistance but determined that Rome was well protected with "a large force of all arms." The Board of Trade Battery had little to do on September 10 and remained in an open field. The battery was well provisioned and watched the Union infantry march down the mountain. The men optimistically anticipated an attack on the flank of Bragg's army. In one of the final events of the day, Stanley reported to headquarters about his deteriorating health. "I have been very sick and confined to my bed all day, but hope to be up tomorrow or next day," an illness that would cause Stanley to give up command in a few days.[50]

On September 11, Rosecrans found that the resistance by Bragg's army, now south of Chattanooga, intensified throughout the day. Negley's division narrowly escaped disaster through the bungling of a Confederate attack at McLemore's Cove. Due to these delays of getting the Confederate forces into position, Negley successfully withdrew his vulnerable division from McLemore's Cove with minor losses. Despite this misstep, Bragg had just shifted from a defensive to offensive strategy. In the meantime, Crittenden, who moved southward in three parallel columns, ran into increased resistance from the Confederate cavalry as he inched southward from Chattanooga. Forrest's cavalry screened Crittenden's advance and shielded the location of the Confederate main force from Rosecrans, although by the end of the day the Union commanders suspected that Bragg had withdrawn to La Fayette and not to Rome.[51]

Stanley sent out three expeditions to develop enemy concentrations, but still had not located Bragg's army. McCook's cavalry finally made the long-delayed expedition to Rome. McCook scouted ahead with two brigades on September 11 just south of Wheeler's headquarters located at Trion Factory, a small town established around a set of cotton mills. The expedition was tentative and posed no real threat but Wheeler had seven regiments of Wharton's division at Trion Factory available to attack the Federal flank or rear, had McCook taken action against the railroad or Rome. In addition, the infantry presence in Rome was sufficient to deal with this reconnaissance. Wheeler had been concerned about a cavalry flanking movement throughout the campaign and explained, "I have several scouts in among the enemy this side of the mountain."[52]

Benjamin Nourse recorded in his diary on September 11: "Last night, the 7th piece went out on picket 16 miles. The rest of the battery came down the mountain today and joined us at night. 'Little muss with capt. tonight.'" Nourse gave no further explanation of the "muss" with Stokes. As the day drew to a close, Alexander McCook felt more isolated and asked Stanley to keep a close eye on the enemy. Garfield sent two additional bits of information—first, it was unlikely that Minty would be allowed to rejoin the main body of cavalry anytime soon, as previously promised, and secondly, Robert Mitchell, Stanley's second-in-command had just returned to duty at army headquarters.[53]

Edward McCook settled into camp near Alpine because he felt this was the only safe location for the night. He was concerned about moving closer toward La Fayette because the local citizens told him Polk's entire infantry corps awaited 12 miles ahead at Trion Factory, screened by Wharton's cavalry division only two miles ahead. Crook agreed with McCook's plan and replied at 5:00 p.m. from the Trion Factory and La Fayette Road requesting that McCook move toward Trion Factory the next morning to occupy Wheeler's attention. Crook needed to complete a reconnaissance mission of his own toward La Fayette and he felt the more enemy cavalry watching McCook, the greater chance he had for success.[54]

September 12—The Momentum Swings in Favor of Bragg

Bragg's botched attack at McLemore's Cove caused the Federal army to pause. So, despite the many earlier reports which suggested that Bragg would fight further south, the new reports, particularly from Stanley and Thomas, indicated that Bragg concentrated his army at La Fayette. The remainder of Thomas's corps moved forward to support Negley's position and Alexander McCook, concerned that he was alone along the flank, cautiously sent reconnaissance expeditions ahead. The cavalry actions of the prior two days had yielded important intelligence for Alexander McCook's southern-most corps. In addition, Wheeler's cavalry increased its activity; as Edward McCook's cavalry scouts pressed toward Trion Factory, they were chased away by large concentrations of Confederate cavalry reported to be "brigade sized." McCook picked up a prisoner who confirmed the intelligence being gathered by the Federal cavalry. McCook flatly reported after his past two days of reconnaissance that Bragg was not retreating, but there was a significant enemy force at Rome. Realizing the need to fully assess the situation, Stanley decided to send his entire cavalry force to determine the enemy's position and numbers at La Fayette on September 13.[55]

While McCook and Thomas were anxious about their situations, Crittenden continued to confidently press southward during the day. Crittenden dismantled Minty's brigade, accompanied at this point with Griffin's section of artillery, even further by sending the 4th U.S. Cavalry to report directly to corps headquarters and then ordered the remainder of Minty's brigade (now only two regiments) to replace John Wilder's mounted infantry brigade on the eastern flank. As the day advanced, Crittenden reached Lee and Gordon's Mill around 11:00 a.m. and received information that Confederate cavalry remained active to the east of his advance. That evening, Garfield tried to temper Crittenden's confidence with some sobering information and presented to him the increasingly serious situation of the disconnected Federal army. Garfield also wanted Minty on the right flank of Crittenden, again providing security along that flank even though the 4th U.S. cavalry had been detached to Crittenden's headquarters duty.[56]

Crittenden still had not grasped the situation near La Fayette by the end of the day and he sent Garfield the results of a heavy skirmish between Wilder's mounted infantry and Pegram's Confederate cavalry at Leet's Tanyard. The major fighting included Pegram's and Armstrong's cavalry divisions but Wilder estimated a brigade of infantry (Brigadier General Otho F. Strahl) defended a wooded area near his location. Pegram reportedly employed four regiments and five artillery pieces, and Wilder's troops moved steadily ahead until it reached the wooded area where infantry was observed. Crittenden discounted Wilder's observation of infantry explaining, "It has always been the plan of the enemy to make stubborn defenses on a retreat, and I do not yet believe that there is a strong force of infantry in the vicinity of La Fayette."[57]

Crittenden had just encountered some of the Confederate forces which planned to attack his corps. Bragg remained frustrated at the missed opportunity at McLemore's Cove, but he saw a new opportunity if he could defeat Rosecrans' scattered corps in detail. While Rosecrans focused on the Confederates at La Fayette, Bragg intended next to strike Crittenden's Twenty-first Corps. The Confederate commander directed Leonidas Polk to move Cheatham's division, reinforced by Hindman's and Walker's divisions, to crush at least John Palmer's Union division. On the morning of September 12, Strahl's presence with the Southern cavalry was part of the intended attack. Again the attack never came because, instead of just facing Palmer's division, Polk faced Crittenden's entire corps while the remainder of his own corps was still marching from its position in McLemore's Cove. Bragg urged Polk to make the attack on Crittenden in a late-night message. Again, on the morning of September 13, no attack came much to the displeasure of Bragg. Polk probably received an order which he could not execute due to the various positions of the Union and Confederate troops, and instead of attacking, he established a defensive position in preparation to receive an attack from Crittenden. "Twice in as many days the Army of Tennessee had allowed certain victory to slip through its grasp," noted historian Peter Cozzens.[58]

Frustrations mounted on the Union side of the line too. Robert Minty felt Rosecrans and Crittenden had dismantled his brigade. The 3rd Indiana Cavalry fell under the command of George Wagner who garrisoned the town of Chattanooga and the 4th U.S. rode away to report to Crittenden. Minty himself was summoned to army headquarters, further revealing his many masters. From his headquarters at Stringer's Creek at 10:30 p.m., Minty dejectedly responded to Goddard's (Rosecrans' assistant adjutant-general) message that he had sent the 4th Michigan Cavalry, along with Griffin's section, as directed. "With the remainder of the brigade I will be at the river at daylight. I have a large train, and the mules are tired out by today's march (27 miles)."[59]

To the south, two sections of the Board of Trade Battery accompanied Long's brigade on a 15-mile reconnaissance mission on September 12 and ran into the enemy. Private Silas Stevens, unaware of the overall tactical situation, recalled an incident in which the five guns were ordered to be unlimbered on the edge of some woods. The enemy was not seen and once the Union cavalry began its probe into the lines of the Confederates, Confederate artillery opened fire, causing no damage to the battery. Soon, a cannon ball came plowing up the ground in front of the battery and the men awaited Stokes' order to "load" which never came. Then, the Confederate battery shifted its fire to Long's troopers near Stokes' position. Still the order to load did not come. "One could hear the force of the shell, as it struck the trees, or the ground—bursting in the air, and finally the report of the enemy's guns hurling these missiles toward our unprotected front." Stokes rode to the guns and ordered them to be limbered. The men expected to be placed in a new position with a clear view of the enemy battery, but they were ordered to the rear at a trot, much to the chagrin of the gunners. Later, they were told that they had just participated in a reconnaissance in force, a new concept to most of the men.[60]

Back at cavalry headquarters, Stanley's illness took a turn for the worse and he had already been too ill to ride with any of the cavalry for several days. George Crook, being the next senior officer in the absence of Mitchell, took command of the cavalry's effort to determine the enemy's position and concentration at La Fayette. At 10 p.m., Crook sent a message for Edward McCook to coordinate his division with the actions of Long's brigade the next day. "If your horses are not too tired, I would like to have you move toward La Fayette at daylight in the morning. I will move in that direction at that time on this road."[61]

September 13—Campbell's Charge at La Fayette

As the sun rose on September 13, Rosecrans suspected that the momentum of the campaign had shifted to Bragg. Rosecrans' three corps remained separated in the mountains and valleys south of Chattanooga and his Reserve Corps slowly moved forward. He desperately needed to concentrate his army before Bragg attacked one of the isolated corps and his orders clearly reflected this shift in strategy. McCook and Stanley planned to march northward to support Thomas' Fourteenth Corps, stationary near McLemore's Cove, and Crittenden's Twenty-first Corps stopped along a line near Lee and Gordon's Mills. Ominous columns of dust, and even smoke, were observed during the day, signaling more movement by the Confederate forces which Rosecrans now believed concentrated near La Fayette.[62]

Alexander McCook wrote to Thomas at 8:15 a.m. that he was moving his corps directly from Alpine to link with Thomas' Fourteenth Corps. He planned a forced march through Dougherty's Gap into McLemore's Cove. McCook, too isolated at his position, wanted to remedy the situation as soon as possible, but he wisely chose to gain additional intelligence regarding the Confederate army at La Fayette before making any dramatic moves. A prisoner captured by the Kentucky cavalry told his captors, "He has never seen so large an army together as the one now concentrated at La Fayette." He saw the top generals in the Confederate army there, including "Bragg, Polk, D.H. Hill, Forrest, Wharton, Harrison, Pegram, Scott, Breckinridge, Preston, Hodge, and Wheeler." He also told the Union officers that Bragg had been definitely reinforced by troops from Virginia.[63]

Edward McCook began the day working in conjunction with Crook and the day would be a frustrating but productive one for the Union cavalry. Crook took control of the cavalry in the field, and he divided the Union cavalry into two columns of two brigades each. (Archibald Campbell's brigade of McCook's division would cooperate with Long's brigade in Crook's reconnaissance to La Fayette.) At 10:00 a.m., McCook's cavalry chased away the Confederate cavalry pickets in front of his division and behind that screen he found a troublesome, but strong, concentration of Wharton's cavalry. At 2:00 p.m., the Confederate cavalry still held a crossroads in front of McCook's advance, stopping any further movement northward. McCook agreed that uniting his cavalry with Crook was a good solution for dealing with the large enemy force, but at this point Crook had already completed his reconnaissance.[64]

Along the roads to the west, Crook's cavalry columns began the mission to find the Confederate forces around La Fayette. Campbell's and Long's brigades moved to La Fayette on two parallel roads which converged on the town. Approaching La Fayette, Long's brigade found only scattered pickets which offered no resistance to the large cavalry force. At 10:00, an explosion of cannons and muskets in the distance surprised Long's troopers. Elijah Watts, 2nd Kentucky, exclaimed, "The effect was electrical! What could it mean? … A halt was ordered. Soon after an aide came hurrying from the head of the column looking dreadfully serious, calling out as he passed: 'Face to the rear!'" In the other column, Campbell's brigade had found and charged the enemy infantry line of John C. Breckinridge's division about three miles south of La Fayette. The 1st Tennessee Cavalry

Opposite: Union cavalry movements, September 12–13, 1863. The Chicago Board of Trade Battery is split between Minty's and Long's brigades.

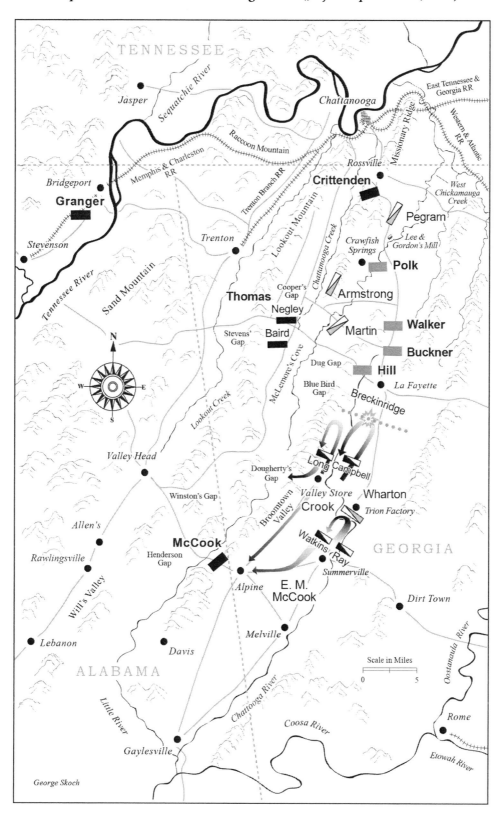

George Skoch

moved to the right flank in support of the 9th Pennsylvania, which had made the initial attack, while the 2nd Michigan followed behind.[65]

Campbell reformed his command and prepared to make a second charge, but Crook arrived on the scene and called off the attack. Crook told Campbell there was more enemy cavalry at the rear of the Union column and since Crook knew Breckinridge's infantry occupied La Fayette, they had achieved their objective. Wharton's cavalry division was somewhere between Edward McCook's brigades and Crook's brigades. Crook decided he was too close to large concentrations of the enemy in the front and rear; with only two brigades he decided he would not be able to make any further progress against the infantry. In front of Crook was Crews' cavalry brigade supporting Adams' Confederate infantry, a force just too large for Crook to move. Campbell rejoined McCook at Alpine at the end of the day and Crook's brigade then moved to Dougherty's Gap.[66]

The Board of Trade Battery had no significant action during the day's fighting. Benjamin Nourse wrote, "Up early and moved to within 2 miles of La Fayette, Ga. Bragg's army (Breckinridge from New Orleans & Vicksburg) in force. Our boys captured the outpost and pickets, then fell back, as we did not wish to bring on an engagement. We came back to our camp. 31 miles is good for a hot day's travel."[67]

Cavalry Actions Cause Bragg to Hesitate

As new and more solid intelligence filtered into army headquarters, Rosecrans became more concerned about his position and ordered Thomas Wood's division to halt at Lee and Gordon's Mill. Then, he sent the remainder of Crittenden's Twenty-first Corps into position on Missionary Ridge. The Reserve Corps still marched ahead and Granger hoped to move into a supporting position the next day. Rosecrans needed Granger's corps to move to Rossville and protect the roads leading to Ringgold and La Fayette, thereby securing Crittenden's left flank. Garfield's concern was evident as he told Granger: "Hold yourself in readiness…." Crittenden was the farthest away from La Fayette and perhaps felt the least risk, but Rosecrans explained that Bragg's army was concentrating near La Fayette behind the mountains. "Hence the necessity of great caution."[68]

McIntyre's 4th U.S. Cavalry and Griffin's Board of Trade section scouted ahead of Crittenden's corps toward La Fayette going between six and twelve miles and found no concentration of Confederates, only enemy cavalry pickets. Wilder's mounted infantry also pushed to within a mile of Leet's Tanyard and only found a small group of Confederate cavalry, perhaps 200 men, which withdrew before the Union force. Finally, Minty remained on duty with two regiments and marched to Lee and Gordon's Mills. The 4th Michigan Cavalry pushed as far south as Crawfish Springs where they found Union infantry and returned to Lee and Gordon's Mill. As the day ended, perhaps the best summary of the situation was by J.C. Van Duzer, head of communications: "[B]y day after tomorrow or Wednesday you may look to hear of Bragg getting hurt. We are in a ticklish place here, but hope to come out with whole skin. Can do nothing but wait."[69]

While the Federal troops feared an attack, the aggressive action by the Federal cavalry for the second day in a row convinced the Confederate commanders that a Union infantry attack was imminent. The initiative which Bragg had gained only a few days earlier was lost just as quickly. The Confederate generals were not in agreement of what action to take.

D.H. Hill explained that at La Fayette, "The Yankee cavalry had, however, captured the infantry pickets, and upon McCook learning that the men belonged to Breckinridge's division, he became aware that Bragg had been re-enforced, and began a precipitate retreat." Hill made no secret of Bragg's mishandling of the situation and stated that Bragg knew the Union army stretched over 60 miles. Hill knew that much of Bragg's army was in position and could have attacked either Thomas' or McCook's corps, which were without support. He bitterly recalled that Bragg hesitated and as a result the attack was delayed for six days. McCook's and Thomas' efforts to close up on one another, Crittenden's advance from the north, and Union cavalry aggressively pushing from the south caused Bragg to pause. Because Bragg hesitated, he allowed Rosecrans the critical time to pull his dispersed army together. Fortunately for the Federal forces, the aggressive actions caused Bragg to enter a "phase of emotional doldrums." Bragg deemed it unwise to stay in close proximity to any one of Rosecrans' corps and he simply withdrew. Rosecrans had been given the gift of time to unite his army while he contemplated Bragg's next move. Bragg, in turn, contemplated how to defeat Rosecrans with a perceived disloyal group of commanders who had failed so badly in the two attempts in the past week. Bragg remained paralyzed from September 13 to September 16 as Rosecrans pulled his army together.[70]

September 14 proved to be a day of re-positioning of the two armies as more dust, smoke and sporadic firing occurred throughout the day. Thomas' corps inched northward establishing a link with Crittenden near Lee and Gordon's Mill without meeting any enemy resistance. Meanwhile, Twentieth Corps marched toward Thomas' right flank, but by a convoluted path due to a misunderstanding from Garfield. McCook had his men on a rapid and difficult march as he hastened to Thomas' flank. McCook complained that backtracking was nine miles longer and would take an additional nine hours. The mistake on the part of army headquarters demonstrated the difficulty of long-range communications. The long, unnecessary march and miscommunications about movement held a heavy toll for those soldiers marching rearward and then northward. A trooper of the 2nd Michigan Cavalry wrote in his diary that the day was a "day of horrors. No water for man or beast after we ascended the mountain. Dust in blinding clouds enveloped us.... After a vain effort to reach a little creek to water our animals we laid down with parched lips and covered in dust." The dust proved a plague to all the soldiers. Robert Burns of Minty's cavalry also described the dust as suffocating as the columns of cavalry moved on their daily expeditions. He also noted that sometimes the dust was so bad the horse in front could not be seen. "It gets in our ears, noses, hair and through and under our clothes."[71]

Granger Arrives at Rossville and the Army Re-Positions

Good news arrived at Federal army headquarters when the first of Granger's Reserve Corps arrived at Rossville and moved to extend the Union left flank to the Tennessee River. At 12:30 p.m., Crittenden reported finding no concentrations of the enemy near him, and his over confidence resonated in his message regarding a potential Confederate attack: "Indeed, I think I can whip them if they do—all of them. We are, I think, in a position that they can turn, but I also think they dare not pass me." Crittenden also explained that his scouts found no Confederates at Ringgold. Garfield ordered Crittenden to place Minty's cavalry along the roads from Ringgold and La Fayette for security and reconnaissance purposes.[72]

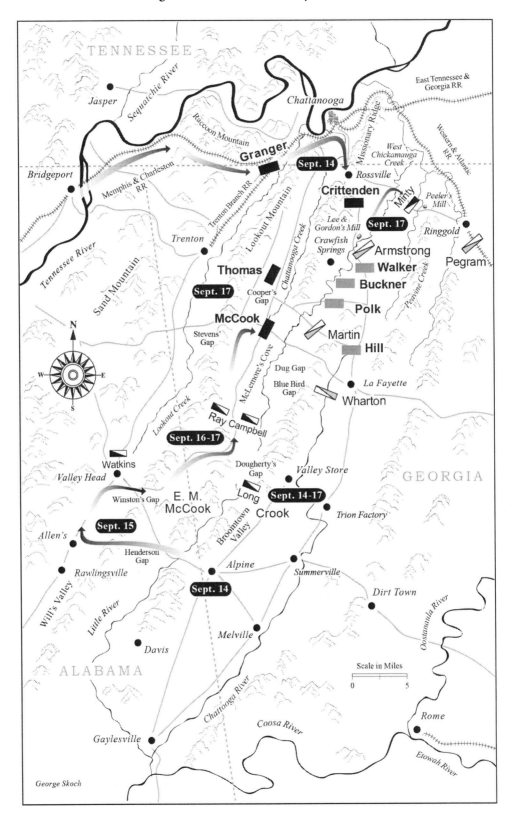

Stanley, now prostrate from his illness, wrote to Garfield about his movement north-ward along a trail shared with the infantry. Crook's cavalry moved toward Dougherty's Gap and did not have to backtrack all the way to Winston's, but Alexander McCook's sup-ply train had to re-ascend Lookout Mountain as Twentieth Corps returned to Winston's in the move northward. The foot soldiers watched the long lines of cavalry move past them throughout the day. Then, Stanley gave up command of the cavalry:"I am still con-fined to my bed, and have had to ride in an ambulance to-day coming over the moun-tain…. General Mitchell is here and will take command of his division in the morning."[73]

In the meantime, Crittenden's corps connected with Thomas' corps on the north near Pond Springs, while Alexander McCook personally reached Thomas' headquar-ters and promised his troops would arrive the next day. Granger's Reserve Corps contin-ued its advance and moved into position near Chattanooga. On September 15 Crittenden reported no enemies observed along his front, but Minty reported something different later in the day: "I have strange reports from the citizens. They say positively that Forrest is at Ringgold, Pegram at Leet's, Buckner at Rock Spring, Cleburne and Longstreet at Dalton." Even Granger, newly arrived on the scene at Rossville, supported Minty's intelligence and reported the citizens in the area saw two divisions of infantry near Graysville the day before marching toward Ringgold. Granger wisely sent a small patrol of mounted infantry in that direction during the day and they returned with intelligence gathered from some citizens that in addition to the infantry, there were four cavalry brigades near Ringgold.[74]

In a serious indictment of Crittenden's dismissiveness of Minty's reconnaissance, Minty's after-action report demonstrated the intelligence he gathered was disregarded by the over confident Crittenden. Minty returned his cavalry to Lee and Gordon's Mill only to be told to move to Pea Vine Valley and encamp near Leet's Crossroads. Minty dutifully followed his orders and bivouacked near Peeler's Mill on Pea Vine Creek, a few miles east of the Chickamauga Creek. Then, Minty received a message from Crittenden's headquar-ters expressing disbelief that Confederate infantry was nearby. Minty recalled: "Same night I reported to Major-General Crittenden the information brought in by these par-ties, and in answer received a letter from Captain Oldershaw, assistant adjutant-general, Twenty-first Army Corps, of which the following is an extract: The major-general com-manding directs me to acknowledge the receipt of your report of this date informing him that Forrest is at Ringgold, Longstreet at Dalton, Pegram at Leet's, and Buckner at Rock Spring; all this would indicate infantry, which the major-general commanding cannot believe." The next day Minty encamped near Reed's Bridge on the Chickamauga Creek, about four miles west of Ringgold.[75]

Mitchell Assumes Command of the Cavalry

Little action occurred over the days of September 14–17 for the Board of Trade Bat-tery on the southern flank with Long's brigade, except for the travel back to Winston's and then moving into the gaps in the mountains. Benjamin Nourse recorded: "14th [Sept.] Up at dawn and climbed the mountains, away across and down into Little Wills Val-ley. 15th [Sept.] Lay in camp all day at the foot of the mountain. Went out foraging, got

Opposite: Union cavalry movements, September 14–17, 1863. The Chicago Board of Trade Bat-tery is split between Minty's and Long's brigades.

corn, sheep, milk, butter, chickens, potatoes & apples. 16th—Up from the valley at 3 oc. p.m. Went up very easy indeed. Then marched 12 miles across and slept. Stood guard. 17th Sept. On top of Lookout Mountain—moved this morning to a spring and camped for the day—and then went out foraging and brought in 15 bushels of potatoes and some corn—captured a rebel horse." Elijah Watts, 2nd Kentucky Cavalry, recalled that the cavalry assisted the Board of Trade Battery over the mountains again "with muscular force every foot of the way, but this was no new experience it had occurred several times before."[76]

John Nourse had more action on September 15. He was detailed along with Corporals Philip Auten, James Hildreth and Private Edward Finnell to collect horseshoes off some dead animals. After collecting the horseshoes, Finnell returned to camp. The remainder of this detail, accompanied by two infantry officers, went in search of a reputed moonshine still. On their way, they ran into a group of bushwhackers. Nourse and his companions, outnumbered, had only revolvers and sabers while the enemy had carbines and muskets. They knew the long guns could pick them off before they got away. So, instead of retreating, the men spurred their horses and "charged them at full gallop, yelling at the top of our voices," wrote Nourse. Nourse could not determine the number of enemy because he did not get close enough to them. When the Union detail charged, the bushwhackers turned and hurried away. After this victory, the men continued on their expedition to find the still. The owner, under gunpoint, took the men to the still where they filled their canteens. The men made the owner drink from each of the containers to ensure the liquor wasn't poisoned and promptly destroyed the still and the remaining liquor. Then, they made the still-owner guide them back to the Union lines, but he was so drunk that he fell off his mule along the way. After reaching camp, the men realized their foolishness of being outside their lines, but they shared their booty with the rest of the men in the battery and forgot the danger.[77]

General Robert Mitchell commanded the First Cavalry Division and assumed overall command of the Union cavalry at the Battle of Chickamauga (Library of Congress).

In regard to the remainder of the cavalry, cavalry headquarters was established in close proximity of Colonel P. Sidney Post's infantry brigade at Valley Head, securing the extreme right flank of Rosecrans' contracting army. Long occupied Dougherty's Gap that morning but the cavalry horses could not remain there too long. There was no forage to be had and the horses would starve if they could not be moved back into the valley. Edward McCook's horses were in little better condition. Sergeant G.W. Baum, 2nd Indiana recorded in his diary that his regiment was not "used up, but I confess we were considerable worse for the wear." Stanley ordered two brigades of McCook's division to move between Dougherty's and Neal's gaps to close up on Alexander McCook's flank. This was relatively easy to accomplish for the cavalry, but the horses needed to be rotated into either Broomtown Valley or McLemore's Cove to be fed.[78]

Stanley finalized the transition of command to Mitchell who reported that David Stanley was "dangerously sick." He continued: "General Stanley will go to the rear to-morrow. He is very sick, and I am fearful that he will have a serious time. Give me specific directions with regard to cavalry movements, and I will endeavor to carry them out. The cavalry are badly used up, both men and horses. We have sent today, and will send tomorrow to Stevenson 300 sick soldiers." Robert Mitchell semi-officially began his command of the cavalry that evening writing to Garfield that Crook was at Dougherty's Gap and he had seen no bodies of enemy near his position. In Mitchell's assessment, more than 2,000 cavalrymen had been lost so far in the campaign due to unserviceable horses and by illness that seemed to be targeting many of the Federal cavalry.[79]

September 16—Bragg Decides to Attack

After the failure to launch two attacks on September 10–11 and September 12–13, Bragg decided to launch a full attack on the Army of the Cumberland. He called his corps commanders together and told them that he planned to make the attack north of the main body of the Federal army, cutting it off from Chattanooga. With his most direct supply line severed, Rosecrans would have to fight, retake Chattanooga, or retreat. These orders essentially laid the plans for the Confederate attack that would begin the Battle of Chickamauga on September 18. At the close of the meeting, the corps commanders returned to their headquarters to await formal marching orders.[80]

The increased enemy activity detected by Granger and Minty alerted the army commanders of the threat to the left flank of the Union army. Rosecrans continued to pull his army together along the west side of Chickamauga Creek and urged Halleck to send him reinforcements. With Granger moving to Crittenden's flank, Minty finally received one of his regiments, 4th U.S. Cavalry which had been detached to the infantry a few days before. Crittenden also agreed to return the 7th Pennsylvania Cavalry, which he had recently appropriated. Minty's brigade pressed three miles ahead on Ringgold Road the evening before and ran into a line of enemy pickets. Early on the morning of September 16, Minty's pickets again found the enemy pressing ahead and when Minty reinforced his line, the Confederate cavalry, which was suspected to be on a strong reconnaissance, withdrew. After dealing with this body of cavalry, his line was tested by another strong enemy reconnaissance from the direction of Leet's Tanyard, to the south. The troopers of the 4th Michigan expected to be attacked and fell into line around Griffin's guns, but no serious fighting occurred. Minty concluded that Colonel John Scott's Confederate cavalry brigade occupied Ringgold and that Brigadier General Henry B. Davidson's cavalry brigade pushed northward from Leet's Tanyard. In the meantime, Minty again expressed his concern about the enemy troops he faced and explained that he did not want to send a scouting force south toward Leet's Tanyard because the Confederate cavalry would probably cut it off and capture his men. In addition, he explained the difficulty in carrying out orders without having a full brigade of cavalry.[81]

Minty followed with another message at noon from his location near Reed's Bridge, relaying that immediately after sending his morning message the Confederate cavalry attacked his line on three different roads. In addition, scouts from the 4th U.S. Cavalry observed an infantry column marching south on the La Fayette Road. If infantry gained the road, Minty would be cut off from direct communications with Crittenden and this would force the Union cavalry to fall back to the west side of Chickamauga Creek at Reed's Bridge. "I still picket the La Fayette road. I have had 1 man killed…. The rebels have been driven on all the roads from 4 to 7 miles."[82]

Minty continued to sound the alert about a large concentration of the enemy nearby, "Strong scouting parties from toward Ringgold and Leet's advanced on me; they were promptly met, driven, and followed. The pickets on the La Fayette and Harrison road, which lies between Pea Vine Ridge and Chickamauga, were attacked from toward La Fayette and my rear threatened." When the enemy stopped their pursuit, the Union cavalry tracked them back toward Leet's Tanyard until they ran into a column of infantry marching toward Ringgold. On receiving the report, General Crittenden answered that the infantry "could be nothing but dismounted cavalry." On September 16 and 17, Minty remained at Reed's Bridge and continued to scout the countryside. The scouts brought back more important information and "reported large bodies of the enemy on our front." Minty was right to be concerned because he was in the path of a major attack by Bragg's infantry. During the day, the 4th U.S. Cavalry clashed with Buckner's infantry near Ringgold while the 7th Pennsylvania encountered some of the infantry in the direction of La Fayette. Both Minty and Wilder would remain critical of Crittenden's over-confidence before the battle and his lack of regard for the intelligence both these officers brought to him.[83]

On the southern side of the line, Bragg was ready to fight and sent orders on September 16 about the attack. Bragg's plan hinged on severing Rosecrans from Chattanooga and the capture of two roads would effectively accomplish this task—the main road from La Fayette to Chattanooga which crossed the Chickamauga Creek at Lee and Gordon's Mill, and the Dry Valley Road which ran along Missionary Ridge just west of the other road. The attack was planned for 5:00 a.m. the next morning, but Bragg cancelled the attack orders just two hours before it took place.[84]

Minty Protects Reed's Bridge and McCook Moves to McLemore's Cove

Rosecrans continued to shift his army on the west bank of the Chickamauga Creek and the apparent threat of attack on the left flank appeared to lessen in his eyes on September 17, but he remained cautious. He ordered his corps commanders to provide a solid screen of pickets in front of his full line, and he pulled his infantry even further north. Crittenden had some "brisk" firing between pickets of his infantry and the 4th Georgia Cavalry, but he believed that only a single cavalry regiment was involved. Crittenden reported his corps in full readiness. Thomas Wood observed clouds of dust moving northward during the day. "The lookout reports the column of dust, when first seen, as moving northward when the firing was heard, and then the column or cloud of dust seemed to cease moving northward." Garfield replied to Wood that the dust resulted from a clash with the 15th Pennsylvania Cavalry and a column of Confederate cavalry near John Palmer's division. All along Crittenden's left flank, a solid screen of Union troops consisted of Wood, Wilder, Minty and finally Granger to the north.[85]

Minty bivouacked his brigade, now with the 7th Pennsylvania Cavalry which returned to his command overnight, at Reed's Bridge and established communications with Granger's Reserve Corps, which extended to Rossville and Graysville. He also established communications with Wilder who assumed a defensive position two miles south at Alexander's Bridge. Minty had some light skirmishing between his scouts and the enemy's pickets throughout the day. His scouting parties rode toward Ringgold and La Fayette and identified large concentrations of the enemy along his front and even observed columns of dust in the distance. Rosecrans wisely placed Minty and Wilder at two of the most important routes coming from the east. Robert Burns wrote his brother on the evening of September 17 that there had been heavy skirmishing over the past few days: "Our horses are saddled all the time and we sleep booted and spurred."[86]

On the Southern flank, Robert Mitchell ordered McCook to establish a line in front of Dug Gap while Crook held Dougherty's Gap. McCook's Second Brigade moved into McLemore's Cove and camped. The concern about his position in front of Dug Gap prompted McCook to order his troopers to also keep their horses saddled and prepared to ride even at night. The precautions were justified. Wheeler received orders on the evening of September 17 to replace the infantry which had previously held the various mountain gaps: Blue Bird, Dug, and Catlett's gaps. D.H. Hill planned to move northward in preparation of the Confederate attack on Rosecrans' army and this left Wheeler the duty of protecting the southern flank and rear of the army.[87]

The table was set for the greatest battle of the west and the Board of Trade Battery would play a key part in the outcome. From September 9–17, the Federal cavalry, supported by the Board of Trade Battery on both flanks, became more active and skirmishes increased. It provided good intelligence about Confederate positions, participated in skirmishes, and its aggressiveness caused Bragg to pause long enough for Rosecrans to concentrate his army. These actions were of immeasurable value to the Union army. The reliable Stanley had given up command of the cavalry over the past few days and he was replaced with Robert Mitchell, a man with only a few months' experience in the mounted forces. This loss to the cavalry was a severe one. Unfortunately, Crittenden did not work well with Minty and because of this, he disregarded the intelligence Minty was giving him about the Confederates moving on his flank. This disregard would put Minty's cavalry and Trumbull Griffin's guns to test as they would face an overwhelming attack on the first day of the Battle of Chickamauga.

CHAPTER FIVE

Battle of Chickamauga and Wheeler's Raid

Griffin's guns raked the approaches so thoroughly that the enemy had to fall back in confusion. —Col. Robert Minty

The Board of Trade Battery would remain split through the end of the Chickamauga Campaign. For the past month, Griffin operated under Minty's command and while the duty was dangerous, no serious engagements had occurred. This was about to change and Griffin's action would add to the most important contribution made by the cavalry in the Battle of Chickamauga. Unfortunately, while there were several men of the battery who gave first-hand accounts, no such accounts have been preserved by those of Griffin's section. Therefore, most of the action and descriptions came from Minty's cavalry regiments. For example, Sergeant James Larson, 4th U.S. Cavalry, had little direct experience with the Chicago Board of Trade Battery before the campaign, but in his description of the fighting on September 18, 1863, he wrote highly of the battery. "The Chicago Board of Trade Battery was composed of well drilled artillerists and it had fine guns too … was equal in every respect to the best drilled battery in the regular army and rendered Minty's brigade great assistance in many tight places." The regular army sergeant's comments spoke volumes in regard to Griffin's contributions on September 18. Griffin's section had been moved into line over the past couple of days while anticipating an attack near Peeler's Mill and Reed's Bridge, despite Crittenden's comments disregarding the intelligence coming from this sector.[1]

Minty at Reed's Bridge and Wilder at Alexander's Bridge

Along Minty's area, Chickamauga Creek was an important obstacle to troop movements. Despite the drought, the stream was difficult to cross, and Reed's Bridge and Alexander's Bridge were vitally important to the rapid movement of Bragg's infantry and cavalry in the anticipated attack. South of Minty's position at Reed's Bridge, Colonel John Wilder and his mounted infantry protected the area near Alexander's Bridge. Two of the Army of the Cumberland's most capable colonels had this important duty. Both Minty and Wilder had detected large concentrations of the enemy over the past few days. Minty began scouting the area near Reed's Bridge and Leet's Tanyard on September 15. Over the next two days, Minty sent reports about the enemy (infantry and cavalry) to Crittenden, but Crittenden downgraded or disregarded these threats. Minty's brigade camped near Reed's Bridge west of Pea Vine Ridge after a hard day's skirmishing on September 16, after which, Minty sent his intelligence report to Crittenden reporting, "The force at Ringgold is, I believe, Scott's brigade. Pegram is at Leet's [Tanyard], with an outpost at Pea Vine Church." On September 17, Minty pushed the enemy back along his front, collecting 23 infantrymen as prisoners. He then sent Crittenden a report that Longstreet's infantry was in the neighborhood, but Crittenden discounted the threat remarking, "They are only some stragglers you picked up." A frustrated Minty concluded his report and returned to his command at Reed's Bridge "with heavy heart" over his inability to convince Crittenden and Rosecrans of the threat to the Union left flank. Many in the cavalry knew they had faced a large concentration of enemy troops for a couple of days and Minty was in position to receive a heavy blow if Bragg could ever mount his attack. Captain Robert Burns, Minty's adjutant general, agreed with Minty's assessment; he wrote to his brother after the battle and related that when Minty told Crittenden of a large Confederate force near his position, Crittenden replied: "Pooh, pooh, don't believe it. Keep good watch. Don't get scared." Even Southern general D.H. Hill commented that never had there been a general so over confident as Crittenden as he unknowingly faced overwhelming odds.[2]

Although the Union forces temporarily occupied Ringgold, they abandoned the town a few days before when Rosecrans concentrated his army and pulled back to the west side of Chickamauga Creek. As a result, a force of Confederate infantry 10,000 men strong returned to Ringgold with Forrest's cavalry screening its advance. Minty's brigade depleted to only two regiments, 4th Michigan and 4th U.S. cavalries accompanied by Griffin's section, and remained underappreciated as the sun rose on September 17. The day before, Minty believed he faced a serious Confederate threat and again requested his other regiments—the 7th Pennsylvania and the 3rd Indiana. Minty had initially established his headquarters at Peeler's Mill, but due to the increasingly intense clashes, with Forrest's cavalry in particular, and heavy skirmishes near that location and along the Harrison and La Fayette Road, he decided to pull back near Reed's Bridge, fearing he could be cut off and isolated from the rest of the Federal army. He still kept pickets and scouts active in Pea Vine Valley, but his cavalry was the only Union force east of Chickamauga Creek, properly named West Chickamauga Creek because East Chickamauga Creek meandered northward from Ringgold. The two branches united a short distance north of the Georgia state line and emptied into the Tennessee River east of Chattanooga. While West Chickamauga Creek lazily flowed northward, it was 10 feet deep in places and had steep and swampy banks, making it a difficult stream to cross. A series of low hills edged the creek. To the rear of Minty's position was Missionary Ridge, about 400 feet high with a very steep northern slope that formed an arc around the southern side of Chattanooga. The southern slope had a more gradual decline.[3]

Minty and Wilder were right to be concerned about the enemy forces near their positions. For two days Bragg had prepared to attack Crittenden's flank north of Lee and Gordon's Mill. The plan called for Brigadier General Bushrod Johnson's strong Confederate division to move west from Leet's Tanyard as it cut the link to Chattanooga. A second Confederate column, Major General William H.T. Walker's corps, intended to march across Alexander's Bridge a couple of miles south of Reed's Bridge. Bragg also planned to seize Rossville from Granger's Reserve Corps in its push west, but Bragg waited two days for reinforcements before ordering the attack.[4]

After reaching Rossville, Granger's corps reconnoitered the area around its position and the surrounding territory on September 17, and Brigadier General James Steedman led an advance in the direction of Ringgold. Steedman nearly reached Ringgold where

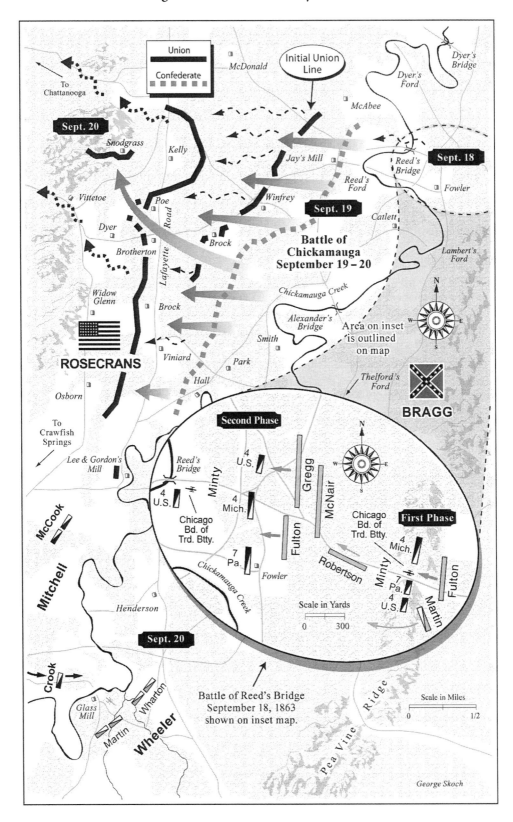

Battle of
Chickamauga
September 19–20

Battle of Reed's Bridge
September 18, 1863
shown on inset map.

George Skoch

the large concentration of Confederate infantry and cavalry awaited orders to attack. This unwelcome occurrence finally prompted Bragg to act. Bragg ordered Pegram's cavalry to strengthen the security at Ringgold and Bragg finally issued orders to attack in the early hours of September 18. Bushrod Johnson's Provisional Division, about 3,700 men strong, would march for Leet's Tanyard, a little south of Minty's position while Walker's corps would move toward Wilder at Alexander's Bridge. Polk's and Buckner's corps planned to attack the Union forces in the vicinity of Lee and Gordon's Mill, and Hill would make a flank attack from the south from the direction of McLemore's Cove. Forrest's cavalry, while not specifically addressed in the orders, would work in conjunction with Johnson's division along the right flank of the Southern Army. Thus, on September 18, Bragg sent his army forward with the objective of severing Rosecrans' connection with Chattanooga by attacking Crittenden's left flank. Minty and Wilder stood in his way.[5]

Minty Finds Bushrod Johnson's Columns

There were three important bridges in the area of Bragg's intended attack—Dyer's Bridge (north of Reed's Bridge), Reed's Bridge, and Alexander's Bridge (south of Reed's bridge). With the bridges about two miles apart, Bragg intended to advance along a six-mile front that featured these three bottlenecks. In addition to the bridges, several fords were important to the rapid crossing of the creek by troops. Reed's Bridge and Alexander's Bridge were about 10 miles west of Ringgold. The day before, Minty had command of only the 4th Michigan and the 4th U.S. Cavalry. Fortunately, the 7th Pennsylvania returned to his command the previous evening. In all, Minty had less than 1,000 officers and men, supported by Griffin's two-gun section, in position along Reed's Bridge Road.[6]

The day would be cloudy and cool and at noon the temperature only reached 62 degrees. Early on September 18, Minty, at his headquarters at James Reed's house just east of Chickamauga Creek, had pickets and patrols out looking for the enemy. Due to the overwhelming evidence of the enemy in the area, at sunrise Trumbull Griffin ordered the section of guns to be harnessed and ready for action. At 6:00 a.m., Minty sent 100 troopers of the 4th U.S. Cavalry toward Leet's Tanyard (a small tannery owned by a Methodist minister and farmer, The Rev. A.I. Leet), and the same number of 4th Michigan and 7th Pennsylvania rode toward Ringgold looking for the enemy. Captain Heber Thompson's command of Pennsylvania troopers rode to Pea Vine Ridge in the early morning fog and then he sent out four-man patrols to the east to search for the enemy. One of the patrols reached a house about 100 yards west of Pea Vine Creek and discovered a Confederate patrol advancing to the west. Thompson's cavalrymen opened fire on the enemy, then moved ahead with 16 troopers while keeping the rest of his men in line watching for more of the enemy. In the meantime, Thompson sent a courier who reached Minty at 7:00 a.m. explaining that he saw a large number of infantry marching in his direction. However, he had not observed infantry, but part of John Scott's cavalry brigade. After sending messages to Gordon Granger, John Wilder, Thomas Wood and Thomas Crittenden about the increased enemy activity, Minty strengthened his pickets along the La Fayette Road and rode forward with the 4th Michigan, a battalion of the 4th U.S., and Griffin's section of

Opposite: The Battle of Chickamauga. Inset MAP shows Minty's and Griffin's first two positions at the Battle of Reed's Bridge, September 18, 1863.

the Chicago Board of Trade Battery. Minty established his defensive line of about 600 troopers along the eastern slope of Pea Vine Ridge, about two miles east of Reed's Bridge and overlooking the small Pea Vine Creek, and prepared to meet Johnson's advancing infantry columns which arrived around 10:00 a.m.[7]

Thompson's men saw light action after initially skirmishing with Scott's cavalry in the morning, but they soon encountered a more deadly threat—soldiers in gray uniforms moving silently through the trees. After firing a few shots at the approaching Confederates, Thompson discovered the strong, advancing skirmish line of the 17th Tennessee Infantry. The advancing infantry drew the immediate attention of Thompson who sent a rider hurrying to Minty with news about the approaching enemy. He then ordered the remainder of his battalion to the west side of the creek and prepared to delay the Confederate advance. Thompson had accomplished what he hoped when Johnson's main column approached amid clouds of dust, stopped, and fell into battle line. A daunting sight, the Confederate infantry fell into line three brigades wide, with the fourth brigade in reserve. Bushrod Johnson's division, supported by Robertson's brigade, gave him about 5,000 men. Johnson also commanded two additional brigades of Hood's infantry which were trailing along behind the column. Not having Forrest's cavalry in advance of the column, Johnson did not know the size of the force he faced and decided on a cautious approach.[8]

Sergeant James Larson, 4th U.S., remarked that the Confederate advance on the morning of September 18 was not a surprise, but "we did not expect it to come off so early." The troopers of the 4th U.S. Cavalry were sitting down to their breakfast and had meat and vegetables cooking in a pot over a campfire. Larson had just started making pancakes when "Boots and Saddles" echoed. The men ran for their horses with part of a pancake in their hands as gunfire echoed in the distance. As the regiment moved to the east, it crossed Reed's Bridge and the column slowed because the bridge was only wide enough for two horses to pass side-by-side. This bridge would be the location of important fighting later in the day. Also hurrying forward were Griffin's two guns which rumbled across Chickamauga Creek and then up the ridge to the forming Federal line. Most likely, Griffin's section crossed Chickamauga Creek at a ford 300 yards south of Reed's Bridge, a crossing specified in the return later in the afternoon. The frail condition of the bridge made crossing with horses, limbers, and heavy guns unsafe.[9]

Fortunately for Minty, Johnson's advance was delayed from the start of the day. Johnson began his advance at 4:00 a.m. from Catoosa Platform, a small rail station a couple of miles southeast of Ringgold. Johnson initially marched to Ringgold and then moved toward Leet's Tanyard. His movement toward Minty's cavalry was delayed by an outdated set of orders directing him to move to Leet's Tanyard instead of Reed's Bridge. After marching three miles, a courier brought Bragg's newly modified orders which directed the infantry column to secure Reed's Bridge and then move southward toward Lee and Gordon's Mill. Once the confusion was sorted, Johnson's column changed direction and marched toward Minty's position. Nathan Bedford Forrest belatedly caught the column at 10:45 a.m. and he rode with about 350 troopers, including Martin's detachment and a 100-man escort of elite cavalry. Martin's detachment was a fragment of the survivors of John Hunt Morgan's ill-fated raid into the north in July.[10]

Thompson's 7th Pennsylvania troopers skirmished with Bushrod Johnson's advancing infantry units near Peeler's Mill with more Southern infantry support following along behind. The 17th Tennessee Infantry of Colonel John Fulton's brigade led the advance and ran into the skirmishers of the 7th Pennsylvania, killing three troopers and mortally

Chickamauga Creek, "ten feet deep in places and had steep and swampy banks, making it a difficult stream to cross" (Library of Congress).

wounding another, but Minty's cavalry fell into an effective fight-retreat-fight method of delaying Johnson's advance. When Forrest arrived on the scene, he ordered Martin's small detachment of Southern cavalry to push Thompson's cavalry westward despite objections from the infantry about having their own cavalry in their front because certainly Johnson already had more than enough infantry. In a puzzling move, Forrest dismounted his cavalry and had them join the infantry, thereby negating the mobility of his force. Johnson's infantry slowly advanced while contending with Minty's stubborn defense bolstered by Griffin's guns. Griffin, in his first position of the day, opened up when the Union skirmishers had been pushed back to the base of Pea Vine Ridge. Griffin, a native of Clinton, New York and printer by trade, kept a steady hand on his two guns which sent shells into the advancing Confederate lines. The size of Bushrod Johnson's division resulted in a "crescent shaped" line of battle converging on Minty's defenders, but the dense woods, hills and streams also aided the Union cavalry by hindering Johnson's advance.[11]

Griffin's guns roared quickly and efficiently as Minty prepared his defensive lines on the ridge. Sergeant Frank Knight, the 33-year-old pre-war railroader, ordered his gun to open fire and would send the first artillery shell in the battle at Reed's Bridge. Griffin had a difficult task as the Confederate columns marched through the densely wooded area. Minty explained that Griffin's guns "did considerable execution" as far as he could observe, but importantly: "This checked the enemy and caused them to deploy. They evidently supposed that there was a strong force opposing them, and they occupied considerable time in getting into position." Minty had little chance of holding back such a large force and he was playing for time, time that Griffin was giving him. The numbers were on Johnson's side as he pushed the Northern troopers off the ridge and back toward Reed's Bridge, "a narrow, frail structure, which was planked with loose boards and fence-rails." Johnson's men began closing in on the Federals on the ridge and Minty ordered Griffin to mount the guns and move back toward Chickamauga Creek to cover the withdrawal. When the troopers in the main line saw Griffin pulling out the guns, they prepared "to do likewise." Minty placed the 4th Michigan on the left of the Pennsylvania cavalrymen while the 4th U.S. moved to the right. Lieutenant Jacob Sigmund, 7th Pennsylvania Cavalry, commanded some of Minty's skirmishers, and as Johnson's troops pressed forward, his skirmishers held their position until they were almost overwhelmed.[12]

Ominous Dust to the North

Johnson's infantry pushed the Union cavalry steadily back toward Reed's Bridge. The Board of Trade Battery and Minty's troopers continued to fire into the advancing Confederate line, but Minty noticed another column of dust moving to the north. Fearing he was about to be flanked while already facing more Confederates than he could handle, at 11:00 o'clock he appealed to John Wilder for reinforcements to guard Dyer's Bridge, which Minty believed was the objective of the newly arriving Confederate column. Wilder, who was not engaged at this point, sent two regiments, 123rd Illinois and the 72nd Indiana, along with a two-gun section of Lilly's Battery to Dyer's Bridge. They arrived at noon and deployed to halt any attempt to flank Minty by that route. The remainder of Wilder's brigade held Alexander's Bridge. At the time the two regiments were sent north, there was no indication these would be needed at Alexander's Bridge; however, Walker's Confederate Reserve Corps attacked Wilder at noon after he had dispatched the reinforcements. Minty and Wilder had secured the three key bridges across Chickamauga Creek, thereby preventing a rapid advance of Johnson's and Walker's Confederates.[13]

While resisting Johnson's advance, Minty had deployed a screen of skirmishers. Sergeant Larson, 4th U.S., one of the first reinforcements to arrive, explained that to attempt to hold off the full might of the Confederate infantry was impractical. Instead, several cavalry companies formed a skirmish line, and when the steady advance of the Confederate infantry continued, it faced a fusillade of Union fire, causing the long gray line to pause before resuming its steady advance. The 4th U.S. companies retreated one company at a time in alphabetical order, and then re-deployed in the rear. Minty made good use of the terrain and the fact that the road leading from Ringgold to Reed's Bridge wound through a narrow pass, which constricted movement through Pea Vine Ridge, greatly benefited the Union defense. As Johnson's infantry pushed forward, Minty boldly decided to advance his skirmishers to meet the advancing line of Confederates while simultaneously withdrawing his main body back toward Reed's Bridge.[14]

Minty held out along Pea Vine Ridge until 12:30 p.m. before retreating further west. By the time Forrest returned from an unsuccessful attempt to find the Federal flank, Minty's cavalry had edged back to the east side of Chickamauga Creek. In the meantime, Johnson's infantry secured Pea Vine Ridge. When Johnson crested the ridge, he observed that he only faced a single brigade of cavalry. The Union troopers watched as the grand advance of Confederate regimental colors fluttered in the wind when

Johnson's troops marched over the ridge toward Reed's Bridge. As the bulk of Johnson's men surged past the ridge around 2:00 p.m., Griffin's guns, concealed among some brush in an ambush position, opened on them again. Minty had withdrawn Griffin's section near Reed's house to the right of the bridge, but the section was in position to shell the enemy as they emerged over the ridge. At Griffin's second position of the day, he fired canister as the enemy troops began moving past the apex of the ridge, causing the advance to halt and reposition. Henry Albert Potter, 4th Michigan, recorded in his diary, "[W]e then rode into a cornfield on our right & on a hill—to support our artillery. From that view I could see clouds of dust a heavy column coming towards us on the left—our guns presently opened up on them—we were answered promptly by the rebels with four pieces—I could see them when they loaded, as soon as the smoke cleared away." So impressive was the Southern advance, that it appeared the "whole brigade would be captured or annihilated," wrote Captain Joseph Vale, 7th Pennsylvania Cavalry. The Union Cavalry retreated westward as they moved out of the dense forests. Near the bridge, the ground leveled and had been planted with crops earlier in the year. Griffin's guns caused the Confederate line to pause. Taking advantage of the more level and cleared terrain, Minty's 4th Michigan and 7th Pennsylvania made a successful mounted charge on the first Confederate troops surging in advance, slowing their progress while the rest of enemy infantry moved along the flanks squeezing the Union cavalry back toward the bridge. Minty realized he could no longer hold his position but much of his brigade was still on the east side of the creek trying to delay Johnson's advance. The enemy pressed the Union position so closely that Griffin's section had an unexpected attack from a detachment of Confederates that approached through a thicket. The attacking enemy troops were "entertained by a hand to hand contest" with the artillerymen as the battery limbered and prepared to withdraw, described Lieutenant Sylvanus Stevens. In the meantime, Minty began preparing his defenses on the west side of the creek in order to provide covering fire once the remainder of the brigade crossed the bridge. The bridge was so narrow that the Union withdrawal had to be finely tuned. Minty directed Captain James McIntyre to withdraw a battalion of the 4th U.S. to cross the bridge "at a sharp walk" and he sent Griffin's guns to cross at a ford 300 yards south of the bridge. He placed the section of artillery into some bushes 300 yards on the west side of Chickamauga Creek on a rise near some old farm buildings, supported by the battalion of the 4th U.S. Cavalry. As the Union withdrawal began and as the Confederate infantry advanced, the 4th Michigan and 7th Pennsylvania cavalries provided the first line of defense. Henry Albert Potter, 4th Michigan Cavalry, recorded the intense action as Johnson pushed Minty rearward: "Order came to fall back—which we did—rejoined the regiment & moved through the woods—our skirmishers soon saw the rebels infantry—we dismounted half of the men and moved upon them—a smart skirmish ensued—but were obliged to fall back by overpowering numbers—formed in line again—again were driven back—passed thro' our camp and past the 'Regulars'—towards the river—which we succeeded in crossing without loss. Formed in a line to cover the retreat of the 4th [Regulars] presently crash! Came the artillery in the midst of us."[15]

Minty Moves Across Reed's Bridge

Sergeant Larson observed Griffin's Board of Trade section arrive on a hill just west of the creek and in a "twinkle" was in position, firing away at the enemy, "right over our

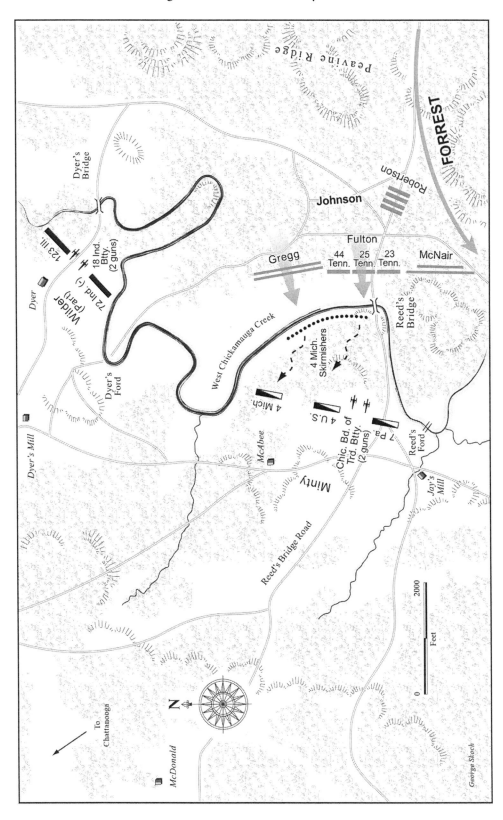

Minty's and Griffin's third position on September 18, 1863.

heads." With the first salvo from Griffin's gun, Larson observed the enemy line ripple and the second shot knocked a wheel from an enemy gun. The enemy hurriedly began re-positioning another gun, and Griffin's guns again sent forth their shells, striking another enemy gun. Larson, impressed with the accuracy of Griffin's firing remarked, "The way our battery sent their shells straight to the mark soon convinced the enemy that they were in danger of having their guns all smashed up if they remained in that place." Having the enemy battery's range, the Confederates rolled the rest of the guns back into the woods by hand.[16]

With Griffin's section in position, the 4th Michigan withdrew across the bridge followed by the 7th Pennsylvania. Finally, the remainder of the 4th U.S. Cavalry under the command of Lieutenant Wirt Davis, a Virginian whose family had severed connections with him due to the war, moved across and stopped long enough on the bridge to pull up the planks making a quick crossing difficult for their enemy. But not all of Minty's command had made it across the river. A squadron of the 4th Michigan had been guarding the Harrison Road, southeast of Reed's Bridge, and was cut off due to the rapid advance of the Confederates. Lieutenant John Simpson, who was commanding the detail, made a determined stand against the Confederates closing on his position before his troopers finally escaped by swimming Chickamauga Creek.[17]

Minty reassembled his command on the west side of the creek as Griffin's guns hammered away, and prepared to delay any movement further westward by Johnson's infantry. With the obstacle of the deep and difficult Chickamauga Creek facing him, Johnson

The Board of Trade Battery fired at the approaching Confederates at Chickamauga Creek (A.R. Waud wartime sketch. From Joseph Brown, *The Mountain Campaign in Georgia*, 1886).

had to decide how best to cross in the face of 1,000 Union cavalry, some with repeating rifles, supported by artillery. Finally, he had had enough waiting and decided to march Fulton's brigade directly toward the bridge. Minty's carbine and artillery fire halted the advance of the Confederate infantry and prevented it from crossing the creek. Minty exclaimed that "Griffin's guns raked the approaches so thoroughly that the enemy had to fall back in confusion." The men of the 23rd Tennessee Infantry ran to the bridge amid shot and shell only to be surprised when they found that the 4th U.S. had stripped its floor planks. At 3:30 p.m., Fulton's infantry again rushed forward. This time the Tennesseans carried planks of their own, torn from James Reed's house and outbuildings, and began to re-floor the bridge under a barrage from Griffin's guns and carbine fire. Once they repaired the bridge, Forrest arrived, thanked the men for their efforts, and then rode ahead. Soon, Fulton's entire brigade followed, prompting Minty to conclude he could not continue to resist further at that location and he wisely withdrew his men to a second elevated position 700 yards farther west. Shortly thereafter, General John Bell Hood arrived on the scene amid the cheers of the Southern infantry.[18]

After falling back again, Minty continued to resist the Confederate advance, however, he was being flanked on all sides by 10 regiments of Confederate infantry, with more in their wake. Also, he received a message from an officer in charge of his supply train informing him, "Colonel Wilder has fallen back from Alexander's Bridge to Gordon's Mills and the enemy are crossing at all points in force." About 4:00 p.m., Minty sent a message to Wilder's troops at Dyer's Bridge to fall back and join him as he retreated closer to Jay's Mill. The cavalry and supporting artillery carriages quickly prepared to move further west but the guns required more time. The horses were taken to the guns but before the guns could be hitched, "A rebel shot carried away a wheel and dropped the end of the axle and the muzzle of one of the guns to the ground. The Sergeant limbered up and dragged the gun from under a running fire and reported with both guns to the command four miles away," wrote Sylvanus Stevens. Upon its arrival at the new position, the first impression suggested the gun was lost, but Griffin ordered the wheel replaced and the gun was found in good condition except for some abrasions from being dragged. Even though the Federal cavalry had been engaged throughout the day, the fighting was so intense that Robert Burns wrote, "I never saw a day to pass so quickly."[19]

Union Cavalry Withdraws

Aware of the action on his left flank, Rosecrans ordered James Steedman to send infantry from the Reserve Corps to support Minty, but Steedman could not get Dan McCook's infantry brigade on the road until 3:30. By that time, the first Confederates along Minty's front were crossing Chickamauga Creek with Hood's division supporting them. About this time, Henry B. Davidson's cavalry brigade of Pegram's division found and forded Fowler's Ford, about a half mile south of Reed's Bridge. Despite the unfolding battle, Crittenden seemed remarkably nonplussed during the day. Because his headquarters was at the same location as Rosecrans', he simply waited for Rosecrans to send him instructions. Thomas Wood, Crittenden's Corps First Division commander, rode to the front after hearing the noise of the battle and smugly discounted the initial reports that Minty and Wilder were under heavy attack. Wood initially thought the fighting was just Confederate cavalry skirmishers. Then, Wood erroneously heard that Minty's brigade had been surrounded and captured and he ordered his infantry forward to meet the threat. Johnson's slow advance combined with Minty's and Wilder's determined defenses thus delayed the Confederate advance for almost a day, giving Rosecrans a chance to prepare for Bragg's move.[20]

Minty, supported by Wilder's two mounted infantry regiments, fell back to Jay's Mill, a steam-powered sawmill about a half a mile west of Reed's Bridge. Minty held this new position for about an hour until Johnson's and Hood's divisions again overwhelmed his troopers. Hood then marched south in the direction of the Alexander farm. As Minty and Wilder retired, they united their commands, forming a single line across La Fayette Road, and engaged the enemy again. This fight continued for more than an hour and the Union line held. Wood moved his infantry forward and met the advancing Confederate infantry, stalling the enemy's advance, but the day's fighting was not over. Finally recognizing the threat, Rosecrans rapidly redirected his troops and prepared for battle. With the Confederate attacks on his left flank, Rosecrans hastened to fill the gap between Crittenden and Granger. The Union line had been shoved back almost to the Chattanooga and Rossville Road, and the Confederates still pushed forward with plenty of infantry, artillery, and cavalry.[21]

Minty's weary troopers fell into line alongside Wilder's brigade at dusk. The two brigades held a line near Viniard's house about a mile and a half north of Lee and Gordon's Mill facing northeast. Two regiments of infantry from Colonel George Dick's brigade of Van Cleve's division moved into line south of Minty and Wilder. At dusk, Hood ordered John Gregg's infantry brigade, just south of Minty's position, to attack the 44th Indiana and 59th Ohio infantries of Dick's brigade. The first attack came about an hour after dark with a second attack soon after, but both were repulsed. When the night attacks failed, the fighting ended for the day and the 10-hour battle was over. The aftermath of the last fighting left everyone nervous about the success of the enemy. Robert Burns explained: "We lay that night where we were in a line within 100 yards of the enemy with our horses a quarter mile in our rear. We could hear the rebels talking in the woods. I never passed such a night. It was cold and bleak. We were allowed no fire and not a man slept, every one of us expecting at the dawn to be annihilated." But the situation still did not suit Minty who, with Wilder, held the left flank of Crittenden's corps. At 2:00 a.m., he rode to headquarters demanding reinforcements before daylight or else the previous day's fighting would have been for nothing. As a result, Major General John Palmer brought up two infantry brigades to relieve Minty and Wilder. Henry Campbell of the 18th Indiana Battery of Wilder's brigade recorded in his diary the movement of Thomas' Fourteenth Corps throughout the night to fill the gap between Crittenden and Granger. Thomas' infantry made a difficult march to be in place to face the enemy the next morning.[22]

By midnight on September 18, Rosecrans' army was concentrating around Lee and Gordon's Mill, and readied itself for a day of vicious fighting. Minty, Wilder and their commands had performed immeasurable service to the Army of the Cumberland. Luck as well as skill aided Minty's and Wilder's important efforts. Halfway between their positions lay Lambert's Ford. The two Union colonels already faced overwhelming odds, and had the Confederates utilized this crossing earlier in the fight, both Minty and Wilder easily would have been flanked. Minty and Wilder held Rosecrans' left flank and gave him time to shift forces to meet what could have been a crushing blow. Bragg faced a critical delay in getting his forces into place and he lost the element of surprise. Because of the action of these two intrepid commanders, the Fourteenth Corps marched throughout the night to be in position to face the Confederate attack the next morning. Whatever would the next day, Minty and Wilder gave Rosecrans what he most needed—time.[23]

By now, there was little doubt in Rosecrans' mind that he had a serious situation on his hands. The intelligence forwarded by Minty and Wilder throughout the day proved beyond doubt that Bragg intended to cut him off from Chattanooga. Minty's brigade, which had fought so hard the day before, spent a fretful and "bitterly cold" night without any campfires. Palmer's infantry division held the position previously occupied by Minty, who moved his command to a position near Lee and Gordon's Mill until noon on September 19 and then moved toward Rossville. Along the way, the cavalry stopped to feed the horses and obtain rations for the men. Minty spent the rest of the day guarding the supply trains coming and going from Chattanooga, and he would end the day near Rossville without participating in the battle. Garfield released Minty from duty with Crittenden's corps, and wanted Minty on reconnaissance duty near Rossville to ensure that Bragg made no further attacks, which would sever Rosecrans' communications with Chattanooga. After accomplishing his reconnaissance, Minty dispelled any concerns, much to the relief of headquarters, and reported that no large force of Confederate cavalry threatened an attack near Chattanooga on the Rossville Road. Minty kept watch on the Confederate movements and bivouacked near Rossville that evening.[24]

Minty Repulses Scott and Screen's Thomas' Infantry

On September 20, Minty's brigade again operated under the command of an infantry commander, this time Gordon Granger in command of the Reserve Corps. In the afternoon, Minty took up Granger's position on the Rossville and Ringgold Road, and found that Granger had already left this position to support Thomas' defense. With Granger gone, Minty's position was vitally important to prevent the enemy from turning the flank of the Union army. The irascible Granger was making one of his most important decisions committing his Reserve Corps to reinforce George Thomas, who was making a desperate defense at Snodgrass Farm and Horseshoe Ridge. After the intense fighting over the past three days, Minty wanted no surprises and sent out reconnaissance patrols in all directions. Minty patrolled the roads leading to Chattanooga which ensured no surprise attacks to the north. Minty moved his brigade to Missionary Mills and then sent strong patrols to Chickamauga Station and Graysville but found no enemy. Later in the afternoon one of the patrols rode to the Red House Bridge and found Colonel John Scott's Confederate cavalry brigade on the west side of the Chickamauga Creek. Minty pulled his brigade together and attacked Scott, which resulted in an hour-long fight before Minty successfully pushed Scott's brigade back over Chickamauga Creek late in the afternoon. Minty concluded in his after-action report: "[F]ound Scott's brigade of cavalry and mounted infantry, about 1,500 strong, moving into position on our side of the creek. I immediately attacked them. After a spirited skirmish of about an hour's duration, drove them across the creek with considerable loss." Minty's cavalry ended the day at McAfee's Church on the Ringgold Road and his men spent a cold night "sitting on the ground bridle in hand." Though not specifically mentioned in any reports, Griffin's section accompanied Minty's brigade and participated in the fighting over the next few days.[25]

The next morning (September 21), Minty held a line a mile in front of Thomas's Fourteenth Corps, screening the Confederate advance. Captain Richard Robbins, 4th Michigan, recalled that the men of the regiment awakened knowing the previous day had been a bad one for the Federal forces, but Thomas' defense at Snodgrass Farm had saved the army.

Like many in the brigade, Robbins was exhausted and his first task of the day was to find out where he was after the back and forth fighting of the previous day. He determined his company started the day in front of Missionary Ridge. Minty's brigade had spent the night just east of Rossville and then moved quickly to Rossville Gap in front of the infantry on Missionary Ridge. Minty sent riders in all directions to determine the location of the enemy and Minty also sent riders to the location of Thomas' headquarters on the previous day only to find him gone. None of the cavalry knew where Thomas had moved overnight. Eventually, the couriers found Thomas on Missionary Ridge. Later, Minty personally rode to Thomas' headquarters and he recalled the conversation with Thomas before being sent to delay the Confederate advance. Minty reported to Thomas who said, "'You should not be there, Colonel.' I replied: 'I know that, General; but there I am.' After a moment's thought, he said: 'Well, as you are there, delay the enemy all you can. Give me as much time as possible to prepare to get ready for them.'" Minty returned to his command and positioned his brigade, supported by Griffin's two guns in the center, at a crossroads about one half mile west of McAfee's Church and planned to delay any enemy advance down the roads. He was soon greeted by Pegram's Division of Scott's and Davidson's Brigades. Minty wrote, "There gave them battle, and, taking advantage of every possible position."[26]

The first echoes of carbines began around 10:00. The Confederates attacked Minty's pickets to his right and front around noon in earnest and by 1:00 p.m. he withdrew to the ridge in front of Thomas' command. Minty believed he faced a double line of infantry which pushed the cavalrymen rearward, but at least some dismounted Confederate cavalry participated in the fight, including the 6th Georgia Cavalry. Robbins explained that soon thereafter the enemy moved forward "probing their way through the brush." The 4th Michigan, 4th U.S. and 7th Pennsylvania supported by the Board of Trade Battery settled into another long day of fighting. Just south of Rossville Gap, the Confederates struck Minty's brigade with a strong force causing the greatest casualties of the day. "I don't believe many who were there will forget it," wrote Robbins. The 7th Pennsylvania Cavalry took the greatest loss with several men in the regiment being killed or wounded.[27]

Robbins noted that Minty's position left him vulnerable to a "blizzard from both sides"—his front, as the Confederate cavalry and infantry moved forward, and from the rear by nervous Union infantrymen after the fighting from the day before. Soon, Minty observed the advance of three Confederate columns, Walker, Hill and Polk, which moved from Missionary Mills, Red House Bridge and Dyer's Ford. Pegram's cavalry division advanced and pushed Minty's cavalry back toward the Union main line. After the fight at Reed's Bridge, Minty was becoming skilled in the "fight, retreat, fight" method of delaying an advance. In addition, the Federal cavalry came under fire from three Confederate batteries, but Barnett's 2nd Illinois Battery counter-fired on the Southern artillery, joined by the Board of Trade guns, lessening the enemy's impact as the cavalry continued the fighting withdrawal. During the skirmishes, Minty's troopers battled Dibrell's cavalry brigade and even shot Nathan Bedford Forrest's horse through the neck as they withdrew toward Thomas' infantry line under the pressure of the Confederate cavalry and Morton's Confederate artillery. After a few hours of skirmishing, the Confederates pushed the cavalry back to Missionary Ridge and just as predicted, as Minty's cavalry withdrew near the Union lines, volleys exploded from the line of Federal infantry in the rear which resulted in fatalities in Minty's cavalry ranks. Minty decided to move his cavalry through the narrow gap and finally made it past Thomas' line, past Missionary Ridge and planned to rest for the night.[28]

The day was not over. That evening, George Thomas informed Minty of his intention to move to Chattanooga during the night and asked Minty to deceive the enemy by taking the place of the infantry in line. Minty's men obediently moved into the passes and along the crest on Missionary Ridge. Thomas received his orders to withdraw at 6:00 p.m. and sent orders at 9:00 to begin pulling the infantry off the ridge. Minty's troops, which had accomplished so much during the campaign and battle, were again called upon to screen the infantry retreat. Captain Richard Robbins knew the next morning would bring more fighting: "For the second time in 24 hours we were left 'out in the cold' to receive the first attack of the enemy on awakening."[29]

On the morning of September 22, the 4th U.S. Cavalry held the most advanced position of Minty's brigade and at 7:00 a.m. the Union troopers met the enemy again. Minty's brigade awoke and began its delaying tactics and inched its way rearward until noon. One of the troopers of the 4th Michigan Cavalry declared Minty's cavalry fire the first, and now, the last shot of the Battle of Chickamauga. Minty proudly noted that it took the Confederates six hours to push his small command four miles from Rossville to Chattanooga. Next, Robert Mitchell ordered all the cavalry, which desperately needed more forage, north of the Tennessee River. At 3:00 a.m. on September 23, Minty crossed the Tennessee River to join the rest of Crook's cavalry for the first time in almost two months. Also of importance, Wilder's brigade was formally attached to the Union cavalry corps reporting to Mitchell. Once across the river, many of the Union cavalry unsaddled their horses for the first time since September 18. While the battle ground to a halt, the Union cavalry fell into its natural role of providing security on the flanks and, in some cases in front of, the infantry. The infantry needed time to organize and the fate of the army depended on the cavalry to prevent a penetration of the line which would unleash the enemy into the rear of the army.[30]

September 19—Day 2: Stokes' Guns Move to Crawfish Springs

While Minty and Wilder desperately fought Confederate infantry columns on September 18, Robert Mitchell's three remaining brigades (with Stokes' five guns) at the front held their positions near McLemore's Cove on the southern flank of the army. Upon receiving orders during the night, the cavalry began to move north to Crawfish Springs to replace Thomas' infantry which held that position on September 18. Meanwhile, the great infantry battle along Chickamauga Creek began on September 19. Throughout the day, Rosecrans and Bragg threw their armies onto the field in a piecemeal fashion and the lines ebbed and flowed. The day before, Wheeler was ordered to move into McLemore's Cove through Dug and Catlett's Gaps and to demonstrate against the enemy. He needed to occupy the attention of the Union forces while Bragg implemented his main attack. On the morning of September 19, Wheeler moved to Owen's Ford on Chickamauga Creek, after leaving a substantial force to protect the mountain gaps.[31]

Crook's and Edward McCook's cavalry forces screened the southern flank and John A. Nourse wrote of his interactions with the local citizens, whom he described as ignorant because they thought Yankee cavalrymen had horns, claws and ate babies. He explained they were very surprised by their appearance. For the bulk of the Union cavalry scattered 15 miles south along the gaps and valleys, Rosecrans' orders drew them back to the main Union concentration forming along La Fayette Road. McCook's cavalry awoke on September 19 after a cold night in the mountains and valleys. Henry Hempstead, 2nd Michigan, wrote: "This morning it is still cold, with a high wind and dust flying in blinding clouds." The three cavalry brigades rode toward Crawfish Springs, Rosecrans' old headquarters and the location of most of the Union army's hospitals. Long's brigade of Crook's Division moved from Rape's Gap into McLemore's Cove during the day and rode toward Crawfish Springs that evening. Only Watkins' brigade had orders to delay until the wounded, sick and prisoners could be transported to Bridgeport. The ride to Crawfish Springs was difficult for the troopers: "We … dashed forward at a gallop three or four miles amid such a cloud of dust that the man in advance could not be seen by those in the rear, and the unlucky horse who fell was sure to be run over by those in the rear," recorded Henry Hempstead.[32]

Shortly after noon, Garfield made an appeal through Alexander McCook, who now had command of the cavalry on the right flank, to hasten Mitchell and the cavalry northward. This would be one of several important messages to Mitchell about the placement of the cavalry in regard to the battle over the next couple of days. Subsequent to this message, Garfield also notified McCook that due to his position on the right flank, Mitchell's cavalry fell under his command. "General McCook will take command of the right and the cavalry, and hold himself in readiness to support either flank," a command that Mitchell would disregard the next day. At 4:00 p.m. Garfield again sent a message to Mitchell to hurry forward. Two hours later Mitchell received further orders to guard the hospitals near Crawfish Springs.[33]

At the end of the day, Edward McCook reached his destination while Crook's brigade moved from Rape's Gap and Dougherty's Gap and stopped south of Crawfish Springs, having a greater distance to ride during the day. Prior to receiving orders to move from Dougherty's Gap, Crook's cavalry observed the beginnings of the battle from the mountaintops. Lieutenant Colonel Elijah Watts, 2nd Kentucky, recalled that from his position in the mountains to the south, "[W]e heard the sound of guns, we were not entirely sure. The dust indicated the line of march from west to east, and we knew the position of the troops in a general way, and of course that a battle was imminent." Mitchell initially had a total of 2,500 cavalry in place near Crawfish Springs with Campbell's and Ray's brigades. In addition, a section of the 1st Ohio Artillery and two sections of the Chicago Board of Trade Battery also accompanied Mitchell's cavalry.[34]

Strength of the Federal Cavalry on the Southern Flank[35]

Command	Officers	Men	Commander
First Brigade, First Division	75	1,242	Archibald Campbell
Second Brigade, First Division	81	1,328	Daniel Ray
Third Brigade, First Division	-	650*	Louis Watkins
Second Brigade, Second Division	-	900†	Eli Long
Total (Officers and Men)	4,276		

Watkins' approximate strength as reported in the court martial records of the event at Cooper's Gap.
†*Long's approximate strength was reported in the after-action report regarding the fight at Glass Mill.*

McCook threw a screen around Crawfish Springs to protect the Union hospitals and the southern flank until Crook's brigade and ultimately, Watkins' brigade, could rejoin the command. During the afternoon and evening of September 19, the hospitals and fields began to fill with the wounded from the day's fighting and due to the location of the hospitals, the narrow road was often congested with ambulances coming from and going to the battle. When the 9th Pennsylvania Cavalry arrived, Captain Thomas McCahan wrote: "I have never seen so many wounded as are coming in...."[36]

While light skirmishing occurred throughout the day, only the 2nd Michigan Cavalry had a more heated skirmish but drove the enemy away from the fords near Glass Mill. Major Leonidas Scranton, commanding the 2nd Michigan, initially moved his regiment to Pond Spring and held his position there for two hours before proceeding to Crawfish Springs. Once Campbell's brigade reached the springs, Campbell ordered the 2nd Michigan to scout the various fords over Chickamauga Creek. Afterward, the regiment remained in position at the fords during the night. The possession of these crossings on Chickamauga Creek by the 2nd Michigan set the stage for a bloody fight the next day. Henry Hempstead of Scranton's regiment explained he observed that the enemy across from Glass Mill seemed to be stronger than his regiment and as a result those assigned to guard the ford did not want to initiate any fighting. "We contented ourselves with picketing the road ... the roar of battle two or three miles to our left was terrific." Hempstead correctly identified the size of the enemy across the creek and by the end of the day his regiment would be opposite the bulk of Wheeler's cavalry corps.[37]

Unfazed by the intense fighting on September 19, the Board of Trade sections moved steadily northward. Benjamin Nourse wrote in his diary on September 19: "Today we started to come down the range, came 20 miles and camped at Stevens Gap. We came through Bloomtown [Broomtown] Cove, most beautiful cove in the mountains—Yesterday our view from the top of the mountain was very fine indeed. The day & sky clear and with the eyes alone we could see the dust in clouds caused by the wagons in Bragg's army." Meanwhile, Rosecrans fought to a draw on September 19, but successfully formed a solid north-south line along La Fayette Road. The day's fighting was hard, but Rosecrans was in a familiar position. His situation was similar to the battles at Iuka, Corinth and Stones River. Rosecrans met with his top commanders in the evening and decided to contract the Federal line farther northward. While this decision would test the command abilities of the cavalry officers on the southern flank, Rosecrans felt confident the next day's fight would end as his previous battles.[38]

September 20: The Engagement at Glass Mill

"The sun arose over the battlefield like a sea of fire," wrote G.W. Baum, 2nd Indiana Cavalry. A heavy fog draped the landscape. September 20 would be a pivotal day in the life of William Rosecrans and a disastrous day for the Army of the Cumberland. For the Union cavalry, the day held an important engagement between Wheeler's cavalry corps and Crook's Second Brigade under command of Colonel Eli Long. So far, Robert Mitchell had successfully moved McCook's division into position along the southern flank of the army. Three Union brigades, Campbell's, Ray's and Long's (which would soon arrive), were in position around Crawfish Springs. McCook's command held a position on the northern portion of Mitchell's defensive line and his men were stretched because Wilder had moved closer to Widow Glenn's House at the end of the fighting the day before. Mitchell directly commanded the remainder of the cavalry in line "farther to the right" by placing one of Archibald Campbell's regiments, 2nd Michigan Cavalry, under his command along with the 2nd Tennessee. Overnight, Campbell (commanding two regiments) was released from duty in Dry Valley and rode with the 1st Tennessee and 4th Indiana cavalries to a ridge a mile or so south of Crawfish Springs, protecting the southern-most most flank of the Federal army. The 2nd Michigan was placed in front of Crawfish Springs and would be the first Union cavalry regiment involved in a fight later that morning. Crook with Long's brigade had yet to arrive at Crawfish Springs.[39]

During the evening of September 19, John C. Breckinridge's infantry division, which had been on the east side of Chickamauga Creek near Crawfish Springs, moved closer to the main infantry battle and Wheeler replaced him. Wheeler had been given orders "to attack the enemy at every opportunity which presented itself." These orders set the stage for the fight near the ford at Glass Mill, located on Chickamauga Creek about two miles south of Lee and Gordon's Mill at a series of deep bends in the creek. The mill, a multi-story building, was used to grind grain for the local farmers. About three-fourths of a mile west of the ford lay the Glenn farm with outbuildings in the middle of several cleared fields. The day before, Negley's division held the Union position on the west side of Chickamauga Creek facing the Confederate division on the opposite side until late in the afternoon when they marched northward just as the Southern infantry also moved north. The respective cavalries of Wheeler and Mitchell moved into position opposite the crossing at the mill.[40]

The location of the hospitals at Crawfish Springs proved to be a problem for Rosecrans. When the hospitals were established, no one expected that the battle would be pulled to the north. This stretched the Union line, which was anchored by these hospitals. In addition, there was such a scarcity of clean water due to the drought and Crawfish Springs offered the most valuable supply needed by the surgeons. Tactically, once the fighting started there was little opportunity to move the hospitals because when the casualties began arriving, the medical staff needed to be prepared to receive them. An important question for the cavalry commanders during the fighting on September 20 was whether their duty centered on protecting the hospitals or joining in the desperate fighting to the north.[41]

The 2nd Michigan Cavalry was in line at daylight on September 20 and skirmished with Colonel Thomas Harrison's Confederate cavalry at the ford near Glass Mill. Amidst the thick fog, the 2nd Michigan had orders to stand "to horse" until after daylight. The Second and Third Battalions claimed the ford from the 8th Texas Cavalry during the early skirmishing and exchanged fire with the enemy throughout the morning. The 2nd Michigan's First Battalion guarded another ford about three-quarters of a mile west, Owen's Ford. The men of the 2nd Michigan thought all was quiet and withdrew about a quarter of a mile to the edge of some cleared fields, equal distance between the ford and the Glenn farmstead directly west. The noise from the main battle reached the cavalry at Glass Mill at 9:00. Sergeant Henry Mortimer Hempstead, 2nd Michigan Cavalry, was settling down for breakfast when Colonel Thomas Harrison again moved his Southern cavalry toward the Union position across the ford at Glass Mill, but this time the advance was made in force. At about 10:00 a.m., the Confederates reappeared, intent on joining in the general Confederate attack. Hempstead recorded in his diary, "I got our mess coffee pot filled and nearly boiled when just as the Captain was inquiring if my coffee was done we were diluted with three or four shells in rapid succession from a battery at very short range, being located just back of the mill and evidently aiming at our camp fire…. [We] had retreated a few steps after the company when another shell burst close to or directly in the fire scattering the brands in every direction."[42]

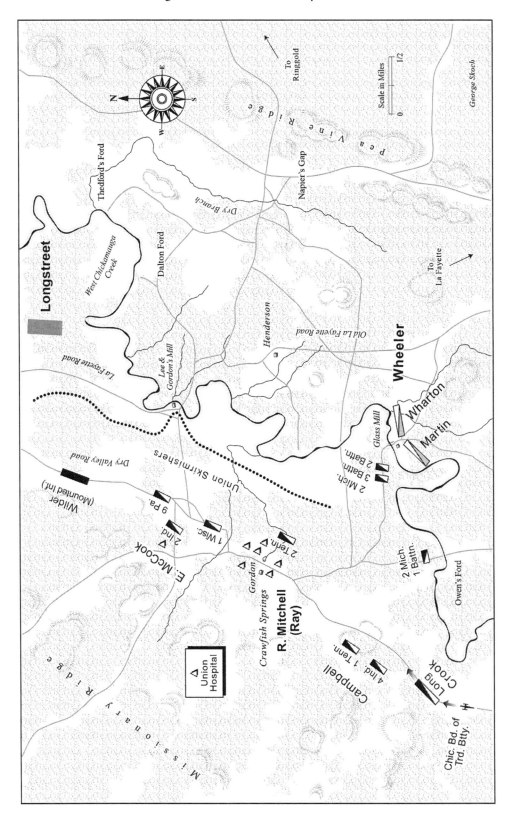

On the southern flank—Long's and Stokes' arrival at Crawfish Springs at 9:00 a.m., September 20, 1863.

Captain Benjamin White's battery of Southern artillery (two three-inch Parrott cannons and two twelve-pounder Howitzers) began firing and the Union cavalry skirmishers were driven back to the main line under a hail of grape and canister. The 2nd Michigan's Second Battalion retreated to the center of the farm and gained some protection by "the house, cabins and corncribs and some trees." Leonidas Scranton, 2nd Michigan, observing his Second Battalion being flanked by a group of 100 Confederates who had crossed the creek, sent forward the Third Battalion, and he was able to drive the Texans back across the creek. The initial Confederate attackers fell back under the protection of their guns, but the Michigan cavalry quickly headed for the rear as "a strong reenforcement again pursued us through the fields and beyond the farm building, but as we got beyond the range of their battery we rallied and held them back until we were reinforced, when we chased them back again." Thomas Colman, 11th Texas, wrote in a letter after the battle that Union cavalry charged like "so many devils." After the initial exchange, Wheeler began his attack with Thomas Harrison's full brigade—3rd Confederate, 3rd Kentucky, 4th Tennessee, 8th Texas, and 11th Texas; shortly thereafter Wheeler added his entire cavalry corps of 6,800 men into the fight—Martin's and Wharton's divisions. Colonel Charles C. Crews, a pre-war Georgia physician, moved his brigade to support Harrison's attack. Crews' command included an Alabama regiment, Malone's, and three Georgia regiments, 2nd, 3rd, and 4th, and brought Wharton's total number of men to about 4,400. Will Martin's division, John T. Morgan's and A.A. Russell's brigades, moved in the rear of Wharton's division until there was room to maneuver to the left. Then, the Confederates advanced across a broad front. Hempstead exclaimed, "Again, they came on with augmented force and swept us before them. We made a stand in the open fields.... We looked around and found on our rear and on our flanks a strong force of cavalry had come up and formed along the edge of the woods, and as our battery was making considerable noise we hoped to hold the force in our front." Hempstead had just observed the arrival of Eli Long's brigade riding hard to join in the fight.[43]

Long's Brigade Joins the Fight

The day began very early for Crook and Long. Mitchell sent orders at 2:00 a.m. directing Crook to hurry his command to Crawfish Springs. When Crook arrived, he met with Mitchell, a commander for whom he had little respect. Mitchell immediately ordered Crook to Glass Mill about two miles from headquarters at Crawfish Springs to reinforce Scranton's 2nd Michigan. Mitchell, with part of McCook's cavalry, remained at Crawfish Springs in defense of the hospitals and lengthy flank south of the Federal infantry. Crook, who did not want to be encumbered with artillery, took a section of the Chicago Board of Trade Battery over his objections and hurried down the road around a juniper thicket to find the 2nd Michigan hotly engaged and falling back. Entering the fight without any intelligence, William Crane, 4th Ohio, wrote in his diary: "We knew not how strong, but supposed this force to be the cavalry." Lieutenant Colonel Elijah Watts, 2nd Kentucky, noted the sound of cannonading greeted Long's advancing cavalry as it moved toward Glass Mill.[44]

Crook arrived at Crawfish Springs at 9:00 a.m. with the 1st Ohio, 3rd Ohio, 4th Ohio, 2nd Kentucky and two sections of artillery. Elijah Watts recalled he was "rested, hopeful, expectant, with an effort to be buoyant." Upon his arrival at Crawfish Springs, he

An 1894 image of the western view of the landscape at Glass Mill. The views are taken facing west about 150 yards from Glass Mill (Louisiana State University, Special Collections: Chickamauga and Chattanooga National Military Park [Ga. and Tenn.] Commission: Louisiana Committee Photographs [Mss. 4504], Louisiana and Lower Mississippi Valley Collections, LSU Libraries, Baton Rouge, Louisiana, USA).

was surprised to find cavalry regiments in columns standing "To Horse" and just waiting. "I was astonished that they were not in line of battle," wrote Watts. He wondered "why Gen. Mitchell had not moved forward with a heavy force and drive the rebels back." When Long's brigade was ordered forward, Watts turned to see the remaining cavalry still calmly waiting by their horses. Watts recalled that Stanley was sick, in an ambulance bound for Nashville, and wrote, "[I]f he was in command things would have been different." Upon reaching the fields near Glass Mill, the 2nd Kentucky passed some Michigan troopers who remarked they were in for a hot time.[45]

Crook found the 2nd Michigan being pressed as Wheeler brought the weight of his corps to bear on Scranton's regiment. The First Battalion of the 2nd Michigan hurried from Owen's Ford to join the rest of the regiment as the fight intensified. Scranton told Crook upon his arrival that the woods ahead were full of Confederates. Once Crook arrived, the Union troopers began again pushing toward the ford, but first, Long had to interpose his relieving force between the 2nd Michigan and the advancing Confederate cavalry. The 2nd Kentucky Cavalry first took up a position on the right side of the road and after advancing a short distance switched to the left side of the road. The three Ohio regiments dismounted and moved to the right of the 2nd Kentucky, which remained mounted. A two-gun section of the Board of Trade Horse Artillery followed the cavalry and unlimbered and began shelling the advancing enemy. The 2nd Kentucky moved slightly forward of the section of artillery on a hill to the left of the guns with "colors flying, guidons, as well as the regimental colors." Watts exclaimed, "There is an immense panorama spread out … but only God knew what was before us." The new Union line formed about one-half mile from Chickamauga Creek and the Confederate battery across the creek began firing at the newly arrived Union guns. The fields ahead of Long's cavalry "swarmed with rebel troops." Crook and Long mistook the dismounted cavalry for Hindman's infantry, which had been in the vicinity the day before. The 2nd Michigan ceased its withdrawal upon Crook's arrival and moved to the right of Long's reinforcements extending the line to meet Wheeler's attack. Scranton observed the reinforcements on his left were soon being forced back leaving him in his original predicament. Next, a company on the left of Henry Hempstead's company "crumbled and broke for the trees" and then Hempstead's company retreated. Scranton's men continued to fall back and he ordered the First Battalion, still firing away, to move back also, but two companies failed to receive the order. Companies A and F unleashed a vicious enfilading volley into the pursuing Confederates who were intent on pushing forward. Soon these two companies hurried to the rear and the entire regiment joined in the retreat to Crawfish Springs.[46]

Captain William Crane, 4th Ohio Cavalry, recorded in his journal that the Ohio cavalry regiments dismounted and advanced to meet the oncoming Confederate attack. The 4th Ohio was greeted with an intense fire from the enemy. The 1st Ohio had the duty of guarding the section of the Board of Trade Battery. Vicious volleys were unleashed by both sides as the lines approached. Crane wrote, "It was tough work, the enemy was very strong, and our lines were slowly driven back…. Many were struck dead & large numbers of wounded carried to the rear until all the ambulances were filled." Crane observed that the 4th Ohio and 2nd Kentucky cavalries took the brunt of the attack, and while Crook

"We got into it quickly and in less than 10 minutes #1 lost all the horses belonging to the cannoneers," Benjamin Nourse wrote (photo depicts a Union field artillery battery, Library of Congress).

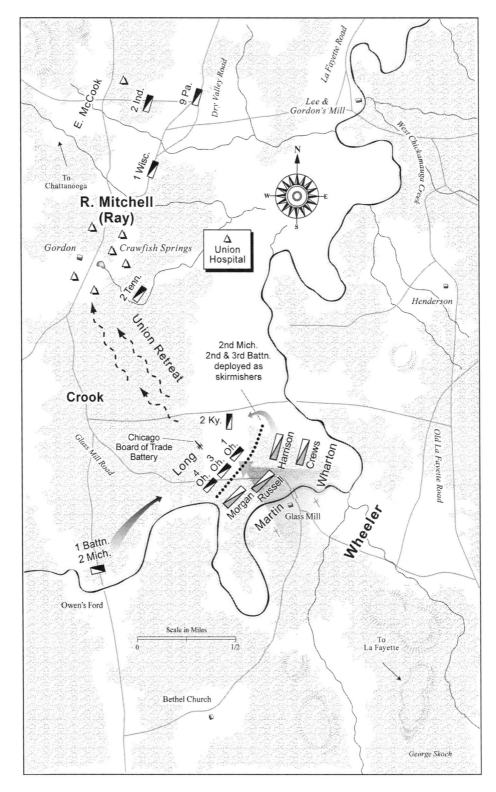

The Battle of Glass Mill, September 20, 1863.

criticized the order to take the Chicago Board of Trade section, many accounts praised the results of this section during the fight. W.L. Curry, 1st Ohio Cavalry, wrote that the brigade was accompanied by "our brave boys" of the battery.[47]

Benjamin Nourse wrote little of the events of the day: "Up at 3 oc. but did not start until 5 oc. and then on the double quick for twenty miles which we made by 10 oc. As we came up to a field, we heard fireing and soon were in the Battle of Chickamauga. We got into it quickly and in less than 10 minutes #1 lost all the horses belonging to the cannoneers…. Oh, the horror of this day and night—I cannot write them."[48]

Elijah Watts, 2nd Kentucky Cavalry, was with the Board of Trade Battery when it arrived on the field, unlimbered on a slight crest of a hill and went into action. Watts understood that the 2nd Kentucky had the duty of protecting the battery. With the 2nd Kentucky to the left of the guns, the 3rd and 4th Ohio Cavalries were dismounted and to the right. Watts lamented that protecting artillery was not pleasant work and that he could never get used to it. He recalled a prisoner, who had been captured while protecting some field artillery, complained to his officer, "Oh, Lieutenant, what's that durned gun <u>worth</u> anyway?" To which, the officer responded, "About $600, I suppose." The soldier retorted, "I'll get pap to pay for it! let's get out of here!" Watts explained the scene on the field: "[T]he thunder of cannon and the roar of musketry amounting in volume and reminding one of the continuous roar of thunder, only different, much nearer, and carrying hundreds to death each moment…. The battery hurled mass after mass of deadly iron missiles into their ranks…. As they came nearer, our battery double shotted with grape and cannister, cut swaths through thin ranks, they were then not over three hundred feet away." The barrage halted the attack temporarily and then, the enemy again attacked. Watts concluded: "We protected the battery, however, that infernal battery, for it had safely retired, before our right gave way."[49]

Private Silas Stevens explained that the section of the battery traveled from Crawfish Springs and the gun was moved into position facing east.

A spot was shown … to place the gun in position, and we drove near this place as possible. Robinson ordered the piece unlimbered and the cannoneers to run the gun by hand over the soft earth, and up onto a hillock, scarce long enough and wide enough to man the piece in one direction. These orders accomplished, we withdrew with the horses to a convenient cover ten paces to the rear. The cannoneers were ordered to fire in the direction to the right of an old dead tree, shown at some distance through an opening in the woods to the front.

In looking around me at the post, I was stationed, beside my horse, I noticed the grass and the bushes had been displaced and trampled upon. Toward the right, a dead horse and army implements, and in every direction many evidences there had been considerable fighting, possibly the day previous. The position of the gun, to my mind, was not especially well chosen. After the first discharge of our gun, not many minutes elapsed before there was a near and quick reply, by the enemy, to our shot. It was plain and evident at once, to us soldiers, the rebels had the range of our position, and undoubtably had been fighting against our forces long before our arrival on the field. The firing was kept up with the gunners at the piece, aiming in the direction of that old tree.

The position of the gun was not favorable as the cannoneers intimated to Robinson, and the piece was withdrawn and another position quickly taken to the right and rear, a little out the range somewhat of the enemies fire. The gun carriage now rested on the solid earth, but the post assigned us was situated amid a heavy growth of timber and bushes, grown along the banks of some stream…. There was no outlook to the front. The enemy noticed, or, was aware of our move and directed their shots toward our new position. We had not replied to a half dozen of their shots, before we were ordered to move the gun to the left of our first position, and farther down the turn of the road, northwards. The ground here falling off considerably toward the creek or wet bottom land. The gun on being unlimbered was run down the incline of the roadway, and off to a much better location than the other two chosen. Here there was a better outlook to the front, and the boys fired with great rapidity. The shots from the rebel guns were out of range, and did not do us harm. At the other posts, they were dangerously near hitting us, at every new shot.

The action seemed to be general now, and the battery against which we had directed our fire had given way to their infantry or dismounted men. There was a rain of shot, shells, and bullets of every kind, very like a hail-storm, as each missile struck the fallen leaves, and the ground around us. At this juncture on the field, there came from the rear, a very unmilitary order, in these words. "Get that battery out of here." … We, whose duty it was to rescue the piece, who heard above the roar of the guns, and screech of the shells, the order, did not hesitate, or delay one moment, in the execution of this imperative order. In the face of a galling fire, we hurried across the field, and down the road to get our gun off the ground. The gunners were ready to comply with our concerted movement in the recovery of the gun. They intimated in limbering up the piece, that the place was getting too hot from the enemies infantry, to sustain longer this unfavorable position against such great odds. The start was at a gallop and the horses made good headway to the cover.

From the same unseen service, a little nearer now, came the command in like voice, this order, "Halt that battery, you'll stampede the Army." In this rapid movement to the rear, we had gained the bend in the road where were stationed the led horses, and the cavalry reserves, and as the road was chocked, of necessity, we came to a halt. In time, these gave way right, and left, and we pursued the road, to the rear, out of easy range of the rebel guns.

One of the dismounted cavalry after the fight informed us, when at the front from the position he was assigned, when number one gun opened on the left, our last position, that the rebs, rose up out of the tall grass, and bushes, and from behind trees, poured a destructive fire into our ranks. And if the battery, had not taken advantage of the order, at the moment given, many would have been killed, or captured, and the gun lost in that neck of the woods, by a rebel capture; their movement and knowledge of our front was so quick and their fire so rapid.

Then the battery was ordered to the rear and again unlimbered in the rear of the Federal line and went to work. W.L. Curry, 1st Ohio, also observed the battery's final re-positioning: "Remained with the rear line and kept up a continuous fire from her guns, and sent shot and shell crashing through the rebel lines."[50]

Much of the result of the fight came from a confusing order. Sergeant John Chapin, 1st Ohio Cavalry, was dismounted and watched as the Confederates charged forward. At about 300 yards, an officer from Crook's staff rode to the 1st Ohio and exclaimed, "Prepare to charge!" Lieutenant Colonel Valentine Cupp, commanding the regiment because Colonel Beroth Eggleston was absent recruiting in Ohio, immediately ordered the 1st Ohio to "sling carbines and draw sabres." The 1st Ohio Cavalry prepared for a suicidal charge into a much superior force. Chapin told a fellow trooper, "If the charge is made not a man can come out alive." Crook saw something was wrong with the 1st Ohio and rode to Cupp and explained the order was to "prepare to resist the charge," not to make a charge. Crook remained close to the troops during the fight and at one point he was almost captured by the advancing Confederate soldiers. By the time the correct order reached the Ohioans, the 1st Ohio was some 30 yards in front of the battery. The regiment was ordered to turn and ride back to the original line, resulting in two turns, during which time the Confederates were constantly firing and charging. The Board of Trade guns fired until the Confederates were 50 yards away and quickly limbered and made its escape. With the artillery safely away, Cupp ordered, "Fours, left about, march!" But before the turn was complete Cupp was shot in the lower abdomen, mortally wounding him. Cupp was gathered off the field and moved to Lee's mansion at Crawfish Springs. As for Chapin, he wrote, just as the about-face was made, "a Confederate officer had the impudence to shoot me with a revolver."[51]

Watts' 2nd Kentucky held the Union left flank during the raging battle. He soon found the Rebel battery exploding with "shot and shell" on his position and Confederate soldiers steadily trotting forward in the attack across a harvested cornfield. Wheeler advanced a line of skirmishers followed by a line of dismounted cavalry, and behind them, a second line of dismounted cavalry. Watts declared the "scene was one of a lifetime, terrific, awe inspiring, frightful!" He bitterly recalled that the thin line of Union cavalry faced the enemy while Mitchell's cavalry remained in the rear:"idle troopers waiting orders." The Kentuckians leveled their carbines and the Chicago Board of Trade Battery fired double canister, momentarily staggering the advance which recovered and steadily moved forward. As the Confederate lines moved closer, the Southern artillery shifted its fire away the Union artillery and focused on the line of Union cavalry. The hammering of the Union carbines echoed across the fields "while the enemy,—I see them now! came steadily for our position, with great gallantry." Many of the troops that advanced on the 2nd Kentucky were armed with muzzle loading Enfield carbines and the two lines exchanged fire but the Federal line held. The Confederate line moved closer and the two lines prepared to fight hand-to-hand. Then, Watts noticed Troop B and D being forced back by the 8th Texas Cavalry advancing from the northeast and instead of backing up, these two Kentucky companies attempted to turn to fall back. When they turned, they were more vulnerable to Confederate attack and were doubled back. The line "folded like a knife." The Texas cavalry pushed forward turning the 2nd Kentucky's flank and this allowed the Confederate attack to surge ahead, which reached the left and rear of the Kentuckians. There was nothing left to do but attempt to save as many troopers as possible. Colonel Thomas Nicholas was in front of the regiment directing the fire while waving his sabre over his head when the regiment folded. Watts also received Crook's order carried by Captain Crane to prepare to charge Wheeler's cavalry just as his regiment was overrun. The 2nd Kentucky recorded the greatest losses of the day suffering eleven men killed, another fifty wounded and two missing.[52]

John A. Wyeth, 4th Alabama Cavalry, described the Confederate side of the fight. The attack by the Confederate cavalry started in earnest when White's artillery opened up on Long's men. The men of the 4th Alabama had a good position to watch the fight because they had been ordered to provide security for the battery. "The Federal guns about five hundred yards away soon got the range and threw a lot of shrapnel," wrote Wyeth. Captain D. Coleman, 11th Texas Cavalry, wrote that he thought the attack would stall, but the collapse of the right and left flanks of the Union line gave energy to a renewed attack until the entire Federal line retreated. Just as the Union soldiers mistook Wheeler's cavalry for infantry, Coleman mistakenly believed the Union cavalry had been supplemented with mounted infantry.[53]

George Guild, 4th Tennessee (CSA) also recalled the battle at Glass Mill. "The enemy knew that we were coming and kept up an incessant shelling of the woods, some of our men being injured by limbs of trees torn off by the cannon balls. We had advanced but a short distance when the skirmishers became hotly engaged, which was the signal for a rapid advance, and we swept through the woods, driving the enemy before us. They rallied at a fence at the edge of the woodland, delivered an effective volley, and fell back across a little field to a new line behind a fence and on the edge of another woodland along an eminence where their artillery was planted. As our line emerged from the wood into the open space this battery, shotted with grape, and the line behind the fence, armed with seven-shooting Spencer rifles, opened on us, and a perfect hailstorm of deadly missiles filled the air. Being commanded to lie down, we did so for a few moments, and then arose and charged across the field. Just here we sustained our heaviest loss, and in a few moments the Fourth Tennessee had forty men shot down as we arose from the ground. As we rushed across the field the line sustaining the battery broke; and as they ran off many were killed and wounded, two or three hundred of them surrendering in a body." Guild would later discover the fight at Glass Mill resulted from the need for the Union troops to protect the hospitals at Crawfish Springs. He continued: "[T]hough we gained the fight and drove them from the field, our loss in killed and wounded was as great as theirs."[54]

Crook was just outmanned as he engaged Martin's and Wharton's divisions. Long's brigade of 900, engaged until noon, was no match for two Confederate cavalry divisions. Crook lost 100 men in a 15-minute interval and he felt many were lost trying to save the Board of Trade Battery guns that Crook had not wanted on the field. He had been overruled by Mitchell who insisted the artillery be moved forward. Long, who was generally not given to discussing his actions on the field, recorded in his autobiography that he was ordered to protect the artillery battery which caused his cavalry to be placed in a position of facing overwhelming odds, and that Long's cavalry was unsupported by the remainder of Mitchell's cavalry division. Mitchell remained at his headquarters at Crawfish Springs as the battle played out at Glass Mill. While many involved in the fight criticized Mitchell for not bringing reinforcements, Mitchell realized he had hospitals, supply trains and a large flank to cover with his cavalry.[55]

Crook rode to the rear with Long's retreating cavalry looking for help, but he got none from Mitchell. Crook found the remainder of the cavalry still standing in a field at Crawfish Springs. Long's brigade fell in line with the rest of the Union cavalry and hastily formed a battle line at the rear of the field in anticipation of Wheeler's attack, which never came. It was unclear what Mitchell intended to do to further delay an attack by Wheeler's division, but Crook wrote in his memoirs that Mitchell abdicated the arrangement of the Federal cavalry's defense after the fight to Crook. Crook had little respect for Mitchell and in his memoirs, he explained that Mitchell asked him to oversee the defenses at Crawfish Springs: "General, you are a military man, I wish you would take charge and straighten things out, and make the necessary dispositions." Crook re-formed the battle line along a slight ridge facing an open field. Wheeler did not follow up his attack from Glass Mill and Mitchell remained in line throughout the afternoon. On the Southern side of the field, Wheeler had just received conflicting orders—one set from Bragg ordering him to Lee and Gordon's Mill and the other from Longstreet telling him to move up and support his infantry. Wheeler chose the former, and fortunately for the Union cavalry, Wheeler decided to backtrack to the east side of Chickamauga Creek and move northward on the eastern bank, a more time-consuming route.[56]

While the fight at Glass Mill was taking place, a dramatic turn of events occurred on the main battlefield. The Confederate infantry penetrated Rosecrans' main line near the Brotherton Farm and rolled up the brigades on both sides. Bragg had just won the Battle of Chickamauga. Wheeler's orders to ride to Lee and Gordon's Mill and to attack the enemy spared Crook and Mitchell from what promised to be a bloody fight. This fight at Glass Mill resulted in a loss in Long's cavalry brigade and the 2nd Michigan of 132 men killed, wounded or missing including the death of Lieutenant Colonel Valentine Cupp. The action would become known as the Battle at Glass Mill, but many in the Union cavalry referred to it as the Battle of Crawfish Springs.[57]

Mitchell Covers the Southern Flank

Soon, Mitchell learned Rosecrans' right flank had been turned and the entire Union army was retreating to Chattanooga. Once the Union line crumbled, it was hard for commanders to get orders because of the confusion on the field. Now, Mitchell made a very difficult decision. He had orders to protect seven hospitals but he needed to remain connected with the army. He initially decided to remain in position around the hospitals, but later in the day he decided to move with the army, abandoning the most severely wounded in the hospitals. At 4:00 p.m. the cavalry started to move away northward, with Colonel Sidney Post's infantry brigade and Long's brigade leading the way, escorting as many of the walking wounded as possible. The remainder of the cavalry followed in line. An hour later the column was gone; at dusk Wheeler's cavalry followed, capturing the hospitals filled with Union wounded. McCook's First Division was placed in charge of the rearguard as Mitchell moved west and then northward, bivouacking between six and nine miles south of Chattanooga. McCook successfully covered the retreat in close proximity to enemy infantry and did not lose a wagon along the way. The column included the ambulances from Crawfish Springs, the cavalry train, and the trains of Twentieth Corps. Later that night, McCook's cavalry fell into a screen in Chattanooga Valley and also held some important mountain gaps including McFarland's Gap. Daniel Ray's brigade fell back to Rocky Ford at the base of Lookout Mountain, just west of Missionary Ridge along the Chattanooga Road, and held its position over night. Long's brigade stopped at McCulloch's Crossroad that night and also set up a defensive line along the Chattanooga Road.[58]

The men of the Board of Trade Battery felt they had had a difficult day and the retreat dimmed any optimism the men had that morning. The battery began the day at Stevens Gap, traveled to Crawfish Springs, immediately thrown into a fight where they were clearly outnumbered, retreated, remained in place, and then ordered to retreat again, all with the increasingly unpleasant knowledge that the army had been defeated. Although the men of the battery expected to be attacked at Crawfish Springs in the afternoon, it did not occur. The men, tired and hungry, not having eaten since early that morning, rode into the twilight, not expecting to eat that night. Private Silas Stevens, especially tired after having been on guard duty the night before, recalled that the withdrawal started at a casual pace, but soon the column became bogged down by other troops marching to the rear. Some of Mitchell's cavalry moved into line in the Chattanooga Valley and some moved into McFarland's Gap on Missionary Ridge. The cavalry regiments eased the retreating soldiers' panic and declared, "There should be no 'Bull Run' here." The Federal horsemen reorganized many of the infantry into stable companies and returned them to their appropriate commands. Crook, occasionally irascible and with a large ego of his own, made no secret of his dislike for Mitchell's handling of the cavalry and this dislike intensified during the day. He wrote in his autobiography, "I was present when Gen. Mitchell made his verbal report to Gen. Rosecrans and to hear him recount the valorous deeds of his command. How he could have the cheek; after what had passed, surpassed my understanding. It was humiliating to see persons wearing the uniforms of general officers be so contemptible." Silas Stevens also lamented that the retreat was a new and unpleasant experience for the men of the battery, an experience which would "remain indelibly stamped on the memory of one's vision forever."[59]

The retreat continued deep into the night for the Board of Trade Battery and the road was packed in a tight formation of retreating troops. There was a short bivouac and

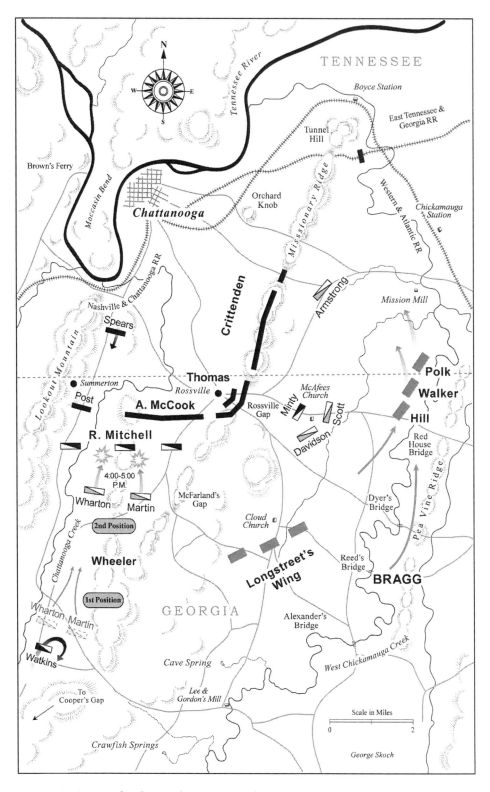

Union cavalry during the retreat to Chattanooga, September 21, 1863.

the men were up early again, but did make time to have a cup of coffee. By 9:00 a.m., the men felt they were safe and in a good position. In the early morning hours of September 21, Robert Mitchell ordered his two divisions to remain in position in Chattanooga Valley guarding the Union right flank. Mitchell ordered: "Prevent the enemy from penetrating our line by way of this valley or along Missionary Ridge." Rosecrans had fallen back during the late afternoon the prior day and in the evening he formed a line resembling a lazy, backward "L." Crittenden's Twenty-First Corps held the left flank on Missionary Ridge, Granger's Reserve Corps had moved to Rossville, Thomas's Fourteenth Corps held the ground near the Rossville Gap and McCook's Twentieth Corps connected with Thomas and formed an east-west line into Chattanooga Valley. Fortunately for Mitchell, Will Martin's cavalry division spent the night at Crawfish Springs and John Wharton's division withdrew to the east side of Chickamauga Creek. This gave Mitchell time to set up his headquarters at Rocky Ford and extend McCook's and Crook's lines from Missionary Ridge across Chattanooga Valley to Lookout Mountain.[60]

The Cavalry Secures the Flanks

Mitchell kept the cavalry in line of battle throughout the day on September 21 while skirmishing with Wheeler. He received some much-needed help from the detached 15th Pennsylvania Cavalry which moved farther west, ascended Lookout Mountain and defended the signal station there. Early in the morning, Edward McCook opened communications with Alexander McCook and George Thomas, and the 2nd Michigan reached Chattanooga after escorting the ammunition and supply trains which had been in the vicinity of Crawfish Springs. On the western flank, Mitchell described: "We have a hell of a front here. We will do the best we can." Mitchell seemed content to command the cavalry for most of the day while sitting astride a rail fence, watching the unfolding developments in front of his lines. The Federal cavalry remained in line all day within sight of their Confederate adversaries. McCook rode to Thomas' headquarters to receive orders and he explained the disposition of his cavalry. McCook skirmished throughout the day and held a firm line, but he noticed a large dust cloud to his front at 4:00 p.m. when the Confederates tried to break the lines. He repulsed "a more determined attempt" to breach his line at 5:00 p.m. but again, the Union line held.[61]

Meanwhile, Crook also spent the day screening the Federal army. Long's brigade spent the night in battle line expecting to fight off a night attack. Early on the morning of September 21, Long ordered his brigade to ride ahead until the enemy was located, an order sent to most of the cavalry commanders. The 1st Ohio Cavalry rode about two miles and spread out and sent skirmishers ahead, locating the enemy line. The opposing forces had a "sharp skirmish" and the cavalry slowly retired, but remained in battle line into the night. W.L. Curry recalled that during the night the Federal and Confederate lines were so close the soldiers spoke to one another. He heard one Rebel soldier call out: "When's you all going down to Atlanta?" and shortly after another asked, "Where is old Granny Burnsides now?" Curry bitterly considered that he had no good reply for his adversaries.[62]

The Board of Trade Battery had continued its retreat into the morning and fell into position with Long's brigade in Chattanooga Valley with the impressive Lookout Mountain just to the west. The battery stopped near an old corn crib, but had no time to start fires for cooking. Some of the men used a smoldering log as their oven, wrapping some sweet potatoes in wet leaves, placing them into the coals and ashes. As they awaited further orders, their breakfast was cooked. Soon the order "Forward!" was given and the battery moved to the north side of Chattanooga Creek on a bluff with a good view to the south. There, the guns were unlimbered and defenses thrown up in case of an attack from the enemy, which was still several miles from Chattanooga. The officers sent orders in preparation of making a determined stand at this location, including sending details to cut trees for better visibility. Long's forces would exchange shots with Confederate probing forces throughout the day, but no serious attacks occurred.[63]

That evening Brigadier General James Spears' brigade of Federal infantry joined Mitchell and would be used to extend the cavalry line even further on the right flank. The Union commanders were very concerned that the enemy would sweep around the west flank and into the rear of the infantry lines. Spears' brigade, part of the Reserve Corps, had only reached Chattanooga late on September 20, had been assigned to security duty a few miles south on Chattanooga Road during the day, and had just received orders to support the cavalry.[64]

Early in the morning of September 22, Long ordered his brigade to very quietly withdraw and then fell into line closer to Chattanooga. W.R. Carter, 1st Tennessee Cavalry, recalled: "Orders were issued immediately for us to fall back with as little noise as possible. The artillery wheels were muffled by wrapping blankets around them, the cavalry, except the rear-guard, was dismounted, and each man was required to carry his saber in his hand to avoid noise, and in this way, we moved some distance along the foot of Lookout Mountain, leading our horses, not being allowed to speak above a whisper." The cavalry withdrew to the rear away from the close proximity of the enemy and again fell into line. Then, the infantry withdrew, leaving the cavalry to again hold the position facing the enemy. The troopers of the 4th Ohio awoke after spending a very short night of hearing the movement of troops in front of their position. They were surprised to find not the enemy in their front, but a regiment of McCook's division. Long's brigade, still stinging from the defeat at Crawfish Springs, slowly withdrew to Chattanooga without further action. Major Peter Mathews, 4th Ohio, recorded skirmishing throughout the day but no major engagements resulted near his location. Spears, Edward McCook and Colonel P. Sidney Post repulsed a determined attack on the withdrawing troops during the day, and successfully reached the newly formed Federal lines.[65]

Benjamin Nourse recorded in his diary: "3 miles south of Chattanooga on the Valley Road was where we were yesterday & today. This morning we were on the road to town early. Stopped at the bridge over Chattanooga Creek & our guns in position in the tan yard. The rebel cavalry came up toward the bridge but were off as soon as charged by our brigade. Genls Rosecrans & Thomas are here and the whole army has fallen inside the creek and are throwing up breastworks. Are tearing down every house to make a line of defense with. The record of these last three days would fill a volume."[66]

Wheeler's Raid

From September 23 to September 30, the battery was primarily on picket duty on the north side of the Tennessee River near Chattanooga. When Minty's brigade re-joined the rest of the cavalry corps, Griffin's section returned to the rest of the battery for the first time in almost two months. Benjamin Nourse recorded that Griffin had lost "2 horses and 3 wheels from gun 3." The reunion was short-lived because the 3rd Section was dispatched to the west of the city on September 24, closer to Bridgeport on a route which took 18 hours due to their guide getting lost along the way. Once the section unlimbered, the enemy across the river greeted them by shooting one of the infantry pickets around the battery. A couple of days later the 3rd Section was relieved by the 2nd Illinois Battery. With the 3rd Section west of Chattanooga, the other two sections moved with the Second Cavalry Division to Smith's Crossroads, the location of Minty's brigade in August.[67]

After the Battle of Chickamauga, Rosecrans entrenched his recently defeated army in Chattanooga. The War Department immediately began to mobilize reinforcements for the Army of the Cumberland which would come over the next month in the form of Henry Slocum's Twelfth Corps and Oliver O. Howard's Eleventh Corps, trailed by a portion of the Army of the Tennessee under command of William T. Sherman. Initially, the bulk of the Union cavalry moved a couple of miles north of the Tennessee River and began providing reconnaissance and security at the various fords along the river while reconditioning their exhausted mounts. Henry Albert Potter, 4th Michigan Cavalry, wrote in his diary at the conclusion of the battle: "Boys tired and horses starving." In a positive move, Wilder's mounted infantry brigade became part of the Second Cavalry Division after the Battle of Chickamauga, placing all the mounted forces under cavalry command, and this provided extra firepower to the cavalry. John Wilder left the army after the recent battle to recuperate and brigade command fell to Colonel Abram O. Miller, 72nd Indiana Mounted Infantry, who was a physician before the war. Miller, an able replacement for Wilder, was a native of Madison County, Indiana, and was raised on a farm at Twelve Mile Prairie in Clinton County, Indiana. He studied medicine at the University of Louisville and graduated in 1856. Miller was appointed colonel of the 72nd Indiana Infantry in August 1862. He was an experienced commander who had fought at the Battle of Rich Mountain, Battle of Mill Springs, the siege of Corinth and the Tullahoma Campaign.[68]

The overall condition of the cavalry after the battle was poor after the extensive campaigning, which took its toll on men and horses. The number of troopers in Union cavalry regiments generally varied between 300–400 men present for duty. The Union cavalry line stretched from Washington, Tennessee, into northern Alabama. Crook had the responsibility of the Union left flank and moved his headquarters to Washington; the various regiments in Long's and Minty's brigades guarded numerous fords along the Tennessee River. Most of Edward McCook's division concentrated near Jasper and Bridgeport, but Archibald Campbell's First Brigade patrolled even farther west in Alabama on the extreme right flank. With threats on the right and the left, the Union cavalry was stretched thin across the wide front and this aided Bragg's and Wheeler's next operation. Fortunately, the new position along the river gave the men of the battery and cavalry corps time to regain their morale and energy after the recent battle.[69]

Union Cavalry Positions September 23, 1863[70]

Command	Commander	Station
First Division	*Col. Edward McCook*	*Sevely Springs**
First Brigade	*Colonel A.P. Campbell*	Sevely Springs/Dallas
Second Brigade	*Colonel Daniel M. Ray*	Sevely Springs/Dallas/Nashville

Command	Commander	Station
Third Brigade	*Colonel Louis D. Watkins*	Sevely Springs /Kelley's Ford/ Nashville
Second Division	*Brig. Gen. George Crook*	*Near Island Ferry*
First Brigade	*Col. Robert Minty*	Forage expedition/Pikeville
Second Brigade	*Col. Eli Long*	Island Ferry, Tennessee
Third Brigade	*Col. William W. Lowe*	McMinnville, Stevenson, Island Ferry

*A few miles, described by one trooper as five miles, north of Chattanooga.

Wheeler's Middle Tennessee Raid

By September 25, there was little doubt the Confederate cavalry had something planned as Bragg attempted to capitalize on his recent victory. Confederate activity had been observed at several locations south of the river but much of the new activity was reported near Bridgeport. Garfield sent orders for McCook's cavalry division to ride immediately to Bridgeport and prepare to repel a likely crossing. This left Crook to guard the Union left flank over a large geographic area and on September 26, his troopers drew five days' rations in preparation of action with the enemy. Then Wheeler struck, crossing the Tennessee River during the night of September 29, and Crook sent a message to Mitchell, "The enemy are endeavoring to cross at Cotton Port Ford, 3 miles from Washington. They are in very heavy force. I am fighting them." Crook later determined from prisoners that Wheeler's success in crossing was cleverly made by selecting a point on the Tennessee River without a known ford, crossing in a location with only a light cavalry guard. A new road had been cut into the river and after dark, Davidson's, Wharton's and Martin's divisions crossed at two locations near Cotton Port. Wheeler's men also carried five to seven days' rations and subsequently a captured prisoner told Crook the raid would extend to the west over the mountains. Of Forrest's cavalry on the raid, Wheeler disparagingly referred to these brigades as mere "skeletons" totaling about 1,500 troopers on worn out horses. However, Wheeler's total force amounted to an impressive 5,000 Confederate cavalrymen riding west into Tennessee.[71]

Crook, with his division scattered at the various locations along the river, was no match for Wheeler's cavalry. He had less than 2,000 men to defend the entire flank. Crook fought with Wheeler for an hour before withdrawing, miraculously saving his supply train. Wheeler made his crossing, crashing into Long's brigade which had suffered a defeat at Glass Mill the week before. The 1st Ohio was thrown back as Wheeler opened on the Union cavalry with artillery and crossed the river, losing only 20 men in the process. Albert Brant, 4th Ohio, exclaimed: "[W]e are in a devil of a fix." Wheeler sent an officer demanding the surrender of the Union cavalry, but Crook declined. While Long battled Wheeler, Minty mounted his brigade and rode toward the point of attack at midnight on September 29.[72]

Minty had had a difficult time over the previous six weeks dealing with Crittenden yet still provided the most valuable cavalry service during the Battle of Chickamauga.

Now, he immediately ran afoul of Crook. At the first indication of Wheeler's crossing, Minty sent three battalions to attempt to delay the movement. Amid a drenching rain, Minty requested permission from Crook to resist the crossing but Crook refused. Next, Crook ordered his division, including Stokes' guns, south to Sale Creek nearer to Chattanooga, but this meant leaving Minty's three battalions to their fate. Minty insisted he move to their support and again Crook refused. This interaction set the tone for relations between Crook and Minty throughout this campaign. Fortunately, the three battalions extracted themselves from behind Wheeler's line and returned to Minty's brigade. Minty bitterly stated: "Our inactivity was very galling."[73]

Wheeler gave his division commanders their orders in a campfire meeting. Wheeler sent Wharton's division directly to McMinnville despite Wharton's opposition to the idea of splitting the command in enemy territory. The relationship between Wharton and Wheeler had deteriorated so badly over the past year that Wharton willingly accepted this assignment because he wanted away from any further direct contact with Wheeler. Once across the river, Wheeler sent one column south through Sequatchie Valley with 1,500 troopers and claimed a 32-wagon supply train while a second column, commanded by John Wharton, moved directly west. On October 2, Wheeler, riding with Martin's division, discovered an 800-wagon supply train at Anderson's Crossroads (20 miles north of Chattanooga) which he handily captured. After selecting the needed supplies, he set fire to the remainder. Mitchell tried to react to the raid and sent a group of scouts to direct Edward McCook's division to the site of the attack. The supply train was desperately needed for Rosecrans' defeated army and this was a severe loss. When McCook's column reached the location of the wagon trains, Colonel Oscar La Grange's 1st Wisconsin Cavalry and Major David Brigg's 2nd Indiana Cavalry rode in advance of the column. The two Federal regiments caught Wheeler's rearguard as the main column withdrew after pillaging the train. McCook ordered the charge of both regiments and "with such vigor" that the enemy fell back. The surprised column swung around preparing to meet the Union cavalry, when a reserve of cavalry charged into the defenders. La Grange exclaimed he scattered Wheeler's "wavering ranks in the wildest rout. Thirty-seven of the enemy were killed and wounded, and 42 made prisoners…. The general himself was closely pursued and narrowly escaped." La Grange and Briggs broke off their pursuit and the Confederate column continued westward.[74]

Meanwhile, Crook pulled his Second Division together, after moving southward to prevent being captured, and set off in pursuit, but only rode about 10 miles before stopping for the first day. Crook would be accompanied by a two-gun (guns number 2 and number 4) section of the Board of Trade Battery, commanded by Captain Stokes. The other guns remained on picket duty. Special orders for the battery included the five days' rations and orders to move fast with little baggage. The guns were taken northward toward Washington to join in the pursuit of Wheeler. Eight horses were hitched to each gun while four horses pulled limber sections with the caissons left behind. The remainder of the equipment of this section stayed in the main battery camp under Lieutenant George Robinson's command. Stokes ordered Sylvanus Stevens to report to him and the Board of Trade Battery section moved over Walden's Ridge and then into Sequatchie Valley, ascending the Cumberland Mountains to the west. This passage over the mountain was accomplished easily compared to the passage in August. This would be the only short day Crook's division would have until October 8 as Crook, in a single-minded, relentless pursuit chased Wheeler at a severe cost to his horses and his men. On October 1,

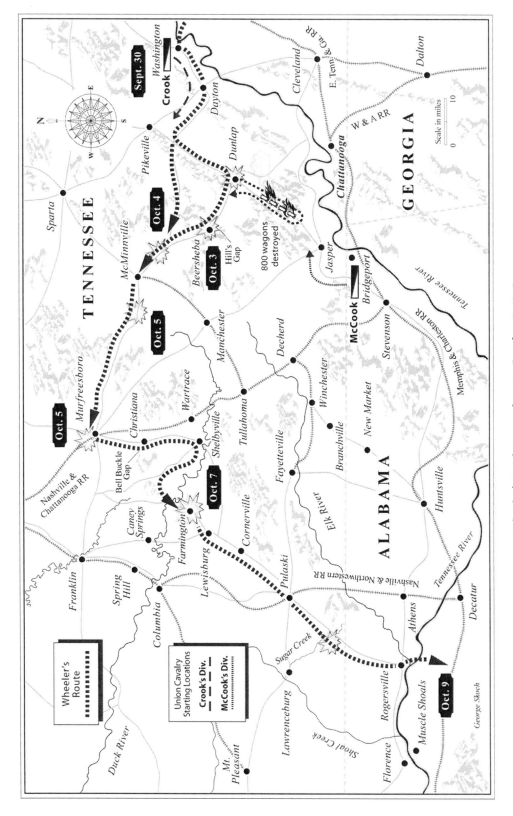

Wheeler's Raid, September 30–October 9, 1863.

McCook's First division, accompanied by Wilder's mounted infantry, mobilized and also began the chase, but McCook lagged behind Crook for much of the pursuit. McCook's movement was hampered because he waited for Campbell's brigade that was unexpectedly delayed, much to the ire of McCook. Wilder's (now Miller's) mounted infantry brigade continued forward and reached Crook's column. By the time the Union cavalry was organized for the pursuit, Wheeler had a 12- to 14-hour head start over Crook and even longer for McCook. Mitchell, cavalry corps commander, did not accompany the cavalry in the initial pursuit but he would join McCook's division a few days later. Mitchell, whose health was failing, was to have a difficult ride over the next week.[75]

Much of Crook's personality could be observed in his actions during Wheeler's raid. The tenacity that Crook demonstrated in this pursuit of Wheeler revealed characteristics that would make him one of the best commanders in the western United States after the war. Crook caught the rear of Wheeler's cavalry at Robinson's Trace, resulting in a small skirmish on October 2. On October 3, Crook again caught the rear guard of Martin's division, in possession of Hill's Gap near Beersheba, and a heated skirmish resulted. Minty's brigade began the skirmish, but the advantage of having mounted infantry attached to the cavalry now yielded good results as Crook ordered Miller's mounted infantry to advance while moving Minty into position to support the advance. Eleven dead enemy soldiers were found after the enemy retreated and the Federals estimated that 25 were killed in total. Darkness ended the fight and Wheeler withdrew. Minty's and Long's men bivouacked for the night "with horses saddled and men under arms." Henry Albert Potter, 4th Michigan Cavalry, simply recorded in his diary, "tired-tired-tired." The hard riding troopers soon exhausted their rations received on September 26 as the cavalrymen pressed ahead with little sleep. The entire pursuit tested the endurance of horse and man.[76]

McMinnville Garrison Destroyed

Still Wheeler rode west, uniting his two columns and capturing the Union garrison and stores at McMinnville on October 3. The Confederates captured almost 600 men, 200 horses and a large amount of supplies. Wheeler's column spent the day destroying the commissary and military stores, a locomotive, rail cars and the Hickory Creek Bridge, but the Union pursuit intensified. Stevens' section of the Board of Trade Battery reached Crook's main column as it fought Wheeler's rearguard near McMinnville. Stevens, who had been detached, finally reached the Union cavalry and his first question upon reaching the halted column was, "Do you have any coffee?" and the reply came, "Yes, Sir." When Crook reached McMinnville, he found the devastation of Wheeler's actions, the garrison having surrendered without a fight. Crook continued his pursuit, and six miles outside of McMinnville on Murfreesboro Road, he encountered Wheeler's rearguard concealed at the edge of some woods. At 6:00 p.m. the enemy formed a strong defensive line and unlimbered the artillery. In return, Lilly's 18th Indiana Artillery and the Board of Trade section unlimbered in an open field and began shelling the enemy. Crook had no time for the delay and he ordered Colonel Eli Long to charge the enemy. The colonel, with his favorite pipe firmly between his teeth, rode at the head of the 2nd Kentucky Cavalry and "made a most gallant charge of some 5 miles, breaking through his lines … driving the remainder into the main column, compelling him to turn round and give me fight." During the pursuit, Crook rotated the lead brigade each day. Minty's brigade led the march on October 4 and Long's brigade moved into the lead position on October 5.[77]

Silas Stevens recalled that the Board of Trade Battery arrived and moved down the west side of the mountain. Arrayed, and in full view, was the impending battle with Wheeler's rearguard. Long's command was already fighting the enemy defenders. Both W.L. Curry, 1st Ohio, and Lucius Wulsin of the 4th Ohio, documented the action of the battery in the fight which knocked out a Confederate battery in the exchange of fire. Having pushed the skirmishers aside, Crook met a defensive line at the edge of some woods. The fight lasted about two hours until sunset before pushing the enemy to the rear. Then, Crook's weary cavalrymen lay down for a night's sleep without supper, although the horses were able to graze. Some of the cavalry stopped at the site of an old camp and found poor rations: "some old crackers, blue with mould, and found them to taste delicious."[78]

The destruction of the Union garrison and depot at McMinnville gained the attention of the supporting cavalry in Middle Tennessee. The 5th Iowa Cavalry, which patrolled near Decherd, learned of the action and immediately set off in pursuit on October 5. The momentum of Wheeler's raid slowed and he was unable to cause destruction at Murfreesboro, settling instead for a "demonstration." Crook began his pursuit at 1:00 a.m., hoping to catch Wheeler and rode about 50 miles during the day. The column reached Murfreesboro at 4:00 in the afternoon and the officers of Crook's command believed their pursuit saved Murfreesboro from the fate that McMinnville suffered just days before. When Crook rode through Murfreesboro, he "found every person at Murfreesborough in great consternation, and overjoyed to see us." On October 6, Wheeler swung south destroying bridges and railroads on his way to the pro–Union town of Shelbyville, which he promptly sacked.[79]

Robert Mitchell finally reached Crook's column and assumed command of the two divisions. Crook sent out scouts while he gave his horsemen a chance to rest. The toll of the pursuit was severe thus far; approximately 500 horses were disabled during the pursuit already and as a result, Crook would continue the next day with fewer troopers. While the troopers rested, the blacksmiths went to work re-shoeing the remainder of the horses, a task badly needed. While the blacksmiths worked, the irony of returning to Murfreesboro where the Board of Trade Battery began the year 10 months ago did not go unnoticed by the battery boys.[80]

Minty chafed under Crook's command. The expedition began poorly when Crook left Minty's three battalions to their fate at Cotton Port and the relationship between Minty and Crook steadily disintegrated over a three-day period starting on October 5. Crook reached McMinnville on October 4 and the next morning Minty came to Crook and asked for 30 minutes for his men to forage their exhausted horses. Minty explained that his men had not had time to obtain grain for their horses the evening before and that the mounts would be ruined, or simply "break down," if they were not allowed to feed on grain. Crook had expected Minty to feed his mounts from a large cornfield as the remainder of the division had done the night before. Because Minty had not accomplished this, Crook denied the request and ordered Minty to advance without forage. Minty was not lax in trying to gather the grain, and he sent two groups of men to find grain in the cornfield. Both groups came back saying there were plenty of stalks but no corn. The Board of Trade Battery had a similar experience and found the field devoid of ears. Silas Stevens found only a bag of ears in the corners of the field during his foraging expedition. To the frustration of Minty, the men who ground the corn for the remainder of the division told him the other regiments had already found the corn and had fed their horses. Because of Crook's decision, Minty lamented the loss of 256 mounts of a total 1,000 he had in his brigade at the time. The next day (October 6), the situation continued to turn sour. Crook sent orders to the division to be ready to move from Murfreesboro at daylight, but it was around 9:00 a.m. before the column began moving out. Minty's brigade did not reach the column at the appointed time because he needed to shoe some of his mounts. Crook would later acknowledge that the condition of the entire division "was bad." Further evidence revealed that Minty had been given permission from headquarters to deal with the horseshoes, but the problem resulted because Crook told Minty's staff there would be prepared rations available the evening before. Crook sent a message that headquarters staff would provide the rations for Minty's men; however, the meals weren't ready until 4:00 a.m. the next morning and this put the shoeing efforts behind schedule. Minty reasoned that his men needed to be fed first and then the horses would be shod. The shoeing only delayed Minty about 30–45 minutes, but the delay further angered Crook. The men of the Board of Trade Battery also had difficulty with rations. Initially the men received spoiled bacon as their meal, but after the demanding trip, the men simply refused to eat the rancid food. Sergeant Frederick Deane, a pre-war clerk and Michigan native, marched to Stokes' tent and told him the men would not stand for it. Stokes then marched to the quartermasters and demanded an explanation. He was told by the chagrined cooks they had not known the meat was spoiled, and the men were re-supplied. In addition, the men received blankets for the first time since leaving Washington. Because they left so fast and so poorly equipped, they had only carried their rations and the tools of war. The next day, the men received their overcoats on the way to Shelbyville.[81]

The Battle at Farmington—October 7

On October 6, the fresh 5th Iowa Cavalry, Lieutenant Colonel Mathewson T. Patrick commanding, which had been serving in Middle Tennessee during the previous Chickamauga Campaign, got into action under brigade command of the very capable Colonel William Lowe. The 5th Iowa, stationed near Winchester, received news about the capture of McMinnville on October 4. Lowe initially moved the regiment from Winchester to Wartrace and as the pursuit continued, the 5th Iowa passed through Tullahoma on the way northward, reaching the Duck River at 3:00 p.m. Wheeler captured the garrison of Union infantry at Wartrace, but a group of Union infantry, which had avoided capture, reported that the enemy cavalry was causing destruction to the railroad. Lowe's fresh regiment found the group of raiders, belonging to Martin's Confederate division, burning a bridge and sent them hurriedly back to the main body of Confederate cavalry.[82]

On the evening of October 6, Wheeler bivouacked south of the Duck River and he rested his command after sacking the town of Shelbyville. Next, he ordered his division commanders to keep an eye out for the pursuing Union cavalry. According to Wheeler, Brigadier General Henry B. Davidson, commanding Forrest's cavalry, was informed of the Union cavalry position and was ordered to keep scouts out to watch for any movement. Davidson would be blamed by Wheeler for the results of the fight which would occur the next day near Farmington. Wheeler wrote, "Unfortunately, he failed to comply with this order, and on the following morning was attacked by a superior force of the enemy. I received two consecutive dispatches ... from General Davidson which indicated that he was moving down Duck River, but on questioning his couriers I ascertained that he was moving toward Farmington. I immediately started at a trot toward Farmington with Martin's division, ordering General Wharton and the wagons to follow me. I reached Farmington just in time to place five regiments of Martin's command in position when the enemy appeared. I had ordered General Davidson to form in column by fours on the pike and to charge the enemy when they were repulsed by Martin's division, General Davidson having officially reported to me that only three regiments of the enemy had been seen during the day. The engagement commenced warmly, but the enemy was soon repulsed. General Davidson had failed to form as stated, and instead had moved for some distance. The enemy soon after came up in strong force with a division of infantry and a division of cavalry. We fought them with great warmth for twenty minutes, when we charged the line and drove it back for some distance." Wheeler concluded his report by claiming 188 losses for the Union cavalry in actions at Farmington while he suffered one quarter of these losses. In the battle, Wheeler would face a single brigade of mounted infantry and a brigade of cavalry. A more realistic report can be found in the only other Confederate report of this engagement written by Colonel George B. Hodge, which detailed the action leading up to the battle at Farmington.[83]

Robert Mitchell reached Crook's division on the evening of October 5 and, with the combined Union cavalry corps, rode in pursuit of Wheeler on the October 6. Mitchell ordered McCook's division to ride west for Unionville on the north side of the Duck River, and Crook's division, including Miller's mounted infantry, to advance toward Farmington on the south side of the river on October 7. As the Union cavalry advanced, a local citizen ran to the column and told the troopers the location of the Confederate cavalry. Crook found Henry Davidson's Confederate cavalry in line behind a fence about three miles from Shelbyville and sent Miller's mounted infantry forward on horseback, pushing the enemy cavalry into a cedar thicket. Next, Long's brigade charged the Confederate cavalry. Long led "a most gallant saber charge, driving the enemy 3 miles, killing and capturing a great many rebels," exclaimed Crook. The enemy made another attempt to halt the Union attack, and the mounted infantry again rode to the front and drove the enemy to Farmington. Long, who had his horse shot from under him at McMinnville a few days before, was wounded with a Minié ball in his side and his horse was again shot during the attack. At this point the Federal cavalry gathered up 70 wounded Confederate troopers and the surgeons went to work on their injuries under some trees near the site of the fight. After retreating, the Confederates again found refuge in a thicket about three quarters of a mile from Farmington and with the mounted infantry in the front and the cavalry on the flank, Crook advanced again. A correspondent for the *Cincinnati Enquirer* described the arrival of the Board of Trade Battery: "A line hurriedly formed, was formed none too soon, their advance was enough to crush us, but not withstanding our fellows opened fire. Just when he was needed more than any other man, Captain Stokes galloped up with his Chicago battery, opened fire rapidly and drove the enemy again on retreat." One Union cavalryman referred to the Confederates moving into position for a "last desperate stand." At this point, Will Martin's division moved into position to support Davidson's retreating cavalry. As Wheeler's cavalry concentrated, Crook realized he was vulnerable to an attack on his flank. Then, Crook sent a rider to bring Minty's brigade to the front.[84]

As Crook continued his fight in a misty rain, he assumed Minty had followed his orders, but he soon found Minty was not at the front with the rest of the troops. This enraged Crook because he now found himself in a precarious position. He had advanced to Farmington against Wheeler's main body of cavalry with what he thought was his entire division (three brigades) only to find one of his brigades missing. Wheeler moved Martin's dismounted cavalry division into a defensive line in another cedar thicket at Farmington and the battle intensified. Part of Wharton's division, which had moved farther south with the supply train and away from the fighting, was ordered to join in the fight. Wheeler's artillery soon opened on the Union column with canister, grape and shell at a distance of about 400 yards. John Toomey, Board of Trade Battery, remarked that the enemy received the attack with a yell. Three guns of the Confederate artillery lay ahead in the open in a bend in the road at the bottom of an incline—two 12-pounder howitzers and a three-inch rifled gun. To be able to depress the muzzles low enough to strike the enemy guns, the Board of Trade Battery had to move 50 yards closer to the enemy.[85]

The correspondent of the *Cincinnati Enquirer* gave a firsthand account of the unfolding battle. "To our right and rear was an old field of four acres forming an impervious hedge around it. Stokes' Chicago battery was placed in position on the pike in one corner of the field, and the 2d brigade, in columns of battalions within the field. The 3d Ohio had been ordered off to the right to guard the flank. Meantime, Miller's command had dismounted, deployed in line on the right and left of the road, and advanced into the cedars. We were not long kept in suspense. A terrific fire opened all along the line. Miller had become engaged, and the Chicago battery gave shot for shot. The enemy used grape and canister on our advancing line and Stokes replied with shell and solid shot against the rebel battery.... A portion of the enemy battery turned on the Chicago battery, and it soon had to send a piece to the rear with a wheel shattered." Due to the nature of the cedar obstructed field, Stokes could only get one gun at a time into position to fire on Wheeler's men. The gun was rolled in position in a slight depression off the road with little visibility. Stokes, seeing this as a poor spot, rolled the gun back onto the road with heavy trees on one side and brush on the other. To the front, there lay a grassy field edged with cedar thickets. As the gun was being positioned, the men were startled by a "ringing shot" from an enemy battery unlimbered straight ahead on the same road, intent on blocking any movement forward. The enemy battery was positioned on a slight knoll. The fire by the enemy targeted Crook and his staff who were observing the field and the enemy positions. After the shot, Lieutenant Sylvanus Stevens took charge of the Board of Trade guns and ordered the horses and limbers to be moved out of sight. To the right, Miller's mounted infantry fired away at the enemy lines. Private Silas Stevens recalled, "The enemy had our range and fired with great precision. Our men replied with equal effect, the distance was not over three hundred yards and from our gun the enemy could be readily seen." Due to the short range, the muzzle of the gun was depressed and solid shot was rammed into the gun. Captain Stokes ordered the Union artillery to fire and "in three shots he disabled one of their pieces, blowing up a caisson, and throwing their ranks into confusion." In return, the fire of the Confederate battery disabled a Chicago Board of Trade gun and by striking the left wheel, "tore off the tire near the ground: broke the spokes, and felloes, and rendered the piece at once unfit for use." All of the men around the gun were struck with debris, but William Tinsley received the most severe injury. Lieutenant Sylvanus Stevens received injuries to both his legs. Orders rang out to pull the gun away and replace it with the second gun. As the fresh gun was pushed into place, a Confederate shell struck the team pulling the first away, killing two horses. John Toomey was riding one of the horses that was struck.[86]

Toomey explained that this was the first time he had ever seen a cannon ball rolling on the ground. It struck his horse in the breast and passed out its flank, instantly killing the horse. The horse fell straight down, pinning Toomey's leg and foot which were still in the stirrup. To make matters worse the unexploded shell lay on the road, not three feet away from him. Stunned, his initial thought was that his leg had been shot off, and seeing the shell so close to his head, he expected it would explode at any second. The shell was still spinning and Toomey distinctly heard the hiss of the fuse. Fortunately for Toomey, his mates came to his assistance and when they lifted the great weight of the horse off his leg, he scurried away from the shell which never exploded. In the meantime, Miller's men continued to fire away in a constant roar. The new gun immediately joined the fight and disabled another of the enemy guns. At this point, Miller's brigade rose and attacked down a hill.[87]

Colonel Abram Miller, commanding the Union mounted infantry brigade, explained that the 17th and 72nd Indiana Mounted Infantry initiated the attack. The 17th Indiana filed into line on the left and 72nd Indiana moved to the right of the road. The 98th Illinois and 123rd Illinois moved in support of these regiments. Miller saw three lines of enemy cavalry before him and overlapping his flanks. Two Union cavalry regiments moved forward on the flanks in support of Miller and the third regiment of Long's cavalry covered the rear. Miller gave the order to charge and the brigade surged ahead. The colonel of 123rd Illinois Mounted Infantry, James Monroe, was mortally wounded in the attack. As Miller continued the advance the Confederate artillery targeted his lines with grape and canister. "[T]he enemy raking my lines … at a range not exceeding 300 yards, the shell[s] exploding in all directions in the thick cedars above our heads and at our feet. While thus closely engaged the enemy, with terrible energy and loud huzzas, charged my lines, but without effect. At this time Captain Stokes opened fire, which partially drew the attention of the enemy's artillery, and seeing the critical condition of affairs, and believing victory could only be obtained by a successful charge, I at once ordered it, which was promptly executed, the whole line impetuously advancing with a shout, driving back the successive lines of the enemy, and resulting in his complete rout, the capture of three pieces of artillery, and the occupancy of the town, when orders were received from General Crook to halt and await further orders." While Wheeler claimed victory, other Confederate reports gave a more accurate accounting. Colonel George Hodge recorded that the remnants of his command reached Wheeler's line at 4:00 and that the Confederate line was "broken" at 5:00 and the retreat began again. Wheeler, realizing he had nothing to gain in a prolonged fight behind enemy lines, withdrew, but Wheeler's assessment of the fight at Farmington attempted to show victory instead of defeat.[88]

R.F. Bunting, chaplain of the 8th Texas, concluded: "But at Farmington were we well nigh ruined." Bunting gave a good description of the battle at Farmington and the aftermath. He wrote in a letter that John Wharton and Thomas Harrison kept the battle from being a worse disaster for Wheeler than it was. A charge by Wharton's cavalry temporarily halted the Union advance long enough for Wheeler to extract his command. As it was, Bunting wrote: "Wheeler's entire force was repulsed and scattered. The attack by Wharton saved Wheeler's cavalry which had been at risk of being a complete and irretrievable route. As it was our loss was severe…. The fight was a disgraceful blunder on the part of Wheeler and demands an investigation."[89]

Hodge's (Third Confederate Cavalry Brigade) after-action report also revealed a significantly different version of the action than Wheeler's report. Hodge had the unenviable task of providing the rearguard action for Davidson's cavalry. Hodge wrote, "For five hours and a half, over 7 miles of country, the unequal contest continued. My gallant brigade was cut to pieces and slaughtered. I had informed the officers and men that the sacrifice of their lives was necessary and they manfully made the sacrifice." The losses claimed by Wheeler and Crook, again, were quite different. Crook reported he lost a total of 111 men for the entire expedition and Abram Miller recorded his loss at 96 for the campaign. Miller also recorded 86 enemy dead and another 270 prisoners during the engagement on October 7 alone. Wheeler claimed a loss of 40–50 men, apparently for just the engagement at Farmington of his command on October 7 and could not have included Hodge's, and perhaps all of Forrest's cavalry.[90]

After the battle, Crook turned his attention to Robert Minty. He preferred charges against Minty for failing to have his brigade in position for the attack at Farmington and for his behavior throughout the raid. Certainly, the two officers disliked each other. Minty was arrested and removed from command, but he pressed for a court martial which took place in February. Minty was cleared in the proceeding and in the meantime, Crook was transferred to West Virginia, effectively separating the two officers. Minty would continue to serve in the cavalry in the west as described by David Stanley as a "most excellent soldier—reliable—always on time and prompt to execute orders."[91]

The Union Cavalry Catches Wheeler's Rearguard at Sugar Creek

The morning after the Battle of Farmington, the Union cavalry took up the pursuit of Wheeler as he rode for the Tennessee River. The Federal cavalry caught Wheeler again at Sugar Creek with the 5th Iowa leading the attack. Both the 3rd Confederate and 9th Tennessee cavalries participated in the fight at Sugar Creek which sent these regiments to the rear. Colonel William W. Lowe, commanding the Union cavalry brigade, reported 85 enemy troopers captured, 13 killed, and some wounded who were able to make an escape. Lowe concluded, "The remnant of his force dispersed in all directions." After driving past the rear guard, the Iowans led the Federal pursuit to Rogersville, Alabama, and rode through the town with their sabers held high. Henry Albert Potter wrote, "Traveled about 35 miles this day—made the longest charge on our record—six miles— came back & encamped two miles from river—thus endeth Wheeler's great cavalry Raid." The Board of Trade Battery stopped at Rogersville.[92]

Wheeler wrote that having accomplished his objective he rode for the safety of his lines. For the Union cavalry, it was the case that they had finally caught up with Wheeler, who rode for his life. Wheeler claimed in his after-action report, "During the trip we captured in action 1,600 prisoners, and killed and wounded as many of their cavalry as would cover our entire loss." Certainly, the destruction of the bridges and railroads, the capture and destruction of the supply depot in McMinnville, and the destruction of the wagon trains all were notable accomplishments for the Confederate cavalry during this raid. Brigadier General Philip D. Roddey's Confederate cavalry brigade moved across the Tennessee River on October 7 in an attempt to assist Wheeler in his raid. Roddey soon found things were not working well for Wheeler. Roddey wrote from Elk River, "At the same point I met several wounded men and stragglers from General Wheeler's corps.... All agreed in the statement that Wheeler had been severely repulsed at Farmington; that he had a valuable wagon train, and was trying to save it by sending it across the river below Decatur; that he was hard pressed."[93]

With Wheeler crossing back into Alabama, the raid was over. After the Union cavalry's pursuit was complete, Rosecrans ordered Mitchell to keep the cavalry away from Chattanooga. There was little chance of forage for the horses and to keep the cavalry in good shape, it needed to be at another location. Crook's division moved to Huntsville and McCook's division was posted at Winchester, Tennessee. The past two months of hard duty had taken a severe toll on the cavalry, and Wheeler's raid had severely tested both horses and men. Mitchell wrote, "My command is, of course, very badly used up. Hard marches, scarcity of shoes (although each man carried two at starting), and miserable, worthless saddles that never should have been bought by the Government, or put on a horse's back after they were bought, have ruined many of the horses." McCook's cavalry division had ridden 225 miles in five days and Crook's division had traveled even farther. Colonel Thomas Jordan, 9th Pennsylvania Cavalry, arrived in Middle Tennessee after recuperating from an illness and found the troopers sleeping without tents. Jordan wisely noted, "For one who dies by the bullet, another 20 die due to exposure and hard service."[94]

Wheeler's raid, after months of relative inactivity for the Confederate general, provided a great deal of excitement and accomplished the destruction of some important supplies and infrastructure in Middle Tennessee. The destruction of Rosecrans' 800-wagon supply train caused a great deal of hardship for the hungry Union soldiers in Chattanooga and Wheeler's raid pulled the entire Union cavalry corps from the Chattanooga area. The 92nd Illinois Mounted infantryman, Albert Woodcock, wrote the hunger of the men at Chattanooga could "not be believed." In addition, the Union cavalry, which had labored since mid–August, was left in absolute exhaustion at the end of the raid. Also notable during the raid, Wheeler's destruction of the railroad bridges delayed the reinforcements bound for Chattanooga until the Confederate cavalry was expelled and the bridges repaired. Finally, until the exact details of Wheeler's raid were known, the initial reports provided a boost in morale for the Confederate infantry at Chattanooga and gave hope that the Confederate cavalry could stop communications and supplies reaching Rosecrans' besieged army.[95]

Mitchell noted the Union cavalry's efforts outweighed any long-term impact of the raid. He recorded, "We captured six pieces of artillery, and, including killed, wounded, prisoners, and deserters, I think they re-crossed the Tennessee River with between 2,000 and 3,000 less men than they started out with." At the end of the campaign, Colonel Robert Minty lost command of his brigade for four months and was court martialed for failure to follow orders. Minty pushed for the trial which took place from February 2 through February 16, 1864. In light of the pressure the Union cavalry had been under for the entire year, it is not surprising that tempers flared particularly during the intense pursuit of Wheeler. The crux of the problem revolved around the question of whether or not Minty had orders to move forward. The court martial found Minty not guilty. Ultimately, Crook's decision to place this well-liked, well-respected colonel under arrest made him very unpopular with Minty's brigade. Robert Burns bitterly wrote that Minty and Wilder were the only brigade commanders to gain any "distinction" and others were jealous of their successes. Burns wrote: "Mitchell and Crook are infantry generals, do not understand the management of cavalry, and would do anything to ruin Minty. Gen. C. has seized the opportunity and did his best."[96]

At the end of the raid, the morale of the Union cavalry was even better than before. They felt they had defeated Wheeler's cavalry, and this was a much-needed boost after the Union army defeat at Chickamauga. Thomas Crofts, 3rd Ohio Cavalry, would write of the campaign: "The campaign had been a remarkable illustration of what men and horses were capable of performing under conditions of deprivation of food and rest ... yet everything was borne cheerfully." The fight at Farmington with only 1,500 Union soldiers was viewed as a Union victory and Wheeler precipitately rode for the friendly confines of the Confederate lines. The pro–Federal press severely criticized Wheeler's raid stating that Wheeler blamed his subordinates for his defeat and that Wheeler's cavalry was more "intent on plundering than military objectives." While the raid through Union-held territory yielded some positive results, the final evaluation showed it to be a failure and it highlighted Wheeler's propensity to claim successes when there were none. "The Confederate cavalry had worn itself out with almost nothing to show for its trouble. Never had Bragg's cavalry been so poorly utilized at such a critical time," wrote historian James Schaefer.[97]

Changes in Command

The performance of the Board of Trade Battery again yielded accolades from the cavalry commanders and the newspapers in Chicago. In particular, George Thomas sent his congratulations for the efforts of the cavalry in dealing with Wheeler: "The brilliant pursuit of the enemy's cavalry under Wheeler by the cavalry command of this army, especially Crook's division and Stokes' Chicago Board of Trade Battery, which were foremost in the fight, deserves honorable mention. The general commanding thanks the cavalry, and particularly General Crook, with the officers and soldiers of his division, and of Stokes' battery, for their valuable services in the pursuit of the enemy, which resulted in driving him in confusion across the Tennessee River."[98]

The end of Wheeler's raid marked the beginning of a period of transition for the cavalry corps of the Army of the Cumberland, and changes were in store for the Chicago Board of Trade Battery, too. David Stanley missed the Battle of Chickamauga and during the subsequent actions had been moved to a Union hospital and returned to his home in Ohio to recuperate from dysentery. Stanley was away from the army for about a month. On October 9, Rosecrans relieved both Alexander McCook and Thomas Crittenden of their commands, and the infantry and artillery components of the army were reorganized. The next day, Brigadier General James A. Garfield left the army to serve in Congress. Stanley still held the position of chief of cavalry for the Army of the Cumberland in October, even though Robert Mitchell had served in that capacity during Stanley's illness. Mitchell's days were also numbered as chief of cavalry. Mitchell wrote on October 14, 1863, "I am out of rations and my horses are breaking down, but will do the best I can. I am as near a dead man on horseback as you ever saw." On October 18, Mitchell again appealed to Rosecrans to be relieved of duty. After only a month in command of the cavalry, Mitchell, who was not seen as a success by many in the cavalry, had had enough and sought to give up command; he left the cavalry corps by the end of the month. Subsequently, Mitchell was also taken to task during the court of inquiry of Alexander McCook's actions during the Battle of Chickamauga for failing to move his cavalry to assist in the battle.[99]

Finally, on October 19, 1863, Rosecrans was relieved of command of the Army of the Cumberland and replaced by George Thomas. Brigadier General Washington Lafayette Elliott was given command of Mitchell's cavalry division. On November 12, 1863,

David Stanley was officially relieved of command of the cavalry and assigned to command the First Division of the Fourth Army Corps, serving under Gordon Granger. Stanley's reassignment to the infantry was decided by George Thomas who had been Stanley's instructor at West Point. Elliott, senior in rank, was named chief of cavalry of the Army of the Cumberland when Stanley was reassigned. On the other side of the line, Nathan Bedford Forrest was transferred to western Tennessee and would no longer cause trouble for the Army of the Cumberland. Wheeler assumed command of the entire Confederate cavalry corps with four divisions of cavalry.[100]

Stokes Leaves the Battery

At the end of Wheeler's Raid, Captain James Stokes was given command of a wing of artillery at Chattanooga and permanently left the Board of Trade Bat-

The new chief of cavalry, General Washington Layette Elliott (Library of Congress).

tery. Stokes was one of the most multi-dimensional characters in the history of the Chicago Board of Trade Battery. It is difficult to characterize this individual, and the events describing his participation and leadership of the battery have been left fairly objective because it is impossible to totally reconstruct the additional parts, and allegations, of his history. Some pre-war information has been left out to this point in this history. We know that Stokes was a U.S. Military Academy trained, experienced soldier, who left the service and went into the business world, ultimately ending up in Chicago working for the Illinois Central Railroad. When the battery was formed, Stokes seemed the ideal individual to command the Board of Trade Battery, because artillery units needed someone knowledgeable about the technical aspects of a battery, including the proper manual of the gun, the mathematics of targeting and quartermaster needs. Stokes had demonstrated initiative in the early parts of the war when he secured the arms in St. Louis from risk of capture from pro–Confederate factions. Once the battery was formed, his success in preparing the battery to effectively fight in battle is without question. The battery performed exceptionally well at Stones River, during the Tullahoma Campaign, and the Chickamauga Campaign. The well-drilled and well-prepared battery speaks volumes about Stokes' ability to prepare the men of the battery to fight in the Civil War.[101]

Stokes began his tenure well and he made an initial favorable impression on the men of the battery. As time went along, grumbling began and increased, with most of the voices preserved in diaries and letters disparaging him. To a certain extent, these comments have to be taken with the understanding that businessmen and clerks were subordinate to a spit and polish West Point trained officer. It would be surprising if there wasn't some grumbling; however, the comments became unified in a dislike of Stokes. The causes of the grumbling ranged from alleged excessive use of alcohol, petty punitive discipline, excessive disciplining and egotistical decisions pertaining to the battery. This has all been outlined in the narrative to this point and anyone reading this has probably already made their decision regarding the qualities of this commander.

There was more to the story about Stokes. For example, in the battery roster Stokes is shown to be 43 years old and an insurance agent, a quite different age and occupation than shown in most of the biographical information about Stokes. He was born in either 1814 or 1815, depending on the source and this made him 47–48 years. And, he was probably an insurance agent as he listed in the battery records, because he had lost his job with the railroad. In a digression, it was generally expressed that Stokes left the army in 1843 due to health reasons or due to an opportunity in business. However, historian Elisabeth Joan Doyle wrote a summary of the work that Stokes did in the Quartermaster Department after he left the Board of Trade Battery and when Stokes uncovered irregularities within the department, his own history came under scrutiny. As General William B. Franklin's command was investigated by Stokes, he fired back stating that Stokes was, by no means, the right person to do an investigation because he left the army in 1843 "under a cloud as to his money matters." More recently, Franklin explained that he had taken money "from the till while in the employ of the Illinois Central Rail Road." Stokes was fired when the managing superintendent of the railroad contacted the president of the company, W.H. Osborne, and asked that Stokes be terminated in 1860. The president, when asked about Stokes, said he was given no specific reason for the firing, but he did fire Stokes. Upon Stokes' dismissal he took $6,300 from the cash drawer without company approval, but left a note stating this was for special service he had performed for the company. Ironically, Ambrose Burnside, the treasurer of the company and future Civil War general, went after Stokes and demanded that he return the money or face arrest. Stokes returned the money and when asked, Osborne said he felt that Burnside's threat of arrest was indeed justified. After looking into Stokes' activities in the company, other irregularities in accounts were attributed to Stokes. Osborne said he would be unwilling to put Stokes into any position of trust. When Burnside was asked about Stokes, he called Stokes "a great knave" who stole several thousand dollars from the railroad. Doyle would conclude that Stokes had to have been a very naïve thief if he intended to steal the money and left a note saying he did; she suggested the entire affair resulted from a substantial personality conflict. However, these events in his past would prompt Stokes' discharge under a cloud and recommendation that he "was an unfit person ... for any position in the military."[102]

By the time he left the battery, he was greatly disliked. Silas Stevens, who detested Stokes, would assess that Stokes' philosophy in regard to promotion was recognition through the prowess of those who served under him. He also thought that Stokes ambitiously sought advancement as something to be achieved over others of his West Point comrades. Ignoring all the events before Stokes joined the battery, perhaps the best assessment came from Private John Fleming in a letter he wrote on November 2. Rumors around the camp pointed to Stokes' resignation and Fleming wrote: "I hope it will prove true, although the battery would lose a splendid officer as a man he is not well liked." Upon his departure from the Board of Trade Battery, Stokes remained a complicated individual with a multi-dimensional record. He was a man who had trained and driven his men to become one of the premier artillery batteries in the west; but he was a man who could be petty, cruel and egotistical, and one who would not be missed by many of the men he commanded.[103]

The Battery Reunites at Washington

When Stokes joined Crook in the pursuit of Wheeler through Middle Tennessee, he left Lieutenant George Robinson with the excess baggage and guns number 3 and number 5. Another section of three guns (guns number 2, number 6, number 7) also remained behind, probably under Griffin's authority. Robinson's section would be under the direct command of General James Spears, described by one of his subordinates as a man of "tyranny and ungentlemanly conduct." Benjamin Nourse's account of the next 30 days would prove this assessment to be correct. With little to do as Rosecrans' army was besieged by a stalemated Army of Tennessee, the men continued to recuperate after the battles on September 18–22. The rations were low, the boots and clothing were worn out, and the weather was starting to turn cold. An attempt to get rations resulted in a return of "5 days, ½ rations to last 10 days. We go out foraging each day but do not get much to eat," wrote Nourse on October 8. Five days later the rations ran out: "No rations—we punch a broken canteen full of holes and then with an ear of corn there on to make meal to keep ourselves alive with, mixing it with water and baking it in the hot ashes—and while baking have to watch it—to prevent it being stolen." Spears appeared to focus on the battery by the end of the first week in October. Nourse wrote, "[T]o please the Genl. we had to hitch up and then after laying around a while, we went to bed again leaving the horses standing at the guns." A few days later, Nourse experienced even more of Spears' unpleasant command abilities: "Genl. Spears was gloriously drunk and ordered out two pieces of our battery to to (sic) go to the river—6 & 7 went and when they got there he ordered 15 shells fired in one place. Of course our gunners knew better than to do so. They fired into the breastworks on the rebel side of the river, but they saw no rebs. Our caisson harnessed up but did not go with the guns. We unharnessed, but when Lieut. Griffin heard the firing we hitched up again—about 1 oc. The guns came back and we unharnessed this time we thought for good but at 3 oc. p.m. the Genl. sent orders to 'meet the returning fire' (drunker) and every thing was packed and we moved out. Two pieces went into the road and into position with three of Lillies Battery in position in our camp ground. All this without a single soldier to support us. I never saw such tomfoolery. At dark the other two guns came back and we pitched our tents and went to bed as usual. All this day in the pouring rain. So much for a drunken fool's spree. Hope we shall soon leave him and his Loyal East Tennesseans. They would be good boys if their officers knew anything—rain, rain." A few days later, two guns were again dispatched on another wild chase.[104]

Still in the vicinity of Washington on October 20, the men received more rations, this time quarter rations. Nourse recorded, "This is hard. One ¼ of a cracker and one thin slice of pork 3 × 2 inches and one pint of weak coffee. Capt. Stokes sent a dispatch by courier this morning saying he had a fight with the rebels and Willie Tinsley & C[harles] A.B. Garnsey were wounded—not seriously." Garnsey was one of the most interesting members of the battery. He was an energetic and innovative individual and was an apprentice dentist at the time of his enlistment. The next day the men of the battery received good news. They were to be relieved by Goodspeed's Ohio Battery and the Board of Trade Battery would be sent closer to Stokes and the other section, but the orders were countermanded before the battery could get away. Little action occurred over the next two weeks, except one of the guns sent some rounds into a Confederate boat on the river.[105]

On November 7, the battery started a movement away from Spears' command to Stevenson, arriving there on November 9. The weather was turning colder. Benjamin Nourse lamented, "Oh we have frosty nights I can tell you. Pretty rough, I can tell you. All I have on is a thin cotton shirt, old thin pants, old jacket without wadding or lining, a very old cap, no boots—it seems as if my feet would freeze in the morning, when I put them into frosty brass stirrups—Thank God we are tough." At Stevenson, without remorse the battery gave up gun number 7, which had been earned during the Battle of Stones River, and again became a six-gun battery. On November 12, the battery continued on its way to Maysville (arriving there on November 15) and the Second Cavalry Division and the other section of guns, unifying the battery after a five week separation. More pleasant news awaited the men. At Maysville, and away from the siege at Chattanooga, there was plenty of rations. The cavalry and the battery would operate away from the concentrating Union forces around Chattanooga thereby missing the important battles at Lookout Mountain and Mission-

Chicagoan and pre-war railroader James B. Finley aided in recruitment for the battery and received a commission in the Michigan artillery in mid–1864 (Chicago History Museum, ICHi-176919).

ary Ridge. The new commanding general, Ulysses Grant, would claim the victories in late November, propelling the Army of Tennessee further south and forcing Bragg to resign his command of the Southern Army. Joseph Johnston would gain command and would lead this army against the Union forces in the upcoming Atlanta Campaign.[106]

George I. Robinson Gains Command of the Battery

Meanwhile, the Board of Trade Battery and the cavalry corps would settle into northern Alabama and Middle Tennessee. Specifically, the battery would remain in Maysville, Huntsville, and Pulaski until March 1864. Reflecting some of the other major changes in the Union forces and especially Stokes' reassignment, Lieutenant George Robinson, nicknamed "Rob" by the men of the battery, assumed command of the battery based on his senior rank. Robinson became aware of Stokes' permanent departure on November 11 and the change in command was acknowledged in the organizational structure of the army on October 21. He sent a letter to the Illinois adjutant general requesting a promotion to the rank of captain and permanent command of the battery, but the commissioning of the next captain would be a long time coming and would not occur until September 1864. In the meantime, the battery was unified and Robinson put his vision of the battery into effect. Benjamin Nourse recorded in his diary: "On the evening of the 17th the Battery was pulled to pieces by Robinson & the men sent from one squad to another. Nearly all are thoroughly changed—Also the gun squads were renumbered according to rank 1 & 6, 2 & 5, 3 & 4. The plan is liked." Robinson reorganized the gun squads and the section compositions into a more organized and efficient manner. (When Robinson took command, the battery reported monthly "returns" or summaries of the number of men present and absent for duty. Those records under Stokes' command were either never completed, submitted or otherwise lost; but Robinson's reports offer a good perspective of the makeup of the battery.)[107]

Board of Trade Returns for October–December 1863
(Present and Absent)

	Officers	Sgt.	Corp.	Buglers	Artificers	Privates	Aggregate
October* (Number Absent 23)	5	8	12	1	2	115	143
November (Number absent 29)	5	8	12	1	2	115	143
December (Number absent 27)	5	8	12	1	2	116	144

*Private Charles Garnsey absent due to a wound inflicted at the Battle of Farmington

The number of men absent over the three-month period ranged from 23 to 29. There was an increase in men absent in November, primarily due to illness requiring the men to enter the hospital for various ailments. With the absences, which ranged from desertions, furloughs, detachments and hospital confinement, the number of men on active service ranged from 114–120 men. This was not a serious matter because the battery prepared for winter quarters, but it was a decrease in the number of active men who started with the battery. Attrition was becoming an important factor as the battery prepared to turn the calendar into 1864. Early in the new year, Robinson would send Lieutenant Henry Bennett, Sergeant Calvin Durand, and Private James Finley back to Chicago to gain new recruits to fill the dwindling ranks. These men set up a tent on the courthouse lawn and easily gained the number of men needed due primarily to the increasing recognition and popularity of the battery.[108]

In the meantime, the battery went into winter quarters, while recuperating after the campaigning over the summer and fall, and the Confederate forces seemed to be doing the same. The battery's camp shifted to Huntsville where the men built houses (about seven feet by 12 feet—four men to a house) which allowed them to stay warm and not sleep on the ground. After building shelters for the men, the next task was barns for the animals which did not go without incident. Private Clark Winslow broke his leg when a roof fell on him while he was tearing down a barn for lumber. (Winslow was later discharged due to disability on June 20, 1864, and the severity of the injury landed him with a disability pension in January 1866.) The new command operated without the stress present under Stokes' command. The men participated in some intra-battery horse races, and in particular, Lieutenant Henry Bennett loaned Benjamin Nourse his horse to ride over a quarter mile course. Nourse lost by two lengths and swore his days of horse racing were over when he lost his $25 bet. As the days passed, the men waited for news of the outcome of the battles at Chattanooga and also, further east, from Virginia as Meade pursued Lee's army.[109]

Supplies slowly reached the battery. Men got new clothes for the first time in three months of active campaigning. The battery also received some new horses to replace some that were worn out. Robinson also set a new schedule for the daily activities:

Reveille: 6 oc	Camp Duties: 9	Water Call: 4
Food Call: 6:15	Roll Call: 12	Feed Call: 4:15
Breakfast: 7	Feed Call: 12:15	Dress Parade: 5
Guard Mounting: 7:45	Dinner: 12 oc	Supper: 5:30
Stable Call: 8	Stable Call: 3	Tattoo: 8
Water & Inspection: 8:45	Inspection of Horses: 3:45	Taps: 8:30

After the battles at Chattanooga, Robinson settled the final accounts and formally assumed the command of the battery. Members of the battery who had been sick trickled back into the command and occasionally a new recruit would arrive. Robinson's command style allowed for fun by the men. On December 15, Nourse wrote: "Tonight the boys are having their usual high time, singing, dancing with banjo, flute and genuine fiddle music." On December 23, the battery began a movement which would result in its arrival in Pulaski, Tennessee, on December 28. The cold and wet trip was highlighted by the passage through the Elk River. Nourse described the crossing: "It rained fast last night and this morning, we started at 8 oc. and crossed the Elk river—We doubled our teams and our caisson came very near going 'off the ford' as it was. The water dashed over the guns and the ammunition chests. Wet all our rations etc. Of course, our legs were wet & our boots full of water. We did not stop & I turned my leg over my horse's head and let the water run out of first one boot and then the other. It was intensely cold today and continued to rain all day. I had a flask of brandy in my valise that I have carried for months and getting it out we four drank it—how we have suffered today with numbness—few at home can guess."[110]

New York native and pre-war clerk George Jewett received a commission in the Michigan artillery in late 1863 (Chicago History Museum, ICHi-176916).

Crook's division concentrated at Pulaski and Long's brigade was detached to operate in the Knoxville area of eastern Tennessee. While the First Cavalry Division (Edward McCook's) was also busy in Eastern Tennessee, Nathan Bedford Forrest began his new command in western Tennessee and Mississippi with a vengeance. His presence in Jackson, Tennessee, on December 6 resulted in an immediate response by the Union forces which mobilized to stop his raids. To this end, Crook's Second Division, excluding Long's brigade, moved westward in Tennessee as part of several Union forces converging on Forrest. But the wily Forrest easily slipped the noose set for him by riding through Collierville and then on to Holly Springs, Mississippi. At the end of the year, Elliott's headquarters was located at Talbott's Station in east Tennessee.

McCook's First Division was also there with a total of 3,916 men present for duty. Crook's Second Division was headquartered at Pulaski with 7,464 men present for duty.[111]

The stay in Pulaski was a cold experience and without the enclosed shelters built in Huntsville, the men suffered through the winter weather. It was so cold that the ink froze at headquarters and the clerks had difficulty in writing. As the year ended, the cavalry of the Army of the Cumberland stretched over a 250 mile front. The corps had a new commander and his leadership style was yet to be determined. McCook's division had heavy fighting in East Tennessee while Crook's had little, but Crook had exhausted his division in the pursuit of Wheeler a few months before. All hoped that 1864 would be a better year and that the war would soon be over. But the cavalry would fight wherever they were needed. Nourse finished his 1863 diary with some thoughtful considerations: "Oh, how good God has been to me through all my goings. I have forgotten Him from day to day, still he has kept me from falling and from sickness, has kept the bullet from me while so many of my companions have fallen by my side, how I thank Him for this, thank Him for giving all at home life and health, thank Him for every thing—I wish I knew how many miles we have traveled since we left Murfrees-boro, Tenn. Where shall I be at the close of 1864? Good bye to 1863." And, welcome 1864.[112]

Battery Losses and Changes July 1–December 31, 1863

Pvt. John J. Carroll	Discharged	November 30, 1863	Disability
Pvt. George D. Jewett	Discharged	November 22, 1863	For promotion
Pvt. Albert Pontius	Discharged	July 23, 1863	Disability
Pvt. Myron S. Sanford	Discharged	December 26, 1863	For promotion
Pvt. John S. Wallace	Died	August 9, 1863	
Capt. James H. Stokes	Detached	October 1863	Artill. wing command

New Recruits	Enlistment Date
Michael Holmes	December 29, 1863
John Kelse	December 10, 1863
Edward F. Kelley	December 12, 1863
Robert Kennedy	December 9, 1863
Martin T. Lynch	December 23, 1863
Henry J. Phillaber/Philliber/Phillibar	December 23, 1863
Leonard Smith	December 10, 1863
Leonard Stahl	December 10, 1863
George L. White	October 22, 1863

CHAPTER SIX

1864 and the Atlanta Campaign

Give them canister, Mr. Griffin.—Col. Robert Minty

The new year gave the Board of Trade Horse Artillery time to become familiar with the new corps commander, Washington L. Elliott, and it also brought more changes for the cavalry corps of the Army of the Cumberland. Elliott was a good commander but he would first struggle under Ulysses Grant, and then William Sherman, who commanded the three Union armies near Chattanooga. The Board of Trade Battery would also lose its division commander early in 1864 when George Crook was transferred to West Virginia. This marked the second departure of divisional commanders in six months and signaled the arrival of the new divisional commander, Brigadier General Kenner Garrard, at Huntsville, Alabama, on February 10, 1864.

In January, Edward McCook had two brigades in Eastern Tennessee which worked under the command of General Samuel Sturgis. Elsewhere, Crook's Second Division, including the Board of Trade Battery, began the year at Pulaski under orders of the chief of cavalry for the Military Division of the Mississippi, William Sooy Smith. Smith initially told Crook to settle his command around Pulaski and Huntsville and prepare for campaigning in the spring. General William Sherman changed Smith's plans when he began the Meridian Campaign in early February. One part of Sherman's plans included Smith leading a large cavalry force against railroads and other Confederate infrastructure. To assist in the raid, Smith pulled some regiments from Crook's Division and assigned them to the cavalry division of Sixteenth Corps, but the Board of Trade Battery remained in the area around Pulaski, not participating in the campaigns to the east or west. On January 28, William Sooy Smith ordered Crook to make a demonstration on Decatur, Alabama, to hold the attention of Roddey's Confederate cavalry while Smith began his cavalry raid in the Meridian Campaign. While the cavalry regiments from the Army of the Cumberland performed well, the lackluster performance of William Sooy Smith in the Meridian Campaign jaded Sherman's outlook on the cavalry. Sherman wrote his wife, "I am down on William Sooy Smith." He wrote, "He could have come to me, and I know it."[1]

In regard to the Board of Trade Horse Artillery, it remained in Pulaski for the first 10 days of the year. Private Tobias Miller wrote in his diary on the first day of January: "Today is as dreary as a soldier's life & the cold as pinching as his hunger … our efforts to be happy have opened memories of the past, now painful to us." The year started very cold, reaching seven degrees below zero on New Year's Eve and reaching no warmer than five degrees during of the day. Little was done in camp and the men concentrated on various activities ranging from going to church to getting drunk due to the boredom. Meanwhile, some of the cavalry regiments, with expiring terms of enlistment, were busy re-enlisting as veterans for the duration of the war. On January 11, the arrival of some liquor resulted in pandemonium in the camp. Benjamin Nourse described: "[O]ur usual quiet camp is a perfect babble of confused sounds—singing, whistling, squealing, laughing from one end to the other of this camp. I pity the sore and aching heads tomorrow—such is life—It makes me think of the song 'All are happy here.' Those drunk and those looking on and laughing." The raucous life at Pulaski was topped off as a young woman rode through camp dressed as a Union soldier and attracted everyone's attention. Tobias Miller remarked, "her language was as unbecoming as her dress," as she momentarily shocked all the artillerymen. The battery set off on a return trip to Huntsville on January 12 and arrived there on January 14, again crossing the Elk River but this time avoiding getting soaked. The men moved back into the small houses they had built in December, but found the windows had been stolen. They repaired the shelters and prepared to finish the winter there. After arriving, the men were busy foraging but found time to play baseball as the weather improved later in the month. The fact that horses were large and potentially dangerous animals was demonstrated on January 17 when Private John Manning was kicked in the temple by his horse. Manning was found "insensible" and badly hurt. Fortunately, he fully recovered from the injury in contrast to Private Samuel Dodd, a pre-war carpenter, who died the year before of erysipelas after being kicked in the head.[2]

Crook's farewell address was read to the men at dress parade on January 23, although he did not physically leave until the first of February. The battery had lost three additional men to promotions recently—Edmund Luff to accept a commission in the 12th Illinois Cavalry, George D. Jewett to accept a commission in the Michigan heavy artillery, and Myron H. Sanford received a commission in the 2nd Massachusetts Heavy Artillery. In addition, Private Joseph Peters was detached to headquarters as an assistant to the chief of staff. In perhaps one of the most significant moves in January, Lieutenant Sylvanus Stevens officially became detached, effectively ending his service in the battery. After being wounded at Farmington, and Robinson's acknowledgment as commanding officer, he had been serving as Acting Assistant Quartermaster for the Department of the Cumberland in Nashville, reporting to Colonel James Donaldson. These losses made the recruitment of new men important and a detachment was sent to Chicago to complete this task. It is also important to note that Governor Richard Yates and Illinois Adjutant General Allen Fuller received a flood of letters from men supporting Robinson as the next captain of the battery. After Stokes' exit, the letters also sought to ensure that the order of succession would be followed and the letters demonstrated a unanimous approval for native New Yorker Lewis Hand, a 27-year-old energetic pre-war clerk, to be commissioned as the next lieutenant. In the meantime, Robinson returned from a trip to Chattanooga bringing two new recruits with him. Robinson brought newly enlisted privates—Martin Lynch and Henry Philliber. Lynch was an Irish-born, 23-year-old cooper from Chicago prior to his enlistment. Fellow Chicagoan Philliber, also a cooper, was 20 years old and a native of Pennsylvania. Private John Fleming chuckled, that because they were new, "as a matter of course we make considerable sport of them." Robinson's purpose in going to Chattanooga was to gain new guns which he successfully achieved. The battery of two James Rifles and four 3-inch guns would receive newer and better guns. The old gun carriages had simply worn out and Robinson, with the support of Crook, lobbied for a total overhaul. George Thomas, who approved the new guns, reportedly declared, "if any company had earned them they had."[3]

The month of February began with Crook leaving by train, but before he left, he spoke with George Robinson. He told Robinson to "thank the command for their good behavior in every particular. So long as he had command of us he never had a single complaint made against the Chicago Board of Trade Battery. He never saw so well drilled or so good a battery in action, as we were. All gentlemen acted the gentleman at all times." The command would await the arrival of their new divisional commander who would arrive a few days later. In the meantime, the old guns were loaded onto a train and sent to Chattanooga, accompanied by an escort of Lieutenant Robinson, Sergeant Abbott Adams, Corporals James Hildreth and Albert Lake, and 12 privates. Of note, James Stokes, who commanded a wing of artillery in the battles at Chattanooga, was assigned by Grant to investigate graft and inefficiency in the quartermaster department. Grant described Stokes as "an old officer of the regular army and also of the Quartermaster's Department. He is eminently fitted for this duty, though a very disagreeable one for him, and particularly so whilst occupying the grade of captain of artillery."[4]

Except for inspections and more baseball games, little of interest occurred until February 10, when the battery rode for Nashville to receive new guns. The battery's second contract surgeon, Dr. W. Richards, left and opened a practice at Rock Island, Illinois, leaving Daniel Jacobs, hospital steward, as the principle medical resource. The battery passed through Shelbyville the next day and encountered some of the men of the Eleventh Corps who had been transferred from the Eastern Theater. Benjamin Nourse described the men as a "dirty, rough looking lot of men. Take no care of themselves, not fit to bear the name of soldier." The unit reached Nashville on February 13 and camped near Stokes' reserve artillery command. The men remained in camp and while they waited for their new guns, they got into mischief. "The boys will run down town and so very often miss roll call. As punishment they have to go on guard every other day until the first of March. Two got drunk and raised 'Ned,' last night—now they are walking up and down the battery tents, hands tied and the placard 'drunkard' on their backs," recorded Benjamin Nourse. Private Lawrence F. Abbott, who had been absent without leave, arrived back in camp on February 22 from Chicago having spent six weeks on the road. Nourse explained, "The provost marshal sent him down. He is to be court martialed."[5]

Finally, on February 24 the battery received their new guns. They had originally expected Rodman cannons, but they received 3" Parrott rifles (10-pounder). The caissons were loaded with 1,000 rounds of case shot, fuse shells and canister rounds. Over the next two weeks, the men familiarized themselves with the new guns and worked on the new harnesses and equipment that had arrived. The battery began marching south again on March 10 and arrived back in Huntsville on March 14, avoiding bushwhackers along the way. Once in camp, the men began the routine of cleaning, drilling and preparing for future action. An unfortunate event occurred on March 25 when someone stole Lieutenant Griffin's revolvers. Nourse described the event. "This afternoon Lieut. Griffin missed his revolvers and we tied [him] up to a tree. Then we went and search a house near camp, finding one of them—then we went in the pioneer camp and by catching several of the…[ex-slaves], we got trace of the other, finding it in the possession of a soldier, but with the engraving filed off." The men tied the prisoner's "arms above his head, stripped him and made one of the black hostlers give him 100 lashes with a mule whip—and then ran him out of camp." The accused, 18 years old, was employed by the quartermaster sergeant. John Fleming explained that Robinson, under orders from superiors, inflicted the punishment that continued after the lashes were administered. The man was cut loose and whipped out of town using a "black snake whip."[6]

Union artillery on parade (Library of Congress).

On the larger scale, General Kenner Garrard arrived for duty as Second Division cavalry commander on February 10. Garrard, a native of Bourbon County, Kentucky, was 36 years old when he was transferred. He was the grandson of the second governor of Kentucky, James Garrard, and his two brothers were also in the Union Army. Garrard was a

graduate of the United States Military Academy, class of 1851. Like many of the professional soldiers of the Union Army, Garrard had served on the western frontier, first in the dragoons, and then transferred to the 2nd U.S. Cavalry. He had been promoted to the rank of captain in 1861 and had served with various individuals who were members of both the Union and Confederate armies, including John Bell Hood, Albert Sidney Johnston, George Thomas and William Hardee. Garrard was serving in Texas at the beginning of the war and was captured by Confederates as the war began. He

The new Second Cavalry Division Commander, General Kenner Garrard (MOLLUS Mass Civil War Collection, United States Army Heritage and Education Center, Military History Institute, Carlisle, PA).

was paroled in September 1861 and appointed commandant at West Point. He was officially "exchanged" and was free to enter the war. He began his active participation in the war by serving as colonel of the 146th New York Infantry and saw extensive action in the eastern theater. He fought at Fredericksburg, Chancellorsville and Gettysburg. He received a commendation for "Gallant and Meritorious Services" at Gettysburg when he assumed command of a brigade after Brigadier General Stephen Weed was killed at Little Round Top. Garrard had a short stay as chief of the Cavalry Bureau and requested field assignment after only two months in that position, "in despair at the graft and corruption he had found there."[7]

Garrard proved to be a very capable cavalry commander, but it should be noted that Thomas was pleased with Garrard as cavalry division commander even though Grant did not consult Thomas about this appointment. Grant's tenure at Chattanooga was not long-lived because he was promoted to the rank of lieutenant general and moved east to become general in chief of all Union armies. On March 12, William Sherman succeeded command of the Military Division of the Mississippi. Not everyone was pleased with Sherman's ascension however, including Andrew Johnson, governor of Tennessee, who thought Thomas should have this position. Unfortunately, the arrival of Sherman signaled disharmony for the cavalry.[8]

On March 26, two important major generals arrived in Huntsville on their way to Chattanooga—Sherman and James McPherson. Sherman was on his way to command three armies in the field: the Army of the Cumberland, the Army of the Ohio, and part of the Army of the Tennessee (commanded by McPherson). In regard to the cavalry corps, Washington Elliott would have overall command of four divisions in the Army of the Cumberland and subsequently George Stoneman would command a division of cavalry attached to the Army of the Ohio. Elliott's corps would include the First Cavalry Division commanded by Edward McCook, the Second Cavalry Division commanded by Kenner Garrard, the Third Cavalry Division commanded by H. Judson Kilpatrick, and the Fourth Cavalry Division commanded by Alvan Gillem. The Board of Trade Battery would remain attached to the Second Cavalry Division.

Brigadier General Kenner Garrard— Second Cavalry Division April 1864

First Brigade	Second Brigade
Colonel Robert Minty	**Colonel Eli Long**
4th Michigan, Lt. Col. Josiah B. Park	1st Ohio, Col. Beroth B. Eggleston
7th Pennsylvania, Col. William B. Sipes	3rd Ohio, Lt. Col. Horace N. Howland
4th United States, Capt. James B. McIntyre	4th Ohio, Lt. Col. Oliver P. Robie

Third Brigade
Colonel John T. Wilder
17th Indiana Mounted Infantry, Lt. Col. Henry Jordan
72nd Indiana Mounted Infantry, Col. Abram O. Miller
98th Illinois Mounted Infantry, Lt. Col. Edward Kitchell
123rd Illinois Mounted Infantry, Lt. Col. Jonathan Biggs
Artillery
Chicago (Illinois) Board of Trade Battery, Lt. George I. Robinson

Camp life continued for the battery into April, but preparation began in earnest for most of the Union forces for what would be called the Atlanta Campaign. This was somewhat of a misnomer because Sherman did not have Atlanta as an objective for the campaign. Instead, his objective was the destruction of the Army of Tennessee under the command of Joseph Johnston. For the battery, part of this preparation was the arrival of 14 new recruits on April 3 which Lieutenant Henry Bennett brought into camp. The next day the battery harnessed and moved to Fayetteville, Tennessee, then on to Lewisburg, and ultimately arrived at Columbia on April 8. The arrival at Columbia resulted from a need to protect the infrastructure from the threat of a Confederate cavalry raid. Little occurred at Columbia except the arrival of 60 new battery horses. While the men waited, cavalry regiments arrived in camp in a piecemeal fashion, some as full regiments, some as companies, some mounted, some dismounted, and many armed with Spencer carbines, the most effective cavalry weapon of the war. Meanwhile, Robinson completed his monthly returns and these showed a slight increase in the number of men present for duty.[9]

Board of Trade Returns for March–May 1864
(Present and Absent)

	Officers	Sgt.	Corp.	Buglers	Artificers	Privates	Aggregate
March (Number Absent 25)	5	8	12	1	2	121	149
April* (Number Absent 20)	5	8	12	1	2	131	159
May (Number Absent 19)	5	8	12	1	2	126	154

*Twenty-one new enlistees recorded for the month.

During this late winter period, Private Silas Stevens was detached to Second Division headquarters to provide clerical duties. Stevens dealt with a variety of issues in his new role, including reports or communications from parents worried about their sons who had not written for some time. He noted one particularly notable item when headquarters received a request for a discharge for one of the soldiers who had no teeth and therefore could not eat much of the army rations, especially hardtack. The soldier felt his dismissal would be "for the good of the service." The response to the request was returned: "The within named soldier will report for duty, to his commanding officer; and if he has no teeth, to eat the hard bread, then he will be obliged to gum it."[10]

Battery Losses And Changes January 1-May 9, 1864

Hector H. Aiken	Discharged	May 9, 1864	For promotion
Frederick A. Chapman	Discharged	May 9, 1864	For promotion
Samuel M. Croft*	Discharged	May 5, 1864	Disability

William B. Gale	Discharged	May 9, 1864	For promotion
Edmund Luff	Discharged	February 20, 1864	For promotion
Daniel B. Richardson	Discharged	April 30, 1864	Transfer to V.R.C. (Veteran Reserve Corps)
Thomas Tinsley	Discharged	March 23, 1864	For promotion
Leonard Stahl	Deserted	January 5, 1864	

*Samuel Croft died May 1864—chronic Diarrhea) "Died," *Chicago Tribune*, May 25, 1864.

Recruits	Enlist. Date	Recruits	Enlist. Date
James B. Appleton	January 4, 1864	Geo. Gackenhiemer	February 2, 1864
Ephraim S. Appleton*	January 16, 1864	James H. Grey/Gray	February 12, 1864
Henry Baker	January 4, 1864	Thomas Hanson	January 11, 1864
Charles Baldwin	March 9, 1864	Robert Johnston	March 10, 1864
George C. Beck	January 23, 1864	William Koehler	February 23, 1864
William Bond	February 2, 1864	August Loschka	February 15, 1864
George Brown	February 29, 1864	George Lunn	January 16, 1864
John Bruckman	January 25, 1864	Albert Merrill	January 25, 1864
Isaac S. Chesbrough	February 8, 1864	Ormango Payne	January 4, 1864
Robert Collins*	January 3, 1864	John Powell	February 18, 1864
John Conners/Connoss*	January 3, 1864	William M. Ragan	January 5, 1864
Michael Dagle*	February 13, 1864	James Stone	January 5, 1864
Alex Drummond*	January 14, 1864	Gustave Stressman	February 2, 1864
Gilbert L. Dunton	January 2, 1864	Frederick W. Weigert	February 10, 1864
Dennis W. Eagan/Edgar	January 5, 1864	Peter Wilson	February 6, 1864
Charles O. Eames	February 25, 1864	Henry C. Wire	February 23, 1864

*Never reached the battery (Chicago Board of Trade Association roster, April 27, 1886, Trumbull Griffin file, Missouri History Museum.

The Beginning of The Atlanta Campaign—May 1864

When the Atlanta Campaign began in early May, it became one of the grandest campaigns of the war and would encompass four bloody months. The Board of Trade Battery distributed 30 days' rations on April 28 in preparation for the campaign and the battery also gave up one wagon to reduce its baggage. The next day half the rations were returned and the men were placed on "⅔ rations of crackers, ⅓ rations of salt meat, double of salt." On April 30, the battery headed east 21 miles to an unknown destination with Minty's and Miller's brigades. Long's brigade would move to the front independently after gaining new mounts and re-equipping in Nashville. Garrard pushed the two brigades forward the second day, outdistancing the 300-wagon division supply train by eight miles. From Benjamin Nourse's perspective, the division had moved too far the first day and the supply wagons were just too heavily loaded. Nourse realized what was unfolding and recorded in his diary, "We are bound for the front surely." The battery moved steadily ahead, travelling 19 miles on May 2, 26 miles the next day, 13 miles over the mountains the following day, and 23 miles on May 5. Most of the cavalry troops pushed ahead of the rest of the column, which reached Bridgeport after marching 19 miles. As the battery continued east, several railroad trains passed and the men observed one train with three cars filled with wounded and another filled with prisoners heading for Nashville. On May 7, the men drew ⅔ rations for the next six days and planned to move over the next set of mountains to Trenton, Chattanooga and then on to La Fayette which they reached on May 10, rejoining the bulk of the cavalry regiments. Here, the cavalry division reached the flank of Sherman's armies.[11]

The cavalry of the Army of the Cumberland and Major General George Stoneman's four brigades of cavalry of the Army of the Ohio were prepared for the campaign. These components of the Union cavalry now faced the cavalry of Joseph Johnston's Army of Tennessee under the command of Joseph Wheeler. Wheeler had three divisions plus two brigades of cavalry. To understand the role of the Chicago Board of Trade Battery in regard to the missions and its day-to-day orders, it is necessary to understand Sherman's attitude toward the cavalry and the cavalry commanders. In regard to the Army of the Cumberland's chief of cavalry Washington L. Elliott, Sherman simply ignored him, sparking Elliott to demand that orders to the cavalry come through him, a request Sherman chose to ignore. Sherman, commanding the armies in the west, by-passed an efficient and experienced commanding officer, choosing to give orders directly to the divisional commanders. In the case of the four divisions of the Army of the Cumberland, he dismissed the Fourth Division commander, Alvan Gillem, as commanding an unimportant, political force which was only suitable to guard the supply line in Tennessee. He saw Edward McCook and his First Division as an effective command. His favorite appeared to be his hand-picked division commander, H. Judson Kilpatrick. Kilpatrick was long known to be brash, impulsive and reckless, with the sobriquet, "Kill-Cavalry Kilpatrick." Kilpatrick's division was generally used in the campaign to secure newly occupied territory. Additionally, Sherman disrespected and disregarded Kenner Garrard as too reserved and unwilling to fight. George Thomas would counsel Sherman that Garrard was, in fact, his best divisional commander but Sherman chose to ignore this advice. As a result, Sherman would under-utilize his largest and best cavalry division, made up of brigades commanded by Minty, Long and Miller, considered by many as among the most exemplary cavalry commanders in the western theater. Finally, Sherman also had command of George Stoneman's Army of the Ohio cavalry and, despite Sherman's opinion that Stoneman allowed others to carry most of the load, he would allow him to make a dash for glory in the campaign, which would virtually destroy two cavalry divisions. Sherman commanded the Union forces in the west, but he still thought he should directly command cavalry divisions on a day-to-day basis. In regard to this history, the Board of Trade Battery would be assigned to Garrard's Second Division for the campaign and would be parceled out as sections to Minty's, Long's and Miller's brigades. In this campaign, the more notable service by the battery would occur at the Battle of Dallas, Battle of Noonday Creek, Battle of Atlanta and Kilpatrick's Raid.[12]

Sherman issued orders for the cavalry's initial advance on the Confederates at Dalton in Special Orders No. 35 on April 25. Stoneman commanded the Union cavalry for the Army of the Ohio which would operate on the left (east) flank of Sherman's forces, and Garrard was ordered to secure McPherson's Army of the Tennessee on the right flank since the Army of the Tennessee's cavalry was still in the Mississippi Valley. Then, Sherman ordered George Thomas to organize McCook's and Kilpatrick's cavalry divisions in the center of the advance. Garrard's Second Division was in the saddle with orders from Sherman to unite with McPherson's army on May 6 or 7 at La Fayette, Georgia. Kilpatrick's division was initially ordered to screen for Hooker's Twentieth Corps. Much to Sherman's unhappiness, both Garrard and Stoneman had not arrived as the campaign began.[13]

In regard to the infantry troops, Schofield's Army of the Ohio was on the left flank, Thomas' Army of the Cumberland in the lead in the center and McPherson's Army of the Tennessee was on the right flank. The campaign was designed to be coordinated with Grant's offensive in the east, but rain hampered Sherman's movements, and the tactical advance didn't start until May 7. With two great Union armies marching simultaneously to strike the "head" and the "heart" of the Confederacy, the Confederates would not be able to shift reinforcements from one location to the other. The first obstacle in the advance was Tunnel Hill through Chetoogeta Mountain, with a 1,400-foot railroad tunnel, about four miles south of Ringgold. Sherman ordered Thomas to capture Tunnel Hill while Schofield moved to Varnell's, about seven miles east of Ringgold. In a demonstration to mislead the Confederates, Schofield and Thomas would advance toward Dalton while the crux of Sherman's plan called for McPherson's Army of the Tennessee to march through Snake Creek Gap 13 miles south of Dalton. McPherson's advance on Resaca through this gap could cut Johnston's supply and escape route to the south. Sherman hoped for a quick fight and planned to flank Johnston from the south and west while he remained behind his strong defenses at Dalton and Rocky Face Ridge.[14]

By May 8, McPherson's army marched toward Snake Creek Gap, about 10 miles west of Resaca, but Garrard's Second Division, which Sherman planned to be working in conjunction, still had not arrived. Sherman urged Garrard to hurry to McPherson. In the meantime, McCook protected the left flank of Schofield's and Howard's infantry corps while Stoneman's cavalry also hurried forward from Kingston, Tennessee. Federal infantry reached the summit of Rocky Face Ridge and attacked the Confederate position from the north along the ridge. Hooker's Twentieth Corps also unsuccessfully attacked Dug Gap a few miles south of Buzzard's Roost while the Fourth and Fourteenth Corps infantry demonstrated along the ridge. But, the important line of march was McPherson's, who seized Snake Creek Gap by the end of the day, but McPherson had only limited reconnaissance ability as he moved toward Resaca with only the 9th Illinois Mounted Infantry screening his advance. Because Garrard's cavalry lagged behind, Sherman ordered Kilpatrick's Third Cavalry Division, which had been screening Hooker's corps, to McPherson's army. Sherman wrote, "Write to General Garrard at all events to keep up with infantry." Garrard, who had been reorganizing in central Tennessee, was not intentionally lagging. He was initially delayed with rain and mud, but since reaching Bridgeport, he was moving as quickly as possible under the direction of Sherman's appointed guide, John Corse.[15]

Thomas and Schofield pressed the enemy on May 9 trying to keep Johnston's attention at Rocky Face Ridge and Buzzard's Roost while McPherson's Army of the Tennessee marched with orders to destroy the Western & Atlantic Railroad at Resaca. Kilpatrick happily worked with McPherson by scouting to the south and east of McPherson's advance and reported no surprises. In response, the Confederates rallied their forces to deal with this surprise arrival of Union troops. At the end of the day, Garrard was still lagging at LaFayette, about 10 miles to the west of Snake Creek Gap and because he had hurried forward, he asked for permission to wait for his forage train to rest and feed his fatigued mounts. But Garrard's desire to rest his horses was not the message Sherman wanted to hear, and this began a conflict which would last for the entire campaign. On the eastern flank, McCook's division, which screened that flank because of Stoneman's delayed arrival, clashed with the enemy in a heated fight.[16]

The next day, May 10, McPherson advanced to within sight of Resaca, but he was unable to reach the railroad. Sherman held Schofield and Howard in their current position and moved the remainder of his troops to support McPherson. Sherman was close to achieving his objective of cutting Johnston from a direct southerly route to Atlanta. He saw an opportunity and exclaimed that the defenses at Dalton would do Johnston no good if the Union army was at Resaca. In regard to the cavalry, Stoneman and Garrard still had not arrived and the five-day delay in these two divisions reaching Sherman's infantry reinforced many of his negative opinions about the cavalry. Sherman gave his opinion of the cavalry in a message to Schofield on May 10: "I am mistrustful of cavalry; it moves so slow." Stoneman, who had a tarnished reputation based on actions at Chancellorsville, missed much of Sherman's scorn. Sherman focused on Garrard and ordered Thomas to demand that Garrard's division "proceed without delay" to McPherson's army. Sherman openly revealed his impressions of Garrard to McPherson: "Garrard has moved so slow that I doubt if he has the dash we need in a cavalry officer." Revealing the problem of Sherman's micromanagement of the cavalry, Garrard, who had just moved 200 miles, responded that McPherson had ordered him on May 9 to remain in LaFayette, and he had not been idle while there. He replied that he had a brigade scouting toward Rome and was awaiting its return. As a result, he was forced to remain in place for the rest of the day, and vowed to ride to McPherson as soon as possible. Garrard's division finally arrived and was present for duty on May 12, as was Stoneman's. Garrard ordered his troopers to push toward Rome to challenge the concentration of Confederates there. Meanwhile, Elliott unhappily sat at cavalry headquarters as Sherman directed the cavalry as he needed.[17]

Total Present for Duty—Army of the Cumberland and Army of the Ohio (Cavalry + Artillery)[18]

	April 30	May 31	June 30	July 31	Aug 31
Garrard's cavalry division	4,798	5,155	4,352	3,992	3,184
McCook's cavalry division	2,426	2,804	2,408	1,817	1,928
Kilpatrick's cavalry division	1,759	1,887	2,717	2,618	2,526
Stoneman's cavalry division*	2,951	2,891	Incomplete[†]	1,899	1,936
Total (Sherman's Records)[‡]	12,455	12,908	12,039	10,517	9,394

*Army of the Ohio.

[†]Records are incomplete. Records show only 128 officers and no men present for duty.

[‡]There is no explanation for the differences in Sherman's total and the cavalry division total. Sherman's total may include cavalry with the Army of the Tennessee, or detached cavalry, e.g., 15th Pennsylvania Cavalry.

The Second Cavalry Division Goes to Rome and the Battle of Resaca

While McCook's division contended with the enemy on the Union left flank, Sherman directed Garrard to send his two brigades southward toward Rome to challenge the enemy there and to find a way across the Oostanaula River. Sherman, who did not think that Johnston would stay and fight at Resaca, wrote to Garrard, "Do this in your own way, but do it thoroughly and well. I will commence crossing McPherson about Lay's Ferry near the mouth of Snake Creek today; he will move on the Rome road; communicate with him but do not wait for him. If it be impossible to cross the Oostanaula with even a raiding force, then threaten Rome, and the Coosa below Rome … the less wheels you have, the better; but I leave it to you—only act with the utmost possible energy and celerity." Sherman believed Johnston was retreating. Garrard pushed his division to Rome with Minty's First Brigade in the lead.[19]

The Board of Trade Battery reached Villanow, Georgia, on May 11 (about 10 miles east of LaFayette, 30 miles north of Rome and 15 miles northwest of Resaca). The battery moved quickly over good sandy roads. Private Silas Stevens described the pleasant march "amid the jangling of the sabre, the clink of the horse's shoes, the champing of the bit, the tinkle of the chains attached to the rowel of the spur, and the frequent bugle blast." The next day, the battery remained stationary as infantry corps marched past and the artillerymen watched as Sherman and Thomas rode south with their staffs. On May 14, the battery again began moving, this time to Rome. The first section went forward with Minty's brigade and the rest of the battery began moving a couple of hours later. The two trailing sections headed to Snake Creek Gap under the command of Lieutenant Trumbull Griffin. Minty's advance covered 24 miles before it reached Armuchee Creek. Minty stopped for the night without a sound so that the enemy would not be alerted. The next morning (May 15), Garrard took one gun with the mounted infantry while a second Parrott accompanied Minty as he drove the enemy from the bridge over the creek. Minty understood his orders to make a demonstration in front of Rome while Garrard with the mounted infantry would attempt to cross the Oostanaula River. Minty clashed with the enemy in a strong position at Farmer's Bridge, which spanned the Armuchee Creek. The capture of the bridge allowed Minty to drive the 12th Alabama Cavalry to the heavily fortified city. The gun of the Board of Trade exchanged fire with the enemy along with Minty's troopers which forced the withdrawal. Minty pushed the enemy to within two miles of Rome, where he "found Jackson's division of cavalry in position supported by a division of infantry. A sharp fire was opened on me by their artillery." Realizing his brigade was not strong enough to challenge the enemy behind fortifications, Minty returned to Farmer's Bridge where he discovered that Garrard had been unable to find a crossing over the river. Nourse described, "Drove the rebel pickets off the bridge. Killing a capt. and 13 men, wounding a lieut. and taking 12 men in out of the cold. We had 3 men of the 4th Mich. Cav. wounded—We drove the rebels up to town and into their rifle pits—then by orders we fell back—The Genl. would not allow us to fire a gun. Bishop Polk's reserve corp of Johnston's Army was there having in position 28 pieces of artillery—The 2nd brigade [mounted infantry] lay in the road to the left of the lane Col. Minty went in on, so as to prevent the rebs from flanking Col. Minty's column. At 3 oc. we fell back." An unclear message to Sherman led him to believe that Farmer's Bridge crossed the Oostanaula River but it only crossed a tributary. Sherman sent Jefferson C. Davis' division to Rome to cross the river, but when he arrived, he also found no way across the formidable river. Garrard and Minty scouted the river for several miles and found no suitable fords or bridges.[20]

With Garrard at Rome, the Battle of Resaca was fought over two bloody days, May 14–15. On May 15, the fighting continued along the Union and Confederate lines and at nightfall the casualties of the two armies were relatively equal; Sherman reported 2,747 and Johnston 2,800 losses at the two-day battle. During the night of May 15, Johnston withdrew and marched for Adairsville. After the previous day's battle, the Union soldiers were surprised on the morning of May 16 to find Johnston gone. In the meantime, the Board of Trade Battery planned to move ahead on May 16, only to be told to unharness because the Union armies in pursuit of the enemy clogged the roads. It did not move until the afternoon and then only marched 10 miles. When camped, the men fed and watered the horses and were greeted with supply wagons. Unfortunately, the wagons only brought feed for the animals and no rations for the men. Wilder's brigade shared some pork with the artillerists, "but no crackers, coffee or sugar. This is rough I tell you," wrote John Nourse. The battery again moved forward at 6:00 p.m. and crossed the river over a pontoon bridge. The battery rode into the night and finally stopped at 3 a.m. As the men finally tried to sleep, two long wagon trains rumbled past their camp, disturbing the sleep again. While the battery advanced, Davis' division at Rome remained outside the town until the Confederates chose to withdraw after the Battle of Resaca.[21]

On to the Etowah River

On May 16, Sherman wired Henry Halleck in Washington that Resaca was in Union hands and that Johnston's army was retreating toward the Etowah River. He explained that Garrard, who commanded two elite brigades (Minty's and Wilder's) and Stoneman's cavalry divisions were pushing ahead attempting to cut off Johnston's retreat. Facing the Union advance was Wheeler's cavalry contesting the pursuit and giving Johnston time to find his next place to make a stand. Edward McCook's and Eli Murray's (commanding Kilpatrick's division due to his wounding on May 13) cavalry divisions marched in front of Sherman's columns developing the route of the Confederate retreat.[22]

The Union infantry marched south through and around Calhoun and then toward Adairsville, about 15 miles south of Resaca. General Joseph Johnston decided to make his next stand at Adairsville, but found the valley where he planned to fight too wide to defend against the large number of Union troops. So, again the march proceeded southward toward Cartersville. Johnston, after consulting with his commanders, decided to march to Cassville, about 10 miles north of the Etowah River, by two roads: one via Kingston and the other directly over the Gravelly Plateau. He hoped to induce the Union armies to also divide and march down the each of the roads. He also wanted to make Sherman believe the majority of his army was entrenched at Kingston so that he could strike the Union column marching down the Cassville Road and destroy it before the other column marching via Kingston came to its aid. As Johnston had hoped, Sherman hurried his three armies forward. He ordered Stoneman and Garrard to cut the railroads to the east and west of Kingston, limiting Johnston's route of retreat and source of supplies and reinforcements; but he sacrificed the important intelligence gathering role of the cavalry.[23]

Minty's cavalry brigade rode toward Kingston on May 17 and the 4th Michigan Cavalry successfully drove the Confederate pickets back to the main line. While following

Sherman's orders to aggressively push the enemy, Minty's troopers fought to within a mile of Kingston, but the aggressiveness came with a price. The next day, Minty continued to drive forward without good intelligence about the position of Johnston's army. The top Federal officers believed that the enemy was in a general withdrawal. Minty followed Garrard's orders and he explained, "General Garrard ordered one battalion Fourth Michigan to move down the Kingston road, and as the enemy was in full retreat, to charge whatever they found." The 4th Michigan found the enemy and drove them two miles until they ran into a line of infantry. The Confederates were firmly in place behind barricades with cavalry support. The infantry unleashed a vicious volley. When Minty's attack was stopped by the Confederate defenses, Ferguson's Confederate cavalry brigade attacked on both flanks, surrounding the 4th Michigan, but the Federals used their sabers to cut their way out, but not before having 13 officers and men killed or mortally wounded, and another eighteen wounded.[24]

The advance to Kingston introduced the men of the Board of Trade Battery to a new level of the war. Benjamin Nourse recorded the impact of the war on civilians on May 17: "The brick house at the river is smashed to pieces by shot and shell that have passed through it. The old man had his head blown off in his own door yard as he was fighting our troops. His son was killed and the old lady's leg was broken by a shell as she was standing at the window shouting on the rebs by waving a white handkerchief." Nourse also described Ferguson's attack on the 4th Michigan: "One battalion of the 4th Mich went down the road towards Rome and captured some prisoners, bringing them back. Five companies of the 17th Ind. went out and cut the Rail Road between Rome and Kingston—Two battalions of the 4th Mich. went to cut the main road but did not succeed. They went within one mile of Kingston but were surrounded and had to cut their way out. They retreated to us (4 miles) on the gallop when Wilder's brigade stopped the rebel advance and they fell back—We lost 34 killed, wounded, and missing. The col. of the 2nd Ga. Cav., commanding a brigade was killed—The Genl. would not let us fire a gun." On a positive note, Miller's mounted infantry successfully carried out Sherman's orders and destroyed the railroad leading to and from Rome on the western flank.[25]

A few miles away at Cassville, Johnston hoped to attack part of Sherman's large force—Howard's Fourth Corps, Hooker's Twentieth Corps and the Twenty-third Corps marching toward Cassville. He also hoped McPherson's two corps and Thomas's Fourteenth Corps were still marching toward Kingston. Johnston had assembled more than 70,000 troops, Hood's, Hardee's, Polk's, and Wheeler's corps, as he prepared to crush Sherman's left flank. Johnston placed Polk's corps north of Cassville with Hood's corps to Polk's right. The plan called for the Federal advance to encounter Polk, and then Hood would attack the flank. After Hood moved into position, he was surprised by reports of Union troops behind him. It was part of McCook's First Division followed by Stoneman's cavalry that generated the alarm. Several thousand Union cavalrymen converging on Hood's exposed flank caused him to postpone his attack. McCook and Stoneman, through this serendipitous encounter, saved many lives at Cassville. The Union cavalry happened on the scene because they were following orders to destroy the railroad between Cass Station and the Etowah River. Reacting to reports that cavalry was in his rear, Hood moved his corps to address this threat and thereby ruined the chance to launch a flank attack on Union infantry approaching the town from the north. Hood's failure to spring the trap caused Johnston to pull the Confederate line—including Hardee's Corps—onto the hills east and south of Cassville. Johnston extended his army along a three-mile front with

Hood on the right, Polk in the center, and Hardee on the left. During the evening, Polk and Hood convinced Johnston of the vulnerability of the Confederate position and Johnston decided to withdraw again.[26]

While the lines of infantry faced each other, Minty's cavalry brigade and a section of guns rode hard for Gillem's Bridge over the Etowah River on May 19. Minty galloped the last five miles to the bridge at the cost of 300 horses being rendered unsuitable for further duty. Realizing the value the bridge held in the pursuit of Johnston, Minty built barricades and breastworks and held the bridge until Eli Murray's Third Cavalry Division moved forward to take over as guards. A section of the Board of Trade Battery was unlimbered and covered the approaches to the bridge. The trailing two sections reached Minty's command and unified the battery. Nourse wrote that Confederates advanced on the bridge but found it too well guarded and broke off the attack. On May 19, Nourse wrote: "We went to Kingston and from there we went on the gallop 4 miles to the river crossing at Etowah bridge before the rebels could set fire to it. We went into position in the front yard of a very fine place, right in the bank of the river. We were well supported by the 'seven shooters' of Wilder's boys—Rebel Genl. Forrest's command were cut off in the bend of the river. They advanced their skirmishers to see if they could cross the bridge, but finding the bridge too well guarded, they drew off and attacked Hooker's left, turning it so as to permit them to cross the river below us and get away—we did want to have a real good fight today—were just in the mood for it—the boys sleep in the ditch." Of course, Forrest was not present for this campaign, but he would be mentioned in more than one account.[27]

If Sherman had issues with Garrard's energy, he should have been pleased with the action over the past two days. The Federal cavalry on the right flank had driven into Kingston with exuberance resulting in the loss of 30 men, Miller's brigade had successfully cut the railroad to the west and Minty had captured the bridge over the Etowah River which would make the crossing a quick and easy endeavor. In all, Garrard captured two bridges and two fords over the Etowah River, and these would be used by Sherman's armies. The cost was men and horses. The loss of 300 horses reflected a serious problem for the campaign. Louis Watkins' cavalry brigade was already dismounted because there were not enough horses. Now, in the early part of the campaign large numbers of horses were becoming unserviceable due to Sherman's order not to spare the horseflesh. Major William Jennings, 7th Pennsylvania Cavalry, recorded many of the horses actually starved to death in May. On May 22, the officers of various regiments reported that 76 horses died of starvation due to daily movements and inability to find forage. From May 26 through June 2, another 134 were lost in one battalion, 101 of this number was due to starvation. The same situation occurred throughout the corps. While soldiers and troopers were lost, so the horses were lost to attrition. Colonel Joseph Dorr, commanding the First Brigade, reported the horses died by the hundreds, generally through starvation, and they were not being replaced fast enough. McCook echoed the other messages when he reported horses dying on duty, writing to Elliott, "five from one company dropped on picket this morning, totally exhausted for want of something to eat." This was just the first three weeks of what would be a four-month campaign. There were not enough horses to replace those lost and this loss greatly reduced the effectiveness of the cavalry later in the campaign. The Board of Trade Battery lost 11 horses in May due to a variety of reasons—scours, overwork, lameness, sore backs, disease, and two killed-in-action.[28]

After reaching the Etowah River, Sherman gave his men a respite. The three days' rest was important for the Board of Trade Battery and allowed the men and horses time to regain the energy needed to continue the campaign. Meanwhile, more changes occurred with the personnel during this lull. Nourse wrote: "Wm. B. Gale and Fred. A. Chapman have received their commission as Lieuts. in the 26th Infantry (colored). They left for Chicago, Illinois. Hector H. Akin's appointment as Capt. in the same regiment was read to us last night. Thos. Tinsley has left for this regiment this morning, Lieut. in the 102nd N.Y. Vol Infantry. Our train and forge with Durand and Knight went back to Kingston— At dress parade Lester & Alcott were made corporals.... My team is in good order ready for another scout or even a raid."[29]

The "Hell Hole"—New Hope Church, Pickett's Mill, Dallas

On May 23, Sherman began the next phase of the campaign as his armies crossed the Etowah River. Sherman expected Johnston to move his army to Allatoona, a formidable geographic obstacle. Several years earlier Sherman had participated in an army survey of the area and he concluded he would not try to assault Johnston at this location. Instead, he decided to advance on Dallas about 15 miles south of the Etowah River and west of Allatoona. Next, Sherman planned to advance on Marietta, 15 miles east of Dallas. By maneuvering around the Allatoona Mountains, he would swing east and cut Johnston off from Atlanta, just as he had planned at Resaca. Meanwhile, Sherman ordered Major General Francis Blair's Seventeenth Corps, accompanied by Colonel Eli Long's cavalry brigade, to the front from their duty in Alabama and Tennessee. When Sherman crossed the Etowah River, Colonel William Lowe, now commanding the Third Cavalry Division, remained in Kingston to protect the Union supply line and to hold the various fords and bridges across the river. The Union cavalry would move toward Dallas with three cavalry divisions—Stoneman on the left, McCook in the center, and Garrard on the right. Johnston countered Sherman's advance by marching two-thirds of his army, Hardee and Polk, to Dallas while he initially retained Hood at Allatoona.[30]

McCook moved forward to cover the advance of Hooker's Twentieth Corps as it demonstrated toward Allatoona while Garrard rode west and south of Dallas, reconnoitering the town. Captain Heber Thompson, 7th Pennsylvania Cavalry, recorded the Confederate cavalry resisted their reconnaissance: "Rebs came up handsomely several times and each time driven back." Garrard found working with McPherson a good experience, but pushing the enemy toward Dallas a difficult one. The relationship between McPherson and Garrard was seen as a positive sign by the men of the battery who also liked McPherson. Silas Stevens described a visit by the general to Garrard: "He was excellently mounted on a coal black horse, and accompanied by a single aide, he presented a beautiful picture of health and haughtiness."[31]

The advance to Dallas resulted in skirmishing throughout the day. On May 24, the third section of the Board of Trade Battery began a 19 mile trek with Minty's brigade. Wilder's Mounted Infantry Brigade and the other two sections of guns followed discretely behind. Minty's column stopped about three miles northwest of Dallas when it ran into an advanced picket near a small stream. The battery went into action, shelling the line of Confederates which headed to the rear. The section fired 44 rounds in this skirmish. Four men were wounded in Minty's brigade but the Federals captured thirty of the enemy. Two of the prisoners were from Lee's Army of Northern Virginia and the men, though only eight miles from home, were on furlough; now they were prisoners and would be sent north to a prison camp. The next day (May 25) began with reveille at 3:00 a.m., and the rain which fell at dusk the day before made the morning pleasant and the road less dusty. By 8:00 the battery had marched eight miles, halting in an orchard. The sound of heavy guns echoed throughout the morning. The hopes of having an early camp in a pleasant orchard were short-lived when the bugler sounded "Mount." To make the day more unpleasant, the skies opened with a downpour so heavy the men riding the horses could not see the animal's heads. The battery moved two miles and fell into line with the rest of Minty's men.[32]

Meanwhile, the actions around McPherson's flank took place in what was to be known as the "hell hole" or the "Dallas Line." This was a rough area in the Georgia countryside where several bloody fights occurred. Private Silas Stevens described the area as one with "bad roads and the country rough and hilly." First Sergeant John Bennett, 4th Michigan Cavalry, noted the impact of the war on the local civilians. He wrote to his wife the sadness he saw among the local citizens. "Whenever we have a fight, we can see women & children cowering nearby scared to death, praying to God to protect them & holding up both hands to us not to hurt them. Little children crying with fear & hunger. This, you know, is hard, even to the wicked. There is thousands of women & children crying for bread…. I really believe they will die of hunger…. May God help them for man will not."[33]

On the morning of May 25, three Confederate corps moved to establish a line east of Dallas; Hood's Corps arrived as Hardee marched toward Dallas and Polk trailed behind. Hood covered the line near New Hope Church, about two miles northeast of Dallas. That afternoon Joseph Hooker's Twentieth Corps advanced and a bloody fight erupted between Hood and Hooker's troops which ended with Hooker withdrawing after suffering about 1,600 casualties. The men of the Board of Trade Battery knew that Hooker was to their left and Private Silas Stevens was riding in the rear on the day of the Battle of New Hope Church. Stevens recalled, "I saw enough of the wounded carried away from the front, by wagon, and ambulance train, to satisfy one's curiosity in that direction." The next day, Edward McCook's cavalry clashed with the enemy at Burnt Church and claimed 80 of the enemy killed and another 52 prisoners.[34]

Resistance stiffened as McPherson pushed to Dallas. Oliver Howard (who would write the after-action report of the Army of the Tennessee) recorded that the Fifteenth and Sixteenth Corps marched through Dallas on May 26. The Federals met the Confederate advanced screen with which Garrard quickly dealt. Garrard, leading the advance, found the enemy on the west side of the town and drove them two miles beyond Dallas until he found a strong line of Confederate forces. McPherson moved his infantry ahead and fell into line with the Fifteenth Corps on the right and Sixteenth Corps on the left. Garrard's cavalry secured McPherson's right flank by extending to the south and west where it fought the Confederate cavalry the next couple of days. Silas Stevens explained that the cavalry extended the right flank and "threw up a rude form of fortification, when the ground was available, and threw out their line of skirmishers, protecting them by rail fences, logs, and dirt dug from the trenches." Tobias Miller recorded in his diary that the "cavalry have been engaged a number of times with slight loss on either side."[35]

May 26–27—Dallas, Georgia

Garrard's division approached the Confederate line some six miles ahead of McPherson. Screening the infantry movements, Garrard advanced directly on Dallas, fighting

Bate's infantry division and the Southern cavalry. He found that Hardee's full corps was also reported moving in the direction of the town. Then, he dismounted and put the cavalry into position along Pumpkin Vine Creek until Fifteenth Corps arrived the next day. Minty's brigade had a sharp skirmish with Ferguson's cavalry brigade, but the 4th Michigan and 7th Pennsylvania charged and drove the enemy three miles. The 4th U.S. Cavalry on special duty with General McPherson missed the action.[36]

The next day a great deal of skirmishing with heavy artillery exchanges occurred in front of Fourth and Sixteenth Corps, resulting in a halt in the infantry advance. The enemy troops attacked the Federal infantry but were repulsed in these probing actions. The most substantial cavalry actions occurred on May 27 with Minty and Miller being engaged in heavy fighting. Having moved about two miles to the rear of Confederate forces on the west flank the night before, Minty's primary action occurred when he moved the 4th Michigan toward the enemy, using the 72nd Indiana and 7th Pennsylvania to hold a strong defensive line. Minty's brigade found the flank of Ferguson's and Armstrong's cavalry line and moved past it, attacking the rear with both artillery and carbines. He advanced with the 4th Michigan and a section of guns into the rear of the enemy and shelled their works. The Confederate forces responded and advanced in force against Minty's command, making repeated attacks while being repulsed by the three regiments and artillery. Garrard proudly wrote that McPherson acknowledged that the cavalry "rendered much service to the Army of the Tennessee" by drawing four infantry regiments from the main battle line to deal with Minty's attack.[37]

The day began for the artillerists of the Board of Trade Battery at 4:30 a.m. and Benjamin Nourse mused, "The morning opened splendidly, but who can tell what will be done before its close?" (Nourse's account described a section of artillery which had not moved with Minty around the flank of the enemy.) The skirmishing began only 30 minutes later. Off to the left the sounds of a serious artillery duel echoed across the countryside. The fighting to the front intensified. The men of the battery drew six days rations and left the horses unharnessed. The respite ended at 10:45 when the orders to mount rang out and the battery moved forward two miles at noon. Unlimbering, the men waited for an attack for about an hour and the artillerymen were not disappointed. The attack came amid an explosion of gunfire and the battery went to work shelling the attacking line. The section threw 67 rounds into Confederate cavalry, but the enemy succeeded in moving past the Union flank, forcing the battery to fall back. Re-positioning, the Board of Trade Battery fell under fire from a single Confederate gun positioned on top of a hill in the front. Nourse explained the gun had been strategically placed. "Said gun was too high up for us to bring our gun to bear on it and a creek at the foot of the hill, with very steep sides, prevented our cavalry from charging them. Their first shell was in range and fell short—the second fell to our left in the woods—the third killed two horses belonging to King & Harvey and only a few feet from me—the fourth shell struck our gun and the limber but did not explode—This was the closest call I have yet had—Will Taylor's wheel horses came nigh down on their knees from fear as the shell passed them." Being at a disadvantageous position, the battery again withdrew to a position near a cotton gin where the fighting ceased. An anonymous account from one of the members of the battery also described the encounter with the enemy guns. "No one was hurt on our side—except two horses killed—although we were pretty badly startled by running into a masked battery one day, posted almost over our heads on a high steep bluff, which gave us a rapid plunging fire, and struck in the midst and all around us, tearing up the ground and 'throwing dust in our eyes.' To use a Southernism, we 'lit eout' lively. A 12-pound solid went so close to my ear, that it roared for six hours afterwards." John Fleming explained the section had been in a pretty "hot place" and that two horses were "turned inside out."[38]

Elsewhere on May 27, the bloody fight at Pickett's Mill occurred about three miles east of New Hope Church, when Oliver Howard was ordered to assault the Confederate position. The terrain was so densely wooded it was difficult to maneuver and observe the enemy. As Howard attacked, he did so in a piecemeal fashion. When each brigade ran into resistance, others moved to the left to try and turn the flank. Cleburne responded each time with his own moves to his right. The Union loss in the disastrous attack totaled 1,600 men in Brigadier General William Hazen's, Colonel William Gibson's and Colonel Frederick Knefler's brigades. Cleburne recorded about 500 casualties among his defenders.

May 28—Dallas, Georgia

Accounts from two different sections have been preserved for the battery's actions on May 28. The first is Benjamin Nourse's diary entry. "Up this morning at daylight and at 6 oc. we started for Dallas, Ga. The horses stood harnessed all night. This makes us 60 hours on picket without being relieved. Moved two miles and stood with 3rd section in the road until 5 oc. when were ordered to unharness, which we did and got water for our coffee & the order came to 'hitch up'—So we lost our supper. We moved 3 miles and stood in the wood until 11 oc. p. m. Then we moved into Dallas—took off the harness from the horses and lay down at 12 ½ to sleep. The center section had been in line with Wilder's brigade all day (filling up a gap in the line left open by the non-arrival of some infantry troops). Lieut. Robinson was with them. They were behind rails so they were out of harm's way—very hot all day." While Nourse was unengaged on May 28, Private Tobias Miller recorded the action with his section which was most likely attached to Wilder's mounted infantry brigade. "Were called at 2 a.m. & moved to the line of battle at 10 a.m. A breastwork was constructed for the section & we took position at 12 M. The skirmishers were soon engaged & at 4 p.m. a general attack was made by the enemy. The section was under heavy fire by both musket & artillery for an hour. No damage done to us & the enemy handsomely repulsed." The enemy made repeated attempts to take this location but each was repulsed.[39]

Johnston took two important actions during the day on May 27. First, he sent Hood to attempt to flank the Federal left, but Hood did not attack when he found he faced a strongly entrenched position. Next, Johnston sent two cavalry brigades and Major General William Bate's and Major General W.H.T. Walker's infantry divisions to develop McPherson's position along the Union right flank on May 28. In what was to be called the Battle of Dallas, Hardee pushed forward but was unsuccessful in a bloody fight with estimated losses of 2,400 for the Union forces and 3,000 for the Confederates. All of William Jackson's Confederate cavalry division was involved in this attack. Armstrong and Ross attacked, with the latter taking the Union line in the flank. Ferguson's brigade moved into the rear where it fought Wilder's mounted infantry brigade which played a significant role in repulsing the attack. Private Silas Stevens recalled that the men heard the Confederates say they "intended to clean out the regiment of Black Soldiers in their front. They came on in a desperate charge with a rebel yell toward our breastworks…." The attacking line met Miller's mounted infantry brigade waiting with Spencer carbines which exploded in a single roar. The charge melted away as the attack failed.[40]

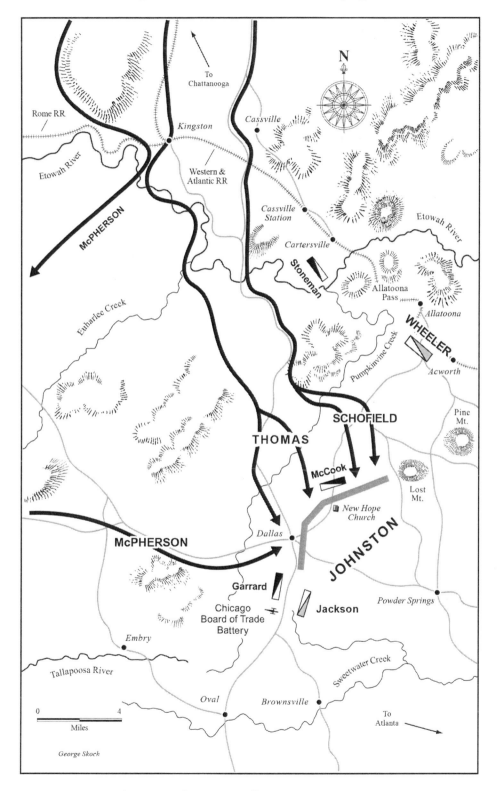

The Union advance on Dallas, Georgia, May 1863.

The last two days of the month were pretty uneventful. On May 29, Nourse recorded in his diary: "[T]he cannoneers went for wheat, green wheat, which they pulled by the roots. As we have no corn or oats for the poor brutes. We stood unharnessed until 6 oc. p. m. then moved 2 miles and waited for the army ammunition train to pass over Pumpkinvine Creek. At 10 oclock we have permission to camp just where we were and quickly improved the opportunity. We might have been asleep one hour ago. Just as well as not. At 12 oclock Lieut. Robinson sent back word to us to unharness and we roused long enough to then lay down again and were undisturbed until morning—No thanks to Griffin or Bennett for it either. It seems as if these fellows tried to make the men as uncomfortable as possible—a sorry Sabbath for us." Tobias Miller's diary agreed with Nourse's assessment of the situation on May 29. Miller's section fell back from the main line and provided security for the wagon train. His guns were quiet throughout the day, but he had time to consider the situation with the animals. The universal concern within the Second Cavalry Division, including the battery, was the condition of the horses. "This is the second day our horses have been without food & there is no prospect saving them from starvation. During ten-mile march at least 200 cav. horses gave out." An anonymous letter appeared in the *Chicago Tribune* dated May 30 from a member of the battery and the account matched Miller's. In part, the letter read: "I am all right and the battery is in good shape. The army has been fighting hard for the last few days, without driving the enemy from his position.... The army has full rations, but our horses have had no grain for three days, nor do I know when they will get any more."[41]

Johnston successfully stopped Sherman's advance near Dallas when he moved his army from Allatoona and formed an arc in front of Sherman. Sherman needed to find a way around this Confederate line, and concluded if the Confederate army was at Dallas, then Allatoona was undefended. Sherman initially wanted to bring Major General Frank Blair's Seventeenth Corps to Rome and then onto Allatoona to seize this important location. On May 31, Blair's infantry and Long's cavalry still lagged several days behind, so Sherman ordered Garrard's division to ride to Allatoona and capture the pass. Sherman told Garrard if he found the enemy along the way to ride over them and seize the pass. Sherman stressed the importance of the mission, "[A]ct boldly and promptly; the success of our movement depends on our having Allatoona Pass." Sherman also sent George Stoneman's division to Allatoona Pass while Edward McCook engaged the enemy in a diversion in his front. Stoneman claimed one end of the pass and Garrard the other. Importantly, at Allatoona was the railroad that Sherman needed.[42]

June 1–15

Sherman now called for his armies to perform a tricky maneuver of extricating McPherson's troops from the enemy he faced, and performing an eastward movement. McPherson moved the Army of the Tennessee from Dallas to New Hope Church by June 2 as both Thomas and Schofield shifted to the east. The shift of the Union Army toward the east continued through June 4, and Johnston moved his army to Lost Mountain, about six miles southeast, to meet the redeployment of Sherman's armies. The new Confederate line, 10 miles long, stretched from Lost Mountain to Brushy Mountain. As the two armies re-positioned Sherman expected Johnston would next fight at Kennesaw Mountain and he was determined to not make any frontal assaults on entrenched Confederate lines.

Sherman's armies were positioned to march in a more southerly direction with Allatoona and the railroad in the rear, but he paused again. He wanted the bridge over the Etowah River to be rebuilt to carry supplies and he wanted Blair's infantry and Eli Long's cavalry ready for the action before he marched again. Long's cavalry brigade arrived on June 6 ready to join the advance.[43]

On June 10, Sherman pushed forward. With the shifts in Sherman's infantry, Garrard rode on the left flank of the army with McPherson, and Stoneman covered the right flank with Schofield's Army of the Ohio. Thomas' Army of the Cumberland advanced in the center and Edward McCook protected the rear of the column. Just as Sherman's advance began on June 10, he sent Garrard a message urging his increased aggressiveness. Sherman had just received a message that his supply line had been attacked near Calhoun. Sherman asked if the enemy could make such progress, why his cavalry could not do the same, but the threats to McPherson's flanks kept Garrard posted on duty near the infantry. By June 11, the Union armies converged on a line of defenses and fell into line about 500 yards from the base of Brushy Mountain, Pine Mountain and Lost Mountain. Sherman's advance was blocked when he found Johnston's army behind firm entrenchments. Garrard's troopers covered 10 miles from north of the Etowah River to the flank of the army. On June 14, Garrard was ordered to try to establish a foothold on the ridge between Brushy Mountain and Kennesaw Mountain and McCook and Stoneman were ordered to reconnoiter Lost Mountain to do the same. Sherman probed the center at Gilgal Church and Lattimer's Farm while he used the cavalry to turn the Confederate line at Lost Mountain, causing Johnston to swing part of his line back to Mud Creek. The Confederate defenders at Lost Mountain were still too strong for the cavalry on the Union right and repulsed the attempt to claim the mountain. By June 17, Johnston had again withdrawn and McCook and Stoneman claimed Lost Mountain.[44]

Board of Trade Horse Artillery

On June 1, the Board of Trade Battery began to move with McPherson's army. The battery withdrew six miles, extracting itself from contact with the enemy troops and found some fields of oats on which their horses could feed. They saw the effects of over-working the cavalry horses along the way. Benjamin Nourse wrote: "The cavalry horses drop down in the road by the dozen. They have been without corn longer than we have. The men who are there dismounted leave saddle and equipments just where their horses fall, taking with them only their carbines and one blanket. Sometimes also their saber." The next day (June 2), the artillerymen were up at 2:00 a.m. and again fed the horses on green oats. The battery moved 14 miles to the railroad over the Etowah Bridge and went into camp. Fortunately, the foraging expeditions resulted in finding corn to feed to "our hungry brutes. It was nice clean corn and you can bet the horses ate lively. 7 days without a single feed of good corn. The rear guard of Johnston's Rebel Army burnt the railroad, pike and pontoon bridges a week ago yesterday (Wednesday)." On June 3, the battery remained stationary and reconditioned the horses. The battery remained in position, providing security for the construction of the bridges over the Etowah River for the next few days.[45]

Private John Fleming wrote to his sister on June 4 from near Cartersville. He apologized for not writing more often since the beginning of the campaign, explaining that the battery had been "marching, day and night, fighting frequently, and in short, we have seen pretty rough service during the campaign." He told his sister that the battery had been in six or seven fights so far and that they had been lucky because none of the men had been killed or seriously wounded.[46]

The fields in the area were planted with oats, rye and wheat, all still green; but very little corn was seen. The horses still had little feed as did the men until the railroad began running again. On June 5, Nourse observed, "The rail road bridge is progressing fast. The train from the north last night brought 300 men and some timber. There are already 3 trestles up. Our rations are short indeed—4 small crackers for 5 days. We robbed the horses of a bag of corn and took it to mill and made cornmeal." The battery camped on the south side of the Etowah River near the burned High Tower Bridge which was being re-built. Sherman remained stationary and Garrard headquartered at Cartersville. The men gained the rest they needed this first week in June and welcoming the men to the south was a turn of hot weather. Nourse noted on June 6, "Hot! Hot!! Hot!!!" and the next day, he wrote, "It is so hot that it had to rain this p.m. to cool the atmosphere." Despite the hot weather, a glorious site greeted the men when the division quartermasters arrived with wagons loaded with provisions. The men increased their rations to full amounts for seven days, although they were still on two-thirds rations of salt pork. Equally pleasant to see were sacks of corn for the animals. The men were also greeted with Blair's fresh Seventeenth Army Corps heading for the front on 10 trains.[47]

The battery was on the move again on June 8 and marched 17 miles through a day of rain. It moved as far as Acworth, a railroad town 10 miles north of Kennesaw Mountain. The battery split duty, with the first two sections moving with Minty's brigade and the third section rode with the mounted infantry brigade. Because Seventeenth Corps marched down the main road, the cavalry traveled on the flanks. Minty moved down the western side of the road and Abram Miller's brigade covered the east. The battery passed through Acworth, passing the Fifteenth and Sixteenth Corps along the way, and the men were surprised that the town had not been burned. The next day (June 9), the third section went to Big Shanty, a railroad station five miles north of Marietta. Big Shanty was so named because it was formed by construction workers' poor houses. The community formed due to its proximity to the railroad, to an abundance of water and its high position. Garrard received orders from Sherman to advance on Confederate positions at this location. He sent Minty's and Miller's brigades, accompanied by two sections of the Board of Trade Battery south from Acworth. Immediately, the advance ran into a strong force of Wheeler's cavalry. Garrard pushed ahead and drove the enemy from two lines of breastworks in the vicinity of Big Shanty defended by Martin's cavalry division. To make matterse worse, the Confederates had strung wire around their position, two feet off the ground. After maneuvering past these obstacles, the Union cavalry found a third line of enemy infantry and dismounted cavalry behind a log-works and again drove the enemy to the rear. At the end of the day, Garrard determined from the prisoners that he faced three cavalry brigades (Martin's division) and one infantry brigade.[48]

Recently, Abram Miller assumed command of the mounted infantry for the first time in the campaign due to Wilder's illness and made a detailed account of the fighting. Minty's brigade led the attack, beginning at 6:00 a.m. and dealt with the initial Confederate resistance until a line of enemy was encountered about a mile north of Big Shanty. Then Abram Miller's mounted infantry got into action. Miller's brigade dismounted about a mile north of Big Shanty and three regiments attacked Martin's defenders. Miller left one regiment in support of the four guns of the Board of Trade Battery. Miller's attack drove a line of skirmishers back to the main Confederate line, positioned along a tree line, behind a "heavy barricade of logs and rails." At this point, Miller halted and realigned his forces, ensuring his flanks were covered and extending the line to the west. Then, he ordered his men to take the Confederate position. The line of blue clad dismounted infantry charged ahead, driving the enemy out of their works, but they retreated 400 yards and fell into a second line of similar works. Miller explained, "Following him up, under a galling fire, I succeeded in driving him from this line also, from which he fell back to a third line of works, on the opposite side of the railroad. Here the [Board of Trade] artillery was brought into requisition, and, after shelling the enemy vigorously for twenty or thirty minutes, I again ordered my line forward, my skirmishers having gained the railroad crossing." Miller drove the enemy from their third line of works and again, the enemy fell back 200 yards into a fourth line of works. At this location, the enemy refused to retreat and stoutly fought with Union troops, but Miller was not to be denied. He ordered his men to charge again, propelling the enemy from their final defensive position. The Confederates withdrew leaving the dead and wounded behind and moved back to the entrenchments at the base of Kennesaw Mountain. Throughout the attack, Minty's cavalry "handsomely supported" the attack, advancing along the flanks of Miller's brigade.[49]

Nourse described what he had heard about the hard-fought clash with Wheeler's cavalry, but his section was not part of the battle. "Our boys made some good shots. One shell went through the eating house. The 3rd brigade made three charges on the rebel works and carried them each time. They returned here to camp at night—Our section would have gone had Lieut. Griffin been well ... the boys fired 53 rounds." Tobias Miller's diary entries echoed Nourse's, except Miller recorded only 40 rounds being fired.[50]

On June 10, for the seventh straight day the rain continued to fall. Garrard's division moved on the left flank of Sherman's armies, which were engaged in a series of movements resulting in Johnston's withdrawal to Kennesaw Mountain. And so began a series of cavalry battles over the next three weeks near Marietta and Kennesaw Mountain. After pushing past Big Shanty and approaching McAfee's bridge, Garrard moved to the vicinity of the old Alabama Road near Noonday Creek. The division remained in this position over the next few weeks and Garrard fought almost daily with Wheeler's cavalry. Significant fights occurred on June 11, 15, 19, 20, 23 and 27. Garrard correctly reported: "The enemy had in every instance the advantage of position, and, as far as I could learn, a superior force."[51]

On June 10, Garrard's division moved to McAfee's Crossroads, a crossroads of Canton and Marietta Road and the Old Alabama Road in Woodstock near the house of Dr. Robert McAfee. The Board of Trade Battery began moving at 9:00 a.m. toward McAfee's Bridge and the advance went smoothly until 2:30 when a halt was called, ending when Long's brigade drove a heavy line of defenders from the front. At 4:00, the division stopped and Nourse noted: "We rode today over level country but could see the Smokey Mountains on our left and Kendrick's Ridge on our right. This state is one vast wheat field—rain on the road—and rain tonight." On June 11, the three sections of the Board of Trade Battery went with the respective cavalry brigades—third section with Miller's mounted infantry, second section with Long's Brigade and first section with Minty's brigade. Benjamin Nourse, part of the first section of guns, moved forward with Minty's brigade and ran into Confederate cavalry which headed for the rear, offering a fighting withdrawal over three miles. Then, Garrard recalled Minty to the location of Miller's mounted infantry, just west of Noonday Creek. The Confederates made a stand at

McAfee's Crossroads and were again driven rearward. Minty and Miller attacked Martin's division at McAfee's Crossroads and pushed it a mile to the south, carrying a line of breastworks in the process. This put the Acworth Road in Federal possession but a counterattack by the Confederates put an end to Minty's advance. Nourse noted: "The rebels flanked us, but it did no good as we had all we wanted. Minty sent for two regiments more but they did not come, and at dark we moved back 2 miles and camped—we captured a man of the 4th Ala Cav. today who told me our shells did more damage to the rebels on the 9th than all the cavalry fighting that day." Long sent the 1st Ohio and 3rd Ohio regiments on reconnaissance missions toward Marietta. In some heavy skirmishing, the two regiments, unsupported, met the enemy and drove in the pickets until superior numbers of the enemy cavalry arrived and the regiments withdrew. Long's casualties amounted to 14 men either wounded or missing in the expedition. Tobias Miller explained that Minty and Miller attempted to encircle the Confederate defenders but failed.[52]

Garrard's division made little progress over the next few days. It rained all day on June 12 and pickets exchanged fire with the enemy throughout the day. The trains reached Acworth, which was good news because the horses were again suffering from lack of grain. The rain continued the next day, as did skirmishing along the picket line. The rain made the area near Noonday Creek unpleasant and the men began to call the area a mud hole. About 30 deserters came into Federal lines during the day and gave themselves over. Tobias Miller recorded: "All tired of the Confederacy." June 13 would prove a fateful day for a detachment of the battery which was out foraging. Corporal Albert Lake, Private Martin Snow and Private Thomas Hanson, unarmed, were on a foraging expedition with a cavalry escort. They left the column for some reason and were captured by the enemy. Benjamin Nourse complained, "They have not come in yet and are no doubt captured—served them right." John Fleming, who served in the same section as John and Benjamin Nourse, offered a kinder comment on the capture. "I pity them, as they will no doubt have a hard time of it." Fleming recalled that he bought his last suit before the war from the store where Snow worked, "White, the clothes dealer under the Fremont House.... Our squad will miss him greatly." On a positive note, new recruit Charles Eames arrived for duty and was placed under Tobias Miller's wing. Miller wrote in his diary that Eames was a "good man." Eames was a mere 16 years old and still a student when he enlisted.[53]

The division ran into a heavy fight on June 15 as it pushed further south on the Marietta Road. The result was a full day's skirmish. Long advanced and at 2:00 p.m., he attacked a force of Wheeler's cavalry, but the enemy proved too strong for him. The Board of Trade Battery remained in camp until noon when the Union forces advanced a couple of miles. The 3rd section, accompanying Long's brigade, had the center position, Miller's mounted infantry had the right position and Minty moved on the left. Long moved too far in advance of the brigades on his flank and took the brunt of the Confederate counter attack, driving the brigade about a half mile to the rear. When the flanking brigades reached Long's new position, the Federal division began driving the Confederates rearward for about a mile. The fighting settled into a general engagement. Nourse described that the Confederate cavalry, "Then halted and threw down the fences for protection—Our section is with Col. Minty who had the left. The center section used cannister with good affect. We fired 50 rounds.—the 1st brigade relieved the the (sic) center, and we remained hitched up all night. I slept well. Our boys had a redoubt for their guns—fine day." Tobias Miller recorded that the cavalry advanced aggressively with the intent to break the center of Wheeler's defenders. "We are confident of success & hope to see the battle won without heavy loss. Our section has the post of honor with Wilder's Brigade. Firing is going on and the division engaged. Our other sections are at work while a position is being found for us." The battle lasted about an hour before he had to retire. Long found that Wheeler's forces were too well fortified and entrenched and he simply could not dislodge him. He lost two killed, sixteen wounded and two missing. "Rebel loss unknown."[54]

Kennesaw Mountain, Noonday Creek and Frustration for the Cavalry—June 16–30

The weather continued to be very hot over the next few days. The Board of Trade Battery moved very little and camped about two miles north of Noonday Creek, described as "a sluggish stream crossed by a wooden bridge coursing along our front to the east," by Private Silas Stevens. Sherman's infantry inched toward the mountains in front and Garrard faced a large force of Confederate cavalry. Throughout the day, the pickets kept a close watch on the enemy but Wheeler's horsemen seemed content to hold their position. Fortunately, a supply train arrived and gave the artillerymen two days' forage for the animals. Not to be outdone by the horses, the next day, the men got two days' rations for themselves. The battery remained relatively stationary and the infantry fights to the west echoed throughout the day. In front of the Second Cavalry Division was a line of hills; the enemy moved an artillery battery in place and dug earthworks to protect it. The rain continued on June 18 as did the artillery firing off to the west, and the battery remained along Noonday Creek which had become a quagmire after the recent rains.[55]

The lull in action was short-lived, because the battery mounted and marched toward Marietta on June 19. On this expedition, Miller's brigade held the center position, moving dismounted down the Marietta Road with the two cavalry brigades on either flank. After moving two miles, the column reached to the north bank of Noonday Creek and found a strong force of Confederate cavalry on the south side of the creek. The Confederates opened fire with a three-gun artillery section positioned in a lunette in a fort built along the pike. The two forces began skirmishing in front of a line of defensive works. Benjamin McGee, 72nd Indiana Mounted Infantry, explained: "We moved forward about a half mile, driving the rebels before us, when suddenly we came upon a large, deep stream, which we could not cross, while just on the opposite bank was a heavy line of works composed of rocks and earth, and behind these works lay a heavy line of infantry ready to slaughter us. Before we got to the stream it began to rain in torrents, which prevented us from seeing clearly what was before us, and we were not aware of our proximity to the creek nor to the rebels on the other side till we ran fully up to the creek." The mounted infantry was in a terrible situation—a rain swollen stream and earthworks built on the elevated banks across the creek with artillery raining shells on the Union soldiers. McGee explained that the Board of Trade Battery was brought forward and relieved the situation somewhat. "[O]ur Board of Trade Battery got into position and opened on the fort. The rebs then let us alone and went to throwing shells at the battery.... In about an hour our battery had disabled the guns in the fort and they quit firing. Our battery then moved around on to a ridge to the right rear of our regiment in order to get a position from which to rake the rebel line of works. From the excessive rains of the past few days their ammunition was bad, and for a time we were in much more danger from our own battery than from the rebs, the shells dropping in our rear and exploding behind us. It was some time before we could get our batterymen to understand what was the matter, and when a shower of grape and canister came pouring down over us, most of the right wing of the regiment wanted to get out of there."[56]

Meanwhile, Benjamin Nourse was surprised when he looked up and saw a battalion of enemy advancing down the road, no more than 100 yards away. "Col. Minty got our guns into position and we put two shells in their ranks that sent them flying to the woods in every direction—We now turned our guns and fired at the cotton gin of which was covered with rebels—our two shells through the barn and gin, killing an officer's horse and making the rebels dust off like potatoes rolling off a table—we now moved to the right and opened with Robinson's section on a rebel battery that was with good aim fireing on the center section. We soon silenced them and drove them off over the hill, they left their gun which they dared not take away until after dark. D. Jouberts was shot through the calf of the leg and Corpl. Miller had his heel shot away by a piece of shell—all this was in the midst of a pouring rain—A genuine Southern rain—The wounded go back to Columbia, Tenn." John Fleming noted that the duel lasted about 30 minutes, "breaking every tree in the vicinity," when the Confederate battery chose to withdraw. Tobias Miller's section had heavy duty during the day along Noonday Creek. The mounted infantry brigade and Miller's section fought at a bridge over the creek beginning at 9:00 a.m. The section remained engaged until it had used all its ammunition. The section withdrew to replenish the ammunition and emptied the second supply of shells. On Miller's return, he was struck in the heel by a fragment of an enemy shell rendering him "helpless" and just prior to this, Desire Joubert was struck in the calf with a Minié ball. Miller was carried away and taken to a surgeon who had to cut away parts of three bones. More surgeries followed and by the end of the month Miller was discharged due to disability from his wound. Fleming explained that Tobias Miller's heel bone was knocked out of his foot and many believed he would have to have the foot amputated. In the more serious case, Joubert would not survive his wound. In total, four guns (numbers 1, 2, 3 and 4) participated in this intense fight which dueled with a Confederate battery.[57]

To make matters worse, the timbre of the communications within the Union cavalry revealed that Sherman felt the organization and performance of mounted forces were not favorable. Sherman's direct control of the cavalry caused tensions throughout his army. Sherman wrote to Ulysses Grant on June 18, "Our cavalry is dwindling away. We cannot get full forage and have to graze, so that the cavalry is always unable to attempt anything. Garrard is over cautious and I think Stoneman is lazy.... Each has had fine chances of cutting in but is easily checked by the appearance of an enemy." Only Edward McCook escaped Sherman's criticism. Cavalry actions centered at Noonday Creek continued for two weeks as Sherman's infantry advanced toward Kennesaw Mountain. The rain continued and Noonday Creek, separating Garrard's cavalry from the Confederate line, became a swamp 400 yards wide. Sherman's letter to Grant during this time of frustration also expressed his dissatisfaction with all his commanders except for McPherson. Unfortunately, during this period he decided to focus on Garrard's cavalry along Noonday Creek.[58]

The Battle of Noonday Creek—June 20, 1864

Garrard's division scouted along the left flank of the army on June 17 and reported directly to Sherman the best way for the infantry to cross Noonday Creek. Garrard also provided intelligence about enemy positions and sent details about rebuilding some bridges which could be used to effectively make a rapid crossing, but Sherman remained unhappy with what he judged to be Garrard's less than aggressive performance. Despite the actions over the past week, Sherman wrote to George Thomas on June 20, "I have sent peremptory orders for Garrard to cross Noonday and attack the enemy's cavalry, and if he don't do it I must get another to command the cavalry. McPherson has a good position and could have advanced today, but we cannot try to turn both flanks at once.... I will in the morning go to that flank and see that Garrard crosses the creek and ridge, and that he threatens the enemy's right flank and attacks any cavalry there." Garrard was not a novice to the cavalry, but a well-respected (at least, by others than Sherman), brave and efficient commander. He had even co-authored a book on the training of the cavalry in 1862, *Nolan's System for Training Cavalry Horses.*[59]

Sherman's order to Garrard stated: "I do not wish to extend the infantry on that flank for good reasons. But the enemy has detached a great part of his cavalry back to our line of railroad where they are doing mischief. Now, if they can cross the Etowah, the Oostanaula, and Connesauga—large streams—it does seem to me you can cross the little Noonday. I therefore order you to cross and advance against the enemy's cavalry toward the Chattahoochee, keeping as far north of Marietta as you please. Take no artillery or wagons with you, and leave all dismounted and ineffective men, but with the balance attack the enemy's cavalry and drive it back and interpose between the enemy and their detached cavalry. We will press the enemy at all points. Stoneman's cavalry is at and beyond Powder Springs."[60]

Garrard promised to make an attack the next day. The result was the most intense cavalry fight in the campaign. Dr. George Parry, veterinary surgeon for the 7th Pennsylvania Cavalry, wrote in his diary that June 20 was "a very exciting day ... severe fighting." Minty's brigade moved across Noonday Creek and pushed the Confederate pickets aside. The Union brigade chased the pickets about two miles, but found the main Confederate defensive line. A heated fight resulted in the loss of 65 men in Garrard's Division. One of the wounded in the fight at Noonday Creek was Private Jarratt Johnston, 1st Ohio Cavalry, who lost a leg when a shell hit him. He pleaded to be taken back to the Union line, but he was left behind. Sherman had left strict orders, "First whip the enemy, and then your wounded are safe."[61]

Minty's cavalry crossed Noonday Creek on the old Alabama Road at 10:00, fell into line and remained there throughout the day. The three sections of the Board of Trade were under the command of Robinson, Griffin and Bennett. Benjamin Nourse, part of Griffin's section, described the fight in his diary: "This morning we were up at daylight (4 oc.) and harnessed. We expected to be shelled, but no rebel music of that kind greeted our ears. We fed our horses wheat for breakfast then the 2nd piece moved out to the hill we shelled from yesterday so as to cover a reconnaissance by the 7th Penn. They did not fire again—at 10 o'clock the First Brigade saddled and moved over the creek—at 3 oc. the swamp was laid with rails so that we could draw our gun carriages across the creek—but if a horse went off the ends of the rails they were lost, had to be left behind—no use to try to get out of the mire." At 3:00 p.m. Minty's brigade was attacked by a heavy force of Confederate cavalry and the 7th Pennsylvania was pushed back. The Pennsylvanians were reinforced with the 4th U.S. Cavalry and the 4th Michigan on the left flank and held their position near Noonday Church. The 4th Michigan and a battalion of the 4th U.S. held the center. Two battalions of the 7th Pennsylvania were positioned on the right flank. Minty's

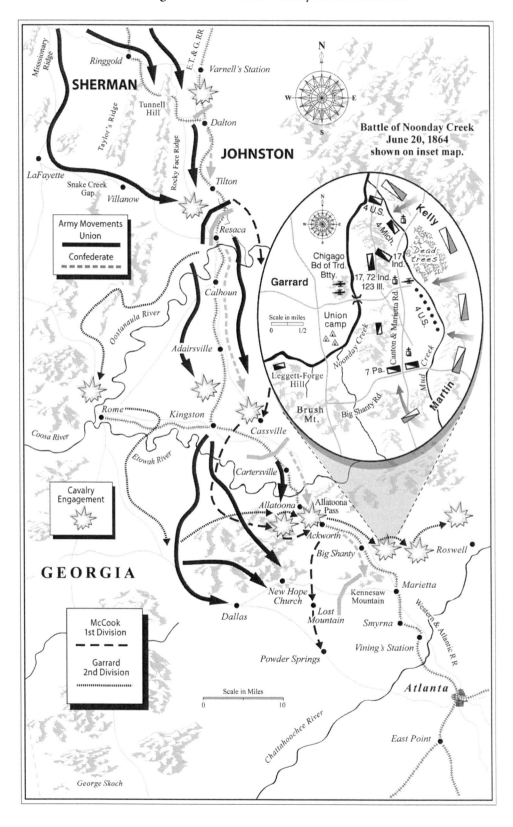

Battle of Noonday Creek
June 20, 1864
shown on inset map.

George Skoch

line held through three charges from six Confederate cavalry brigades which began flanking the Union troopers. Minty called for a section of the Chicago Board of Trade Battery, commanded by Minty's comrade from the Reed's Bridge action, Trumbull Griffin, to delay the Confederate flanking action on his line and the artillery began shelling the advancing cavalry. Colonel Moses Hannon's brigade of Confederate cavalry turned and advanced on Griffin's guns. Minty, seeing the situation unfold, calmly rode to Griffin and said, "Give them canister, Mr. Griffin." Griffin's section was posted without any support at the rear of a field on the Marietta Road. As the attack drew closer, Lieutenant Griffin told Minty he was afraid he would lose his guns. Minty replied: "Those men need to be checked—pour in your canister." Minty said the battery boys worked the guns "nobly." Griffin ordered the guns to keep firing but again expressed his concern for his guns and asked permission to withdraw. Minty exclaimed, "No sir, you will not; give them another round or two." Benjamin Nourse explained, "As soon as we were over the creek the rebels opened on us and then charged full force on the 4th Michigan cavalry, before they could dismount or even form a line—of course they fell back a short distance, then formed and charged them with the saber—our guns were quickly at the front and repulsed the second rebel charge with cannister. The 4th Mich. sat, and fired from their horses. The rebels had plenty of men and had us in a very narrow place with only one line of retreat open to us. So, they supported their third charge with dismounted men, a heavy line on each side of the charging columns." At that point, a charge wedged in one of the guns making it inoperable, but the other cannon continued to fire and successfully stopped the attack. Next, Miller's mounted infantry provided support and reinforced the Union troopers already in line. Nourse exclaimed, "We had to fall back lively—here Silas E. Peckham was shot through the thigh—our gun got a cartridge foul and we returned across the creek to draw the charge—the second gun and lead horses came back also. The third brigade now went over the creek dismounted and formed a line to cover the retreat of the mounted cavalry—and to receive with us the fourth charge, our six guns now being 'in battery' [i.e., in line firing with all six guns]. We opened again and with the 7 shooters of the mounted infantry, the rebels were terribly cut up—the rebs now ran two guns up a little rise of ground but we were turned on them and before they could load we scattered them, both men and horses, nor did they return for their guns."[62]

John Fleming, also of Griffin's section, explained this was the most difficult position the battery had experienced since the Battle of Stones River. Fleming humorously stated that Minty's brigades fought three enemy divisions "and although we had the impudence to show fight to this force, they came near taking us on under their protecting care. No. 1 piece was disabled and moved to the rear, leaving our piece and it having no support whatever. The rebel cavalry charged on our gun twice but we gave them grape and cannister lively and when they commenced to get the upper hand, we limbered up and galloped off and barely saved our gun at that. At one time the rebs were within 150 yards of us and no one between our gun and them." The guns blazed away and at that point, Silas Peckham, the 24-year-old ex-farmer, while still mounted was shot in the leg. Fortunately, none of the horses assigned to this gun had been shot and this allowed the gun to be withdrawn. But a Confederate battery saw the withdrawing gun as a prime target and opened fire. In return, the other guns of the Board of Trade Battery had been positioned in the

Opposite: The Atlanta Campaign, May—July 9, 1864. The inset MAP shows the cavalry battle of Noonday Creek June 20, 1864.

rear and returned fire on the Confederate gunners, allowing Fleming's gun time to reach the full battery. Then, the disabled gun had been cleared and all six guns went to work shelling the enemy forces until Minty extracted his command.[63]

As Miller's men fought, the attacks ended and Miller's support allowed Minty to withdraw from the field with a loss of 65 men. Johnston's line and two divisions of Confederate cavalry were just too strong for Minty's brigade, but the action temporarily silenced Sherman's criticisms. Minty's record of the action: "Was attacked by Wheeler with six brigades, viz: Allen's, Iverson's, Anderson's, Hannon's, Williams's, and Dibrell's. About 500 men of Seventh Pennsylvania and Fourth Michigan, with Lieutenant Griffin's section of Chicago Board of Trade Battery, fought Williams's, Hannon's, and Anderson's brigades for over two hours. The Seventh Pennsylvania and Fourth Michigan each made one saber charge, and two battalions of Fourth Michigan repulsed three saber charges made by Anderson's brigade of regular cavalry. Colonel Miller reported to me with three regiments from his brigade. I directed him to form on the hills around the bridge over Noonday. One battalion Fourth U.S. Regulars checked the advance of Allen's and Iverson's brigades on my right flank and enabled me to fall back on Colonel Miller. The six brigades of rebels dismounted and charged my new line. The artillery, which I had placed in position across the creek, opened on them and they were repulsed." After the heavy fighting, Minty knew he could not hold his position and returned to the north side of the creek. Minty heralded Griffin's action and John C. McLain, 4th Michigan Cavalry, described the importance of Miller's brigade which waited for Confederate cavalry to follow Minty's troopers. McLain wrote in his diary that night, "Wilders [Miller's] brigade were waiting for them behind a rail barrack and it was dark by the time they came up and did not see what was in front and for a short time it was warm place." General Jacob Cox exclaimed the action was "one of the most hotly contested cavalry fights of the war," and Joseph Johnston referred to this as the "most considerable cavalry affair of the campaign." Benjamin Nourse concluded his diary entry, "At dark the lines withdrew across the creek right through the creek, water up to their necks. A pouring rain has fallen all the time of this engagement. We lost 70 men—took 12 prisoners—we camped in the mud up to our ears."[64]

Silas Stevens, clerk at cavalry headquarters, greeted Garrard accompanied by his aides, "flushed, excited, and covered in mud" at the end of the battle and Garrard exclaimed upon entering the rooms: "Stevens, we have had a great fight this afternoon." Stevens transcribed Garrard's report which would be transmitted to Sherman. "The orders were to cross at any fording place, at the risk of horse and rider, miring in the bottom land beyond. Those who succeeded in this venture took up the line of battle, under cover of the guns of the Battery, occupying a favorable position, and fired with their usual rapidity and precision." The firing prompted an attack on the Federal position "with a large and impetuous force." Stevens stated that several of the battery were wounded but he recalled most were able to return to duty.[65]

Garrard struck back directly at Sherman after the fight at Noonday Creek. Garrard wrote his impression of the situation at Noonday Creek and willingness to abdicate his command if Sherman found his performance unsatisfactory. Garrard explained, "Please inform the major-general commanding the army that his communication of last night has been received. His instructions to cross Noonday Creek have, in anticipation, been complied with four times, and attempted another, within the last ten days. I have in that time attacked the enemy's cavalry five times, and have always found it superior to me in numbers, and always they have had the advantage in position. Yesterday I lost 65 men in the fight." Garrard was positioned within four miles of the main force of Confederate cavalry and he flatly told Sherman if he was unsatisfied with his command to replace him. "I regret exceedingly that on several occasions the major-general commanding has seen fit to write as if he were dissatisfied with my activity and zeal. It is impossible to do all that might be desired, but the same consideration should be had for the cavalry, which cannot advance over natural advantages and a strong enemy, that is given to the infantry, which has not overcome the numerous difficulties before them.... My service with the cavalry this campaign has been very unsatisfactory, for I have been made to feel more than once that it was not equal to the occasion, when I feel confident that both men and officers of the command have been earnest and zealous in the discharge of their duties and have well and faithfully done all in their power to accomplish what was asked of them. Should the general commanding desire a change in the command of this division, I will most cheerfully yield it and take command of a brigade of infantry. The Noonday is not the obstacle to my advance on these roads, but the superior force of the enemy in strong positions."[66]

Continued Action with McPherson's Corps

The maps showed Noonday Creek as a small and insignificant obstruction, but that was only part of the picture. Due to excessive rain, the problem was the approach to the creek which was 700 yards of swamp according to James Larson, 4th U.S. Cavalry, who described the terrain, "So soft a man could not walk on it, far less a horse." The swampy area around the creek had to be covered with rails if any artillery or wagons were expected to move. McPherson met with Sherman on June 21 and returned to Garrard with new orders and gave him the reassurance he needed: "The general is well satisfied with your operations yesterday, and what he wants and expects is that you will keep the rebel cavalry in your front occupied, and be certain that they do not send a large force to our rear." Even Garrard's subordinates knew Sherman was dissatisfied with him. Captain Heber Thompson, 7th Pennsylvania Cavalry, wrote, "It is evident that the authorities (Sherman and McPherson) are dissatisfied with Genl. Garrard and disposed to find fault with him without occasion. Sherman yesterday wrote to General Garrard making great complaint of our inactivity and inefficiency, forsooth! ... Such an absurd letter as that, one would not expect from Genl. Sherman, though lately it must be confessed, our confidence in his Generalship has been greatly weakened."[67]

McPherson was much more collegial and supportive of Garrard and had been throughout the campaign. On June 23, McPherson wrote to Garrard that his actions were very "satisfactory" for the day after Garrard had stopped a Rebel attack along McPherson's flank. W.L. Curry, 1st Ohio Cavalry, reported the Confederates "wheeled into line and with a yell charged down the hill.... Our whole division was lying in line dismounted, and at the command they raised up, rushed forward with a yell, opened up with their carbines, and the volleys were deafening ... volley after volley was poured into them." McPherson then informed Garrard that his cavalry would be needed to support a movement for the Seventeenth Corps the next day. Garrard had found a friend in McPherson.[68]

By the end of June 24, Garrard pushed to within two miles of Marietta and Sherman's infantry inched steadily closer to Johnston's Confederates entrenched in an arc around Marietta. The stage was set for the Battle of Kennesaw Mountain on June 27. The battle would be carried by McPherson's and Thomas' armies. Garrard and one division of infantry were ordered to feint toward Marietta with orders to contain Johnston's cavalry, and Schofield and Stoneman were to feint on the extreme west end of the Union line. The Union advance began at 8:00 a.m. but by 11:30 a.m. the attack had stalled. At the end of the day the Union casualties were about three times that of the Confederate defenders—about 3,000 Union losses compared to about 1,000 Confederate losses in this Confederate victory.[69]

Little of note occurred with the Board of Trade Battery until June 25 as the hot weather continued. Corporal Albert B. Lake was reduced from the rank of corporal at dress parade due to disobedience of orders, resulting in the capture of his detail on June 14. Walter Riddle, a Scottish-born, pre-war shoemaker, was promoted in his place. The next day, the battery advanced five miles closer to Marietta, finally claiming the south side of Noonday Creek in the process. On June 27, the battery ascended Black Jack Ridge and unlimbered on the left flank of the Seventeenth Corps, opposite the Confederate line. The battery went to work in a long and difficult day. Four guns of the battery faced the Confederate battery behind heavy breastworks and shelled it for six hours. In the return, the Confederate battery fired at the Board of Trade Battery but neither battery could dislodge the other. The Confederate shells generally landed above the Board of Trade Battery, throwing debris over the horses and men, but doing no damage. The weather was so hot, the men had to take frequent breaks to preserve their energy and to let the guns cool. Fleming explained that he had "short sleeves rolled to his shoulder, and the perspiration rolling off freely, loading the gun, and then dropping in a plowed field to dodge the shells for although you can see a shell coming sometimes, and always can hear it humming through the air, you cannot know where it may strike." This was the longest prolonged fire of the war for the battery. John Nourse wrote: "We could not get at them without a good deal of pounding ... but they changed position three times which argues well for the directness of our fire." The battery's work was designed to occupy the enemy while Thomas' and McPherson's attacks at Kennesaw Mountain unfolded but by 2:00 the battery was sent back to its camp. The battle was over.[70]

On June 28, the battery remained stationary and Nourse commented that it was "[a]ctually too hot to fight." The fate of Corporal Lake and his detail was learned from a prisoner from the 4th Georgia Cavalry. The prisoner explained: "Lake, Hanson & Snow were captured by a Lieut. and five men of his co & he described the boys so accurately that we are sure he was truthful—he even told the contents of their pockets—Photos, etc.—they were taken near Gov. Brown's farm and are now safe in Dixie. O this war, this war, this cruel war." The battery remained stationary with little action through the end of the month.[71]

Sherman decided any further frontal assaults on Johnston's lines would be futile. Instead, he decided to supply his armies and again try to flank Johnston by swinging to the west around Kennesaw Mountain, attempting to isolate Confederate forces from the south. Sherman reasoned that if Johnston remained on Kennesaw Mountain, then he could strike the railroad south of this position. The two armies remained in place for a few days and on July 1, Sherman began to maneuver his flanks around Kennesaw Mountain toward the Chattahoochee River. Stoneman's and McCook's divisions claimed the village of Sweetwater Town, about 10 miles south of Kennesaw Mountain on July 2. In the meantime, Garrard's division protected the flanks and rear of McPherson's army. Johnston had temporarily stopped Sherman's advance, but he was slowly being swallowed by the Union armies in front of his lines. To his rear was the Chattahoochee River and his line of retreat; this river was also the last significant geographic obstacle before Atlanta.[72]

Board of Trade Battery Moves on to Roswell—July 2-July 14

At 10:00 the next morning, Sherman wired Halleck that he had possession of Kennesaw Mountain and Johnston had withdrawn because of the flanking movement to the west. Immediately Garrard and McCook, who had been cooperating with George Stoneman, were ordered to push for the Chattahoochee River. By the end of the day, Marietta was in the hands of the Union army, but Johnston stopped at Smyrna to give his wagons time to move south. After two days of relatively minor fighting, Johnston withdrew again, this time into the well-prepared defenses north of the Chattahoochee. To get around Johnston, Garrard's cavalry was ordered to Roswell, site of the next bridge east from Johnston's River Line. McCook was ordered to secure the river between the Federal infantry and Garrard's right and to be prepared to join Garrard should he run into trouble. The advantage of numbers was now apparent. Should Wheeler try to strike Sherman's rear from the east, he would face two Union cavalry divisions with infantry support. In addition, George Stoneman, who was already near the Chattahoochee River near Campbellton on the Union right, was prepared to cross the river and attack Johnston's rear and communications. In the meantime, the infantry moved forward, engaging the Confederates along the Smyrna line on July 4 when Sherman ordered Howard's Fourth Corps to continue the advance in the face of an entrenched line of enemy infantry. Howard's attack was repulsed. The Union attack collapsed part of the enemy line, but the Confederates successfully delayed the Federals long enough to get their wagons across the river.[73]

For the Board of Trade Battery, July began with the company in camp on July 1. The next day, the top cavalry commanders, including George Robinson, met at Big Shanty and returned with orders for the battery and division to withdraw two miles nearer Big Shanty. A long-departed member of the battery appeared in camp, Private John Buckingham. Buckingham, part of Sylvanus Stevens' foraging detail, was captured south of Nashville on December 14, 1862, and had been absent since. He was exchanged in June 1863, but he had been in a hospital and detailed to barracks duty in St. Louis since that time. He had finally regained his health to such an extent as to allow him to return to duty. On July 3, the battery again marched southward about eight miles through Marietta and then took a sharp turn east in the direction of Roswell. While advancing to Roswell, the column ran into a screen of Confederate cavalry and the two opposing forces skirmished as Federals continued east. Miller's mounted infantry handled much of the fighting and the artillery was not used. The next day each of the three artillery sections accompanied each of the three cavalry brigades. The troopers ran into another strong force of the enemy, believed to be infantry. Again, Miller's brigade was called forward and the Federals and Confederates battled throughout the afternoon. Nourse's section alone fired 85 rounds during the fighting. The arrival of Oliver Howard's Fourth Corps settled the fight in favor of the soldiers in blue. Nourse recorded: "[T]he rebs charged our skirmish line three times during the day but did not drive it once—Our Division took many prisoners."[74]

On July 5, Garrard's Second Division approached Roswell, about 10 miles east of Marietta. The Confederate defenders withdrew from the town and burned the bridge over the Chattahoochee. Minty's brigade led the column accompanied by a section of Board of

Trade guns. After the previous day's fighting, all was clear and the column marched nine miles and camped three miles west of Roswell. Private Silas Stevens described the river as a "formidable stream, with high banks and steep sides, covered with a heavy growth of bushes, and stout trees, with a rapid difficult water to cross." Garrard took possession of Roswell the next day and on July 7, Garrard's troopers burned wool and cotton mills and machine shops. McCook joined Garrard on the left flank on July 6 while along the Union right flank George Stoneman had not yet reached the Chattahoochee River because of enemy entrenchments. Garrard's success at Roswell, in which he destroyed over $1 million dollars' worth of Confederate factories, made a favorable impression on Sherman. When Garrard arrived in Roswell, he found a French flag flying over some of the mills and a claim by a French citizen, Theophile Roche, that he owned the mills. This was a lie perpetrated by the mill owners for whom Roche worked. Garrard discovered that the mills manufactured blankets and Confederate uniforms. Despite Roche's protestations that he was not part of the Confederacy, but a French citizen, the factories were burned. The more distressing part of the event related to the women who worked in the factory. Sherman ordered Garrard, "[T]o arrest for treason all owners and employees, foreign and native, and send them under guard to Marietta, whence I will send them North. Being exempt from conscription, they are as much governed by the rules of war as if in the ranks." Records show approximately 400 women from Roswell and 100 women from the New Manchester Mill at Sweetwater (burned by Stoneman's troopers on July 9) were deported to various locations in the north. In addition, Garrard secured positions the Union infantry would use to cross the river. Private Silas Stevens, who clerked in Garrard's headquarters, recalled that Sherman gave Garrard the authority to hang Theophile Roche if he so chose.[75]

Nourse wrote on July 7: "Col. Miller went up to Roswell today with a detail of men and the Mills are burning now. The Col. gave out all the cloth and the provisions to the girls—who were employed there. 15 buildings were burnt—one building alone employed 800 girls—There are three mills down with power enough to give motion to the machinery of six such mills as the 'Bay state' mills of Mass.—These mills and the whole country around here is owned by King & Co.—they own all the stores, provisions, etc., etc. They allowed no liquor sold in the town—and in truth ran every thing to suit themselves—had their own paper currency which circulated all through this section as better than Confederate scrip—the Kings left town with their hard money in a wagon the night before we came in … it is half a mile to the river—the town had 1000 inhabitants besides the factory girls." On July 8, the Board of Trade Battery was reunited and moved into Roswell with the cavalry division. The next morning the cavalry division provided security for the crossings over the river. Two sections moved on to a bluff overlooking a ford at Roswell while to the west Minty's and Miller's brigades, supported by the third section of Board of Trade guns, crossed the river, driving the enemy pickets away in the process. The battery did some shelling, firing 25 rounds, on the opposite bank but the fighting was surprisingly light. Later in the day, the Fourth Corps crossed the river at the secured fords.[76]

The crossing of the Chattahoochee continued on July 10. Sixteenth Corps crossed, followed by Twenty-third Corps. Benjamin Nourse recorded in his diary that the previous day's fighting made the eleventh engagement of the campaign, so far. The battery remained stationary through July 13, but of note, a quartermaster train of three wagons, commanded by Quartermaster Sergeant Calvin Durand and which left camp on July,

10 returned without five men of the detail. Among those presumed captured was Sergeant Durand. Nourse commented: "Calvin Durand started with three wagons for our camp and he rode on ahead with a Lieut. of the first brigade and three men. the wagons have all come in but not the men—and we know they are safely in Dixie ere this—good bye Cal.—I hope they will find the other boys."[77]

Durand served as quartermaster sergeant for essentially the entire war and on July 10 he had the misfortune of being sick. Still, he was driven by his duty to keep the battery well-provisioned. He started for Roswell with four loaded wagons and he was accompanied by Private William Shipley, a pre-war carpenter from Chicago. As the wagons rumbled eastward, Durand began to feel increasingly unwell, to such an extent that he feared he could not stay in the saddle. He decided to take a rest before starting out and sent Shipley along with the wagons and teamsters. Durand was feeling good about the situation when Shipley returned shortly and told Durand that the wagons and the

Charles Brewster, a New Hampshire native, enlisted at 19 years old and was a pre-war clerk in Chicago (Chicago History Museum, ICHi-176926).

cavalry escort had become separated. Durand recalled, "I was disgusted, but quickly left my bed, threw the saddle upon my horse, and starting with him and the wagons, soon found the right road, and told him to move on rapidly with the wagons, and I would ride ahead, overtake the rear guard and bring back an escort." Durand proceeded ahead and after a five-mile ride, he saw the rear of the division supply train and this eased his concern of traveling unescorted so near enemy territory. Then, as he rounded a bend in the road, he saw a dozen mounted men ahead, sitting in the road and facing Durand. Durand concluded the party intended to ambush the column, but finding the train too heavily guarded decided to pick up stragglers. Durand was unsure of what to do. If he tried to run away, he would have been shot, captured, or drawn the raiders toward the four supply wagons behind him. He decided to give himself up, saving the wagons and the teamsters in the process. Durand soon found himself in the hands of a party of Southern cavalry scouts, which was better than irregulars. Durand was taken to Andersonville Prison where he found Lake, Snow, and Hanson from the Board of Trade Battery who were captured a few days earlier (and this group would be joined by Coleman Brown who would be captured in August). Of this group, Snow and Lake would die in the prison. Durand would be exchanged in March 1865 and had a long and difficult time as a prisoner of war, nearly dying himself.[78]

The grueling campaign was taking its toll on both armies. William Allen Clark of the 72nd Indiana Mounted Infantry wrote, "I am getting tired of this Campaign. We have been either in the saddle or on the skirmish line almost every day since the 10th of May." By July, Sherman had been given authority to make his actions independent of any concerns about keeping the enemy occupied as a way to support Grant's actions in the east. Sherman established headquarters at Vining's Station along the Western & Atlantic Railroad just north of the Chattahoochee River, putting Atlanta within striking distance. Both Sherman and Johnston understood that although Sherman had a larger army, it was vulnerable and deep in enemy territory. If his tenuous supply line was severed, Sherman could be in trouble. Sherman, as commander of the Military Division of the Mississippi, used two additional military actions to occupy the attention of Confederate troops in Mississippi, Alabama and Tennessee. In Sherman's eyes, Nathan Bedford Forrest was the most disruptive enemy force and he felt it was imperative to keep Forrest away from the vulnerable Union supply lines. In early June, Sherman sent Brigadier General Samuel Sturgis to deal with this threat, but in the process, Sturgis was defeated in the Battle of Brice's Crossroads. The Union losses totaled over 2,200 men killed, wounded or missing compared to slightly less than 500 for Forrest. Next, he sent Major General A.J. Smith and Brigadier General Joseph Mower on an expedition to Tupelo to deal with Forrest. These two generals are two of the least known and best generals in the western theater, and their expedition ended quite differently. Lieutenant General Stephen Lee and Forrest were defeated at the Battle of Tupelo on July 14 and 15. The Union infantry held Forrest's attention and even wounded the famed Confederate general on July 15. Both of these expeditions had the two-fold objectives of trying to destroy Forrest and diverting the enemy's resources away from Sherman's supply line.[79]

As Sherman began to besiege Atlanta, he alerted Henry Halleck about his next steps. Instead of directly attacking Johnston's entrenchments, he proposed to destroy all the railroads leading to Atlanta and therefore, starving Johnston into abandoning the city. This was a tricky maneuver but it would save many lives. Sherman had hinted at this strategy, and now he proposed to put his cavalry to work to accomplish this task. The months of July and August would signal a beginning of Sherman's decision to use his cavalry in a much more offensive series of raids behind enemy lines.[80]

Union Cavalry Raids—July and August 1864

Raid	Date	Location	Outcome
Rousseau's Raid	July 10–22, 1864	Loachapoka and Opelika, Alabama	Success
Stoneman's Raid	July 10–15, 1864	Atlanta & West Point	Failure
Garrard's Raid	July 21–24, 1864	Covington, Georgia	Success
McCook's Raid	July 27–Aug 3, 1864	Lovejoy's Station, Georgia	Failure
Stoneman's Raid	July 27–Aug 6, 1864	Macon, Georgia	Failure
Kilpatrick's Raid	August 18–22, 1864	Jonesborough, Georgia	Failure

The Cavalry Raids Begin

The first raid made by Lovell Rousseau was a great success and the raid deep into Alabama began Sherman's strategy to destroy all the railroads leading to the city. Next, he ordered George Stoneman to take his cavalry across the Chattahoochee River and destroy the railroad "below" Atlanta. If Stoneman failed to destroy the railroad, Sherman was confident Rousseau would succeed. Sherman believed Stoneman would return from the raid, which began on July 10, within five days and then he planned to feint to the right and swing his army to the left (east). Sherman reasoned he would weaken Johnston's center and left flanks with the move, and if Johnston moved his army to the east, then Sherman would rush Atlanta. If Johnston took the offensive, Sherman was prepared to use Peach Tree Creek as a formidable defensive obstacle. While waiting for Stoneman to return from his raid, the Union army rested until Sherman was informed on July 15 that Stoneman's attempt to destroy the railroad south of Atlanta failed. Stoneman tried to capture a bridge to cross the Chattahoochee at Newnan (10 miles from the railroad) but was met with artillery fire. Rather than force a crossing, Stoneman burned the bridge and camped at Villa Rica, where he re-shoed his horses. Sherman's entire command awaited the return of Stoneman who had not shown much cooperation or energy in his assignment. Sherman, however, showed no obvious concern about the abortive raid and was confident Rousseau would accomplish the task. Afterward, McCook and Stoneman were assigned duty protecting the crossings along the Chattahoochee River and Garrard was ordered to cooperate in the movement of McPherson's army.[81]

Stoneman's reputation was dealt another blow on July 20 when Thomas discovered the extent of his efforts in the failed raid. Thomas wrote, "The Stoneman raid turns out to be a humbug. I sent you his last report yesterday afternoon and hope it was received. It seems that when twenty-five of the enemy are seen anywhere, they are considered in force." However, Sherman thought it might be time for Stoneman and McCook to strike in the rear of Hood's army in another determined raid.[82]

Sherman began his infantry movement southward on July 17 and brought the Fourteenth and Twentieth Corps across the Chattahoochee. Garrard's cavalry screened McPherson's advance during the day and found little opposition. Next, Sherman ordered Garrard to push forward and destroy the railroad between Decatur and Stone Mountain in cooperation with McPherson's infantry. Garrard began the mission on the evening of July 18, and Sherman reported, "General Garrard's cavalry at once set to work to break up road and was re-enforced by Brig. Gen. Morgan L. Smith's division of infantry, and they expect by night to have five miles of road effectually destroyed." The expedition was successful and Sherman had to be pleased with Garrard's performance during the day. By the end of July 18, Sherman's armies moved two to five miles with their right flank under Thomas on the Chattahoochee River. McPherson was on the left flank, and Schofield held the center.[83]

The Board of Trade Battery remained in the vicinity of Cross Keys and McAfee's Bridge until July 17. The next day, Garrard led an expedition to destroy the Augusta & Atlanta Railroad between Decatur and Stone Mountain. One section of guns, which saw some light action during the expedition, accompanied the column in its successful destruction of six miles of track. Meanwhile, Sherman ordered a general advance on Atlanta, and Garrard was pulled from railroad destruction and ordered to protect the left flank and rear from any actions of the Confederate cavalry. Meanwhile on the Confederate side of the line, big changes were taking place. On the evening of July 17, a telegram relieving Johnston of command arrived at his headquarters. In Johnston's place, President Davis appointed John Bell Hood and promoted him to full general. Hood was selected in part because Jefferson Davis correctly believed he was more likely to take offensive action than many of the other possible commanders.[84]

The Union Forces Destroy the Railroad on the East

On July 20, two sections of the Board of Trade Battery moved 10 miles and camped at Cross Keys, filling a gap between McPherson's and Thomas' infantry. Nourse described the terrain: "The country is thinly settled, poor soil, sandy, rolling ground, covered with small pine and black jack trees, a very poor place to live in." The battery continued on and reached Decatur on July 21. Benjamin Nourse regarded his surroundings and wrote: "The rebs burnt the depot, warehouse, trains & forage when they left here—poor people here are short of food. Always the same old story." At division headquarters, Garrard received abrupt orders to destroy the railroad near Covington and he took Lieutenant Robinson's section of guns and set off on the expedition. The other two sections camped near the jail in Decatur that night on the inglorious duty of providing protection for McPherson's supply trains. When Robinson departed, he took all the forage with him because he expected hard riding. The details of Robinson's section during the successful expedition have not been preserved. Little heavy fighting occurred in the raid and Robinson returned with most of the cavalry intact. Unknown to Robinson and his gunners, the battery left at Decatur was to be in a fight for its life the next day.[85]

On July 20 the new Confederate commander of the Army of Tennessee attacked Thomas's Army of the Cumberland after it crossed Peachtree Creek. Although the Union infantry was hard pressed, it successfully repulsed the attack of the aggressive Hood which resulted in a large loss of 2,600 men compared to 2,100 for Thomas. While the battle was fought, McPherson pressed within a couple miles of Atlanta, but Sherman was frustrated that none of his subordinate army commanders could break through for a quick victory. So, he began the process of isolating the city. Over the night of July 20–21, he had ordered Garrard to destroy more thoroughly the railroad to Augusta. Garrard was ordered to proceed to Covington, about 30 miles east of his headquarters at Decatur to destroy the Georgia Railroad at Lithonia, 10 miles west of Covington, and then destroy the Yellow River Bridge, a 555-foot trestle, about five miles west of Covington. Next, Garrard focused on destroying the railroad and bridge over the Ulcofauhachee River. By destroying this section of railroad Sherman ensured no supplies or reinforcements could be moved quickly from Virginia by way of Augusta, a rumor Grant had just communicated to Sherman. Sherman chided Garrard to be aggressive in his actions. Sherman reminded Garrard he had met with little resistance along his flank and erroneously concluded the enemy cavalry was a long way to the west of the armies. Then, he stressed the importance of the mission and specifically told Garrard the loss of 25 percent of his command should be contemplated and expected. Finally, Sherman told him to start on July 21, and he had two days to complete his task.[86]

But Sherman's orders to begin a raid at Covington angered McPherson and were abrupt for Garrard. McPherson, who had been attacked during the day, felt he should have some input before pulling his cavalry away, and retorted, "[I] will simply remark in closing, that I have no cavalry as a body of observation on my flank, and that the whole rebel army, except Georgia militia, is not in front of the Army of the Cumberland." Garrard, on the other hand, received Sherman's orders at 1:30 a.m. which directed him to begin this raid the next day. Garrard replied that he had regiments strung along a 10-mile front and he would have to pull his command together which also had skirmished throughout the day. He replied, "I desire to succeed, as you place so much importance in having it done, and I will endeavor to do it." Garrard decided to start for the bridges with five regiments at 5 a.m. the next morning while the remainder of his command caught up before starting the destruction of the railroad.[87]

The condescension in Sherman's orders was obvious to Garrard, but Garrard was to have a successful three days in the saddle. One section of Board of Trade Battery guns (guns number. 3 and 4) under the command of George Robinson accompanied the expedition. Garrard began the raid by scattering the Confederates at McAfee's Bridge and then rode east. True to his word, Garrard rode for the 555-foot trestle bridge over the Yellow River, and the 92nd Illinois Mounted Infantry burned it. Then, the 250-foot covered bridge over the Ulcofauhachee (or Alcovy) River was burned. Next, part of the column rode through Oxford and captured a train and locomotive at Conyers before setting both afire. The depot was also burned as the column rode away. The Union column descended on Covington and burned the depot there. Garrard proceeded to claim the quartermaster and commissary stores and burned what his troopers couldn't carry. Another two trains were burned there also, and by destroying the bridge over the Yellow River, another two trains were stranded along the railroad. Garrard also burnt 2,000 bales of cotton and turned his attention to a new, 30-building hospital which was set afire.[88]

Garrard's troopers encountered civilians who were fleeing before the Union cavalry who thought their personal possessions were not safe from the marauding cavalry. Over 1,000 sick and wounded Confederate soldiers were in hospitals at Oxford and Covington, and many escaped into the woods and hills. Those who remained in the hospitals were undisturbed by the raiders. Then, Garrard's troopers began destroying the railroad for six miles as ordered by Sherman and within the timeframe given. Garrard's division rode 90 miles and had two men killed during the raid. Garrard's only real resistance came at Loganville where 50 Confederate soldiers, hastily assembled, awaited Minty's brigade. The small band was quickly dispersed once Minty advanced. When Garrard returned to the Union line, he found the Battle of Atlanta had been fought, but he also was greeted with what he needed most—praise from Sherman, "I am rejoiced to hear that you are back safe and successful…. I will give you time to rest and then we must make quick work with Atlanta. I await your report with impatience, and in the meantime tender you the assurance of my great consideration." Sherman so welcomed Garrard's return that he ordered Major General Grenville Dodge to make a demonstration on Wheeler's cavalry to distract him so that Garrard would be unimpeded on his return.[89]

A Bloody Day at Decatur—Board of Trade Battery

While Garrard followed Sherman's orders to destroy the Georgia Railroad at Covington, Hood attacked McPherson's exposed left flank. The terse message McPherson sent to Sherman regarding lack of cavalry support on the evening on July 21 proved prophetic, and a coordinated attack by Hardee's Corps and Wheeler's cavalry began around noon on July 22. Sherman's abrupt orders resulted in Garrard's absence along McPherson's flank and prompted McPherson to convince Sherman to forego, at least temporarily, using part of McPherson's infantry to further destroy the railroad. Instead, McPherson put two brigades on his left flank, preventing a disaster when Hardee's infantry appeared unexpectedly. Although there were delays in launching the attack, Hood outmaneuvered Sherman on July 22 and launched a furious attack with Benjamin Cheatham's corps making a frontal assault. The Union line was tested by this attack, but held. Meanwhile, two divisions and a brigade of Joseph Wheeler's cavalry attacked John Sprague's Union infantry brigade (about 1,000 men) at Decatur. Wheeler's cavalry approached the Federal wagon trains of three infantry corps parked around Decatur, where Sprague had the unenviable duty of guarding a thousand wagons. Wheeler planned to deal with the Union supply train and then attack the rear of the Federal infantry. Sprague was successful in withdrawing while avoiding being encircled by the Confederate cavalry and this prevented Wheeler from swinging into the rear of McPherson's infantry. Sprague, greatly outnumbered, had two batteries to assist in the repulse, including the four guns of Chicago Board of Trade Battery, which played an important role in stemming the attack.[90]

Three regiments of John Sprague's brigade (63rd Ohio, 25th Wisconsin and 35th New Jersey) arrived in Decatur on July 21, replacing Garrard's cavalry which Sherman had sent east on the raid. His fourth regiment, 43rd Ohio, remained in Roswell. Sprague placed his regiments in position to hold the town, supported by a section of 1st Michigan artillery and four guns of the Board of Trade Battery. Upon his arrival, Sprague dispersed pickets along all the routes leading to the town. Around noon on July 22, the movement of a large force of Confederate troops was detected and this was confirmed as Wheeler attacked Sprague's position from two roads—one directly to the south and the other from the southwest. Four companies of the 25th Wisconsin and four companies of the 63rd Ohio had advanced about a half mile south of town looking for the enemy. Two additional companies of the 25th Wisconsin were on picket duty and three remaining companies, along with two companies of the 63rd Ohio supported the 1st Michigan Battery just south of the railroad near the house of Dr. Hoyle. Three companies of the 63rd Ohio supported the two sections of the Board of Trade guns on an elevation just north of the jail on the southern edge of the town while the last company of the 63rd Ohio was at the courthouse on provost duty. The 35th New Jersey covered the roads leading to the southeast. The large concentration of infantry supply trains (XV, XVI, XVII corps) remained on the north edge of town. Two divisions and a brigade of Confederate cavalry was pitted against three Union regiments supported by artillery and battle opened around noon.[91]

One of the most tried and true officers of the Board of Trade Battery was Lieutenant Trumbull Griffin. Griffin seemed destined to be in the middle of whatever fighting was occurring and he made notable contributions in several engagements in the war. With Robinson off on Garrard's raid, Griffin commanded the four guns at Decatur and he was ably supported by Lieutenant Henry Bennett. Sprague ordered Griffin and Bennett to camp on the crest of a hill south of the Decatur courthouse and on the north side of the railroad north of the town jail and at that location it was supported with three companies of the 63rd Ohio. This positioned the four guns behind three infantry regiments and the two-gun section of the 1st Michigan Artillery. This seemed a good placement and Board of Trade gunners settled in for a rather non-eventful day. Benjamin Nourse described, "This morning each one lay in his bed as long as he choose. There is no feed for the horses and beside that all are tired. We did some washing and got ready for marching again—We have to improve every chance we get or suffer by neglect. At 12 m. it was rumored through the camp that the rebs were advancing. Stragglers brought in word. So, the brigade of infantry & a section of the 3rd [1st] Mich. battery that were here on train guard, got out and into line and position. The Johnnies opened on them— We had received no orders to harness but our knowledge of war told us to be up and awake." Suddenly, Griffin noticed activity within the infantry and artillery in front and these units began falling into a line of battle. Griffin hurried forward to determine the

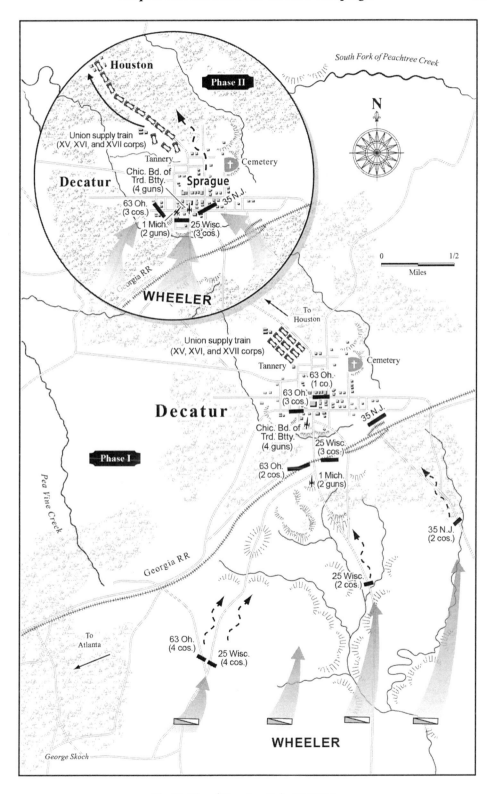

The Battle of Decatur, July 22, 1864.

unfolding situation and found Sprague directing his troops. Sprague calmly told him that the enemy was approaching his line from the south, but he didn't think it was a large force, only enemy cavalry. Sprague, cautious but unconcerned, was trying to determine what was unfolding. So, Griffin returned to the battery and heard an occasional shot, but also, being cautious, he ordered the horses harnessed and the limbers and caissons hitched just in case. Just as the hitching was completed around 1:00, an explosion of artillery and gunfire echoed across the countryside. "So we harnessed and hitched up the moment the skirmishing commenced, but before we got hitched up the shells came right into camp, lighting all round us—our guns opened fire (from where they stood) on the rebels who were coming at a brisk walk across the hill in front (to the south). Our caisson got out into the road—ready for retreat or advance. The wagon trains of the 17th, 15th & 23rd army corps were here, but they got to rear without the loss of a single wagon. It was wonderful to see the men drive and they can thank their stars the road was wide and all the fences down. they drove at a tearing gallop three and four abreast, no stop for any obstruction—the rebels came on by the thousand and the infantry and Mich. battery, fled before them away to the rear. They went without looking at our boys while we gave the rebels canister fearfully, which checked them and allowed the Mich. battery to bring off two guns but they lost their battery wagon and baggage wagons," wrote Nourse. The enemy, Wheeler's cavalry, was driving Sprague's regiments back toward the town. Soon, Wheeler's artillery moved into position and opened fire, the shells falling just left of the Board of Trade Battery. Sprague sent two companies of the 63rd Ohio forward and told Griffin to advance one section, leaving Lieutenant Henry Bennett in command of the section which remained stationary. Griffin hurried forward 100 yards, only to be directed to return to his original position. As the fighting intensified, the infantry regiments and the section of 1st Michigan guns were already in the process of withdrawing before the large enemy force. Griffin hurried back to Bennett's section, unlimbering the guns as the infantry streamed to the rear. The enemy emerged, no more than 300 yards ahead, on the heels of the withdrawing infantry. The Board of Trade Battery opened fire on the Confederate line with canister, effectively stalling the attack, as Sprague's infantry line began forming around the battery. The enemy re-grouped and again pushed directly ahead while swinging around both flanks. A lieutenant colonel of one of the infantry regiments told Griffin he could not hold his position because a strong force was moving on his right flank and that Griffin should withdraw the guns. The four guns limbered and headed for the courthouse square in Decatur. Griffin pulled one section back a short distance behind Bennett's new position on the courthouse lawn because should the enemy attack prove successful, then Griffin would be in position to cover Bennett's withdrawal. This is exactly what happened and as Bennett moved his guns to the courthouse, he came under fire from enemy artillery and cavalry. He quickly got his guns into action and halted the enemy fire. Meanwhile, Griffin's guns in the rear fired away in support of the infantry and Bennett.[92]

Just as things seemed to be under control, a large group of enemy troops appeared off to the right and prepared to make a concentrated attack on Bennett and the 63rd Ohio, while the 35th New Jersey faced the same situation to the east. At the same time, Wheeler was advancing in front of the 25th Wisconsin Infantry. Griffin's section turned its guns to the west, causing the enemy to pause. Still the enemy pressed ahead on both flanks. Nourse explained, "Then the rebs came on again and again we stopped them—but it was no use for we had no support and they stretched their wings and so flanked us on both sides. We

The battery rumbled into position and opened fire ("Going into action," Library of Congress).

drew back a 100 yds to a cross street and so placed the guns, as to rake both streets. Here we did good work with canister, but having no support here. (All the infantry having gone to the rear.) The rebs came up on both sides of us through lots, behind fences, houses etc. and shot our men like dogs, dropping them all round the guns with not a soldier to help us and not a shot from the Mich. battery which had gone to the rear." The Board of Trade Battery blazed away, trying to halt the attack, but after 25 rounds, Griffin saw the position was untenable and ordered the guns withdrawn. Bennett relayed the orders to mount and then both sections withdrew about 400 yards. The battery again opened fire, but immediately realized it could not hold this position either, and withdrew once more into a new line where Sprague's brigade was forming about a mile north of town at the intersection of the Roswell and Pace's Ferry Roads. Here, the battery retained its position as Union infantry (accompanied by another large supply train, this one 400-wagons long) began to arrive and stabilized the position. Wheeler chose not to attack the newly reinforced line. Nourse summarized the end of the fight: "We stood for about three minutes then moved back one mile—where we found the infantry and Mich. battery had halted and were in line—to sum it up—We lost 8 men wounded out of 32 and all this occurred in less than 30 minutes time—but we stopped the rebels long enough to allow all the ammunition & commissary trains for the 3 army corps to get safely to the rear. The rebs did not get a single supply wagon—I don't know what our General will say when he returns and finds us so badly used— The rebel force was Wheeler's Division of Cavalry and one battery. We are thankful their artillery firing was so poor or they might have killed us all." Leaving no one behind, all the wounded were collected and removed to the rear.[93]

Wheeler had little to say in his after-action report about the fighting at Decatur, but he included a few lines about this attack. He advanced his dismounted cavalry and first met the two regiments of infantry. Wheeler pushed the infantry to the rear capturing a number of prisoners by his account. Then, as he advanced against the reforming lines, "we received a most galling fire from both infantry and artillery," probably referring to the action near the courthouse. The Union descriptions of being in a cross fire were correct and Wheeler planned this type of action, placing one line in an oblique attack on the Union right and left flanks and reaching the rear of the line. After firing into the Union defenders, Wheeler ordered both his wings and his troops in the front to attack simultaneously. At first, it seemed the Union line would hold but the Confederates pushed forward, driving the defenders through the town. Wheeler described the attack and the result: "At first the galling fire made the most exposed portion of my line waver, but, quickly rallying, the onset was renewed, and with a triumphant shout the entire line of works was carried. Some 225 prisoners, a large number of small-arms, 1 12-pounder gun, 1 forge, 1 battery wagon, 1 caisson, and 6 wagons and teams, together with the captain of the battery and most of his men, were captured and brought off." Wheeler carried the day but there can be little doubt this was a hard-fought engagement.[94]

Lieutenant Henry Shier, 1st Michigan Artillery, explained that two Confederate batteries, from the left and the right, initially targeted his section forcing it to the rear. Sprague ordered Shier to fall back to a position that was already occupied by the Board of Trade guns near the jail, but he unlimbered a short distance to the right and opened fire in conjunction with the Chicago guns. Then, the position was threatened and Shier withdrew another 150 yards to the courthouse and fired again, before falling back to the final position. Not mentioned in the Board of Trade Battery accounts was some much-needed support from the 63rd Ohio Infantry. Sprague ordered Major John Fouts to a ridge north of the town, but Bennett's section was still firing away. As the enemy approached, the guns were mounted and prepared to make a hasty get-away. Then, Bennett's guns got entangled in a "heap of old iron" just as the enemy converged on the section. Seeing the dire events unfold, Companies G and H fixed bayonets and charged into the enemy, forcing them back while Bennett's section made its escape. Bennett, though a quiet member of the battery, was one of the most reliable and capable officers.[95]

Griffin ended his account: "I cannot close this report without mentioning the name of Lieut. Henry Bennett. His conduct with his section at the court-house, as well as during the whole engagement, was such as to deserve the highest praise and entitle him to the warmest regard of all who witnessed it. Did he not exhibit something more than ordinary coolness and courage on this occasion, I should not under the circumstances have noticed his bravery. I feel it also to be a duty to mention the names of Sergeants Randolph, Salisbury, Deane, and Adams, and Gunners Close, J.D. Howard, John Howard, and Wolcott as men who are entitled to great credit for their conduct upon that day, and to whom I am indebted for much of the efficiency of the battery." Griffin also acknowledged the courage of Private Thomas McClelland, who was shot in the left arm which had to be amputated. McClelland told Griffin that he wasn't so concerned about his arm as much as his disappointment in being forced to retreat. Griffin acknowledged the bravery of all the men in battery who acted "nobly and manfully, and appeared to vie with each other in their exhibition of coolness and bravery." The four guns fired about 125 rounds in the battle. The casualties for the battery totaled eight men and one horse.[96]

A letter from an unnamed member of the battery appeared in the *Chicago Tribune* and added details to the casualty list[97]:

First Position (ridge south of town):	
E.C. Field, it is feared, mortally.	Charley Holyland, foot.
Will Tinsley, severely, right hip.	George Jackenhamer, in the wrist.
Corporal Andrew Close, lower jaw.	
Second Position (town square):	
Tom McClelland, arm, amputated.	J.D. Toomey, right hip.
J.B. Appleton, right leg.	

John Fleming gave further details about the wounded men. Field was shot through the lower abdomen. McClelland was shot with a Minié ball in the left arm, leaving it badly broken. Close was also hit with a Minié ball in the jaw. Fleming remarked that the fight was the worst he ever experienced and fortunately only one horse was shot, which allowed the guns to be withdrawn without a loss. Fleming mused that the fight occurred exactly two years from his enlistment and sarcastically added, "wasn't it celebrated."[98]

The author of a *Chicago Tribune* account gave a description of the fight. "[I]n that, our first position, we had five men wounded. The infantry that should have stood and supported us, ran like cowards and prayers and curses could not rally them. We were forced to fall back to the Court House, only a few yards, and then we managed to get a few men to stand and sharpshoot for us. When the Rebels saw us falling back, they took advantage of it, and formed a triangle on our right and left, getting a terrible cross line on us, wounding three more of our boys. We had to fall back and evacuate the city." A writer for the *Cincinnati Commercial* accompanied Sprague's brigade and wrote in his column: "The section of the Michigan battery joined the section of the Chicago Board of Trade batteries, and the rebels did not seem to be eager to advance into the range of the guns, Lieut. Bennett, who was a stranger to us, won our admiration for his cool, energetic bravery, and will always obtain a hearty greeting from Col. Sprague's brigade."[99]

Included in the list of the wounded was Private John Toomey. The attack came as the men were having their noon meal. Toomey's section opened fire with canister "with terrible effect" but the battery had little infantry support. The enemy attacked "over fences and around buildings," prompting the withdrawal. The battery re-formed on an elevation in the rear and held this position despite the losses. Just at the end of the battle, Toomey was shot in the hip and had to be carried off the field. Toomey urged a comrade to remove the ball, which he reluctantly did by inserting two knife blades into the wound, grasping the ball, and removing it. Afterward, Toomey was away from the battery for three months recuperating. James Appleton's and George Gackenhiemer's wounds would keep them away from the battery for four months.[100]

When the battery reached its final position, General James W. Reilly's infantry brigade, part of the Army of the Ohio, arrived and fired into the attackers. The next day Nourse bitterly remarked in his diary, "Col. Sprague told us we could go. So we left him after saving his brigade and artillery—for all this, he did not so much as thank us or express the least regret at our loss…. Shall we ever receive any credit for yesterday's work? I doubt." Nourse was glad to return to his duty with Garrard's cavalry. However, Nourse's anger might have been misplaced because Sprague recorded in his report that the Chicago Board of Trade Battery "served and worked with admirable skill and rapidity during the action." Other accounts from the battery gave a better accounting of Sprague. The anonymous author of the *Chicago Tribune* account of the fight stated Sprague "thanked us very kindly, and told us we saved his command and train." Sprague also sent a note recognizing the battery's action to General Logan and the battery was given a post of honor in recognition of its actions. Wheeler, who had pushed into the center of town, withdrew and went to the aid of Hardee's infantry. Almost 30 years later, Sprague was awarded the Medal of Honor for organizing the defense of Decatur on July 22. The Battle of Decatur is often presented as almost a footnote to the Battle of Atlanta, but this fight held great significance for Sherman's armies. The loss of the entire supply trains for the Army of the Tennessee and the Army of the Ohio would have been staggering for McPherson and Schofield and would have stopped these two armies in their tracks. Sprague deserved this recognition, and his brigade along with the Board of Trade Battery fought hard, paying a high price for an important place in history.[101]

The toll in this infantry and cavalry battle at Atlanta, which was primarily fought with McPherson's Army of the Tennessee and Hood's Army of Tennessee, was heavy with over 3,700 Union casualties and 5,500 Confederate casualties. Hood replaced Joseph Johnston because it was thought he would fight, and fight he did; but he was losing more men than Sherman, men he could ill afford to lose. Certainly, one of the biggest losses for Sherman's command in this fight was the death of James McPherson. McPherson had shown, perhaps, a unique ability to work with Sherman and had served as a buffer between Garrard and Sherman.[102]

Preparation for McCook's and Stoneman's Raids

Sherman had, so far, called for three cavalry raids in July. Rousseau and Garrard had been very successful, and only Stoneman had failed to find the Chattahoochee River crossing that would have enabled him to strike the Atlanta & West Point Railroad. An additional benefit from Rousseau's raid was the addition of 2,000 cavalry to Sherman's armies. Sherman's reward for Garrard's "perfectly successful" expedition was an opportunity for his men to rest after the three-day raid, and Stoneman was ordered to take Garrard's position on the Union left flank while Rousseau's provisional division assumed responsibility for the Union right flank in cooperation with McCook.[103]

After the Battle of Atlanta on July 22, Hood moved his army into the inner defenses of Atlanta and Sherman asked the rhetorical question of General John Logan, who temporarily commanded the Army of the Tennessee after McPherson's death, "What next?" On July 25, Sherman revealed the answer. He put together a plan which would send an infantry column to the south of the city to occupy the attention of the Confederates and then swing much of his cavalry south of the city, cutting off the railroad coming into Atlanta from Macon. The Atlanta & West Point and the Macon & Western Railroads united at East Point and continued to Atlanta on a single track. If the Union cavalry could destroy the railroad at East Point and move southward, the last rail line into Atlanta would be closed.[104]

On July 25, Sherman issued his orders. Garrard's division and Rousseau's former division, now commanded by the 8th Indiana's Colonel Thomas Harrison, were included in the raid, but because both commands had had hard duty, their roles were initially planned only as support. Only McCook's and Stoneman's divisions would attempt to cut the railroads. McCook, positioned on the west flank, would travel west and then swing south and rendezvous with Stoneman at Lovejoy's Station, well south of East Point.

Stoneman, on the east flank, would begin his raid at Decatur and feint toward Augusta. He would then swing south and meet McCook. It was later decided that Harrison's cavalry would accompany McCook. Garrard would occupy the Confederate cavalry's attention south of Decatur but not participate in the raid on the railroad. Sherman wanted two to five miles of rails destroyed during the raid.[105]

Sherman wrote to Halleck about his strategy: "At the same time I send by the right a force of about 3,500 cavalry, under General McCook, and round by the left about 5,000 cavalry, under Stoneman, with orders to reach the railroad about Griffin. I also have consented that Stoneman (after he has executed this part of his plan), if he finds it feasible, may, with his division proper (about 2,000), go to Macon and attempt the release of our officers, prisoners there, and then to Anderson[ville] to release the 20,000 of our men, prisoners there. This is probably more than he can accomplish, but it is worthy of a determined effort." Sherman's exact orders for Stoneman were: "[H]ave received your letter of July 26, asking permission after breaking good the railroad below McDonough to push on [to Macon], release the officers there, and afterward to go to Anderson[ville] and release the men confined there. I see many difficulties, but, as you say, even a chance of success will warrant the effort, and I consent to it. You may, after having fulfilled my present orders, send General Garrard back to the left flank of the army, and proceed with your command proper to accomplish both or either of the objects named." It was these orders which caused so much confusion and controversy after the raid was over.[106]

On July 24, the Board of Trade Battery reunited after Garrard's raid and the fighting at Decatur. Those who remained at Decatur were told of Garrard's results and Benjamin Nourse summarized: "They tore up and burnt the Augusta rail road for 10 miles, burnt two bridges over 400 feet long and three trains (loaded) of cars, burnt the depot, Confederate warehouses filled with sacked grain, rifle manufactory, 1500 × 2000 and over 400,000$ worth of baled cotton, and brought back 200 prisoners, 500 negroes and 1700 head of horses and mules. Our section brought 15 head of stock, (two of the largest mules I ever saw) tobacco, meal, sugar & leather. The Division lost only 3 men killed, none wounded." In return, Lieutenant Robinson and his section discovered the losses after the fighting at Decatur. Nourse wrote that Robinson "is sorry that so many men are gone. Who is not?" The next day the cavalry division moved to Decatur. On July 26, the impact of the fighting at Decatur continued for those who had escaped injury when the camp learned that Thomas McClelland had his arm amputated above the elbow due to his wounds. McClelland, a druggist before the war, would survive his injuries but would have a series of misfortunes after the war. Nourse asked, "What could anyone do?" The battery took up a collection and gathered over $700 for him.[107]

On the eve of the new cavalry raids, several important command changes occurred within the Army of the Cumberland. Fourth Corps Commander, Oliver Howard, was promoted to command the Army of the Tennessee after McPherson's death. This decision caused some dissension within the command of the Union army. Some felt John Logan should have been offered command. The other officer particularly unhappy was Joseph Hooker who had performed well after arriving in the west in the fall of 1863, and he complained that Howard was his junior in rank. Hooker immediately asked to be relieved of command of the Twentieth Corps and his request was granted. In the cavalry, Judson Kilpatrick, recuperated from his wound, returned to command the Third Cavalry Division.

Garrard's Support of Stoneman's Raid

George Stoneman began his raid the same day Edward McCook planned to begin his raid. Stoneman intended to swing around the east side of Hood's army and meet with McCook near Lovejoy's Station. Sherman, temporarily pleased with Garrard's latest action, ordered Stoneman not to over-use Garrard's exhausted horses. Stoneman rode with three brigades totaling about 2,000 men while Garrard's division of 3,500 men also served under Stoneman's command. On July 27, Stoneman, a major general, met with Garrard, a brigadier general, and ordered him to Flat Rock, or Flat Shoals, to occupy the Confederate cavalry's attention. Captain William E. Crane, 4th Ohio, wrote sarcastically of the role Garrard's cavalry was to play; "[W]e attract the enemy's attention toward ourselves—Stoneman to do the raiding & we the fighting." This plan would allow Stoneman to start his raid unencumbered and divert the enemy's attention away from his march into the Confederate rear. The Board of Trade Battery began the expedition at 3:00 a.m. and would move 30 miles during the day. Nourse recorded: "3 oc. this morning found us harnessed and ready to move out. the first brigade and 1st section have the advance. We went into Decatur & halted for Stoneman's Div. to take the advance—moving, we kept a south east course all day and at dark halted at Flat Rock ford on South River—30 good miles today. Col. Minty captured 6 wagons and one ambulance at the bridge. All of said property belonging to the so-called Southern Confederacy—they were burnt. Stoneman had taken a road to the left or east of us—tonight we are 7 miles from Jonesboro, Ga. a town on the Macon & Atlanta R.R. I suppose we shall cut the road tomorrow." Garrard spent the first day without much resistance, and reached his destination at 2:00 p.m. after riding 20 miles or so. Garrard ordered his command to form a horseshoe shaped defensive line on the north side of the South River. Immediately, Brigadier General Alfred Iverson's three brigades of Confederate cavalry rode to meet Garrard's force and attacked at about 10:00 p.m. that evening when a few picket shots erupted into an explosive fight. About midnight Wheeler arrived to take command of the Confederate forces.[108]

Despite Garrard's diversion, Wheeler was aware that Stoneman continued his march intent on destroying the railroad somewhere south of Atlanta. Wheeler ordered one brigade to stay in Garrard's front while two other brigades pursued Stoneman. Confederate reinforcements, brigades of Colonel George Dibrell and Colonel Robert Anderson, converged on Garrard's position. At 8:00 a.m. on July 28, the Confederates opened with two 12-pounder howitzers on the Federals. The Board of Trade Battery returned fire. Private John Fleming's section was ordered to address the Confederate artillery. Fleming explained that the section moved into position to fire on the Southern guns, under a "shower of bullets," but once the guns got into action, it silenced the enemy artillery after firing 50 rounds. The author of *Sherman's Horsemen*, David Evans, wrote, "Everyone knew they were in a tight place. A captured Confederate intimated Garrard was surrounded by seven brigades of Wheeler's cavalry." In addition, it was possible Rebel infantry was already closing in from Atlanta. At 10:00 a.m. a Confederate officer approached the Union line under a flag of truce demanding Garrard's unconditional surrender. After an extended conversation, Garrard, whom Sherman thought timid, replied, "Tell your general that as soon as I get ready I will walk out of here." Then, the Confederate officer was escorted back across the lines.[109]

Garrard made his boast a reality and his division broke out of its position by initially moving a strong force to the southeast side of the line. Benjamin McGee, 72nd

Indiana Mounted explained that prior to the full attack, "[T]wo pieces of artillery (Board of Trade) were run down to Long's position on the river and opened on the rebels vigorously on the east and south. They replied, and for a time the music was lively." Then, Garrard formed his real attack on the northern side of the line. McGee continued, "The balance of the artillery was brought up and two pieces unlimbered and put in position, and when everything was ready the artillery opened out. We jumped over our works and without uttering a word started on a keen run." Nourse, who had a poor night's sleep on the muddy ground, wrote: "At day light we were ready to move but the rebel Genl. Wheeler had brought his cavalry all around us. They drove in our pickets and as soon as they see well fighting commenced—fighting untill 11 oclock a.m. then the 123rd Illinois charged dismounted supported by the 7th Penn & 4th regular cavalry on the flanks. Our gun fired over their heads as they went across the fields. They quickly cleared the road and our Division quietly moved out and back 7 miles to Lithonia on the Augusta & Atlanta R.R. the Rebels did not follow us. They dare not cross South River. the Div. lost 12 men—the 2nd Sect. was with the 2nd brigade and did some good shooting." Garrard formed a skirmish line, placed Abram Miller's brigade of mounted infantry in the center, Minty's cavalry on the flanks, and Eli Long's cavalry behind. Then the line of blue surged forward, pushing back north toward Latimer's Crossroads. In 20 minutes, Garrard had cut his way out and the Confederates did not pursue. On the evening of July 30, Garrard's column returned to the main Union lines fulfilling his orders and providing time for Stoneman to initiate his raid.[110]

But Stoneman was not destined to be successful in his raid despite Sherman's initial conclusion that the railroad was cut south of Atlanta. Sherman notified Henry Halleck that Stoneman had cut the railroad and had two days' head start on the Confederates. In fact, the rails cut south of Atlanta were the result of McCook's efforts and not Stoneman's. He was correct, however, that Garrard had given Stoneman a head start. After Minty's return from Flat Shoals, he talked with Kilpatrick. Kilpatrick spoke of Stoneman, "Mark me, Minty, I know Stoneman like a book. He will go to the proper spot like a cannon ball, but when he gets there, like a shell, he will burst." The battery remained in camp on July 29 but the following day, it marched 40 miles, passing through Lithonia and shifting toward Stone Mountain, only to return to Cross Keys.[111]

As the days dragged on, Sherman worried about McCook and Stoneman still absent on their respective expeditions. Sherman's fickleness toward Garrard continued. His irritability about the cavalry was focused on Garrard who, just days before, was in Sherman's good graces for his success at Covington and Yellow River. Now Garrard was in the doghouse again despite the fact Garrard reported he was surrounded by superior Confederate force, which was not true in fact. Sherman focused on the small losses of his command and the fact he had not destroyed any of the railroad even though Garrard acted properly under Stoneman's and Sherman's own orders. This manner of evaluation of military effort recalled William Rosecrans' communication to Henry Halleck who disregarded the achievements of the Tullahoma Campaign because they were not "written in letters of blood." Sherman's unhappiness during the day resulted in a letter to Thomas and Howard exclaiming, "I must have a bolder commander for General Garrard's cavalry and want General Thomas to name to me General Kilpatrick or some good brigadier for the command." Thomas came to Garrard's defense urging Sherman to reconsider, "I think if you will bear with Garrard you will find in a short time he will be the best cavalry commander you have."[112]

Perhaps Sherman would have been more tolerant of Garrard's actions if he was aware of orders given to him by Stoneman. Sherman seemed to have expectations that Garrard would have a more active role in Stoneman's raid despite his own orders and was frustrated that Garrard made no further progress than Flat Rock. Sherman seemed to expect Garrard to accompany Stoneman to McDonough, but Stoneman gave no such directions. Stoneman, in his haste for glory, followed what he perceived to be Sherman's orders of assigning Garrard to light duties since he had so recently been on a raid of his own. To round out this lack of understanding, Garrard was equally frustrated and said so in his after-action report: "On the 27th the division was placed under General Stoneman, who ordered it to Flat Rock, and abandoned it to its fate." Sherman's greater concern was the fate of McCook, who was stranded at Lovejoy's Station waiting for Stoneman who would never arrive. In Sherman's message about the cavalry raid, he clearly and correctly envisioned McCook with no bridge to re-cross the river, facing Wheeler, deep in enemy territory and alone.[113]

Historians do not agree about Stoneman's decisions during his raid and the ultimate outcome. Stoneman had imagined a greater raid than originally planned by Sherman. Sherman's original plan was to destroy the last railroad from the south leading into Atlanta, but Stoneman imagined the glory of sweeping through enemy territory releasing Union prisoners at Macon and then Andersonville. Sherman had agreed, but Stoneman needed to destroy the railroad first. By-passing his obligations at Lovejoy's Station, Stoneman reached the outskirts of Macon on July 30, about 90 miles south of Atlanta but a determined defense of militia, citizens and reserves prevented his entry into the town. He initially considered riding to Florida, but then headed north. He ran into Wheeler's cavalry north of Macon on July 31, and he ordered two of his brigades to breakout on their own while he and the last brigade covered the escape. Stoneman was forced to surrender with 700 of his men and Capron's brigade would be shattered as it fought its way back to the Union lines.[114]

It is also important to note the exceptional performance of the Confederate cavalry during the McCook and Stoneman raids. Wheeler and Jackson were drawn in three different directions and still effectively contained the Union raids. This is a testament to the Southern cavalry and their commanders. This was one of the premier defensive actions of the war and the result was saving the last lifeline to Atlanta and the destruction of two full Union cavalry divisions along the way. Certainly, this was one of Joseph Wheeler's best actions of the war. Sherman's conclusion of the cavalry expeditions beginning on July 27 and 28 was: "General McCook is entitled to much credit for thus saving his command, which was endangered by the failure of General Stoneman to reach Lovejoy's. But on the whole the cavalry raid is not deemed a success, for the real purpose was to break the enemy's communications, which though done was on so limited a scale that I knew the damage would soon be repaired."[115]

Sherman, ever the practical general, with half of his cavalry essentially gone, ordered Garrard to the left flank and ordered up Kilpatrick's Third Division to the right flank. What remained of McCook's cavalry was sent to the Marietta area for garrison duty. After all these efforts, Sherman still had to find a way to cut the last railroad to Atlanta, and now Wheeler was looking at the vulnerable supply line in the rear of the Union armies. Sherman temporarily reviewed the use of his cavalry and wrote to Henry Halleck, "I will use my cavalry hereafter to cover the railroad, and use infantry and artillery against Atlanta." Sherman was not to follow his own advice.[116]

A New Month—August 1, 1864

In late July, Sherman moved his armies back to the west and attempted to get around Hood's flank. Schofield's Army of the Ohio moved from the left to the Union right flank, Howard's Army of the Tennessee occupied the center and Thomas's Army of the Cumberland held the left flank. When Schofield moved, Sherman assigned the duty of occupying the vacated trenches east of the city to Garrard's cavalry. This was hapless duty for cavalrymen, but the Confederate cavalry had been manning the lines with the infantry for many months. Fortunately, not all of Garrard's cavalry were destined for the trenches. Much of Garrard's cavalry remained in the trenches for only two weeks, and the rest for the horses was needed.[117]

On August 8, Brigadier General Washington L. Elliott reported the condition of the cavalry for Sherman's armies at Atlanta:

Strength of the Cavalry
(Army of the Cumberland)—August 8, 1864[118]

Total Present for Duty	Officers	Men	Total
McCook's Division	67	949	1,016
Garrard's Division	199	4,177	4,376
Kilpatrick's Division	162	2,826	2,988

For the next two and half weeks, the Board of Trade Battery remained with the Second Cavalry Division in line with the Union armies besieging Atlanta. A message from Nashville arrived reporting Private Desire Joubert's leg was amputated due to his injuries on June 19. A few days later, the men learned that Edward Field died due to his wounds received at Decatur. Field died during a move of the field hospitals. Nourse wrote: "The army changed its line and the hospitals had to be changed also. The surgeon knew that Edward could not be moved in an ambulance so he detailed 4 men to carry him—they bore him as easily as possible but he died while on the way to the new hospital, just as he was on the stretcher—he is buried near the R.R. track 3 miles from Atlanta." He lamented that everything possible was done to save his life and he philosophically mused, "[S]o they go one after another, good boys all." The constant shelling by heavy artillery continued daily and by mid-month great fires swept through Atlanta. On August 16, word that Desire Joubert had died reached the battery. Joubert had been hit in the leg with a shell fragment during the fighting at Noonday Creek, resulting in gangrene, and his ultimate death. John Fleming also recorded Joubert's death on the eve of Kilpatrick's Raid; he mused "One by one they go, but now are only 70 of original number doing duty in the battery," less than half the original number of enlistees.[119]

After McCook's and Stoneman's raids, McCook's division was dismounted and sent to join Louis Watkins' brigade in the rear to protect the supply line at Kingston and Cartersville, Georgia, and Calhoun, Tennessee. When horses became available, McCook's troopers were sent to Nashville to be remounted. On August 10, Wheeler began a month-long raid into Tennessee that would challenge the reserves and defenses in the rear of Sherman's armies. Sherman rallied his troops in the rear to deal with Wheeler but he believed the raid to be more of a nuisance than a threat. The removal of Wheeler and much of Confederate cavalry from the Atlanta area, and Schofield's reluctance to send his infantry on an expedition to cut the railroad south of Atlanta, helped persuade Sherman to allow another cavalry raid. Kilpatrick, whose aggressive tendencies found favor with Sherman, was able to persuade Sherman to try another raid. Not everyone supported this plan, including George Thomas. Washington Elliott issued orders for both Kilpatrick and Garrard on August 14 to develop the Confederate positions in preparation for the raid. Garrard was ordered to push hard on the left flank and to give battle with the Confederate cavalry "without too much risk." Kilpatrick was also ordered to the same duty on the western flank, but before any raid was ordered Sherman wanted to hear from both Garrard and Kilpatrick about what they were facing.[120]

By mid–August, Sherman decided to give Eli Long command of the Second Division. Sherman had just lost the bulk of two of his four cavalry divisions on ill-fated raids on Hood's communications, but Garrard's performance was supported by top army commanders—Thomas, McPherson and by his immediate commanding officer, Elliott. Kilpatrick's fighting spirit convinced Sherman to attempt to break the railroad south of Atlanta which would take place from August 18 through August 22. Prior to the raid, Sherman explained his reasoning to allow Kilpatrick to lead, "[H]e will fight. I do believe he, with his own and General Garrard's cavalry, could ride right round Atlanta and mash the Macon road all to pieces, but I don't want to risk our cavalry." Sherman chose to send Garrard's best two brigades while not including Garrard himself in the raid. George Robinson, commanding the Board of Trade Battery, related that during the planning of the raid, Garrard told Sherman that he did not think the raid would be successful unless all of the cavalry was used to destroy the railroads. Sherman was not prepared to commit all of his cavalry and Garrard's reluctance gave Sherman the opportunity to exclude Garrard from the raid. After the war, when addressing the details of the raid, Robinson remarked, "[E]vents, proved that his [Garrard's] judgment was pretty nearly correct."[121]

Kilpatrick's Raid—the Advance

Kilpatrick left the Union lines on the evening of August 18. He rode with over 4,500 troopers from his own Third Cavalry Division and Second Cavalry Division's two brigades. Eli Long (who was probably not aware he had been promoted to the rank of brigadier general that day) and Minty commanded the two Second Division brigades. Once the expedition was completed, Kilpatrick planned to return to the Union right flank. In light of Stoneman's failed raid, Kilpatrick's objective was to destroy enough track to put the railroad out of commission for two weeks. The Second Division's force included 871 men and 54 officers of Colonel Robert Minty's brigade (4th Michigan, 7th Pennsylvania and 4th U.S.) and another 1,308 men and 75 officers of Long's brigade (1st, 3rd and 4th Ohio cavalries). (The 46-year-old Col. Beroth Eggleston would gain command of Long's brigade when Long was wounded during the expedition. Before the war, he was a businessman, postmaster and farmer near Chillicothe, Ohio.) The Chicago Board of Trade Battery (four guns) commanded by Robinson also accompanied the expedition with Lieutenant Henry Bennett and 88 enlisted men. Kilpatrick sent a communication to each of the regiments outlining the objective of the raid and concluded: "Let each soldier remember this & resolve to accomplish this, the great object for which so much is risked, or die trying."[122]

Second Cavalry Division On Kilpatrick's Raid[123]

Commands	Officers	Men	Total	Guns
First Brigade, Col. R.H.G. Minty	54	871	925	....
Second Brigade, Col. Eli Long	75	1,308	1,383	....
Chicago Board of Trade Battery, Lieutenant G. Robinson	2	88	90	4
Total	131	2,267	2,398	4

The Board of Trade Battery received orders to begin its movement at 11:00 p.m. on August 17. Nourse recorded: "Numbers 1, 3, 4 & 5 with 8 horses each and the caisson limbers with 6 horses—2 days rations were issued—and we moved at two oclock with the 1st, & 2nd brigades under Col. Minty—the moon shone clear and bright and traveling was very pleasant. We rode until 9 oc. a.m." The raid began on August 18 and Kilpatrick ran into the pickets of the 6th Texas Cavalry at Camp Creek, three miles south of Sandtown. Just after midnight, Kilpatrick pushed General "Sul" Ross's 400 troopers aside at East Point and away from the road with Lieutenant Colonel Fielder Jones' Second Brigade as the rest of the Union column passed. At daylight, Kilpatrick began destroying the Atlanta & West Point Railroad five miles further at Red Oak, about eight miles south of the Chattahoochee River. Benjamin Nourse described: "At 6 oc. p.m. we were under way going from Sand Town towards the Montgomery R.R. Skirmishing with the rebel cavalry commenced at 9 oc. but the 98th Illinois soon drove them. Kilpatrick's Division now got at the road, tore up and burnt the rails for miles. I shall never forget how the road looked when we came up to it. (I had been more than half asleep on my horses.) the fire was in a cut and the banks of red clay. It looked in the gray of morning like a very firey furnace. As our guns came up and crossed the track, the well known sound of a 12# shell struck our ears—(sound and shell) and over us it went striking in the woods and burying itself in the earth. Their next one came nearer us, but struck no one, but by the time it came my turn to cross the track and in full view and easy range of the rebel guns—I went over at a

General Hugh Judson Kilpatrick commanded the Third Cavalry Division (Library of Congress).

trot. A shell passed and burst just in front of me but not a piece struck any of us. Our two brigades passed without any one being hurt." After the late-night surprise, General Ross reorganized his cavalry and attacked Kilpatrick while he was attending to the destruction of the rails. However, the numbers of Union cavalry were just too great and the Federals repulsed his attack.[124]

Robinson's guns got into this fight near Red Oak/Bank. A Confederate battery greeted Kilpatrick's forces upon their arrival. Robinson unlimbered the guns on open ground south of the railroad and targeted the enemy battery. In the meantime, Minty's brigade wheeled into position on both sides of the guns and the 4th Michigan advanced through the smoke, fog, and darkness, driving the enemy defenders to the rear. After driving away the first enemy force, the column resumed its march towards Jonesborough only to run into another battery and force of Confederate cavalry. Again, Minty's brigade moved his troopers ahead at a trot on the right and left of the road and the Board of Trade Battery remained in the center, on the road. The skirmishers pushed ahead and when the Federals reached the crest of a low hill, the main line of enemy forces was seen behind rough barricades positioned around a Confederate battery. As soon the Union cavalry crested the hill, the enemy battery opened fire. Robinson hurried his first section in line and returned fire from a position on the road. Shortly thereafter, the second section unlimbered on the left of the road and joined in. In the meantime, Minty's dismounted troops surged toward the defenders. Robinson explained, "A few well directed and well timed shells from us, and their battery withdrew, quickly followed by their cavalry, leaving only a strong skirmish line to check our advance." The cavalry remounted and advanced, only to find another such position a mile ahead. The process was repeated several times. The Board of Trade Battery dismounted one of the enemy guns in this subsequent fighting.[125]

Then, Kilpatrick marched for his real objective—Jonesborough. The flamboyant Kilpatrick was in his element as described by Captain William E. Crane, 4th Ohio Cavalry: "I found Kilpatrick flying about in lively style, swearing at everything & issuing half a dozen orders in a breath." Again, Ross reformed his cavalry and began a fight-withdraw-fight strategy to slow Kilpatrick who pressed toward Jonesborough. A significant fight took place at the Flint River Bridge where Ross attempted to burn the bridge over the river while trying to delay the Union column. The enemy resistance stiffened and had a good defensive position at the Flint River. Robinson noticed that the enemy artillery had been positioned so that it could cover the bridge over the river. The enemy artillery had been delayed in getting over the stream and then Ross attempted to burn the bridge, but he was too late. As Union cavalry arrived, Robinson wheeled a section of guns into place, driving the enemy troops away from the bridge. In return, the Confederate battery opened on the Board of Trade section, but the shells sailed over the heads of the gunners, succeeding in only disturbing the horses. Henry Bennett's two-gun section arrived and went into a firing position on a knoll on the left of the road. When Bennett opened fire, Robinson moved his section to the left of Bennett's guns on a ridge and the four guns quickly silenced the Confederate battery. Robert Burns wrote that the very first shot from Robinson's guns "struck a rebel artilleryman, burst inside him, blowing him to atoms." The *New York Herald* exclaimed that Bennett's section of guns "dried up" the Confederate artillery and sent it to the rear. Long's cavalry surged across the river and drove the Confederate line defending the bridge and approach to the river, while the Board of Trade Battery dueled with Confederate guns.[126]

While on the way to Red Oak, Kilpatrick decided he needed a diversion to keep the Confederates from focusing all their efforts on the main column. He ordered his 309-man,

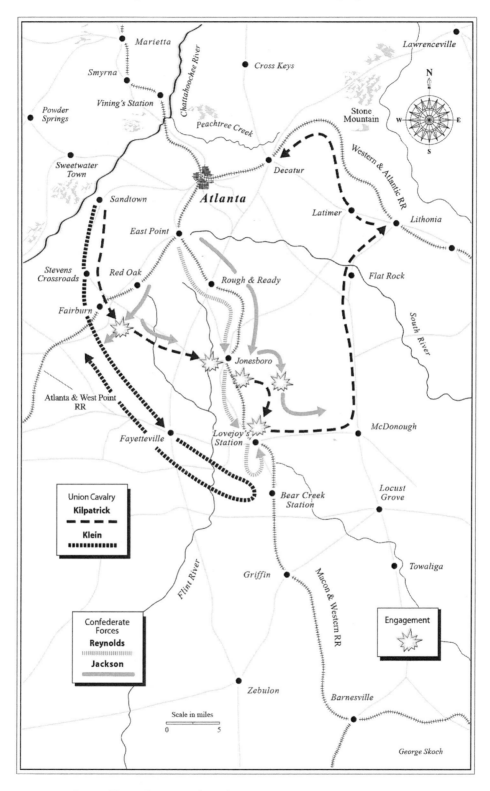

Kilpatrick's Raid During the Atlanta Campaign, August 18–22, 1864.

two-regiment First Brigade (3rd Indiana and 5th Iowa), under command of the veteran Lieutenant Colonel Robert Klein, to ride to Fairburn, five miles west of Red Oak, and destroy the railroad there. Upon completing this task, Klein was to rejoin Kilpatrick at Griffin. Klein's ruse worked perfectly. Frank Armstrong's Confederate cavalry was posted at Jonesborough and rode to meet Klein's feint, leaving Jonesborough lightly defended. When Kilpatrick reached Jonesborough, he found the telegraph and railroad at Bear Creek Station, 10 miles south of Jonesborough, were already destroyed by Klein's command. Armstrong's and Samuel Ferguson's cavalry had ridden through Jonesborough at 1:00 p.m. to attack Klein. Klein destroyed about 300 yards of track at Bear Creek Station and after setting a train afire rode northward, destroying sections of track along the way. Two miles south of Lovejoy's Station, a train filled with Confederates was observed heading in his direction. Facing infantry and cavalry, and not finding Kilpatrick, Klein decided it was time to try to get his two regiments back to the Union lines. Klein rode west for Fayetteville and when he was within two miles of the town, he saw Confederates, part of Frank Armstrong's Mississippi Cavalry, across the road in front of him. He had been cut off, but Klein, a former Prussian soldier, decided his only hope lay ahead. Then, he ordered "charge" and the column slammed into and then through the thin Southern line. Klein reached the Union lines on August 20.[127]

For Kilpatrick's main column, moving into Jonesborough was no easy task, even after driving the enemy away from the Flint River Bridge. The Union troopers could see over the trees the church spires and the railroad station. After the Confederate battery withdrew, Robinson's guns continued the barrage on the wooded area on the east side of the river. Minty sent the 4th Michigan to claim the bridge, supported by the 7th Pennsylvania, while the Board of Trade guns hammered the enemy positions. Robinson recalled, "I said to Col. Minty, who happened to be near me, that I thought if the enemy had any additional force it should have shown itself there, that I believed we had got them already scared, and with his permission I would move two of my guns across and on to the skirmish line." Minty agreed and Robinson moved the guns steadily ahead by hand, alternately firing canister and shell, as needed. The enemy battery made no further appearance and this allowed Robinson to focus on the enemy troops. Robinson explained, "Our line now moved forward boldly, preceded by a strong line of skirmishers and two guns of the battery on the skirmish line." In the meantime, the enemy resistance lessened. Then, Kilpatrick descended on Jonesborough, skirmishing with the remnants of the defenders. "The most annoyance that we were then receiving was from that part of their force located under and around the water tank, and I directed a shell at it which went through it near the bottom, and the water from it compelled them to vacate its immediate vicinity." Next, Robinson focused on the buildings near the railroad. "The freight depot was quite an extensive structure, with a small dome or tower in the centre of the roof, resembling more, however, the ventilators we often see on barns through the country in the northern states. I then directed a shell, with short fuse, at the roof of the depot, which struck it near the centre and well down near the eaves, and exploded inside, and the little tower seemed to jump bodily about ten or fifteen feet into the air and then rolled down the roof and dropped to the ground. A cloud of smoke soon rose through the aperture in the roof, followed by flame, and the depot was soon ablaze, which quickly spread to the adjacent warehouses and a train of cars on the further side, all of which we afterwards learned were filled with commissary stores and the household goods of refugees."[128]

The major part of the town consisted of a main street with a row of stores, residences and railroad buildings on either side. Bennett's section of guns was placed so that they could obliquely fire on the enemy defenders and then open up. The other two guns moved opposite the railroad depot and started firing from the west of the railroad. The two sections only had to fire a few shells down the main street before the defenders scurried out of town. Robinson continued: "We … went forward at the gallop, the cannoneers mounting the limber-chests and the trails of the pieces, and went into position at the spot just vacated by the center of the enemy's line, and again commenced shelling the rear of his column down the road. Thus these two gun-detachments were the first Yankee troops to enter the town. A few dismounted rebels, left behind, took refuge in the buildings on our right and front and let into us pretty lively from the windows for a moment or two, but a couple of shells sent crashing through the building soon silenced them, and the 4th Michigan coming up we ceased firing."[129]

The main column of the Union cavalry spent the next six hours destroying the railroads around Jonesborough. Minty's 4th U.S. and 4th Michigan moved north of the town, guarding the crossroads and forming a screen to prevent any attacks from Atlanta. W.L. Curry, 1st Ohio Cavalry, described the scene around Jonesborough, "The sky was lighted up with burning timbers, buildings and cotton bales; the continuous bang of carbines, the galloping of staff officers and orderlies up and down the streets carrying orders and dispatches, the terrified citizens peering out their windows, the constant marching of troops changing positions" all accompanied by Kilpatrick's divisional band playing patriotic Union music. Hampering the efforts to destroy the railroad, the sky opened and a downpour of rain commenced. Robinson lamented: "[I]t *did* rain as if it had been husbanding a six months' supply for this particular time, and unmindful of a reserve for any future occasion." The rain hampered further destruction of the railroad because the wet crossties would not burn and without a fire, the rails could not be bent. The cavalrymen settled for tearing up the railroad and scattering the crossties. In all, about a mile or two of railroad was destroyed.[130]

Benjamin Nourse described the action of the battery on August 18–19: "One mile west of the town [Jonesborough] we had a stiff fight. The two brigades dismounted and charged the rebs and quickly drove them through the town—28 miles today—We set fire to the depot, cars, track, warehouses, court house, stores, and shops—also to one house because the owner cut the well rope and dropped both bucket and rope down the well. He ought to have been shot. The rebel cavalry charged the town twice during the night but our Spencers kept them off."[131]

Later that night, Colonel Eli Murray's Third Brigade of Kilpatrick's Division was attacked a mile from Lovejoy's Station by Brigadier General Daniel Harris Reynolds' Arkansas infantry, which had been transported part of the way by railcars. Reynolds was joined with Brigadier General William "Red" Jackson's cavalry. It was the 10th Ohio Cavalry's turn to be surprised as they rode along the track and was hit by a volley from Reynolds's infantry. Kilpatrick suspended his rail destruction and sent his entire command to face the Confederate force converging on his position. The two lines faced each other under a heavy rain, which made the situation even worse for both sides. Kilpatrick, in his own particular style, worsened the situation as the Southern guns and the Union battery counter-fired. Due to the darkness, it was somewhat difficult to locate the various guns, but Kilpatrick insisted that his band play Union songs while positioned near the Union artillery. John Nourse recorded: "Our cannoneers were quite indignant and used their ramrods to drive the band out of the battery."[132]

Kilpatrick faced cavalry and infantry from the south, and train whistles were heard coming from the north. Kilpatrick did not want a pitched battle behind enemy lines.

So, he called his commanding officers to a meeting on the porch of a house and he discussed his escape route. He decided to feint his withdrawal by a northerly route and then ride west. Unknown to Kilpatrick, in addition to Reynolds's infantry, Ferguson's, Ross' and Armstrong's Confederate cavalry brigades were also riding toward him. He made the decision to extract his command and begin moving east on the Stockbridge Road toward McDonough, then turned south and west on the Fayetteville Road. Two guns of the Board of Trade Battery accompanied Minty's brigade and the other two traveled with Long's brigade. Benjamin Nourse noted, "Towards morning we left the town and moved 7 miles—halted just long enough to get a cup of coffee."[133]

Kilpatrick's Raid—Fight at Nash Farm

The Union column was riding south toward the Fayetteville Road when the 3rd Texas Cavalry attacked the 3rd Ohio Cavalry serving as rearguard, sending it rushing for the Union column. The 3rd and 4th Ohio cavalries formed a solid line and stopped the Confederate attack and then moved to regain the column, but Ross had discovered the true route of Kilpatrick's retreat. He was not riding north; he was riding south. Ross sent this information to Reynolds, who ordered his infantry back down the railroad to Lovejoy's Station, correctly anticipating Kilpatrick would turn west. Kilpatrick, in his movement to the west, struck the railroad about a mile north of Lovejoy's Station at 11:00 a.m. on August 20. As he moved south toward the station he ran into Reynolds's infantry. What ensued was to be known as the Battle of Nash Farm. Kilpatrick found himself battling infantry in his front with cavalry attacking his rear in this hard-fought battle.[134]

Order of Battle, August 20, 1864[135]
Union Forces
Major General Judson Kilpatrick

Second Cavalry Division

1st Cavalry Brigade—Colonel Robert Minty	2nd Cavalry Brigade— Eli Long/ Beroth B. Eggleston
4th Michigan Cavalry—Major Frank Mix	3rd Ohio Cavalry—Colonel Charles B. Seidel
7th Pennsylvania Cavalry—Major Wm. Jennings	4th Ohio Cavalry—Lt Colonel Oliver P. Robie
4th U.S. Cavalry—Captain James B. McIntyre	1st Ohio Cavalry—Colonel Beroth B. Eggleston
Chicago Board of Trade Battery (4 guns)—Lieutenants Henry Bennett and George Robinson	

Third Cavalry Division

1st Cavalry Brigade—Lt. Colonel Robert Klein	2nd Cavalry Brigade—Lieutenant Colonel Fielder Jones
3rd Indiana Cavalry—Major Alfred Gaddis	8th Indiana Cavalry—Major Thomas Herring
5th Iowa Cavalry—Major John Morris Young	2nd Kentucky Cavalry—Major Owen Starr
10th Ohio Cavalry—Lt Colonel Thomas Wakefield Sanderson	

3rd Cavalry Brigade—Colonel Eli Houston Murray

92nd Illinois Mounted Infantry—Colonel Smith D. Atkins (Major Albert Woodcock)

3rd Kentucky Cavalry—Lt Colonel Robert H. King

5th Kentucky Cavalry—Colonel Oliver L. Baldwin

10th Wisconsin Battery Light Artillery—Captain Yates V. Beebe

Confederate Forces

Cavalry Division—Brigadier General William Hicks Jackson

Armstrong's Brigade— Brig. General Frank Armstrong	Ross's Brigade— Brig. General Lawrence S. Ross
1st Mississippi Cavalry—Col. R.A. Pinson	1st Texas Legion–Colonel Edwin R. Hawkins
2nd Mississippi Cavalry–Major J.J. Perry	3rd Texas Cavalry–Lt Colonel Jiles S. Boggess
28th Mississippi Cavalry–Major Joshua T. McBee	6th Texas Cavalry–Lt Colonel Peter F. Ross
Ballentine's (Mississippi)–Lt Colonel William L. Maxwell	9th Texas Cavalry–Colonel Dudley W. Jones
Company "A" 1st Confederate Cavalry–Captain James Ruffin	

Ferguson's Brigade—Brig. General Samuel Wragg Ferguson

2nd Alabama Cavalry–Colonel John N. Carpenter

56th Alabama Cavalry–Colonel William Boyles

9th Mississippi Cavalry–Colonel H.H. Miller

11th Mississippi Cavalry–Colonel R.O. Perrin

12th Mississippi Cavalry Battalion–William M. Inge

Artillery–Captain John Waties

Croft's Battery, Georgia Light Artillery (Columbus Artillery)–1st Lt Alfred J. Young

King's Battery, Missouri Light Artillery (Clark Artillery)–Captain Houston King

3rd Battalion, South Carolina Light Artillery (Palmetto Battalion)–Lt R.B. Waddell

Confederate Infantry Brigade–
Brigadier General Daniel Harris Reynolds

1st Arkansas Mounted Rifles (dismounted)

2nd Arkansas Mounted Rifles (dismounted)

4th Arkansas Infantry

9th Arkansas Infantry

25th Arkansas Infantry

48th Tennessee Infantry (Attached to Reynolds' brigade)

As Kilpatrick's column approached Lovejoy's Station, he discovered a line of Reynolds' infantry. A volley from some of Jackson's cavalry stopped the Union advance.

Reynolds' brigade charged ahead as Minty and Long deployed their regiments, dismounted, into a battle line. One volley killed Minty's horse under him and the Union cavalry was pushed back through a 400-yard-long cornfield. The 7th Pennsylvania Cavalry was hit particularly hard during the fight. T.F. Dornblaser recorded the Confederate infantry poured a volley into his company killing four and wounding several others, including Dornblaser. Long deployed his brigade as Minty's forward command was roughly pushed to the rear, but they rallied on Long's position. As Minty realigned, the Second Brigade troopers began throwing up rough barricades. The cornfield gave the Chicago Board of Trade Battery a treeless field of fire and the gunners began to fire double loaded canister, "opening a galling fire" on the enemy attack, wrote Joseph Vale, 7th Pennsylvania Cavalry. Once the battery began firing "the cavalry raised the cheer, and I felt better," recalled George Robinson. Robinson's shots cleared the cornfield of enemy soldiers while ripping the corn to shreds. Robinson soon noticed the ground was so soft that recoils of the guns resulted in trenches being formed around the wheels. The battery boys had to physically lift the guns out of the ruts after a couple of shots. With the enemy troops under cover, the battery slowed its shelling, but suddenly, the enemy line exploded from the woods. Robinson explained they "let us have it, seemingly with a confidence that they had us within their grasp, and it looked a little that way to me, for this first revealed to me that my flanks were not protected and that my support had fallen back. One of my guns had broken down and the limber been sent to the rear, but I quickly changed front to the right by drawing back my right piece and running forward the left, and again gave them canister, and splinters, rails and rebels flew promiscuously in our front, and that flank was soon cleared when we discovered that we were being fired into from the woods on the left, now almost to our rear, but not by so much of a force, and we drew back our left piece and opened on them in that direction and soon drove back the comparatively small force that had moved down there under cover of the fence, woods and standing corn … now having a temporary breathing spell, and my men reporting ammunition nearly gone, one man killed, a number of others badly wounded, a number of horses shot and one gun hanging by the trunnions beneath the axle, I concluded to get out of that cornfield with what there was left, and so fell back and went into position on line with the cavalry a short distance beyond the east end of the cornfield."[136]

In the fight, Robinson mentioned one of the guns had a broken trail and could not fire. Benjamin Nourse wrote his account of the fight: "We drove into a cornfield and opened just where we could find a place to unlimber—We were supported by the first & second brigades—we gave them 10 rounds from each piece, then fell back—My gun trail was broken and we had to leave it on the field—for a little while—then getting up a wagon we cut the wheels to pieces and put the gun in the wagon, bound to bring it off some way or other. In the 15 minutes that we were in that field—our loss was Thos. Wygant— was killed—Geo. White, Camberg, Phillips & Fitz wounded." The battle with the infantry took a heavy toll on the Union battery as men began to fall and over 75 percent of the horses were killed in the first few minutes of the fight. As the battery began to pull back, they could not withdraw the damaged gun. Then, the 3rd Ohio Cavalry charged ahead and temporarily stopped the infantry advance and pulled the gun off the field by hand. The dismounted gun was loaded onto an ammunition wagon.[137]

A creditable Union defensive line took shape. A battalion of the 4th Michigan held the right flank of the Union line, and left to right were the 3rd Ohio, 1st Ohio and 92nd Illinois. The 3rd and 5th Kentucky cavalries fell into line behind. Finally, Fielder Jones'

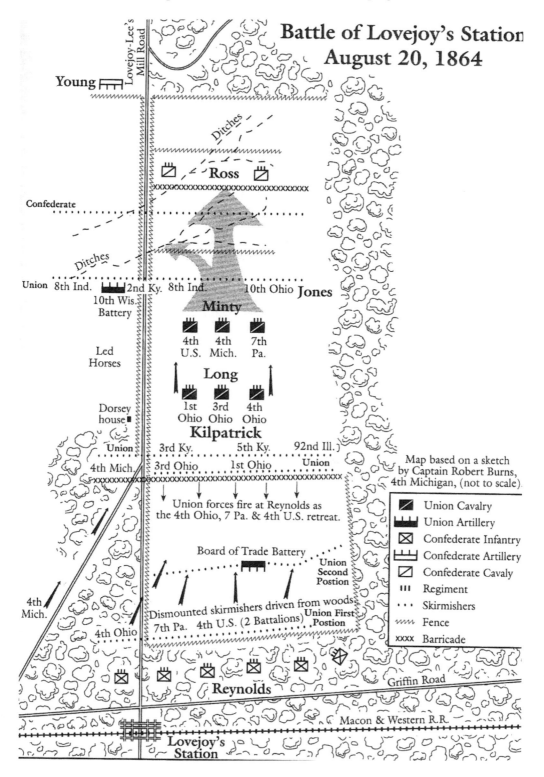

Battle of Lovejoy's Station
August 20, 1864

Young

Lovejoy-Lee's Mill Road

Ditches

Ross

Confederate

Ditches

Union 8th Ind.   2nd Ky. 8th Ind.   10th Ohio **Jones**
10th Wis.
Battery
Minty

4th   4th   7th
U.S.   Mich.   Pa.

Led
Horses
Long

1st   3rd   4th
Ohio   Ohio   Ohio

Dorsey
house
Kilpatrick

Union   3rd Ky.   5th Ky.   92nd Ill.
4th Mich. 3rd Ohio   1st Ohio   Union

Union forces fire at Reynolds as
the 4th Ohio, 7 Pa. & 4th U.S. retreat.

Map based on a sketch
by Captain Robert Burns,
4th Michigan, (not to scale).

▨	Union Cavalry
⊞	Union Artillery
⊠	Confederate Infantry
⊞	Confederate Artillery
▨	Confederate Cavalry
ııı	Regiment
···	Skirmishers
∿∿	Fence
xxxx	Barricade

Board of Trade Battery
Union
Second
Postion

4th
Mich.

4th Ohio

Dismounted skirmishers driven from woods
7th Pa. 4th U.S. (2 Battalions) Union First
Postion

Reynolds

Griffin Road

Macon & Western R.R.

Lovejoy's
Station

The Battle of Lovejoy's Station (*Sherman's Horsemen* by David Evans, Indiana University Press, 1996, page 439).

8th Indiana, 2nd Kentucky and 10th Ohio completed the Union defense in a third defensive line. As all the Union regiments joined in the fight, the Confederate infantry began to push ahead. So close were the two lines, the cavalry resorted to using their revolvers, but the Union defense stopped Reynolds' advance. When things seemed to be working out for the Union cavalry, an explosion of gunfire was heard in the rear as Ross' Texas cavalry attacked the 10th Ohio Cavalry which was assigned duty of protecting the Lovejoy-Lee's Mill Road. The battle, thus far, had been hard fought and rapid. The fight in the rear and in the front made a continuous roar.[138]

It took only 20 minutes for the combined Confederate forces to encircle Kilpatrick, producing a critical situation. Kilpatrick went to Minty to discuss the next action. Kilpatrick said, "[W]e are surrounded. You know what is in our front; Jackson with 5,000 cavalry is in rear of our left, and Pat Cleburne with 10,000 infantry is closing on our right." Despite Kilpatrick's exaggeration of the number of troops he faced, he wanted Minty and Eli Murray's brigades to charge side-by-side and cut through Ross' cavalry on the northeast. Minty agreed to follow any orders, but suggested a charge by column of fours. Kilpatrick replied, "Form in any way you please." In the meantime, the Confederate cavalry formed three lines of defenders behind hastily thrown up barricades.[139]

While this conference was taking place, Robinson recalled, "The enemy's artillery opened on us, and I was directed to put two guns in position to engage it, and sent Lieut. Bennett in charge, who by the way was a reliable and gallant soldier in any emergency. Completing arrangements and instructing my sergeant the movements he should make with the limbers, wagon and ambulance in case we succeeded in cutting our way through, I joined Bennett with the other gun, and found that he had already disabled one piece of the rebel battery, so that we were now equal in number, they having three and we three."[140]

Leaving a line of skirmishers facing the infantry to the south, the Union cavalry again got into their saddles and formed north of the cornfield. Robinson described the preparation for the charge: "Col. Minty rides to the front and center of the first brigade and gives the command, 'Draw, sabre!' and as the twelve hundred blades leaped and swung into the air, the flash of sunlight upon each one of them seemed to reflect the courageous countenance and confident expression of him who now more tightly grasped its hilt." The Union cavalry brigades, all riding in columns of four, charged Ross' cavalry line. W.L. Curry, 1st Ohio Cavalry, wrote, "It Twas a glorious sight, with horses stamping, and champing the bits as if eager for the fray, standards and guidons flung to the breeze, with the dashing here and there of staff officers carrying orders, the serious faces of the commanders, the stern, quick commands of the officers as the squadrons are forming." Then, Minty yelled, "Charge!" The horses leapt ahead and as they charged, the Confederate artillery boomed, but the distance was quickly covered by the charging horses. Minty led the Union charge, the horsemen riding with sabers drawn raced forward, and they were irresistible.[141]

Benjamin Nourse described the next actions: "and the whole command now formed in solid column by regiments for a charge—with the 1st & 2nd brigades of the 2nd Division in the advance. The men threw away all extra clothing and traps of all kinds, horseshoes, blankets, haver sacks, ammunition, carbines, camp utensils and clothing. At the sound of the bugle away they went, standing in the saddle with a yell all along the line— they were over the rebels like straw but the details of the scene are too horrible to write.... We followed closely the cavalry—stopping our gun limber long enough to hitch onto a rebel gun from which all the cannoneers were either killed or had fled. We brought it away with us—a brass 6# [gun].” The Confederate defenders fell under the onslaught of the Union cavalry, and those who could run did so before the large body of Union cavalry. Kilpatrick would claim four guns, three of which were destroyed and one captured, three battle-flags, and an ordnance train, in addition to a large number of enemies killed and captured.[142]

Naturally observing the enemy artillerists, Robinson remarked, “The gunners of their battery took flight or were sabred at their pieces, and the guns fell into our possession, one of which was brought off by using the only spare limber that I had with me, the others, following instructions, having gone hurriedly down the road and when we reached there the battery was too far in advance to then be halted.” The 4th Ohio fought its way through the Confederate line and as long-time comrades of the Board of Trade Battery, the troopers were concerned about the fate of Robinson’s men in this attack. The regiment was “reforming, when some one cried to go back for the artillery. Turning, we had gone but a short distance, when ‘make way for the artillery’ was heard, and out came all the artillery.”[143]

The Union cavalry had successfully punched a hole through the encirclement, but the charge had disorganized the regiments which took some time to get back into shape. Luck is important, and Kilpatrick was lucky. As his command re-formed a few miles away, Brigadier General Frank Armstrong’s cavalry arrived at Lovejoy’s Station. If he had arrived sooner, the results of the charge might have been quite different; however, Armstrong did mount a determined pursuit. The 1st, 3rd and 4th Ohio cavalries formed the rearguard and Long placed the 3rd Ohio as the rear-most regiment along a road on the banks of Walnut Creek, a few miles northeast of Lovejoy’s Station. The Ohioans faced the 1st Mississippi Cavalry which crossed the creek and then charged across a cornfield. The 3rd Ohio fired with their Spencer carbines, but this did not stop the Mississippians who threw the Ohio cavalry into disorder. During the fight, Long was wounded and his horse was killed under him and the horse of the 3rd Ohio’s commanding officer, Colonel Charles Seidel, was also killed.[144]

The Board of Trade Battery and King’s Battery exchanged fire as the cavalry battle continued. Robinson explained, “While aiding in repelling a charge, one of my guns burst, and in another a shell became wedged about half way down the bore, and we could neither ram it home nor blow it out, and had to send the piece to the rear, leaving me only one serviceable, and ammunition for that nearly exhausted. Leaving this in charge of Lieut. Bennett, I rode forward seeking to find Col. Minty to request of him that Kilpatrick’s battery be sent back to relieve me, but not finding him readily I rode back and found that Long’s brigade, having exhausted its ammunition, was being withdrawn, and as we pushed on we soon found Minty ‘s brigade in position ready to take our place in covering the retreat.” When gun number 5 exploded, all the spokes were cut above the wheel hub and all the cannoneers were thrown to the ground, but no one was seriously injured. All that remained of the gun was a small piece of the breach. The remainder of the cannon was thrown out of sight. Upon further consideration, Robinson had no idea why the gun exploded. His only explanation was that it was being used beyond its capacity.[145]

To their rear were two of Minty’s regiments, 4th Michigan and 7th Pennsylvania. The Ohioans passed through this line. Minty’s regiments greeted the Confederate cavalry with a volley from their Spencer carbines and what followed was described as “the hardest fighting that we had seen during the raid.” Minty’s men repelled three different charges before he was forced to give way. After a one hour and 45 fight, Minty and

Eggleston, now in command of Long's brigade, ordered their men back into the saddle and rode after Kilpatrick who was leading the rest of the column northward. Almost immediately, heavy rain drenched the troopers. The retreat continued until midnight when the men, at last, rested.[146]

Kilpatrick's weary Union cavalry rode for Covington, near the eastern most Union lines. The column continued northward, across muddy roads, through unfriendly towns and across rain-swollen streams; all the while with Confederate cavalry on their heels. Benjamin Nourse noted the action during the day and the exhaustion that night: "[W]e again moved back through McDonald [McDonough] and across the river. Here we lay down to get a few hours sleep, right in the mud and wet through—we did not unhitch the horses but let them stand in their tracks and we slept well for 2½ hours—the first we have had in 4 days and 4 nights—40 miles today." The next day, Nourse mentioned the loss of the gun with the broken trail. "Sunday—Off early, crossed Walnut Creek, which was very high on account of the heavy rains. The water came up over my saddle and the limbers floated—we lost our mule team, wagon and the gun that was dismounted—the current was too strong for the poor animals—only one man went down—in fact all the wagons were burnt after it was found that ours was lost."[147]

The Union cavalry had a difficult crossing at the rain-swollen river. Kilpatrick abandoned his wagons in getting across. Robinson clashed with Kilpatrick when he was ordered to throw his damaged cannon (gun number 1) into the river. Kilpatrick exclaimed, "Damn the gun! Destroy the wagon." Robinson responded likewise, "I would dam the river by throwing the damned gun into it." Robinson wrote some 20 years after the war: "Some of my men, dumped the gun from the wagon and into the river, cut down the wagon and set fire to it, and have frequently, though mentally, damned Kilpatrick from then till now." Private John Fleming reasoned that no dishonor was attached to the losses of gun number 1 and number 5 during the raid, because neither had been captured. Kilpatrick finally reached David Stanley's Fourth Corps lines northeast of Atlanta on August 22, absolutely exhausted. Minty's brigade recorded 106 casualties and Eggleston's 94. In Kilpatrick's division, the Second Brigade recorded 49 casualties, and Third Brigade only 15. Garrard's men did the hardest fighting during the expedition, but the numbers were only a fraction of the losses recorded in McCook's and Stoneman's earlier raids. Joseph Vale, 7th Pennsylvania Cavalry, sarcastically wrote of Kilpatrick, "Kilpatrick seemingly to be desirous of complementing the Second Division by giving it the precedence whenever a fight was imminent, no matter whether in the front or rear!"[148]

Second Cavalry Division, Casualties (Kilpatrick's Raid)[149]

Command*	Killed		Wounded		Wounded & Missing		Missing		Total	
	O	M	O	M	O	M	O	M	O	M
First Brigade	....	....	....	1		....	....	....	1	1
4th U.S. Cavalry	....	10	1	10	1	4	....	16	2	40
7th Pennsylvania Cavalry	....	5	....	12	1	11	2	13	3	41
4th Michigan Cavalry	....	2	1	6	....	....	....	9	1	17
Total	....	17	2	29	3	15	2	38	7	99

Command*	Killed		Wounded		Wounded & Missing		Missing		Total	
	O	M	O	M	O	M	O	M	O	M
Second Brigade	....	....	2	....	....	....	....	....	2	....
1st Ohio Cavalry	....	4	....	13	....	....	....	2	....	19
3d Ohio Cavalry	1	7	....	30	....	5	....	2	1	44
4th Ohio Cavalry	....	3	2	16	....	....	2	5	4	24
Total	1	14	4	59	....	5	2	9	7	87
Chicago Board of Trade	....	1	....	4	....	....	....	1	....	6
Grand Total	1	32	6	92	3	20	4	48	14	192

*(O = officers; M = men)

The casualties for the Board of Trade Battery included two men deceased, Thomas Wygant and George White. Wygant was killed in action with a gunshot through his body and White was mortally wounded by receiving a gunshot through the hips. Four other privates were wounded: John Camberg, Howard Phillips, Thomas Fitzwilliam and Fred Weigert (who was severely wounded). For Camberg, this was his second wound, the first was received in the Battle of Stones River, and would mark the end of the war for him. He was sent to a hospital in Nashville and discharged on a surgeon's certificate in January 1865. Phillips would return to duty after a three-month recuperation on November 21, 1864. Weigert was sent to the hospital due to his wounds and did not return to the battery by the end of the war. The battery records do not indicate that Fitzwilliam was away from the battery due to his wounds.[150]

Kilpatrick rode to Sherman's headquarters and explained the complete success of his raid. He exaggerated the ease in which he had pushed aside the Confederates and trumpeted the accomplishments of the expedition. He assured Sherman that the railroad was destroyed to such an extent it would take 10 days to repair. Sherman summed up the mission from his point of view on August 23, just one day after Kilpatrick's return: "I think the rebels have already repaired the Macon [rail]road." On August 17, Sherman noted that Kilpatrick had exclaimed how "comparatively easy" it would be to destroy the railroad "effectually." Kilpatrick had exclaimed, "Such an opportunity to strike the enemy a terrible blow has never offered." In the end, this raid, like the two before it, proved to be ineffective. The practical and professional soldier Eli Long concluded that the railroad was unlikely to destroyed by a raiding party such that Hood would be unable to rebuild it quickly, just as Garrard had counseled before the raid. Long's assessment applied to not only Kilpatrick, but also Stoneman and McCook. The raids were ill-conceived and had only a minimal chance for success from the start.[151]

Once back within the Union lines, the aftermath of the raid settled on the Board of Trade Battery. For the men in the raid, they lamented the loss of their guns and tried to console themselves with a captured cannon, but Nourse remarked that having a captured gun was good "but it will not repay us for the fine one[s] lost." In contrast, some good news reached some of the top cavalry officers. Robert Minty and John Wilder received their long-overdue promotions of brigadier general. On a more somber side, Long was in the hospital after being shot in the arm during the raid. The battery lost one additional man, Coleman Brown, who was captured at Jonesborough. In addition, two more men were lost in the battery. The first was Robert Piersall, the native Canadian, who had his thumb amputated after having it severely injured by his mule. The Irish-born Thomas DeCoursey also had his thumb amputated, after it had been previously injured (bitten) and "mortified."[152]

The toll the raid took on the battery was significant and the men spent the next few days trying to get the equipment back into working order. Inspectors arrived to look over the condition of the equipment, in particular the carriages and caissons. On August 25, the battery was declared a four-gun battery due to the loss of two guns during the raid and would remain as such through the end of the war. Nourse commented, "We now have 8 horses on the guns and are a 4 gun battery at last." The battery was again on the move the next day in close proximity to Fourth Corps and the campaign continued to take a terrible toll on the animals. "Our old horses dropped on the road by the dozen today," wrote Nourse. The battery continued to advance with the infantry over the next few days and had no involvement with the important Battle of Jonesborough on August 30 and September 1. The men only saw the aftermath. "The rebel wounded fill the woods all around us—They are left right on the grass—in the shade of the trees. I see many hard sights. Poor fellows I pity them. Some of them are fairly butchered. One poor boy had his limb cut off square—the surgeon ought to be shot—that would do so crude a job. We pick up rebel stragglers by the dozen."[153]

The Battle of Jonesborough was a decisive victory for the Federals and resulted in Hood's abandonment of Atlanta, but the principal objective of the campaign—destruction of the Confederate army—remained unmet. Although Sherman had six corps within range of Hardee, he failed to bring the full might of his armies on the defenders at Jonesborough. As a result, Hardee was able to withdraw. A letter from a member of the battery was printed in the *Chicago Tribune* reflecting the end of the campaign. Written on September 15, it stated: "No more roaring of cannon or whistling of bullets, for a while at least. In short, the campaign is over." For the rest of the month, the battery, like most of Sherman's armies, remained relatively stationary. On September 9, the men found that George White, who joined the battery in October 1863 and who was wounded at Decatur, died on August 26. Importantly, James H. Stokes was finally mustered out of the Board of Trade Battery and remained in the volunteer army working on the defenses at Washington, D. C., returning to the rank of captain. This allowed for promotions to occur within the battery, in particular, George Robinson would finally be promoted to the rank of captain. Officially, Stokes was mustered out on August 22, but practically, the men weren't aware of this until September 12. In addition to this move, Private Isaac S. Chesbrough was notified that he would be discharged for promotion. Chesbrough had only been with the battery since February. Andrew Close, who was wounded in the jaw in the Battle of Decatur, was discharged for a commission in the War Department.[154]

Battery Losses and Changes May 10-September 30, 1864

Pvt. Andrew J. Close	Discharged	September 15, 1864	For promotion	
Pvt. Frederick G. Deane	Discharged	September 30, 1864	For promotion	
Pvt. James B. Finley	Discharged	July 15, 1864	For promotion	14th Michigan Battery

Pvt. Samuel Lord	Discharged	August 18, 1864	Disability	
Corp. Tobias Miller	Discharged	June 30, 1864	Disability	
Pvt. Clark Winslow	Discharged	June 20, 1864	Disability	
Pvt. Thomas H. Watson	Discharged	August 30, 1864	-	
Capt. James H. Stokes	Mustered out	August 22, 1864	Re-assignment	
Lt. Trumbull Griffin	Promoted	August 22, 1864	To 1st Lieutenant	
Sgt. Lewis Hand	Promoted	August 22, 1864	To Lieutenant	
Lt. George I. Robinson	Promoted	August 22, 1864	To Captain	
Pvt. Thomas Hanson	Captured	June 14, 1864		
Corp. Albert B. Lake	Captured	June 14, 1864		
Pvt. Martin Snow	Captured	June 14, 1864		
Pvt. Edward C. Field	Died	August 1, 1864	Wounds	
Pvt. Desire Joubert	Died	August 2, 1864	Wounds	
Pvt. George White	Died	August 28, 1864	Vining Station	
Pvt. Thomas Wiggant/ Wygant	Died	August 29, 1864	Lovejoy's Station	

Recruits	Enlist. Date	Recruits	Enlist. Date
John Austin*	September 30, 1864	Thomas J. Gates	September 26, 1864
David Burr	September 30, 1864	James Ivis	September 27, 1864
George Baer	September 30, 1864	William H. Johnson	September 26, 1864
Leonard Cottrell	September 26, 1864	Francis Kent	September 27, 1864
Sylvester Crum	September 26, 1864	Jeremiah Linehan	September 29, 1864
Michael Carmichael	May 31, 1864	Michael Lynch	August 26, 1864
David Chapman	September 29, 1864	Charles H. Richards	August 1, 1864
Henry Dippe	September 30, 1864	Robert McMorn	September 26, 1864
Anthony Dean*	May 31, 1864	James F. Reed	September 29, 1864
William Delany*	September 17, 1864	William Simpson	September 30, 1864
Charles Fuller	September 22,1864	Frank J. Steiger	September 27, 1864
Dennis Wood	September 22, 1864		

*Never reached the battery. (Chicago Board of Trade Association roster, April 27, 1886, Trumbull Griffin file, Missouri History Museum.)

Total Losses of Artillery Horses During the Atlanta Campaign[155]
Key: A—no. at start; B—received during campaign; C—no. on hand; D—Loss

Command	A	B	C	D
Fourth Army Corps	658	81	478	261
Fourteenth Army Corps	613	228	304	537
Twentieth Army Corps	600	139	447	282

Command	A	B	C	D
11th Indiana Battery	133	11	76	68
18th Indiana Battery	157	110	94	173
Chicago Board of Trade Battery	*201*	....	*126*	*75*
10th Wisconsin Battery	83	30	70	43
Total	2,445	599	1,595	1,439

In addition, George Robinson reported the total number of battery losses during the campaign as 22–one killed in action, three wounded who had since died, thirteen additional wounded and five missing. Robinson exclaimed in all encounters with the enemy artillery that the battery had successfully silenced the enemy guns (three of which were disabled) or drove them from the field. Robinson also noted the exemplary service of Henry Bennett and Trumbull Griffin, and Robinson should have included himself. He also deserved recognition for commanding the battery in a variety of difficult fights. Robinson, Griffin and Bennett proved worthy officers and escaped much of the earlier command problems.[156]

Board of Trade Returns for July–September 1864*

(Present and Absent)
Officers, Enlisted Men, and Aggregate
Sgt. Corp. Buglers Artificers Privates

	Officers	Sgt.	Corp.	Buglers	Artificers	Privates	Aggregate
July	5	8	12	1	2	126	154
(Number absent 27)							
August	5	7	12	1	2	118	144
(Number absent 22)							
September	4	7	11	1	2	116	141
(Number absent 33)							

*Illinois State Archives

CHAPTER SEVEN

The Nashville Campaign

[T]errible, death everywhere—poor troops, poor rebels
lay so thick we can hardly drive our horses up the hill without
stopping every rod to remove them. —Benjamin Nourse

At last, the Atlanta Campaign was over and Sherman received praise from the dignitaries in the North for his capture of the city. The Union armies in the east were bogged down besieging Lee's army in Virginia and a close-run presidential election loomed in the near future. Sherman would write in his memoirs that the capture of Atlanta made the election a certainty for Lincoln, who had had a tough political campaign against George McClellan. But Sherman would not be spared the criticism from future historians who observed that his objective entering the campaign was the destruction of the Army of Tennessee, not the capture of Atlanta. Hood's army remained a powerful adversary while Sherman accepted praise for his victory. Historian Albert Castel observed that Sherman outnumbered the Confederate army and that Sherman was poised to strike a decisive blow to the retreating army but "did not close his fist." With Atlanta in his hand, Sherman still faced the problem of dealing with Hood's large Confederate army nearby.[1]

The Situation Further to the West

Sherman also faced the formidable mounted forces of the Confederacy under the command of Wheeler who was raiding in Tennessee, but in regard to cavalry, Sherman's biggest concern was to the west. Nathan Bedford Forrest, like Hood in many ways, was one of the most aggressive and controversial commanders in the war. Forrest spent the last year in Mississippi and Tennessee improving those skills as a corps commander. Forrest was so effective that Sherman believed he could have been the most important impediment to the Union armies' advance in the Atlanta Campaign. As the campaign for Nashville developed, it would be Forrest who would lead the cavalry in the campaign. Wheeler's losses and his need to move eastward left the cavalry duties in Middle Tennessee to Forrest, commanding about 7,000 cavalry.[2]

There was still a lot of military action in August and September 1864 despite the Union capture of Atlanta. In the west, Sterling Price began his Missouri raid on August 28 as he swept a 12,000 man Confederate column, supplemented by local pro–Southern forces, through the state. The last battle during the raid did not occur until the end of October. In the east, Jubal Early was active in the Shenandoah Valley in August and the Union siege of Richmond and Petersburg extended into the autumn. Along the Gulf of Mexico coast, the Union army and navy had just concluded a campaign against Mobile on August 23, successfully capturing Fort Gaines and Fort Morgan. The Federal navy forced the Confederate navy to surrender and effectively closed one of the Confederacy's last two open ports. The resources of the north, coupled with Union victories in 1864, resulted in the Union armies totaling twice the number of soldiers as the Confederate States and this stretched the ability of the Southern forces to defend what remained of the Confederacy. Outside of Virginia, the greatest concentration of Union and Confederate forces lingered in the vicinity of Atlanta where the Army of Tennessee had about 40,000 men present and available for duty. At the conclusion of the Atlanta Campaign, the all-too-common policy of casting blame continued in the command ranks of the Confederate forces. Seeking solace after the recent defeats in Georgia, Hood put the blame for the loss of the campaign on Joseph Johnston for his defensive strategy and he felt he had gained an army "enfeebled in number and in spirit by long retreat and by severe and apparently fruitless losses." He proudly stated that when he took command, and through his offensive efforts, the "tone constantly improved and hope returned"; but not all in the Southern army agreed with Hood's assessment. General Lawrence "Sul" Ross of the Confederate cavalry wrote to his wife on September 14: "They all call loudly for the Old hero Genl. Johnston…. When Johnston left this army, I think it was the finest and best army I ever heard of to the number, but now it is hacked and the men will not charge Breastworks, and it is 20,000 men weaker now than when he left." In regard to the recent loss of Jonesborough, Hood blamed that loss on another top-ranking Confederate officer, William Hardee, who made a "disgraceful effort" even though Hardee faced six Union corps compared to only two for the Confederate forces. There is little doubt that Hood faced a situation where the odds were stacked against him, but he had striven for this position. In the meantime, Hood was given command of the new Department of Tennessee and Georgia.[3]

Sherman, at conclusion of the Atlanta Campaign, moved his army to Atlanta and gave his troops a month's rest. Sherman received a message from Grant on September 20 asking his opinion regarding the next actions for his army. With the closure of Mobile to outside commerce and trade, only one other Confederate port remained open—Wilmington, North Carolina. Sherman suggested that Grant march south toward Wilmington, that Major General Edward Canby should hold the Mississippi River, and Sherman would march his army across Georgia, in a bold "march to the sea." While this was a very risky move by Sherman, he explained: "I would not hesitate to cross the State of Georgia with 60,000 men…. Where a million of people live my army won't starve…."[4]

On the Southern side of the line, Hood felt that only offensive actions and victories would restore the fighting spirit to the Army of Tennessee. He faced two choices—prepare to resist Sherman's further movement south or take the war to the Union forces. He had just criticized Johnston for a weak campaign of defensive actions. Clearly, he could not take the same strategy. Besides, Jefferson Davis desired an offensive war with the Confederate forces striking into Tennessee and Kentucky. Hood chose to advance northward and he explained, "Something was absolutely demanded, and I rightly judged that an advance, at all promising success, would go far to restore its fighting spirit." Hood's cavalry had been unable to cut Sherman's supply line for any extended period of time and this left only one option: offensive actions for the infantry. He decided to march his forces around Sherman's right flank in a northern advance while destroying the railroad leading to Atlanta. This bold move by a smaller force would accomplish Hood's desire for offensive action by striking where Sherman was most vulnerable.[5]

On September 18, Hood set his army in motion and moved to the vicinity of Palmetto along the Chattahoochee River and resupplied his army. On September 25, Jefferson Davis, a friend and supporter, arrived for a two-day visit of reviewing the troops, speech-making, and consultation about Hood's next moves. Hood told Davis he planned to attack Sherman's supply line north of Atlanta and he hoped that a mobile Confederate army could avert a major battle while pulling the bulk of the Federal army from Atlanta. Most importantly, Hood hoped that Sherman would split his army, making the odds more even, and then, Hood could defeat a wing of the Federal army on his chosen ground.[6]

Hood Begins His March North

To support Hood's northward offensive, the Southern forces across the states in the west made a concerted effort to occupy the Union forces. Brigadier General James R. Chalmers' cavalry division in Mississippi began destroying the Memphis & Charleston Railroad east of Memphis. Sterling Price had surged out of Arkansas and rode across the state of Missouri. Hood had Wheeler's cavalry concluding a raid on the railroads extending through Tennessee and Alabama. Philip Roddey's cavalry command was instructed to begin attacking the supply lines in northern Alabama. In addition, the northward march by the Army of Tennessee would destroy the railroad directly north of Atlanta and, finally, Hood gained agreement to send Forrest's cavalry into Alabama and Tennessee to strike the railroad in yet another raid. The overall understanding of the Southern mounted forces included cooperation between Forrest and Wheeler, but Wheeler's command was in such poor condition after his recent raid, Forrest knew he had little hope of support from Wheeler.[7]

Hood began his offensive on September 29 while Forrest attacked the railroad in Tennessee. Hood, in the trail of the recent Atlanta Campaign, converged on Lost Mountain, west of Marietta on October 3. Hood's advance met with little initial resistance and on October 4, A.P. Stewart's infantry destroyed the railroad at Acworth and Big Shanty, gathering up about 400 prisoners assigned to protect the railroad. Next, Hood, in need of supplies of his own, marched toward Allatoona to capture the supply depot and destroy the bridge over the Etowah River, making a Federal pursuit a longer and more difficult process. Major General Samuel French's division attacked the Federal garrison at Allatoona on October 5 but despite some initial success, French received information from Armstrong's cavalry brigade that a large Federal force advanced on his position. The information, while probably premature, caused French to withdraw before he could capture the supply depot or burn the bridge. In these initial moves, Hood destroyed about 10 miles of track between Atlanta and Marietta; but on October 6, Hood, believing the Union forces were moving toward him, began a series of moves, picking off small Union garrisons along the way. He moved across the Coosa River and moved up the west bank of the Oostanaula River until he reached the railroad between Resaca and Mill Creek Gap on October 13. Hood again began destroying the tracks and then captured about 1,000 Union troops at Tilton, Dalton and Mill Creek Gap. By this time, Washington Elliott's Federal cavalry arrived and pursued the Confederate army as the opposing cavalries skirmished daily. Elliott's cavalry successfully clashed with the 8th Texas Cavalry near Rome in mid–October claiming the Texans' colors as a prize. Then, Hood turned southwest and headed for Gadsden, Alabama, while the Federal cavalry and infantry followed in his path.[8]

Sherman initially expected Hood would march west into Alabama but when he decided to strike the railroad leading directly to Atlanta, Sherman, while postponing his march to the sea, set his troops in motion. Sherman moved five infantry corps in pursuit of Hood while leaving Slocum's Twentieth Corps in the Atlanta vicinity. As he marched ever northward, Hood wanted Sherman to divide his forces so that he might destroy them in detail, but he perceived that the bulk of the Federal armies was in pursuit. He was not ready for pitched battle. On the Union side of the line, Sherman soon realized that Hood wanted to draw the Federal armies northward. Sherman wanted to march across Georgia and he decided to send George Thomas, whom he thought was a slow but reliable commander, to Nashville to deal with the new threat there. At Gadsden, Hood re-supplied his armies and discussed his next moves with his superior, Pierre Beauregard. While action took place in Georgia and Alabama, George Thomas prepared to meet Hood in Tennessee.[9]

The Federal Army Pursues Hood

Sherman had the unenviable task of chasing Hood who did not want to offer battle and who had a variety of potential targets. Garrard's Second Cavalry Division relayed the path of Hood's march back to army headquarters as it trailed the Confederate column past Rome, Georgia. Sherman unsuccessfully attempted to reach the flank of Hood's army with Twenty-third Corps but Garrard closed on some of Jackson's cavalry screening for Hood, claiming two artillery pieces and some prisoners in the skirmish. Sherman successfully reinforced the Union garrison at Resaca but Hood had more success on the railroad and garrison at Dalton. When Sherman arrived at Resaca on October 14, he felt he could mount an attack and catch Hood in a flanking movement. Sherman spread his pursuing columns to attack but Hood successfully slipped the noose. "Hood, however, was little encumbered with trains, and marched with great rapidity.... He evidently wanted to avoid a fight."[10]

By mid–October, George Thomas continued aligning his troops in preparation to meet Hood's advance into Alabama or Tennessee. Succeeding in expelling the Confederate cavalry after the recent raids, he now faced 35,000 infantry accompanied by the same cavalry which he fought a few weeks before. He pulled two cavalry commands into service—Croxton's First Brigade of Edward McCook's First Division and Hatch's division of the District of Western Tennessee. Thomas also called for the cavalry in Kentucky to move to Nashville. Meanwhile, Sherman's armies still trailed Hood's Southern army. During this pursuit the Board of Trade Battery followed along but saw little action.[11]

Now in Alabama, Hood halted in Gadsden on October 20, and he contemplated his next move if Sherman continued his pursuit. Sherman also chose to stop and consider his next action while his men repaired the railroad. Sherman correctly summarized the situation: "Hood's movements and strategy had demonstrated that he had an army capable of endangering at all times my communications, but unable to meet me in open fight. To follow him would simply amount to being decoyed away from Georgia, with little prospect of overtaking and overwhelming him. To remain on the defensive would have been bad policy for an army of so great value as the one I then commanded, and I was forced to adopt a course more fruitful in results than the naked one of following him to the southwest." Sherman wanted to be marching for the sea and he could chase Hood all winter. When Hood pulled out of Gadsden, heading west, Sherman decided he had had enough. On October 22, Hood reached Guntersville along the Tennessee River, with Wheeler's cavalry on the flanks and rear of the Army of Tennessee. Four days later, Sherman sent Stanley's Fourth Corps to Chattanooga under the authority of George Thomas, now in Nashville. Four days after that, he ordered Schofield's Twenty-third Corps in the same direction, also under Thomas' command.[12]

Over the next month, the Army of Tennessee and Thomas' forces in Tennessee would align to face each other along the Tennessee River. Sherman pulled the bulk of his infantry forces back to Atlanta in anticipation of the historic march to the sea which would begin in mid–November. The stage was set. Hood's Army of Tennessee would begin the campaign in November 1864 accompanied by Forrest's cavalry corps supplemented by Jackson's division (two brigades). This force would face Thomas with two infantry corps and variously assembled cavalry forces. A.J. Smith's XVI Corps, still fighting in Missouri, would join Thomas as soon as possible, and Thomas would draw in the forces of Rousseau's District of Tennessee and Steedman's District of the Etowah. In addition, Thomas had the garrison of Nashville to add to his strength. Initially, Croxton's and Capron's brigades with Hatch's Division made up the active Union cavalry forces. By mid–December, Richard Johnson's and Joseph Knipe's divisions would be added to the Union mounted forces in Middle Tennessee. In the meantime, several important actions would occur at Decatur, Columbia, Spring Hill and Franklin.

On the last day of October, Thomas summarized the situation that he faced in a message to Henry Halleck. Hood had crossed the Tennessee River at Florence and it became apparent that Tennessee was the next target for the Southern army. Croxton would soon be reinforced by Hatch's Division. Stanley's Fourth Corps marched for Pulaski and even though Schofield was still in Resaca, he had orders to move to Tennessee with all haste. Thomas bravely wrote, "With Schofield and Stanley I feel confident I can drive Hood back." Thomas had received 12 new regiments over the past couple of weeks and they had been distributed to the various garrisons across the state and re-filling brigades which needed men. That meant that Thomas had no great reserve of troops to call on to meet Hood's advance. Still, the decisions were made and the details of the campaign would be determined when Hood decided exactly where he would attack, a location still unclear to all.[13]

The Chicago Board of Trade Battery—October 1864

The Board of Trade Battery joined in the pursuit of Hood on October 2, stayed on the move for the entire month, and saw some light skirmishing on October 13. The battery moved steadily northwest and ended the month 20 miles east of Gadsden, Alabama, on Terrapin Creek, near a community called Ladiga. Benjamin Nourse's diary revealed that the first day's journey met with an immediate delay after traveling 18 miles, because on the way to Vining's Station, Peach Tree Creek was a torrent which had swept away the bridge over it. The battery stopped that afternoon until a pontoon bridge could be built. Early the next day (October 3), the battery was joined by Elliott and his staff. The battery crossed the pontoon bridge and ended the day four miles south of Powder Springs.

October 4 again saw the battery traveling north, arriving at Marietta at noon, where the men were greeted with a column of smoke coming from Big Shanty; the rails and cross-ties were burning after the Confederate advance. The Fourth Corps followed the battery north and some light skirmishing occurred along the way. Rumors circulated around camp, correct for once, that Hood was trying to capture the Union supply depot at Allatoona, 40 miles to the north. The next day the battery moved only seven miles as the Confederate rear guard stiffened its resistance, but the battery was not put to work. Little movement occurred until October 9 when the battery moved to Acworth, and reached Kingston on October 12. The Second Cavalry Division ran into the Confederate cavalry seven miles from Rome and won the fight, capturing two cannons in the process. The battery reached Resaca on October 15, a village consisting of only seven houses, and found that the Confederates had destroyed the railroad for 22 miles. Nourse described a cruel and foolish event by one of the Federal soldiers. "One of the accidents so often occurred last night—a soldier snapped his gun at a…[ex-slave] lieing asleep by the road—dead— that's all—he forgot his gun was loaded." The foolishness continued the next day when a member of the 7th Pennsylvania Cavalry stole George Robinson's horses. Upon discovering what had the happened, the commander of the regiment returned the horses along with an apology.[14]

The next day (October 17) the battery proceeded through Snake Creek Gap and ran into a major obstacle of trees felled by the enemy, intending to delay the Federal pursuit. "At the pass the rebels delayed the troops several hours by having cut all the trees so that they lapped one another in their fall and the only way to get through or out was to cut every tree. About 2000 trees were felled in the gap of 7 miles—and not much more than 200 feet wide—we are in camp at Villanow—We took all the good horses in the battery to fix out our section for tonight. The left section goes to Chattanooga tonight with the wagon trains—the whole army will follow Hood tomorrow towards the Coosa river." Nourse's section marched all night and the pursuit continued, reaching Gaylesville, Alabama, on October 25. The next day, the men discovered that Elliott had been relieved of command and that James Wilson would command all the cavalry in the West. Elliott would be reassigned to division command in Fourth Corps. Good news arrived in regard to Abram Miller, who had so ably commanded Wilder's Brigade, when it was announced that he had been promoted to the rank of brigadier general. Nourse wrote, "[G]ood—he has well earned it." The section returned to Rome and then moved on to the Etowah River, where on the last day of the month, Kilpatrick's division took the horses of Long's Second Division. Kilpatrick would accompany Sherman on his march to the sea and Sherman showed no compunction in taking the good mounts from other divisions to support his own expedition, leaving the Second Division dismounted.[15]

Board of Trade Battery—November-December 14, 1864

Little occurred for the battery in November. It is interesting to note that the Board of Trade Battery, which had been previously designated as horse artillery, lost that name in the official reports. Hence forth, the battery would be shown as Illinois Light Artillery, Chicago Board of Trade Battery, but no practical changes occurred within the operations of the unit. The battery marched to Chattanooga and reached there on November 6. Upon arrival, the men were met by Captain Robinson who told them they were ordered to Nashville. The men loaded the guns, wagons and themselves onto a train on November 13 and began the movement to Nashville, arriving the next day. The battery was greeted by fellow battery comrades, Lieutenant Sylvanus Stevens and Private Charles LeSur—Stevens, still a member of the battery, serving with the quartermaster department, and LeSur who had been discharged due to a disability. The battery languished in Nashville for the rest of the month and several absent members arrived for duty including, "Phillips, Baker, Jackenheimer [sic], Toomey, Rockwood, and Appleton," wrote Nourse. Howard Phillips had been wounded at Nash Farm. George Gackenhiemer, James Appleton and John Toomey were wounded at Decatur. Of importance, Sergeant Lewis B. Hand was promoted to the rank of second lieutenant and Trumbull Griffin was finally promoted to first lieutenant on December 1, filling these two positions. When Griffin was promoted to first lieutenant, this left Henry Bennett as the only second lieutenant and provided the opportunity for Hand's advance. These were long overdue promotions for worthy officers and Robinson told Allen Fuller, Illinois adjutant general, as much. On the last day of the month, Sylvanus Stevens' brother, E.B., arrived with supplies from home. Each pair of men received "3# nice butter, ½ peck green apples, ½ peck Dr. apples, 1 gal cranberries, ¾ # codfish—2# fine cheese and Mrs. S.[ylvanus] H. Stevens brought us 50 cans of peaches and strawberries. Mrs. S. brought me a large box from home with boots, socks, apples, pickles, turkey, papers, etc." The battery was reminded of the war when they received new horses, which brought the promise of further action. Immediately after noon, the orders rang out to get ready to move. "No wagons or saddles and new unruly horses. Much of our good things were lost or had to be left on the ground."[16]

While the Board of Trade Battery had an uneventful month, Hood's Army of Tennessee pressed forward toward Nashville on November 21. Since that time, cavalry fights were frequent and daily as Hood marched to Columbia. Significant military action took place at Spring Hill on November 29 and the bloody battle of Franklin occurred on November 30 resulting in serious losses for the attacking Confederates and moderate losses for the Federals. Schofield and Stanley marched with their corps for Nashville after the Battle of Franklin. Once these units reached Nashville, Thomas, who had cobbled together an army which also included A.J. Smith's wing of Sixteenth Corps and infantry from James Steedman's Department of Etowah along with the Nashville garrison, prepared to meet Hood's advancing army.

The expectation that Hood would attack, or even by-pass, Nashville resonated with those in the city and the Board of Trade Battery moved a short distance south, but the Union forces moving from Franklin had no problem reaching Nashville. The battery moved to Lebanon Pike, barricades and earthen works were constructed around the guns west of the pike, and the small defensive area was christened "Fort Stevens." Then, as with all the Union troops at Nashville, they awaited the attack by Hood and in the meantime, the men built shelters to help them deal with the cold weather. From December 9 through December 12, the weather turned so bad that no fighting would take place. On December 9, Nourse wrote, "Snow this morning 4 in. deep, then rain—freezing as fast as it fell. very cold." The next day was no better, "Cold, colder, very cold—ice that the boys are skating on—sharp wind." On December 11, Nourse continued his analysis, "Ice so hard that it will bear up a horse anywhere. very slippery—cold wind. Cloudy." The weather began improving on December 13 and thawing continued on December 14. Then, Thomas sent orders to attack Hood's line on December 15.[17]

In early December, the Board of Trade Battery was temporarily assigned to John

Croxton's First Brigade of Edward McCook's First Cavalry Division. At the time of the Battle of Nashville, McCook and his other two brigades were in Kentucky dealing with Hylan Lyon's Kentucky raid. Eli Long's Second Division remained in Louisville awaiting mounts and necessary equipment before returning to the field. This meant that Croxton would act as a semi-independent brigade in the battle with Board of Trade designated as his artillery support. The story of the Board of Trade Battery, an integral part of the Union cavalry in the heartland and the Battle of Nashville, would show the value of the cavalry, the importance of a new chief of cavalry who worked well with the commanding general of the armies, and the final evolution in the Union mounted forces in the Civil War.[18]

The Battle of Nashville

The Board of Trade Battery was attached to General John Croxton's brigade at the Battle of Nashville (Library of Congress).

The Battle of Nashville reflected, in many ways, the state of the Civil War. Hood faced a force almost twice the size of his army and he desperately needed to win the battle. He had marched to the outskirts of Nashville, the second most heavily defended city in the nation, and halted. He had been unsuccessful in his objective of defeating the smaller components of the Union forces at Spring Hill, Franklin and Murfreesboro (where the bulk of his cavalry was still positioned), and offensive actions against entrenched enemy positions at Nashville were impractical. He received no significant numbers of reinforcements and to return south would be to admit defeat, something he would not do. In addition, he had little hope of pushing into Kentucky with the large Union army in his rear at Nashville. He had only two options: remain in winter quarters and prepare for a spring offensive, if Thomas would grant him this respite, or defeat Thomas, defensively, when the Union armies attacked his position. Finally, Thomas made the decision for Hood when he issued his orders to attack on December 15.

On the morning of December 15, the weather continued to moderate but this was accompanied by a dense fog which made visibility limited. Thomas' plan called for an early attack, but the fog delayed this for several hours. Thomas ordered Steedman's District of the Etowah troops to attack the eastern portion of Hood's line, holding it in place, while the major attack was directed to the western flank by A.J. Smith's Sixteenth Corps, Thomas Wood's Fourth Corps, and Wilson's reinvigorated cavalry corps (now 12,000 men strong). The attack on the western flank would be made in a large wheeling movement which would push James Chalmers' cavalry division, really just Edmund Rucker's brigade, out of the way while attacking the Confederate infantry along that flank. Facing

Thomas, Hood placed Cheatham's infantry corps on the eastern flank, extending to the Nolensville Road with his left near Franklin Pike. Stephen D. Lee held the Confederate center, uniting with Benjamin Cheatham on his right, and extending to Granny White Pike on the left. A.P. Stewart's corps held the position with Lee on his right and his left aligned along Hillsboro Pike. This left Rucker's cavalry brigade to hold a position west of Stewart's line and Chalmers' other cavalry brigade, Biffle's, on the eastern flank. Though outnumbered, Hood had the advantage of holding the high ground and to defeat Hood, the Union army needed to march up hills devoid of cover and into the sights of the Confederate guns.[19]

Wilson had spent all his time since gaining command of the cavalry in the west assembling, organizing, equipping and mounting his forces. Wilson's cavalry, which would mostly operate dismounted during the battle, marched south of the Cumberland River near Charlotte Pike and prepared to attack Hood's lines in conjunction with the infantry. Finally, the fog lifted and the attacking Union forces on the western flank pushed toward the waiting lines of Confederate soldiers. The Union cavalry operated with about 12,000 men, consisting of Richard Johnson's Sixth Division, Edward Hatch's Fifth division, Joseph Knipe's Seventh Division, and Croxton's First Brigade (accompanied by the Board of Trade Battery). The cavalry forces went into battle with Johnson, Croxton, and Hatch from right to left, extending from the Cumberland River to the flank of A.J. Smith's infantry. Knipe would bring up the rear as the reserve. Johnson, with Battery I, 4th U.S. Artillery, and Croxton, with the Board of Trade Battery, would face Rucker's Cavalry Brigade on the first day of the battle.

Croxton's First Cavalry Brigade, First Cavalry Division
Brig. Gen. John T. Croxton

8th Iowa, Col. Joseph B. Dorr
4th Kentucky (mounted infantry), Col. Robert M. Kelly
2nd Michigan, Lt. Col. Benjamin Smith
1st Tennessee, Lt. Col. Calvin M. Dyer
Artillery—Illinois Light Artillery, Board of Trade Battery, Capt. George I. Robinson

Croxton had served under Hatch and Johnson at various times during the past month, but now he operated semi-independently. After getting his troopers ready to advance at 4:00 a.m. Croxton's initial movements did not go smoothly and he became entangled with two brigades of John McArthur's infantry division. He began the day outside the fortifications near the Nashville & Northwestern Railroad to the right of Hatch's division and the left of Johnson's. He waited until the infantry began the attack and then he rode forward, riding between the railroad and Charlotte Pike. He sent out skirmishers in advance of his main force and then began to hurry ahead. A sharp skirmish resulted just before noon and Croxton paused along a ridge overlooking a valley, observing the enemy in position on the ridge ahead. When McArthur's infantry began its wheeling movement, Croxton continued ahead and crossed Richland Creek, threatening Edmund Rucker's right flank in the process. With Johnson also pushing ahead and Croxton along his flank and rear, Rucker had little choice but to withdraw.[20]

With Rucker's first withdrawal, Croxton continued his advance trying to hold a line between the advancing forces. He found a Confederate artillery battery in place on

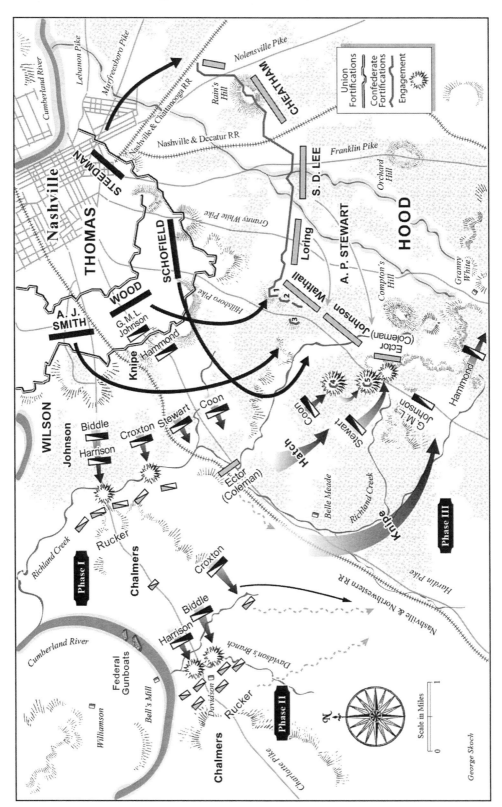

The Battle of Nashville, December 15, 1864.

George Skoch

Charlotte Pike which proved too tempting a target to pass. George Monlux, 8th Iowa Cavalry, watched as the Confederate battery fired on the Union troops and then, the Board of Trade Battery "came quietly marching along the pike." The veteran Federal battery moved forward and when they came in range of the Confederate battery it increased to a gallop, stopping about 500 yards away from the enemy guns. The guns had barely stopped as the battery boys hurried the horses out of range of the enemy artillery. The guns were unlimbered and moved into place while men carried the shells from the caissons to the guns. Then, the guns exploded in a deadly barrage. The gunners were swabbing the guns even before the recoil had stopped. "Every man had his work and they did it with amazing rapidity." Monlux noted the speed in which the men worked, sending three shells in a minute and the duel lasted only a few minutes. In the meantime, Croxton ordered his regiments into line with the 2nd Michigan on the right and the 8th Iowa in support. The two batteries had been within plain sight of each other and Monlux described it "as no grander sight" in the war. The Federal cavalrymen were temporarily mesmerized by the workings of the two batteries. This would mark the main action of the battery during this battle. Then, Croxton observed a line of Confederate cavalry on the hills to his front and he ordered two regiments to dismount and charge up the hill. Despite having to push through some dense cane brakes, the enemy was "driven at the first dash." This action widened the void in the Confederate left flank between Coleman's (Ector's) infantry brigade and Chalmers. An officer in Coleman's brigade, Lieutenant J.T. Tunnel observed a "vast body of cavalry maneuvering to our left front" followed by infantry. Coleman held out "as long as he could and ordered his men to run the two miles back to the main Confederate line." Just to Croxton's left, Hatch's division fought with the Confederate infantry throughout the day and captured two of the five redoubts on the Confederate left in conjunction with Smith's infantry. Thomas achieved a remarkable victory in the first day of the battle. The Confederate defenders on the west flank had been roughly handled and only the early darkness of the December night stopped the fighting. At the close of the day, Hood decided to shorten his lines and fight again the next day in the hills north of Brentwood.[21]

The night was cold and unpleasant. Iowa cavalryman Henry Kratzer McVey and his comrades gathered up the wounded after dark in the area of Croxton's brigade and tried to make them comfortable. Some were slightly wounded but some were beyond help. "I saw one man with his head shot clear off but his under jaw. Another a piece of shell had struck him in the back of the head and came out his face. His hair was cut as though some one had struck him in the head with a sharp ax. One poor fellow had been shot with a musket ball clear through his temples. His eyeballs were laying on his cheeks and he was still talking."[22]

There are few further details of the Board of Trade Battery's participation in first day of the Battle of Nashville. Neither Croxton, nor the battery, were pressed in this overwhelming Union victory. Benjamin Nourse recorded in his diary: "The cavalry drove the rebels steadily until dark—5 miles were made. We did not get into action, only so far as to get into position and load—did not fire—The army has moved all along the line and have driven the whole rebel horde from their lines and works capturing much artillery and many prisoners—at night we ran into the rebel pickets but they shot too high and no one was hurt—we moved back to a fort and got to where we could cook some coffee at 10 o'clock … terrible, death everywhere—poor troops, poor rebels lay so thick we can hardly drive our horses up the hill without stopping every rod to remove them." Nourse's

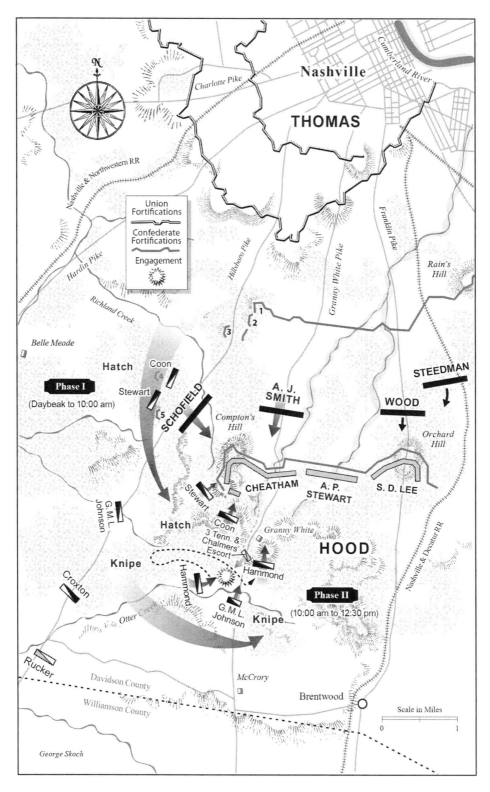

The Battle of Nashville, December 16, 1864.

account indicated that the battery was not in action and is contrary to Monlux's account. If both authors were correct, it is likely that Monlux described the actions of a section of guns while Nourse's section was not involved in the cannonading.[23]

The fighting began early on the second day of the battle as opposing cavalry forces exchanged volleys. The Northern cavalrymen knew the Southern troops were not defeated and Henry Hempstead, 2nd Michigan Cavalry, recalled a prisoner boldly told them that Hood, who had selected his position well, would repay them for the prior day's losses. For the most part, the Union cavalry, particularly Hatch's division and Croxton's brigade, began the day along Hillsboro Pike. As Wilson prepared for the day's fighting, he ordered Hatch to connect with the right flank of Schofield's infantry. Knipe's division went to the right of Hatch, and Croxton with the Board of Trade Battery would remain unengaged in its role as a reserve. Johnson's division would begin the day west of Nashville on Charlotte Pike, some distance away from the main concentration of the forces.[24]

Nourse wrote in his diary: "Yesterday our division captured 1200 prisoners, 18 pieces of artillery and 200 wagons. The main line of the rebels was driven two miles—by 7 oc the whole line was engaged—We moved ½ miles and stood until 3 oc when the rebels lines were broken by a charge and we moved across the fields to the Brentwood Pike and charged five miles—then camped on the pike—We captured guns, wagons, & everything else—rain all the afternoon and will rain all night."[25]

Johnson's division would cover the area to the right of Croxton's brigade while Hatch and Knipe had heavy fighting. The Federal cavalry made significant contributions to the ultimate victory at Nashville and by late afternoon, attacks by Smith's infantry and Hatch's and Knipe's cavalry divisions resulted in the Confederate collapse on the western flank. The Confederate army was routed and streamed south toward Franklin. Thomas had achieved a complete victory at Nashville and this battle essentially marked the end of the Army of Tennessee. The end of the battle, however, meant the pursuit of Hood's army which would continue for the next 10 days.

Hood Retreats

Hood's retreat would take the Confederate army over much of the same path that led Hood to Nashville and at the end, Hood would offer his resignation, which was accepted. The Federal pursuit continued through December 26 when the remnants of the Army of Tennessee, only 15,000 men strong, would cross the Tennessee River. The lead elements in the pursuit were Union cavalry brigades and heated fights occurred throughout the retreat. The first and probably the toughest day for the Confederate army occurred on December 17. The Confederate rearguard had heavy fighting with Union cavalry at Hollow Tree Gap, north of Franklin, and two fights south of Franklin. All the fights were dominated by the mounted Union forces. The Board of Trade Battery and Croxton's brigade had duty on the extreme eastern flank and missed the significant fighting on December 17.[26]

On December 18, the Southern retreat continued over muddy roads in weather cold and wet. The Board of Trade Battery camped on Columbia-Franklin Pike after reaching the main body of Union cavalry. The pursuit continued the following day but the swollen streams allowed the Confederate troops time to re-group and provide a more determined

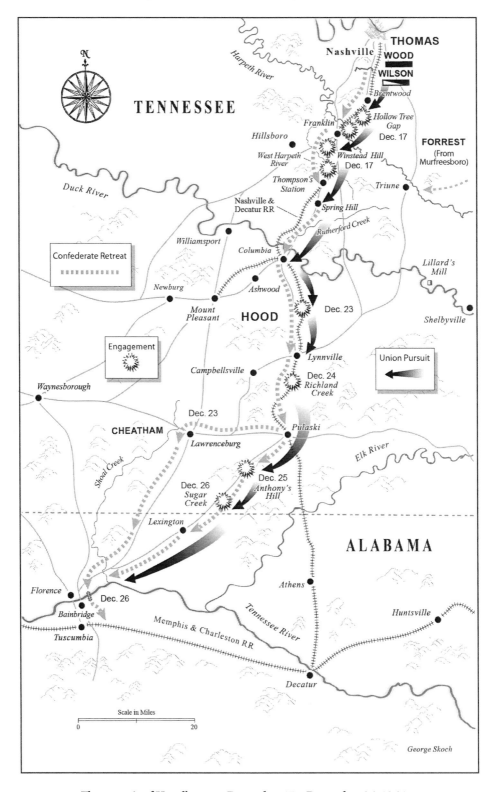

The pursuit of Hood's army, December 17—December 26, 1864.

rearguard action. Importantly, Forrest with a portion of his cavalry arrived from Murfreesboro to supplement the Confederate mounted forces. Once the Confederate army marched past Columbia, Hood would assign Forrest, with Walthall's infantry division, the duty of holding back Wilson's cavalry with a force of about 5,000 men. On December 19, Wilson re-organized his troops and decided to move forward with Harrison's, Hammond's, Croxton's, Coon's and Stewart's brigades and the rest of the Union cavalry was sent back to Nashville. The continued pursuit was a miserable affair. The Board of Trade Battery did not move that day but on December 20, Nourse recorded: "Moved at 3 p.m. Moved through Spring Hill and out on the Columbia Pike. Forded creek and camped after dark—did not get wet crossing the stream—raining fast and freezing hard—ice on everything—ice, ice, ice, everything is covered

General Nathan Bedford Forrest commanded the rearguard during Hood's retreat after the Battle of Nashville (Library of Congress).

with a coating of ice—very disagreeable indeed—We could make no fire and lay down wet, cold and hungry—could pitch no tent—frozen—lay under the large canvas—pity us." By nightfall, the Union forces reached the Duck River, near Columbia, but the river was so swollen a pontoon bridge was needed to cross. The next day the Board of Trade Battery languished on the banks of the river and the weather conditions were no better. "Today is clear and cold as ice…. We got some dry straw and will go to bed early—This is hard on our horses—Our harness is covered with a coat of ice and mud frozen on." The horses' legs became covered with mud which froze in the evening, softening the hoofs and stripping the hair from the animals' legs. General James Wilson recalled, "[I]n all my experience I have never seen so much suffering." During the two-week period of the pursuit of Hood, over 5,000 Federal mounts were disabled. There was no change in position the next day, and the weather remained cold. Nourse wrote: "All the forenoon was taken with thawing out the harnesses—This afternoon we had a row with the officers about carrying wood for their fires—14 men were arrested. But we carried our point." No further explanation was given for the disagreement or the outcome of the arrests. The traveling was miserable in the cold, muddy and icy conditions, and Private John Toomey's horse slipped, throwing the surprised private over its head, severely injuring his hands and knees in the process. Toomey, who had survived several close calls so far in the war, traveled the next few days in an ambulance.[27]

Fortunately, the pontoon bridges were constructed and the Union pursuit again continued. On December 23, the battery moved across the river after waiting until 7 p.m. for an opportunity to cross. Overnight, Wilson issued marching orders for December 24: Croxton's brigade would lead the column, followed by Hammond, Hatch (Coon and Stewart) and Harrison in that order. In front of them was the Confederate rearguard attempting to slow the relentless pursuit to give Hood time to move his army across the Tennessee River. The Federal cavalry had achieved important recognition among the troops in the West during this campaign and the next morning Thomas Wood declared he had never seen so many cavalry troops in a single location. As the Federal horsemen mounted and rode south, they passed Wood's corps and Wilson heard the infantry "splitting their throats with cheer after cheer" for the long columns of Federal horsemen.[28]

Richland Creek—the Board of Trade Battery Gets in the Fight

The most significant action by the Board of Trade Battery in this campaign occurred on December 24 when a fierce skirmish erupted with Forrest's cavalry while Hood's infantry continued its slow march southward. Forrest spent the night at Pulaski and moved northward early in the morning to set up a defensive line. On the other side of the line after riding three miles, Croxton's brigade, leading the advance that day, ran into Forrest's cavalry about 10 miles north of Pulaski. The Board of Trade Battery's advance was unimpeded until about noon when it reached a gap in two hills held by Confederate troops supported by two 12-pound guns. The battery unlimbered and began to shell the Confederate defenders. Then, Croxton continued his advance and the Kentuckian ordered the guns to proceed in a leapfrog manner—moving two guns forward, while two guns fired, pushing the defenders steadily toward Pulaski. Ross' brigade had the Confederate rearguard duty and at one point fended off a charge by the Federal cavalry. It appeared the Union horsemen were going to break through the Confederate line when the 6th Texas cavalry "hastily forming, met and hurled them back, administering a most wholesome check to their ardor." This initial skirmish lasted two hours before Forrest pulled his men back another two miles and again fell into position, this time at Richland Creek near Buford's Station on the Nashville & Decatur Railroad eight miles north of Pulaski. Walthall's infantry marched through the mud into a supporting position, should Forrest be driven from his defensive line.[29]

To the north of Richland Creek was a plain and the creek proved an important obstacle, described by a Confederate cavalryman as "deep & boggy," which needed to be crossed at a ford or bridge. Forrest aligned much of his cavalry on the north side of the creek. Armstrong's brigade, supported by six pieces of artillery, held the forward position on the pike facing the Union cavalry. Ross' brigade held the east flank; Chalmers' and Buford's divisions were on the west flank. John Morton placed one section of artillery on the north side of the creek and the other section was placed on the south side of the creek covering the road over the covered bridge. The forward section was unlimbered on the main road and in line with Buford's, Chalmers' and Ross' cavalry. Forrest described: "After severe artillery firing on both sides two pieces of the enemy's artillery were dismounted," but if Forrest was referring to the artillery supporting Croxton's leading brigade, he was incorrect about the dismounted guns. The two lines converged when the Federals attacked and the Board of Trade guns went into action. Nourse explained that during the fights, the forward guns had simply exhausted the ammunition. "[T]hey fired on us and we returned with two guns—then as we got out of ammunition # 3 & # 4 came up and 'at them'—we filled our chests and then reopened on them—in about a half an hour their troops had got over the bridge and we followed at a charge capturing many preventing them from burning the bridge—which was already on fire—during the fight we were at a disadvantage being in a hollow—We lost George Crane killed—I came within a second of losing my life." As the skirmish developed, Croxton's brigade moved into position on the west flank and the supporting Union troops filled in the battle line. Coon and Stewart advanced on the eastern flank, pushing forward to the edge of the creek. When the Federal cavalry marched forward, Forrest ordered Armstrong and Ross to the south side of the stream to stem the Union advance on the eastern flank. In the meantime, Buford and Chalmers battled the Federals on the western end of the line. Isaac Rainey, 7th Tennessee Cavalry (CSA), received orders to burn the bridge over the creek as the fight intensified: "We pilled fence rails on both ends and set fire to them. Our cavalry all this time gallopin' over the bridge." With both flanks being turned, Forrest needed to withdraw to the south side of the creek. Then, the Union artillery opened fire on those attempting to burn the bridge, forcing them to the rear. As the groups setting fire to the bridge moved to escape, the Union cavalry rode over the bridge, not 200 yards behind. A counter charge by Armstrong's cavalry brigade stopped the Union pursuit temporarily and allowed the Confederates to withdraw. The rear section of Morton's battery also opened fire on the Federal troops, assisting in halting the pursuit. The battle lasted two hours when the Federal cavalry successfully turned both flanks and Forrest ordered his men to head for Pulaski. The quick action by the Federals, including the battery, saved the bridge over the creek. The 9th Indiana Cavalry passed over the bridge after the fight and Sergeant Daniel Comstock wrote, "No one will forget the little knot of dead and dying artillerymen and horses by the road-side, maimed and mangled by a bursting shell, a gory, ghastly sight."[30]

On the Union side of the line, not everything had worked well for the Federals and Croxton was clearly displeased with Colonel Joseph Dorr, commanding the 8th Iowa. Dorr had not kept up with the rest of the brigade and he was supposed to be covering the right flank. Croxton repeatedly sent for the regiment to move into the battle, but it did not appear. Croxton fumed: "Had it been up (and I know no good reason why it was not, as the firing indicated clearly the position of the brigade), we would, without doubt, have captured the enemy's artillery and many prisoners." For the cavalrymen on both sides, it was a bitter Christmas Eve and more fighting awaited the next day.[31]

Later in the fight, General Abraham Buford received a carbine wound to his leg which ended his participation in the campaign and plagued him for months after the fight. The wound forced Buford from the field and his staff left with him; this caused more problems for Chalmers who assumed supervisory control of Buford's division in addition to his own. Forrest was with Walthall during part of the fight and while waiting, an excited courier arrived. The messenger told Forrest: "General the enemy are now in our rear." Forrest looked at the young man and replied, "Well ding it, aint we in theirs?" Seeing the Federals held the better position, Forrest ordered the withdrawal. Wilson sent a pursing force of Union cavalry after the retreating Confederate column. Forrest, adept at fighting off the enemy, took advantage of the terrain and held off the Federal pursuit. The hilly, wooded countryside was conducive to rearguard action by Forrest. One trooper of the 1st Mississippi Cavalry recalled the "turnpike itself, threading the valleys, depressions, and gorges, offered many advantageous positions for defense." The Confederate rearguard again withdrew, selecting a new defensive position in the rear. The fight along Richland Creek ended the day's fighting as the main Confederate column ambled southward into Alabama and the Union cavalry prepared to press forward again the next day. Further away, Hood's wagon train rumbled ever southward often traveling on dirt, or now muddy, county roads.[32]

On December 25, the fighting between Forrest's and Wilson's cavalry continued. Wilson drove Forrest from Pulaski but a few miles south of town Forrest ambushed the Union cavalry at Anthony's Hill. This was a heated fight in which Walthall drove a wedge into Thomas Harrison's advanced brigade, but the supporting Union cavalry troops moved into line and pushed the attackers to the rear. Afterwards, Forrest again withdrew toward Sugar Creek a few miles to the south. The Board of Trade Battery was not involved in this fight. Nourse recorded: "Yesterday, we drove the rebels twenty-one miles—and being in the advance—gives us the rear today—lively work today—by 9 oc. we were well out and passed through Pulaski Tenn at 11½ oc.—here the advance had to charge the bridge over Elk River—they lost five men—rain all day—at Pulaski the pike ceases—and we have only mud roads—from the bridge the road was strewn with ammunition wagons, caissons, tents, forges, 34 wagons left in the mud, muskets, etc.— 14 wagon loads of musket ammunition—oxen, mules, etc. etc.—they threw 7 guns in the Elk River and 17 in the Duck River—toward night they made a stand in the mountains & charged down—capturing one gun from Company M 4th regular artillery— cowardice—or they would never have got the gun—the poor rebs are in a hard fix—bare foot and hungry. I saw the remains of a dog that some poor devil had stripped the skin from to rap round his poor feet. We pick up the stragglers by the hundreds." Another ambush occurred the next morning along Sugar Creek, and this time Hammond's brigade received the brunt of the attack. As with the prior day's fighting, the Federal cavalry re-grouped and Forrest again headed south.[33]

This was the last skirmish of the Confederate withdrawal and by the end of the month the battery reached Waterloo, Alabama, on the north side of the Tennessee River just east of Eastport. The battery moved south through muddy roads finding Confederate property scattered all along the way. When the battery arrived in Waterloo, the men saw an impressive sight of 12 Federal transports and gunboats on the river loaded with rations for the men and forage for the animals. Nourse reflected on the past year as 1864 passed into 1865, the last year of the war. "I have road horseback this year 1697 miles and by rail 1523 miles—good healthy exercise—last year 1480 miles—1862 353 miles horseback. 300 miles by rail—I am hearty and well—have been all the yr." The battery settled into winter quarters and would remain in the vicinity of Gravelly Springs and Waterloo, 15 miles west of Florence, Alabama, and 10 miles east of Eastport Mississippi, until March 1865.[34]

Henry Small, a pre-war clerk, worked at James Wilson's corps headquarters in late 1864 through the end of the war (Chicago History Museum, ICHi-176925).

Board of Trade Returns for November 1864–January 1865[35]

(Present and Absent)
Officers, Enlisted Men, and Aggregate
Sgt. Corp. Buglers Artificers Privates

	Officers	Sgt.	Corp.	Buglers	Artificers	Privates	Aggregate
November	4	6	9	1	2	127	149
(Number absent 15)							
December	5	7	12	1	2	135	162
(Number absent 18)							
January	5	7	12	1	2	135	162
(Number absent 33)							

At the end of the campaign, George Robinson had the unpleasant duty of writing to George Crane's family regarding his death. Crane, a pre-war carpenter from Chicago with light hair and blue eyes, had enlisted in March 1863 and proved himself a worthy soldier. Crane's uncle replied to Robinson in January, thanking him: "I am very thankful to you for your kind letter." Thanks were also expressed in the letter to Sergeant John Howard who also had written to the family.[36]

Battery Losses and Changes October 1—December 31, 1864

Isaac Chesbrough	Discharged	October 21, 1864	
Frederick Gregory	Discharged	November 13, 1864	
Thomas McClelland	Discharged	October 13, 1864	Disability
Edward F. Wood	Discharged	November 5, 1864	
George Crane	KIA	December 24, 1864	Pulaski, TN

Recruits	Enlist. Date	Recruits	Enlist. Date
David Bettschen	October 4, 1864	John McGrath	October 4, 1864
Byron Bicknell	October 8, 1864	John McConnelong	October 13, 1864
Richard Blackmoor	October 6, 1864	Don McGee	October 1, 1864
John Bancroft	October 6, 1864	William Mescall	December 6, 1864
Addison Chapin	October 13, 1864	David Main	October 6, 1864
Thomas Collaghau/Gallaghan*	October 1, 1864	James McNally	October 5, 1864
William Eastland	October 13, 1864	William Otery	October 6, 1864
Charles Fowler	October 4, 1864	Tallman Selly	October 1, 1864
David Gitchel	December 8, 1864	Alexander Smith	December 29, 1864
George Hand	October 6, 1864	George Tank	October 3, 1864

Recruits	Enlist. Date	Recruits	Enlist. Date
John Harrup	October 18, 1864*	Charles Wilson	October 20, 1864
Andrew Hall	October 6, 1864	George Wilson	October 5, 1864
Oscar Ingersoll	No date	Samuel Wilson	October 5, 1864
William H. Jackson	December 22, 1864	John Webb	October 6, 1864
Michael Leary	October 4, 1864	David Wain	October 6, 1864
John McLean	October 3, 1864	Wells Sheeks	October 3, 1864

*Never reached the battery. (Chicago Board of Trade Association roster, April 27, 1886, Trumbull Griffin file, Missouri History Museum.)

CHAPTER EIGHT

Wilson's Raid
and the End of the War

*[T]he division only 1200 men, commenced the descent of the ridge,
first at a walk, then trot, then a charge.*—Benjamin Nourse

Waterloo, Alabama, was merely a landing on the Tennessee River in 1865 with a dozen houses, one store and a blacksmith shop. The men of the battery prepared their winter quarters, repaired and refurbished their harnesses and equipment, drilled new recruits, and watched the transports and gunboats steam past. Being on the bank of the river proved a muddy experience and daily the men trudged through a deep mire in camp. The battery supply wagons had been separated from the battery since December 15 and the wagons finally caught up on January 10. Wilson and his staff, who had been in Huntsville since the end of the pursuit of Hood's army, arrived to establish cavalry headquarters nearby. On January 13, the battery was inspected by Wilson who did not even dismount, but simply rode by the men and guns, telling them to move to Gravelly Springs the next day. In true army fashion, the men set out the next morning, but after only traveling two miles, they received new orders to return to Waterloo.[1]

On February 28, lieutenants Lewis Hand's and Henry Bennett's resignations were accepted and the battery lost two important officers. John Nourse wrote to his sister stating that Hand's and Bennett's reasons for resignation were essentially the same—a sibling already in the army and a dependent parent. Robinson sent his recommendation that sergeants Menzo Salisbury and Abbott Adams be promoted lieutenants, but the Illinois adjutant general, Isham N. Haynie, disapproved the promotions. On March 15, Haynie told Robinson that he needed to justify these promotions over Sergeant William Randolph. Unknown to Robinson, Sylvanus Stevens, who was not present with the battery, was telegramming friends in Chicago with recommendations of his own—Adams and Randolph. Others, John Hancock and J.H. Woodworth, were recommending Private Homer Baker be promoted over several superior officers. Not to be outdone, a petition, signed by over 100 people from the Chicago area, none of whom were members of the battery, was sent to the governor urging that Randolph and Adams be given the promotions. Certainly, the machinations of Stevens' promotions from private to first lieutenant without having been elected to the position by the battery members, came to full bloom in the efforts to secure promotions through influence. In fact, one letter sent by a civilian, John Wilson, reminded the adjutant general of this occurrence: "I am very sure that you will not let this happen again." Governor Richard Oglesby, who received a flurry of letters, referred this matter back to the adjutant general with instructions to gain some agreement from Robinson. In the meantime, Robinson justified the recommendation of

Salisbury over Randolph due to merit. Salisbury was appointed first sergeant previously over Randolph due to his "having proven himself" more worthy and by the fact that Randolph had declined the promotion at that time. By the time Robinson received Haynie's reply the campaign would be under way and at the end of the campaign, the war would be over. No promotion was ever officially made. Still at Waterloo, the battery remained with little to do until March 9. Private John Conklin, who began his service as a corporal and subsequently resigned that rank, left the battery for headquarters duty in the Military Division of Mississippi. A few days later, while awaiting orders to advance, word reached the camp that Private Anthony Dean died in the hospital at Nashville on March 16 due to gangrene poisoning. Dean had been mustered into the battery (October 1864) but never physically arrived.[2]

The Final Campaign: Wilson's Raid and the Battle of Selma

The state of the war for the Confederate troops was dismal as 1865 began, but the South was not defeated and intended to fight as long as possible. On the other hand, the Northern forces in the west focused on the last large concentrations of Confederate forces. To that end, Grant planned cooperative operations in 1865—Stoneman would raid from East Tennessee into North Carolina, proceeding toward Columbia, South Carolina, destroying railroads and other military facilities in the state which Sherman's march had missed. General Edward Canby would attack the Confederate military bases near Mobile and drive into the state from the south. In conjunction with these expeditions, Grant ordered a cavalry raid deep into the heart of the South under Wilson's command. Thomas gave Wilson the outline of the plan to strike Tuscaloosa, Selma and Montgomery, destroying the infrastructure which supported the Confederate army, and he allowed Wilson to design the specifics. Due to the condition of the horses and the poor overall condition of the roads, the raid did not begin until March 22. Wilson decided to use three of his best divisions in the raid—Upton's, Long's, and McCook's divisions. Of course, the Board of Trade Battery accompanied Long's division in this final campaign of the war.[3]

The Board of Trade Battery moved across the Tennessee River on March 9 at Waterloo on the transports *Swallow* and *Westmoreland*, and remained relatively stationary for the next two weeks. For the common soldier the move portended an advance, but where was still unknown. The rest of the cavalry division crossed a few days later. The Second Cavalry Division's supply train proceeded south on March 21 and the battery and cavalry began marching along the river the next day, traveling 22 miles over poor and swampy conditions. All three cavalry divisions moved forward on March 23. Long's and McCook's divisions marched to Elyton (present day Birmingham) by the way of Cherokee Station, Frankfort, Russellville, Thorn Hill and Jasper before reaching Elyton on March 29. The weather was good during this part of the raid but the roads were in poor condition, making the traveling difficult. The Board of Trade Battery had a difficult trip beginning March 27 when George Robinson received orders to move off the road to allow the pontoon train to pass. It was needed to cross some of the swollen streams. Unfortunately, the train moved only a short distance when it became stuck in the mud. This was the beginning of delays for the next three days as the battery tried to re-gain its place with the cavalry brigades. The battery remained bogged down on March 27 and the next morning it started early, again finding the pontoon train stuck in the road. The men had

General James Wilson commanded the cavalry in the west. Wilson is in the center of the photo, reclining on the second step with his saber visible (National Archives).

to cut a path around the train and finally reached division headquarters at noon. The battery was ordered to join Minty's brigade but without a guide, Robinson did not know which route Minty took. The battery reached the rain-swollen Black Warrior River that evening and camped for the night, after picking up several deserters from the Confederate cavalry along the way. Crossing streams was particularly difficult due to the need to keep the gunpowder dry. This meant the powder had to be removed from caissons and carried by hand to prevent the water from ruining it, or else the column had to wait for pontoon bridges to be constructed. Crossing the Black Warrior River, Benjamin Nourse recorded: "A wild, rough, swift stream. Saw many men and mules drown before my eyes. I was afraid to go in, but my team behaved splendidly and we went over without a single misstep." John Toomey confirmed Nourse's account, also recalling men and horses being drowned while crossing the river. Then, the first part of the mission was accomplished with the destruction of iron works in Elyton. "Up at 3 oc.—At daylight we moved to the Cahawba [Cahaba] river—which stream we crossed on the ties of the R.R. bridge, 40 feet above the water, taking off all the horses and running the carriages over by hand—this forenoon we passed through Irondale—the Green Mountain Iron works were burned. In the afternoon the Central Iron Works were burned. 18 miles today," wrote Benjamin Nourse. Trumbull Griffin ordered the horses to be blindfolded and moved across the bridge, while the men rolled the guns over by hand.[4]

On March 29, the river was crossed and the battery joined the division, camping that evening about 18 miles from Elyton. The battery proceeded to Elyton, but when it reached within four miles of the town, Robinson found the swollen rivers made it impossible to get the guns across. Long saw the predicament and ordered Robinson to take the guns on a 36-mile circuitous route, reaching Elyton at 8 p.m. only to find the division had already moved south again. The battery camped that night at Elyton. Robinson went in search of Minty the next day and upon finding him after dark, agreed upon a plan to join the cavalry brigade. On April 1, Robinson ordered a 49-mile journey for the battery, finally reaching Plantersville, and not a moment too soon.[5]

Benjamin Nourse described the details of the long ride during the day:

> Bugle call at 3 oc. a.m. started at daylight passing through Montevalle and Randolph, camped near Planters Station at 11.30 p.m., 47 miles today, a very long march and I am so ill I can barely sit on my horse. In fact it has been perfect agony for me to be in my saddle since 9 oc. this forenoon—all day we have been driving the rebels before us. Although our 'guns' have not been brought into action—the cavalry being quite strong enough to dislodge the rebs from every stand they made—the pine leaves on the ground are very dry and the fireing of powder has set the whole country in a blaze and thousands of cords of pinewood along the R.R. track has been on fire also destroying all the rails and trees for miles and miles of track. One spot was so very hot that I was actually afraid a spark might light in some limber chest and blow us to atoms—we drove through the fire at a fearful gallop—all the horses keeping their feet well and we met with no accident but it was hot, I tell you. The road side and woods adjoining have been scattered with the bodies of dead rebels and many a one got his burial by fire that should have been put under the sod—but what's the odds? none—dead men roast well and greasy rebels burn up quite thoroughly. The stench at times was fearful—dead and burning horses also helped to fill the air with foul smells. Just at dusk the rebs made a firm stand at Planters Station throwing the rail fence across the road as they had done many times before today—the 17th Indiana Mounted Infantry of our brigade charged the rebs—and had to accomplish it by dismounting—as the woods were too heavy to charge mounted through—they quickly drove the troops of the rebel Genl. Rody, capturing three pieces of artillery and 200 prisoners. Also a train of cars loaded with forage—work ahead for tomorrow—and only a few hours sleep tonight.[6]

The surreal scene of traveling through a forest on fire was not lost on Nourse, nor on his comrade John Toomey who described the inferno in the woods that required the horses to gallop through the blaze. Fortunately, none of the horses stumbled as the battery hurried through the fire. Toomey recalled "it was a miracle no caisson was blown up."[7]

While the battery was trying to catch up with the main column, Wilson learned that Forrest's cavalry corps was moving to Tuscaloosa and he dispatched Croxton's brigade in that direction with orders to capture the town and burn the military school, foundry and other important infrastructure. Then, he told Croxton to re-join the column at Selma. Croxton's mission drew Jackson's division away from Forrest's main force, at least temporarily. Meanwhile, Long's division reached Montevallo, a town 40 miles south of Elyton, on March 31. Emory Upton's division reached there the evening before and had subsequently destroyed Red Mountain Iron Works, Cahawba Valley Mills, Bibb Iron Works, Columbiana Works and other military property. Upton continued forward and ran into a force of Roddey's cavalry on a ridge a few miles south of town. The Federals charged ahead causing a precipitous retreat by the Southern defenders. A mile ahead, a stronger defensive line was encountered and again the Union cavalry prevailed, but the cost was 50 Union troopers. There was no report of the losses for Roddey's command, but Wilson reported 100 prisoners from Edward Crossland's Kentucky brigade.[8]

The next day (April 1), Croxton, while on his mission to Tuscaloosa, discovered Forrest's main body of cavalry was passing to the east through Trion. Croxton moved to Trion, intent on following the main Confederate column, but he soon found Jackson's cavalry division attempting to encircle his brigade. Jackson attacked that morning and Croxton fought his way out, withdrawing 10 miles. The next day, he took up his orders to attack Tuscaloosa before re-joining the column. While Croxton initially delayed

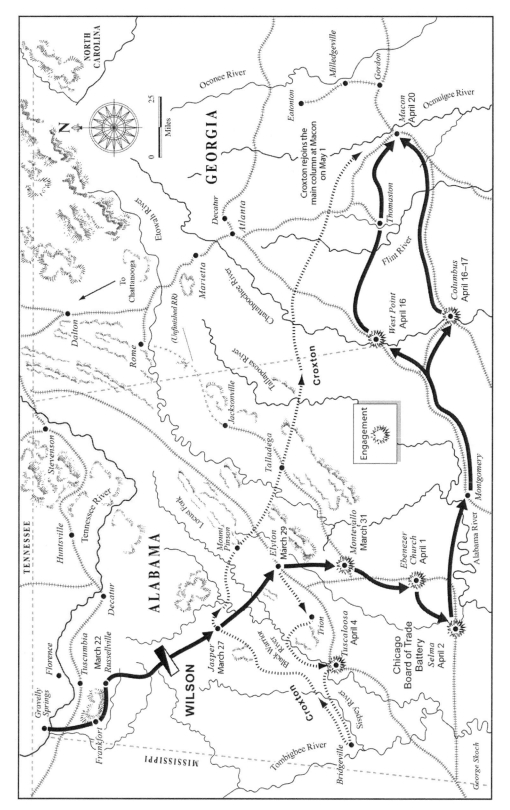

Wilson's Raid, March 22–April 20, 1865.

Jackson, Wilson intercepted a communication from Forrest which gave the locations of the various Confederate forces. Then, Wilson ordered McCook's Second Brigade, Oscar LaGrange commanding, to capture the bridge over the Cahaba River at Centerville, the only crossing north of Selma. Wilson hoped to keep Forrest and Jackson separated while Croxton re-joined McCook. McCook tried in vain to find Croxton, but he successfully burned the bridge over the river, destroying all the boats in the area. Meanwhile, Wilson closed in on Selma with his other two divisions.[9]

Again, the Board of Trade Battery was trying to join Minty's brigade on April 1, and another day of fighting would mark the second of three days fighting between Union and Confederate troops. This time the fighting occurred near Plantersville and Ebenezer Church. The Union column began the day 10 miles south of Montevallo and pushed toward Selma. Croxton and McCook (LaGrange) engaged Jackson's division to the west and Upton and Long directed their columns south. Wilson discovered that Forrest was personally commanding the Confederate defense north of Selma and fighting unfolded when the Union cavalry struck the Confederates on the north side of a creek at Ebenezer Station five miles north of Plantersville. The 17th Indiana Mounted Infantry charged Chalmers' Division, supported by Armstrong's brigade, while Upton attacked on the right flank with Andrew Alexander's brigade. Edward Winslow's brigade took up the pursuit as Upton turned the flank. In all, Wilson's two divisions captured two guns and more than 300 prisoners and succeeded in driving the Southern cavalry beyond Plantersville.[10]

The Battle of Selma—April 2, 1865

In 1865, Selma remained a key location for the Confederacy, a mere 50 miles west of one of the most pro–Southern locations in the country and the first capital of the Confederacy—Montgomery. Selma was located on the north bank of the Alabama River with six roads leading in and out of the town and two railroads passing through the town— Alabama & Tennessee and Alabama & Mississippi Railroads. More importantly Selma's factories supplied the Southern armies with material needed to carry on the war, including 24 buildings comprising the arsenal, the Confederacy's primary gun factory, machine shops and many other manufacturing shops and small factories which produced everything from uniforms to cannons. Being such an important part of the Confederacy's war effort, Selma boasted a semi-circle line of outer fortifications stretching entirely around the northern part of the town. Closer to the town, an inner line of fortification had been started but not yet completed. Attacking from the north meant that a force would have to approach the fortifications and earthworks across open fields which had the trees removed to provide for a clear field of fire. On the northeast approach, an attacking force would have to move through a swamp to reach the fortifications. Waiting within the fortifications were 3,000 Confederate troops and 32 cannons.[11]

Upton and Long ended the previous day near Plantersville and the two columns advanced toward Selma the next morning (April 2) at daylight with Long's division leading the way along the Summerfield Road. Upton's division moved south along Range Line Road pushing enemy pickets aside. Long reached the enemy defenses at 3:00 p.m., but Upton had a more difficult approach to Selma, moving through the swamps which extended between the roads leading to the city, and did not arrive until an hour later. The swamps meant that the Union attacks would be made separately along the two roads leading from the north. Wilson planned to strike with Long's division in a diagonal

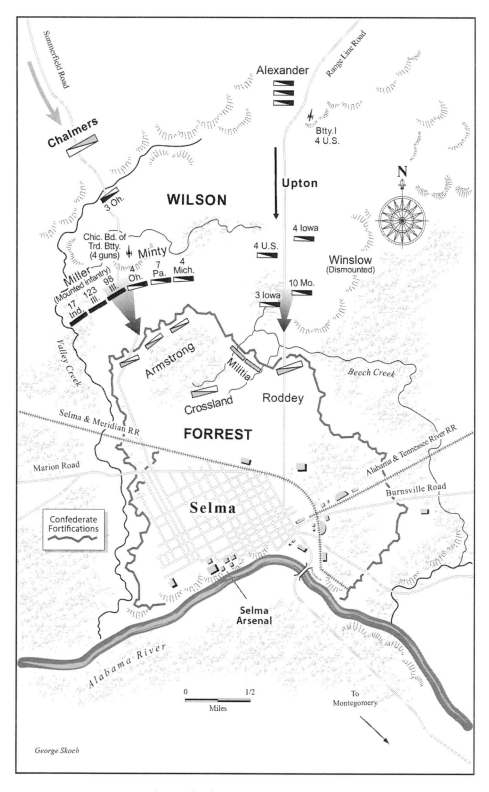

The Battle of Selma, April 2, 1865.

southeast thrust across the Summerville Road, while Upton's division attacked from the north. However, Wilson explained, before Upton could get his troops aligned, "Chalmers attacked General Long's picket posted on the creek to cover his rear. Long, without waiting for the signal, with admirable judgment, immediately began the attack with two dismounted regiments from each brigade, 1,160 men in all, himself, Colonels Miller and Minty, gallantly leading their men."[12]

George Robinson had striven to unite the battery with the cavalry brigades and reached Minty's brigade only the day before. Robinson sent his weary artillerists on the road at 7:30 a.m. and the guns rumbled along until 3:00 that afternoon. Robinson placed his guns into line with Long's division about two miles north of the town on Summerfield Road. The battery's position on a hill was about 1,400 yards from the outer line of enemy works. At 4:30 p.m. Robinson met with Long and was told that Long planned an immediate attack. In the meantime, the Union line began receiving artillery fire from the works. Confederate artillery was placed strategically along the fortifications, including inside four strong forts. Long told Robinson to direct his fire "so as to produce the most effect upon the enemy and to render the most assistance to the advance of the line making the assault." Robinson decided to use his two sections in a leap frog manner, advancing one section in conjunction with the dismounted attack by the cavalrymen, while the other section continued to fire on the enemy works. Robinson reasoned "that my fire could be directed with more precision and effect." Misunderstanding the timing of the attack, Robinson hurried one section forward about 400 yards which exposed it to an immediate fire from artillery from both flanks. Then, chagrined, Robinson realized the Union cavalry movement he had observed was not an attack, just some re-positioning. This left the section exposed, and Robinson ordered the section back to its original position without any casualties. Once back in line, Long gave Robinson the honor of signaling the attack and with a shot from the guns, the Union cavalry surged toward the Confederate defenses. At the battery's position, both sections replied to the Southern guns. Once Long ordered the attack, Robinson ordered both sections forward 400 yards and opened fire again. Trumbull Griffin commanded one section while Robinson directed the other. Robinson remarked that each section advanced along with an attacking line of cavalry and fired on the enemy until the enemy guns were "silenced by the close approach of our men to the works, which in a moment more were in their possession." Long had such confidence in the Board of Trade Battery that he allowed the guns to fire over the heads of his attacking line.[13]

Long's charge surged over 500 yards of open ground, "leaping over and tearing up the stockade in front of the works, pushed through the ditch over the parapet, and swept everything before them." Long's attack struck Armstrong's brigade which manned the works with 1,500 men. As the men streamed across the open fields, the Confederate fire was intense but the Federal troops kept running forward until they clashed with the defenders in a hand-to-hand fight. Long's men were victorious and Armstrong's defenders hurried back to the inner defenses. Off to the left Upton's troops also surged ahead, launching an attack of their own but met with very little resistance and claiming "many prisoners." With the collapse of the outer fortifications, the Board of Trade Battery advanced forward. From this new position, Robinson found he could enfilade much of the outer defensive line to his left (northeast), easing Upton's attack. The cavalrymen to his right had successfully carried the outer works and also turned their fire on the defenders to the left. With Robinson and the cavalry firing from the flank, this caused "the enemy to seek shelter outside of the breast-works and between them and the palisades, under the protection of which he was endeavoring to make his escape." Robinson directed two guns to fire down the adjusting Confederate line and he sent Griffin with two guns inside the works. Robinson rode with Griffin's section and the two officers picked a good position for the guns. Griffin's job was to fire on the enemy guns in the inner works near the town which had begun firing on the Federal cavalry now in place in the outer works. Just as Griffin moved forward, a column of mounted Union cavalry wheeled into position to carry on the attack. Griffin quickly moved past the traffic and unlimbered his guns, putting the section into action. With the Confederates now hurrying toward the inner works, the second section arrived and the battery went to work. Robinson wrote that the battery "opened upon the inner line of works, which, like the first, was soon in the possession of our troops, and rendering further firing unnecessary." Silas Stevens, who worked at cavalry headquarters, observed the battery on the Summerfield Road: "Well to the front: without cover or protection of any kind, from the enemies' guns posted on the breastworks, and from their incessant musketry fire, pouring into our ranks on the right of the line. The boys began firing at once. Their aim was directed toward the rebel works at short range. They fired with usual rapidity, great precision, and coolness, without let or hindrance. A short artillery duel ensued."[14]

When the Confederate defenders fell back to the inner works and prepared to carry on the fight, the 4th U.S. Cavalry charged the works, but could not carry them. Again, the Federals rallied and this time the 17th Indiana and 3rd Ohio joined in the fight and under the guns of the Board of Trade Battery carried the inner works just after dark. This ended the day for the Board of Trade Battery and the fighting at Selma. This would also be the last event in which the battery would fire their guns against the enemy in the war. Robinson recorded no casualties in the battle. Wilson wrote, "[I]n the confusion Generals Forrest, Adams, Buford, and Armstrong, with about half of their forces, escaped by the road toward Burnsville; Lieutenant-General [Richard] Taylor had left at 3 p.m. on the cars." Wilson claimed 2,700 prisoners (150 of which were officers), 26 field pieces and one 30-pounder Parrott. Another 70 heavy guns, factories, warehouses and other material fell in Union hands which were all destroyed, along with 25,000 bales of cotton. In the attack, Long was severely wounded in the scalp, Abram Miller was shot through the leg, Colonel George Dobb, 4th Ohio, was killed in action and Colonel Jonathan Biggs, 123rd Illinois, was shot through the chest. Long lost 46 men killed in action and another 200 wounded in the attack. This costly attack was a dramatic Union victory in the heart of the South and sounded the death knell for the Confederacy in the west. Wilson remained in Selma for the next eight days (until April 10). In the meantime, Croxton and McCook advanced to re-join the command and the cavalry corps spent the next few days recuperating and destroying the factories, arsenal and foundries.[15]

Eli Long had to be carried off the field and in his after-action report, he mentioned the work of the Board of Trade Battery. "The Chicago Board of Trade Battery, commanded by Capt. George I. Robinson, occupied a position on the hill in the rear of my line. Their rapid and effective firing contributed greatly to the demoralization of the enemy. It was afterward reported to me that this battery did good and efficient service in assisting the driving of the enemy through and beyond the town. Although not personally cognizant of the part it took throughout the entire action, I have no doubt from the manner in which it had always executed its work hitherto that it did everything possible to be done." At the end of the campaign, Minty wrote "Captain Robinson,

Chicago Board of Trade Battery, one of the most industrious and untiring officers in the service."[16]

Benjamin Nourse left a long and detailed account of his day on April 2: "Day never to be forgotten so long as life and brain remains in this body—Only 2 hours and 30 minutes to lay on good old 'Mother Earth' last night but we did not get under way until 8 oc. (All this time we might have slept.) We started for Selma, Ala at a brisk walk.... Six miles from Selma we turned to the right and crossed fields to the Summerfield road and then came up to the works round the city. The division was at once dismounted and formed on the hills and as we sat on our horses, we saw the last train of cars leave Selma—I was so tired that after dismounting I lay right down in the dust in the road, putting first a blanket under me and had a good nap for half an hour. The battery was fireing all the time but I heard it not. By this time every thing being ready the division only 1200 men, commenced the descent of the ridge, first at a walk, then trot, then a charge over morass—trees, pickets, ditch, up the works and even into the lines and redoubts. Every reb ran before them.... We captured 2300 men and all the artillery, not a piece being drawn off. It was a terrible charge and a grand, glorious sight. We were fireing over their heads all the time until the lines were taken, then we followed into the city at a gallop."[17]

The Board of Trade Battery reorganized the next morning. The previous night's battle had ended by 7:00 p.m. and the town was plundered. Both Northern soldiers and Southern citizens joined in the shameful looting of the town. The next day with order restored, Robinson was put in charge of dealing with the enemy artillery. He destroyed "one 30-pounder Parrott gun; five 14-pounder iron guns; four 12-pounder light guns; three 3-inch rifled guns; three 12-pounder howitzers; two 6-pounder rifled brass guns; two mountain howitzers for a total of twenty guns and carriages, 20 guns, with carriages." Robinson removed the trunnions, cylindrical protrusions on the guns used to mount the guns, and spiked the guns making them permanently useless. In addition, Robinson destroyed over 4,000 rounds of ammunition. Silas Stevens also observed that after the battle the town was sacked without restraint. Looting continued by local citizens and ex-slaves into the next day: "[F]inishing the job of plundering the stores that did not burn, also the rebel commissary—not a thing is left in the stores."[18]

With Long out of action due to his wound, Minty took command of the division and sent instructions for the various commands to prepare for the next phase of the campaign. The battery moved into camp near North and Lauderdale Streets, near the depot, and joined in the destruction of military facilities over the next few days. The Union troops had no compunction of putting the ex-slaves to work. "Gangs ... are at work piling lumber, tow & pouring oil over the wood work in the arsenal & yards, tearing down the out buildings so as to prevent the spread of fire to dwellings & near—throwing ammunition into the river," wrote Benjamin Nourse. After the battle, the various forces tried to care for the wounded of both armies while the Union soldiers destroyed artillery, carriages, breastworks, machine shops, foundries and the arsenal. The blaze lit up the sky and John Toomey recalled that the "illumination from the great arsenal as it went up was simply grand." Stevens remarked that the destruction of the Confederate-supporting facilities in Selma, culminating in the explosion of the arsenal, was a perfect symbol for a war of fire and sword. Forrest and Wilson communicated via flags of truce and met to discuss an exchange of prisoners, but in the end no agreement was made. The battery moved again on April 10 at 3:00 p.m., traveling 16 miles before stopping at midnight at Benton and the next day the movement to Montgomery continued all day. The battery camped on the evening of April 12 only eight miles from Montgomery. Benjamin Nourse explained this had been a grueling movement, "Only 3½ hours sleep out of 108 hours, pretty hard for both man & horse."[19]

Unaware of Lee's surrender at Appomattox, Wilson marched with abandon into Montgomery. With McCook's division in advance bridges were destroyed on the way. The column arrived in the city on the morning of April 12 and received the surrender of the city after the Confederate forces had evacuated. This spared the destruction of the town. Afterward, the Union column rode for Columbus, Georgia, on April 14. Upton's division lead the advance on Columbus while Oscar LaGrange's brigade rode for West Point. On April 16, Columbus did put up a defense in a feeble attempt to stop Wilson's onslaught but it was overwhelmed by Upton's division in an attack which was completed after dark. Upton claimed 1,200 prisoners and 52 field guns in this Union victory. Twenty miles to the north, LaGrange's brigade captured Fort Tyler at West Point and claimed a large amount of railroad material, including 19 train engines and 340 railroad cars.[20]

The Board of Trade Battery was on the move with the rest of Wilson's cavalry but would not be placed into fighting situations. The battery passed through Montgomery on April 13, a day after the city surrendered. McCook's division led the advance and after the pillaging at Selma, the Federal officers made sure such an event did not occur again. The battery, part of the rearguard, continued onward toward Columbus the next day, but being at the end of the column it did not move until after 3:00 p.m. and continued until 11:00 p.m. The movement continued without incident and reached eight miles west of Columbus on April 16. Benjamin Nourse wrote on April 17, "Bugle blew at the regular time (3 oc) this morning at 7 oc. moved on the city which had been taken last night by the brigade of Brig. Genl. Winslow of the 4th Division. They charged the bridge and a heavy earthwork in front of the same, which had 10 pieces of artillery and 5000 men. It was a quick movement and in an hour (10 p.m.) the works, artillery, bridge, arsenal & city was ours and prisoners. All was so quickly and so quietly done that the townspeople knew nothing of it." Again, as the battery passed through the town now heading for Macon, all the private property was again under guard. The situation for the Confederate forces was simply dismal after the string of defeats, seemingly from all quarters. Nourse recorded, "[A]ll day long we pick up rebel wagons and stragglers, scattered all along the route." On April 20, the battery reached Macon after traveling 42 miles. Nourse recorded: "A flag of truce met the advance 8 miles from Macon but Col. Minty of the 4th Mich. Cavalry who was in command of the advance paid them, or it, no respect. He gave the bearers 5 minutes to get out of they (sic) way, which they did in a lively manner—then we charged to the city meeting the rebel cavalry driving them before us into and through the city. Not many shots were fired—none killed—they surrendered like cowards." The Board of Trade Battery's Private Joseph Peters penned Minty's reply to the Confederate flag of truce before he attacked the town. Once at Macon, the battery and the division went into camp for the last time in this campaign. On April 21, orders arrived from Sherman to cease the conflict.[21]

George Robinson completed his report of Wilson's Raid by summarizing that the battery moved some 600 miles, ranging from 21 to 49 miles per day, or an average of about 30 miles per day over many wet, muddy, poor roads. Robinson declared that he believed this "almost unprecedented in the movements of artillery."[22]

Board of Trade Returns for March–May 1865[23]

(Present and Absent)
Officers, Enlisted Men, and Aggregate
Sgt. Corp. Buglers Artificers Privates

	Officers	Sgt.	Corp.	Buglers	Artificers	Privates	Aggregate
March–May*	3	8	12	1	2	136	162

*(March Number absent 24; April and May Number absent 25)

Final Events

The capture of Macon ended Wilson's Raid and, for all intents and purposes, the war for the Chicago Board of Trade Battery. The last shell fired in anger came at Selma and now 250 miles to the east, the conflict which had started four years ago ended. The battery went into camp in a wooded area about two miles from Macon and a couple of days later the men heard the first rumors that Lee had surrendered two weeks earlier at Appomattox. This was good news, but only a short time later the men heard the terrible news of Lincoln's assassination. The rumor of the assassination was met with disbelief, but on May 3, it was confirmed accompanied by outrage. Still seething, Nourse wrote: "President Lincoln is actually dead—killed by a man named Booth—We got it through the New York Herald only 5 days from New York and these d___d rebels say they have heard all the Northern news through that paper during the whole war. It is awful to hear. The soldiers swear—about the death of Lincoln—there would be no mercy shown to any rebs if we could only have a fight—we all pray that this truce of Sherman & Johnston may come to an end and so we go at it again—Oh, for a good fight to last two or three days."[24]

The 4th Michigan Cavalry left camp on May 9 riding hard to the south. Nourse asked, "Is the truce over? Pray so." The next day the rumors indicated that the 4th Michigan had orders to stop a train carrying Jefferson Davis and some staff officers on the way to Mobile. Glorious news reached camp on May 12—"The war is over!!! The advance brings in word that the boys have Jeff." The next day (May 13) Jefferson Davis arrived in camp. "Today Jeff C. Davis, President of the so called Southern Confederacy, with his whole family and several of the leading members of the rebellion, were brought into camp under guard of the 4th Mich. Cav. they were captured 105 miles south of here—Jeff rode horseback, and the Postmaster Genl. drove the team of six mules that drew the wagon containing Mrs. Davis and the children, also an iron safe contain some gold—They stopped right at our tent for half an hour, and we had a good look at them—The little girl is very pretty—The boys received some beautiful magnolia blossoms from them, and will try to keep for mementoes—At 9 oc. the whole party were sent north under a strong guard. At the hotel where they took supper the crowd was immense, but very orderly—No bad talk by any of the rebels—Our seven shooters were too much for them—My first and last look at Jeff—(God's curse rest on all such as he)—How easy it would have been for me to have shot him dead with my pistol as he sat on his horse, not forty feet from me—Col. Minty, commander of our brigade would not receive him, nor go out to hold any communication but kept him sitting on his horse until his report to his superior officer was ready to be handed in." John Toomey also gave a description of the scene with Davis' family: "Mrs. Davis was sitting in an ambulance wagon by the side of her husband and as an encouragement was reading to him from the Bible." None of the Union soldiers had much sympathy for Davis and Toomey referred to him as the "arch traitor." Benjamin Nourse wrote that he was treated with the "utmost contempt by all the officers." This would mark that last significant military event in the life of the Board of Trade Battery. Trumbull Griffin explained that at least some of the men of the battery were present with the 4th Michigan when it captured Davis. Griffin wrote that the commanding officer of the cavalry regiment selected two men from each of the gun squads to join in the expedition and these men were present when Davis was captured.[25]

On May 23, the Board of Trade Battery, 4th Ohio, 98th Illinois, 123rd Illinois, 72nd Indiana and 4th Michigan regiments all began the long-awaited march home. The column reached Atlanta on May 27 and continued northward traveling through places very familiar to the men. They reached Chattanooga and waited a few days until the battery papers were properly authorized for discharge. On June 7, some of the men of the battery accompanied the guns on the train destined for Nashville, but the rest of the men still marched overland with the Second Cavalry Division and arrived on June 15. At Nashville, the men were greeted with the arrival of Charles Durand, Coleman Brown and George Hanson who had been released from the prisoner of war camp. Before going home, the men turned over their horses and this was difficult duty because the mounts and the men had been through so much together. For example, Benjamin Nourse wrote: "I turned in Lady Clyde—dear creature good bye—many a hard mile you have carried me—many a night have I gone hungry to bed that you might have something to eat. I wish I could take you home with me." Finally, on June 23, the men loaded onto rail cars for the long ride to Chicago and arrived in Michigan City on June 27 where they were greeted with "many of our dear Chicago friends, and a committee from the 'Board of Trade of Chicago.'"[26]

The Michigan Central train was supposed to arrive from Indianapolis at 11:00 that evening but the train was late by an hour and hundreds of well-wishers anxiously awaited. When the train arrived, the battery returned "covered in honor and glory, and bearing aloft the proud colors, bullet-torn and storm-tattered, which were intrusted to their charge when they first went forth from the city to do battle for Liberty and the Republic," according to the *Chicago Tribune*. The next day the men dressed in civilian clothes and for many this was the first time in three years. Nourse concluded his diary with a summary of his service: "O happy day! I was discharged from the United States Service this noon; receiving all pay and emoluments due me. There from—$231.60. This endeth the first lesson—Chicago Board of Trade Battery in three years marched by road—5268 miles, Traveled by rail—1231 miles, Total 6499." William Sherman would acclaim: "These are the gallant fellows, who, he had declared, had easily detected at the first glance he gave them—men of bravery and muscle, soldierly height and bearing, and of a courage which shrank from no danger, and daring which made death contemptible."[27]

Private John Toomey recalled the hardships of the three years of service. "I wish to say however that no human mind can conceive, except a soldier, the many privations & hardships that must of necessity be encountered by an army in the field and in my experience this was no exception…. The Board of Trade battle flag contained the important engagements in the west: Stone River, Elk River, Chickamauga, Farmington, Dallas, Decatur, Atlanta, Lovejoy, Nashville, and Selma."[28]

Battery Losses and Changes January 1–June 30, 1865

Lt. Henry Bennett	Resigned	February 18, 1865	
Lt. Lewis Hand	Resigned	February 18, 1865	

Battery Losses and Changes January 1–June 30, 1865 *cont.*			
Pvt. George Bowers	Discharged	June 3, 1865	
Pvt. John C. Camberg	Discharged	January 21, 1865	Wounds
Pvt. David Chapman	Discharged	June 6, 1865	Disability
Pvt. Gilbert Dunton	Discharged	June 19, 1865	Disability
Pvt. George Gavitt	Discharged	January 19, 1865	Disability
Pvt. Frank Packard	Discharged	January 19, 1865	Disability
Pvt. Daniel Richardson	Discharged	March 16, 1865	Disability
Pvt. Charles Frink	Mustered Out	May 18, 1865	
Pvt. William Otey	Mustered Out	May 23, 1865	
Pvt. Lambert Schommer	Mustered Out	May 29, 1865	
Pvt. James H. Gray/Grey	Died	January 7, 1865	Jeffersonville, IN

Recruits	Enlist. Date	Recruits	Enlist. Date
John Connoss	January 3, 1865	Lambert Schommer	January 4, 1865
William Darbin*	January 1, 1865	Thomas Wilson	January 3, 1865
Edward Leaming	January 1, 1865	Richard Wells	January 3, 1865

*Never reached the battery. (Chicago Board of Trade Association roster, April 27, 1886, Trumbull Griffin file, Missouri History Museum.)

When the war was over, the men of battery, while re-entering community life in Chicago, never forgot their experiences of the past three years. In November a group of the battery went to their old battlegrounds and hospitals and retrieved the bodies of those who had died in the war, just as they had done with those who died at Stones River.[29]

Summary of Three Years of Service

Almost three years after enlisting, the men of the Chicago Board of Trade Battery were mustered out of service after becoming one of the most prominent artillery units in the west. One hundred fifty-one men made up the original battery and over three years another 85 recruits joined. Of this complement of men, 42 were discharged, of which 17 received promotions. Thirteen men were disabled due to wounds and four men were transferred to other branches of service. Five men were sent to the infamous Andersonville prison. Due to the unfortunate loss of records, the exact reconciliation of these individuals may never be complete, but the performance of this battery was without question. The battery made an immediate contribution with its action in the Battle of Stones River which secured the center of Rosecrans' reforming line and continued from there. The battery participated in 11 significant actions—Stones River, Elk River, Chickamauga (Reed's Bridge and Glass Mill), Farmington, Dallas, Decatur, Atlanta, Lovejoy, Nashville and Selma. In addition, it played an active part in 26 other actions as part of the Army of Cumberland, including Resaca, Kennesaw Mountain, Peach Tree Creek, Marietta, Vining Station, Noonday Creek, and Stone Mountain. Finally, the battery had another 42 minor actions in its day-to-day activities while on reconnaissance, outpost duty and other duties.[30]

The summary of the battery's service was a long and honored one[31]:

Chicago Board of Trade Independent Battery,
Light Artillery and Record of Service

1862

Moved to Louisville, September 9–11	Expedition on Franklin Pike and skirmish, Dec. 14
Pursuit of Bragg into Kentucky, October 1–16	Advance on Murfreesboro, December 26–30
Lawrenceburg, October 11	Battle of Stone's River, Dec. 30–31 and Jan. 1–3, 1863
Moved to Bowling Green, and duty there till Dec. 4	
March to Nashville, December 4–7	

1863

Duty at Murfreesboro till June	Pea Vine Ridge, September 18 Reed's Bridge, September 18
Scouts on Manchester Pike, June 13	Battle of Chickamauga, fight at Glass Mill, Sept. 19–21
Battery changed from Mounted Field to Flying Horse Artillery and assigned to 2nd Cavalry Div., March 1863	Guarding fords above Chattanooga till Oct. 1
Tullahoma Campaign, June 23–July 7	Operations against Wheeler, October 1–17
Morris Ford, Elk River, July 2	Thompson's Cove, October 3
Occupation of Middle Tennessee till Aug. 16	McMinnville, October 4
Expedition to Huntsville, July 13–22	Murfreesboro, October 5
Chickamauga Campaign, Aug. 16-Sept. 22	Near Shelbyville and Farmington, October 7
Alpine, September 3 and 8	Sugar Creek, October 9
Ringgold, September 11	March to Decherd, October 10–15
Reconn. toward Lafayette/skirmish, Sept. 13	Then to Maysville

1864

Maysville, Huntsville, and Pulaski, till March	Lovejoy's Station, August 20
Refitted with 3-inch Parrotts, Feb. 24, 1864	Chattahoochee River Bridge and Turner's Ferry, Aug. 26-Sept. 2
Moved to Huntsville, March 10	At Cross Keys till September 21
Moved to Columbia, April 4–8	Operations Hood and Forest, Sept. 29–Nov. 3
Atlanta Campaign, May 1 to September 8	Near Lost Mountain, October 4–7
On right flank of army, May 11–17	New Hope Church, October 5
Battle of Resaca, May 14–15	Dallas, October 7
Tanner's Bridge, Oostenaula River, May 15	Rome, October 10–11
Kingston, May 19	Narrows, October 11
Near Dallas, May 24	Coosaville Road, near Rome, October 13
Operations about Dallas, May 25–June 5	Near Summerville, October 17
Acworth, June 8	Little River, October 20
Near Big Shanty, June 9	Leesburg, October 20–21
Operations about Marietta and against Kennesaw Mountain, June 10–July 2	Ladiga, Terrapin Creek, October 28
McAfee's Cross Roads, June 11	Moved to Chattanooga, November 3–5
Noonday Creek, June 15 and 19	To Nashville, November 13
Powder Springs, June 20	Line of Shoal Creek, November 16–20
Noonday Creek, June 27	Nashville Campaign, November–December
Nickajack Creek, July 2–5	Fouche Springs, November 23
Marietta and Roswell, July 3	Columbia, Duck River, November 24–27
Rottenwood Creek, July 4	Nashville during Hood's investment, Dec 1–15
Chattahoochee River, July 6–10	Battle of Nashville, December 15–16
Raid to Atlanta & Augusta R. R., July 13–20	Pursuit of Hood, December 17–28
Raid to Covington, July 22–24 (Center Sect.)	Richland Creek, December 24
Decatur, July 22	Lynnville, December 24
Red Oak, August 19	Pulaski, December 25
Flint River, August 19	At Gravelly Springs, till March 1865
Jonesborough, August 19	

1865 (Chicago Board of Trade Independent Battery *cont.*)	
At Gravelly Springs till March Wilson's Raid to Macon, March 22–April 24 Ebenezer Church, April 1 Selma, April 2 Montgomery, April 12	Capture of Columbus, April 16 Macon, April 20 Duty at Macon till May 23 Moved to Nashville, then to Chicago, June 23–27 Mustered out, June 30, 1865

Officially the battery lost ten enlisted men killed or mortally wounded and another nine died due to disease for a total of nineteen deaths. Piecing together the casualty reports which remain, the list of deaths include:

Deaths (killed, mortally wounded, died of disease)	
William Bagley	Gunshot through arm
Theodore Baker	Typhoid fever
Andrew Baskerville	General disability (died on way to Chicago after being discharged)
Augustus Carver	Gunshot through hips
George Crane	Killed in action
Samuel Croft	Died in Chicago of chronic diarrhea in 1865
Anthony Dean	Died of gangrene poisoning (never reached the battery)
Charles De Costa	General disability
Thomas De Coursey	Died in hospital in Louisville
Samuel Dodd	Kicked in head
Edward Field	Gunshot through the body
Andrew Finney	Killed in action
James Gray/Grey	Died in hospital in Jeffersonville
Desire Joubert	Gunshot though the leg
Albert Lake	Died in prison of war camp
Martin Snow	Died in prison of war camp
Thomas Stagg	Killed in action

Deaths (killed, mortally wounded, died of disease)	
James B. Wallace	Died of dysentery
George White	Gunshot through hips
William H. Wiley	Killed in action
Thomas Wygant	Killed in action
Hector Aiken	Killed in action at Battle of Petersburg (after leaving battery)

Hector Aiken was not part of the battery when he died and should not be formally reported as a battery loss but it is worthy of mention. Also, Anthony Dean enlisted after serving in another unit, but never arrived at the battery. He died in the Nashville hospital on March 16, 1865, never reaching his new unit. James Gray also enlisted in the battery after his prior service in the 88th Illinois Infantry. Gray would die in the Joe Holt hospital in Jeffersonville, Indiana, early in 1865. Remarkably, the number of deaths due to illness and those of battle wounds were almost the same. This is not representative of many other units in the war which often had much greater numbers of death due to illness. For example, the 1st Regiment Illinois Light Artillery, Batteries A–M, had about a 3:1 ratio of deaths due to illness compared to deaths due to battle injuries. It is notable that efforts by the post-war Chicago Board of Trade Battery Association retrieved the bodies of their fallen comrades using zinc-lined containers, or otherwise accounted for them. They were determined to bring their comrades home.[32]

In addition, about 30 men were discharged due to physical disabilities and another 17 were discharged for promotions or reassignment. Some additional men were reassigned temporarily to other duties within the Army of the Cumberland. The lingering effects of life in the war often resulted in an under-reporting of the total casualties. Certainly, for the men who were wounded, many would never be the same after the war and those who had certain diseases would suffer from these for years after the war. Fortunately, many of the wounded survived the war and lived productive lives. Among those wounded and for whom records exist are:

Wounded (Non-Lethal)

Abbott Adams	James Appleton	James Bloom
John Camberg	John Carroll	Andrew Close
Thomas Fitzwilliam	George Gackheimer	Charles Garnsey
Turnbull Griffin	Charles Holyland	Jackson Howard
Thomas McClelland	Tobias Miller	William O'Dell
Ormango Payne	Silas Peckham	Henry Philliber
Howard Phillips	Sylvanus Stevens	William Tinsley
John Toomey	Frederick Weigert	

The battery had several men captured during the conflict and again, many returned home after the harrowing experience of being imprisoned in the Civil War, but Albert Lake and Martin Snow would die in prison.

Captured		
South of Nashville:		
Homer Baker	John Buckingham	Francis Richmond
John Sleman	Thomas Tinsley	Thomas Williams
Near Murfreesboro:		
Lawson Andrews	James Hildreth	Charles Johnston
Charles Maple		
Atlanta Campaign:		
Coleman Brown	Calvin Durand	Thomas Hanson
Albert Lake	Martin Snow	

The story of the Chicago Board of Trade Battery was told throughout the war in various newspapers and the exploits of the battery made it one of the most famous artillery units in the war. After the war, most newspaper accounts referred to the battery as "famous." The list of battles and skirmishes in which the battery was involved proved an adequate justification for this sobriquet. Taking into consideration the original enlistees and the recruits throughout the war, the battery fielded about 240 men. After three years

Chicago Board of Trade Battery Association meeting, May 30, 1901 (Chicago History Museum, ICHi-176918).

of conflict, the men formed a relationship that would carry on long after the war. And certainly, there are 240 different stories of each of the men who fought with this battery—some were model stories of a normal life and some were tragedies; but without doubt the men moved into the later years of the 19th century and into the 20th century as builders of this great country. The men of the Board of Trade Battery spread across the country after the war and made productive lives. Many returned to the business lives they had before the war as grain speculators, wholesale grocers, newspapermen, printers, farmers, lumbermen, bakers, architects, dentists, designers and railroadmen.

The unit lived on long after the war in the form of the Chicago Board of Trade Battery Association with regular meetings, reunions and annual events. A solemn funeral was held in Chicago for the fallen of the Chicago based artillery units on January 7, 1866. At this ceremony the efforts of the Board of Trade Battery were recognized and bodies of those who had died in the war had been retrieved or settled into what would become national cemeteries, with the exception of one man, Albert Lake, who died as a prisoner of war. In 1901, the association installed a monument honoring the battery in Rosehill Cemetery. The simple stone monument included dates of service, battles and miles traveled during the war. The association initially discussed a monument as early as 1868, and then later seriously planned its installation in 1891 and needed to collect $10,000 for stone. At the unveiling of the monument, William S. Warren, president of the Chicago Board of Trade, spoke: "Let us make the dedication of this monument a fresh starting point to ever glory in the achievements of these men, the cause for which they fought and bled and died, and the results of their self-sacrifice."[33]

Monument erected in 1901 at Rosehill Cemetery in Chicago in honor of the battery (Chicago History Museum, ICHi-176917).

"After war peace!

Peace through their labors to the living. These 'have fought their last fight';
the salvos of artillery which soon shall sound from the guns they loved so well shall not
awake them. The grass shall grow in the spring time, the birds of summer shall sing their sweet-
est notes, the bright glories of autumn shall tint the foliage above them, and the white snow of
winter shall lie on their graves; but these shall sleep on in peace."[34]

—Dr. O.H. Tiffany

CHAPTER NINE

Post-War Biographical Information

The war concluded in May 1865 and the surviving members of the battery returned home to continue their lives. The experience of the previous three years would always be a part of each man, but it was time to move forward. These men had been part of the business community in Chicago and most returned to that way of life, but the comradery made lasting friends of these men. Included in this final section are short post-war accounts of the officers, sergeants, and those whose voices echoed through the previous pages.

Captains

James H. Stokes left the battery permanently in late summer of 1863 and initially commanded a wing of artillery in the Chattanooga Campaign. Officially, he still held the rank of captain of the Chicago Board of Trade Battery and this meant no one could be promoted captain. In February 1864, he was promoted to the rank of lieutenant colonel of volunteers and assigned to the Quartermaster Department where he was involved in inspecting the New Orleans quartermaster activities. He remained in this capacity until August 1864, when he was reassigned at the rank of captain to the staff of Assistant Adjutant General, U.S. Volunteers, and served in the Washington, D.C., area. In July 1865, he was promoted to the rank of brigadier general, and he was mustered out of service the following month. He returned to Chicago where his health began to fail. In 1867, he lost some sight in his left eye which he attributed to his service in Florida in the 1840s. He began managing an estate in Chicago two years after. In 1875, his left eye hemorrhaged and had to be removed. Shortly after this procedure, he began having additional problems with his right eye which ultimately resulted in blindness. Although Stokes tried to get a pension due to his disability, he was unsuccessful and died impoverished in 1890 in New York.[1]

When **George Irving Robinson** enlisted, he was 22 years old and he successfully recruited many who would also enlist in the battery. He was elected to the rank of first lieutenant and remained in this position until Stokes left the battery in 1863. Then, he served as nominal captain of the battery without that rank until August 1864 when he was promoted captain. Robinson was respected by the men he commanded and operated in an efficient and professional manner. While still a lieutenant, Robinson, an avid learner, routinely toured the other batteries in the Army of the Cumberland and observed how they were organized and operated. When Stokes left the battery, Robinson applied this knowledge to the Board of Trade Battery with welcome results. Robinson was one of the men and he treated them with more consideration than did Stokes. He allowed the men more time for entertainment while in camp, but still gained respect and obedience. By the end of the war, the professional soldiers, Minty and Long, held Robinson in high esteem as a trustworthy and skilled commander on whom they could rely. He turned down an opportunity to join the regular army at the end of the war.[2]

Before Robinson's enlistment, he worked in a firm of wholesale grocers and, upon the completion of the war, he returned to the business with Durand Bros. & Powers. There was an opportunity to expand this venture and Robinson went to Milwaukee to manage the new business there. As the business succeeded, it was renamed Durand, Robinson & Co. and in 1879, Robinson bought the business in Milwaukee, now renamed the George I. Robinson, Co. He began his business career in Chicago as a porter at the age of 16 and owned his own successful business 20 years later. He was active in the business and social life in Milwaukee. He was a member of the Episcopal Church and a Republican. Robinson and wife Jane Adams Porter Robinson had five children, two boys and three daughters, all of which graduated from the University of Wisconsin. Robinson died of stroke in January 1909 at the age of 68.[3]

Lieutenants

Next to Robinson, **Trumbull Dorrance Griffin** is probably the best-known officer of the Board of Trade Battery. Griffin offered remarkable and historical service with the battery during the Battle at Reed's Bridge, the Battle of Noonday Creek and Battle of Atlanta. He earned the respect of Minty who liked and respected Griffin and knew he could be counted on when needed. Griffin was 28 years old at his enlistment and a native of New York. Two of Griffin's brothers also served in the Civil War, one an officer in a Wisconsin infantry regiment and the other an officer in the 4th Michigan Cavalry. Griffin had worked with various newspapers before the war and indicated his profession as printer upon his enlistment. After the war, Griffin relocated to St. Louis where he began the *St. Louis Market Reporter* and was for many years a member of the Merchants' Exchange. He retired from the newspaper business in the late 1870s. Griffin married Mary Davis, a native of Chillicothe, Ohio, and the daughter of a prominent merchant of that city. The couple had three children, Margery, Dorrance, and Everett. Griffin died in St. Louis on February 21, 1912.[4]

After the Battle of Farmington, **Sylvanus Harlow Stevens** served detached from the battery with the quartermaster department in Nashville for the remainder of the war. Stevens, like Stokes maintained his rank in the battery, which prevented others from being promoted. Late in the war, Stevens returned to the battery and was mustered out with the others. It is important to note that Stevens' wife, Juliet Eleanor (nee Brawner), whom he married in 1852, accompanied him through much of the war and also assisted in nursing the men of the battery when necessary. While ambitious, Stevens was well-liked and respected by many in the battery. After the war, Stevens remained in Nashville as a civilian and worked with the government to deal with excess war supplies and equipment. In 1867, he started a wagon manufacturing business in Nashville and in September 1869 he moved to Humboldt, Kansas. The following spring, he opened a lumber business which he sold a few years later. Then, he entered the grain business in Humboldt. During this time, he served as mayor for two years and served one term in the state legislature. He remained at this location until 1881 when he again moved to Chicago and served as chief grain inspector for the Flax Department of the Chicago Board of Trade. Stevens pursued his career and focused on his family—his wife, two sons and two daughters, and community. He was a member of the Episcopal Church. He died on December 19, 1902, in Chicago.[5]

Henry Bennett was a quiet but reliable officer. Little direct communications were recorded by Bennett, except for one letter which was sent to his grandfather, that was discovered after the war. Bennett's prior experience with artillery made him an invaluable member of the battery. Bennett served in all the major actions, including the Battle of Stones River, Battle of Atlanta and Kilpatrick's Raid where he made notable contributions. Upon returning to Chicago in February 1865, Bennett, a carpenter by training, took advantage of rapid growth in Chicago and began contracting work as part of the Grannis & Bennett Company. Two years later he was in business for himself and continued contracting work in Chicago through 1876. At one point he had 250 men working for him and he became a princi-

Sylvanus H. Stevens, an important personage in forming and commanding the battery (Post war image, Chicago History Museum, ICHi-176922).

pal contractor in the city. On December 13, 1866, Bennett married Mary F. Vreeland, daughter of another established contractor in Chicago. In 1876, he moved to Silver Lake, Kansas, a few miles north of Topeka, to begin stock raising, but he continued with his contracting business which included constructing a building for the state insane asylum, many other state buildings, churches, hospitals, banks and Santa Fe Railroad buildings. He also built the east wing of the state house of government. His business expanded outside Kansas and he even spent time in Mexico constructing railroad buildings. His health began to fail in 1908 and his two sons took over much of the burden of the construction business. He and his wife had two daughters and two sons. He was a member of the Methodist-Episcopal Church, a mason, member of Rotary and the Capitol Commercial Club. Bennett died on January 26, 1924 at the age of 82, after several months of illness.[6]

Lewis B. Hand was an energetic member of the battery and was unanimously selected for the last promotion to lieutenant in the battery. Hand brought experience when the battery was organized. At the end of the war, he returned to Chicago and entered several business pursuits. He ultimately became a grain inspector for the Chicago Board of Trade. In May 1877, he began rooming at the European Hotel on Sherman Street in Chicago. He came under the care of a physician (Dr. A.J. Baxter) for urinary stricture and after some time, Hand stopped seeing the doctor. Baxter had observed the condition had been improving. Ten days later Baxter was informed that Hand had an operation in his hotel room by another physician and during the operation for bladder stones,

Hand died. The case received notoriety in the papers because Hand was aestheticized with ether, followed by chloroform. The friends of the 40 year old demanded an investigation but the unfortunate event was done. It was subsequently discovered that Hand died due to paralysis of the heart. Hand was buried in Joliet.[7]

Unfortunately, First Lieutenant **Albert F. Baxter**, who was one of the first to enlist in the battery, resigned in November 1862. He was well-liked by the men and was presented a sword early in his tenure by the men of the battery. Baxter was so ill that he resigned and then he undoubtedly returned to Chicago, but little is known about him from this point. Baxter's brother Henry was discharged also in November due to consumption and Albert's resignation was due to general physical disability.[8]

Sergeants

Two sergeants had short lives after the war. **Myron S. Sandford** and **Frederick Deane** both died within two months of each other in Chicago. Sanford left the battery in March 1864 and joined the 2nd Massachusetts Heavy Artillery with the rank of second lieutenant. He resigned his commission in September 1865 and returned to Chicago to work as a clerk for the railroad. On April 5, 1867, Sanford committed suicide presumably due to excess alcohol consumption and due to his gambling on grain prices. The newspaper article reporting his death stated that he was respectably connected but alcohol was his downfall. Two months earlier, Frederick G. Deane, the pre-war clerk, also died. Deane also left the battery and received a promotion to the rank of lieutenant in the 13th Michigan Light Artillery. He resigned his commission on June 5, 1865, and died in Chicago in 1867 of "brain fever."[9]

Smith Martin Randolph was the battery ordance sergeant and had studied architecture in Chicago in 1854 with his older brother, Mahlon. In 1859, Randolph moved to Missouri as part of another firm but as the war approached, Smith joined the Dubuque Elevator Company which supplied the army with grain. Mahlon and Smith raised a company for Bissell's Engineering Regiment but Smith remained with the grain company. Then, when the call came for the Board of Trade Battery, he enlisted. When the war ended, he joined Mahlon's firm in St. Louis, Randolph Brothers, which designed public and private buildings in the area. Next, Randolph was appointed police commissioner and he became the president of the police board. After the great Chicago fire, Randolph left St. Louis and continued his architecture business in Chicago, rebuilding many buildings. He made heavy mercantile and manufacturing buildings his specialty and later made advances in building construction using reinforced concrete. He married in 1870 but his wife died in 1876. In 1882, he married Harriet Maher Smith, who had a daughter who would be called Dolly Randolph, and the couple had two sons and one daughter together. Randolph died in Chicago in 1924. Smith's brother, **Sergeant William Randolph**, also served in the battery. Just prior to his enlistment, he married Theodosia Merrill. Randolph was one of the potential final appointments as lieutenant in 1865, but the promotion was never finalized. Randolph returned to Chicago and entered business like many from the battery. In 1870 he moved to Godfrey, Illinois, as a bookkeeper and he continued in the insurance business in St. Louis until he moved to Madison, Wisconsin, as an auditor for the insurance company. William had four sons and two daughters. William died in a hospital after a two-month illness at the age of 74 in Madison in April 1914.[10]

Sergeant Frank Knight might have been the hardest working of all the men of the battery after the war. Knight's life of adventure began when he ran away from home at 17 to work on a ship carrying cotton from New Orleans to Boston. He arrived in Chicago in 1852 and began working for the railroad which would prove to be his life's vocation. He started as an agent and worked his way up to conductor. Then, at the age of 32, he joined the Chicago Board of Trade Battery. Knight married Sarah Potter in what he called a "romantic marriage." After the war he returned to the railroad, working until he was 94 years old and during that time he worked for 56 years for the same employer. He missed only two weeks when he had pneumonia when he was in his 70s and he took only three vacations.

If Knight was a dedicated railroader, then **Philip L. Auten** was a dedicated lumberman. Auten was the son of a log-

Sergeant Frank Knight ordered his gun to fire the first artillery shell in the Battle of Chickamauga (Chicago History Museum, ICHi-176923).

ger and saw mill owner on the Susquehanna River. He completed his education at Wesleyan Seminary at Williamsport and moved to Chicago and went to work for Jemson & Roberts Lumber Company where he was foreman of the yard. In 1861, he took the same position with Jacob Beidler Lumber Company where he stayed until he enlisted in the Board of Trade Battery. After the war he returned to his position with Beidler until 1872 when he went to work at Ford River Lumber Co. In 1876, he formed a partnership with H.G. Billings. Three years later, Auten bought an interest in the Ford River company, where he remained until 1896. He even became co-owner of the Pittsburg Pirates baseball team for a few years in the 1890s. He retired and concentrated on his own business interests. Auten married Isabel Seydel and the couple had one son and one daughter. He died at the age of 79 in Pasadena on March 7, 1919, after suffering ill health.[11]

George W. Bowers was born in Summit County, Ohio, on July 29, 1840, and in 1848 the family moved to Joliet, Illinois, where they continued farming. Bower was the third of eight children and he was educated in Illinois. He began his career engaged in boating on the Erie Canal and Mississippi River. When the war broke out, Bowers enlisted in the three-month unit, McAllister's Battery of light artillery. This made him an important part of the Board of Trade Battery when he enlisted. Fortunately, he successfully made it through the war without a serious wound. He returned to Illinois after the war and while there, married Helena Hess in 1868. The couple remained in Illinois until 1871 when he moved to York County, Nebraska, and began homesteading. He focused on cultivation, but soon added stock raising to his operation. The Bowers had two sons and one daughter. In politics, he became a Populist. He was justice of the peace and held other county offices. He belonged to the Grand Army of the Republic, and was a member of the Congregational Church. He died in York in January 1918 at the age of 82.[12]

Henry Bradford Chandler was born in at Lunenburg, Vermont, in March 1840. He completed his education in Vermont and in 1857 he relocated to Chicago where he worked as a clerk in his brother's flour and feed store, Chandler & Baker. He remained in his job until 1860 when he went to Pike's Peak to prospect for gold. In the fall of 1861, he returned to Chicago and went to work with his brother, C.R. Chandler, in the general commission business. He enlisted in the battery and was promoted to the rank of sergeant. He returned to Chicago and spent 10 years as a commercial traveler in Michigan, Wisconsin, Illinois and Iowa. Afterwards, he became a traveling representative of the Union Knife Company of Naugatuck, Connecticut, and later became the manager of the Chicago branch of the company. He was deeply involved with fraternal organizations and Freemasons. He was also a member of George H. Thomas Post, Grand Army of the Republic and, politically, he was a Republican. In 1867 he married Eunice Sherman of Newton, Massachusetts, and the couple had two daughters. Chandler continued his career in Chicago and died there on January 19, 1915.[13]

John A. Howard received a great deal of notoriety after the war because he was one of the small detachments of the battery which accompanied the 4th Michigan Cavalry when they captured Jefferson Davis. After the war, Howard returned to Chicago, was married, and had a son. Howard died suddenly of a stroke while sweeping his porch on January 5, 1897. He was born in New York City and had been one of the first to enlist in the battery. For much of his life he was a manager for the U.S. Express Company, a shipping firm with a branch office in Chicago. When Howard died, the notice of his death was printed in a large number of newspapers from coast-to-coast due to his participation in Davis' capture. He was noted for being an individual of exceptional energy.

Menzo Salisbury also returned to Chicago at the end of the war. Though recommended for promotion to the rank of lieutenant in 1865 and battery records would show him as commissioned, he was never mustered into that rank. Salisbury proved an exceptional member of the battery during the war. In 1870, he worked for a commission house and in 1880, he worked for the Chicago Board of Trade. In his later years, he became a manager in the dry goods business in both wholesale and retail. His first wife died in 1885 leaving a substantial estate and at that point, Salisbury worked for Witheral & Co. In 1886, he married Bessie Dean. He died on February 25, 1920, and was buried in Evanston, Illinois.[14]

Along with Menzo Salisbury, **Sergeant Abbott Adams** was also commissioned, but never mustered at the rank of lieutenant. Presumably, both Salisbury and Adams acted as lieutenants in the last campaign of the war, but they were never formally approved. Abbott Livermore Adams, a clerk, enlisted at the age of 22 and was a native of New Hampshire. His family moved to Chicago in 1853 where he completed his education. Adams stood almost six feet tall with brown hair and gray eyes. He had served in a 100-day unit with Battery A, 1st Illinois Light Artillery in 1861. When he joined the Board of Trade Battery, he brought some much-needed experience to the new unit and he proved invaluable. After the war, Abbott worked at the United States Depository until 1868 when he entered the lumber business of A.T. King & Company. He was employed with King, Adams & Lord, and Adams, Hastings & Co. until 1891 when he began managing real estate. Adams was a responsible individual and a congenial friend to many and on his headstone was carved: "He was a good man." He died in Chicago on February 7, 1907, at the age of 64 years old.[15]

Other Members of the Battery

After reading through the various "voices" of the battery, it seemed appropriate to include a little of the post-war lives of those who had preserved the history of the battery.

Born at Clintonville, New York, May 7, 1840, **Sergeant Calvin Durand** was educated at a boarding school in Keeseville to which he walked every Monday morning. The youngest of five sons and a daughter, Durand taught school early in his adult life. He came to Chicago in 1859 to join his brothers in business as a porter. Durand was captured and spent time in two of the most notorious Confederate prisons—Andersonville and Libby. Durand nearly died when he contracted a deadly fever but he survived long enough to be exchanged in March 1865. He returned to Chicago and after some time, reentered the business world as part of Durand & Powers Co., but the effects of prison life remained with him for years. He was a major figure in the business and social communities of Chicago and eventually became the head of the Durand Kasper Company, a large wholesale grocery firm. He was a member of the Union League, University and the Onwentsia clubs. Durand and his wife had six children and the couple were married for 40 years. On October 31, 1911, at Lake Forrest, Calvin Durand died a mere nine weeks after his wife's death, attributed to heart failure, but his son said he died of a broken heart.[16]

John Caskey Fleming, the prolific and articulate recorder of the actions of the battery, left a complete account of much of three years of war. Fleming provided a positive impression of the events from 1862 through 1865 in his letters. When the war concluded, he returned to Chicago and began work as a clerk in a grocery store and later became a bookkeeper for a coal company. In 1884, he went to work as a sales agent, and later sales manager, for the Carnegie Corporation and remained in that position until his retirement in 1901. His primary duty was the sales of Carnegie steel in the Chicago area and he was very successful. He married Isabella Creighton of Chicago and the couple had one daughter. He died in Chicago on October 3, 1932, at the age of 89 years.[17]

Tobias Charles Miller, who provided a good summary of much of the action of the battery in the war, was discharged in June 1864 after receiving a serious wound in the Battle of Decatur, but his time in the war was not over. His cousin, General John F. Miller, commanded the Federal garrison at Nashville in 1864 and Tobias received a promotion to the rank of captain and served on Miller's staff until the end of the war. After the war he was appointed U.S. Marshall, headquartered at Nashville, and later he began working as an internal revenue collector. He married Miss Malona Hanks, a close relative of Nancy Hanks, in 1868. Upon his retirement, he entered the lumber business in the South and finally moved to California in 1882 where he served in state government. He died in 1898.[18]

Benjamin and John Nourse, two brothers, left a complete chronicle of the events of the battery. Benjamin was called Ben by some but generally "Frank" by his friends, and he was a Massachusetts native, born on February 25, 1843. Like many in the battery, he returned home at the end of the war and went into business, but he never forgot his experiences in the battery. He initially became a clerk in a wholesale grocery firm and later became the manager of a baking powder firm. He married and had five children. Importantly, he became very active in the Board of Trade Battery Association, the Grand Army of the Republic and even served in the Police Battery in the Chicago riots in 1877. He remained in the militia battery in Chicago for some years afterward. He was

Left: John A. Nourse, post war lumberman, left a lasting chronicle of the Board of Trade Battery (Chicago History Museum, ICHi-014380). *Right:* Benjamin F. Nourse returned to business in Chicago, serving in the militia and in the police battery in the city. His legacy and record of the battery remains an important part of the history of the war (Chicago History Museum, ICHi-176914)

instrumental in the establishment of a Board of Trade Battery monument which was placed at Rosehill Cemetery and in the annual meetings of the battery association. He and his comrades penned the definitive record of the battery in the *Historical Sketch of the Chicago Board of Trade Battery*. He was forever changed by the war, and forever embraced his comrades and the memories of the service provided by "battery boys" of the Chicago Board of Trade Battery. He died suddenly on June 18, 1903, at the age of 60. Benjamin's brother, **John Aiken Nourse,** recorded that the family moved to Bloomington, Illinois, in 1852 and was educated in the Bloomington public schools. The family relocated to Chicago and John was just 17 years old when he enlisted. After the war he returned to Chicago. In 1872 he married Clara E. Swift and the couple had three daughters—Hattie, Ida, and Clara. He began working for Rogers & Co., coal dealers, weighing coal in 1866, but this was work which did not suit him. Then, he worked as a bookkeeper, a job at which he did not feel proficient, for Wheelok, Dean, & Hermann, lumber dealers, in 1867. He shifted to the outside work of the lumber business and found his vocation. Nourse's first exposure to yellow pine, a primary lumber product, came with his time in the war. In 1871, Mears, Bates & Co. opened a lumberyard under Nourse's management. In 1880, Sawyer-Goodman Co. opened a lumber yard and Nourse managed that enterprise. The second year, the business sold 40 million board-feet of lumber and continued this amount of business until 1897 under Nourse's management and sales efforts. The business closed in 1900 and Nourse retired for three years and then began Nourse-Taylor Lumber Co. with its main offices in the Chamber of Commerce building. In 1910, the Taylor partnership dissolved and Nourse continued in business on his own. Nourse died at the age of 68 of apoplexy while in his garden at Willmette, a suburb of Chicago, on June 16, 1913. He was Republican in politics. He was member of the George H. Thomas Post, G.A.R. and the Cleveland Lodge A.F. and A.M. Club.[19]

Silas Stevens would leave one of the most complete summaries of the battery's events in a series of letters he wrote to his brother after the war. Stevens was the younger brother of Lieutenant Sylvanus Stevens. He initially served with the battery, but later served as a clerk in division headquarters. After the war, he returned to Chicago and worked as a clerk with some commission merchants. He went to Maine, his birthplace, in 1867 and for two years traveled in California and the Pacific Northwest. In 1877, he also opened a business devoted to numismatic and philatelic interests and gained a national reputation for his expertise in these endeavors. Next, he found real estate to be a lucrative occupation in 1878. Stevens' life was not without controversy in both his real estate dealings and in his dubious transactions with currency. He remained in Chicago and died in April 1919.[20]

John David Toomey had the misfortune of being injured and wounded several times during the war, including being shot by a spent ball at the Battle of Stones River and being shot by a live round at Decatur which had to be extracted using two knives. This resilient young man returned to Chicago after the war and entered the business world again. Toomey, a carpenter before the war, had several occupations including a box builder and, later in life, a grocer. He married Jane Edgar in 1877; he gained stepchildren by the marriage and he and his wife had two additional children. Toomey died at home on January 27, 1907. He was active in the GAR, Knights Templar, and other lodge organizations.[21]

Appendix I:
Roster of the Chicago Board of Trade Battery

This roster is a consolidation of the rolls found in the *Historical Sketch of the Chicago Board of Trade Battery*, Illinois State Archives, and Report of the Adjutant General of the State of Illinois. NOTE: There are discrepancies between the three sources in several items. For those differences which seemed significant, both entries are included separated by "/". Also of importance, the Adjutant General's report showed many of the recruits' mustered out dates as July 3, 1865, in contrast to the battery records which showed June 30, 1865. These entries can be found in Adjutant General's report.

	Residence	Date of Rank or Enlistment	Date of Muster	Remarks	Occupation	Age	Height	Hair Color	Eye Color	Nativity
Captains										
Stokes, James H.	Chicago	July 31, 1862	July 31, 1862	Mustered out Aug. 22, 1864; Appointed to command artillery on Right Wing, October 1863 by Gen. Grant	Insurance Agent	45				Maryland
Robinson, George I.	Chicago	Aug. 22, 1864	Oct. 14, 1864	Mustered out June 30, 1865	Clerk	24	5' 11"	Black	Hazel	Rhode Island
1st Lieutenants										
Robinson, George I.	Chicago	July 31, 1862	July 31, 1862	Promoted Captain Aug. 22, 1864	Clerk	22	5' 11"	Black	Hazel	Rhode Island
Baxter, Albert F.	Chicago	July 31, 1862	-	Resigned Nov. 18, 1862–disability	Clerk	24/25	6'	Black	Dark	Massachusetts
Stevens, Sylvanus H.	Chicago	Nov. 18, 1862	Dec. 8, 1862	Mustered out June 30, 1865	Merchant	34	6'	Light	Blue	Maine
Griffin, Trumbull D.	Chicago	Aug. 22, 1864	Dec. 1, 1864	Mustered out June 30, 1865	Printer	28	5' 10"	Dark	Hazel	New York
2nd Lieutenants										
Griffin, Trumbull D.	Chicago	July 31, 1862	July 31, 1862	Promoted Senior 1st Lt. Nov. 30, 1864; wounded at Battle of Stones River, Dec. 31, 1862	Printer	24/26	5' 10"	Dark	Hazel	New York
Bennett, Henry	Chicago	July 31, 1862	July 31, 1862	Resigned Feb. 18, 1865	Mechanic	22/26	5' 11"	Dark	Hazel	Illinois
Hand, Lewis B.	Chicago	Aug. 22, 1864	Dec. 1, 1864	Resigned Feb. 18, 1865	Clerk	-	5'4"	Dark	Hazel	New York

	Residence	Date of Rank or Enlistment	Date of Muster	Remarks	Occupation	Age	Height	Hair Color	Eye Color	Nativity
Adams, Abbott L.	Chicago	June 22, 1865	Not mustr'd	M. O. June 30, '65. as Serg't	Clerk	-	5'11"	Brown	Gray	New Hampshire
Salisbury, Menzo/ Mezo H.	Chicago	June 22, 1865	Not mustr'd	M. O. June 30, '65. as Serg't	Clerk	-	5'7"	Black	Black	New York
Stevens, Sylvanus H.	Chicago	Nov. 18, 1862	Dec. 8, 1862	Promoted to 1st Lt.	Merchant	34	6'	Light	Blue	Maine
1st Sergeants										
Stevens, Sylvanus H.	Chicago	Nov. 18, 1862	Dec. 8, 1862	Promoted to 2nd Lt. Dec. 8, 1862	Merchant	34	6'	Light	Blue	Maine
Hand, Lewis B.	Chicago	Aug. 22, 1864	Dec. 1, 1864	Promoted to 2nd Lt. Dec. 11, 1864	Clerk	-	5'4"	Dark	Hazel	New York
Salisbury, Menzo H.	Chicago	June 22, 1865		Promoted to 2nd Lt.	Clerk	-	5'7"	Black	Black	New York
Q. M. Sergeants										
Durand, Calvin	Chicago	Aug. 1, 1862	July 31, 1862	Mustered out June 30, 1865, as Co. Q. M. Sergeant; captured July 10, 1864, POW	Merchant	22	5'7"	Dark	Hazel	New York
Sanford, Myron S.	Chicago	Aug. 1, 1862	July 31, 1862	Discharged for prom. Dec. 26, 1863	Merchant	30	5'8"	Light	Blue	Massachusetts
Ordnance Sergeants										
Randolph, Smith M.	Chicago	Aug. 1, 1862	July 31, 1862	Mustered out June 30, 1865	Architect	25	5'9"	Light	Blue	New Jersey
Sergeants										
Adams, Abbott L.	Chicago	Aug. 1, 1862	July 31, 1862	M. O. June 30, '83, as Serg't; Com. 2nd Lt; not mustered; wounded at the Battle of Stones River	Clerk	22	5'11"	Brown	Gray	New Hampshire

	Residence	Date of Rank or Enlistment	Date of Muster	Remarks	Occupation	Age	Height	Hair Color	Eye Color	Nativity
Auten, Philip L.	Chicago	Aug. 1, 1862	July 31, 1862	M. O. June 30 '65, as Serg't	Clerk	22	5'10"	Black	Black	Pennsylvania
Bowers, George	Chicago	Aug. 1, 1862	July 31, 1862	Discharged June 3, 1865	Seaman	26	5'6"	Brown	Hazel	Ohio
Chandler, Henry B.	Chicago	Aug. 1, 1862	July 31, 1862	M.O. June 30 '65, as Serg't.	Merchant	22	5'10"	Brown	Blue	Vermont
Deane, Frederick G.	Chicago	Aug. 1, 1862	July 31, 1862	Sergeant, Discharged for prom. Sept. 30, 1864	Clerk	21	5'6"	Dark	Hazel	Michigan
Howard, John A.	Chicago	Aug. 1, 1862	July 31, 1862	M.O. June 30 '65 as Sergt.	Designer	30	5'9"	Black	Gray	Pennsylvania
Hand, Lewis B.	Chicago	Aug. 1, 1862	July 31, 1862	Prom. 1st Sgt. then 2nd Lt.	Clerk	25	5'4"	Dark	Hazel	New York
Knight, Frank	Chicago	Aug. 1, 1862	July 31, 1862	M.O. June 30 '65 as Sergt.	Clerk	32	5'11"	Light	Blue	Rhode Island
Randolph, William	Chicago	Aug. 1, 1862	July 31, 1862	M.O. June 30 '65 as Sergt.	Clerk	22	5'10"	Black	Gray	New Jersey
Salisbury, Menzo H.	Chicago	Aug. 1, 1862	July 31, 1862	M.O. June 30 '65 as 1st Sergt., Com. 2nd Lt, not mustered	Clerk	-	5'7"	Black	Black	New York

Corporals

	Residence	Date of Rank or Enlistment	Date of Muster	Remarks	Occupation	Age	Height	Hair Color	Eye Color	Nativity
Auten, Philip L.	Chicago	Aug. 1, 1862	July 31, 1862	M. O. June 30, '65, promoted Serg't May 8, 1864	Clerk	22	5'10"	Black	Black	Pennsylvania

	Residence	Date of Rank or Enlistment	Date of Muster	Remarks	Occupation	Age	Height	Hair Color	Eye Color	Nativity
Aiken, Hector H.	Chicago	Aug. 1, 1862	July 31, 1862	Disch. for prom. May 9, 1864, Capt. 29th USCT; KIA Battle of Petersburg July 23, 1864	Clerk	26	5'7"	Brown	Blue	Vermont
Baker, Theodore E.	Chicago	Aug. 1, 1862	July 31, 1862	Died Murfreesboro, June 1, 1863	Merchant	27	5'6"	Brown	Blue	Ohio
Brown, William W.	Chicago	Aug. 1, 1862	July 31, 1862	Mustered out June 30, 1865, as corp'l	Tin Smith	23	5'8"	Brown	Blue	Canada
Chandler, Henry B.	Chicago	Aug. 1, 1862	July 31, 1862	M.O. June 30, '65, promoted Serg't Dec. 13, 1864	Merchant	22	5'10"	Brown	Blue	Vermont
Carver, Augustus H.	Chicago	Aug. 1, 1862	July 31, 1862	Died at Nashville, Jan. 30, 1863, wounded at Battle of Stones River Dec. 31, 1862	Clerk	25	5'8"	Brown	Blue	New York
Close, Andrew J.	Chicago	Aug. 1, 1862	July 31, 1862	Disch. for prom. Sept. 15, 1864; wounded at the Battle of Decatur July 22, 1864	Carpenter	22/25	5'6"	Brown	Blue	New York
Conklin, John K.	Chicago	Aug. 1,1862	July 31,1862	Mustered out June 30, 1865	Printer	28	5'10"	Light	Blue	New York
Daily, James W.	Chicago	Aug. 1, 1862	July 31,1862	Mustered out June 30, 1865, as corp'l.	Shoemaker	23	5'9"	Brown	Blue	Michigan
Dupries/ Dupuis, Frederick	Chicago	Aug. 1, 1862	July 31,1862	Mustered out June 30, 1865	Engineer	19	5'10"	Brown	Blue	Canada
Ford, Seth L.	Chicago	Aug. 1, 1862	July 31,1862	Mustered out June 30, 1865	Printer	21	5'7"	Light	Blue	New York

	Residence	Date of Rank or Enlistment	Date of Muster	Remarks	Occupation	Age	Height	Hair Color	Eye Color	Nativity
Hildreth, James H.	Chicago	Aug. 1, 1862	July 31, 1862	Mustered out June 30, 1865	Clerk	22	6'	Light	Blue	Massachu-setts
Holyland, Charles	Chicago	Aug. 1, 1862	July 31, 1862	Mustered out Aug. 22, 1865 to June 30, 1865	Engineer	25	5'7"	Light	Dark	New York
Howard, Jackson D.	Chicago	Aug. 1, 1862	July 31, 1862	Mustered out June 30, 1865	Clerk	25	5'7"	Brown	Blue	New York
Howard, John A.	Chicago	Aug. 1, 1862	July 31, 1862	M.O. June 30 '65, promoted Sergt. Dec. 10, 1864	Designer	30	5'9"	Black	Gray	Pennsylvania
Kieley, James	Chicago	Aug. 1, 1862	July 31, 1862	M.O. June 30 '65 as corp'l.	Carpenter	19	5'10"	Brown	Gray	Ireland
Lake, Albert B.	Chicago	Aug. 1, 1862	July 31,1862	Captured June 14, 1864, near Wood-stock, GA; Died en route to prisoner exchange—Feb. 23, 1865	Clerk	21	5'8"	Light	Blue	Illinois
Lester, Austin A.	Chicago	Aug. 1, 1862	July 31, 1862	M.O. June 30 '65 as corp'l.	Clerk	22	5'9"	Black	Blue	New York
Le Suer/Lesur, Charles	Chicago	Aug. 1, 1862	July 31,1862	Disch. Apr. 5 '63 as corp'l, disability	Clerk	25	5'7"	Brown	Black	New York
Luff, Edmund	Chicago	Aug. 1, 1862	July 31,1862	Corp'l. Disch. for prom. Feb. 20, 1864; Captain 12 Ill. Cav.	Clerk	21	5'11"	Brown	Gray	New York
Miller, Tobias C.	Chicago	Aug. 1, 1862	July 31,1862	Disch. June 30 '64 as corp'l, disability; wounded at Noonday Creek June 19, 1864,	Clerk	23	5'10"	Brown	Gray	Illinois

	Residence	Date of Rank or Enlistment	Date of Muster	Remarks	Occupation	Age	Height	Hair Color	Eye Color	Nativity
Olcott, William M.	Chicago	Aug. 1, 1862	July 31, 1862	M.O. June 30 '65 as corp'l.	Clerk	23	5'7"	Brown	Hazel	New York
Peters, Joseph G.	Chicago	Aug. 1, 1862	July 31, 1862	Mustered out June 30, 1865	Clerk	20	5'8"	Black	Blue	New York
Rockwood, Frank B.	Chicago	Aug. 1, 1862	July 31, 1862	Mustered out June 30, 1865	Merchant	22	5'6"	Brown	Black	Massachusetts
Riddell, Walter	Chicago	Aug. 1, 1862	July 31, 1862	M.O. June 30 '65 as corp'l.	Shoemaker	27	5'6"	Dark	Hazel	Scotland
Seaton/Sexton, Joseph M.	Chicago	Aug. 1, 1862	July 31, 1862	M.O. June 30 '65 as corp'l.	Railroader	21	5'7½"	Brown	Black	Ohio
Toomey, John D.	Chicago	Aug. 1, 1862	July 31, 1862	M.O. June 30 '65 as corp'l.	Carpenter	19	5'8"	Black	Brown	Ohio
Tinsley, Thomas	Chicago	Aug. 1, 1862	July 31, 1862	Discharged for prom. Mar. 23, 1864	Clerk	28	5'5"	Light	Blue	New York
Wolcott, George H.	Chicago	Aug. 1, 1862	July 31, 1862	M.O. June 30 '65 as corp'l.	Merchant	28	5'9"	Black	Gray	Maine
Young, Henry C.	Chicago	Aug. 1, 1862	July 31, 1862	M.O. June 30 '65 as corp'l.	Clerk	23	5'6"	Black	Hazel	Massachusetts
Privates										
Abbott, Lawrence F.	Chicago	Aug. 1, 1862	July 31, 1862	Mustered out June 30, 1865	Clerk	21	5'6"	Brown	Black	New York
Adams, Abbott L.	Chicago	Aug. 1, 1862	July 31, 1862	M. O. June 30, '63, promoted Serg't Aug. 1, 1862; Com. 2nd Lt; not mustered	Clerk	22	5'11"	Brown	Gray	New Hampshire

	Residence	Date of Rank or Enlistment	Date of Muster	Remarks	Occupation	Age	Height	Hair Color	Eye Color	Nativity
Aiken, Hector H.	Chicago	Aug. 1, 1862	July 31, 1862	Corp'l Aug. 1862; Discharged for prom. May 9, 1864	Clerk	26	5'7"	Brown	Blue	Vermont
Alexander, John S.	Chicago	Aug. 1, 1862	July 31, 1862	Mustered out June 30, 1865	Boatman	32/22	5'8"	Brown	Gray	New York
Andrews, Lawson M.	Chicago	Aug. 1, 1862	July 31, 1862	Deserted Mar. 3, 1863	Butcher	25	5'9"	Black	Blue	Vermont
Auten, Philip L.	Chicago	Aug. 1, 1862	July 31, 1862	M. O. June 30, '65, promoted corporal Oct. 4, 1862, M.O. as Serg't	Clerk	22	5'10"	Black	Black	Pennsylvania
Avery, William O.	Chicago	Aug. 1, 1862	July 31, 1862	Discharged May 18, 1863; detached to Rosecrans HQ Feb. 1863	Clerk	27	5'5"	Black	Black	New York
Bagley, William N.	Chicago	Aug. 1, 1862	July 31, 1862	Died at Cincinnati, Feb. 8, 1863, wounds	Seaman	28	5'10"	Black	Black	New York
Baker, Homer	Chicago	Aug. 1, 1862	July 31, 1862	Mustered out June 30, 1865; taken prisoner Dec. 14, 1862	Grocer	23	5'7"	Black	Blue	Ohio
Baker, Theodore E.	Chicago	Aug. 1, 1862	July 31, 1862	Died Murfreesboro, June 1, 1863; promoted to corporal at organization	Merchant	27	5'6"	Brown	Blue	Ohio
Barry, Robert	Chicago	Aug. 1, 1862	July 31, 1862	Mustered out June 30, 1865	Bookkeeper	29	5'6"	Brown	Blue	England
Baskerville, Andrew	Chicago	Aug. 1, 1862	July 31, 1862	Discharged Jan. 8, 1863; died en route to Chicago	Clerk	22	5'11"	Black	Black	New York

	Residence	Date of Rank or Enlistment	Date of Muster	Remarks	Occupation	Age	Height	Hair Color	Eye Color	Nativity
Baxter, Albert F.	Chicago	Aug. 1, 1862	July 31, 1862	Prom. 1st. Lt. at organization	Clerk	24/25	6'	Black	Dark	Massachusetts
Baxter, Henry J.	Chicago	Aug. 1, 1862	July 31, 1862	Discharged Nov. 3, 1862, disability	Clerk	29	5'9"	Brown	Black	Massachusetts
Beach, John D.	Chicago	Aug. 1, 1862	July 31, 1862	Mustered out June 30, 1865	Clerk	28	6'	Brown	Light	New York
Bennett, Henry	Chicago	Aug. 1, 1862	July 31, 1862	Promoted 2nd Lt. at org.	Mechanic	22/26	5'11"	Dark	Hazel	Illinois
Bloom, James W.	Chicago	Aug. 1, 1862	July 31, 1862	Mustered out June 30, 1865; Wounded at the Battle of Stones River Dec. 31, 1862	Clerk	22	5'10"	Light	Blue	New York
Bowers, George	Chicago	Aug. 1, 1862	July 31, 1862	Discharged June 3, 1865; promoted Serg't Aug. 1, 1862	Seaman	26	5'6"	Brown	Hazel	Ohio
Bradley, Charles M.	Chicago	Aug. 1, 1862	July 31, 1862	Mustered out June 30, 1865	Clerk	24	5'6"	Black	Blue	New York
Brewster, Charles H.	Chicago	Aug. 1, 1862	July 31, 1862	Mustered out June 30, 1865; detailed to 2nd Cav. Div. HQ. May 13, 1865	Clerk	19	5'5"	Brown	Hazel	New Hampshire
Brown, Coleman	Chicago	Aug. 1, 1862	July 31, 1862	Mustered out June 30, 1865; captured Aug. 19, 1864	Printer	22	5'7"	Brown	Gray	New York
Brown, William W.	Chicago	Aug. 1, 1862	July 31, 1862	Mustered out June 30, 1865, as corp'l	Tin Smith	23	5'8"	Brown	Blue	Canada
Buckingham, John/James H.	Chicago	Aug. 1, 1862	July 31, 1862	Mustered out June 30, 1865; captured Dec. 14, 1862	Carpenter	30/31	5'7"	Light	Blue	Pennsylvania

	Residence	Date of Rank or Enlistment	Date of Muster	Remarks	Occupation	Age	Height	Hair Color	Eye Color	Nativity
Burdell/Berdel, William	Chicago	Aug. 1, 1862	July 31, 1862	Mustered out June 30, 1865; bugler	Clerk	23	5'9"	-	-	Illinois
Camburg/Camberg, John C.	Chicago	Aug. 1, 1862	July 31, 1862	Wounded at Stones River Dec. 31, 1862 and Lovejoy's Station Aug. 20, 1864; absent at M. O. of battery	Printer	23	5'9"	Light	Hazel	Norway
Carroll, John J.	Chicago	Aug. 1, 1862	July 31, 1862	Discharged Nov. 30, 1863, disability; wounded Dec. 14, 1862	Printer	24	5'5"	Brown	Blue	Rhode Island
Carver, Augustus H.	Chicago	Aug. 1, 1862	July 31, 1862	Promoted corp'l Aug. 1, 1862; Died at Nashville, Jan. 30, 1863, wounds	Clerk	25	5'8"	Brown	Blue	New York
Chandler, Henry B.	Chicago	Aug. 1, 1862	July 31, 1862	M.O. June 30, '65, as Serg't.; promoted corp'l Mar. 14, 1864	Merchant	22	5'10"	Brown	Blue	Vermont
Chapman, Frederick A.	Chicago	Aug. 1, 1862	July 31, 1862	Discharged May 9, 1864, for prom. in Colored Troops, captain 29th USCT	Clerk	19	5'5"	Black	Blue	New York
Close, Andrew J.	Chicago	Aug. 1, 1862	July 31, 1862	Appointed artificer August 1862; promoted to corp'l June 16, 1863; Discharg. for prom. Sept. 15, 1864	Carpenter	22/25	5'6"	Brown	Blue	New York
Conklin, John K.	Chicago	Aug. 1, 1862	July 31, 1862	Promoted to corp'l Feb. 23, 1863; Mustered out June 30, 1865	Printer	28	5'10"	Light	Blue	New York

	Residence	Date of Rank or Enlistment	Date of Muster	Remarks	Occupation	Age	Height	Hair Color	Eye Color	Nativity
Cooper, George A.	Chicago	Aug. 1, 1862	July 31, 1862	Discharged Nov. 13, 1862, disability	Printer	20	5'7"	Brown	Blue	New York
Crocker, William	Chicago	Aug. 1, 1862	July 31, 1862	Discharged Nov. 13, 1862, disability	Tradesman	45	5'11"	Sandy	Gray	New York
Croft, Samuel M.	Chicago	Aug. 1, 1862	July 31, 1862	Discharged May 5, 1864, disability	Clerk	21	5'7"	Black	Black	New York
Daily, James W.	Chicago	Aug. 1, 1862	July 31, 1862	Mustered out June 30, 1865; promoted corp'l Dec. 10, 1864	Shoemaker	23	5'9"	Brown	Blue	Michigan
Deane, Frederick G.	Chicago	Aug. 1, 1862	July 31, 1862	Promoted sergeant Aug. 1, 1862; Discharged for prom. Sept. 30, 1864	Clerk	21	5'6"	Dark	Hazel	Michigan
DeCosta/Decoster, Charles W.	Chicago	Aug. 1, 1862	July 31, 1862	Died Nashville, Feb. 2, 1863	Seaman	24	5'11"	Light	Blue	England
DeCourser/ DeCoursey Thomas	Chicago	Aug. 1, 1862	July 31, 1862	Mustered out June 30, 1865; died in hospital in Louisville, date unknown	Railroader	22	5'10"	Brown	Blue	Ireland
Dodd, Samuel	Chicago	Aug. 1, 1862	July 31, 1862	Died at Murfreesboro, Mar. 21, 1863	Carpenter	35	6'3"	Brown	Gray	Pennsylvania
Downer, Andrew N.	Chicago	Aug. 1, 1862	July 31, 1862	Discharged Nov. 13, 1862, disability	Lumberman	27	5'5"	Black	Blue	New York
Dubois, Stafford A.	Chicago	Aug. 1, 1862	July 31, 1862	Mustered out June 30, 1865	Dentist	19	5'7"	Light	Light	Michigan
Dupuis/Dupries, Frederick	Chicago	Aug. 1, 1862	July 31, 1862	Promoted corp'l Aug. 1, 1862; Mustered out June 30, 1865	Engineer	19	5'10"	Brown	Blue	Canada

	Residence	Date of Rank or Enlistment	Date of Muster	Remarks	Occupation	Age	Height	Hair Color	Eye Color	Nativity
Durand, Calvin	Chicago	Aug. 1, 1862	July 31, 1862	Mustered out June 30, 1865; Co. Q. M. Sergeant Nov. 14, 1862; POW	Merchant	22	5'7"	Dark	Hazel	New York
Dwight, Charles	Chicago	Aug. 1, 1862	July 31, 1862	Detailed with Special Inspector, Louisville, Dec. 14, 1864; Mustered out June 30, 1865	Clerk	22	5'6"	Brown	Black	Illinois
Eakins, William	Chicago	Aug. 1, 1862	July 31, 1862	Mustered out June 30, 1865	Clerk	18	5'11"	Dark	Blue	Ireland
Erby/Erbey, Conrad W.	Chicago	Aug. 1, 1862	July 31, 1862	Mustered out June 30, 1865	Engineer	19	5'7"	Brown	Blue	Michigan
Everts, John J.	Chicago	Aug. 1, 1862	July 31, 1862	Discharged Nov. 4, 1862, disability	Engineer	27	5'9"	Brown	Black	New York
Fassett, Henry S.	Chicago	Aug. 1, 1862	July 31, 1862	Mustered out June 30, 1865	Clerk	21	5'8"	Black	Hazel	Ohio
Favor, Frederick J.	Chicago	Aug. 1, 1862	July 31, 1862	Discharged, Jan. 16, 1863	Railroader	48	5'9"	Brown	Blue	New Hampshire
Field, Edward C.	Chicago	Aug. 1, 1862	July 31, 1862	Died at Atlanta, Aug. 1, 1864, wounded at the Battle of Decatur July 22, 1864	Tinner	19	6'	Light	Blue	Illinois
Finley, James B.	Chicago	Aug. 1, 1862	July 31, 1862	Discharged for prom. July 15, 1864; promoted to commission in 14th Michigan Battery	Railroader	31	5'7"	Red	Blue	Ohio
Finnell, Edward	Chicago	Aug. 1, 1862	July 31, 1862	M. O. June 30, 1865, appointed artificer Aug. 1, 1862	Blacksmith	26	5'5"	Black	Black	Ireland

	Residence	Date of Rank or Enlistment	Date of Muster	Remarks	Occupation	Age	Height	Hair Color	Eye Color	Nativity
Finney, Andrew	Chicago	Aug. 1, 1862	July 31, 1862	Killed at Murfreesboro, Dec. 31, 1862	Railroader	37	5'9"	Brown	Blue	Massachusetts
Fitzwilliam, Thos. F.	Chicago	Aug. 1, 1862	July 31, 1862	Wounded Lovejoy's Station, Aug. 20, 1864; Mustered out June 30, 1865	Printer	20	5'10"	Black	Gray	Ireland
Fleming, John C.	Chicago	Aug. 1, 1862	July 31, 1862	Mustered out June 30, 1865	Clerk	18	5'11"	Brown	Blue	Alabama
Ford, Seth L.	Chicago	Aug. 1, 1862	July 31, 1862	Promoted corp'l Aug. 1, 1862; Mustered out June 30, 1865	Printer	21	5'7"	Light	Blue	New York
Foster, Richard C.	Chicago	Aug. 1, 1862	July 31, 1862	Mustered out June 30, 1865	Guilder	25	5'5"	Brown	Gray	England
Frink/Fink, Charles	Chicago	Aug. 1, 1862	July 31, 1862	Mustered out May 18, 1865	Pressman	20	5'7"	Brown	Blue	New York
Gale, William B.	Chicago	Aug. 1, 1862	July 31, 1862	Discharged as corp'l. May 9, '64; promoted to commission in 26th USCT, wounded at Petersburg	Clerk	26	5'8"	Black	Black	Massachusetts
Garnsey, Charles A. P.	Chicago	Aug. 1, 1862	July 31, 1862	Mustered out June 30, 1865, wounded at Farmington	Student	20	5'8½"	Black	Black	Illinois
Gavitt, George W.	Chicago	Aug. 1, 1862	July 31, 1862	Discharged Jan. 19, 1865, disability (surgeon's certificate)	Painter	29	5'8½"	Brown	Blue	Connecticut
George, William	Chicago	Aug. 1, 1862	July 31, 1862	Mustered out June 30, 1865	Cooper	22	5'6"	Black	Black	Michigan

Name	Residence	Date of Rank or Enlistment	Date of Muster	Remarks	Occupation	Age	Height	Hair Color	Eye Color	Nativity
Gilmore, John J.	Chicago	Aug. 1, 1862	July 31, 1862	Mustered out June 30, 1865	Carpenter	30	5'5½"	Light	Blue	Ireland
Gregory, Frederick W.	Chicago	Aug. 1, 1862	July 31, 1862	Discharged Nov. 13, 1862, disability (surgeon's certificate)	Railroader	21	5'7½"	Brown	Black	New York
Griffin, Trumbull D.	Chicago	Aug. 1, 1862	July 31, 1862	Prom. 2nd Lt at org.	Printer	24/26	5'10"	Dark	Hazel	New York
Grosch, Jacob	Chicago	Aug. 1, 1862	July 31, 1862	Appointed artificer, Discharged Jan. 16, '63	Blacksmith	25	5'10"	Black	Black	Germany
Hall, John D./B.	Chicago	Aug. 1, 1862	July 31, 1862	M.O. June 30 '65; promoted corp'l Nov. 17, 1864 .	Clerk	21	5'8"	Brown	Blue	England
Hand, Lewis B.	Chicago	Aug. 1, 1862	July 31, 1862	Prom. 1st Sgt. Aug. 1862; then 2nd Lt.	Clerk	25	5'4"	Dark	Hazel	New York
Hanssen/Hansen/Hanson, George	Chicago	Aug. 1, 1862	July 31, 1862	Mustered out June 14, 1865	Bar Tender	30	5'6"	Brown	Light	Sweden
Harvey, James J.	Chicago	Aug. 1, 1862	July 31, 1862	Mustered out June 30, 1865	Railroader	20	5'6"	Brown	Blue	Michigan
Hildreth, James H.	Chicago	Aug. 1, 1862	July 31, 1862	Promoted corp'l; Mustered out June 30, 1865	Clerk	22	6'	Light	Blue	Massachusetts
Hogan, Edward	Chicago	Aug. 1, 1862	July 31, 1862	Mustered out June 30, 1865	Guilder	20	5'7"	Light	Hazel	England

	Residence	Date of Rank or Enlistment	Date of Muster	Remarks	Occupation	Age	Height	Hair Color	Eye Color	Nativity
Holyland, Charles	Chicago	Aug. 1, 1862	July 31, 1862	Mustered out Aug. 22, 1865 to June 30, 1865; Promoted corp'l Aug. 1862; wounded at Battle of Decatur July 22, 1864; Detailed to A.G.O. Washington Oct. 21, 1864	Engineer	25	5'7"	Light	Dark	New York
Hotchkiss, Sylvester C.	Chicago	Aug. 1, 1862	July 31, 1862	Mustered out June 30, 1865	Carpenter	22	5'10"	Light	Blue	Michigan
Howard, Jackson D.	Chicago	Aug. 1, 1862	July 31, 1862	Promoted corp'l; Mustered out June 30, 1865	Clerk	25	5'7"	Brown	Blue	New York
Howard, John A.	Chicago	Aug. 1, 1862	July 31, 1862	M.O. June 30 '65 as Sergt.; promoted corp'l July 1, 1863	Designer	30	5'9"	Black	Gray	Pennsylvania
Jacobs, Daniel D.	Chicago	Aug. 1, 1862	July 31, 1862	Appointed hospital steward; Mustered out June 30, 1865	Clerk	40	5'8"	Brown	Black	Massachu-setts
Jewett, George D.	Chicago	Aug. 1, 1862	July 31, 1862	Discharged for prom. Nov. 22, 1863	Clerk	23	5'7"	Black	Black	New York
Johnston, Charles W.	Chicago	Aug. 1, 1862	July 31, 1862	Mustered out June 30, 1865	Engineer	28	5'9"	Light	Gray	Ohio
Joubert, Desire/ Deyer	Chicago	Aug. 1, 1862	July 31, 1862	Died at Nash-ville, Aug. 2, 1864, wounded at Noonday Creek June 19, 1864	Mechanic	24	5'8"	Brown	Black	New York

	Residence	Date of Rank or Enlistment	Date of Muster	Remarks	Occupation	Age	Height	Hair Color	Eye Color	Nativity
Kennedy, John	Chicago	Aug. 1, 1862	July 31, 1862	M.O. June 30 '65; appointed artificer August 1862	Black-smith	31	5'6"	Black	Blue	Ireland
Kieley/Kiely, James	Chicago	Aug. 1, 1862	July 31, 1862	M.O. June 30 '65, promoted corp'l Nov. 10, 1864	Carpenter	19	5'10"	Brown	Gray	Ireland
King, Frederick W.	Chicago	Aug. 1, 1862	July 31, 1862	Detailed to Cav. HQ May 10–22, 1865; Mustered out June 30, 1865	Lumber Merchant	22	5'6"	Brown	Blue	New York
Knight, Frank	Chicago	Aug. 1, 1862	July 31, 1862	M.O. June 30 '65; promoted Sergt. Sept. 22, 1862	Clerk	32	5'11"	Light	Blue	Rhode Island
Lake, Albert B.	Chicago	Aug. 1, 1862	July 31, 1862	Captured June 14, 1864; promoted corp'l Aug. 1862; died POW	Clerk	21	5'8"	Light	Blue	Illinois
Lawson, Julius	Chicago	Aug. 1, 1862	July 31, 1862	Mustered out June 30, 1865	Cigar Maker	28	6'	Light	Blue	Sweden
Leet, John B.	Chicago	Aug. 1, 1862	July 31, 1862	Mustered out July 1, 1865; detailed to Grant's HQ Oct. 31, 1863	Druggist	20	5'6"	Brown	Blue	Pennsylvania
Lester, Austin A.	Chicago	Aug. 1, 1862	July 31, 1862	M.O. June 30 '65 as corp'l.	Clerk	22	5'9"	Black	Blue	New York
Lesur/Lesuer, Charles	Chicago	Aug. 1, 1862	July 31, 1862	Disch. Apr. 5 '63 as corp'l, disability	Clerk	25	5'7"	Brown	Black	New York
Little, George W.	Chicago	Aug. 1, 1862	July 31, 1862	Mustered out June 30, 1865	Clerk	22	5'5"	Brown	Hazel	Vermont

	Residence	Date of Rank or Enlistment	Date of Muster	Remarks	Occupation	Age	Height	Hair Color	Eye Color	Nativity
Lock, Samuel/James A.	Chicago	Aug. 1, 1862	July 31, 1862	Mustered out June 30, 1865	Clerk	24	5'5"	Brown	Blue	Pennsylvania
Loutensleger/Loutensleiger/ Lontenslegen, Louis	Chicago	Aug. 1, 1862	July 31, 1862	Mustered out June 30, 1865	Barber	19	5'6"	Black	Hazel	Germany
Lord, Samuel R. B.	Chicago	Aug. 1, 1862	July 31, 1862	Discharged Aug. 18 '64, disability	Farmer	23	5'9¼"	Brown	Blue	Massachusetts
Luff, Edmund	Chicago	Aug. 1, 1862	July 31, 1862	corp'l; Discharged for prom. Feb. 20, 1864	Clerk	21	5'11"	Brown	Gray	New York
Manning, John D.	Chicago	Aug. 1, 1862	July 31, 1862	Mustered out June 30, 1865	Bookkeeper	22	5'5"	Light	Blue	New York
Maple, Charles H.	Chicago	Aug. 1, 1862	July 31, 1862	Discharged May 31, 1863, to take commission	Clerk	19	5'5"	Light	Hazel	Illinois
Marlow/ Malau, William C.	Chicago	Aug. 1, 1862	July 31, 1862	Mustered out June 30, 1865	Sail maker	42	5'7"	Brown	Blue	Denmark
McClelland/ McClernand, Thos. A.	Chicago	Aug. 1, 1862	July 31, 1862	Discharged Oct. 13 '64, disability; wounded at Battle of Decatur July 22, 1864	Druggist	19	5'6"	Black	Black	Mississippi
McDonald, John	Chicago	Aug. 1, 1862	July 31, 1862	Mustered out June 30, 1865	Clerk	18	5'6"	Brown	Blue	New Jersey
McElevey, Albert	Chicago	Aug. 1, 1862	July 31, 1862	Mustered out June 30, 1865	Clerk	19	5'5½"	Brown	Gray	Ohio
McMunn, David/ Daniel H.	Chicago	Aug. 1, 1862	July 31, 1862	Discharged Nov. 26 '62 disability, appointed artificer August 1862	Saddler	50	5'10"	Brown	Blue	Ohio

	Residence	Date of Rank or Enlistment	Date of Muster	Remarks	Occupation	Age	Height	Hair Color	Eye Color	Nativity
Miller, Tobias C.	Chicago	Aug. 1, 1862	July 31, 1862	Discharged June 30 '64 as corp'l, disability	Clerk	23	5'10"	Brown	Gray	Illinois
Nourse, Benjamin F.	Chicago	Aug. 1, 1862	July 31, 1862	Mustered out June 30, 1865	Clerk	19	5'5"	Dark	Gray	Massachusetts
Nourse, John A.	Chicago	Aug. 1, 1862	July 31, 1862	Mustered out June 30, 1865	Clerk	18	5'4"	Brown	Hazel	Massachusetts
Odell, William H.S.	Chicago	Aug. 1, 1862	July 31, 1862	Mustered out June 30, 1865	Clerk	21	5'7"	Black	Black	New York
Olcott, William M.	Chicago	Aug. 1, 1862	July 31, 1862	Mustered out June 30 '65 as corp'l.	Clerk	23	5'7"	Brown	Hazel	New York
Orr, John	Chicago	Aug. 1, 1862	July 31, 1862	Mustered out June 30, 1865	Carpenter	18	5'9"	Light	Gray	New York
Packard, Frank	Chicago	Aug. 1, 1862	July 31, 1862	Discharged Jan. 19 '65, disability	Clerk	29	5'11"	Black	Black	New York
Pearsall, Richard/ Robert N.	Chicago	Aug. 1, 1862	July 31, 1862	Mustered out June 30, 1865	Cooper	29	5'7"	Brown	Black	Canada
Pease, Ira A.	Chicago	Aug. 1, 1862	July 31, 1862	Discharged Nov. 31 '62, disability	Clerk	18/19	5'7"	Brown	Blue	New York
Peck, George W.	Chicago	Aug. 1, 1862	July 31, 1862	Mustered out June 30, 1865	Clerk	21	5'7"	Black	Blue	Vermont
Peters, Joseph G.	Chicago	Aug. 1, 1862	July 31, 1862	Mustered out June 30, 1865; promoted corp'l Aug. 1862; detailed to 2nd Div. Cav. HQ, Nov. 26, 1864	Clerk	20	5'8"	Black	Blue	New York

	Residence	Date of Rank or Enlistment	Date of Muster	Remarks	Occupation	Age	Height	Hair Color	Eye Color	Nativity
Peterson, Morris	Chicago	Aug. 1, 1862	July 31, 1862	Mustered out June 30, 1865	Tailor	22	5'6"	Light	Blue	Illinois
Phillips, Howard W.	Chicago	Aug. 1, 1862	July 31, 1862	Mustered out June 30, 1865; wounded at Lovejoy's Station August 20, 1864	Clerk	26	5'6"	Light	Blue	Michigan
Phillips, Samuel T.	Chicago	Aug. 1, 1862	July 31, 1862	Discharged Nov. 31 1862, disability	Tobacconist	19	5'6"	Brown	Blue	England
Probst, Henry	Chicago	Aug. 1, 1862	July 31, 1862	Mustered out June 30, 1865	Clerk	19	5'3"	Brown	Hazel	Ohio
Randolph, Smith N.	Chicago	Aug. 1, 1862	July 31, 1862	Mustered out June 30, 1865; promoted ordnance Sergt.	Architect	25	5'9"	Light	Blue	New Jersey
Randolph, William	Chicago	Aug. 1, 1862	July 31, 1862	Mustered out June 30 '65 as Sergt.	Clerk	22	5'10"	Black	Gray	New Jersey
Richardson, Daniel B.	Chicago	Aug. 1, 1862	July 31, 1862	Tr. to V. R. C. Apr. 30 '64. Discharged Mar. 16 '65, disability	Clerk	31	5'11"	Black	Black	Vermont
Richmond, Francis R.	Chicago	Aug. 1, 1862	July 31, 1862	Mustered out June 30, 1865	Cooper	19	5'5"	Brown	Blue	Michigan
Riddell, Walter	Chicago	Aug. 1, 1862	July 31, 1862	Mustered out June 30 '65; promoted Corp'l. July 24, 1864	Shoemaker	27	5'6"	Dark	Hazel	Scotland
Rockwood, Frank B.	Chicago	Aug. 1, 1862	July 31, 1862	Mustered out June 30, 1865; promoted corp'l Aug. 1862	Merchant	22	5'6"	Brown	Black	Massachusetts
Rockwood, Frederick S.	Chicago	Aug. 1, 1862	July 31, 1862	Mustered out June 30, 1865	Clerk	22	5'6"	Black	Black	Massachusetts

	Residence	Date of Rank or Enlistment	Date of Muster	Remarks	Occupation	Age	Height	Hair Color	Eye Color	Nativity
Rutledge, James A.	Chicago	Aug. 1, 1862	July 31, 1862	Mustered out June 30, 1865	Lumberman	24	5'7"	Brown	Blue	Canada
Salisbury, Menzo H.	Chicago	Aug. 1, 1862	July 31, 1862	M.O. June 30 '65; promoted 1st Sergt. August 1862, Com. 2nd Lt, not mustered	Clerk	23	5'7"	Black	Black	New York
Sanford, Myron S.	Chicago	Aug. 1, 1862	July 31, 1862	Disch. for prom. Dec. 26, 1863; promoted to Q.M. Sergt. Aug. 1862	Merchant	30	5'8"	Light	Blue	Massachusetts
Seaton/Sexton, Joseph M.	Chicago	Aug. 1, 1862	July 31, 1862	M.O. June 30 '65; promoted corp'l. Dec. 10, 1864	Railroader	21	5'7½"	Brown	Black	Ohio
Shipley, William H.	Chicago	Aug. 1, 1862	July 31, 1862	Mustered out June 30, 1865	Carpenter	21	5'11"	Brown	Black	Illinois
Sleaman/Sleman, John B.	Chicago	Aug. 1, 1862	July 31, 1862	On detached service at M. O. of Battery; detached to A.G.O. Washington Nov. 30, 1863	Clerk	24	5'5"	Brown	Blue	Canada
Small, Henry N.	Chicago	Aug. 1, 1862	July 31, 1862	Mustered out June 30, 1865; detailed to Cavalry Corps HQ Dec. 15, 1864–May 27, 1865	Clerk	21	5'8"	Light	Blue	Pennsylvania
Snow, Martin V. B.	Chicago	Aug. 1, 1862	July 31, 1862	Captured June 14, 1864; promoted corp'l Aug. 1862; died in prison Wilmington, NC, Mar. 17, 1865	Clerk	22	5'6"	Dark	Gray	Vermont

	Residence	Date of Rank or Enlistment	Date of Muster	Remarks	Occupation	Age	Height	Hair Color	Eye Color	Nativity
Stagg, John S.	Chicago	Aug. 1, 1862	July 31, 1862	Killed at Murfreesboro, Dec. 31, 1862	Carpenter	22/24	5'11"	Light	Gray	England
Steele, Valentine	Chicago	Aug. 1, 1862	July 31, 1862	Mustered out June 30, 1865	Tobacconist	23	5'7"	Light	Dark	New York
Stevens, Loyal A.	Chicago	Aug. 1, 1862	July 31, 1862	Mustered out June 30, 1865	Printer	24	5'10"	Brown	Gray	New York
Stevens, Silas C.	Chicago	Aug. 1, 1862	July 31, 1862	Mustered out June 30, 1865; detailed HQ Cavalry Corps, Jan. 13, 1865	Clerk	24	5'6"	Brown	Gray	Maine
Stevens, Sylvanus/ Sylvester H.	Chicago	Aug. 1, 1862	July 31, 1862	Prom. Sgt., then 1st Lieutenant	Merchant	34	6'	Light	Blue	Maine
Taylor, William L.	Chicago	Aug. 1, 1862	July 31, 1862	Mustered out June 30, 1865	Clerk	19	5'9"	Red	Hazel	Maine
Tinsley, Thomas	Chicago	Aug. 1, 1862	July 31, 1862	Promoted corp'l Aug. 1862; Discharged for promotion Mar. 23, 1864–Lt. 102nd N. Y. Infantry	Clerk	28	5'5"	Light	Blue	New York
Tinsley, William H.	Chicago	Aug. 1, 1862	July 31, 1862	Wounded, absent at M. O. of Battery; wounded at Battle of Decatur July 22, 1864	Clerk	26	5'7"	Light	Blue	New Hork
Toomey, John D.	Chicago	Aug. 1, 1862	July 31, 1862	M.O. June 30 '65 as corp'l; wounded at Battle of Decatur July 22, 1864	Carpenter	19	5'8"	Black	Brown	Ohio
Wagner, Matthias	Chicago	Aug. 1, 1862	July 31, 1862	Mustered out June 30, 1865	Harness maker	31	5'7"	Brown	Gray	Prussia

	Residence	Date of Rank or Enlistment	Date of Muster	Remarks	Occupation	Age	Height	Hair Color	Eye Color	Nativity
Wallace, James S./ John	Chicago	Aug. 1, 1862	July 31, 1862	Died in hospital at McMinnville Aug. 9, 1863	Farmer	18	5'6"	Light	Blue	Illinois
Watson, Thomas H.	Chicago	Aug. 1, 1862	July 31, 1862	Discharged Aug. 30, 1864 (provided substitute)†	Book-keeper	21	5'8"	Light	Brown	New York
Weeks/Wicks, Charles	Chicago	Aug. 1, 1862	July 31, 1862	Mustered out June 30, 1865	Clerk	21	5'7"	Light	Blue	New York
Wygant/Wiggant, Thomas	Chicago	Aug. 1, 1862	July 31, 1862	Killed at Lovejoy, GA August 20, 1864	Steamfitter	18	5'4"	Brown	Blue	New York
Wiley, William H.	Chicago	Aug. 1, 1862	July 31, 1862	Killed at Murfreesboro, Dec. 31, 1862	Clerk	24	5'7"	Brown	Hazel	New York
Williams, Thomas N.	Chicago	Aug. 1, 1862	July 31, 1862	Mustered out June 30, 1865	Clerk	20	5'11"	Brown	Gray	Pennsylvania
Williams, William	Chicago	Aug. 1, 1862	July 31, 1862	Mustered out June 30, 1865	Painter	24	5'7"	Brown	Blue	New York
Wilson, Stephen H.	Chicago	Aug. 1, 1862	July 31, 1862	Mustered out June 30, 1865	Clerk	21	5'4"	Dark	Hazel	Ohio
Winslow, Clark A.	Chicago	Aug. 1, 1862	July 31, 1862	Discharged June 20 '64, disability	Carpenter	35	5'10"	Brown	Blue	New York
Wolcott, George H.	Chicago	Aug. 1, 1862	July 31, 1862	M.O. June 30 '65; promoted corp'l. Aug. 1862	Merchant	28	5'9"	Black	Gray	Maine
Wood, Edward F.	Chicago	Aug. 1, 1862	July 31, 1862	Discharged Nov. 5, 1864	Clerk	24	5'5"	Brown	Blue	New York
Worrell, Robert	Chicago	Aug. 1, 1862	July 31, 1862	Mustered out June 30, 1865	Printer	20	5'10"	Brown	Blue	Pennsylvania

	Residence	Date of Rank or Enlistment	Date of Muster	Remarks	Occupation	Age	Height	Hair Color	Eye Color	Nativity
Young, Henry C.	Chicago	Aug. 1, 1862	July 31, 1862	M.O. June 30 '65; promoted corp'l. Dec. 10, 1864	Clerk	23	5'6"	Black	Hazell	Massachusetts
Recruits										
Appleton, James B.	Chicago	Jan. 4, 1864	Jan. 31, 1864	Mustered out June 30, 1865; wounded in Battle of Decatur July 22, 1864	Laborer	23	5'10"	Dark	Black	Maine
Appleton, Ephraim S.*	Chicago	Jan. 16, 1864	Jan. 31, 1864	-	Laborer	18	5'3"	Light	Brown	Maine
Austin, John*	Niles	Sept. 30, 1864	Sep. 30, 1864	-	Saddler	22	5'8"	Fair	Hazel	Indiana
Baer, George J.	Chicago	Sep. 30, 1864	Sep. 30, 1864	Mustered out June 30, 1865	Carpenter	18	5'5½"	Fair	Blue	Germany
Baker, Henry	Chicago	Jan. 4, 1864	Jan. 31, 1864	Mustered out June 30, 1865	Farmer	18	5'8"	Brown	Blue	Illinois
Baldwin, Charles	Chicago	Mar. 9, 1863	Mar. 19, 1863	Mustered out June 30, 1865	Clerk	19	5'9"	Dark	Dark	Connecticut
Bancroft, John L	Chicago	Oct. 6, 1864	Oct. 6, 1864	Mustered out May 21, 1865	Printer	25	5'3½"	Light	Blue	England
Beck, George C.	Chicago	Jan. 23, 1864	Jan. 31, 1864	Mustered out June 30, 1865	Fruit Dealer	20/26	5'9"	Light	Blue	Ohio
Bettschen/Bettshan, David	Wauconda	Oct. 3, 1864	Oct. 4, 1864	Mustered out June 30, 1865	Farmer	21	5'8½"	Brown	Gray	Canada

Name	Residence	Date of Rank or Enlistment	Date of Muster	Remarks	Occupation	Age	Height	Hair Color	Eye Color	Nativity
Bicknell, Byron H.	Good Farm	Oct. 8, 1864	Oct. 8, 1864	Mustered out June 30, 1865; detailed to Cavalry Corps HQ April 24, 1865—May 22, 1865	Tel. operator	20	5'5½"	Brown	Blue	Vermont
Blackmoor, Richard K.	Rich	Oct. 1, 1864	Oct. 1, 1864	Mustered out June 30, 1865	Cooper	21	5'5½"	Dark	Gray	Ireland
Bond, William	Chicago	Feb. 2, 1864	Feb. 29, 1864	Mustered out June 30, 1865	Farmer	19	5'8"	Dark	Blue	Indiana
Brown, George	Chicago	Feb. 29, 1864	Feb. 29, 1864	Mustered out June 30, 1865	-	18	5'8"	Dark	Gray	New York
Bruckman, John	Chicago	Jan. 25, 1864	Jan. 31, 1864	Mustered out June 30, 1865	Confectioner	27	5'10"	Light	Brown	Germany
Burns, James*	Chicago	Mar. 12, 1863	-	Deserted Mar. 18, 1863	Clerk	23	5'8"	Light	Blue	New York
Burr, David	Elk Grove	Sep. 30, 1864	Sep. 30, 1864	Mustered out June 30, 1865	Clerk	19	5'6½"	Dark	Hazel	Indiana
Campbell, James M.	Orange/Troy, OH	Aug. 2/12, 1862	Sep. 16, 1862	Transf. from Co. K 102d Ohio V. I., Dec. 2,1862; M.O. June 30, 1865; appointed artificer Dec. 2, 1862	Harness maker	29	5'8½"	Brown	Hazel	Ohio
Carmichael, Michael	Chicago	May 31, 1864	Oct.21, 1864	Mustered out June 30, 1865; re-mustered from 100 days service	Seaman	33	5'9"	Light	Blue	Scotland
Chapin, Addison S.	Chicago	Oct.13, 1864	Oct.13, 1864	Mustered out June 30, 1865	Clerk	22	5'4½"	Light	Gray	Pennsylvania

Name	Residence	Date of Rank or Enlistment	Date of Muster	Remarks	Occupation	Age	Height	Hair Color	Eye Color	Nativity
Chapman, David A.	Chicago	Sep. 29, 1864	Sep. 29, 1864	Discharged June 6, 1865, disability	Carpenter	23	5'7"	Dark	Gray	New York
Chesbrough, Isaac S.	Chicago	Feb. 8, 1864	Feb. 29, 1864	Discharged Oct. 21, 1864	Farmer	25	5'6¼"	Dark	Blue	North Carolina
Clark, William W.‡	Chicago	July 23, 1862	-	Stricken from rolls Aug. 1, 1862	Carpenter	22	5'7"	Light	Blue	New York
Collaghau/Callaghan, Thomas*	Niles	Oct. 1, 1864	Oct. 1, 1864	-	Carpenter	38	5'7"	Dark	Blue	Ireland
Collins, Robert *	Barrington	Jan. 3, 1864	Jan. 3, 1864	-	Laborer	21	5'8"	Brown	Hazel	Ireland
Conners/Connoss, John*	Elk Grove	Jan. 3, 1865	Jan. 3, 1865	-	Clerk	23	5'6½"	Brown	Gray	New York
Cottrell, Leonard	Cicero	Sep. 26, 1864	Sep. 26, 1864	Mustered out June 30, 1865	Farmer	20	5'8½"	Light	Hazel	New York
Crane, George	Chicago	Mar. 17, 1863	Mar.19, 1863	Killed near Pulaski, TN, Dec. 24, 1864	Carpenter	26	5'11"	Light	Blue	New York
Crum, Sylvester	McHenry	Sep. 26, 1864	Sep. 26, 1864	Mustered out June 30, 1865	Farmer	28	5'6"	Light	Gray	New York
Dagle, Michael*	Chicago	Feb. 13, 1864	Feb. 29, 1864	-	Farmer	24	5'6"	Brown	Blue	Ireland
Darbin, William*	Spring Bay	Jan. 1, 1865	Jan. 1, 1865	Mustered with Mercantile Battery	Laborer	23	5'6½"	Light	Blue	Ireland
Dean, Anthony*	Chicago	May 31, 1864	Oct. 21, 1864	Re-mustered from 100 day service; died at Nashville	Laborer	32	5'5"	Dark	Blue	Prussia

	Residence	Date of Rank or Enlistment	Date of Muster	Remarks	Occupation	Age	Height	Hair Color	Eye Color	Nativity
Delany, William*	Hyde Park	Sept. 17, 1864	Sep. 17, 1864	-	Laborer	35	5'8½"	Brown	Dark	Ireland
Dippe, Henry	Chicago	Sep. 30, 1864	Sep. 30, 1864	Mustered out June 30, 1865	Basket maker	21	5'6"	Light	Blue	Germany
Drummond, Alex*	Chicago	Jan. 14, 1864	Jan. 31, 1864	-	Moulder	26	5'5"	Light	Blue	Scotland
Duffy, John*	Chicago	Mar. 9, 1863	-	Deserted Mar.16, 1863	Blacksmith	32	5'10"	Brown	Gray	Ireland
Dunton, Gilbert L.	Chicago	Jan. 2, 1864	Jan. 31, 1864	Disch. June 19, 1865, disability	Sail maker	21/31	5'8½"	Sandy	Blue	New York
Eagan/Edgar, Dennis E.	Chicago	Jan. 5, 1864	Jan. 13, 1864	Mustered out June 30, 1865	Trunk maker	22	5'5½"	Black	Gray	Ireland
Eames, Charles O.	Chicago	Feb. 25, 1864	Feb. 29, 1864	Mustered out June 30, 1865	Scholar	16	5'5"	Dark	Gray	New York
Eastland, William	Chicago	Oct. 13, 1864	Oct. 13, 1864	Mustered out June 30, 1865	Peddlar	29	5'5"	Light	Blue	New York
Foster, James K.*	Chicago	Mar. 10, 1863	-	Deserted Mar. 16, 1864	Clerk	31	5'8"	Dark	Hazel	Pennsylvania
Fowler, Charles K.	Chicago	Oct. 4, 1864	Oct. 4, 1864	Mustered out June 30, 1865	Carpenter	25	5'6½"	Dark	Dark	New York
Fuller, Charles*	Hyde Park	Sep. 22, 1864	Sep. 22, 1864	-	Brakeman	19	5'6¾"	Light	Blue	Indiana
Garritson, Derk H.	Thornton	-	-	Transferred to Co. A 1st Ill L. Artillery	-	-	-	-	-
Gates, Thomas J.	New Milford	Sep. 26, 1864	Sep. 26, 1864	Mustered out June 30, 1865	Clerk	18	5'8"	Brown	Brown	Illinois

	Residence	Date of Rank or Enlistment	Date of Muster	Remarks	Occupation	Age	Height	Hair Color	Eye Color	Nativity
Gitchel, David	Chicago	Dec. 8, 1864	Dec. 8, 1864	Mustered out July 20, 1865, to date June 30, 1865	Farmer	18	5'4½"	Light	Gray	Michigan
Grey/Gray, James H.	Chicago	Feb. 12, 1864	Feb. 29, 1864	Died at Jeffersonville, IN, Jan. 1/7, 1865	Paper hanger	34	5'4"	Brown	Black	Canada
Guckenheimer/ Gackenhiemer, George	Chicago	Feb. 2, 1864	Feb. 2, 1864	Mustered out June 30, 1865; Wounded at the Battle of Decatur July 22, 1864	Cigar maker	18	5'7"	Brown	Brown	Germany
Hall, Andrew J.	Chicago	Oct. 6, 1864	Oct. 6, 1864	Mustered out May 23, 1865	Printer	29	5'6½"	Dark	Blue	New York
Hand, George H.	Chicago	Oct. 6, 1864	Oct. 6, 1864	Mustered out July 13, 1865	Lawyer	27	5'9"	Dark	Blue	Ohio
Hanson Thomas	Chicago	Jan. 11, 1864	Jan. 29, 1864	Mustered out June 14, 1865; captured June 1864	Clerk	22	5'6"	Dark	Gray	Maine
Harrup, John*	Seward	Oct. 18, 1864	Oct. 18, 1864	-	Laborer	37	5'4"	Sandy	Hazel	England
Holmes, Michael	Chicago	Dec. 29, 1863	Dec. 31, 1863	Mustered out June 30, 1865	Tailor	39	5'7¾"	Auburn	Gray	Ireland
Ingersoll, Oscar L.	-	-	-	Mustered out June 30, 1865		31				
Ivis/Ives, James	Chicago	Sep. 27, 1864	Sep. 27, 1864	Mustered out June 30, 1865	Painter	22	5'9¼"	Dark	Gray	New York
Jackson, William H.	Hanover	Dec. 22, 1864	Dec. 22, 1864	Mustered out June 30, 1865; detailed to Cav. Corps HQ (A. Q. M.) June 1, 1865	Clerk	25	5'10"	Dark	Brown	Tennessee

	Residence	Date of Rank or Enlistment	Date of Muster	Remarks	Occupation	Age	Height	Hair Color	Eye Color	Nativity
Johnson, William H.	Chicago	Sep. 26, 1864	Sep. 26, 1864	-	Farmer	18	5'5½"	Light	Blue	Illinois
Johnston Robert	Chicago	Mar. 10, 1863	Mar.19, 1863	Mustered out June 30, 1865	Farmer	34	5' 9"	Brown	Blue	Ireland
Keating, Robert	Chicago	Dec. 9, 1863	Dec. 30, 1863	-	Laborer	28	5' 5"	Brown	Blue	Ireland
Kelly/Kelley/Kiely, Edward F.	Chicago	Dec. 12, 1863	Dec. 30, 1863	Transf. to 45th IL. Infantry	Clerk	18	5'7½"	Brown	Hazel	Ireland
Kelse/Kelsey, John	Moline	Dec. 10, 1863	Dec. 11, 1863	Mustered out June 30, 1865	Brewer	28	5'6½"	Brown	Hazel	Sweden
Kent, Francis	Chicago	Sep. 27, 1864	Sep. 27, 1864	Mustered out June 30, 1865	Laborer	19	5'11"	Light	Blue	Illinois
Kinger, Charles C.	Chicago	Mar. 12, 1863	Mar.19, 1863	Mustered out June 30, 1865	Butcher	23	5'7"	Sandy	Blue	Germany
Koehler, William	Chicago	Feb. 23, 1864	Feb. 29, 1864	Mustered out June 30, 1865	Saddler	26	5'7"	Dark	Dark	Germany
Lanahan/Linehan, Jeremiah	Chicago	Sep. 29, 1864	Sep. 29, 1864	Mustered out July 11, 1865, to date June 30, 1865	Carver	18	5'3"	Light	Gray	Ireland
Leaming, Edward	Spring Bay	Jan. 1, 1865	Jan. 1, 1865	Mustered out June 30, 1865	Brakeman	18	5'4"	Light	Blue	Pennsylvania
Leary, Michael	Chicago	Oct. 4, 1864	Oct. 4, 1864	-	Laborer	24	5'10½"	Light	Blue	Ireland
Lewis, Alexander	Chicago	Mar. 7, 1863	Mar.19, 1863	Mustered out June 30, 1865	Carriage maker	32	5'6"	Dark	Blue	Michigan
Loschka, August	Chicago	Feb. 15, 1864	Feb. 29, 1864	Mustered out June 30, 1865	Blacksmith	22	5'4"	Hazel	Gray	Germany

	Residence	Date of Rank or Enlistment	Date of Muster	Remarks	Occupation	Age	Height	Hair Color	Eye Color	Nativity
Lunn, George	Chicago	Jan. 16, 1864	Jan. 31, 1864	Mustered out Nov. 6, 1865 to date June 30, 1865	-	27	5'11"	Gray	Blue	Ireland
Lynch, Martin T.	Chicago	Dec. 23, 1863	Dec. 23, 1863	Mustered out June 30, 1865	Cooper	23	5'10"	Dark	Blue	Ireland
Lynch, Michael	Springfield	Aug. 26, 1864	Aug. 26, 1864	-	Stone cutter	35	5'5½"	Brown	Blue	Ireland
Main, David M.	Chicago	Oct. 6, 1864	Oct. 6, 1864	-	Farmer	19	5'5"	Dark	Hazel	Canada
McConnelong/ McConneloug/ McConloe, John M.	Chicago	Oct. 13, 1864	Oct. 13, 1864	Mustered out July 20, 1865, to date June 30, 1865	Farmer	18	5'7½"	Brown	Blue	Maryland
McGhee/McGee/ McKee, Don A./B.	Chicago	Oct. 1, 1864	Oct. 1, 1864	Mustered out June 30, 1865	Laborer	21	5'10"	Dark	Hazel	New York
McGrath, John J.	Chicago	Oct. 4, 1864	Oct. 4, 1864	Mustered out June 30, 1865	Clerk	20/28	5'8"	Fair	Blue	Illinois
McLean/McLane, John C.	Wauconda	Oct. 3, 1864	Oct. 4, 1864	Mustered out June 30, 1865	Farmer	28	5'11"	Light	Blue	Scotland
McMinn/McMorn, Robert	Chicago	Sep. 26, 1864	Sep. 26, 1864	-	Farmer	44	5'1½"	Light	Blue	Pennsylvania
McNally, James	Chicago	Oct. 5, 1864	Oct. 5, 1864	-	Shoemaker	26	5'8"	Dark	Gray	Ireland
Merrill, Albert	Chicago	Jan. 25, 1864	Feb. 29, 1864	Mustered out June 30, 1865	Machinist	18	5'8"	Brown	Blue	Ohio
Mescall, William J.	Orland	Dec. 6, 1864	Dec. 22, 1864	Mustered out June 30, 1865	Mason	24	5'11"	Dark	Blue	Ireland
Otery/Otney, William	Chicago	Oct. 6, 1864	Oct. 6, 1864	Mustered out May 23, 1865	Laborer	19	5'6"	Dark	Black	England

	Residence	Date of Rank or Enlistment	Date of Muster	Remarks	Occupation	Age	Height	Hair Color	Eye Color	Nativity
Payne, Ormango	Chicago	Jan. 4, 1864	Jan. 31, 1864	Mustered out June 30, 1865; wounded in battle	Farmer	18	5'9"	Dark	Blue	Massachusetts
Peckham, Silas C.	Chicago	Mar. 12, 1863	Mar.19, 1863	Mustered out June 30, 1865; wounded in Battle of Noonday Creek June 20, 1864	Farmer	22	5'9"	Light	Blue	New York
Philliber/Phillaber/ Phillibar, Henry J./T.	Chicago	Dec. 23, 1863	Dec. 23, 1863	Mustered out June 30, 1865; wounded in battle	Cooper	20	5'7"	Light	Blue	Pennsylvania
Pontius, Albert C.	Chicago	Mar. 12, 1863	Mar.19, 1863	Discharged July 23, 1863, disability; surgeon's certificate	Clerk	19	5'9"	Light	Blue	Pennsylvania
Powell, John	Chicago	Feb. 18, 1864	Feb. 29, 1864	-	Mechanic	37	5'11"	Brown	Gray	Pennsylvania
Probst, Henry C. L.	-	-	-	Transf. to 45th IL Infantry	-	-	-	-	-	-
Ragan, William M.	Chicago	Jan. 5, 1864	Jan.31,1864	Mustered out June 30, 1865	Farmer	17	6'	Dark	Gray	Illinois
Reed, James F.	Chicago	Sep. 29, 1864	Sep. 29, 1864	-	Mechanic	26	5'4"	Light	Blue	Missouri
Richards, Charles	Chicago	Aug. 1, 1864	Aug. 1, 1864	Mustered out July 11, 1865, to date June 30, 1865	Blacksmith	40	5'10"	Gray	Blue	Massachusetts
Schommer, Lambert	Schaumberg	Jan. 4, 1865	Jan. 4, 1865	Mustered out May 29, 1865	Carpenter	35	5'6"	Brown	Blue	Germany
Selly, Talman/Tolman	Chicago	Oct. 1, 1864	Oct. 1, 1864	Mustered out June 30, 1865	Farmer	22	5'8"	Light	Blue	New York

	Residence	Date of Rank or Enlistment	Date of Muster	Remarks	Occupation	Age	Height	Hair Color	Eye Color	Nativity
Sheeks, Wells/Wills W.	Chicago	Oct. 3, 1864	Oct. 4, 1864	Mustered out July 11, 1865, to date June 30, 1865	Soldier	20	5'9½"	Dark	Hazel	Indiana
Simpson, William	Elk Grove	Sep. 30, 1864	Sep. 30, 1864	Mustered out June 30, 1865	Soap maker	42	5'10"	Light	Gray	Scotland
Smith, Alexander	Hanover	Dec. 29, 1864	Dec. 29, 1864	Mustered out June 30, 1865	Paper maker	18	5'4½"	Light	Gray	England
Smith, Christian	Chicago	Mar. 13, 1864	Mar.13, 1864	Mustered out June 30, 1865	Chair maker	26	5'8"	Sandy	Blue	Germany
Smith, James*	Chicago	Mar. 9, 1863	-	Deserted Mar. 16, 1863	Clerk	29	5'7"	Brown	Blue	England
Stahl, Leonard*	Rock Island	Dec. 10, 1863	Dec. 11, 1863	Deserted Jan. 5, 1864	Brewer	28	5'10½"	Brown	Blue	Germany
Steiger, Frank J.	Cicero	Sep. 27, 1864	Sep. 28, 1864	Mustered out June 30, 1865	Trunk maker	29/20	5'9"	Light	Blue	Austria
Stone, James	Chicago	Jan. 5, 1864	Jan. 31, 1864	Mustered out June 16, 1865	Carpenter	22/32	5'8"	Brown	Blue	Michigan
Stressman, Gustave	Chicago	Feb. 2, 1864	Feb. 3, 1864	Mustered out June 30, 1865	Cigar maker	20	5'10"	Brown	Gray	Prussia
Tanso/Tank, George	Chicago	Oct. 3, 1864	Oct. 3, 1864	Mustered out July 11, 1865, to date June 30, 1865	Cooper	30	5'7½"	Dark	Gray	Germany
Wain, David M.*	Chicago	Oct. 6, 1864	Oct. 6, 1864	-	-	-	-	-	-	-
Webb, John/Job	Chicago	Oct. 6, 1864	Oct. 6, 1864	Mustered out June 30, 1865	Mason	20	5'5"	Dark	Gray	England

	Residence	Date of Rank or Enlistment	Date of Muster	Remarks	Occupation	Age	Height	Hair Color	Eye Color	Nativity
Weigert, Frederick W.	Chicago	Feb. 10, 1864	Feb. 29, 1864	Wounded in Battle of Lovejoy's Station Aug. 20, 1864, absent at M.O. of Battery	Farmer	37	5'6"	Dark	Gray	Saxony
Wells, Richard T.	Elk Grove	Jan. 3, 1865	Jan. 3, 1865	-	Brickmaker	30	5'8½"	Dark	Hazel	Ohio
White, George L.	Jacksonville	Oct. 22/27, 1863	Oct. 27, 1863	Died at Vining Station, Aug. 28, 1864, wounded at the Battle of Decatur July 22, 1864	-	21	-	-	-	-
Wilson, Charles	Chicago	Oct. 20, 1864	Oct. 20, 1864	Mustered out June 30, 1865	Laborer	25	5'3"	Dark	Hazel	England
Wilson, George W.	Chicago	Oct. 5, 1864	Oct. 5, 1864	Mustered out June 30, 1865	Laborer	18	5'5½"	Dark	Hazel	Ohio
Wilson, Peter	Chicago	Feb. 6, 1864	Feb. 29, 1864	-	Seaman	28	5'7"	Light	Blue	Norway
Wilson, Samuel O.	Chicago	Oct. 5, 1864	Oct. 5, 1864	Mustered out June 30, 1865	Farmer	20	5'8½"	Light	Blue	Ohio
Wilson, Thomas	Palatine	Jan. 3, 1865	Jan. 3, 1865	-	Laborer	21	5'6½"	Dark	Hazel	Ohio
Wire, Henry C.	Chicago	Feb. 23, 1864	Feb. 29, 1864	Mustered out May 23, 1865	RR conductor	35	5'8"	Light	Light	Connecticut
Wood, Dennis	Hyde Park	Sep. 22, 1864	Sep. 24, 1864	-	Brakeman	18	5'7¾"	Brown	Blue	New York

*Never reached the battery;
†Special Orders 246; Adjutant General's Office Washington, July 23, 1864—copy in Illinois State Archives files.
‡Stricken from battery records; M.O. = mustered out.

Appendix II:
Battery Losses*

(From battery casualty returns from the Illinois State Archives, Chicago Board of Trade Battery files)

Name	Casualty	When	Where	Nature of Wound or Disability	Date of Death or Discharge
Aiken, Hector	Discharged			War Dept. Order #172 to accept promotion	5/9/64
Avery, William O.	Discharged			War Dept. Order #221	5/18/63
Bagley, William	Wounded/ Died	12/20/62	Nashville	Gunshot wound to arm, died in hospital in Cincinnati	2/8/63
Baker, Theodore	Died		Murfreesboro	Typhoid fever	6/1/63
Baskerville, Andrew	Died			General disability, died on the way to Chicago	
Baxter, Albert	Discharged			Physical disability	11/18/62
Baxter, Henry	Discharged			Consumption	11/3/62
Carroll, John	Wounded/ Discharged	12/14/62	Nashville	Gunshot through the spine and shoulder; discharged	11/30/63
Carver, Augustus	Wounded/ Died	12/31/62	Stones River	Gunshot through hips, died at Nashville	1/30/63

*This table shows losses, i.e., soldiers who would no longer be carried on battery roster due to death or discharge. It does not show those who were wounded, ill, or otherwise absent from the battery for any period of time. Entries in italics indicate additional documented losses not shown in battery records held at the Illinois State Archives.

Name	Casualty	When	Where	Nature of Wound or Disability	Date of Death or Discharge
Chapman, Frederick				War Dept. Order #172 to accept promotion	5/9/64
Close, Andrew	Discharged			War Dept. Order #305, *for promotion*	9/15/64
Cooper, George A.	Discharged			Rheumatism; died in Detroit, date unknown	11/13/62
Crane, George	*Killed*	*12/24/64*	*Pulaski*		*12/24/64*
Crocker, William	Discharged			General disability	11/13/62
Croft, Samuel	Discharged			General disability; died in Chicago in 1865, chronic diarrhea	5/5/64
Dean, Anthony	*Died*			*Gangrene poisoning in Nashville hospital*	*3/65*
De Costa, Charles	Died		Nashville	*In hospital in Nashville*	2/2/63
DeCoursey, Thomas	*Died*			*In hospital in Louisville; shown as mustered out in 1865*	1865
Dodd, Samuel	Died	*3/31/63*	Murfreesboro	Kicked by horse	3/31/63
Downer, Andrew	Discharged			General disability	11/13/62
Everts, John J.	Discharged			Paralysis	11/4/62
Favor, Frederick	Discharged			General disability	1/16/63
Field, Edward	Wounded/ Died	7/22/64	Decatur	Gunshot through the body; died	8/1/64
Finley, James B.	Discharged			By Army of the Cumberland Order #193 to accept promotion	7/13/64
Finney, Andrew	Killed	12/31/62	Stones River	By solid shot	12/31/62
Gale, William B.	Discharged			War Dept. Order #172 to accept promotion	5/9/64
Gray/Grey, James	*Died*			*In hospital, Jeffersonville, Indiana*	*1/65*
Gregory, Frederick /Ferdinand	Discharged			Hernia	11/13/62
Grosch, Jacob	Discharged			General disability	1/16/63

Name	Casualty	When	Where	Nature of Wound or Disability	Date of Death or Discharge
Jewett, George D.	Discharged			War Dept. Order #566 to accept promotion	11/22/63
Joubert, Desire	Wounded/ Died	6/19/64	Noonday Creek	Gunshot through leg; died in Nashville hospital	8/2/64
Lake, Albert	*Captured/ Died*	*6/14/64*	*Woodstock*	*POW—Died on the way to exchange*	*1865*
Leet, Edmund	Discharged			War Dept. Order #84 to accept promotion	2/20/64
Lesuer, Charles	Discharged			General disability	4/5/63
Lord, Samuel	Discharged			Chronic diarrhea	8/18/64
Maple, Charles	Discharged			Special Order #128 to accept promotion	5/31/63
McClelland, Thomas	Wounded	7/22/64	Decatur	Left arm shattered and amputated; discharged	10/13/64
McMunn, David	Discharged			Fever	11/20/62
Miller, Tobias	Wounded/ Discharged	6/19/64	Noonday Creek	Shell wound to foot, discharged	7/30/64
Packard, Frank	Discharged			General disability	1/19/64
Pease, Ira	Discharged			General disability	11/13/62
Phillips, Samuel	Discharged			General disability	11/13/62
Pontius, Albert	Discharged			General disability	7/18/63
Richardson, Daniel	Discharged			Disability, arm fractured, *8/30/63* in the Cumberland Mountains	4/30/64
Sanford, Myron	Discharged			War Dept Order 572	12/26/63
Snow, Martin V. B.	*Captured/ Died*	*6/14/64*	*Woodstock*	*Died in prison, Wilmington, NC— POW*	*3/17/1865*
Stagg, John	Killed	12/31/62	Stones River	By shell	12/31/62
Stokes, James	Discharged			Promotion	8/22/64
Tinsley, Thomas	Discharged			Discharged for promotion	5/23/64
Wallace, James	Died		McMinnville	Dysentery	8/9/63
Watson, Thomas	Discharged			Spec. Orders from War Department	8/30/64

Name	Casualty	When	Where	Nature of Wound or Disability	Date of Death or Discharge
White, George	Wounded/ Died	8/20/64	Wounded at Lovejoy, GA	Died in field hospital	8/28/64
Wiley, William	Killed	12/31/62	Stones River	By solid shot	12/31/62
Winslow, Clark	Discharged			Leg fractured on *Dec. 2, 1863 at Huntsville*	6/20/64
Wygant, Thomas	Killed	8/20/64	Lovejoy, GA	Gun shot through the body	8/20/64

Chapter Notes

Chapter One

1. Aretas A. Dayton, "The Raising of Union Forces in Illinois during the Civil War," *Journal of the Illinois State Historical Society*, Vol. 34, No. 4 (Dec. 1941), pp. 409–412; Abraham Lincoln, *Collected Works*, Marion Dolores Pratt and Lloyd A. Dunlap, assistant editors (New Brunswick, NJ: Rutgers University Press, 1953), 296–297; Israel Washburn, Jr,. et. al., *The War of the Rebellion. A Compilation of the Official Records of the Union and Confederate Armies*, Series III, Volume 123, No. 2, 180 [Hereafter referred to as *Official Record.*]; Robert P. Golonka, "Mobilizing the Illinois Spirit for the Civil War," Master's Thesis, Paper 762, Loyola University 1949, p. 63.

2. *Historical Sketch of the Chicago Board of Trade Battery* (Chicago: The Henneberry Co. Publishers, 1902), 18 [Hereafter referred to as *Historical Sketch*]; J.N. Reese, *Report of the Adjutant General to the State of Illinois*, Vol. VIII (Springfield: Journal Company, Printers and Binders, 1901), 732; "The Chicago Board of Trade," *Chicago Tribune*, July 22, 1862, p.1, col. 1; Edward Jerome Dies, *Through Three Wars* (Chicago: Board of Trade Post of the American Legion, 1928), 9; Chester Arthur Legg, "The Board of Trade in the City of Chicago in the Civil War," Part of Chicago Board of Trade Collection of addresses and papers describing the services rendered by the Board of Trade of the City of Chicago in the Civil War, Chicago History Museum, p. 12; "The Board of Trade Battery," *Chicago Tribune*, June 27, 1865.

3. A.T. Andreas, *The History of Chicago*, Volume II (Chicago: The A.T. Andreas Company, Publishers, 1885), 346.

4. John Moses and Joseph Kirkland, *The History of Chicago*, Vol. I (Chicago and New York: Munsell & Co., Publishers, 1895), 307–311, 316–318; A.T. Andreas, *The History of Chicago*, 337–339, 344.

5. *Historical Sketch*, 17–18; "The Board of Trade Battery," *Chicago Tribune*, July 23, 1862, p. 1, col. 1; "The News," *Chicago Tribune*, July 24, 1862, p.1, col.1; Address of Henry H. Taylor, Chicago Board of Trade papers, Chicago History Museum; "Board of Trade Battery and Regiment," *Chicago Tribune*, February 27, 1864; "Well Done for the Dry Goods Clerks," *Chicago Tribune*, July 24, 1862, p. 4; Theodore J. Karamanski, *Rally 'Round the Flag: Chicago and the Civil War* (Lanham, MD: Rowman & Littlefield Publishers, Inc., 2006), 114.

6. "Great War, Mass Meeting," *Chicago Tribune*, July 26, 1862, p.1, col. 1; "What Are the Railroads Doing," *Chicago Tribune*, July 29, 1862, p. 1, col. 1; Benjamin F. Nourse, Diary, July 22, 1862, Rubenstein Library, Duke University; Charles H. Taylor, ed. *The History of the Board of Trade of the City of Chicago*, Vol. III (Chicago: Robert O. Law Company, 1917), 146–147; John Nourse, journal entry July 23, John A. Nourse papers, 1862–1922, Chicago History Museum [Note: transcriptions of Benjamin Nourse's diary are held at Duke University and John Nourse's diary/journal are held at the Chicago History Museum. These transcriptions are very similar but there have significant differences between the two. For this work, John Nourse's diary is referred to as a "journal" as a way to more clearly distinguish it from Benjamin's diary]; A.T. Andreas, *The History of Chicago*, 331–332.

7. *Historical Sketch*, 19.

8. *Historical Sketch*, 20; John A. Nourse, Journal August 7, 8, 13 15, 1862; B.F. Nourse, August 7, 8, 15 diary entries; James C. Hazlett, Edwin Olmstead, and M. Hume Parks, *Field Artillery Weapons of the Civil War* (Urbana and Chicago: University of Illinois Press, 2004), 149–150; Ken Baumann, *Arming the Suckers 1861–1865* (Dayton, OH: Morningside House, Inc., 1989), 33–34; [Some records show the cannons being received on Aug. 22].

9. John Nourse, Journal, July 22; John Robertson, "Re-Enlistment Patterns of Civil War Soldiers," *The Journal of Interdisciplinary History*, Vol. 32, No. 1 (Summer, 2001), pp. 20, 23; William C. Shaw, compiler, *Illustrated Roster of the Department of Illinois Grand Army of the Republic* (n. p.: n. p. 1914), 45.

10. Calvin Durand, "Calvin 'Cam' Durand Jr.," Stones River Technical Information Center, Regimental Records, NPS, p. 47; *The Belmont Chronicle*, "The Chicago Churches" August 7, 1862, p. 1, col. 7.

11. Muster and Descriptive Roll, Chicago Board of Trade, Records of the Illinois Adjutant General (301.018, 2S, 15B, F 6) Illinois Archives, Springfield, IL.

12. Tobias Miller, Aug. 14, 1862 letter, Tobias Charles Miller diary and letters, 1862–1866, Chicago History Museum; William L. Willis, "O.H.

Miller," in *History of Sacramento County California* (Los Angeles: Historic Record Co., 1913) 668–669.

13. Descriptive Roll, Illinois State Archives.

14. *Historical Sketch*, 19–20.

15. *Ibid.*

16. "Death Under the Knife: A Case for the Coroner," July, 11, 1877, *Chicago Tribune*, p. 2, Col. 4–5; Descriptive Rolls, Illinois State Archives; *Industrial Chicago: The Manufacturing Interests. Vol. 3* (Chicago: The Goodspeed Publishing Co., 1894), 505.

17. John Gibbon, *Artillerist Manual* (New York: D. Van Nostrand, 1860), 250–255, 342, 348.

18. John, Gibbon, *Artillerist Manual*, 168, 350.

19. George W. Cullum, *Biographical Register of the Officers and Graduates of the U.S. Military Academy*, Vol. 2 (New York: D. Van Nostrand, 1868–79), 596; *Twenty-Second Annual Reunion of the Association of the Graduates of the United States Military Academy, June 12th, 1891* (Saginaw: Seaman & Peters, Printers and Binders, 1898), 189; [Stokes' birthdate is also recorded as 1814 and 1816 in some records].

20. Descriptive Roll, Illinois State Archives.

21. George W. Cullum, *Biographical Register*, 596; *Twenty-Second Annual Reunion of the Association of the Graduates*, 189.

22. Sarah Gould Downs Durand, *Calvin Durand, A Memorial* (Chicago: Lakeside Press, 1912), 47; *History of Milwaukee, Wisconsin, The Western Historical Company* (Chicago: A.T. Andreas Proprietor, 1881), 1190; Descriptive Roll, Illinois State Archives; "Robinson, George Irving Jan. 14, 1909, Milwaukee," In Memoriam, R-Z (1886–1917) Box 1, File 19, Military Order of the Loyal Legion of the United States, Wisconsin Commandery, Mss-0938, Milwaukee County Historical Society.

23. Descriptive Roll, Illinois State Archives; Massachusetts Town & Vital Records, 1838.

24. Walter B. Stevens, *Centennial History of Missouri (The Center State) One Hundred Years In The Union 1820–1921*, Vol. 6 (St. Louis-Chicago: The S.J. Clarke Publishing Company, 1921), 504; Trumbull Griffin, Biographical information entered on Battery Roster, Trumbull Griffin papers, Missouri History Museum; 1860 U. S Census Records; "Patriotic," *Chicago Tribune*, August 5, 1862, p. 2.

25. William E. Connelley, *A Standard History of Kansas and Kansans*, Vol. IV (Chicago and New York: Lewis Publishing Co., 1918), 1754–1755.

26. Sarah Gould Downs Durand, *Calvin Durand*, 46.

27. John A. Nourse, Journal Sept. 9–10; Sarah Gould Downs Durand, *Calvin Durand*, 47, John C. Fleming, Letter September 12, 1862, John C. Fleming Papers, Box 1, Folder 3, Newberry Library, Chicago.

28. Benjamin Nourse, Diary, Sept. 11–14; Frances Bailey Hewitt, compiler, *Genealogy of the Durand, Whalley, Barnes and Yale Families* (Chicago: Privately Printed at the Lakeside Press, 1912), 111–113; Sarah Gould Downs Durand, *Calvin Durand*, 45–47; Tobias Miller, Letter Aug. 14; John Nourse, Journal September 12–15; John C. Fleming, Letter Sept. 14, Box 1; Folder 4.

29. Sarah Gould Downs Durand, *Calvin Durand*, 48–49; Muster and Descriptive Roll, Chicago Board of Trade, Records of the Illinois Adjutant General; Benjamin Nourse, Diary, September 14, 1862.

30. James C. Hazlett, *Field Artillery Weapons of the Civil War*, 30–41, 213–219; 4th Quarter (December) 1863 Ordnance Summary Statements, for independent Chicago batteries, Jan. 24, 1864, National Archives; Philip Katcher, *American Civil War Artillery 1861–1865* (Oxford: Osprey Publishing, 2002), 18, 21; Janice E. McKenney, *The Organizational History of Field Artillery 1775–2003* (Washington, D.C.: Center of Military History United States Army, 2007), 52; John Fleming, Letter September 12.

31. John C. Fleming, Letter Sept. 14; William B. Dickson, compiler, *History of the Carnegie Veterans Association* (Montclair, NJ: Montclair Press, 1938), 70–71.

32. *Historical Sketch*, 20; Benjamin Nourse, Diary, September 16; Nicky Hughes, "Fort Boone and the Civil War Defense of Frankfort," *The Register of the Kentucky Historical Society*, Vol. 88, No. 2 (Spring 1990), p. 148; John A. Nourse, Journal entry September 16.

33. Horatio Wright, *Official Records*, Series 1, Volume 16, Part 1, 662; Benjamin Nourse, Diary, September 14.

34. Horatio Wright, *Official Records*, Series 1, Volume 16, Part 2, 662.

35. John C. Fleming, Letter October 7, Box 1; Folder 2; F.A. Lord, Letter to Professor Emerson, April 20, 1869, Beloit University, Civil War Collection, Beloit College Archives, Civil War—Students—Personal Sketches F to W; Muster and Descriptive Roll, Chicago Board of Trade, Records of the Illinois Adjutant General, Illinois State Archives; Chicago Board of Trade Association roster, April 27, 1886, Trumbull Griffin file, Missouri History Museum.

36. F.A. Lord, *ibid.*.

37. Dallas Irvine, compiler, *Military Operations of the Civil War: A Guide-index to the Official Records* (Washington: General Services Administration, 1977), 51; William C. Davis, Meredith L. Swentor, eds. *Bluegrass Confederate: The Headquarters Diary of Edward O. Guerrant* (Baton Rouge: Louisiana State University Press, 1999), 157; Braxton Bragg, *Official Records*, Series 1, Volume 16, Part 2, 930; George Brent, *Official Records*, Series 1, Volume 16, Part 2, 935, 941; Joseph Wheeler, *Official Records*, Series 1, Volume 16, Part 1, 898; Kenneth Hafendorfer, *They Died by Twos and Tens* (Louisville: KH Press, 1995), 753; Compiled Service Records Showing Records of Service of Military Units, "Chicago Board of Trade Battery," National Archives and Records Administration, Microcopy 594, Roll 14.

38. John C. Fleming, Letter October 17, Box 1, Folder 8; Benjamin Nourse, Diary, October 11, 1862.

39. George Knox Miller, *An Uncompromising Secessionist The Civil War of George Knox Miller, Eighth (Wade's) Confederate Cavalry*, Richard M. McMurry, editor (Tuscaloosa: University of

Alabama Press, 2007), 93; Braxton Bragg, *Official,* Series 1, Volume 16, Part 1, 1088, 1093.

40. Don Carlos Buell, *Official Records,* Series 1, Volume 16, Part 1, 51.

41. Henry Halleck, *Official Records,* Series 1, Volume 16, Part 2, 623, 626–627; Don Carlos Buell, *Official Records,* Series 1, Volume 16, Part 2, 619.

42. Henry Halleck, *Official Records,* Series 1, Volume 16, Part 2, 638; John Lillyett, Letter April 14, 1863, Don Carlos Buell Papers, 1818–1898, Correspondence, Letters Received, Mss A B928, 15, Filson Historical Society, Louisville, KY.

43. Braxton Bragg, *Official Records,* Series 1, Volume 16, Part 1, 1087, 1094; George Knox Miller, *An Uncompromising Secessionist,* 93.

44. Benjamin Nourse, Diary, October 16–31, 1862; Sarah Gould Downs Durand, *Calvin Durand,* 53; Lucille Detraz Skelcher and Jane Lucille Skelcher, "Descendants of the Dumonts of Vevay," *Indiana Magazine of History,* Volume 34, No. 4 (December, 1938), p. 409; John A. Nourse, Journal October 16–31, 1862; John C. Fleming, Letter October 17, 1862.

45. Kirby Smith, *Official Records,* Series 1, Volume 16, Part 2, 958, 967, 975; Joseph Wheeler, *Official Records,* Series 1, Volume 16, Part 2, 976–977; Braxton Bragg, *Official Records,* Series 1, Volume 16, Part 2, 952; John Crittenden, letter to wife, October 25, 1862, Crittenden, John Crittenden letters (1862–1865), Record Group 765, Auburn University, Auburn, Alabama.

46. Peter Cozzens, *No Better Place to Die: The Battle of Stones River* (Urbana and Chicago: University of Illinois Press, 1991), 3; Basil W. Duke, *History of Morgan's Cavalry* (Cincinnati: Miami Printing and Publishing Company, 1867), 270; Braxton Bragg, *Official Records,* Series 1, Volume 16, Part 1, 1093, 1095–1107; Leonidas Polk, *Official Records,* Series 1, Volume 16, Part 1, 1096–1107; William Hardee, *Official Records,* Series 1, Volume 16, Part 1, 1095–1107.

47. Kirby Smith, *Official Records,* Series 1, Volume 16, Part 2, 975; Braxton Bragg, *Official Records,* Series 1, Volume 16, Part 2, 974; Stanley Horn, *The Army of Tennessee* (Norman: University of Oklahoma Press, 1952), 189.

48. James Negley, *Official Records,* Series 1, Volume 16, Part 2, 613, 619; Alfred P. James, "General James Scott Negley," *Western Pennsylvania Historical Magazine,* Volume 14, Number 2 (April 1931), 77.

Chapter Two

1. Don Carlos Buell, *Official Records,* Series 1, Volume 16, Part 2, 652; William Rosecrans, *Official Records,* Series 1, Volume 16, Part 2, 653; George Thomas, *Official Records,* Series 1, Volume 16, Part 2, 657; Henry Halleck, *Official Records,* Series 1, Volume 16, Part 2, 642, 663; L. Thomas, *Official Records,* Series 1, Volume 16, Part 2, 642.

2. James B. Fry, *Official Records,* Series 1, Volume 16, Part 2, 643; Don Carlos Buell, *Official Records,* Series 1, Volume 16, Part 2, 641, 644–647.

3. Ephraim Otis, "The Murfreesboro Campaign," In *Campaigns in Kentucky and Tennessee include the Battle of Chickamauga, 1862–1864, Papers of the Military Historical Society of Massachusetts* Vol. VII (Boston: Military Historical Society of Massachusetts, 1908), 296–297; Basil Duke, *Morgan's Cavalry* (New York: The Neale Publishing Co., 1909), 193–194.

4. John Nourse, Journal entry November 3–5, John A. Nourse papers, 1862–1922, Chicago History Museum; Benjamin F. Nourse, Diary, November 4, 9, 1862, Rubenstein Library, Duke University; Board of Trade Standard, photographic image, Chicago History Museum.

5. John Nourse, Journal entry November 12–14.

6. Frances Bailey Hewitt, compiler, *Genealogy of the Durand, Whalley, Barnes and Yale Families* (Chicago: Privately Printed at the Lakeside Press, 1912), 111–113.

7. John C. Fleming, Letter November 23, 1862, John C. Fleming Papers, Box 1; Folder 12, Newberry Library, Chicago; Benjamin Nourse, Diary, November 16, 1862; *Chicago Tribune,* "The Board of Trade Battery. Gen. Rosecrans Allows Them to Carry Their Flag," January 24, 1863.

8. Fleming, *Ibid.*; John A. Nourse, Journal November 15–17, 1862; *Chicago Tribune,* "Board of Trade Battery," August 18, 1862.

9. John C. Fleming, Letters October 17, November 2, 23, Box 1, Folder 10, 12; John Nourse, letter, Nov. 23, 1862; Tobias Miller, Letter November 27, 1862, Tobias Charles Miller diary and letters, 1862–1866, Chicago History Museum. [It is unclear which Granger, Robert S. or Gordon, that Fleming is referring to in his letters. He specifically refers to Major General Granger and that could only be Gordon Granger.]

10. Tobias Miller, letter November 7, 1862; J.A. Nourse, letter 1, undated; Benjamin Nourse, Diary, November 28–29, 1862.

11. John A. Nourse, journal November 28–29; John Toomey, "Account of the Chicago Board of Trade Battery," George Thomas Post, GAR, Stones River Technical Information Center, NPS.

12. John Grier Stevens, *The Descendants of Samuel Stevens with Histories of Allied Families* (Baltimore: Edward Brothers, Inc., 1968), 107–108.

13. Calvin Durand, "Calvin 'Cam' Durand Jr.," Stones River Technical Information Center, Regimental Records, NPS, p. 53; Benjamin Nourse, Diary, December 4–7, 1862; John Nourse, Letter December 10, 1862; Gordon Granger, Letter to colonel commanding, December 5, 1862, George I. Robinson papers, Chicago History Museum.

14. John A. Nourse, Journal December 7, 1862; Allen Fuller, Letter to Griffin, December 7, 1862, Trumbull Dorrance Griffin papers, Missouri History Museum, St. Louis; Trumbull Griffin, Letter to Allen Fuller, December 2, 1862, Chicago Board of Trade Collection, Muster Out Rolls & Misc. Letters, Illinois State Archives; Mrs. S.H. Stevens, Letter to Allen Fuller, December 18, 1862, Illinois State Archives.

15. Benjamin Nourse, Diary, December 9–10, 1862.

16. Sylvanus Stevens, *Official Records*, Series 1, Volume 20, Part 1, 80; Benjamin Nourse, Diary, December 12–13, 1862; John C. Fleming, Letter December 15, 1862, Box 1, Folder 16.

17. *Ibid.*; Sylvanus Stevens, GAR, George Thomas Post, Autobiographies, Chicago History Museum.

18. Sylvanus Stevens, *Official Records*, Series 1, Volume 20, Part 1, 80; Calvin Durand, "Calvin 'Cam' Durand Jr.," 54–55; Benjamin Nourse, Diary, December 14, 1862; John A. Nourse, Journal December 14, 1862; *Chicago Tribune*, "From Nashville," December 19, 1862; James Negley, *Official Records*, Series 1, Volume 20, Part 2, 176.

19. S.H. Stevens, GAR, Autobiography.

20. William S. Rosecrans, *Official Records*, Series 1, Volume 20, Part 2, 118; Henry Halleck, *Official Records*, Series 1, Volume 20, Part 2, 117–118.

21. Henry Halleck, *Official Records*, Series 1, Volume 20, Part 2, 123–124; William Rosecrans, *Official Records*, Series 1, Volume 20, Part 2, 118.

22. Benjamin Nourse, Diary, December 15–25, 1862; *Historical Sketch of the Chicago Board of Trade Battery* (Chicago: The Henneberry Co. Publishers, 1902), 12.

23. William Rosecrans, *Official Records*, Series 1, Volume 20, Part 2, 219–222; James Negley, *Official Records*, Series 1, Volume 20, Part 2, 224–225; H.W. Graber, *The Life Record of H.W. Graber, A Terry Texas Ranger, 1861–1865* (n.p.: H.W. Garber Publisher, 1916), 186–187.

24. William Rosecrans, *Official Records*, Series 1, Volume 20, Part 2, 285.

25. William Hardee Papers, Hardee Family Papers, "Report of the Battle of Murfreesboro," (1862–1962), LPR121, p. 17, Alabama Department of History and Archives, Montgomery.

26. William Rosecrans, *Official Records*, Series 1, Volume 20, Part 1, 184, 189–190; C. Goddard, *Official Records*, Series 1, Volume 20, Part 2, 242; Jefferson C. Davis, *Official Records*, Series 1, Volume 20, Part 1, 262.

27. Leonidas Polk, *Official Records*, Series 1, Volume 20, Part 1, 685–686; Joseph Wheeler, *Official Records*, Series 1, Volume 20, Part 1, 958; Edward Longacre, *A Soldier to the Last: Maj. Gen. Joseph Wheeler in Blue and Gray* (Washington, D.C.: Potomac Books, Inc., 2007), 73; Robert Burns, Letter, January 11, 1863, Robert Burns Letterbook, MSS M642, Minnesota Historical Society, St. Paul, MN; John Fitch, "Battle of Stone River," In *Annals of the Army of the Cumberland* (Philadelphia: J. B, Lippincott & Co., 1863), 385.

28. Alexander McCook, *Official Records*, Series 1, Volume 20, Part 1, 253; W.D. Bickham, *Rosecrans' Campaign with the Fourteenth Army Corps, of the Army of the Cumberland* (Cincinnati: Moore, Wilstach, Keys & Co., 1903), 162; Thomas Crittenden, *Official Records*, Series 1, Volume 20, Part 2, pp. 243–44; Ebenezer Hannaford, "In the Ranks at Stone River," *Harper's Magazine*, 27 (1863), p. 810; Thomas Wood, *Official Records*, Series 1, Volume 20, Part 1, 457.

29. Benjamin Nourse, Diary, December 25, 1862.

30. John A. Nourse, Journal December 27, 1862; John C. Fleming, Letter December 25, 1862, Box 1, Folder 17.

31. George Knox Miller, *An Uncompromising Secessionist*, 113–114; John Berrien Lindsley, editor, *The Military Annals of Tennessee*, Confederate (Nashville: J.M. Lindsley & Co., Publishers, 1886), 714–715; Patrick Cleburne, *Official Records*, Series 1, Volume 20, Part 1, p. 843; Edward Longacre, *A Soldier to the Last*, 73; Robert D. Jackson, letter January, n.d., 1863, Robert D. Jackson family papers, 1857–1914: LPR290, Alabama Department of History and Archives; John W. DuBose, *General Joseph Wheeler and the Army of Tennessee* (New York: The Neale Publishing Co., 1912), 120; Isaac Ulmer, Letter, December 26, 1862, Isaac Barton Ulmer Papers, #1834, Southern Historical Collection, The Wilson Library, University of North Carolina at Chapel Hill.

32. Benjamin Nourse, Diary, December 27, 1862.

33. Patrick Cleburne, *Official Records*, Series 1, Volume 20, Part 1, 843; William Henry Harder, Diary 1861–1865, December 27, 1862, Microfilm 574, Tennessee State Library and Archives; S. A. M. Wood, *Official Records*, Series 1, Volume 20, Part 1, 896; Thomas Crittenden, *Official Records*, Series 1, Volume 20, Part 2, 243–244; Thomas Wood, *Official Records*, Series 1, Volume 20, Part 1, 458.

34. Robert Minty, *Official Records*, Series 1, Volume 20, Part 1, 623; Thomas Wood, *Official Records*, Series 1, Volume 20, Part 1, 458–459; Milo Hascall, *Official Records*, Series 1, Volume 20, Part 1, 466.

35. James Negley, *Official Records*, Series 1, Volume 20, Part 2, 246; George Thomas, *Official Records*, Series 1, Volume 20, Part 2, 248; Braxton Bragg, *Official Records*, Series 1, Volume 20, Part 1, 672–673.

36. William Hazen, *Official Records*, Series 1, Volume 20, Part 2, 253; Lyne Starling, *Official Records*, Series 1, Volume 20, Part 2, 253; Alexander McCook, *Official Records*, Series 1, Volume 20, Part 2, 254; John Daeuble Journal, John Daeuble Papers (1839–1864), Mss. A D123 1, Filson Historical Society, Louisville; Benjamin Nourse, Diary, December 28, 1862.

37. Julius Garesché, *Official Records*, Series 1, Volume 20, Part 2, 255; Alexander McCook, *Official Records*, Series 1, Volume 20, Part 2, 257.

38. John A. Nourse, Journal December 28, 1862.

39. William Rosecrans, *Official Records*, Series 1, Volume 20, Part 1, 182.

40. Julius P. Garesché, *Official Records*, Series 1, Volume 20, Part 2, 257–258; George Brent, *Official Records*, Series 1, Volume 20, Part 2, 464; Braxton Bragg, *Official Records*, Series 1, Volume 20, Part 2, 467.

41. Benjamin Nourse, Diary, December 29, 1862; John C. Fleming, Letter January 9, 1863, Box 1, Folder 18; George W. Cullum, *Biographical Register of the Officers and Graduates of the U.S. Military Academy*, Vol. 2 (New York: D. Van Nostrand, 1868–79), 437.

42. Joseph Mitchell, *Official Records*, Series 1,

Volume 20, Part 1, 626; Robert Burns Letter Book, January 11, 1863, M642, Minnesota Historical Society, St. Paul; Julius P. Gareché, *Official Records*, Series 1, Volume 20, Part 2, 263–265.

43. Lewis Zahm, *Official Records*, Series 1, Volume 20, Part 1, 636; William Rosecrans, *Official Records*, Series 1, Volume 20, Part 1, 191; Charles Anderson, *Official Records*, Series 1, Volume 20, Part 1, 345.

44. Silas Stevens, Letter September 17, 1903, Silas Curtis Stevens letters, 1903–1918, Folder 5, pp. 3–4; John Nourse, Journal, Dec. 30, 1862; John Fleming, Letter January 9, 1862.

45. William Rosecrans, *Official Records*, Series 1, Volume 20, Part 1, 192.

46. William Rosecrans, *Official Records*, Series 1, Volume 20, Part 1, 192; Henry M. Kendall, *The Battle of Stones River* (District of Columbia: Military Order of the Loyal Legion United States, 1903), 9; Edwin C. Bearss, Cavalry Operations: Battle of Stones River, Unpublished, Stones River National Park, Technical Information Center, Murfreesboro, TN, 1959, 59; James Knight, Letter January 3, 1863, Federal Collection Box F 25, Folder 8, Tennessee State Library and Archives, Nashville.

47. William Hardee Papers, Hardee family papers, "Report of the Battle of Murfreesboro," [1862–1962] LPR121, p. 17, Alabama Department of History and Archives; Peter Cozzens, *No Better Place to Die: The Battle of Stones River* (Urbana and Chicago: University of Illinois Press, 1991), 60; Grady McWhiney, *Braxton Bragg and the Confederate Defeat*, Volume I (New York and London: Columbia University Press, 1969), 347–348.

48. John Wharton, *Official Records*, Series 1, Volume 20, Part 1, 966; Braxton Bragg, *Official Records*, Series 1, Volume 20, Part 1, 663–664: George Brent, Diary, December 30, 1862, Braxton Bragg Papers, Mss. 2000, Series II, Box 4, Folder 22, Western Reserve Historical Society, Cleveland, Ohio.

49. Peter Cozzens, *No Better Place to Die: The Battle of Stones River* (Urbana and Chicago: University of Illinois Press, 1991), 75–76.

50. Peter Cozzens, *No Better Place to Die*, 79–80; Nathaniel Cheairs Hughes, Jr., *General William J. Hardee: Old Reliable* (Baton Rouge: Louisiana State University, 1965), 141.

51. Peter Cozzens, *No Better Place to Die*, 81–83; Richard Johnson, "Losing a Division at Stones River," In *Battles and Leaders of the Civil War*, Volume 5 edited by Peter Cozzens (Urbana and Chicago: University of Illinois Press, 2002), 296.

52. *Ibid.*, *New York Daily Tribune*, "From General Rosecrans's Army: A Terrible Battle at Murfreesboro," January 3, 1863, p. 1; L.B. Williams, *A Revised History of the 33rd Alabama Volunteer Infantry Regiment: In Cleburne's Elite Division, Army of Tennessee, 1862–1865* (Auburn, AL: Auburn University Printing Service, 1998), 31; Thomas W. Cutrer, *Our Trust is in the God of Battles: The Civil War Letters of Robert Franklin Bunting, Chaplain, Terry's Texas Rangers* (Knoxville: University of Tennessee Press, 2006), 112.

53. Peter Cozzens, *No Better Place to Die*, 92–100; Mathew Askew, Letter—January 21, 1863, Askew Family Correspondence, MMS 1380, Bowling Green State University, Bowling Green, Ohio; Alexis Cope, *The Fifteenth Ohio Volunteers and Its Campaigns, 1861–1865* (Columbus, Ohio: Published by Author, 1916), 234–237; Alexander Stevenson, *Battle of Stones River near Murfreesboro*, Tennessee (Boston: J.R. Osgood and Company, 1884), 39; Joab Stafford, *Official Records*, Series 1, Volume 20, Part 1, 343.

54. P. Sidney Post, *Official Records*, Series 1, Volume 20, Part 1, 269–70; Charles B. Humphrey, *Official Records*, Series 1, Volume 20, Part 1, 267; Alfred Tyler Fielder Diaries, December 31, 1862 entry, Ac #341, Box 1, Tennessee State Library and Archives.

55. William Henry Harder, Diary, 1861–1865, December 31, 1862, Microfilm 574, Tennessee State Library and Archives, Nashville pp. 46–56; John M. Routt, Microfilm 824, Confederate Collection, Reel 4 (Box 11, Folder 15), Tennessee State Library and Archives.

56. Peter Cozzens, *No Better Place to Die*, 156–159; Lanny Smith, *The Stone's River Campaign: 26 December 1862–5 January 1863, Army of Tennessee* (n.p.: Lanny Smith, 2010), 328; Daniel Wait Howe, Diary, December 31, 1862, Daniel Wait Howe Papers, 1824–1930, Collection #M 0148 Box 1, Folder 15, Indiana Historical Society; J.J. Womack, *A Civil War Diary of Captain J.J. Womack, Company E 16th Tennessee Volunteers* (McMinnville, TN: Womack, 1961), 78.

57. John Fleming, Letter January 9, 1863; Benjamin Nourse, Diary, December 31, 1862; James Morton *Official Records*, Series 1, Volume 20, Part 1, 243; James Stokes, *Official Records*, Series 1, Volume 20, Part 1, 251; Silas Stevens, Letter September 17, 1903, pp. 9–10; Jackson D. Howard, "From The Board or Trade Battery," January 14, 1863, *Chicago Tribune*; John A. Nourse, Diary, December 31, 1862.

58. John A. Nourse, Journal December 31, 1862; John Toomey, "Account of the Chicago Board of Trade Battery," GAR papers; James H. Stokes, Letter, January 8, 1863, Stones River Technical Information Center; Silas Stevens, Letter September 17, 1903, pp. 10–12, 19–20; Dean S. Thomas, *Cannons: Introduction to Civil War Artillery* (Arendtsville, PA: Thomas Publications, 1985), 3–4; [The exact origin of the seventh gun may be in question, but Benjamin Nourse specifically noted that the gun was one taken by the Confederates from an Ohio battery. Why this gun was not returned to that battery remains a mystery and most official reports do not mention the origin of the gun.]

59. William Rosecrans, *Official Records*, Series 1, Volume 20, Part 1, 194; Henry Freeman, "Some Battle Recollections of Stone's River," In *Military Essays and Recollections, State of Illinois*, Vol. III (Chicago: Dial Press, 1899), 232–233.

60. Lanny Smith, *The Stone's River Campaign*, 376–378; Compiled Service Records Showing Records of Service of Military Units, "Chicago Board of Trade Battery," National Archives and Records Administration, Microcopy 594, Roll 14.

61. Alanson J. Stevens, *Official Records*, Series 1, Volume 20, Part 1, 580; Samuel Beatty, *Official Records*, Series 1, Volume 20, Part 1, 584; Henry Fales Perry, *History of the Thirty-eighth Regiment Indiana Volunteers Infantry* (Palo Alto, Cal., F.A. Stuart Printer, 1906), 60–61; United States Army, Ohio Infantry Regiment, 94th, *Record of the Ninety-fourth Regiment, Ohio Volunteer Infantry, in the War of the Rebellion* (Cincinnati: The Ohio Valley Press, n.d.), 28; Lanny Smith, *The Stone's River Campaign*, 388–390; Tobias Miller, Letter Jan 8, 1863; W.D. Bickham, *Rosecrans' Campaign with the Fourteenth Army Corps*, 222; Henry Haymond, Letter to mother, January 7, 1863, Haymond (Henry) Papers, 1863, Pearce Civil War Collection, Navarro College.

62. Lanny Smith, *The Stone's River Campaign*, 387–394; Lyman Bridges, *Official Records*, Series 1, Volume 20, Part 1, 245; Silas Stevens, Letter September 17, 1903, pp. 13, 24; Tobias Miller, Letter Jan 8, 1863; John A. Nourse, Letter No. 4; Benjamin Nourse, Diary, December 31, 1862; James Stokes, *Official Records*, Series 1, Volume 20, Part 1, 251; James Morton *Official Records*, Series 1, Volume 20, Part 1, 243.

63. "From the 84th Regiment," *Macomb Weekly Herald*, January 30, 1863, p. 1.

64. John Carroll, "The Artillery at Murfreesboro—Letter from the 5th Regulars," *The Morning Leader* (Cleveland), January 16, 1863; Frank Reed, "Army Correspondence: Experience of a Tuscarawas Boy at the Battle of Murfreesboro—Eating a Dead Horse," *The Ohio Democrat* (New Philadelphia), January 30, 1863.

65. Benjamin Nourse, Diary, December 31, 1862, January 9, 1863; John Toomey, "Account of the Chicago Board of Trade Battery"; Lyman Bridges, *Official Records*, Series 1, Volume 20, Part 1, 245; Silas Stevens, Letter September 17, 1903, pp. 13, 24; Tobias Miller, Letter Jan 8, 1863; John A. Nourse, Letter No. 4; James Stokes, *Official Records*, Series 1, Volume 20, Part 1, 251; James Morton *Official Records*, Series 1, Volume 20, Part 1, 243; Jackson Howard, "From The Board or Trade Battery," *Chicago Tribune*, January 14, 1863; "Honors to the Gallant Dead," *Chicago Tribune*, March 23, 1863.

66. Tobias Miller, Letter January 8, 1863; Mathew Ector, *Official Records*, Series 1, Volume 20, Part 1, 927–928; Robert Harper, *Official Records*, Series 1, Volume 20, Part 1, 946–947; James Stokes, letter—Friday 8th, 1865, Chicago Board of Trade File, Technical Information Center, Stones River National Battlefield.

67. Lyman Bridges, *Official Records*, Series 1, Volume 20, Part 1, 245–246; Calvin Hood, *Official Records*, Series 1, Volume 20, Part 1, 247–248; W.D. Bickham, *Rosecrans' Campaign with the Fourteenth Army Corps*, 223.

68. James Stokes, *Official Records*, Series 1, Volume 20, Part 1, 251; Tobias Miller, Letter January 8, 1863; Benjamin Nourse, Diary, December 31, 1862.

69. Lyman Bridges, *Official Records*, Series 1, Volume 20, Part 1, 246; James Morton, *Official Records*, Series 1, Volume 20, Part 1, 243.

70. "With a Confederate," *The Angola Record* (Angola, New York), July 30, 1896, p. 2.

71. Tobias Miller, Letter January 8, 1863; Benjamin Nourse, Diary, December 31, 1862; Compiled Service Records Showing Records of Service of Military Units, "Chicago Board of Trade Battery," National Archives and Records Administration, Microcopy 594, Roll 14; *The Gate City News* (Keokuk), "Further Particulars of the Great Battle," January 8, 1863; *The Weekly Pioneer and Democrat* (St. Paul, MN), "We Achieve Victory," January 9, 1863, p. 5; William Rosecrans, *Official Records*, Series 1, Volume 20, Part 1, 194.

72. Silas Stevens, Letter January 2, 1904, pp. 7–10; F.A. Lord, Letter to Professor Emerson, April 20, 1869, Beloit University, Civil War Collection, Beloit College Archives, Civil War—Students—Personal Sketches F to W.

73. James Morton, *Official Records*, Series 1, Volume 20, Part 1, 243; Benjamin Nourse, Diary entry, January 1, 1863; Lyman Bridges, *Official Records*, Series 1, Volume 20, Part 1, 246.

74. John Toomey, "Account of the Chicago Board of Trade Battery"; James Morton, *Official Records*, Series 1, Volume 20, Part 1, 243.

75. James Stokes, *Official Records*, Series 1, Volume 20, Part 1, 251; John Nourse, Journal entry January 1, 1863.

76. Braxton Bragg, *Official Records*, Series 1, Volume 20, Part 1, 667.

77. John A. Nourse, Journal, January 2, 1863; Benjamin Nourse, Diary, January 2, 1863.

78. Edwin Bearss, "The Union Artillery and Breckinridge's Attack," Research Project #2, The Battle of Stones River, United States Parks Services, 1959, pp. 21–22; Lanny Smith, *The Stone's River Campaign*, 498–502.

79. Charles Harker, *Official Records*, Series 1, Volume 20, Part 1, 504; John Mendenhall, *Official Records*, Series 1, Volume 20, Part 1, 455; Milo Hascall, *Official Records*, Series 1, Volume 20, Part 1, 472–474; Seymour Race, *Official Records*, Series 1, Volume 20, Part 1, 475; Cullen Bradley, *Official Records*, Series 1, Volume 20, Part 1, 479; Edwin Bearss, "The Union Artillery and Breckinridge's Attack," p. 22; "Death of S.O. Kimberk," *The Summit County Beacon* (Akron, Ohio), November 12, 1868, p. 3.

80. Silas Stevens, Letter January 2, 1904, pp. 16–17.

81. J.N. Reese, *Report of the Adjutant General to the State of Illinois*, Vol. VIII (Springfield: Journal Company, Printers and Binders, 1901), 734; Benjamin Nourse, Diary, December 31, 1863. [These details are contrary to the account recorded in the Nourse diary which records the event as occurring on the first day of the battle and Nourse attributes the gun as one abandoned by an Ohio battery. The post-war account seems more plausible but if it was a gun from the Ohio battery there is no explanation why it wasn't returned to the proper unit. The

Board of Trade Battery would proudly claim the status of being a 7-gun unit but the details of this event is sketchy, at best.]

82. Larry Daniel, *Days of Glory*, 219–222; John C. Breckinridge, "Murfreesboro," *Southern Historical Society Papers*, Vol. 5, Number 5 (May 1878), pp. 211–213; H. H. G. Bradt, *History of the Services of the Third Battery Wisconsin Light Artillery in the Civil War of the United States, 1861–1865* (Berlin, Wisconsin: Courant Press, 1902), 17; George Brent, "Journal of George Brent," January 2, 1863, Braxton Bragg Papers, MS 2000, Series II, Box 4, Folder 22, Western Reserve Historical Society, Cleveland Ohio; John M. Hollis, Diary, January 1 and 2, 1863, John M. Hollis Papers, MS.3222, Box 1, Folder 1, University of Tennessee Libraries, Special Collections, Knoxville.

83. Benjamin Nourse, Diary, January 2, 1863; M.B. Butler, *My Story of the Civil War and the Under-ground Railroad* (Huntington, IN: The United Brethren Publishing Establishment, 1914), 275–277; Compiled Service Records Showing Records of Service of Military Units, "Chicago Board of Trade Battery," National Archives and Records Administration, Microcopy 594, Roll 14; James Morton, *Official Records*, Series 1, Volume 20, Part 1, 244; Edwin Bearss, "The Union Artillery and Breckinridge's Attack," 16–18.

84. Edwin Bearss, "The Union Artillery and Breckinridge's Attack," chapter 1, pp. 32–40, chapter 2, p. 25; Silas Stevens, Letter January 2, 1904, 17–25.

85. Edwin Bearss, "The Union Artillery and Breckinridge's Attack," Appendix I.

86. Silas Stevens, Letter January 2, 1904, pp. 17–25; M.B. Butler, *My Story of the Civil War*, 277–78; Edwin Bearss, "The Union Artillery and Breckinridge's Attack," chapter 2, pp. 35–44, chapter 3, pp. 1–8.

87. Tobias Miller, Letter January 8, 1863; James Stokes, *Official Records*, Series 1, Volume 20, Part 1, 251.

88. Benjamin Nourse, Diary, January 2, 1863.

89. Joe Onofrey and Jim Roubal, "The Life of a Civil War Soldier 'Traveling Trunk'" (Gettysburg: National Park Service, 2008), 72; John Fleming, Letter January 9, 1863; James Negley, *Official Records*, Series 1, Volume 20, Part 1, 408; Benjamin Nourse, Diary, January 3, 1863.

90. *The Inland Printer*, Vol. V (Chicago: The Inland Printer Co., 1887), 531; Chicago Board of Trade Association roster, April 27, 1886, Trumbull Griffin File, Missouri History Museum; *Chicago Tribune*, "From the Chicago Board of Trade Battery," January 17. 1863, p. 2.

91. John A. Nourse, Journal December 31, 1862; John Fleming, Letter January 9, 1863; Returns of Casualties, Discharges, etc., Illinois Adjutant General Records, Illinois State Archives; John Toomey, "Account of the Chicago Board of Trade Battery"; "Latest Telegraphic News," *Cincinnati Daily Commercial*, January 7, 1863, p. 3, c. 4; John A. Nourse, letter No. 4; Returns of Casualties, Discharges, etc., Chicago Board of Trade Battery, Illinois State

Archives; Benjamin Nourse, Diary, January 2, 1863; John Fleming, Letter January 9, 1863; William Rosecrans, *Official Records*, Series 1, Volume 20, Part 1, 224; Tobias Miller, Letter January 8, 1863; *Chicago Tribune*, "The Murfreesboro Battle," January 6, 1863, p. 1, column 5; *Evansville Daily Journal*, "Termination of the Fight," January 9, 1863; George I. Robinson, Letter to support Loyal A. Stevens pensions claim, undated, George Robinson papers, Chicago History Museum; Boyd L. Dastrup, *King of Battle: A Branch History of the U.S. Army's Field Artillery* (Fort Monroe, VA: Office of the Command Historian, 1992), 106.

92. Silas Stevens, Letter January 2, 1904, p. 33.

Chapter Three

1. *Chicago Tribune*, "Aid for the Sick and Wounded Soldiers, January 7, 1863; *Chicago Tribune*, "The Board of Trade Battery," February 11, 1863; *Chicago Tribune*, "The Florence Nightingales of the North," March 19, 1863; Silas Stevens, Letter to brother, Folder 7, Silas Stevens papers, Chicago History Museum.

2. John A. Nourse, Journal entries January 4–31, 1863, John A. Nourse papers, 1862–1922, Chicago History Museum.

3. Benjamin Nourse, Diary, January 4–31, 1863, Rubenstein Library, Duke University; John Fleming, Letter January 18, 1863, John C. Fleming Papers, Box 1, Folder 19, Newberry Library, Chicago; 1st and 2nd Quarter 1863 Ordnance Summary Statements, for independent Illinois batteries, Jan. 24, 1864, Quarterly returns of ordnance and ordnance stores on hand in Regular and Volunteer Army organizations 1862–1867, 1870–1876) Record Group: 156/159; Microfilm/Pamphlet No: M 1281.

4. John Fleming, Letters January 18 and February 10, Box 1, Folder 19, 20; *Historical Sketch of the Chicago Board of Trade Battery* (Chicago: The Henneberry Co. Publishers, 1902), 18; J.N. Reese, *Report of the Adjutant General to the State of Illinois*, Vol. VIII (Springfield: Journal Company, Printers and Binders, 1901), 732; Muster and Descriptive Roll, Chicago Board of Trade, Records of the Illinois Adjutant General (301.018, 2S, 15B, F 6) Illinois Archives, Springfield, IL; Charles Goddard, Letter to Colonel Morrison, January 12, 1863, Chicago Board of Trade Battery, Miscellaneous Letters, Records of the Adjutant General, Illinois State Archives; John A. Nourse, Letter No. 6; *Chicago Tribune*, "The Board of Trade Battery. Gen. Rosecrans Allows Them to Carry Their Flag," January 24, 1863; *Chicago Tribune*, "The City: Died," February 3, 1863; *Chicago Tribune*, "Death of Corporal Carver," Board of Trade Battery, February 6, 1863; Silas Stevens, Letter to brother, Folder 8; Chicago Board of Trade Association roster, April 27, 1886, Trumbull Griffin file, Missouri History Museum.

5. Edwin Bearss, "The History of Fortress Rosecrans," United States Department of Interior, Research Report, Stones River National Military

Park, 1960; Lenard E. Brown, "Fortress Rosecrans: A History, 1865–1990," *Tennessee Historical Quarterly*, Vol. 50, No. 3 (Fall 1991), p. 138.

6. Glenn W. Sunderland, *Lightning at Hoover's Gap* (New York, South Brunswick, London: Thomas Yoseloff, 1969), 23–26; Larry Daniel, *Days of Glory, The Army of the Cumberland 1861–1865* (Baton Rouge: Louisiana State University Press, 2006), 227; William Rosecrans, *Official Records*, Series 1, Volume 20, Part 2, 328.

7. *Official Records,* Series 1, Volume 20, Part 2, 345.

8. Stephen Z. Starr, *The Union Cavalry in the Civil War: The War in the West, Volume III* (Baton Rouge: Louisiana State University, 2007), 225.

9. *Official Register of the Officers and Cadets of the U.S. Military Academy* (West Point, NY: U.S. Military Academy, 1852), 7; David Stanley, *An American General—The Memoirs of David Sloan Stanley,* Samuel W. Fordyce IV, ed. (Santa Barbara, California: The Narrative Press, 2004), 49–50.

10. John Toomey, "Account of the Chicago Board of Trade Battery," George Thomas Post, GAR, Stones River Technical Information Center, NPS.

11. E.B. Stevens, Letter to Allen Fuller, January 24, 1863, Muster out and Miscellaneous letters, Chicago Board of Trade Collection, Illinois State Archives; John Nourse, Journal entry February 18; *Chicago Tribune*, "Why It Hates Them," February 6, 1863.

12. Benjamin Nourse, Diary entries, February 5, 8, 18; Silas Stevens, Letter to brother, Folder 7, p. 5.

13. Benjamin Nourse, Diary entries, March 12, 15; John A. Nourse, Journal entries, March 4, 9; John Fleming, letter to father, February 18, 1863, Box 1, Folder 21; Silas Stevens, Letter to Brother, Folder 7; [Presumably the "W.A." refers to Worrell and Auten.]

14. Silas Stevens, Letter to Brother, Folder 7.

15. Benjamin Nourse, Diary entries, March 8, 14, 1863; John A. Nourse, Journal March 2, 1863 and Letter No. 8; John Fleming, Letter to Dear Sister, March 16, 1863, Folder 26.

16. Benjamin Nourse, Diary entries, March 2, 22, 1863, postscript to diary March 6, 1867; George I. Robinson papers, Capt. Thrall Special Orders No. 59, March 3, 1863, Chicago History Museum; Letter from James H. Stokes to Griffin, undated, Trumbull Griffin Papers, Missouri History Museum, St. Louis; John A. Nourse, Letter No. 8; *Chicago Tribune*, "From Rosecrans' Army," March 11, 1863; Fleming letter, *ibid.*.; John Fleming, Letter to Father, March 22.

17. Recruitment papers, George I. Robinson papers, Chicago History Museum; *Historical Sketch of the Chicago Board of Trade Battery*, 77–80; J.N. Reese, *Report of the Adjutant General to the State of Illinois*, 730–731; Muster and Descriptive Roll, Chicago Board of Trade, Records of the Illinois Adjutant General, March 19, 1863 (301.018, 2S, 15B, F 6) Illinois Archives, Springfield, IL; "Robinson, George Irving Jan. 14, 1909, Milwaukee," In Memoriam, R-Z (1886–1917) Box 1, File 19, Military Order of the

Loyal Legion of the United States, Wisconsin Commandery, Mss-0938, Milwaukee County Historical Society.

18. James H. Stokes, Letter to Griffin, undated, Trumbull Griffin Papers; *Chicago Tribune*, "Recruits for the Board of Trade Battery, February 27, 1863"; *Chicago Tribune*, "Chicago Board of Trade Battery," March 11; George Baker Anderson, *Landmarks of Rensselaer County, New York*, Volume 2 (Syracuse: D. Mason & Co., 1897), 149.

19. Larry Daniel, *Days of Glory*, 234–235; Stephen Z. Starr, *The Union Cavalry in the Civil War*, 231–232; John Fleming, Letters March 22, 23, 1863.

20. Tobias Miller, Letter to brother, April 20, 1863; John Nourse, Journal entry, April 14, 1863; Benjamin Nourse, Diary entries, April 20, 21, 26, 1863; *Chicago Tribune*, "Captured," April 16, 1863; John Fleming, Letter to Uncle March 23, April 12, 1863; *A General Catalogue of the Officers and Graduates from Its Organization in 1837–1864* (Ann Arbor: University of Michigan, 1864), 29.

21. George I. Robinson, Letter to Allen Fuller, April 7, 1863, Chicago Board of Trade Battery Records, Muster out Rolls and Misc. Letters, Illinois State Archives.

22. *Chicago Tribune*, "Stokes' Battery," May 23, 1863; John A. Nourse, Letter to father, May, 30, 1863, Letter number 11; John Fleming, letter to mother, May, 17, 1863.

23. William S. Rosecrans, *Official Records*, Series I, Vol. 23, Part 1, 418.

24. David Stanley, *Official Records*, Series 1, Vol. 23, Part 1, 334–335; David Stanley, *An American General*, 158–159; Earnest East, "Lincoln's Russian General," *Journal of the Illinois State Historical Society*, Vol. 52 (1959), No. 1, 106–122; Don Carlos Buell, *Official Records*, Series 1, Vol. 16, Part 2, 71; Trumbull Griffin, War summary, Trumbull Dorrance Griffin papers, Missouri History Museum, St. Louis.

25. William Henry Powell, editor, *Officers of the Army and Navy (volunteer) Who Served in the Civil War* (Philadelphia: L.R. Hamersly, 1893), 313.

26. David Stanley, *Official Records*, Series 1, Vol. 20, Part 1, 619; Marshall Thatcher, *A Hundred Battles in the West: The Second Michigan Cavalry* (Detroit: Thatcher, 1884), 124.

27. "Echo of the War: Letter From Henry Bennett of Topeka Is Unearthed," *The Topeka Daily State Journal*, May 31, 1909, p.10, col. 3–4.

28. William Lamers, *The Edge of Glory: A Biography of General William S. Rosecrans, U.S.A.* (New York: Harcourt, Brace & World, Inc., 1961), 253; Benjamin Nourse, Diary entry, May 1, 1863; John Nourse letter #10, May 3, 1863.

29. Benjamin Nourse, Diary entries, May 18, 26–29, 1863; John A. Nourse, Letter number 11, May 30, 1863; Silas Stevens, Letter to brother, Folder 8.

30. John Nourse, Journal entry June 4, 1863; Michael Bradley, "Tullahoma: The Wrongly Forgotten Campaign," *Blue & Gray*, Volume XXVII (2010), Number 1: 22; John A. Nourse, May 30, 1863 letter

to Father; Tobias Miller, Letter to dear sister May 20, 1863; Benjamin Nourse, Diary entry, June 1, 1863; Return of Casualties, Chicago Board of Trade Battery, Illinois State Archives; John Fleming, Letter to mother, June 7, 1863.

31. Benjamin Nourse, Diary entries, June 8–11, 15, 1863; John Nourse, Journal entries, June 4–9, 1863; John Nourse, Letter to father, June 21, 1863.

32. John Nourse, Letter to father, June 21, 1863; Benjamin Nourse, Diary entries, June 12–14, 1863; John Turchin, *Official Records*, Series 1, Vol. 20, Part 1, 380; John Fleming, Letter to Sister, Folder 1–40; Frederick Lord, Letter to Professor Emerson April 20, 1869, Beloit University.

33. John Nourse, Journal entry June 16, 19, 1863; Benjamin Nourse, Diary entries, June 15–16, 1863; John Fleming, Letter to Mother, June 7, 1863; Silas Stevens, Letter to brother, Folder 8.

34. Benjamin Nourse, Diary entries, June 16–18, 1863.

35. Benjamin Nourse, Diary entry, June 21, 1863.

36. *Ibid.*; W.L. Curry, *Four Years in the Saddle: History of First Regiment Ohio Volunteer Cavalry* (Columbus: Champlin Printing Co., 1898), 22, 99; Tobias Miller, Letter to dear sister, May 20, 1863; Michael Bradley, "Varying Results of Cavalry Fighting: Western Flank vs. Eastern Flank," *Blue and Grey*, Volume XXVII (2010), Number 1, 21.

37. Larry J. Daniel, *Days of Glory: The Army of the Cumberland*, 267; William Rosecrans, *Official Records*, Series 1, Volume 23, Part 1, 404–405; Michael Bradley, "Tullahoma: The Wrongly Forgotten Campaign"; William Lamers, *The Edge of Glory*, 275.

38. Stephen Z. Starr, *The Union Cavalry in the Civil War: The War in the West, Volume III* (Baton Rouge: Louisiana State University, 2007), 225.

39. Henry Mortimer Hempstead, Diary, June 23, 1863, Hempstead, Henry Mortimer Papers, Bentley Historical Library, University of Michigan, Ann Arbor; Michael Bradley, *Tullahoma: The 1863 Campaign for the Control of Middle Tennessee* (Shippensburg, Pennsylvania: White Mane Publishing Company, 1999), 51–52; Thomas McCahan, Diary, June 24, 1863, Thomas McCahan Papers Historical Society of Pennsylvania, Philadelphia; *National Tribune*, "Tullahoma Campaign," May 6, 1882; John Randolph Poole, *Cracker Cavaliers: The 2nd Georgia Cavalry Under Wheeler and Forrest* (Macon, Georgia: Mercer University Press, 2000), 78.

40. David Stanley, *Official Records*, Series 1, Volume 23, Part 1, 538–540; David A. Powell, *Failure in the Saddle* (New York and California: Savas Beatie, 2010), 5–6; Thomas Jordan, Letter to Wife—June 26, 1863, Thomas J. Jordan Civil War Letters Box Number: 1, Folder 12, Historical Society of Pennsylvania, Philadelphia, Pennsylvania; Edward G. Longacre, *A Soldier to the Last: Maj. Gen. Joseph Wheeler in Blue and Gray* (Washington: Potomac Books Inc., 2007), 103.

41. Joseph Vale, *Minty and the Cavalry: A History of Cavalry Campaigns in the Western Armies* (Harrisburg, Pennsylvania: Edwin K. Myers, Printer

and Binder, 1886), 174–175; David Stanley, *Official Records*, Series 1, Volume 23, Part 1, 539; Robert Brandt, "Lightning and Rain in Middle Tennessee: The Campaign of June–July 1863." *Tennessee Historical Quarterly*, vol. 52, no. 3, 1993, pp. 158–169.

42. Stephen Z. Starr, *The Union Cavalry in the Civil War, Volume 3: The War in the West, 1861–1865* (Baton Rouge: Louisiana State University Press, 1985), 245–246; John Allan Wyeth, *With Sabre and Scalpel: The Autobiography of a Soldier and Surgeon* (New York and London: Harper Brothers Publishers, 1914), 214; William B. Sipes, *Official Records*, Series 1, Volume 23, Part 1, 565; Michael Bradley, *Tullahoma: The 1863 Campaign*, 76; David Stanley, *Official Records*, Series 1, Volume 23, Part 1, 539; George Steahlin, "Stanley's Cavalry: Minty's Sabre Brigade at Guy's Gap," *National Tribune*, May 27, 1882, p. 1, col. 5.

43. Richard J. Brewer, "The Tullahoma Campaign: Operational Insights," Master's Thesis, U.S. Army Command and General Staff College, Leavenworth, KS., 1978, 142; David Stanley, *Official Records*, Series 1, Volume 23, Part 1, 540–541; John Allan Wyeth, *With Sabre and Scalpel*," 232; *Cleveland Morning Leader*, "Letter from the 3d Ohio Cavalry," August 14, 1863.

44. T.F. Dornblaser, *Sabre Strokes of the Pennsylvania Dragoons* (Philadelphia: Lutheran Publication Society, 1884), 118–119; Thomas Crofts, *History of the Service of the Third Ohio Veteran Volunteer Cavalry* (Toledo: Stoneman Press, 1910), 108.

45. John A. Nourse, Journal entries June 24–30, 1863; James Stokes, *Official Records*, Series 1, Volume 23, Part 1, 578–579; Sylvanus Stevens, *Official Records*, Series 1, Volume 23, Part 1, 580; John Fleming, Letter to father July, 8, 1863.

46. Stevens, *Ibid.*; Stokes *Ibid.*; John A. Nourse, Letter No. 13, July 9, 1863.

47. Stokes, *Ibid.*; Richard Brewer, "The Tullahoma Campaign: Operational Insights," Master's Thesis, U.S. Army Command and General Staff College, Leavenworth, KS., 1978, 146; John Turchin, *Official Records*, Series 1, Volume 23, Part 1, 554–556; Silas Stevens, Letter to brother, Folder 9.

48. Stokes, *Ibid.*; Silas Stevens, Letter to brother, Folder 9.

49. Calvin Durand, "Calvin 'Cam' Durand Jr.," Stones River Technical Information Center, Regimental Records, NPS, p. 57; Stephen Starr, *The Union Cavalry in the Civil War*, 237; Richard J. Brewer, "The Tullahoma Campaign," 73.

Chapter Four

1. Jack Welsh, *Medical Histories of Confederate Generals* (Kent, Ohio: Kent State University Press, 1995), 23; Peter Cozzens, *This Terrible Sound: The Battle of Chickamauga* (Urbana and Chicago: University of Illinois Press, 1992), 27–28.

2. Robert S. Brandt, "Lightning and Rain in Middle Tennessee," In *The Battle of Stones River and The Fight for Middle Tennessee*, Timothy Johnson, ed.

(Nashville: Tennessee Historical Society, 2012), 133; Phil Sheridan, *Official Records*, Series 1, Volume 23, Part 2, 519; William Rosecrans, *Official Records*, Series 1, Volume 23, Part 2, 555; Henry Halleck, *Official Records*, Series 1, Volume 23, Part 2, 556; John W. Taylor, *Official Records*, Series 1, Volume 23, Part 2, 601; David Stanley, *Official Records*, Series 1, Volume 23, Part 2, 538, 541, 548.

3. George Thomas, *Official Records*, Series 1, Volume 23, Part 2, 551; Kinloch Falconer, *Official Records*, Series 1, Volume 23, Part 2, 938; Edward G. Longacre, *A Soldier to the Last: Maj. Gen. Joseph Wheeler in Blue and Gray* (Washington: Potomac Books Inc., 2007), 109; James A. Garfield, *Official Records*, Series 1, Volume 23, Part 2, 527; Henry Halleck, *Official Records*, Series 1, Volume 23, Part 2, 552; John W. DuBose, *General Joseph Wheeler and the Army of Tennessee*, 188.

4. Braxton Bragg, *Official Records*, Series 1, Volume 23, Part 1, 584; David Stanley, *Official Records*, Series 1, Volume 23, Part 1, 538, 541; Thomas McCahan, Diary, September 10, 1863, Thomas McCahan Papers (Am. 6092) Historical Society of Pennsylvania, Philadelphia; Benjamin Nourse, Diary entry, July 4, 1863, Rubenstein Library, Duke University; James H. Stokes, *Official Records*, Series 1, Volume 23, Part 1, 579; Silas Stevens, Letter April 25, 1904, Folder 10, Silas Stevens papers, Chicago History Museum.

5. John A. Nourse, Journal entries July 5–11, 1863, John A. Nourse papers [manuscript], 1862–1922, Chicago History Museum; Silas Stevens, Letter, Folder 9.

6. James A. Garfield, *Official Records*, Series 1, Volume 23, Part 2, 527; David Stanley, *Official Records*, Series 1, Volume 23, Part 2, 548; *Nashville Daily Press*, "Court-Martialed," July 16, 1863; Court Martial Record, August 14, 1863, RG 94, 4th Kentucky Cavalry, Orders and Correspondence books, National Archives; 4th U.S. Cavalry, Correspondence July 16, 1863 and September 4, 1863, RG 391, Entry 731, 4th U.S. Cavalry regimental books, National Archives; Silas Stevens, Letter April 25, 1904, Folder 10; Benjamin Nourse Diary entry, July 12, 1863.

7. David Stanley, *An American General—The Memoirs of David Sloan Stanley*, Samuel W. Fordyce IV, ed. (Santa Barbara, California: The Narrative Press, 2004), 167–168; John Beatty, *The Citizen Soldier: The Memoirs of a Civil War Volunteer* (Lincoln and London: Bison Books University of Nebraska Press, 1998), 303; Mary Jane Chadick, *Incidents of the War: The Civil War Journal of Mary Jane Chadick*, Nancy Rohr, ed. (Huntsville: Silver Thread Publishing, 2005), 110; James Garfield, *Official Records*, Series 1, Volume 23, Part 2, 527; W.S. Rosecrans, *Official Records*, Series 1, Volume 23, Part 2, 529; W.L. Curry, *Four Years in the Saddle: History of First Regiment Ohio Volunteer Cavalry* (Columbus: Champlin Printing Co., 1898), 106; Robert D. Richardson, "Rosecrans' Staff at Chickamauga: The Significance of Major General William S. Rosecrans' Staff on the Outcome of the Chickamauga

Campaign." Master's Thesis, Command and General Staff College, Fort Leavenworth, Kansas, 1989, 62.

8. Charles Perry Goodrich, July 16–18, 1863, *Letters from Home from the First Wisconsin Cavalry*; Julius Thomas, July 17, 1863, diary entry; John McLain, Diary entries, July 20–30, 1863; Robert Merrill, "July 7, 1863," *Robert Sidney Merrill, Co. K. 1st Wis. Cav.* (Cedarsburg, WI.: MSG Publishing, 1995); W.R. Carter, *History of the First Regiment of Tennessee Volunteer Cavalry*, 79; *Staunton Spectator*, "Huntsville, Ala." July 28, 1863, p. 2; *Alexandria Gazette*, "From the Army of the Cumberland," July 25, 1863, p. 3; *Washington City Evening Star*, "The Taking of Huntsville," July 25, 1863, p. 4; Thomas Speed, "Cavalry Operations in the West Under Rosecrans and Sherman," In *Battle and Leaders of the Civil War*, Vol. 4 (New York: The Century Company, 1884, 1888), 415.

9. *The Abingdon Virginian*, "Interesting Letter," August 7, 1863, p. 2; Benjamin Nourse, Diary, July 13–22; John Fleming, Letter to father, July 17, 1863, John C. Fleming Papers, Newberry Library, Chicago; John Fleming, Letter to mother July 27; Capt. W.B. Curtis orders to Sylvanus Stevens, July 22, Letters sent, Second Cavalry Division, RG 393 Item 2500, National Archives and Records Administration; John Lynch, Letter July 31, 1863, Morris Fitch Papers, Bentley Historical Library, University of Michigan.

10. *Staunton Spectator*, "Huntsville, Ala." July 28, 1863, p. 2; *Alexandria Gazette*, "From the Army of the Cumberland," July 25, 1863, p. 3; *Washington City Evening Star*, "The Taking of Huntsville," July 25, 1863, p. 4; Thomas Speed, "Cavalry Operations in the West Under Rosecrans and Sherman," In *Battle and Leaders of the Civil War*, Vol. 4 (New York: The Century Company, 1884, 1888), 415; John Nourse, Journal entry, July 29, 1863; John Fleming, Letter to Father, August 3, 1863.

11. David Stanley, *Official Records*, Series 1, Volume 23, Part 2, 548–549; William Sinclair, *Official Records*, Series 1, Volume 23, Part 2, 568; Joseph Vale, *Minty and the Cavalry: A History of Cavalry Campaigns in the Western Armies* (Harrisburg, PA.: Edwin K. Myers, Printer and Binder, 1886), 196; Isaac Skillman, Diary, August 9, 1863, MMS1083, Bowling Green State University, Bowling Green, Ohio; John Nourse, Journal, August 1–3; John Beatty, *The Citizen Soldier*, 306–307; I.R. Conwell, Diary entry, August 2, 1863, Conwell Diary, S2753, F3, Indiana Historical Society, Indianapolis.

12. Benjamin Nourse, Diary, July 30, 1863; Descriptive rolls, Chicago Board of Trade Battery, Illinois State Archives, Springfield; John Fleming, Letter to father, August 3, 1863; "A Hero," *Chicago Tribune*, July 25, 1863.

13. William Sinclair, *Official Records*, Series 1, Volume 23, Part 2, 567–568; G.P. Thruston, *Official Records*, Series 1, Volume 23, Part 2, 568; John Nourse, Journal entry, July 31, 1863; Benjamin Nourse, Diary, August 1–3, 1863.

14. Simon Buckner, *Official Records*, Series 1, Volume 23, Part 1, 842; John Scott, *Official Records*,

Series 1, Volume 23, Part 1, 840–842; George Hartsuff, *Official Records*, Series 1, Volume 23, Part 1, 829–831; Thomas Jordan and J.P. Pryor, *The Campaigns of Lieut.-Gen. Nathan B. Forrest of Forrest's Cavalry* (New Orleans, Memphis, New York: Blelock & Co., 1868), 293–295.

15. William Rosecrans, *Official Records*, Series 1, Volume 30, Part 3, 4; Edward McCook, *Official Records*, Series 1, Volume 23, Part 2, 595.

16. William Rosecrans, *Official Records*, Series 1, Vol. 30, Part 3, 274–275.

17. Braxton Bragg, *Official Records*, Series 1, Volume 23, Part 2, 954; Simon Buckner, *Official Records*, Series 1, Volume 23, Part 2, 946, 962.

18. William Rosecrans, *Official Records*, Series 1, Volume 23, Part 2, 607; Braxton Bragg, *Official Records*, Series 1, Volume 23, Part 2, 957.

19. William Rosecrans, *Official Records*, Series 1, Volume 23, Part 2, 590; William Rosecrans, *Official Records*, Series 1, Vol. 30, Part 3, 3, 11; Henry Halleck, *Official Records*, Series 1, Volume 23, Part 2, 592–593; Ambrose Burnside; *Official Records*, Series 1, Volume 23, Part 2, 592.

20. Edward McCook, *Official Records*, Series 1, Vol. 30, Part 3, 43; Benjamin Nourse, Diary, August 16–20, 1863; John Fleming, Letter to Isaac, August 9, and letter to mother, August 15, 1863.

21. John Fleming, Letter to sister August 28, 1863; Sylvanus Stevens, Letter, Folder 10.

22. Compiled Service Records Showing Records of Service of Military Units, "Chicago Board of Trade Battery," National Archives and Records Administration, Microcopy 594. Roll 14; "From the Chicago Board of Trade Battery," *Chicago Tribune*, September 5, 1863; Eli Long, Autobiography, Eli Long Papers, U.S. Army and Heritage Education Center; Thomas Crofts, *History of the Service of the Third Ohio Veteran Volunteer Cavalry* (Toledo: Stoneman Press, 1910), 111.

23. Thomas Crofts, *Ibid.*

24. John Fleming, Letter to mother, August 15, 1863; Compiled Service Records Showing Records of Service of Military Units, "Chicago Board of Trade Battery," National Archives and Records Administration, Microcopy 594. Roll 14.

25. Robert Minty, Official Records, Series 1, Vol. 30, Part 1, 920–921.

26. Robert Minty, *Official Records*, Series 1, Vol. 30, Part 1, 921; Joseph Vale, *Minty and the Cavalry*, 206–207; T.F. Dornblaser, *Sabre Strokes of the Pennsylvania Dragoons* (Philadelphia: Lutheran Publication Society, 1884), 122–123.

27. E.A. Otis, *Official Records*, Series 1, Vol. 30, Part 3, 107; Thomas L. Crittenden, *Official Records*, Series 1, Vol. 30, Part 3, 117; Robert Minty, *Official Records*, Series 1, Vol. 30, Part 3, 125; Horatio Van Cleve, *Official Records*, Series 1, Vol. 30, Part 3, 125; Robert Burns, Letter, August 25, 1863, Robert Burns Letterbook, MSS M642, Minnesota Historical Society, St. Paul, MN; John McLain, Diary entry, August 21, 1863, Diary entry, February 13, 1863, John McLain, Papers (c.00111), Michigan State University Archives & Historical Collections, East Lansing,

Michigan; Journal of 4th Michigan Cavalry, August 20, RG 94, Entry 112, National Archives; Joseph Vale, *Minty and the Cavalry: A History of Cavalry Campaigns in the Western Armies* (Harrisburg, Pennsylvania: Edwin K. Myers, Printer and Binder, 1886), 213.

28. Thomas Crittenden, *Official Records*, Series 1, Vol. 30, Part 3, 137, 153; Horatio Van Cleve, *Official Records*, Series 1, Vol. 30, Part 3, 140, 190; Robert Minty, *Official Records*, Series 1, Vol. 30, Part 3, 139; P.P. Oldershaw, *Official Records*, Series 1, Vol. 30, Part 3, 140; Alva Griest, Diary entry, August 22, 1863; William B. Hazen, *Official Records*, Series 1, Vol. 30, Part 3, 138; Robert Minty, *Official Records*, Series 1, Vol. 30, Part 3, 139; Horatio Van Cleve, *Official Records*, Series 1, Vol. 30, Part 3, 139.

29. George E. Flynt, *Official Records*, Series 1, Vol. 30, Part 3, 234; James Garfield, *Official Records*, Series 1, Vol. 30, Part 3, 236; William Rosecrans, *Official Records*, Series 1, Vol. 30, Part 3, 242; Edward McCook, *Official Records*, Series 1, Vol. 30, Part 3, 240–241.

30. W.W. Mackall, *Official Records*, Series 1, Vol. 30, Part 4, 579; J.L. Abernathy, *Official Records*, Series 1, Vol. 30, Part 3, 254–255; T.H. Mauldin, *Official Records*, Series 1, Vol. 30, Part 4, 574; David Powell, *The Chickamauga Campaign: A Mad Irregular Battle* (El Dorado Hills, CA: Savas Beatie, 2014), 105; William Rosecrans, *Official Records*, Series 1, Vol. 30, Part 3, 279; George Thomas, *Official Records*, Series 1, Vol. 30, Part 3, 282; Peter Cozzens, *This Terrible Sound: The Battle of Chickamauga* (Urbana and Chicago: University of Illinois Press, 1992), 45; George Burroughs, *Official Records*, Series 1, Vol. 30, Part 3, 285; Jonathan Pratt, *Official Records*, Series 1, Vol. 30, Part 3, 315; Edward McCook, *Official Records*, Series 1, Vol. 30, Part 1, 894; George Baum, Diary entry, September 2, 1863, Book 10, M 674 B1 F3, Baum Diaries, Indiana Historical Society; "The First Wisconsin Cavalry," Quiner Scrapbooks: Correspondence of the Wisconsin Volunteers, 1861–1865, Volume 10, Wisconsin Historical Society, Madison; Benjamin Nourse, Diary, September 1, 1863; Peter Williamson, Letter to Wife, September 7, 1863, Williamson, Peter J. 1823–1907, Special Collections Division of the Nashville Public Library; Marshall P. Thatcher, *A Hundred Battles in the West: The Second Michigan Cavalry* (Detroit: L.F. Kilroy, Printer, 1884), 138.

31. Benjamin Nourse, Diary, September 2–4, 1863.

32. D.S. Stanley, *Official Records*, Series 1, Vol. 30, Part 3, 331; William Garrett, *Reminiscences of Public Men in Alabama* (Atlanta: Plantation Publishing Company's Press, 1872), 230.

33. G.W. Baum, Diary entry, September 3, 1863; I.R. Conwell, Diary entry, September 3, Conwell Diary, S 2753, F. 3, Indiana Historical Society; Marshall P. Thatcher, *A Hundred Battles in the West: The Second Michigan Cavalry* (Detroit: L.F. Kilroy, Printer, 1884), 140; Edward McCook, Orders—September 2, 1863, RG 393, Number 2527, Letters Sent First Cavalry Division, National Archives;

W.R. Carter, *History of the First Regiment of Tennessee Volunteer Cavalry* (Knoxville: Gaut-Ogden Co., Printers and Binders, 1902), 83; Benjamin Nourse, Diary, September 4, 1863; Elisha Peterson, Letter to parents, September 29, 1863, Elisha Peterson Manuscript, Sec. A Box 104, Rubenstein Library, Duke University.

34. Benjamin Nourse, Diary, September 6; Silas Stevens, Folder 10.

35. R.B. Mitchell, *Official Records*, Series 1, Vol. 30, Part 3, 331–332; O.F. Strahl, *Official Records*, Series 1, Vol. 30, Part 4, 588; Peter Cozzens, *This Terrible Sound,* 49–50; Ephraim Dodd, *Diary of Ephraim Shelby Dodd*, 22–23.

36. E.S. Burford, *Official Records*, Series 1, Vol. 30, Part 4, 584–586; W.E. Wailes, *Official Records*, Series 1, Vol. 30, Part 4, 585; W.W. Mackall, *Official Records*, Series 1, Vol. 30, Part 4, 584; Thomas Connelly, *Autumn of Glory: The Army of Tennessee 1862-1865* (Baton Rouge: Louisiana State University Press, 1971), 171; John Fleming, Letter—August 28, 1863; Lawry C. Edwards, "Confederate Cavalry At Chickamauga: What Went Wrong," Master's Thesis, U.S. Army Command and General Staff College, Fort Leavenworth, Kansas, 1990, 124–125; George Wm. Brent, *Official Records*, Series 1, Vol. 30, Part 4, 579; Kinloch Falconer, *Official Records*, Series 1, Vol. 30, Part 3, 580; Braxton Bragg, *Official Records*, Series 1, Vol. 30, Part 4, 583–584; William W. Mackall, *Official Records*, Series 1, Vol. 30, Part 4, 584; Peter Cozzens, *This Terrible Sound: The Battle of Chickamauga* (Urbana and Chicago: University of Illinois Press, 1992), 45; Doyle D. Broome, "Intelligence Operations of The Army of The Cumberland During The Tullahoma And Chickamauga Campaigns," Master's Thesis, U.S. Army Command and General Staff College, Leavenworth, KS., 1989, 73.

37. George L. Hartsuff, *Official Records*, Series 1, Vol. 30, Part 3, 319; Robert Minty, *Official Records*, Series 1, Vol. 30, Part 3, 306–307, 316–317; *Rome Tri-Weekly Courier*, "Summary of the Latest News," September 3, 1863, p. 2; *Alexandria Gazette*, "Gen. Burnside Telegraphs," September 5, 1863, p. 4. Col. 2; Journal of the 4th Michigan Cavalry, September 2, 1863; John McLain, Diary, September 2, 1863.

38. J.A. Garfield, *Official Records*, Series 1, Vol. 30, Part 3, 322–323.

39. Alexander McCook, *Official Records*, Series 1, Vol. 30, Part 3, 345–346; Silas Stevens Folder 10.

40. George Crook, *Official Records*, Series 1, Vol. 30, Part 1, 917–918; W.L. Curry, *Four Years in the Saddle: History of First Regiment Ohio Volunteer Cavalry* (Columbus: Champlin Printing Co., 1898), 108–109; William Sinclair, *Official Records*, Series 1, Vol. 30, Part 3, 375; David Stanley, *Official Records*, Series 1, Vol. 30, Part 3, 374.

41. Frank S. Bond, *Official Records*, Series 1, Vol. 30, Part 3, 444; W.S. Rosecrans, *Official Records*, Series 1, Vol. 30, Part 3, 442; Edward Summers, Letter to Arthur Johnson, November 2, 1863, Edward Summers Letter, MS 2714, Special Collections, University of Tennessee, Knoxville.

42. G.W. Baum, Diary entry, September 8, 1863, 52; David Stanley, *Official Records*, Series 1, Volume 30, Part 3, 468; Edward McCook, National Archives, Letter—September 7, 1863, Record Group 393, Part 2, Number 2527, Correspondence; I.R. Conwell, Diary entry, September 8, 1863; Henry Mortimer Hempstead, Diary entries, September 7–8, 1863; Daniel Prickitt diary, September 8, 1863, ed. Edwin Stoltz, Bowling Green State University; Julius Thomas Diary, September 8, 1863, Julius E. Thomas Diary, 1863–1864, Julius E. Thomas Collection, MS.2720, University of Tennessee, Knoxville; Edward McCook, Orders—September 7, 1863, RG 393, Number 2527, Letters Sent First Cavalry Division, National Archives; Peter Williamson, Letter to Wife, September 7, 1863; John Allan Wyeth, *Life of General Nathan Bedford Forrest* (New York and London: Harper & Brothers Publishers, 1899), 238–239; W.B. Corbitt, September 8, 1863, Subseries 1.1 Civil War-era documents, 1860–1865, Box 2, Folder 37 Manuscript, Archives, and Rare Book Library, Emory University; David A. Powell, *Failure in the Saddle* (New York and California: Savas Beatie, 2010), 54; David Powell, *The Chickamauga Campaign: A Mad Irregular Battle* (El Dorado Hills, CA: Savas Beatie, 2014), 108, 131; Walter Brian Cisco, *States Rights Gist: A South Carolina General of the Civil War* (Gretna, LA: Pelican Publishing, 2008), 96; William Rosecrans, *Official Records*, Series 1, Vol. 30, Part 3, 467–468; David Stanley, Telegrams sent August 28–31, Telegrams Sent by Chief of Cavalry, RG 393, Entry 2463, National Archives; Henry Mortimer Hempstead, Diary entries, September 7–8, 1863; William Rosecrans, *Official Records*, Series 1, Vol. 30, Part 3, 467–468; David Stanley, Telegrams sent August 28–31, Telegrams Sent by Chief of Cavalry, RG 393, Entry 2463, National Archives.

43. Benjamin Nourse, Diary, September 8, 1863.

44. James Negley, *Official Records*, Series 1, Vol. 30, Part 3, 446, 447–449; James Garfield, *Official Records*, Series 1, Vol. 30, Part 3, 451, 468–469; William H. Sinclair, *Official Records*, Series 1, Vol. 30, Part 3, 469–470; Edward McCook, *Official Records*, Series 1, Vol. 30, Part 3, 469; G.P. Thruston, *Official Records*, Series 1, Vol. 30, Part 3, 452.

45. N.B. Forrest, *Official Records*, Series 1, Vol. 30, Part 4, 628; E.S. Burford, *Official Records*, Series 1, Vol. 30, Part 4, 627; Archer Anderson, *Official Records*, Series 1, Vol. 30, Part 4, 627; George Brent, *Official Records*, Series 1, Vol. 30, Part 3, 627; Joseph Freeman, Letter, Freeman to his sister, September 16, 1863, MS.0806, Special Collections, University of Tennessee, Knoxville; Thomas B. Wilson, "Reminiscences," 1904, Collection Number: 01736-z, The Southern Historical Collection at the Louis Round Wilson Special Collections Library, University of North Carolina, p. 57.

46. George Crook, *Official Records*, Series 1, Vol. 30, Part 1, 917–918; Robert Mitchell, *Official Records*, Series 1, Vol. 30, Part 1, 891–892; G.W. Baum, Diary entry, September 9, 1863; Elijah Watts, "Chickamauga Campaign" (hand written account, undated), Watts, Elijah S., Papers. 1861–1907,

Mss./A/W349; John W. Rowell, *Yankee Cavalrymen* (Knoxville: University of Tennessee Press, 1971), 143; Thomas Crofts, *History of the Service of the Third Ohio Veteran Volunteer Cavalry* (Toledo: Stoneman Press, 1910), 112; Nancy Pape-Findley, *The Invincibles: The Story of Fourth Ohio Veteran Volunteer Cavalry* (Tecumseh, Michigan; Blood Road Publishing: 2002), 158; Robert Merrill, Diary, September 9, 1863, *Robert Sidney Merrill, Co. K. 1st Wis. Cav.* (Cedarsburg, WI.: MSG Publishing, 1995).

47. Elijah Watts, "Chickamauga Campaign."

48. John Nourse, Letter written between September 7 and 26, 1863; Eli Long, *Official Records*, Series 1, Vol. 30, Part 1, 927; Benjamin Nourse, Diary, September 9, 1863.

49. David S. Stanley, *Official Records*, Series 1, Vol. 30, Part 1, 887–888; Julius Thomas, Diary, September 9, 1863; D.G. Reed, *Official Records*, Series 1, Vol. 30, Part 1, 889; David Powell, *The Chickamauga Campaign: A Mad Irregular Battle*, 138–139; David Powell, *Failure in the Saddle*, 71; Thomas W. Cutrer, *Our Trust is in the God of Battles: The Civil War Letters of Robert Franklin Bunting, Chaplain, Terry's Texas Rangers* (Knoxville: University of Tennessee Press, 2006), 196; Benjamin Nourse, Diary, September 9, 1863.

50. David Stanley, *Official Records*, Series 1, Vol. 30, Part 1, 889; W.B. Corbitt, Diary, September 10–11, 1863; Frank Vogel, "Diary of Frank Vogel," Frank L. Vogel Collection, MS 67-111: Accession Box 12 Folder 6, Archives of Michigan, Michigan Historical Center, Lansing, Michigan, p. 5; Benjamin Nourse, Diary, September 10, 1863.

51. Peter Cozzens, *This Terrible Sound*, 66–67; Henry Halleck, *Official Records*, Series 1, Vol. 30, Part 3, 530; William Palmer, *Official Records*, Series 1, Vol. 30, Part 3, 532–33; Smith Atkins, *Official Records*, Series 1, Vol. 30, Part 3, 538; James Garfield, *Official Records*, Series 1, Vol. 30, Part 3, 539–541; George Thomas, *Official Records*, Series 1, Vol. 30, Part 3, 538–539; Alexander McCook, *Official Records*, Series 1, Vol. 30, Part 3, 539; Thomas Crittenden, *Official Records*, Series 1, Vol. 30, Part 3, 545; Robert E. Harbison, "Wilder's Brigade in the Tullahoma and Chattanooga Campaigns of the American Civil War," Master's Thesis, U.S. Army Command and General Staff College, Fort Leavenworth, Kansas, 2002, p. 60.

52. Joseph Wheeler, *Official Records*, Series 1, Vol. 30, Part 4, 636.

53. James Garfield, *Official Records*, Series 1, Vol. 30, Part 3, 551; Alexander McCook, *Official Records*, Series 1, Vol. 30, Part 3, 551; Benjamin Nourse, Diary, September 11, 1863.

54. George Crook, *Official Records*, Series 1, Vol. 30, Part 3, 552–553; Edward McCook, *Official Records*, Series 1, Vol. 30, Part 3, 552.

55. Edward McCook, *Official Records*, Series 1, Vol. 30, Part 3, 569; *Rome Tri-Weekly Courier*, "From the Front," September 12, 1863, p. 2; George Thomas, *Official Records*, Series 1, Vol. 30, Part 3, 563–564.

56. James Garfield, *Official Records*, Series 1, Vol. 30, Part 3, 577; C. Goddard, *Official Records*, Series 1, Vol. 30, Part 3, 574; John Wilder, *Official Records*, Series 1, Vol. 30, Part 3, 575; Thomas L. Crittenden, *Official Records*, Series 1, Vol. 30, Part 3, 575; Journal of the 4th Michigan Cavalry, September 10, 1863, National Archives and Records Administration.

57. Thomas Crittenden, *Official Records*, Series 1, Vol. 30, Part 3, 577–578; Robert E. Harbison, "Wilder's Brigade in the Tullahoma and Chattanooga Campaigns of the American Civil War," pp. 60–61; William Sylvester Dillon, Diary, September 12–13, 1863, Dillon Diary, Small Manuscripts, Archives and Special Collections, J.D. Williams Library, The University of Mississippi; Thomas W. Davis, "The Civil War Diary of Thomas W. Davis," Chattanooga—Hamilton County Bicentennial Library, Chattanooga.

58. Peter Cozzens, *This Terrible Sound*, 82–85; George Brent, *Official Records*, Series 1, Volume 30, Part 2, 50; Steven E. Woodworth, *Six Armies in Tennessee: The Chickamauga and Chattanooga Campaigns* (Lincoln and London: University of Nebraska Press, 1998), 75–76; David Powell, *The Chickamauga Campaign: A Mad Irregular Battle*, 200–201.

59. C. Goddard, *Official Records*, Series 1, Vol. 30, Part 3, 590; Robert Minty, *Official Records*, Series 1, Vol. 30, Part 3, 590.

60. Silas Stevens, Letter, Folder 10; Benjamin Nourse, Diary, September 12.

61. David Stanley, *Official Records*, Series 1, Vol. 30, Part 3, 589; Robert Mitchell, *Official Records*, Series 1, Vol. 30, Part 1, 892; Edward McCook, *Official Records*, Series 1, Vol. 30, Part 1, 895–896; Archibald Campbell, *Official Records*, Series 1, Vol. 30, Part 1, 899–900; Leonidas S. Scranton, *Official Records*, Series 1, Vol. 30, Part 1, 901–902; Roswell Russell, *Official Records*, Series 1, Vol. 30, Part 1, 903–904; David Briggs, *Official Records*, Series 1, Vol. 30, Part 1, 908–909; G.W. Baum, Diary entry, September 12, 1863.

62. J.R. Fitch, *Official Records*, Series 1, Vol. 30, Part 3, 598; George Thomas, *Official Records*, Series 1, Vol. 30, Part 3, 598.

63. Alexander McCook, *Official Records*, Series 1, Vol. 30, Part 3, 598–600, 603–604.

64. Edward McCook, *Official Records*, Series 1, Vol. 30, Part 3, 616 and Part 1, 895; G.W. Baum, Diary entry, September 13; David Powell, *Failure in the Saddle*, 79–80; David Powell, *The Chickamauga Campaign: A Mad Irregular Battle*, 207; William Sinclair, *Official Records*, Series 1, Vol. 30, Part 3, 615–616.

65. George Crook, *Official Records*, Series 1, Vol. 30, Part 1, 918; Robert Mitchell, *Official Records*, Series 1, Vol. 30, Part 1, 892; Elijah Watts, "Chickamauga Campaign"; Thomas Crofts, *History of the Service of the Third Ohio Veteran Volunteer Cavalry*, 112; Benjamin Nourse, Diary, September 13, 1863; James Thompson, Diary entry, James Thomson Papers. 1861–1865 (VFM 2167) Ohio Historical Society, Columbus, Ohio.

66. George Crook, *Official Records*, Series 1, Vol. 30, Part 1, 918; Leonidas Scranton, *Official Records*,

Series 1, Vol. 30, Part 1, 901–902; Archibald Campbell, *Official Records*, Series 1, Vol. 30, Part 1, 899–900; David Powell, *The Chickamauga Campaign: A Mad Irregular Battle*, 208.

67. Benjamin Nourse, Diary, September 13, 1863.

68. P.P. Oldershaw, *Official Records*, Series 1, Vol. 30, Part 3, 608; C. Goddard, *Official Records*, Series 1, Vol. 30, Part 3, 607; James A. Garfield, *Official Records*, Series 1, Vol. 30, Part 3, 613.

69. John Wilder, *Official Records*, Series 1, Vol. 30, Part 3, 609; J.C. Van Duzer, *Official Records*, Series 1, Vol. 30, Part 3, 596; Thomas L. Crittenden, *Official Records*, Series 1, Vol. 30, Part 3, 609; John McLain, Diary, September 13, 1863.

70. George W. Brent, Journal—September 15, 1863, William Palmer Collection of Braxton Bragg Papers, Western Reserve Historical Society, Cleveland; Peter Cozzens, *This Terrible Sound*, 86; Thomas Connelly, *Autumn of Glory*, 189; D.H. Hill, *Official Records*, Series 1, Vol. 30, Part 2, 139; John Randolph Poole, *Cracker Cavaliers*, 86; W.B. Corbitt, Diary entry, September 14, 1863; D.H. Hill, "Chickamauga-The Great Battle of the West," *Century*, Vol. 33, No. 6 (April, 1887), pp. 944–945; W.L. Curry, *Four Years in the Saddle*, 110; W.M. Polk, "General Bragg and the Chickamauga Campaign," *Southern Historical Society Papers*, Vol. 12, January–December 1884, 378–390, pp. 381–383; Steven E. Woodworth, *Six Armies in Tennessee: The Chickamauga and Chattanooga Campaigns*, 77.

71. George Flynt, *Official Records*, Series 1, Vol. 30, Part 3, 625; J.J. Reynolds, *Official Records*, Series 1, Vol. 30, Part 3, 625; George Thomas, *Official Records*, Series 1, Vol. 30, Part 3, 624; J.M. Connell, *Official Records*, Series 1, Vol. 30, Part 3, 625–626; Samuel Bachtell, *Official Records*, Series 1, Vol. 30, Part 3, 623; George Brent, *Official Records*, Series 1, Vol. 30, Part 3, 624; James Garfield, *Official Records*, Series 1, Vol. 30, Part 3, 628–629; Alexander McCook, *Official Records*, Series 1, Vol. 30, Part 3, 627–628; Thomas Speed, *Union Regiments of Kentucky*, Volume I (Louisville: The Courier Journal Job Printing, Co., 1897), 122–123.

Henry Mortimer Hempstead, Diary entry, September 15, 1863; Elijah Watts, "The Chickamauga Campaign"; Roberts Burns, Letter, September 17, 1863, Robert Burns Letterbook, MSS M642, Minnesota Historical Society, St. Paul, MN; James Garfield, *Official Records*, Series 1, Vol. 30, Part 3, 628–629; Alexander McCook, *Official Records*, Series 1, Vol. 30, Part 3, 627–628.

72. James Garfield, *Official Records*, Series 1, Vol. 30, Part 3, 633; Gordon Granger, *Official Records*, Series 1, Vol. 30, Part 3, 631; Thomas Crittenden, *Official Records*, Series 1, Vol. 30, Part 3, 631–632; Robert Minty, *Official Records*, Series 1, Vol. 30, Part 1, 922; Robert E. Harbison, "Wilder's Brigade in the Tullahoma and Chattanooga Campaigns of the American Civil War," 64–65.

73. David Stanley, *Official Records*, Series 1, Vol. 30, Part 3, 637; Edward McCook, *Official Records*, Series 1, Vol. 30, Part 3, 637; Robert Mitchell, *Official Records*, Series 1, Vol. 30, Part 1, 890; Edward

McCook, *Official Records*, Series 1, Vol. 30, Part 1, 895–896; Archibald Campbell, *Official Records*, Series 1, Vol. 30, Part 1, 899; Jonathan Pratt, *Official Records*, Series 1, Vol. 30, Part 3, 637–638; William E. Crane, "William E. Crane's Daily Journal," September 15, 1863, Mss 980, Cincinnati History Library & Archives; Chesley Mosman, *The Rough Side of War: The Civil War Journal of Chesley A. Mosman*, Arnold Gates, ed. (Garden City, NY: The Basin Publishing Co., 1987), 80.

74. Gordon Granger, *Official Records*, Series 1, Vol. 30, Part 3, 651; George Wagner, *Official Records*, Series 1, Vol. 30, Part 3, 652; J.J. Reynolds, *Official Records*, Series 1, Vol. 30, Part 3, 647; George Flynt, *Official Records*, Series 1, Vol. 30, Part 3, 647; Thomas L. Crittenden, *Official Records*, Series 1, Vol. 30, Part 3, 650; Robert Minty, *Official Records*, Series 1, Vol. 30, Part 3, 650–651; W.N. Pickerill, *History of the Third Indiana Cavalry* (Indianapolis, Aetna Printing Co., 1906), 60–62.

75. Robert Minty, *Official Records*, Series 1, Vol. 30, Part 1, 922; Joseph Vale, *Minty and the Cavalry*, 217.

76. Benjamin Nourse, Diary, September 14–17, 1863; Elijah Watts, "Chickamauga Campaign."

77. John Nourse, Journal, September 15, 1863.

78. David Stanley, *Official Records*, Series 1, Vol. 30, Part 3, 652–653; P. Sidney Post, *Official Records*, Series 1, Vol. 30, Part 3, 648; G.W. Baum, Diary entry, September 15, 1863; Benjamin Nourse, Diary, September, 14–17, 1863; Elijah Watts, "Chickamauga Campaign."

79. Robert Mitchell, *Official Records*, Series 1, Vol. 30, Part 3, 653; David S. Stanley, *Official Records*, Series 1, Vol. 30, Part 3, 653; George Crook, *Official Records*, Series 1, Vol. 30, Part 3, 654–655; William H. Sinclair, *Official Records*, Series 1, Vol. 30, Part 3, 654–655; William Rosecrans, *Official Records*, Series 1, Vol. 30, Part 1, 106; William Crane, Diary, September 15, 1863.

80. Peter Cozzens, "*This Terrible Sound: The Battle of Chickamauga*," 101–103.

81. Robert Minty, *Official Records*, Series 1, Vol. 30, Part 3, 679; Thomas Crittenden, *Official Records*, Series 1, Vol. 30, Part 3, 679; Journal of the 4th Michigan Cavalry, September 16, 1863, National Archives.

82. Robert Minty, *Official Records*, Series 1, Vol. 30, Part 3, 680; Journal of the 4th Michigan Cavalry, September 16, 1863, RG 94, 4th Michigan Cavalry Regimental Books, National Archives.

83. Robert Minty, *Official Records*, Series 1, Vol. 30, Part 1, 922; Joseph Vale, "Address of Captain Joseph Vale," In *Pennsylvania at Chickamauga and Chattanooga*, George W. Skinner, editor (Harrisburg, Pennsylvania: William Stanley Ray, State Printer of Pennsylvania, 1897), 302–303; Joseph Vale, *Minty and the Cavalry*, 220.

84. Kinloch Falconer, *Official Records*, Series 1, Vol. 30, Part 4, 660; W.F. Mastin, *Official Records*, Series 1, Vol. 30, Part 4, 658; Thomas Connelly, *Autumn of Glory*, 193.

85. Thomas Crittenden, *Official Records*, Series

1, Vol. 30, Part 3, 708–709; Thomas Wood, *Official Records*, Series 1, Vol. 30, Part 3, 710–711; William Fuller, *Official Records*, Series 1, Vol. 30, Part 3, 701; J.C. Van Duzer, *Official Records*, Series 1, Vol. 30, Part 3, 701; James Garfield, *Official Records*, Series 1, Vol. 30, Part 3, 711.

86. Thomas Wood, *Official Records*, Series 1, Vol. 30, Part 3, 712; Robert Minty's, *Official Records*, Series 1, Vol. 30, Part 1, 922; Robert Minty, *Official Records*, Series 1, Vol. 30, Part 3, pp. 709–710; Journal of the 4th Michigan Cavalry, September 16, 1863; Robert Burns, September 17, 1863.

87. George H. Purdy, *Official Records*, Series 1, Vol. 30, Part 1, 910; Robert Mitchell, *Official Records*, Series 1, Vol. 30, Part 3, 716; *Official Records*, Series 1, Vol. 30, Part 1, 892–893; Edward McCook, *Official Records*, Series 1, Vol. 30, Part 1, 895, 898; Edward McCook, *Official Records*, Series 1, Vol. 30, Part 3, 716–717; Archibald Campbell, *Official Records*, Series 1, Vol. 30, Part 1, 899; George Brent, *Official Records*, Series 1, Vol. 30, Part 4, 662.

Chapter Five

1. James Larson, *Sergeant Larson, 4th Cavalry* (San Antonio: Southern Literary Institute, 1935), 179.

2. Robert Burns, Letter, October 30, 1863, Robert Burns Letterbook, MSS M642, Minnesota Historical Society, St. Paul, MN; D.H. Hill, "Chickamauga: The Great Battle of the West," In *Battles and Leaders in the Civil War, Vol. III* (New York: The Century Co., 1888), 643; Robert Minty, *Minty's Sabre Brigade: The Part They Took in the Chattanooga Campaign* (Wyandotte, MI: The Herald Steam Presses, 1892), 9; D.L. Haines, "Record of the Fourth Michigan Cavalry," Bentley Historical Library, University of Michigan; William G. Robertson, et. al, *The Staff Ride Handbook for the Battle of Chickamauga: 18–20 September 1863* (U.S. Army Command and General Staff College, Command Studies Institute, Fort Leavenworth, KS, 1992), 173.

3. Joseph Vale, *Minty and the Cavalry: A History of Cavalry Campaigns in the Western Armies* (Harrisburg, Pennsylvania: Edwin K. Myers, Printer and Binder, 1886), 221–224.

4. Peter Cozzens, *This Terrible Sound*, 89; David Powell, *Failure in the Saddle* (New York and California; Savas Beatie, 2010), 92–93.

5. Braxton Bragg, *Official Records*, Series 1, Volume 30, Part 2, 31; David Powell, *The Chickamauga Campaign: A Mad Irregular Battle* (El Dorado Hills, CA: Savas Beatie, 2014), 250–254; Newton Cannon, *The Reminiscences of Newton Cannon: First Sergeant, CSA*, Campbell Brown, editor (Franklin, TN: Carter House Association, 1963), 31–33.

6. Charles Eugene Belknap, ed., *History of the Michigan Organizations at Chickamauga, Chattanooga, and Missionary Ridge* (Lansing: Robert Smith Printing Co., 1899), 276–277.

7. Robert Minty, *Official Records*, Series 1, Volume 30, Part 1, 923; David Powell, *Failure in the Saddle*, 2010), 104; *Obituary Record of the Graduates of Yale University, Deceased from June 1910, to July 1915* (New Haven: Yale University Press, 1915), 40–43; William G. Robertson, et. al., *The Staff Ride Handbook for the Battle of Chickamauga*, 173; Joseph Vale, *Minty and the Cavalry*, 224.

8. Robert Burns, Letter—October 30, 1863; John McLain, Diary entry, September 18, 1863, John McLain, Papers (c.00111), Michigan State University Archives & Historical Collections, East Lansing, Michigan; Robert Minty, *Official Records*, Series 1, Volume 30, Part 1, 923; David Powell, *Failure in the Saddle*, 104; *Obituary Record of the Graduates of Yale University, Deceased from June 1910, to July 1915* (New Haven: Yale University Press, 1915), 40–43; William G. Robertson, et. al., *The Staff Ride Handbook for the Battle of Chickamauga*, 173; David Powell, *The Chickamauga Campaign: A Mad Irregular Battle*, 253, 257–258.

9. James Larson, *Sergeant Larson, 4th Cavalry*, 174–176.

10. David Powell, *Failure in the Saddle*, 96; Thomas Franklin Berry, *Four Years with Morgan and Forrest* (Oklahoma City: Harlow-Ratliff Company, 1914), 235; David Powell, *Failure in the Saddle*, 100–104; Mike West, "Like the Army of Tennessee, Bushrod Johnson Faced Both Glory, Despair," *Murfreesboro Post*, November 9, 2008; James W. Rabb, *Confederate General Lloyd Tilghman* (Jefferson, NC: McFarland and Co., Publishers, 2006), 68.

11. Robert Minty, *Official Records*, Series 1, Volume 30, Part 1, 923; T.F. Dornblaser, *Sabre Strokes of the Pennsylvania Dragoons* (Philadelphia: Lutheran Publication Society, 1884), 131–132; David Powell, *Failure in the Saddle*, 104–105; Trumbull D. Griffin, Typeset document, B241, Papers of Trumbull Dorrance Griffin (ca. 1836–1912), 1862–1911, Missouri Historical Museum, St. Louis, MO; Joseph Vale, *Minty and the Cavalry*, 225.

12. Robert Minty, *Official Records*, Series 1, Volume 30, Part 1, 923; T.F. Dornblaser, *Sabre Strokes of the Pennsylvania Dragoons* (Philadelphia: Lutheran Publication Society, 1884), 131–132; David Powell, *Failure in the Saddle*, 104–105; Journal of 4th Michigan, September 18, 1863, RG 94, National Archives and Records Administration; Robert Minty, "Minty's Sabre Brigade: Chickamauga," *National Tribune*, U.S. Army Heritage and Education Center; Robert Burns, Letter to Davidson, Oct. 20, 1863; "Frank Knight," *The Index-Journal* (Greenwood, South Carolina), June 16, 1922, p. 3.

13. Robert Minty, "The Fourth Michigan Cavalry," In *History of the Michigan Organizations at Chickamauga, Chattanooga, and Missionary Ridge*, Charles Eugene Belknap, ed. (Lansing: Robert Smith Printing Co., 1899), 91; Robert Minty, "Minty's Saber Brigade: Chickamauga," *National Tribune*, March 3, 1892; Robert E. Harbison, "Wilder's Brigade in the Tullahoma and Chattanooga Campaigns of the American Civil War," Master's Thesis, U.S. Army Command and General Staff College, Fort Leavenworth, Kansas, 2002, 70–71; Peter Cozzens, *This Terrible Sound*, 104; Robert Minty,

Official Records, Series 1, Volume 30, Part 1, 923; Henry Campbell, Diary entry, September 18, 1863, *Three Years in the Saddle: A Diary of the Civil War*, Unpublished (n.d.), Wabash College, Crawfordsville, Indiana.

14. James Larson, *Sergeant Larson, 4th Cavalry*, 177–178.

15. Robert Minty, "The Fourth Michigan Cavalry," 91; Robert Minty, *Official Records*, Series 1, Volume 30, Part 1, 923; David Powell, *The Chickamauga Campaign: A Mad Irregular Battle*, 262–265; Joseph Vale, *Minty and the Cavalry: A History of Cavalry Campaigns in the Western Armies* (Harrisburg, Pennsylvania: Edwin K. Myers, Printer and Binder, 1886), 227; Henry Albert Potter, Diary entry, September 18, 1863, MS 91–480 Henry Albert Potter Collection, Accession Box 461 Folder 2, Archives of Michigan, Michigan History Center; Joseph Vale, *Minty and the Cavalry*, 222, 226- 227; R.B. Robbins, "At Reed's Bridge," *National Tribune*, November 14, 1895; "Chickamauga Battlefield," *The Abbeville Press and Banner*, September 04, 1895, p. 1, col. 7; Undated letter by Sylvanus H. Stevens to Edgar D. Swain, Chickamauga and Chattanooga National Military Park; Robert Minty, "Minty's Saber Brigade: Chickamauga," *National Tribune*.

16. James Larson, *Sergeant Larson*, 179; Charles Greeno, "Address of Lieut.-Col. Charles L. Greeno," In *Pennsylvania at Chickamauga and Chattanooga*, George W. Skinner, editor (William Stanley Ray, State Printer of Pennsylvania, 1897), 314.

17. Robert Minty, "The Fourth Michigan Cavalry," 91; Joseph Vale, *Minty and the Cavalry*, 227; Robert Minty, *Official Records*, Series 1, Volume 30, Part 1, 923; David Powell, *Failure in the Saddle*, 107; Charles Gatewood, *Lt. Charles Gatewood and His Apache Wars Memoir*, Louis Kraft, ed. (Lincoln: University of Nebraska Press, 2005), 214.

18. John McLain, Diary, September 18, 1863; David Powell, *Failure in the Saddle*, 109; David Powell, *The Chickamauga Campaign: A Mad Irregular Battle*, 264; Joseph Vale, *Minty and the Cavalry*, 227; George F. Steahlin, "Address and Historical Sketch," In *Pennsylvania at Chickamauga and Chattanooga*, George W. Skinner, editor (Harrisburg, Pennsylvania: William Stanley Ray, State Printer of Pennsylvania, 1897), 310.

19. Robert Burns, Letter, letter October 30, 1863; Joseph Vale, "Address of Captain Joseph Vale," In *Pennsylvania at Chickamauga and Chattanooga*, George W. Skinner, editor (Harrisburg, Pennsylvania: William Stanley Ray, State Printer of Pennsylvania, 1897), 304; Robert Minty, *Official Records*, Series 1, Volume 30, Part 1, 923; Undated letter by Sylvanus H. Stevens to Edgar D. Swain.

20. Robert Burns, Letter—October 30, 1863; Joseph Vale, *Minty and the Cavalry* 229–230; Charles Eugene Belknap, *History of the Michigan Organizations at Chickamauga*, 278; Robert Minty, "Minty's Saber Brigade, The Part They Took in the Chattanooga Campaign," *National Tribune*, March 3, 1892; Ethan Rafuse, "In the Shadow of the Rock: Thomas L. Crittenden, Alexander M. McCook, and the 1863 Campaigns for Middle and East Tennessee," In *The Chickamauga Campaign*, Steven E. Woodworth, ed. (Carbondale and Edwardsville: Southern Illinois University Press, 2010), 21; John Wilder, *Official Records*, Series 1, Volume 30, Part 3, 724–725; Charles Eugene Belknap, *History of the Michigan Organizations at Chickamauga*, 278; Robert Burns, Letter, October 30, 1863; Joseph Vale, *Minty and the Cavalry*, 229–230.

21. Joseph Vale, *Minty and the Cavalry*, 230; Abram Miller, *Official Records*, Series 1, Volume 30, Part 1, 464–465; Bushrod Johnson, *Official Records*, Series 1, Volume 30, Part 1, 452–453; Thomas Wood, *Official Records*, Series 1, Volume 30, Part 3, 728; David Powell, *The Chickamauga Campaign: A Mad Irregular Battle*, 297.

22. George F. Steahlin, "Address and Historical Sketch," 310; Robert Burns, Letter—October 30, 1863; James R Carnahan, "Personal Recollections of Chickamauga" In *Sketches of War History: 1861–1865*, Vol. I Ohio, MOLLUS (Cincinnati, Robert Clarke & Co. 1888), 407; Henry Campbell, Diary entry, September 18, 1863, *Three Years in the Saddle: A Diary of the Civil War*; Israel Webster, "Chickamauga: Going into Action with Hands Full of Bacon and Coffee," *National Tribune*, July 2, 1891; George Dick, *Official Records*, Series 1, Volume 30, Part 1, 822–823.

23. Clement Evans, *Confederate Military History*, Volume IV (Atlanta: Confederate Publishing Co., 1899), 247–248.

24. James Garfield, *Official Records*, Series 1, Volume 30, Part 1, 73; C. Goodard, *Official Records*, Series 1, Volume 30, Part 1, 76; Charles Eugene Belknap, ed., *History of the Michigan Organizations at Chickamauga, Chattanooga, and Missionary Ridge* (Lansing, Robert Smith Printing Co., 1899), 94; C. Goddard, Sept. 19 Orders, Letters and Orders Received by Chief of Cavalry, RG 393, Entry 2469, National Archives and Records Administration; Robert Mitchell, *Official Records*, Series 1, Volume 30, Part 3, 744–745; James Garfield, *Official Records*, Series 1, Volume 30, Part 3, 741.

25. Joseph Vale, "Address of Captain Joseph Vale," In *Pennsylvania at Chickamauga and Chattanooga*, George W. Skinner, editor (Harrisburg, Pennsylvania: William Stanley Ray, State Printer of Pennsylvania, 1897), 307; George F. Steahlin, "Address and Historical Sketch," p. 310; Joseph Vale, *Minty and the Cavalry*, 235; Henry Albert Potter, Diary, September 20, 1863; Stirling D. Popejoy, "The Second Tennessee Cavalry in the American Civil War," Master's Thesis, 2014, U.S. Army Command and General Staff College, Fort Leavenworth, KS, 61; Robert Minty, *Official Records*, Series 1, Volume 30, Part 1, 923–924; John McLain, Diary entry, September 20, 1863, McLain Papers (c.00111), Michigan State University Archives & Historical Collections, East Lansing.

26. Joseph Vale, *Minty and the Cavalry* 240; Robert Minty, "The Fourth Michigan Cavalry," Charles Eugene Belknap, ed., In *History of the Michigan*

Organizations at Chickamauga, Chattanooga, and Missionary Ridge (Lansing: Robert Smith Printing Co., 1899), 95; David A. Powell, *The Chickamauga Campaign—Barren Victory*, 10; Richard Robbins, "Reminiscences," Richard Robbins Papers, Bentley Historical Library, University of Michigan; Journal of 4th Michigan Cavalry, September 21, 1863, National Archives.

27. Robert Minty, *Official Records*, Series 1, Volume 30, Part 1, 151–152, 924; Richard Robbins, "Reminiscences"; George Thomas, *Official Records*, Series 1, Volume 30, Part 1, 254; Joseph Vale, "Address of Captain Joseph Vale," In *Pennsylvania at Chickamauga and Chattanooga*, George W. Skinner, editor (Harrisburg, Pennsylvania: William Stanley Ray, State Printer of Pennsylvania, 1897), 308; George F. Steahlin, "Address and Historical Sketch," 311; Robert Burns, Letter, October 30, 1863; Joseph Vale, *Minty and the Cavalry*, 235; John Watson Morton, *The Artillery of Nathan Bedford Forrest's Cavalry* (Nashville, Tennessee and Dallas, Texas: Publishing House of the M.E. Church, 1909), 126; David A. Powell, *The Chickamauga Campaign—Barren Victory*, 14–15; Mamie Yeary, *Reminiscences of the Boys in Gray* (Smith and Lamar Publishing House: Dallas, 1912), 547.

28. Minty, *Ibid.*; Vale, *Ibid.*, Richard Robbins, "Reminiscences"; Michael Bower Cavender, *The First Georgia Cavalry in the Civil War: A History and Roster* (Jefferson, NC: McFarland and Company Publishing, 2016), 77; Eddy W. Davison and Daniel Foxx, *Nathan Bedford Forest: In Search of the Enigma* (Gretna, LA: Pelican Publishing Company, 2007), 172.

29. Robert Minty, "The Fourth Michigan Cavalry," 95; Robert Minty, *Official Records*, Series 1, Volume 30, Part 1, 924; Richard Robbins, "Reminiscences"; George Thomas, *Official Records*, Series 1, Volume 30, Part 1, 255; Terry H. Cahal, Letters, September 30, 1863, Confederate Collection, Box 8, Folder 17, Tennessee State Library and Archives; Robert Burns, Letter October 30, 1863; Glenn Tucker, *Chickamauga: Bloody Battle in the West* (Dayton, OH: Press of Morningside Bookshop, 1984), 374–375.

30. Richard Robbins, "Reminiscences"; Robert Burns, Letter—October 30, 1863; Robert Merrill Diary, September 23, 1863; August Yenner, Diary entry, September 27, 1863, Augustus L. Yenner, 1837–1924, Papers, Western Michigan University, Kalamazoo, Michigan; C. Goddard, *Official Records*, Series 1, Volume 30, Part 1, 166–167; John L. Herberich, *Masters of the Field: The Fourth United States Cavalry in the Civil War* (Atglen, PA; Schiffer Publishing Co., 2015), 128.

31. Benjamin T. Smith, *Private Smith's Journal: Recollections of the Late War,* Clyde C. Walton ed. (Chicago: R.R. Donnelley & Sons Company, 1963), 89–90; John W. DuBose, *General Joseph Wheeler and the Army of Tennessee* (New York: The Neale Publishing Co., 1912), 199; Nathan Forrest, *Official Records*, Series 1, Volume 30, Part 2, 524.

32. Henry Hempstead, Diary entry, September 19, 1863; Julius Thomas Diary entry, September 19, 1863; Thomas Harrison, *Official Records*, Series 1, Volume 30, Part 1, 548; John A. Nourse, Letter to parents, September 23, 1863, John A. Nourse papers, 1862–1922, Chicago History Museum; John W. Rowell, *Yankee Cavalrymen* (Knoxville: University of Tennessee Press, 1971), 145; Henry Mortimer Hempstead, Diary entry, September 19, 1863, Hempstead, Henry Mortimer, 1832–1916, Papers, Bentley Historical Library, University of Michigan, Ann Arbor.

33. James A. Garfield, *Official Records*, Series 1, Volume 30, Part 1, 68, 76, 963; J.R. Hayden, *Official Records*, Series 1, Volume 30, Part 1, 344.

34. Elijah Watts, "Chickamauga Campaign" (hand written account, undated), Watts, Elijah S., Papers. 1861–1907, Mss./A/W349, Filson Historical Society; John W. Rowell, *Yankee Cavalrymen*, 145; Archibald Campbell, *Official Records*, Series 1, Volume 30, Part 1, 899–900; Edward McCook, *Official Records*, Series 1, Volume 30, Part 1, 895–896; Frank S. Bond, *Official Records*, Series 1, Volume 30, Part 3, 743; Eli Long, *Official Records*, Series 1, Volume 30, Part 1, 927; Robert Minty, *Official Records*, Series 1, Volume 30, Part 3, 744.

35. Robert Mitchell, *Official Records*, Series 1, Volume 30, Part 3, 743; Robert Mitchell, *Official Records*, Series 1, Volume 30, Part 1, 893; George Crook, *Official Records*, Series 1, Volume 30, Part 1, 919; William T. Hoblitzell Court Martial, July 1864, Record Group (RG) 153, Adjutant General's Office, Court Martial Case Files, 1809–1854, Case Number NN-2774, National Archives, Washington, D.C.

36. John Andes and Will McTeer, *Loyal Mountain Troopers: The Second and Third Tennessee Volunteer Cavalry in the Civil War* (Maryville, Tennessee: Blount County Genealogical and Historical Society, 1992), 65; Benjamin T. Smith, *Private Smith's Journal: Recollections of the Late War*, 90–91; Edward McCook, *Official Records*, Series 1, Volume 30, Part 1, 894; Thomas McCahan, Diary, September 19, 1863, Thomas McCahan Papers (Am. 6092) Historical Society of Pennsylvania, Philadelphia.

37. Henry Hempstead, Diary entry, September 19, 1863; Leonidas Scranton, *Official Records*, Series 1, Volume 30, Part 1, 901–902; Joseph Wheeler, *Official Records*, Series 1, Volume 30, Part 2, 520; Archibald Campbell; *Official Records*, Series 1, Volume 30, Part 1, 900; David A. Powell, *The Chickamauga Campaign—Glory or the Grave: The Breakthrough, the Union Retreat to Chattanooga* (Eldorado Hills, CA: Savas Beatie, 2015), 26.

38. David A. Powell, *The Chickamauga Campaign—Glory or the Grave*, 27, 35; Benjamin Nourse, Diary, September 19, 1863.

39. Edward McCook, *Official Records*, Series 1, Volume 30, Part 1, 896; G.W. Baum, Diary entry, September 20, 1863; Edward McCook, Archibald Campbell, Daniel Ray, Louis Watkins, George Crook, Eli Long Reports, *Official Records*, Series 1, Volume 30, Part 1, 895–926; Archibald Campbell, *Official Records*, Series 1, Volume 30, Part 1, 900; William G. Robertson, et. al, *The Staff Ride*

Handbook for the Battle of Chickamauga: 18–20 September 1863 (U.S. Army Command and General Staff College, Command Studies Institute, Fort Leavenworth, KS, 1992), 176.

40. Ed Porter Thompson, *History of the Orphan Brigade* (Louisville, KY.: Lewis N. Thompson, 1898), 212; Joseph Wheeler, *Official Records*, Series 1, Volume 30, Part 2, 520; George Kryder, Letter to wife, September 25,1863, MS 163 George Kryder (1834–1925), Letters, 1862–1865; Edward McCook, Archibald Campbell, Daniel Ray, Louis Watkins, George Crook, Eli Long Reports, *Official Records*, Series 1, Volume 30, Part 1, 895–926.

41. David Rubenstein, "A Study of the Medical Support to the Union and Confederate Armies During the Battle of Chickamauga: Lessons and Implications for Today's U.S. Army Medical Department Leaders," Master's Thesis, U.S. Army Command and General Staff College, Fort Leavenworth, KS, 1990.

42. Henry Mortimer Hempstead, Diary, September 20, 1863; Thomas Colman, Letter October 5, 1863, Colman-Hayter Family Papers (C0084); The State Historical Society of Missouri Research Center-Columbia.

43. Henry Mortimer Hempstead, Diary entry, September 20, 1863; James Hagan, "3rd Alabama Cavalry," SG024911, Alabama Department of History and Archives, Montgomery; L.S. Scranton, *Official Records*, Series 1, Volume 30, Part 1, 902; Peter Cozzens, *This Terrible Sound*, 464; David Powell, *Failure in the Saddle*, 160; David A. Powell, *The Chickamauga Campaign—Glory or the Grave*, 465–469; Thomas Colman, *ibid*.

44. William E. Crane, "William E. Crane's Daily Journal of Life in the Field during the War of the Rebellion," September 20, 1863 entry, Mss. 980, Cincinnati Historical Society, Cincinnati Museum Center; Elijah Watts, "Chickamauga Campaign"; George Crook, *General George Crook: His Biography* (Norman & London: University of Oklahoma Press, 1960), 105.

45. Robert B. Mitchell, Letter September 20, Letters Sent, Chief of Cavalry, RG 393, Number 151 (2460) National Archives, Washington, D.C.; Elijah S. Watts, "Chickamauga Campaign."

46. Charles Eugene Belknap, ed., *History of the Michigan Organizations at Chickamauga, Chattanooga, and Missionary Ridge* (Lansing: Robert Smith Printing Co., 1899), 78; George Crook, *General George Crook: His Biography*, 105–107; Joseph Wheeler, *Official Records*, Series 1, Volume 30, Part 2, 521; L.S. Scranton, *Official Records*, Series 1, Volume 30, Part 1, 902; Eli Long, *Official Records*, Series 1, Volume 30, Part 1, 927; Franklin F. Moyer, Letter September 29, 1863, *Journal and Letters of Franklin F. Moyer*, Robert H. Wieser, editor (Dayton: Robert Wieser Publisher, 2008); Elijah Watts, "Chickamauga Campaign."

47. Eli Long, "Autobiography," Eli Long Papers, Civil War Collection, Box 1, USAHEC, Carlisle, Pennsylvania; Nancy Pape-Findley, *The Invincibles: The Story of Fourth Ohio Veteran Volunteer Cavalry*

(Tecumseh, Michigan; Blood Road Publishing, 2002), 162; William E. Crane, Diary, September 20, 1863; Benjamin Nourse, Diary entry, September 20, 1863; W.L. Curry, *Four Years in the Saddle: History of First Regiment Ohio Volunteer Cavalry* (Columbus: Champlin Printing Co., 1898), 111.

48. Benjamin Nourse, Diary, September 20, 1863.

49. Elijah Watts, "Chickamauga Campaign."

50. W.L. Curry, *Four Years in the Saddle*, 111; Silas Stevens, Folder 11; Nancy Pape-Findley, *The Invincibles*, 162.

51. W.L. Curry, *Four Years in the Saddle*, 111; Whitelaw Reid, *Ohio in the War: Her Statesmen, Her Generals, and Soldiers*, Volume I, 751; John Chapin, "At Chickamauga," In *Reunions of the First Ohio Volunteer Cavalry* (Columbus, Ohio: Landon Printing, Co., 1891), 15–17.

52. Henry Mortimer Hempstead, Diary, September 20, 1863; Elijah S. Watts, "Chickamauga Campaign"; David Powell, *Failure in the Saddle*, 165.

53. John Allan Wyeth, *The Life General Nathan Bedford Forrest* (New York and London: Harper and Brothers Publisher, 1899), 247; D. Coleman, Diary entry, September 20, 1863, D. Coleman Diary, 1863–1864, Collection Number: 03317-z, The Southern Historical Collection at the Louis Round Wilson Special Collections Library, University of North Carolina.

54. George Guild, *A Brief Narrative of the Fourth Tennessee Cavalry Regiment* (n.p.: Nashville, 1913), 27–28.

55. Robert Mitchell, *Official Records*, Series 1, Volume 30, Part 1, 893–894; George Kryder, Diary, September 25, 1863, MS 163 George Kryder (1834–1925), William T. Jerome Library, Bowling Green State University, Bowling Green, Ohio; David A. Powell, *Failure in the Saddle*, 160; Eli Long, "Autobiography" and "Synopsis of the Military Career of Brevet Major-General Eli Long," Eli Long Papers, Civil War Collection, Box 1, USAHEC, Carlisle, Pennsylvania; Elisha Peterson, Letter to parents September 29, 1863, Elisha Peterson manuscript, Sec. A Box 104, Rubenstein Library, Duke University; Eli Long, Letter to Ex-soldiers of OVC, Sept. 20, 1892, Long Correspondence Folder, Eli Long Papers, U.S. Army Heritage and Education Center.

56. George Crook, *General George Crook: His Biography*, 106–107; David Power, *Failure in the Saddle*, 168–169; 1st Ohio Cavalry, Morning reports. Company G, September 20, 1863, RG 94, E 112–115, National Archives, Washington, D.C.; William Crane, September 20; Leonidas S. Scranton, *Official Records*, Series 1, Vol. 30, Part 1, 901–902.

57. 1st Ohio Cavalry, Morning reports. Company G, September 20, 1863, RG 94, E 112–115, National Archives, Washington, D.C.; William Crane, September 20; George Crook, *General George Crook: His Biography*, 106; Joseph Wheeler, *Official Records*, Series 1, Volume 30, Part 2, 521; Leonidas S. Scranton, *Official Records*, Series 1, Vol. 30, Part 1, 901–902: Eli Long, *Official Records*, Series 1, Vol. 30, Part 1, 927.

58. Robert Mitchell, *Official Records*, Series 1,

Volume 30, Part 1, 893; Edward McCook, *Official Records*, Series 1, Volume 30, Part 1, 896; Roswell Russell, *Official Records*, Series 1, Volume 30, Part 1, 905; Daniel Ray, *Official Records*, Series 1, Volume 30, Part 1, 908; Michael Hendrick Fitch, *The Chattanooga Campaign*, Wisconsin History Commission (n.p.: Democrat Printing Co., State Printer March 1911), 124; John W. Rowell, *Yankee Cavalrymen*, 148; David Powell, *Failure in the Saddle*, 171; Roswell Russell, *Official Records*, Series 1, Volume 30, Part 1, 905; John Andes and Will McTeer, *Loyal Mountain Troops*, 65; Chesley Mosman, *The Rough Side of War: The Civil War Journal of Chesley A. Mosman*, Arnold Gates, ed. (Garden City, NY: The Basin Publishing Co., 1987), 84–85; Leroy S. Mayfield, "Letters and Diaries of Leroy S. Mayfield," *Indiana Magazine of History*, Vol. 39, no. 2 (June 1943): 144–91, p. 161.

59. Marshall P. Thatcher, *A Hundred Battles in the West*, 147; Archibald Campbell, *Official Records*, Series 1, Volume 30, Part 3, 754; Charles Eugene Belknap, ed., *History of the Michigan Organizations at Chickamauga* 79; George Crook, *General George Crook: His Biography*, 107; Silas Stevens, Folder 11.

60. William Sinclair, *Official Records*, Series 1, Volume 30, Part 3, 768; David A. Powell, *The Chickamauga Campaign—Barren Victory*, 8; Silas Stevens, *Ibid.*

61. John Williams, *Leaves of a Trooper's Diary* (Philadelphia: Published by Author, 1869), 69–70; Henry Mortimer Hempstead, Diary, September 21, 1863; Smith Cozens, "Company L on Lookout Mountain," In *History of the Fifteenth Pennsylvania Volunteer Cavalry*, J.C. Reiff, ed. (Philadelphia, Pennsylvania: Society of the Fifteenth Pennsylvania Cavalry, 1906), 287–291; Robert Mitchell, *Official Records*, Series 1, Volume 30, Part 1, 155, 893, 896; Edward McCook, *Official Records*, Series 1, Volume 30, Part 1, 896; Daniel Ray, *Official Records*, Series 1, Volume 30, Part 1, 907; G.W. Baum September 21, 1863, Book 10, M 674 B1 F3, Baum diaries, Indiana Historical Society, Indianapolis; George Hazzard, *Hazzard's History of Henry County, Indiana, 1822–1906*, Volume 1 (New Castle, Indiana: George Hazzard Publisher, 1906), 118; Chesley Mosman, *The Rough Side of War*, 86.

62. W.L. Curry, *Four Years in the Saddle*, 112–113.

63. Silas Stevens, Folder 11; Robert Mitchell, After action report, RG 393, Entry 960, part 3, National Archives.

64. Edward McCook, *Official Records*, Series 1, Volume 30, Part 1, 896; Charles Greeno, "Address of Lieut.-Col. Charles L. Greeno," In *Pennsylvania at Chickamauga and Chattanooga*, George W. Skinner, editor (William Stanley Ray, State Printer of Pennsylvania, 1897), 312–313; Robert Mitchell, *Official Records*, Series 1, Volume 30, Part 3, 767; James Spears, *Official Records*, Series 1, Volume 30, Part 1, 884.

65. Nancy Pape-Findley, *The Invincibles*, 164–165; *Wyandot Pioneer*, "Army Correspondence," December 25, 1863, p. 1 col 40; W.R. Carter, *History of the First Regiment of Tennessee Volunteer Cavalry*, 9; Edward McCook Report, September 30, 1863, RG 393, Number 2527, Letters Sent First Cavalry Division, National Archives; Silas Stevens, Folder 12.

66. Benjamin Nourse, Diary, September, 22, 1863; Robert Mitchell, Chickamauga after-action report, RG 393.

67. Benjamin Nourse, Diary, September 23–30; John Fleming, Letter to father, September 23, 1863, Fleming Papers, Newberry Library.

68. Robert E. Harbison, "Wilder's Brigade in the Tullahoma and Chattanooga Campaigns of the American Civil War," Master's Thesis, U.S. Army Command and General Staff College, Fort Leavenworth, Kansas, 2002, pp. 49–50, 91–93; Henry Albert Potter, Diary entry, September 24, 1863; Robert Mitchell, Abram O. Miller, *Official Records*, Series 1, Volume 30, Part 3, 804.

69. Chris Beck, *Official Records*, Series 1, Volume 30, Part 3, 833–834; Daniel Ray, *Official Records*, Series 1, Volume 30, Part 3, 952; Louis Watkins, *Official Records*, Series 1, Volume 30, Part 3, 900; W.T. Hoblitzell, *Official Records*, Series 1, Volume 30, Part 3, 920; Robert Mitchell, *Official Records*, Series 1, Volume 30, Part 3, 856–867; Silas Stevens, Folder 12; Chris Beck, *Official Records*, Series 1, Volume 30, Part 3, 833–834.

70. Robert Mitchell, *Official Records*, Series 1, Volume 30, Part 3, 836.

71. William H. Sinclair, *Official Records*, Series 1, Volume 30, Part 3, 857, 880; Joseph Wheeler, *Official Records*, Series 1, Volume 30, Part 2, 723; Edward G. Longacre, *A Soldier to the Last: Maj. Gen. Joseph Wheeler in Blue and Gray* (Washington: Potomac Books Inc., 2007), 123; *New York Times*, "Wheeler's Raid Into Tennessee," December 27, 1863; George Crook, *Official Records*, Series 1, Volume 30, Part 3, 952; Stephen Z. Starr, *The Union Cavalry in the Civil War: The War in the West*, Volume III (Baton Rouge: Louisiana State University, 2007), 292; Thomas W. Cutrer, *Our Trust is in the God of Battles: The Civil War Letters of Robert Franklin Bunting, Chaplain, Terry's Texas Rangers* (Knoxville: University of Tennessee Press, 2006), 202; William Gibbs Allen, "Memoirs," Civil War Collection (Confederate), Box 12, Folder, p. 3, Tennessee State Library and Archives, Nashville; William H. Sinclair, *Official Records*, Series 1, Volume 30, Part 3, 857, 880.

72. Lucien Wulsin, *The Fourth Regiment Ohio Veteran Volunteer Cavalry* (Cincinnati: Fourth Ohio Volunteer Cavalry Association, 1912), 38; Nancy Pape-Findley, *The Invincibles*, 171; John McLain, Diary entry, September 30, 1863, John McLain, Papers (c.00111), Michigan State University Archives & Historical Collections; W.L. Curry, *The Raid of the Confederate Cavalry through Central Tennessee, October 1863* (Columbus: The Ohio Commandery of the Loyal Legion, MOLLUS, 1908), 4–6; Thomas W. Davis, "The Civil War Diary of Thomas W. Davis," Chattanooga—Hamilton Country Bicentennial Library.

73. Robert Minty, "Picketing and Scouting," August 31, 1893, *National Tribune*; "An Incident

after Chickamauga," *National Tribune*, March 9, 1893; W.L. Curry, *The Raid of the Confederate Cavalry through Central Tennessee,* 6; John Fleming. Letter, October 7, 1863.

74. Robert Mitchell, Letter to James Garfield, October 3, 1863, Letters sent by chief of cavalry, RG 393, Entry 2460, National Archives; John W. DuBose, *General Joseph Wheeler and the Army of Tennessee* (New York: The Neale Publishing Co., 1912), 208–209; Thomas W. Cutrer, *Our Trust is in the God of Battles*, 203; Wilbur F. Mims, *War History of the Prattville Dragoons* (Prattville, Alabama: n.p., n.d.), 10–11; Jesse Hyde, Diary entry, October 2, 1863, Kentucky Historical Society, Jesse Hyde Diary, SC 1274, Frankfort; Aaron Aster, *Civil War along Tennessee's Cumberland Plateau* (Charleston: History Press, 2015), 107; G.W. Baum, Diary entry, October 2, 1863, Book 10; John T. Young, Letter November 20, 1863, Walter King Hoover Papers, Civil War Collection Box 2, folder 11, Tennessee State Library and Archives, Nashville; Robert Merrill, "October 2, 1863," *Robert Sidney Merrill, Co. K. 1st Wis. Cav.* (Cedarsburg, WI.: MSG Publishing, 1995); Edward McCook Report—October 23, 1863, RG 393, Number 2527, Letters Sent First Cavalry Division, National Archives.

75. George Crook, *Official Records*, Series 1, Volume 30, Part 2, 684–685; John Fleming, Letter October 7, 1863; Silas Stevens, Folder 12; Journal of the 4th Michigan Cavalry, October 2, 1864.

76. W.L. Curry, *Four Years in the Saddle: History of First Regiment Ohio Volunteer Cavalry* (Columbus: Champlin Printing Co., 1898), 136; Lucien Wulsin, *The Fourth Regiment Ohio*, 40; G.W. Baum, Diary entry, October 4, 1863; Joseph Wheeler, *Official Records*, Series 1, Volume 30, Part 2, 724; Henry Albert Potter, Diary entry, October 3, 1863; Robert Burns, Letter, October 30, 1863; Abram Miller, *Official Records*, Series 1, Volume 30, Part 2, 693; Alva Griest, Diary entry, October 4, 1863, *Three Years in Dixie: Personal Adventures, Scenes and Incidents of the March—The Journal of Alva C. Griest*, Journal Entry, Alva Griest Collection, William Henry Smith Memorial Library, Indiana Historical Society, Indianapolis, Indiana; George Crook, *Official Records*, Series 1, Volume 30, Part 2, 685; Joseph Wheeler, *Official Records*, Series 1, Volume 30, Part 2, 723.

77. Robert Burns, Letter October 30, 1863; Eli Long, Autobiography, Eli Long Papers, United States Army Heritage and Education Center, Carlisle, PA; "Military Synopsis of the Military Career," pamphlet, Eli Long Papers, United States Army Heritage and Education Center, Carlisle, PA; W.L. Curry, *Four Years in the Saddle*, 137; George Crook, *Official Records*, Series 1, Volume 30, Part 2, 685–686; W.C. Dodson, *Campaigns of Wheeler and his Cavalry, 1862–1865* (Atlanta: Hudgins Publishing Company, 1899), 124; Henry Campbell, Diary entry, October 4, 1863, *Three Years in the Saddle: A Diary of the Civil War* (Unpublished, n.d.), Wabash College, Crawfordsville, Indiana; Robert H.G. Minty Court Martial Case File, 1864, Case Number NN-1210, National Archives, Washington.

78. Robert Burns, Letter October 30, 1863; W.L. Curry, *Four Years in the Saddle*, 137; W.L. Curry, "The Raid of the Confederate Cavalry through Central Tennessee, October 1863," 9–10; W.L. Curry, "The Raid of the Confederate Cavalry through Central Tennessee," *Journal of the United States Cavalry Association*, Volume 19 (1908/1909), 823; Trumbull D. Griffin, Typeset document, B241: Papers of Trumbull Dorrance Griffin (ca. 1836–1912), 1862–1911, Missouri Historical Museum, St. Louis, MO; Silas Stevens, Folder 12.

79. G.W. Baum, Diary entry, October 5, 1863; W.L. Curry, *Four Years in the Saddle*, 137; James Hagan, "3rd Alabama Cavalry," SG024911, Alabama Department of History and Archives, Montgomery; Joseph Wheeler, *Official Records*, Series 1, Volume 30, Part 2, 724; George Crook, *Official Records*, Series 1, Volume 30, Part 2, 686.

80. W.L. Curry, "The Raid of the Confederate Cavalry through Central Tennessee," 12.

81. Robert H.G. Minty Court Martial Case File, 1864, Case Number NN-1210, National Archives, Washington; Silas Stevens, Folder 12.

82. George Healy, Letter October 15, 1863, George Healy Papers (Box 006, Folder 22), State Historical Society of Iowa, Des Moines; Charles Alley, Diary entry, October 6, 1863, Charles Alley Diary 1861–1865, Western History Collection, University of Oklahoma, Norman; Edward Walter Letter, November 19, 1863, McEwen Family Papers A 269, Missouri Historical Museum, Special Collections, St. Louis; Robert Mitchell letter to Garfield October 7, 1863, Letters sent by Chief of Cavalry, RG 393, Entry 2460, National Archives; Eugene Marshall, Diary entry, October 6, 1863, Eugene Marshall Papers, RL.00850, David M. Rubenstein Rare Book & Manuscript Library, Duke University.

83. Joseph Wheeler, *Official Records*, Series 1, Volume 30, Part 2, 724.

84. George Crook, *Official Records*, Series 1, Volume 30, Part, 2, 686; Thomas Crofts, *History of the Service of the Third Ohio Veteran Volunteer Cavalry* (Toledo: Stoneman Press, 1910), 114; Whitelaw Reid, *Ohio in the War: Her Statesmen, Her Generals, and Soldiers*, Volume I, 861; John Stutsman, Letter November 10, 1863, Civil War Times Illustrated Collection, USAHEC, Carlisle, Pennsylvania; John W. Rowell, *Yankee Cavalrymen* (Knoxville: University of Tennessee Press, 1971), 153; Michael Brown, McCook Report, October 23, 1863, Michael Brown Letters, Civil War Collection, United States Army Heritage and Education Center; Robert Mitchell, *Official Records*, Series 1, Volume 30, Part 2, 670; Lucien Wulsin, *The Fourth Regiment Ohio*, 46; *Chicago Tribune*, "From North Alabama," November 5, 1863.

85. John Toomey, "Account of the Chicago Board of Trade Battery," GAR, George Thomas Post, Autobiographies, Chicago History Museum; George Crook, *Official Records*, Series 1, Volume 30, Part 2, 686–687; *Chicago Tribune*, "From North Alabama"; J.N. Reese, *Report of the Adjutant General to the State of Illinois*, Vol. VIII (Springfield: Journal Company, Printers and Binders, 1901), 736.

86. *Chicago Tribune*, "From North Alabama,"; John Toomey, "Account of the Chicago Board of Trade Battery."

87. John Toomey, "Account of the Chicago Board of Trade Battery."

88. R.F. Bunting, Undated (1863–1865) biography of John A. Wharton, Wharton, John Austin Papers, 1862–1866, Accession Number, 25–0567, Galveston and Texas History Center, Rosenberg Library, Galveston, TX., p. 10; Alva Griest, Diary entry, October, 1863; Henry Campbell, Diary entry, October 7, 1863, *Three Years in the Saddle*; George Hodge, *Official Records*, Series 1, Volume 30, Part 2, 726; Abram Miller, *Official Records*, Series 1, Volume 30, Part 2, 694; George Crook, *Official Records*, Series 1, Volume 30, Part 2, 686–687.

89. Thomas W. Cutrer, *Our Trust is in the God of Battles*, 212; Benjamin Franklin Batchelor and George Batchelor, *Batchelor-Turner Letters, 1861–1864: Written by Two of Terry's Texas Rangers*, H. J. H. Rugeley, editor (Austin: The Streck Company, 1961), 71; R.F. Bunting, "John A. Wharton," p. 11.

90. J. K. P. Blackburn, *Reminiscences of the Terry Rangers* (n.p.: University of Texas, 1919), 46; George Hodge, *Official Records*, Series 1, Volume 30, Part 2, 726; George Crook, *Official Records*, Series 1, Volume 30, Part 2, 686–687; Samuel J. Martin, *General Braxton Bragg, CSA* (Jefferson, NC: McFarland and Company, 2011), 341.

91. Robert Burns, Letter October 30, 1863; George Crook, *Official Records*, Series 1, Volume 30, Part 2, 686–687.

92. William W. Lowe, *Official Records*, Series 1, Volume 30, Part 2, 690; George Healy, October 15, 1863 letter; Henry Albert Potter, Diary entry, October 9, 1863.

93. Phillip D. Roddey, *Official Records*, Series 1, Volume 30, Part 2, 729; Joseph Wheeler, *Official Records*, Series 1, Volume 30, Part 2, 725.

94. G.W. Baum, Diary entry, October 9, 1863; Robert Mitchell, *Official Records*, Series 1, Volume 30, Part 2, 673; Thomas Jordan, Letter to Wife October 25, 1863, Thomas J. Jordan Civil War Letters [2066] Box Number: 1, Folder 13, Historical Society of Pennsylvania, Philadelphia, Pennsylvania; Charles Alley, Diary entry, October 9, 1863, Tennessee State Library and Archives, Nashville, Tennessee; Edwin Stuart, "The Federal Cavalry with the Armies in the West: 1861–1865," *Journal of the United States Cavalry Association*, Volume XVII (October 1906), No. 62: 195–259.

95. Horace McLean, Letter October 20, 1863, McLean, Horace letters (1862–1864), Auburn University, Auburn; Dan Butterfield, *Official Records*, Series 1, Volume 30, Part 2, 714.

96. W.L. Curry, *Four Years in the Saddle*, 141; Robert Mitchell, *Official Records*, Series 1, Volume 30, Part 2, 673; Robert Burns, Letter October 30, 1863; Paul Magid, *George Crook: From the Redwoods to Appomattox* (Norman: University of Oklahoma Press, 2011), 167–171; James Larson, *Sergeant Larson, 4th Cavalry*, 206.

97. Thomas Crofts, *History of the Service of the Third Ohio Veteran Volunteer Cavalry*, 115; Peter Cozzens, *The Shipwreck of Their Hopes: The Battle for Chattanooga* (Urbana and Chicago University of Illinois Press, 1994), 19, 34–35; James Arthur Schaefer, "The Tactical And Strategic Evolution of Cavalry During The American Civil War," Ph.D. Dissertation, The University of Toledo, 1982, 173; Henry Campbell, *The Years in the Saddle*, news clipping, p. 124; Edward Longacre, *A Soldier to the Last*, 123; George Walsh, *Those Damn Horse Soldiers* (New York: A Tom Doherty Associates Book, 2006), 235.

98. Henry Cist, *Official Records*, Series 1, Volume 30, Part 2, 667; *Chicago Tribune*, "How Wheeler's Cavalry Were Driven Out of Tennessee," November 4, 1863.

99. Robert Mitchell, *Official Records*, Series 1, Volume 30, Part 4, 371, 462; David Stanley, *An American General*, 172; Allan Peskin, *Garfield: A Biography* (Kent, Ohio: Kent State University Press, 1999), 212.

100. William McMichael, *Official Records*, Series 1, Volume 31, Part 3, 126; David Stanley, *An American General—The Memoirs of David Sloan Stanley*, Samuel W. Fordyce IV, ed. (Santa Barbara, California: The Narrative Press, 2004), 171; Benson Bobrick, *Master of War: The Life of George H. Thomas* (New York: Simon and Schuster, 2009), 38.

101. Muster and Descriptive Roll, Chicago Board of Trade, Records of the Illinois Adjutant General (301.018, 2S, 15B, F 6) Illinois Archives, Springfield; George W. Cullum, *Biographical Register of the Officers and Graduates of the U.S. Military Academy*, Vol. 2 (New York: D. Van Nostrand, 1868–79), 596–597; Jack Welsh, *Medical Histories of Union Generals*. (Kent, Ohio: Kent State University Press, 2005), 321–322; Ezra J. Warner, *Generals in Blue: Lives of Union Commanders* (Baton Rouge: Louisiana State University Press, 1992), 472.

102. Elisabeth Joan Doyle, "'Rottenness in Every Direction': The Stokes Investigation in Civil War New Orleans," *Civil War History*, Volume 18, Number 1 (March 1972): 24–41, pp. 24–41; William M. Ferraro, *The Papers of Ulysses S. Grant: Aug. 16-Nov. 15, 1864*, Vol. 12 (Carbondale and Edwardsville: University of Southern Illinois Press, 1984), 186.

103. Silas Stevens, Folder 12; John Fleming, Letter, November 2, 1863.

104. John A. Nourse, Letter to sister, October 8, 1863; George Cooper, et. al. *Official Records*, Series 1, Volume 31, Part 3, 330–331; Benjamin Nourse, Diary, October 3, 1863. [In the absence of official records, there is some question whether four or five guns remained behind or whether two or three guns accompanied Stevens on Wheeler's raid.]

105. Benjamin Nourse, Diary, October 20–21, 1863; Clyde D. Foster, *Evanston's Yesterdays* (Evanston: n.p., 1956), 191–192.

106. Benjamin Nourse, Diary, November 19, 1863; John Fleming, Letter November 19, 1863.

107. Nourse, *Ibid.*; Fleming, *Ibid.*; Silas Stevens Folder 12; Robinson letter to Allen C. Fuller, Nov. 11, 1863; Murry Nelson letter to Allen C. Fuller, Feb

20, 1864, Illinois State Archives; George Robinson to Allen C. Fuller, October 24, 1864; Chicago Board of Trade Battery monthly returns, Illinois State Archives; George Thomas, *Official Records*, Series 1, Volume 31, Part 1, 809; *Chicago Tribune*, "To Be Promoted," February 25, 1864.

108. George Robinson, Monthly Returns, Chicago Board of Trade Battery, Illinois State Archives; Sarah Gould Downs Durand, *Calvin Durand, A Memorial* (Chicago: Lakeside Press, 1912), 60–61.

109. Benjamin Nourse, Diary, November 10–December 8, 1863; John Fleming, Letter, December 1, 1863; Chicago Board of Trade Association roster, April 27, 1886, Trumbull Griffin file, Missouri History Museum; Clark Winslow, pension file—75,308, National Archives.

110. Benjamin Nourse, Diary, December, 24–31, 1863.

111. Robert Mitchell, *Official Records*, Series 1, Volume 30, Part 2, 673.

112. Benjamin Nourse, Diary, December 31, 1863; John Toomey, "Account of the Chicago Board of Trade Battery," GAR Autobiography; Silas Stevens, Folder 14.

Chapter Six

1. William Smith, *Official Records*, Series 1, Volume 32, Part 2, 40, 250; George Thomas, *Official Records*, Series 1, Volume 32, Part 2, 102–103; Ulysses Grant, *Official Records*, Series 1, Volume 32, Part 2, 110; William Sherman, *Official Records*, Series 1, Volume 32, Part 1, 172; Lafayette McCrillis, *Official Records*, Series 1, Volume 32, Part 1, 305; William T. Sherman, *Home Letters of General Sherman* (New York: Charles Scribner's Sons, 1909), 285.

2. Benjamin Nourse, Diary, January 1864, Rubenstein Library, Duke University; John Fleming, Letter January 18, 1863, John C. Fleming Papers, Letter Jan 8, 1864, Newberry Library, Chicago; Tobias Miller, Diary, January 1–17, 1864, Tobias Charles Miller diary and letters [manuscript], 1862–1866, Chicago History Museum; Chicago Board of Trade, Casualty lists, Illinois State Archives; Record Group 94: Records of the Adjutant General's Office, 1762–1984 Series: Registers of Deaths of Volunteers, 1861–1865 File Unit: Illinois, G–J, National Archives p. 106.

3. Muster rolls and Descriptive rolls, Chicago Board of Trade Battery, Illinois State Archives; Benjamin Nourse, Diary, January 18–31, 1864; Joseph Peters, GAR autobiography, Thomas Post, Chicago History Museum; (William Randolph, Letter to Allen Fuller, January 12, 1864; James H. Stokes Letter Richard Yates, January 24, 1864; John Wilson, Letter to Richard Yates, February 20, 1864; George Robinson, Letter to Richard Yates, February 27, 1864; Trumbull Griffin, Letter to Richard Yates, February 27, 1864; Trumbull Griffin, Letter to Allen Fuller, February 27, 1864; George Robinson, Letter to Allen Fuller, March 2, 1864; George

Crook, Letter to Allen Fuller, April, 1864; John Wilson, Letter to Allen Fuller, February 20, 1864,) in Miscellaneous Letters, Chicago Board of Trade Battery, Illinois State Archives; *Chicago Tribune*, "Promoted," November 19, 1863; Tobias Miller, Diary, January 25, 1864; John Fleming, Letter to brother, February 9, 1864; "Our Honored Dead," *Chicago Tribune*, January 8, 1866.

4. Benjamin Nourse, Diary, February 1–9, 1864; Ulysses Grant, *Official Records*, Series 1, Volume 32, Part 2, 335; Tobias Miller, Diary, March 1, 1864.

5. Benjamin Nourse, Diary, February 10–23, 1864; "Dr. W. Richards," *The Rock Island Argus* (Rock Island, Illinois), May 9, 1864, p. 1.

6. Benjamin Nourse, Diary, February 24–March 25, 1864; Ken Baumann, *Arming the Suckers 1861–1865* (Dayton, OH: Morningside House, Inc., 1989), 34; Tobias Miller, Diary, March 3, 1864; John Fleming, Letter to brother, Feb. 9 1864, March 29, 1864.

7. *Harper's Weekly*, "General Kenner Garrard," February 11, 1865; Frances Densmore, "Garrard Family in Frontenac," *Minnesota History*, Volume 14, No. 1 (March 1933), p. 31–43; David Evans, "Kenner Garrard's Georgia Romp," *America's Civil War*, March 2002, Volume 15, Issue 1, 44–50.

8. Andrew Johnson, *Official Records*, Series 1, Volume 32, Part 3, 105.

9. Benjamin Nourse, Diary, April 29, 1864; John A Nourse, Letter to Father April 24, 1864; Tobias Miller, Diary, April 4–8, 1864; John Fleming, Letter to Father, April 3 and 21, 1864.

10. Silas Stevens, Letter to brother, Folder 14, Silas Stevens papers, Chicago History Museum.

11. Benjamin Nourse, Diary, April 28-May 10, 1864; Kenner Garrard, *Official Records*, Series 1, Volume 38, Part 3, 803; Tobias Miller, Diary, April 29-May 7, 1864; John Fleming, Letter to Mother May 6, 1864.

12. John Schofield, *Official Records*, Series 1, Volume 32, Part 3, 569; James McPherson, *Official Records*, Series 1, Volume 32, Part 3, 561; Joseph Johnston, *Official Records*, Series 1, Volume 32, Part 3, 866; James Alex Baggett, *Homegrown Yankees: Tennessee's Union Cavalry in the Civil War* (Baton Rouge: Louisiana State University, 2009), 12, 40–41, 78, 82; Alexander Eckel, *History of the Fourth Tennessee Cavalry* (Johnson City, Tennessee: Overmountain Press, 2001), 28, 47, 106; George E. Pond, "Kilpatrick's and Dahlgren's Raid to Richmond," In *Battles & Leaders*, Volume 4 (New York: The Century Company, 1888), 95–96; Stephen Z. Starr, *The Union Cavalry in the Civil War: The War in the West, Volume III* (Baton Rouge: Louisiana State University, 2007), 447–473.

13. R.M. Sawyer, *Official Records*, Series 1, Volume 32, Part 3, 497.

14. William Sherman, *Official Records*, Series 1, Volume 38, Part 4, 26, 38.

15. William Sherman, *Official Records*, Series 1, Volume 38, Part 4, 85; Kenner Garrard, *Official Records*, Series 1, Volume 38, Part 4, 29; John Corse, *Official Records*, Series 1, Volume 38, Part 4, 53, 85.

16. H. Judson Kilpatrick, *Official Records*, Series

1, Volume 38, Part 4, 96–97; James McPherson, *Official Records*, Series 1, Volume 38, Part 4, 104–106.

17. James McPherson, *Official Records*, Series 1, Volume 38, Part 4, 107.

18. William Sherman, *Official Records*, Series 1, Volume 38, Part 1, 115–117.

19. Kenner Garrard, *Official Records*, Series 1, Volume 38, Part 2, 803; Robert Minty, *Official Records*, Series 1, Volume 38, Part 2, 811; Robert B. Leach, "The Role of Union Cavalry During the Atlanta Campaign," Master's Thesis, U.S. Army Command and General Staff College, Fort Leavenworth, Kansas, 1994, 39–40.

20. Robert Minty, *Official Records*, Series 1, Volume 38, Part 2, 811; Silas Stevens, Folder 15; Tobias Miller, Diary, May 12, 14, 1864; Joseph Vale, *Minty and the Cavalry: A History of Cavalry Campaigns in the Western Armies* (Harrisburg, Pennsylvania: Edwin K. Myers, Printer and Binder, 1886), 281; Benjamin Nourse, Diary, May 11–15, 1864; Albert Castel, *Decision in the West: The Atlanta Campaign of 1864* (Lawrence: University Press of Kansas, 1992), 196; Kenner Garrard, *Official Records*, Series 1, Volume 38, Part 2, 803.

21. John Nourse, Journal, May 16, 1864.

22. William Sherman, *Official Records*, Series 1, Volume 38, Part 4, 201; L.M. Dayton, *Official Records*, Series 1, Volume 38, Part 4, 209.

23. Albert Castel, *Decision in the West: The Atlanta Campaign of 1864*, 194–197.

24. John Bennett, Letter to wife, June 5, 1864, Bennett, John, B. Papers, Bentley Historical Library, University of Michigan, Ann Arbor; Kenner Garrard, *Official Records*, Series 1, Volume 38, Part 2, 803; Robert Minty, *Official Records*, Series 1, Volume 38, Part 2, p. 811; Joseph Vale, *Minty and the Cavalry*, 285; Heber Thompson, Diary Entry—May 18, 1864, Heber Thompson Diary, Civil War Roundtable Collection, USAHEC, Carlisle, Pennsylvania.

25. Kenner Garrard, *Official Records*, Series 1, Volume 38, Part 2, 803; Benjamin Nourse, Diary May 17–18, 1864.

26. Albert Castel, *Decision in the West: The Atlanta Campaign of 1864*, 198–202; Edward McCook, *Official Records*, Series 1, Volume 38, Part 4, 255; Larry J. Daniel, *Days of Glory: The Army of the Cumberland, 1861–1865* (Baton Rouge: Louisiana State University Press, 2006), 399; Robert Minty, *Official Records*, Series 1, Volume 38, Part 2, 812.

27. Benjamin Nourse, Diary, May 19, 1864; Tobias Miller, Diary, May 20, 1864; Robert Minty *Official Records*, Series 1, Volume 38, Part 2, 812.

28. John Bennett, Letter to wife, June 5, 1864; Trumbull Griffin, Letter May 31, 1864 to George J. Harrison, Illinois Artillery, Chicago Board of Trade Battery Letters Concerning Loss of Equipment, USAHEC, Earl M. Hess Collection, Box 2, Folder 12.

29. Benjamin Nourse, Diary, May 20–22, 1864; Tobias Miller, Diary, May 21, 1864.

30. W.L. Elliott, *Official Records*, Series 1, Volume 38, Part 2, 747; Sherman, *Official Records*, Series 1, Volume 38, Part 4, 278; Daniel Butterfield, *Official Records*, Series 1, Volume 38, Part 4, 296.

31. Silas Stevens, Folder 15.

32. Benjamin Nourse, Diary, May 24–25, 1864; Tobias Miller, Diary, May 23–24, 1864.

33. Stevens Folder, 15; John Bennett, Letter to wife, June 5, 1864, Bennett, John, B. Papers, Bentley Historical Library, University of Michigan, Ann Arbor; Albert Castel, *Decision in the West: The Atlanta Campaign of 1864*, 249.

34. Silas Stevens, Folder 15; W.L. Elliott, *Official Records*, Series 1, Volume 38, Part 2, 746–747; Edward McCook, W.L. Elliott, *Official Records*, Series 1, Volume 38, Part 2, 753.

35. Silas Stevens, Folder 15; Tobias Miller, Diary, May 26, 1864.

36. Kenner Garrard, *Official Records*, Series 1, Volume 38, Part 2, 804; Robert Minty, *Official Records*, Series 1, Volume 38, Part 2, 811.

37. Oliver Howard, *Official Records*, Series 1, Volume 38, Part 3, 34; Kenner Garrard, *Official Records*, Series 1, Volume 38, Part 2, 804; Robert Minty, *Official Records*, Series 1, Volume 38, Part 2, 811, Joseph Vale, *Minty and the Cavalry*, 300.

38. John Fleming, Letter to sister June 4, 1864; Benjamin Nourse, Diary, May 27, 1864; *Chicago Tribune*, "From the Board of Trade Battery," June 15, 1864.

39. Tobias Miller, Diary, May 28, 1864; Joseph Vale, *Minty and the Cavalry*, 300; Benjamin Nourse, Diary, May 28, 1864.

40. Silas Stevens, Folder 15.

41. *Chicago Tribune*, "From the Board of Trade Battery," June 9, 1864; John Fleming, Letter to sister, June 4, 1864; Benjamin Nourse, Diary, May 29, 1864; Tobias Miller, Diary, May 29, 1864.

42. William Sherman, *Official Records*, Series 1, Volume 38, Part 4, 367; W.L. Elliott, *Official Records*, Series 1, Volume 38, Part 4, 378; Kenner Garrard, *Official Records*, Series 1, Volume 38, Part 5, 60.

43. William Sherman, *Official Records*, Series 1, Volume 38, Part 4, 385, 408–409.

44. L.M. Dayton, *Official Records*, Series 1, Volume 38, Part 4, 445–446, 480; William Sherman, *Official Records*, Series 1, Volume 38, Part 4, 449–450; J.C. Van Duzer, *Official Records*, Series 1, Volume 38, Part 4, 479; Kenner Garrard, *Official Records*, Series 1, Volume 38, Part 4, 478; Edward McCook, *Official Records*, Series 1, Volume 38, Part 4, 501; Edward McCook, *Official Records*, Series 1, Volume 38, Part 2, 756.

45. Benjamin Nourse, Diary, June 1–4, 1864; Tobias Miller, Diary, June 1–4, 1864.

46. John Fleming, Letter to sister, June 4, 1864.

47. Benjamin Nourse, Diary, June 5–7, 1864; Tobias Miller, Diary, June 5–7, 1864; *Chicago Tribune*, "From the Board of Trade Battery," June 15, 1864.

48. Kenner Garrard, *Official Records*, Series 1, Volume 38, Part 2, 804; Robert Minty, *Official Records*, Series 1, Volume 38, Part 2, 812; Robert Minty, "The Sabre Brigade," *The National Tribune*, March 1, 1894, p. 1.

49. A.O. Miller, *Official Records*, Series 1, Volume 38, Part 2, 848–849; John Bennett letter to wife June 14, 1864.

50. Tobias Miller, Diary, June 9, 1864; Silas Stevens, Folder 15; Benjamin Nourse, Diary, June 8–9, 1864.

51. Kenner Garrard, *Official Records*, Series 1, Volume 38, Part 2, 804.

52. Tobias Miller, Diary, June 10–11, 1864; Robert Minty, *Official Records*, Series 1, Volume 38, Part 2, 812; Eli Long, *Official Records*, Series 1, Volume 38, Part 2, 837; [Dr. Robert McAfee also petitioned and was granted permission for the construction of a bridge over the Chattahoochee River].

53. Tobias Miller, Diary, June 12–14, 1864; *Chicago Tribune*, "Capture of Three Members of the Board of Trade Battery," June 26, 1864; Benjamin Nourse, Diary, June 12–14, 1864; John Fleming, Letter to Dear Parents June 15, 1864; (Lake would ultimately die in prison due to chronic diarrhea in Feb. 1865, Pension files Aug. 9, 1877, A.B. Lake papers, Stones Rivers NPS).

54. Tobias Miller, Diary, June 15; Robert Minty, *Official Records*, Series 1, Volume 38, Part 2, 812; Eli Long, *Official Records*, Series 1, Volume 38, Part 2, 848; Benjamin Nourse, Diary, June 15.

55. Benjamin Nourse, Diary, June 16–18, 1864; Tobias Miller, Diary, June 16–18, 1864; Silas Stevens, Folder 15.

56. Benjamin F. McGee, B.F., *History of the 72d Indiana Volunteer Infantry of the Mounted Lightning Brigade*, William Ray Jewell, ed. (Lafayette, IN: S. Vater & Co., 1882), 314–316.

57. John Fleming, Letter to parents June 25, 1864; Benjamin Nourse, Diary, June 19, 1864; Tobias Miller, Diary, June 19-September 1; Robert Minty, *Official Records*, Series 1, Volume 38, Part 2, 812; *Chicago Tribune*, "Board of Trade Battery," June 30, 1864.

58. William Sherman, *Official Records*, Series 1, Volume 38, Part 4, 507; Edward McCook, *Official Records*, Series 1, Volume 38, Part 2, 756.

59. William Sherman, *Official Records*, Series 1, Volume 38, Part 4, 535; Kenner Garrard and Lewis Edward Nolan, *Nolan's System for Training Cavalry Horses* (New York : D. Van Nostrand, 1862), 1–120.

60. William Sherman, *Official Records*, Series 1, Volume 38, Part 4, 542.

61. Kenner Garrard, *Official Records*, Series 1, Volume 38, Part 4, 505–506; W.L. Curry, *Four Years in the Saddle: History of First Regiment Ohio Volunteer Cavalry* (Columbus: Champlin Printing Co., 1898), 83–84; *The Catalogue and History of Sigma Chi* (Chicago: Published by the Fraternity, 1890), 169; George Parry, Diary entry, June 20, 1864, George F. Parry Family Volumes, Collection 3694, Record Number: 10325, Historical Society of Pennsylvania, Philadelphia, Pennsylvania.

62. Robert Minty, "Noonday Church," *National Tribune*, January 31, 1895, 3; Heber Thompson, Diary entry, June 20, 1864; Robert Minty, "The Sabre Brigade," *The National Tribune*, March 1, 1894, p. 1; Benjamin Nourse, diary June 20, 1862.

63. John Fleming, Letter to Parents June 25, 1864.

64. Joseph Vale, *Minty and the Cavalry*, 315–319; Robert Minty, *Official Records*, Series 1, Volume 38,

Part 2, 812–813; John McLain, Diary entry, June 20, 1864, John McLain Papers (c.00111), Michigan State University Archives & Historical Collections, East Lansing; Joseph Johnston, *Narrative of Military Operations Directed during the Civil War* (New York: D. Appleton, 1874), 339; Benjamin Nourse, diary, June 20, 1862.

65. Silas Stevens, Folder 15.

66. Kenner Garrard, *Official Records*, Series 1, Volume 38, Part 4, 556.

67. James McPherson, *Official Records*, Series 1, Volume 38, Part 4, 557; Kenner Garrard, *Official Records*, Series 1, Volume 38, Part 4, 556; W.L. Curry, *Four Years in the Saddle: History of First Regiment Ohio Volunteer Cavalry* (Columbus: Champlin Printing Co., 1898), 170; James Larson, *Sergeant Larson, 4th Cavalry*, 249; Benjamin Nourse, Diary entry, June 20, 1864; Robert B. Leach, "The Role of Union Cavalry during the Atlanta Campaign," 54; Heber Thompson, Diary, June 21, 1864.

68. James McPherson, *Official Records*, Series 1, Volume 38, Part 4, 579; W.L. Curry, *Four Years in the Saddle,* 170.

69. William Clark, *Official Records*, Series 1, Volume 38, Part 4, 605; William Whipple, *Official Records*, Series 1, Volume 38, Part 4, 602–603.

70. Benjamin Nourse, November 27, 1864; John Fleming, Letter to Mother, June 30, 1864.

71. *Chicago Tribune*, "All Safe," July 9, 1864; Benjamin Nourse, Diary, June 28, 1864.

72. William Sherman, *Official Records*, Series 1, Volume 38, Part 4, 645 and Part 5, 61–62.

73. W.L. Elliott, *Official Records*, Series 1, Volume 38, Part 4, 643; William Sherman, *Official Records*, Series 1, Volume 38, Part 4, 645; William Sherman, *Official Records*, Series 1, Volume 38, Part 5, 24–25.

74. Benjamin Nourse, Diary, July 1–4, 1864; Silas Stevens, Folder 16; John Fleming Letter to Father, July 12, 1864; Chicago Board of Trade Association roster, April 27, 1886, Trumbull Griffin file, Missouri History Museum.

75. Silas Stevens, Folder 16; William Sherman, *Official Records*, Series 1, Volume 38, Part 5, 29–30, 42; Dianna Avena, *Roswell: History, Haunts and Legends* (Charleston, SC: History Press, 2007), 23–28; William Sherman, *Official Records*, Series 1, Volume 38, Part 5, 73.

76. Silas Stevens, Folder 16; John Fleming, Letter to father July 12, 1864; B.F. McGee, *History of the 72d Indiana*, 334; Benjamin Nourse, Diary, July 5–9, 1864.

77. Benjamin Nourse, Diary, July 10 -13, 1864; John Fleming, Letter to Father July 12, 1864.

78. Calvin Durand and Sarah Gould Downs Durand, *A Memorial* (Chicago: Privately Printed, 1912), 63–96.

79. William Allen Clark, "Please Send Stamps: The Civil War Letters of William Allen Clark," Part IV, Edited by Margaret Black Taturn, *Indiana Magazine of History*, XCI (December, 1995), p. 424; Benjamin H. Pike, "I Have Commited (sic) a Wrong by Coming Here," *Civil War Times Illustrated* (Jun 2000): pp. 16, 68–77; Heber Thompson, Diary, entry

June 24, 1864; Charles Treadway, "The Letters of Charles Wesley Treadway," *Foot Prints: Past and Present*, Vol. 9 (Olney, Ill.: Richland County Genealogical and Historical Society, 1986), 140–141; Michael Ballard, *The Battle of Tupelo, Mississippi—July 14 & 15, 1864* (Tupelo, Mississippi: Northeast Mississippi Historical & Genealogical Society, 2009), 10–28.

80. William Sherman, *Official Records*, Series 1, Volume 38, Part 4, 66.

81. William Sherman, *Official Records*, Series 1, Volume 38, Part 5, 108, 142; George Stoneman, *Official Records*, Series 1, Volume 38, Part 5, 145–146; Alex Sackett, Letter July 10, 1864, Private Alex Sackett Letters (N16/3/5; B/HF), State Historical Society of Iowa, Des Moines.

82. George Thomas, *Official Records*, Series 1, Volume 38, Part 5, 196, William Sherman, *Official Records*, Series 1, Volume 38, Part 5, 198.

83. L.M. Dayton, *Official Records*, Series 1, Volume 38, Part 5, 166–167; William Sherman, *Official Records*, Series 1, Volume 38, Part 5, 167–170; William Clark, *Official Records*, Series 1, Volume 38, Part 5, 168; J.C. Van Duzer, *Official Records*, Series 1, Volume 38, Part 5, 179.

84. William T. Clark, *Official Records*, Series 1, Volume 38, Part 5, 194.

85. Benjamin Nourse, Diary, July 17–21, 1864.

86. David Evans, *Sherman's Horsemen* (Bloomington: Indiana University Press, 1996), 177; William Sherman, *Official Records*, Series 1, Volume 38, Part 5, 209; Robert Ramsey, *Official Records*, Series 1, Volume 38, Part 5, 207.

87. Kenner Garrard, *Official Records*, Series 1, Volume 38, Part 5, 221; James McPherson, *Official Records*, Series 1, Volume 38, Part 5, 219.

88. John Fleming, Letter to Dear Parents, July 25, 1864; Kenner Garrard, *Official Records*, Series 1, Volume 38, Part 2, 809; William E. Crane, "William E. Crane's Daily Journal of Life in the Field during the War of the Rebellion," July 22, 1864 entry, Mss. 980, Cincinnati Historical Society, Cincinnati Museum Center.

89. William Clark, *Official Records*, Series 1, Volume 38, Part 5, 240; Kenner Garrard, *Official Records*, Series 1, Volume 38, Part 2, 809; William Sherman, *Official Records*, Series 1, Volume 38, Part 2, 811; David S. Evans, "Kenner Garrard's Georgia Romp," *America's Civil War*, March 2002, Volume 15, Issue 1, pp. 44.

90. Joseph Wheeler, *Official Records*, Series 1, Volume 38, Part 3, 952–953; John Sprague, *Official Records*, Series 1, Volume 38, Part 3, 507; George I. Robinson, *Official Records*, Series 1, Volume 38, Part 2, 854; David Allison, *Attacked on All Sides* (North Charleston: CreateSpace Independent Publishing Platform, 2018), 40–42. [The records about the number of Union supply wagons and the actual Confederate forces remains cloudy. In regard to the supply trains, the wagons were from the three corps of the Army of the Tennessee and could have totaled 1,000 wagons. In regard to Wheeler's forces, Wheeler's report does not indicate which units participated in the attack. He mentioned in his after-action report that just a few days earlier his command amounted to "two divisions of cavalry, under Generals Kelly and Iverson, and one small brigade, under General Williams." Historian Albert Rauber found that Wheeler commanded 25 regiments on July 22.]

91. David Allison, *Attacked on All Sides*, 98–102; Charles Anderson, Hand sketched map, Charles Anderson papers, Atlanta History Center.

92. Trumbull D. Griffin, *Official Records*, Series 1, Volume 52, 109–110; John Fleming, Letter to Parents, July 25,1864: Map -1864, Army of the Ohio, Maps Folder, DeKalb History Center, Decatur Georgia; Benjamin Nourse, Diary, July 22, 1864.

93. Trumbull Griffin, *Ibid.*, David Allison, *Attacked on All Sides*,116.

94. Joseph Wheeler, *Official Records*, Series 1, Volume 38, Part 3, 953; Benjamin Nourse, Diary, July 22, 1864.

95. John Fouts, *Official Records*, Series 1, Volume 38, Part 3, 517; Henry Shier, *Official Records*, Series 1, Volume 38, Part 3, 537.

96. Trumbull D. Griffin, *Official Records*, Series 1, Volume 52, 109–110.

97. *Chicago Tribune*, "Board of Trade Battery," August 4, 1864.

98. John Fleming, Letter to Parents July 25, 1864.

99. *Chicago Tribune*, "The Board of Trade Battery," August 3, 1864; *New York Times*, "Wheeler's Attack Upon Decatur His Repulse, "August 6, 1864, Page 1.

100. John Toomey, "Account of the Chicago Board of Trade Battery," GAR Autobiography; Chicago Board of Trade Association roster, April 27, 1886, Trumbull Griffin file, Missouri History Museum.

101. Benjamin Nourse, Diary, July 22–23, 1864; Joseph Wheeler, *Official Records*, Series 1, Volume 38, Part 3, 952–953; John Sprague, *Official Records*, Series 1, Volume 38, Part 3, 507; George I. Robinson, *Official Records*, Series 1, Volume 38, Part 2, 854; *Chicago Tribune*, "The Board of Trade Battery," August 3, 1864; David Evans, *Sherman's Horsemen*, 94.

102. Albert Castel, *Decision in the West: The Atlanta Campaign of 1864*, 411; George McVeigh diary July 22–23, 1864, Box 1, vol. 2, George McVeigh papers, Louisiana State University Libraries Special Collections.

103. William Sherman, *Official Records*, Series 1, Volume 38, Part 5, 240.

104. William Sherman, *Official Records*, Series 1, Volume 38, Part 5, 238, 248–249.

105. L.M. Dayton, *Official Records*, Series 1, Volume 38, Part 5, 255–256.

106. William Sherman, *Official Records*, Series 1, Volume 38, Part 5, 260–261, 265.

107. Benjamin Nourse, Diary, July 24–26, 1864; *Chicago Tribune*, "A Friendly Souvenir," November 20, 1864; *Chicago Tribune*, "Bankruptcy Matters, April 21, 1877, p. 6; *Inter Ocean*, "Speculation Unsettled His Mind," April 20, 1887, p. 7.

108. William E. Crane, "William E. Crane's Daily

Journal," July 27, 1864; Benjamin Nourse, Diary, July 27, 1864.

109. John Fleming, Letter to parents August 3, 1864; David Evans, *Sherman's Horsemen*, 213; James Larson, *Sergeant Larson, 4th Cavalry* (San Antonio: Southern Literary Institute, 1935), 267.

110. B.F. McGee, *History of the 72d Indiana*, 354; Benjamin Nourse, Diary, July 29, 1864; Kenner Garrard, *Official Records*, Series 1, Volume 38, Part 2, 803–804.

111. Benjamin Nourse, Diary, July 28–31, 1864; William Sherman, *Official Records*, Series 1, Volume 38, Part 5, 309; Robert Minty, "Picketing and Scouting," *National Tribune*, May 31, 1894, pp. 1–2.

112. William Sherman, *Official Records*, Series 1, Volume 38, Part 5, 310; George Thomas, *Official Records*, Series 1, Volume 38, Part 5, 311.

113. Kenner Garrard, *Official Records*, Series 1, Volume 38, Part 2, 804.

114. Robert W. Smith, *Official Records*, Series 1, Volume 38, Part 2, 916.

115. William Sherman, *Official Records*, Series 1, Volume 38, Part 1, 77; Henry H. Belfield, "My Sixty Days in Hades. In Hades, not in Hell,—Andersonville was Hell," *Military Essays And Recollections Papers Read before the Commandery of the State of Illinois, Military Order of the Loyal Legion of the United States*, Vol. III (Chicago: The Dial Press, 1899), 451–452; John McElroy, "The Atlanta Campaign," *National Tribune*, June 17, 1909, p. 2, column 4–5.

116. William Sherman, *Official Records*, Series 1, Volume 38, Part 5, 340.

117. L.M. Dayton, *Official Records*, Series 1, Volume 38, Part 5, 327; Joseph Vale, *Minty and the Cavalry*, 332–333; Robert Minty, "Picketing and Scouting," *National Tribune*, May 31, 1894, 2.

118. W.L. Elliott, *Official Records*, Series 1, Volume 38, Part 5, 433.

119. Benjamin Nourse, Diary, August 1–16, 1864; U.S. Army Adjutant General's Office, Letter April 27, 1874, A.B. Lake Pension application form, Stones Rivers, National Parks Service; *Chicago Tribune*, "Died in Hospital," August 10, 1864; John Fleming, Letter to Father August 17, 1864.

120. William Sherman, *Official Records*, Series 1, Volume 38, Part 5, 442; John Schofield, *Official Records*, Series 1, Volume 38, Part 5, 442; George Thomas, *Official Records*, Series 1, Volume 38, Part 5, 490; William Sherman, *Official Records*, Series 1, Volume 38, Part 5, 489; William Sherman, *Official Records*, Series 1, Volume 38, Part 5, 507; W.L. Elliott, *Official Records*, Series 1, Volume 38, Part 5, 494.

121. W.L. Elliott, *Official Records*, Series 1, Volume 38, Part 5, 509, 524; George Thomas, *Official Records*, Series 1, Volume 38, Part 5, 524; William Sherman, *Official Records*, Series 1, Volume 38, Part 5, 521; George I. Robinson, "With Kilpatrick Around Atlanta," *War Papers, Commandery of Wisconsin MOLLUS*, Volume 1 (New York: Nostrand Van Allen, 1891), 206–209.

122. Joseph Vale, *Minty and the Cavalry*, 338; William Sherman, *Official Records*, Series 1, Volume 38, Part 5, 551; William E. Crane, "William E. Crane's Daily Journal," August 18, 1864; David Evans, *Sherman's Horsemen*, 407–408; *Portrait And Biographical Album of Sedgwick County, Kan.* (Chicago: Chapman Brothers, 1888), 469–471.

123. Robert Minty, *Official Records*, Series 1, Volume 38, Part 2, 824.

124. David Evans, *Sherman's Horsemen*, 412–413; William E. Crane, "William E. Crane's Daily Journal," August 19, 1864; Albert Castel, *Decision in the West*: The Atlanta Campaign of 1864 (Lawrence: University Press of Kansas, 1992), 471; Benjamin Nourse, Diary, August, 17–19, 1864.

125. George I. Robinson, "With Kilpatrick Around Atlanta," 209–210; George Robinson, *Official Records*, Series 1, Volume 38, Part 2, 852.

126. David Evans, *Sherman's Horsemen*, 412–413; William E. Crane, "William E. Crane's Daily Journal," August 19, 1864; Albert Castel, *Decision in the West*, 471; Robert Burns, Letter August 28, 1864" In Joseph Vale, *Minty and the Cavalry*, p. 359; George Robinson, "With Kilpatrick Around Atlanta," 210–211; *New York Herald*, "Sherman: Additional Details of Kilpatrick's Raid Around Atlanta," September 2, 1864; Lucien Wulsin, *The Fourth Regiment Ohio Veteran Volunteer Cavalry* (Cincinnati: Fourth Ohio Volunteer Cavalry Association, 1912), 55–56.

127. *Roster and Record of Iowa Soldiers in the War of the Rebellion*, Volume IV (Des Moines: Emory H. English, State Printer, E.D. Chassell, State Binder 1910), 858; Albert Castel, *Decision in the West*, 471–472.

128. George Robinson, "With Kilpatrick Around Atlanta," 211–213.

129. George Robinson, "With Kilpatrick Around Atlanta," 213–214.

130. George Robinson, "With Kilpatrick Around Atlanta," 214–215.

131. Benjamin Nourse, Diary, August 18–19, 1864.

132. David Evans, *Sherman's Horsemen*, 431,432; W.L. Curry, "Raid of the Union Cavalry by General Judson Kilpatrick Around the Confederate Army in Atlanta, August 1864," in *Sketches of War History 1861–1865*, Vol. VI, Theodore F. Allen, Edward McKee, and J. Gordon Taylor, eds. (Cincinnati: Monfort & Company, 1908), 263–264; Robert Winn letter August 24, 1864, Winn-Cook Family: Papers, 1861–1875 (Mss. A W776), Filson Historical Society, Louisville, Kentucky; J.A. Nourse, Letter to Minty February 3, 1903, Robert Minty Papers, Box 1, Folder 3, Civil War Collection, USAHEC, Carlisle, Pennsylvania.

133. Hugh Judson Kilpatrick, *Official Records*, Series 1, Volume 38, Part 2, 858–859; Benjamin Nourse, Diary, August 18–19, 1864.

134. David Evans, *Sherman's Horsemen*, 402–403; Hugh Judson Kilpatrick, *Official Records*, Series 1, Volume 38, Part 2, 858–859.

135. Daniel T. Elliott and Tracy M. Dean, *The Nash Farm Battlefield: History and Archaeology* (Savannah, Georgia: The Lamar Institute, 2007), 10–11.

136. George Robinson, "With Kilpatrick Around Atlanta," 218–219; Joseph Vale, *Minty and the Cavalry*, 345.

137. Eli Long, *Official Records*, Series 1, Volume 38, Part 2, 839–840; Robert Minty, *Official Records*, Series 1, Volume 38, Part 2, 814; David Evans, *Sherman's Horsemen*, 441; William E. Crane, "Bugle Blasts," *Sketches of War History 1861–1865* (MOLLUS, Ohio, Volume 1) (Cincinnati: Robert Clarke, 1888), 233–51, 247; T.F. Dornblaser, *My Life Story for Young and Old* (USA: Privately printed, 1930), 64; J.A. Nourse, Letter to Minty February 3, 1903, USAHEC; Benjamin Nourse, Diary, August 20, 1864.

138. W.L. Curry, "Raid of the Union Cavalry Commanded by General Judson Kilpatrick around the Confederate Army at Atlanta," 265.

139. David Evans, *Sherman's Horsemen*, 446; Hugh Judson Kilpatrick, *Official Records*, Series 1, Volume 38, Part 2, 859; W.S. Scott, "Kilpatrick's Raid Around Atlanta, August 18 -22, 1864," *Journal of the Association of the United States Cavalry*, Volume 3 (1890), 268; Robert Minty, "Raiding Hood's Rear," *National Tribune*, January 22, 1903.

140. George Robinson, "With Kilpatrick Around Atlanta," 220.

141. David Evans, *Sherman's Horsemen*, 438–450; W.L. Curry, *Four Years in the Saddle: History of First Regiment Ohio Volunteer Cavalry* (Columbus: Champlin Printing Co., 1898), 181; George I. Robinson, "With Kilpatrick Around Atlanta," 222–223.

142. George I. Robinson, *Official Records*, Series 1, Volume 38, Part 2, 852–853; Benjamin Nourse, Diary, August 20, 1864; Judson Kilpatrick, *Official Records*, Series 1, Volume 38, Part 2, 859; John McLain, Diary entry, August 20, 1864, John McLain Papers (c.00111), Michigan State University Archives & Historical Collections, East Lansing.

143. Lucien Wulsin, *The Fourth Regiment Ohio*, 59; George I. Robinson, "With Kilpatrick Around Atlanta," 221–223.

144. Joseph Vale, *Minty and the Cavalry*, 350–351; David Evans, *Sherman's Horsemen*, 458–9; L.K. Dunn, Letter August 24, 1864, Dunn Family Papers, 1854–1977 (D923, folder 4–6), Filson Historical Society, Louisville; W.L. Curry, Letter to J.A. Nourse—March 10, 1903, Robert Minty Papers, Box 1, Folder 5, Civil War Collection, USAHEC, Carlisle, Pennsylvania.

145. George I. Robinson, *Official Records*, Series 1, Volume 38, Part 2, 852–853; George I. Robinson, "With Kilpatrick Around Atlanta," 223.

146. James Thompson Diary, August 20, 1864, James Thomson Papers. 1861–1865 [VFM 2167] Ohio Historical Society, Columbus, Ohio; David Evans, *Sherman's Horsemen*, 458–459; J.A. Nourse, Letter to Minty February 3, 1903, USAHEC, Carlisle, Pennsylvania.

147. Benjamin Nourse, Diary, August 20–21, 1864.

148. John Fleming, Letter to parents Sept. 13, 1864; M.T. Patrick, *Official Records*, Series 1, Volume 38, Part 5, 615; Joseph Vale, *Minty and the Cavalry*, 343; David Evans, *Sherman's Horsemen*, 467; George I. Robinson, "With Kilpatrick Around Atlanta," 225–226.

149. Robert Minty, *Official Records*, Series 1, Volume 38, Part 2, 827.

150. Casualties and Discharge reports, Board of Trade Battery, Illinois State Archives; Benjamin Nourse, Diary, August 18, 1864; John Fleming, Letter to parents, September 13, 1864; Chicago Board of Trade Association roster, April 27, 1886, Trumbull Griffin file, Missouri History Museum.

151. William Sherman, *Official Records*, Series 1, Volume 38, Part 5, 641; Eli Long, "Letter from General Long," *Journal of the United States Cavalry Association*, Vol. 3, 1890, p. 430.

152. Benjamin Nourse, Diary, August 22–24, 1864; John A. Nourse, Letter to sister, August 10, 1864; John Fleming, Letter to mother, August 22, 1864.

153. Benjamin Nourse, Diary, August 25–September 3, 1864.

154. *Chicago Tribune*, "Deserved Promotion," September 22, 1864; *Chicago Tribune*, "From the Board of Trade Battery," September 24, 1864; John Fleming, Letter to parents September 13, 1864; George W. Cullum, *Biographical Register of the Officers and Graduates of the U.S. Military Academy*, Vol. 2 (New York: D. Van Nostrand, 1868–79), 597; Richard M. McMurry, *Atlanta 1864: The Last Chance for the Confederacy* (Lincoln and London: University of Nebraska Press, 2000), 173–174; Benjamin Nourse, Diary September 2–12, 1864; Chicago Board of Trade Association roster, April 27, 1886, Trumbull Griffin file, Missouri History Museum.

155. John Brannan, *Official Records*, Series 1, Volume 38, Part 1, 186.

156. George I. Robinson, *Official Records*, Series 1, Volume 38, Part 2, 854–55.

Chapter Seven

1. Albert Castel, *Decision in the West: The Atlanta Campaign of 1864* (Lawrence: University Press of Kansas, 1992), 542; William Sherman, *Personal Memoirs of Gen. W.T. Sherman*, Vol. 2 (New York: Charles L. Webster & Co., 1890), 109–110; Abraham Lincoln, *Official Records*, Series 1, Volume 38, Part 1, 87; Ulysses Grant, *Official Records*, Series 1, Volume 38, Part 1, 87.

2. S.D. Lee, *Official Records*, Series 1, Volume 32, Part 3, 864; S.D. Lee, *Official Records*, Series 1, Volume 39, Part 2, 675; David Powell, *Failure in the Saddle* (New York and California; Savas Beatie, 2010), 212.

3. John B. Hood, *Official Records*, Series 1, Volume 38, Part 3, 636; Joseph Johnston *Official Records*, Series 1, Volume 38, Part 3, 637; Samuel W. Melton, *Official Records*, Series 1, Volume 38, Part 5, 965; John B. Hood, *Official Records*, Series 1, Volume 38, Part 5, 1021, 1023; L.S. Ross, *Personal Civil War Letters of General Lawrence Sullivan Ross with other letters*, transcribed and compiled by Perry

Wayne Shelton, edited by Shelly Morrison (Austin: Shelly and Richard Morrison, 1994), 68; Thomas L. Livermore, *Numbers and Losses in the Civil War in America, 1861–1865* (Boston and New York: Houghton, Mifflin and Co., 1901), 47; Eric Jacobson and Richard Rupp, *for Cause, for Country: A Study of the Affair at Spring Hill and the Battle of Franklin* (Franklin, Tennessee: O'More Publishing, 2007), 19.

4. William Sherman, *Personal Memoirs,* 114–115; William T. Sherman, *Official Records,* Series 1, Volume 39, Part 2, 411–412.

5. William Sherman, *Personal Memoirs,* 134; Christopher N. Schloemer, "General John Bell Hood: His Leadership During the 1864 Tennessee Campaign," *Saber and Scroll,* Vol. 5: Issue 2 (2016), p. 24; John B. Hood, *Official Records,* Series 1, Volume 38, Part 1, 801; John B. Hood, "The Invasion of Tennessee," In *Battles and Leaders of the Civil War,* Volume IV (New York: The Century Co., 1888), 427.

6. John B. Hood, *Advance and Retreat* (New Orleans: G.T. Beauregard, 1880), 254; John B. Hood, *Official Records,* Series 1, Volume 39, Part 1, 801.

7. John B. Hood, *Official Records,* Series 1, Volume 39, Part 2, 860; Braxton Bragg, *Official Records,* Series 1, Volume 39, Part 2, 867; Richard Taylor, *Official Records,* Series 1, Volume 39, Part 2, 873; James Chalmers, *Official Records,* Series 1, Volume 39, Part 2, 876.

8. John B. Hood, *Official Records,* Series 1, Volume 39, Part 1, 801–802; Jefferson Davis, *Official Records,* Series 1, Volume 39, Part 3, 782; C.K. Stribling, Letter, October 16, 1864, In *Batchelor-Turner letters, 1861–1864,* written by two of Terry's Texas Rangers, Annotated by H. J. H. Rugeley (Austin, TX: The Steck Company, 1961), 86–87; Lawrence Sul Ross, Letter, October 23, 1864, Ross Family Papers, Manuscript #0014, The Texas Collection, Baylor University, Waco, TX; Lawrence Sullivan Ross, "Personal Civil War letters of General Lawrence Sullivan Ross: with other letters," transcribed and compiled by Perry Wayne Shelton, Master's Thesis, Baylor University, 1938, pp. 68–69; Richard McMurry, *John Bell Hood and the War for Southern Independence* (Lexington: The University Press of Kentucky, 1982), 158; Daniel Prickitt, Diary, October 13, 1864, Daniel Prickitt, 3rd Ohio Cavalry, Diary, ed. Edwin Stoltz, Bowling Green State University; W.B. Corbitt, Diary, October 31, 1864, Civil War-era documents, 1860–1865, Box 2, Folder 37, Emory University.

9. N.B. Forrest, *Official Records,* Series 1, Volume 39, Part 3, 812, 815–817; William Sherman, *Official Records,* Series 1, Volume 39, Part 1, 581; Stewart Bennett, "The Storm Broke in All Its Fury: The Struggle for Allatoona Pass," In *The Tennessee Campaign of 1864,* edit. Steven Woodworth and Charles Grear (Carbondale: Southern Illinois University Press, 2016), 45; Samuel French, *Official Records,* Series 1, Volume 39, Part 1, 813; William Sherman, *Personal Memoirs,* 144; Mark A. Smith, "Sherman's Unexpected Companions: Marching Through Georgia with Jomini and Clausewitz," *The Georgia Historical Quarterly,* Vol. 81, No. 1 (Spring 1997), pp. 10–14.

10. William T. Sherman, *Official Records,* Series 1, Volume 39, Part 1, 581–582; Willard Warner, *Official Records,* Series 1, Volume 39, Part 3, 324; John Crittenden, Diary, October 22, 1864, John Crittenden Papers, Auburn University Libraries, Special Collections and Archives.

11. George Thomas, *Official Records,* Series 1, Volume 39, Part 3, 318–319; John Croxton, *Official Records,* Series 1, Volume 39, Part 3, 318; L.M. Dayton, *Official Records,* Series 1, Volume 39, Part 3, 325; W.L. Elliott, *Official Records,* Series 1, Volume 39, Part 3, 327.

12. William T. Sherman, *Official Records,* Series 1, Volume 39, Part 1, 582–583 and Part 3, 333; L.M. Dayton, *Official Records,* Series 1, Volume 39, Part 3, 511; G.T. Beauregard, *Official Records,* Series 1, Volume 39, Part 3, 841; Robert Winn, Letter to Sister, October 21, 1864, Winn—Cook Family Papers, 1861–1875, Mss. A W776, Filson Historical Society, Louisville, Kentucky; George Healy, Letter to Mother et. al., October 18, 1864, George Healey Papers, State Historical Society of Iowa, Des Moines, 1F 006: F22 N14/3/4B/HU.

13. George H. Thomas, *Official Records,* Series 1, Volume 39, Part 3, 535.

14. Benjamin Nourse, Diary, October 1–16, 1863, Rubenstein Library, Duke; Frederick H. Dyer, *A Compendium of The War of The Rebellion* (Des Moines, The Dyer Publishing Company, 1908), 1044.

15. Benjamin Nourse, Diary, October 16–31, 1864.

16. Benjamin Nourse, Diary, November 1–30, 1864; *Chicago Tribune,* "The City: Promotions," December 24, 1864; Trumbull D. Griffin, Letter to Allen Fuller, November 12, 1864, Chicago Board of Trade Battery, Miscellaneous Letters, Illinois State Archives; George Robinson, Letter to Allen Fuller, Nov. 19, 1864, Illinois State Archives; Trumbull Griffin, Letter Griffin to Gov. Yates, Nov. 30, 1864, Illinois State Archives; George H. Thomas, *Official Records,* Series 1, Volume 45, Part 1, 95.

17. Benjamin Nourse, Diary, December, 1–14, 1864.

18. George H. Thomas, *Official Records,* Series 1, Volume 45, Part 1, 96.

19. James H. Wilson, *Official Records,* Series 1, Volume 45, Part 1, 551.

20. W.R. Carter, *History of the First Regiment of Tennessee Volunteer Cavalry,* 228; Isaac R Sherwood, *Memoirs of the War* (Toledo: The H.J. Crittenden, Co., 1923), 149; James Chalmers, *Official Records,* Series 1, Volume 45, Part 1, 765; George Monlux, "To My Comrades Co. I, 8th Iowa Cavalry," Personal narrative, State Historical Library of Iowa, Des Moines, p. 58.

21. John Croxton, *Official Records,* Series 1, Volume 45, Part 1, 572; W.R. Carter, *History of the First Regiment of Tennessee Volunteer Cavalry,* 227; George Monlux, "To My Comrades Co. I, 8th Iowa Cavalry," p. 58; Homer Mead, *The Eighth Iowa*

Cavalry in the Civil War (Carthage, IL: S.C. Davidson, Publisher, 1927), 44; David R. Logsdon, *Eyewitnesses at the Battle of Nashville*, 46; J.T. Tunnell, "Ector's Brigade in the Battle of Nashville," *Confederate Veteran*, Volume 12, p. 348; George Thomas, *Official Records*, Series 1, Volume 45, Part 2, 194.

22. Ambrose Armitage, *Brother to the Eagle: The Civil War Journal of Sgt. Ambrose Armitage, 8th Wisconsin Infantry*, Alden Carter, ed. (United States: Booklocker, Inc, 2006), 519: Henry Kratzer McVey, *Two Years and Two Days: A Writ of My Civil War Experiences* (Jefferson County, Iowa: n.p. 2001), 19-20.

23. Benjamin Nourse, Diary, December 15, 1864.

24. Henry M. Hempstead, Journal, December 16, 1864, Bentley Historical Library, University of Michigan; James H. Wilson, *Official Records*, Series 1, Volume 45, Part 1, 551-552; Bruce Catton, *This Hallowed Ground: A History of the Civil War* (New York: Vintage Books, 2012), 367.

25. Benjamin Nourse, Diary, December 16, 1864.

26. Benjamin Nourse, Diary, December 17, 1864,

27. John Toomey, "Account of the Chicago Board of Trade Battery, George Thomas Post, GAR; Benjamin Nourse, Diary, December 18-21, 1864; James H. Wilson, *Under the Old Flag*, Volume II (New York and London: D. Appleton and Company, 1912), 143.

28. James Wilson, *Under the Old Flag*, Volumes II, 136.

29. Benjamin Nourse, Diary, December 24, 1864; J.A. Creager, "Ross's Brigade of Cavalry," *Confederate Veteran*, Volume 28, No. 8 (August 1920), 292; Scott Walker, *Hell's Broke Loose in Georgia* (Athens & London: University of Georgia Press, 2005), 213.

30. N.B. Forrest, *Official Records*, Series 1, Volume 45, Part 1, 757-758; J.G. Deupree, "The Noxubee Squadron of the First Mississippi Cavalry, C.S.A. 1861-1865," In *Publications of the Mississippi Historical Society*, Volume II, Dunbar Rowland, ed. (Jackson, MS: Democrat Printing Co., 1918), 117-118; J. Harvey Mathes, *Great Commanders: General Forrest* (New York; D. Appleton and Company, 1902), 326; Derek Smith, *In the Lion's Mouth*, 189; D.W. Sanders, "Hood's Tennessee Campaign," *Confederate Veteran*, Volume 15, No. 9 (September 1907), p. 403; John Morton, *The Artillery of Nathan Bedford Forrest's Cavalry* (Nashville and Dallas: Publishing House of the M.E. Church, South Smith & Lamar, Agents, 1909), 294; James Wilson, *Under the Old Flag*, 140; D.W. Comstock, *Ninth Cavalry*, 40; Benjamin Nourse, Diary, December 24, 1864.

31. James H. Wilson, *Official Records*, Series 1, Volume 45, Part 2, 334; John Croxton, *Official Records*, Series 1, Volume 45, Part 1, 574.

32. L.S. Ross, *Official Records*, Series 1, Volume 45, Part 1, 772; Douglas Hale, *The Third Texas Cavalry in the Civil War* (Norman: University of Oklahoma Press, 1993), 264-265; George L. Griscom, *Fighting with Ross' Texas Cavalry Brigade, C.S.A.: The Diary of George L. Griscom, adjutant, 9th Texas Cavalry Regiment*, edited by Homer L. Kerr (Hillsboro, TX: Hill Junior College Press, 1976), 197; William Johnson Worsham, *The Old 19th Tennessee Regiment, C.S.A. June 1861-April 1865* (Knoxville, TN: Press of Paragon Printing company, 1902), 259; Stephen S. Kirk, *Sul Ross' Sixth Texas Cavalry: Six Shooters & Bowie Knives* (Independence, MO: Two Trails, 2008), 113; J.G. Deupree, "The Noxubee Squadron of the First Mississippi Cavalry, C.S.A. 1861-1865," 118; Eddy Davison and Daniel Fox, *Nathan Bedford Forrest: In Search of the Enigma* (Gretna, LA: Pelican Publishing Co., 2007), 373; Jack Welsh, *Medical Histories of Confederate Generals* (Kent, OH: Kent State University Press, 1995), 31.

33. Benjamin Nourse, Diary, December 25-26, 1864.

34. Benjamin Nourse, Diary, December 27-31, 1864.

35. Chicago Board of Trade Returns, Illinois State Archives

36. H.D. Crane, Letter to Robinson, January 19, 1865, George Robinson Papers, Chicago Historical Society.

Chapter Eight

1. Benjamin Nourse, Diary, January 1-31, 1865, Rubenstein Library, Duke University.

2. George Robinson, Letter to Haynie, March 15, 1864, Robinson papers, Chicago Historical Society; John Nourse, Letter to sister, March 5, 1865, John A. Nourse papers, 1862-1922, Chicago History Museum; Telegram, Sylvanus Stevens to Charles Randolph, March 9, 1865, Misc. Letters, Illinois State Archives; The following letters are also included in Misc. Letters, Chicago Board of Trade Battery, Illinois State Archives: William Bross et. al., Letter to Gov. Oglesby from March 10, 1865, Misc. Letters, Illinois State Archives; Gov. Oglesby letter to adjutant general March 13, 1865, Misc. Letters, Illinois State Archives; James H. Dole, et. al., Letter to governor, March 1865, Misc. Letters, Illinois State Archives; John Wilson, Letter to Allen Fuller, February 20, 1865; William Randolph, Letter to Gov. Oglesby, March 2, 1865; George Robinson, Letter to Haynie, June 13, 1865; Chicago Board of Trade Association roster, April 27, 1886, Trumbull Griffin file, Missouri History Museum.

3. George Thomas, *Official Records*, Series 1, Volume 49, Part 1, 342-343.

4. Trumbull Griffin, Record of the Chicago Board of Trade Battery, Griffin, Trumbull Dorrance, papers, Missouri History Museum; Silas Stevens, Letter to brother, Folder 22, Silas Stevens papers, Chicago History Museum; John Fleming, Letter to Sarah, March 13, 1865, John C. Fleming Papers, Box 1, Folder 19, Newberry Library, Chicago; John Nourse, Letter to Sister, March 5, 1865; John Toomey, "Account of the Chicago Board of Trade Battery," George Thomas Post, GAR; Benjamin Nourse, Diary, March 9- 23, 1865; James H. Wilson, *Official Records*, Series 1, Volume 49, Part 1, 350.

5. George Robinson, *Official Records*, Series 1, Volume 49, Part 1, 469.

6. Benjamin Nourse, Diary, April 1, 1865.

7. John Toomey, "Account of the Chicago Board of Trade Battery"; Silas Stevens, Folder 22.

8. James H. Wilson, *Official Records*, Series 1, Volume 49, Part 1, 350.

9. Edward McCook, *Official Records*, Series 1, Volume 49, Part 1, 416; Thomas P. Clinton, "The Military Operations of Gen. John T. Croxton in West Alabama, 1865," In *Transactions of the Alabama Historical Society*, v.4, 1899–1903, Thomas P. Owen, editor (Tuscaloosa: Printed for the Society, 1904): 449–463, pp. 449–451; John Croxton, *Official Records*, Series 1, Volume 49, Part 1, 420.

10. James H. Wilson, *Official Records*, Series 1, Volume 49, Part 1, 351; Jim Bennett, "The Yankees Came: Wilson's Raid Across Alabama and Georgia, March and April 1865," *Newsletter*, Birmingham Historical Society, March/April 2015: 1–11.

11. Stephen L. Bowman, "Ahead of Its Time: Wilson's Cavalry Campaign of 1865," *Army History*, No. 23 (Summer 1992), p. 14; Jim Bennett, "The Yankees Came," 7–8; Perry D. Jamieson, *Spring 1865: The Closing Campaigns of the Civil War* (Lincoln: University of Nebraska Press, 2015), 204–205; Theodore Scribner, "Selma," *New York Herald*, April 22, 1865, p. 8; Silas Stevens, Folder 23.

12. James H. Wilson, *Official Records*, Series 1, Volume 49, Part 1, 351; *Burlington Weekly Hawk-eye*, "General Wilson's Cavalry Raid," April 25, 1865; Silas Stevens, Folder 23.

13. George Robinson, *Official Records*, Series 1, Volume 49, Part 1, 469–470; Theodore Scribner, "Selma," *New York Herald*, April 22, 1865; *Chicago Tribune*, "Wilson's Raid Ebenezer Church and Selma," May 6, 1865; John Toomey, "Account of the Chicago Board of Trade Battery"; Trumbull Griffin, Record of the Chicago Board of Trade Battery; *Daily Illinois State Journal*, "Telegraphic: More Particulars of Wilson's Raid," May 6, 1865, p. 1.

14. George Robinson, *Official Records*, Series 1, Volume 49, Part 1, 470; William D. Whipple, Wilson's Raid, *Memphis Appeal*, December 27, 1865; Silas Stevens, Folder 23.

15. James H. Wilson, *Official Records*, Series 1, Volume 49, Part 1, 351.

16. Eli Long, *Official Records*, Series 1, Volume 49, Part 1, 439; Robert Minty, *Official Records*, Series 1, Volume 49, Part 1, 444.

17. Benjamin Nourse, Diary, April 2, 1865.

18. Robert Minty to Robinson, Letter, April 3, 1865, George Robinson letters, Chicago History Museum; Benjamin Nourse, Diary, April 3, 1865; George Robinson, *Official Records*, Series 1, Volume 49, Part 1, 470; S. Ellen Phillips, "Remeniscences (sic) of the War and Episode of Wilson's Raid near Selma, Ala, April 1865," Alabama Department of Archives and History; Silas Stevens, Folder 23.

19. Benjamin Nourse, Diary, April 7–12, 1865; John Toomey, "Account of the Chicago Board of Trade Battery"; James H. Wilson, *Under the Old Flag*, Volume 2 (New York: D. Appleton and Company, 1912), 241–243.

20. James H. Wilson, *Official Records*, Series 1, Volume 49, Part 1, 352, 364.

21. Benjamin Nourse, Diary, April 13–20, 1865; Joseph Peters, GAR papers, George Thomas Post, Chicago History Museum; Silas Stevens, Folder 24.

22. George Robinson, *Official Records*, Series 1, Volume 49, Part 1, 471.

23. Chicago Board of Trade, Company returns, Illinois State Archives.

24. Benjamin Nourse, Diary, April 21-May 8, 1865.

25. Trumbull Griffin, Record of the Chicago Board of Trade Battery; Benjamin F. McGee, *History of the 72d Indiana Volunteer Infantry of the Mounted Lightning Brigade*, William Ray Jewell, ed. (LaFayette, IN: S. Vater & Co., 1882), 601; Benjamin Nourse, Diary, May 9–13, 1865; John Toomey, "Account of the Chicago Board of Trade Battery"; John Nourse, Letter from Francis, partial, without date or salutation, John Nourse' papers, Chicago History Museum; "Jeff Davis' Captors," *Washington Times* (Washington, D.C.), January 10, 1897, p. 1.

26. Benjamin Nourse, Diary, May 23–July 3, 1865.

27. *Ibid.*; *Chicago Tribune*, "The Board of Trade Battery," June 27, 1865.

28. Trumbull Griffin, Record of the Chicago Board of Trade Battery; John Toomey, "Account of the Chicago Board of Trade Battery."

29. *Daily Illinois State Journal*, "From Chicago: The Board of Trade Battery," November 24, 1865, p. 2.

30. "Our Honored Dead," *Chicago Tribune*, January 8, 1866.

31. Frederick H. Dyer, *A Compendium of the War of the Rebellion* (Des Moines, Ia.: The Dyer publishing Company, 1908) Part 3, 1044.

32. "Board of Trade Association Meeting," *Chicago Tribune*, November 24, 1865.

33. "Unveil Shaft to Dead," Chicago Tribune, May 31, 1901; "Our Honored Dead," *Chicago Tribune*, January 8, 1866; "The Board of Trade Battery Monument," *Chicago Tribune*, August 21, 1868.

34. "Our Honored Dead," *Chicago Tribune*, January 8, 1866.

Chapter Nine

1. George W. Cullum, *Biographical Register of the Officers and Graduates of the U.S. Military Academy*, Vol. 2 (New York: D. Van Nostrand, 1868–79), 596–597; *Twenty-Second Annual Reunion of the Association of the Graduates of the United States Military Academy, June 12th, 1891* (Saginaw: Seaman & Peters, Printers and Binders, 1898), 189; Elisabeth Joan Doyle, "Rottenness in Every Direction": The Stokes Investigation in Civil War New Orleans," *Civil War History*, Volume 18, Number 1 (March 1972): 24–41, pp. 40–41.

2. "Robinson, George Irving Jan. 14, 1909,

Milwaukee," In Memoriam, R-Z (1886-1917) Box 1, File 19, Military Order of the Loyal Legion of the United States, Wisconsin Commandery; Mss-0938, Milwaukee County Historical Society.

3. A.T. Andreas, *History of Milwaukee, Wisconsin* (Chicago: The Western Historical Company, 1881), 1190; Ellis Baker Usher, *Wisconsin: Its Story and Biography, 1848-1913*, Volume 8 (Chicago and New York: The Lewis Publishing Co., 1914), 2202.

4. "T.D. Griffin is Dead," *St. Louis Globe-Democrat* (St. Louis, Missouri), February 22-23, 1912; Walter B. Stevens, *Centennial History of Missouri (The Center State) One Hundred Years In The Union 1820-1921*, Vol. 6 (St. Louis-Chicago: The S.J. Clarke Publishing Company. 1921), 504.

5. "Colonel Sylvanus H. Stevens," *The Inter Ocean* (Chicago, Illinois), August 26, 1900, p. 35; "Death of Col S.H. Stevens," *Humboldt Union*, December 27, 1902; John Grier Stevens, *The Descendants of Samuel Stevens with Histories of Allied Families* (Baltimore: Edward Brothers, Inc., 1968), 185-204.

6. William E. Connelley, *A Standard History of Kansas and Kansans*, Vol. IV (Chicago and New York: Lewis Publishing Co., 1918), 1754-1755; "Bennett Dies," *Topeka State Journal*, Jan. 26, 1924, p. 1.

7. "Death Under the Knife," *Chicago Tribune*, July 1, 1877, p. 2; "City Brevities," *The Inter Ocean*, July 12, 1877, p. 8; "Late City Items," *The Inter Ocean*, July 11, 1877, p. 4; "The City: Lewis B. Hand," *Chicago Tribune*, July 12, 1877.

8. Chicago Board of Trade, Casualty lists, Illinois State Archives.

9. "Resolution of Respect," *Chicago Tribune*, February 2, 1867; *Annual Report of the Adjutant General of the State of Michigan*, Vol. 1 (Lansing: John A. Kerr, Printers, 1866), Appendix, 33; "The West," *The Weekly Republican* (Plymouth, Indiana), April 12, 1867, p. 6.

10. U.S. Census, 1870, 1880, 1900, 1910; "William Randolph Dies at Hospital," *Wisconsin State Journal* (Madison, Wisconsin), April 30, 1914, p. 5; "William Randolph," *Wisconsin State Journal* (Madison, Wisconsin), May 1, 1914, p. 15; John W. Leonard, ed., *The Book of Chicagoans* (Chicago: A.N. Marquis & Company, 1905), 475-476; Alfred Theodore Andreas, *History of Chicago: From the Fire of 1871 until 1885* (Chicago: A.T. Andreas, Publisher, 1886), 70.

11. George Woodward Hotchkiss, *History of the Lumber and Forest Industry of the Northwest* (Chicago: George W. Hotchkiss Co., 1898), 695-696;

"Quits the Railroad at 94—Frank Knight," *The Index-Journal* (Greenwood, South Carolina), June 16, 1922, p. 3; "Elected a Chicago Man," *The Inter Ocean*, Chicago, December 7, 1892, p. 6.

12. *Memorial and Biographical Record of Butler, Polk, Seward, York and Filmore Counties, Nebraska* (Chicago: Geo. A. Ogle & Co., 1899), 714-715.

13. George W. Warvelle, ed., *Illinois Historical Compendium of Freemasonry in Illinois*, Vol. II (Chicago: The Lewis Publishing Company (1897), 255-256; George Chandler, *The Chandler Family: The Descendants of William and Annis Chandler* (Worcester, MA: Press of Charles Hamilton, 1883), 1268.

14. "Probate Matters," *The Inter Ocean* (Chicago, Illinois), November 8, 1885, p. 15; "Jeff Davis's Captor," *Indianapolis Journal*, January 10, 1897, p. 2; "Telegraphic News," *Pioche Weekly*, Pioche, NV, January 28, 1897.

15. Alexander L. Stevenson, William Eliot Furness, and Joseph Stockton, *Memorials of Deceased Companions of the Commandery of the State of Illinois Military Order of the Loyal Legion of the United States* (Chicago: MOLLUS, 1912), 402-405.

16. *Calvin Durand Sarah Gould Downs Durand: A Memorial* (Chicago: Lakeside Press, 1912), 31-34; "Calvin Durand Dies of Grief for Wife," *Chicago Eagle*, November 1, 1911; "Grief Kills Calvin Durand," *Chicago Tribune*, November 1, 1911, p. 7.

17. William B. Dickson, compiler, *History of the Carnegie Veterans Association*. (Montclair, NJ: Montclair Press, 1938), 70-71.

18. William L. Willis, "O.H. Miller," in *History of Sacramento County California* (Los Angeles: Historic Record Co., 1913), 668-669.

19. John W. Leonard, ed., *The Book of Chicagoans* (Chicago: A.N. Marquis & Company, 1905), 434-435; "Long and Honored Career in the Lumber Business," *Lumber Trade Journal*, Vol. 55 No. 12 (June 15: 1909): 15; "John A. Nourse Disposed of Interest in Nourse & Taylor Lumber Co.," *The Lumber World*, Vol. 50, No. 8 April 15, 1910, p. 16.

20. John Grier Stevens, *The Descendants of Samuel Stevens with Histories of Allied Families* (Baltimore: Edward Brothers, Inc., 1968), 169-184; "Long Criminal Chain," *New York Tribune*, May 24, 1908, p. 5; Illinois Supreme Court, *Reports of Cases at Common Law and in Chancery*, Vol. 107 (Springfield: H.W. Rokker Printer, 1884), 29-32.

21. U.S. Census 1880, 1900; "John D. Toomey," *The Inter Ocean* (Chicago, Illinois), January 28, 1907, p. 2.

Bibliography

Primary Sources

Published

Andes, John, and Will McTeer, *Loyal Mountain Troopers: The Second and Third Tennessee Volunteer Cavalry in the Civil War*. Maryville, Tennessee: Blount County Genealogical and Historical Society, 1992.

Armitage, Ambrose. *Brother to the Eagle: The Civil War Journal of Sgt. Ambrose Armitage, 8th Wisconsin Infantry*, Alden Carter, ed. United States: Booklocker, Inc, 2006.

Batchelor, Benjamin Franklin, and George Batchelor. *Batchelor-Turner Letters, 1861–1864: Written by Two of Terry's Texas Rangers*, H.J.H. Rugeley, editor. Austin: The Streck Company, 1961.

Chadick, Mary Jane. *Incidents of the War: The Civil War Journal of Mary Jane Chadick*, Nancy Rohr, ed. Huntsville: Silver Thread Publishing, 2005.

Cutrer, Thomas W. *Our Trust is in the God of Battles: The Civil War Letters of Robert Franklin Bunting, Chaplain, Terry's Texas Rangers*. Knoxville: University of Tennessee Press, 2006.

Davis, William C., and Meredith L. Swentor, eds. *Bluegrass Confederate: The Headquarters Diary of Edward O. Guerrant*. Baton Rouge: Louisiana State University Press, 1999.

Dodd, Ephraim. *Diary of Ephraim Shelby Dodd*. Austin: Press of E.L. Steck, 1914.

Goodrich, Charles Perry. *Letters from Home from the First Wisconsin Cavalry*, Richard N. Larson, editor. Madison: State Historical Society of Wisconsin, n.d.

Griscom, George L. *Fighting with Ross' Texas Cavalry Brigade, C.S.A.: The Diary of George L. Griscom, adjutant, 9th Texas Cavalry Regiment*, edited by Homer L. Kerr. Hillsboro, TX: Hill Junior College Press, 1976.

Lincoln, Abraham. *Collected Works*, Marion Dolores Pratt and Lloyd A. Dunlap, assistant editors. New Brunswick, N.J: Rutgers University Press, 1953.

Merrill, Robert. *Robert Sidney Merrill, Co. K. 1st Wis. Cav.* Cedarsburg, WI.: MSG Publishing, 1995.

Miller, George Knox. *An Uncompromising Secessionist: The Civil War of George Knox Miller, Eighth (Wade's) Confederate Cavalry*, Richard M. McMurry, editor. Tuscaloosa: University of Alabama Press, 2007.

Moyer, Franklin F. *Journal and Letters of Franklin F. Moyer*, Robert H. Wieser, editor. Dayton: Robert Wieser Publisher, 2008.

Ross, L.S. *Personal Civil War Letters of General Lawrence Sullivan Ross with other letters*, transcribed and compiled by Perry Wayne Shelton, edited by Shelly Morrison. Austin: Shelly and Richard Morrison, 1994.

Scribner's, Theodore. "Selma." *New York Herald*, April 22, 1865.

Sherman, William T. *Home Letters of General Sherman*. New York: Charles Scribner's Sons, 1909.

Williams, John. *Leaves of a Trooper's Diary*. Philadelphia: Published by Author, 1869.

Womack, J.J. *A Civil War Diary of Captain J.J. Womack, Company E 16th Tennessee Volunteers*. McMinnville, TN: Womack, 1961.

Unpublished

Alabama Department of History and Archives
James Hagan, "3rd Alabama Cavalry"
William Hardee Papers, Hardee Family Papers
Robert D. Jackson family Papers
S. Ellen Phillips Papers

Atlanta History Center
Charles Anderson Papers

Auburn University
John Crittenden Papers

Baylor University
Ross Family Papers

Beloit University
F.A. Lord Letter, Civil War Collection

Bowling Green State University
Askew Family Correspondence
George Kryder Letters
Daniel Prickitt Diary
Isaac Skillman Diary

Chicago History Museum
Chicago Board of Trade Light Artillery Battery, United States Army (1862–1865)
Edward Jerome Dies, "Through Three Wars"
Chester Arthur Legg, "The Board of Trade in the City of Chicago in the Civil War"
Tobias Miller Papers
Diary
Letters
John A. Nourse Papers
Journal

Diary
Letters
Joseph G. Peters, GAR, George Thomas Post, Civil
War, Autobiographies
George I. Robinson Papers
Silas Curtis Stevens Letters
Sylvanus Stevens, GAR, George Thomas Post, Auto-
biographies
Henry H. Taylor, Address
John Toomey, GAR, George Thomas Post, Auto-
biographies

*Chickamauga and Chattanooga National Military
Park*
Sylvanus Stevens Letter, Chicago Board of Trade Bat-
tery file

Cincinnati History Museum Center
William E. Crane's Daily Journal, Mss 980

DeKalb History Center, Decatur
Map collection

Duke University, Rubenstein Library
Eugene Marshall Diary
Benjamin F. Nourse Diary
Elisha Peterson Manuscript

Emory University
W.B. Corbitt, Diary

Filson Historical Society
Don Carlos Buell Papers, 1818–1898
John Daeuble Journal
Dunn Family Papers
Elijah Watts Papers
Winn-Cook Family Papers

Galveston, Rosenberg Library
Wharton, John Austin Papers

*Hamilton County Bicentennial Library,
Chattanooga*
Thomas W. Davis Diary

Historical Society of Pennsylvania
Thomas J. Jordan Civil War Letters
Thomas McCahan Diary
George Parry Diary

Illinois State Archives
Commissions, Discharges, Muster-in Rolls
Miscellaneous Letters
George Crook Letter
Calvin Durand Letter
Charles Goddard Letters
Trumbull Griffin Letters
Murry Nelson Letter
William Randolph Letter
George Robinson Letters
James Stokes Letters
John Wilson Letters
Muster and Descriptive Rolls
Muster-out Rolls and Miscellaneous Letters
Return Lists
Returns of Casualties

Indiana Historical Society
George Baum Diary
I.R. Conwell Diary

Alva Griest Diary
Daniel Wait Howe Papers

Kentucky Historical Society
Jesse Hyde Diary

Louisiana State University
George McVeigh, diary and letter

Michigan History Museum, Archives of Michigan
Henry Albert Potter Collection
Frank Vogel Diary

*Michigan State University Archives & Historical
Collections*
John McLain Diary

Milwaukee County Historical Society
George I. Robinson Papers
Military Order of the Loyal Legion of the United
States Collection

Minnesota Historical Society
Robert Burns Letters

Missouri History Museum
Trumbull Griffin papers
Edward Walter Letter

National Archives
Compiled Service Records Showing Service of Mili-
tary Units—Illinois
Court Martial Records, RG 94
Court Martial Records, RG 153
Journal of the 4th Michigan Cavalry, RG 94
Letters Sent, 1st Cavalry Division, RG 393, Number
2527
Letter and Orders Received by Chief of Cavalry, RG
393, Entry 2469
Letters Sent, Chief of Cavalry, RG 393, Number 151
Letters sent, Second Cavalry Division, RG 393
Edward McCook, Chickamauga after action report,
RG 393
Robert Mitchell, Chickamauga after action report,
RG 393
Ordnance Summary Statements for independent Illi-
nois batteries, Microcopy 594
Quarterly returns of ordnance and ordnance stores
on hand in regular and volunteer army organizations 1862–1867, 1870–1876; Record Group:
156/159; Microfilm/Pamphlet No: M 1281
Register of Deaths of Volunteers, Illinois adjutant
general, PG 94
Telegrams Sent by Chief of Cavalry, RG 393, Entry
2463
1st Ohio Cavalry, Morning reports, RG 94
3rd Ohio Cavalry, Morning Reports RG 94
4th Kentucky Cavalry, Orders and Correspondence
books
4th Ohio Morning Reports, RG 94
4th U.S. Cavalry, RG 391, Entry 731, regimental
books

Navarro College, Pearce Civil War Collection
Henry Haymond Papers

Newberry Library
John Fleming Letters

Ohio Historical Society
James Thompson Diary

Special Collections Division of the Nashville Public Library
Peter Williamson Letters

State Historical Society of Iowa, Des Moines
George Healy Papers
George Monlux Papers
Alex Sackett Letters

State Historical Society of Missouri
Colman-Hayter Family Papers

Stones River National Battle Field Technical Information Center
Philemon Baldwin Papers
Calvin Durand, "Calvin 'Cam' Durand Jr.
Albert Lake Papers
James H. Stokes Letter

Tennessee State Library
William Gibbs Allen Papers
Terry H. Cahal, Letters
Alfred Tyler Fielder Diaries
William Henry Harder Diary
Walter King Hoover Papers
James Knight Letter
John M. Routt Papers

United States Army Heritage and Education Center
Michael Brown Letters
Earl M. Hess Collection
Eli Long Papers
Robert Minty Papers
John Stutsman Letter
Heber Thompson Diary

University of Michigan, Bentley Historical Library
John Bennett Papers
Morris Fitch Papers
D.L. Haines Papers
Henry Mortimer Hempstead Papers
Richard Robbins Papers

The University of Mississippi
William Sylvester Dillon Diary

University of North Carolina, The Wilson Library
Isaac Barton Ulmer Papers
D. Coleman Diary

University of Oklahoma
Charles Alley Diary

University of Tennessee Libraries
Joseph Freeman Letter
John M. Hollis Diary
Edward Summers Letter
Julius E. Thomas Diary

Wabash College
Henry Campbell Diary

Western Michigan State University
August Yenner Diary

Western Reserve Historical Society
George Brent Diary (Braxton Bragg Papers, Mss 2000)

Wisconsin Historical Society
Quiner Scrapbooks

Government Publications

Reese, J.N. *Report of the Adjutant General to the State of Illinois*, Vol. VIII. Springfield: Journal Company, Printers and Binders, 1901.
United States Census Records, 1850–1930.
The War of the Rebellion. A Compilation of the Official Records of the Union and Confederate Armies, [Hereafter referred to as *Official Records*.]

Journal Articles

Bennett, Jim. "The Yankees Came: Wilson's Raid Across Alabama and Georgia, March and April 1865." *Newsletter*, Birmingham Historical Society (March/April 2015): 1–11.
Bowman, Stephen L. "Ahead of Its Time: Wilson's Cavalry Campaign of 1865." *Army History*, No. 23 (Summer 1992): 12–20.
Bradley, Michael. "Tullahoma: The Wrongly Forgotten Campaign." *Blue & Gray*, Volume XXVII (2010), Number 1: 22.
Bradley, Michael. "Varying Results of Cavalry Fighting: Western Flank vs, Eastern Flank," *Blue and Grey*, Volume XXVII (2010), Number 1, 21.
Brandt, Robert S. "Lightning and Rain in Middle Tennessee: The Campaign of June-July 1863." *Tennessee Historical Quarterly*, vol. 52, no. 3, 1993:158–169.
Brown, Lenard E. "Fortress Rosecrans: A History, 1865–1990." *Tennessee Historical Quarterly*, Vol. 50, No. 3 (Fall 1991): 135–141.
Clark, William Allen. "'Please Send Stamps': The Civil War Letters of William Allen Clark," Part IV, ed. Margaret Black Tatum, *Indiana Magazine of History*, Volume 91, Issue 4 (1995): 407–437.
Crane, William E. "Bugle Blasts," *Sketches of War History 1861–1865*, MOLLUS, Ohio, Volume 1. Cincinnati: Robert Clarke, 1888: 233–51.
Creager, J.A. "Ross's Brigade of Cavalry." *Confederate Veteran*, Volume 28, No. 8 (August 1920): 290–292.
Dayton, Aretas A. "The Raising of Union Forces in Illinois during the Civil War." *Journal of the Illinois State Historical Society* (1908–1984), Vol. 34, No. 4 (Dec. 1941): 401–438.
Densmore, Frances. "Garrard Family in Frontenac." *Minnesota History*, Volume 14, no. 1 (March 1933): 31–43.
Doyle, Elisabeth Joan. "Rottenness in Every Direction": The Stokes Investigation in Civil War New Orleans." *Civil War History*, Volume 18, Number 1 (March 1972): 24–41.
East, Earnest. "Lincoln's Russian General." *Journal of the Illinois State Historical Society*, Vol. 52 (1959), No. 1: 106–122.
Evans, David S. "Kenner Garrard's Georgia Romp." *America's Civil War*, Volume 15, Issue 1 (March 2002): 44–50.
Hannaford, Ebenezer. "In the Ranks at Stone River." *Harper's Magazine*, 27 (1863): 810.
Hill, D.H. "Chickamauga-The Great Battle of the West," *Century*, Vol 33, No. 6 (April, 1887): 944–945.

Hughes, Nicky. "Fort Boone and the Civil War Defense of Frankfort." *The Register of the Kentucky Historical Society,* Vol. 88, No. 2 (Spring 1990): 148–162.

James, Alfred P. "General James Scott Negley." *Western Pennsylvania Historical Magazine,* Volume 14, Number 2 (April 1931): 69–91.

"John A. Nourse Disposed of Interest in Nourse & Taylor Lumber Co.," *The Lumber World,* Vol. 50, No. 8 (April 15, 1910): 16.

"Long and Honored Career in the Lumber Business," *Lumber Trade Journal,* Vol. 55, No. 12 (June 15, 1909): 15.

Long, Eli. "Letter from General Long." *Journal of the United States Cavalry Association,* Vol. 3 (1890): 430.

Mayfield, Leroy S. "Letters and Diaries of Leroy S. Mayfield." *Indiana Magazine of History,* Vol. 39, no. 2 (June 1943): 144–191.

Pike, Benjamin H. "I Have Commited (sic) a Wrong by Coming Here." *Civil War Times Illustrated* (June 2000): 16, 68–77.

Polk, W.M. "General Bragg and the Chickamauga Campaign," *Southern Historical Society Papers,* Vol. 12 (January–December 1884): 378–390.

Robertson, John. "Re-Enlistment Patterns of Civil War Soldiers." *The Journal of Interdisciplinary History,* Vol. 32, No. 1 (Summer, 2001): 15–35.

Sanders, D.W. "Hood's Tennessee Campaign," *Confederate Veteran,* Volume 15, No. 9 (September 1907): 401–404.

Schloemer, Christopher N. "General John Bell Hood: His Leadership During the 1864 Tennessee Campaign." *Saber and Scroll,* Vol. 5: Issue 2 (2016): 24.

Scott, W.S. "Kilpatrick's Raid Around Atlanta, August 18–22, 1864." *Journal of the Association of the United States Cavalry,* Volume 3 (1890): 268.

Skelcher, Lucille Detraz and Jane Lucille Skelcher. "Descendants of the Dumonts of Vevay." *Indiana Magazine of History,* Volume 34, No. 4 (December, 1938): 409–416.

Smith, Mark A. "Sherman's Unexpected Companions: Marching Through Georgia With Jomini and Clausewitz." *The Georgia Historical Quarterly,* Vol. 81, No. 1 (Spring 1997): 10–14.

Starr, Stephen Z. "The Third Ohio Volunteer Cavalry: A View from the Inside," *Ohio History,* Volume 85, Number 4 (Autumn 1976): 306–318.

Stuart, Edwin. "The Federal Cavalry with the Armies in the West: 1861–1865." *Journal of the United States Cavalry Association,* Volume XVII, No. 62 (October 1906): 195–259.

Treadway, Charles. "The Letters of Charles Wesley Treadway," *Foot Prints: Past and Present,* Vol. 9, Olney, Ill.: Richland County Genealogical and Historical Society, 1986: 140–141.

Tunnell, J.T. "Ector's Brigade in the Battle of Nashville," *Confederate Veteran,* Volume 12: 348–349.

Newspapers

The Abbeville Press and Banner (South Carolina)
Alexandria Gazette (Virginia)
The Angola Record (Angola, New York)
The Belmont Chronicle (St. Clairsville, Ohio)
Burlington Weekly Hawk-eye (Iowa)
Chicago Eagle
Chicago Tribune
Cleveland Morning Leader
Daily Illinois State Journal (Springfield)
Harper's Weekly
Humboldt Union (Kansas)
The Index-Journal (Greenwood, South Carolina)
Indianapolis Journal
The Inter Ocean (Chicago)
Macomb Weekly Herald (Macomb, Illinois)
Memphis Appeal
Murfreesboro Post
Nashville Daily Press
National Tribune (Washington)
Pioche Weekly (Pioche, Nevada)
The Rock Island Argus (Rock Island)
Rome Tri-Weekly Courier (Georgia)
Sacramento Daily Union
St. Louis Globe-Democrat
Staunton Spectator (Virginia)
The Summit County Beacon (Akron)
The Topeka Daily State Journal
Washington City Evening Star (DC)
Washington Times (DC)
Weekly Republican (Plymouth, IN)
Wisconsin State Journal (Madison)
Wyandot Pioneer (Ohio)

Other Sources

Allison, David. *Attacked on All Sides.* North Charleston: CreateSpace Independent Publishing Platform, 2018.

Anderson, George Baker. *Landmarks of Rensselaer County, New York,* Volume 2. Syracuse: D. Mason & Co., 1897.

Andreas, Alfred Theodore. *History of Chicago: From the Fire of 1871 until 1885.* Chicago: A.T. Andreas, Publisher, 1886.

Andreas, A.T. (Alfred Theodore). *The History of Chicago,* Volume II. Chicago: The A.T. Andreas Company, Publishers, 1885.

Andreas, A.T. (Alfred Theodore). *History of Milwaukee, Wisconsin.* Chicago: The Western Historical Company, 1881.

Annual Report of the Adjutant General of the State of Michigan, Vol. 1. Lansing: John A. Kerr, Printers, 1866.

Aster, Aaron. *Civil War along Tennessee's Cumberland Plateau.* Charleston: History Press, 2015.

Avena, Dianna. *Roswell: History, Haunts and Legends.* Charleston, SC: History Press, 2007.

Baggett, James Alex. *Homegrown Yankees: Tennessee's Union Cavalry in the Civil War.* Baton Rouge: Louisiana State University, 2009.

Ballard, Michael. *The Battle of Tupelo, Mississippi—July 14 & 15, 1864.* Tupelo, Mississippi: Northeast Mississippi Historical & Genealogical Society, 2009.

Baumann, Ken. *Arming the Suckers 1861–1865*. Dayton, OH: Morningside House, Inc., 1989.

Bearss, Edwin. "Cavalry Operations—Battle of Stones River," Unpublished, Stones River National Park, Technical Information Center, Murfreesboro, TN, 1959.

Bearss, Edwin. "The History of Fortress Rosecrans," United States Department of Interior, Research Report, Stones River National Military Park, 1960.

Bearss, Edwin. "The Union Artillery and Breckinridge's Attack," Research Project #2, The Battle of Stones River, United States Parks Services, 1959.

Beatty, John. *The Citizen Soldier: The Memoirs of a Civil War Volunteer*. Lincoln and London: Bison Books University of Nebraska Press, 1998.

Belfield, Henry H. "My Sixty Days in Hades. In Hades, not in Hell,—Andersonville was Hell," In *Military Essays and Recollections Papers Read before the Commandery of the State of Illinois, Military Order of the Loyal Legion of the United States*, Vol. III. Chicago: The Dial Press, 1899.

Belknap, Charles Eugene ed., *History of the Michigan Organizations at Chickamauga, Chattanooga, and Missionary Ridge*. Lansing: Robert Smith Printing Co., 1899.

Bennett, Stewart. "The Storm Broke in All Its Fury: The Struggle for Allatoona Pass," In *The Tennessee Campaign of 1864*, Steven Woodworth and Charles Grear, edit. Carbondale: Southern Illinois University Press, 2016.

Berry, Thomas Franklin. *Four Years with Morgan and Forrest*. Oklahoma City: Harlow-Ratliff Company, 1914.

Bickham, W.D. *Rosecrans' Campaign with the Fourteenth Army Corps, of the Army of the Cumberland*. Cincinnati: Moore, Wilstach, Keys & Co., 1903.

Blackburn, J.K.P. *Reminiscences of the Terry Rangers*. n.p.: University of Texas, 1919.

Bobrick, Benson. *Master of War: The Life of George H. Thomas*. New York: Simon & Schuster, 2009.

Bradley, Michael. *Tullahoma: The 1863 Campaign for the Control of Middle Tennessee*. Shippensburg, Pennsylvania: White Mane Publishing Company, 1999.

Bradt, H.H.G. *History of the Services of the Third Battery Wisconsin Light Artillery in the Civil War of the United States, 1861–1865*. Berlin, Wisconsin: Courant Press, 1902.

Brandt, Robert S. "Lightning and Rain in Middle Tennessee," In *The Battle of Stones River and The Fight for Middle Tennessee*, Timothy Johnson, ed. Nashville: Tennessee Historical Society, 2012.

Breckinridge, John C. "Murfreesboro," *Southern Historical Society Papers*, Vol. 5, Number 5, May 1878.

Brewer, Richard J. "The Tullahoma Campaign: Operational Insights," Master's Thesis, U.S. Army Command and General Staff College, Leavenworth, KS., 1978.

Broome, Doyle D. "Intelligence Operations of the Army of the Cumberland During the Tullahoma and Chickamauga Campaigns," Master's Thesis, U.S. Army Command and General Staff College, Leavenworth, KS., 1989.

Butler, M.B. *My Story of the Civil War and the Underground Railroad*. Huntington, IN: The United Brethren Publishing Establishment, 1914.

Cannon, Newton. *The Reminiscences of Newton Cannon: First Sergeant, CSA*, Campbell Brown, editor. Franklin, TN: Carter House Association, 1963.

Carnahan, James R. "Personal Recollections of Chickamauga" In *Sketches of War History: 1861–1865*, Vol. I Ohio, MOLLUS. Cincinnati: Robert Clarke & Co. 1888.

Carter, W.R. *History of the First Regiment of Tennessee Volunteer Cavalry*. Knoxville: Gaut-Ogden Co., Printers and Binders, 1902.

Castel, Albert. *Decision in the West: The Atlanta Campaign of 1864*. Lawrence: University Press of Kansas, 1992.

The Catalogue and History of Sigma Chi. Chicago: Published by the Fraternity, 1890.

Catton, Bruce. *This Hallowed Ground: A History of the Civil War*. New York: Vintage Books, 2012.

Cavender, Michael Bower. *The First Georgia Cavalry in the Civil War: A History and Roster*. Jefferson, NC: McFarland, 2016.

Chandler, George. *The Chandler Family: The Descendants of William and Annis Chandler*. Worcester, MA: Press of Charles Hamilton, 1883.

Chapin, John. "At Chickamauga," In *Reunions of the First Ohio Volunteer Cavalry*. Columbus, Ohio: Landon Printing, Co., 1891.

Cisco, Walter Brian. *States Rights Gist: A South Carolina General of the Civil War*. Gretna, LA: Pelican Publishing, 2008.

Clinton, Thomas P. "The Military Operations of Gen. John T. Croxton in West Alabama, 1985," In *Transactions of the Alabama Historical Society*, v.4, 1899–1903, Thomas P. Owen, editor. Tuscaloosa: Printed for the Society, 1904.

Connelley, William E. *A Standard History of Kansas and Kansans*, Vol. IV. Chicago and New York: Lewis Publishing Co., 1918.

Connelly, Thomas. *Autumn of Glory: The Army of Tennessee 1862–1865*. Baton Rouge: Louisiana State University Press, 1971.

Cope, Alexis. *The Fifteenth Ohio Volunteers and Its Campaigns, 1861–1865*. Columbus, Ohio: Published by Author, 1916.

Cozens, Smith. "Company L on Lookout Mountain," In *History of the Fifteenth Pennsylvania Volunteer Cavalry*, J.C. Reiff, ed. Philadelphia, Pennsylvania: Society of the Fifteenth Pennsylvania Cavalry, 1906.

Cozzens, Peter. *No Better Place to Die: The Battle of Stones River*. Urbana and Chicago: University of Illinois Press, 1991.

Cozzens, Peter. *The Shipwreck of Their Hopes: The Battle for Chattanooga*. Urbana and Chicago University of Illinois Press, 1994.

Cozzens, Peter. *This Terrible Sound: The Battle of Chickamauga*. Urbana and Chicago: University of Illinois Press, 1992.

Crofts, Thomas. *History of the Service of the Third Ohio Veteran Volunteer Cavalry*. Toledo: Stoneman Press, 1910.

Crook, George. *General George Crook: His Biography*. Norman & London: University of Oklahoma Press, 1960.

Cullum, George W. *Biographical Register of the Officers and Graduates of the US Military Academy*, Vol. 2. New York: D. Van Nostrand, 1868–1879.

Curry, W.L. *Four Years in the Saddle: History of First Regiment Ohio Volunteer Cavalry*. Columbus: Champlin Printing Co., 1898.

Curry, W.L. *The Raid of the Confederate Cavalry through Central Tennessee, October 1863*. Columbus: The Ohio Commandery of the Loyal Legion, MOLLUS, 1908.

Curry W.L. "Raid of the Union Cavalry by General Judson Kilpatrick Around the Confederate Army in Atlanta, August 1864," In *Sketches of War History 1861–1865*, Vol. VI, Theodore F. Allen, Edward McKee, and J. Gordon Taylor, eds. Cincinnati: Monfort & Company, 1908.

Daniel, Larry. *Days of Glory, The Army of the Cumberland 1861–1865*. Baton Rouge: Louisiana State University Press, 2006.

Dastrup, Boyd L. *King of Battle: A Branch History of the U.S. Army's Field Artillery*. Fort Monroe, VA: Office of the Command Historian, 1992.

Davison, Eddy W. and Daniel Foxx. *Nathan Bedford Forest: In Search of the Enigma*. Gretna, LA: Pelican Publishing Company, 2007.

Deupree, J.G. "The Noxubee Squadron of the First Mississippi Cavalry, C.S.A. 1861–1865," In *Publications of the Mississippi Historical Society*, Volume II, Dunbar Rowland, ed. Jackson, MS: Democrat Printing Co., 1918.

Dickson, William B., compiler. *History of the Carnegie Veterans Association*. Montclair, NJ: Montclair Press, 1938.

Dies, Edward Jerome. *Through Three Wars*. Chicago: Board of Trade Post of the American Legion, 1928.

Dodson, W.C. *Campaigns of Wheeler and his Cavalry, 1862–1865*. Atlanta: Hudgins Publishing Company, 1899.

Dornblaser, T.F. *Sabre Strokes of the Pennsylvania Dragoons*. Philadelphia: Lutheran Publication Society, 1884.

DuBose, John W. *General Joseph Wheeler and the Army of Tennessee*. New York: The Neale Publishing Co., 1912.

Duke, Basil. *Morgan's Cavalry*. New York: The Neale Publishing Co., 1909.

Duke, Basil W. *History of Morgan's Cavalry*. Cincinnati: Miami Printing and Publishing Company, 1867.

Durand, Sarah Gould Downs. *Calvin Durand Sarah Gould Downs Durand: A Memorial*. Chicago: Lakeside Press, 1912.

Dyer, Frederick H. *A Compendium of the War of the Rebellion*. Des Moines, The Dyer Publishing Company, 1908.

Eckel, Alexander. *History of the Fourth Tennessee Cavalry*. Johnson City, Tennessee: Overmountain Press, 2001.

Edwards, Lawyn C. "Confederate Cavalry at Chickamauga: What Went Wrong," Master's Thesis, U.S.

Army Command and General Staff College, Fort Leavenworth, Kansas, 1990.

Elliott, Daniel T., and Tracy M. Dean. *The Nash Farm Battlefield: History and Archaeology*. Savannah, Georgia: The Lamar Institute, 2007.

Evans, Clement. *Confederate Military History*, Volume IV. Atlanta: Confederate Publishing Co., 1899.

Ferraro, William M. *The Papers of Ulysses S. Grant: Aug. 16-Nov. 15, 1864*, Vol. 12. Carbondale and Edwardsville: University of Southern Illinois Press, 1984.

Fitch, John. "Battle of Stone River," In *Annals of the Army of the Cumberland*. Philadelphia: J. B, Lippincott & Co., 1863.

Fitch, Michael Hendrick. *The Chattanooga Campaign, Wisconsin History Commission*. n.p.: Democrat Printing Co., State Printer, 1911.

Foster, Clyde D. *Evanston's Yesterdays*. Evanston: n.p., 1956.

Freeman, Henry. "Some Battle Recollections of Stone's River," In *Military Essays and Recollections, State of Illinois*, Vol. III. Chicago: Dial Press, 1899.

Garrett, William. *Reminiscences of Public Men in Alabama*. Atlanta: Plantation Publishing Company's Press, 1872.

Gatewood, Charles. *Lt. Charles Gatewood and His Apache Wars Memoir*, Louis Kraft, ed. Lincoln: University of Nebraska Press, 2005.

A General Catalogue of the Officers and Graduates from Its Organization in 1837–1864. Ann Arbor: University of Michigan, 1864.

Gibbon, John. *Artillerist Manual*. New York: D. Van Nostrand, 1860.

Golonka, Robert P. "Mobilizing the Illinois Spirit for the Civil War," Master's Thesis, Paper 762, Loyola University, 1949.

Graber, H.W. *The Life Record of H.W. Graber, A Terry Texas Ranger, 1861–1865*. H.W. Graber Publisher, 1916.

Greeno, Charles. "Address of Lieut.-Col. Charles L. Greeno," In *Pennsylvania at Chickamauga and Chattanooga*, George W. Skinner, editor. Harrisburg, PA: William Stanley Ray, State Printer of Pennsylvania, 1897.

Guild, George. *A Brief Narrative of the Fourth Tennessee Cavalry Regiment*. Nashville: n.p., 1913.

Hafendorfer, Kenneth *They Died by Twos and Tens*. Louisville: KH Press, 1995.

Hale, Douglas. *The Third Texas Cavalry in the Civil War*. Norman: University of Oklahoma Press, 1993.

Harbison, Robert E. "Wilder's Brigade in the Tullahoma and Chattanooga Campaigns of the American Civil War," Master's Thesis, U.S. Army Command and General Staff College, Fort Leavenworth, Kansas, 2002.

Hazlett, James C., Edwin Olmstead, M. Hume Parks. *Field Artillery Weapons of the Civil War*. Urbana and Chicago: University of Illinois Press, 2004.

Hazzard, George. *Hazzard's History of Henry County, Indiana, 1822–1906*, Volume 1. New Castle, Indiana: George Hazzard Publisher, 1906.

Herberich, John L. *Masters of the Field: The Fourth*

United States Cavalry in the Civil War. Atglen, PA: Schiffer Publishing Co., 2015.

Hewitt, Frances Bailey, compiler. *Genealogy of the Durand, Whalley, Barnes and Yale Families.* Chicago: Privately Printed at the Lakeside Press, 1912.

Hill, D.H. "Chickamauga: The Great Battle of the West," In *Battles and Leaders in the Civil War, Vol. III.* New York: The Century Co., 1888.

Historical Sketch of the Chicago Board of Trade Battery. Chicago: The Henneberry Co. Publishers, 1902.

History of Milwaukee, Wisconsin, The Western Historical Company. Chicago: A.T. Andreas Proprietor, 1881.

Hood, John B. *Advance and Retreat.* New Orleans: G.T. Beauregard, 1880.

Hood, John B. "The Invasion of Tennessee," In *Battles and Leaders of the Civil War, Volume IV.* New York: The Century Co., 1888.

Horn, Stanley. *The Army of Tennessee.* Norman: University of Oklahoma Press, 1952.

Hotchkiss, George Woodward. *History of the Lumber and Forest Industry of the Northwest.* Chicago: George W. Hotchkiss Co., 1898.

Hughes, Jr., Nathaniel Cheairs. *General William J. Hardee: Old Reliable.* Baton Rouge: Louisiana State University, 1965.

Illinois Supreme Court, *Reports of Cases at Common Law and in Chancery,* Vol. 107. Springfield: H.W. Rokker Printer, 1884.

Industrial Chicago: The Manufacturing Interests, Vol. 3. Chicago: The Goodspeed Publishing Co., 1894.

The Inland Printer, Vol. 5. Chicago: The Inland Printer Co., 1887.

Irvine, Dallas, compiler. *Military Operations of the Civil War: A Guide-index to the Official Records.* Washington: General Services Administration, 1977.

Jacobson, Eric, and Richard Rupp. *For Cause, for Country: A Study of the Affair at Spring Hill and the Battle of Franklin.* Franklin, Tennessee: O'More Publishing, 2007.

Jamieson, Perry D. *Spring 1865: The Closing Campaigns of the Civil War.* Lincoln: University of Nebraska Press, 2015.

Johnson, Richard. "Losing a Division at Stones River," In *Battles and Leaders of the Civil War,* Volume 5, Peter Cozzens, ed. Urbana and Chicago: University of Illinois Press, 2002.

Johnston, Joseph. *Narrative of Military Operations Directed during the Civil War.* New York: D. Appleton, 1874.

Jordan, Thomas, and J.P. Pryor. *The Campaigns of Lieut.-Gen. Nathan B. Forrest of Forrest's Cavalry.* New Orleans, Memphis, New York: Blelock & Co., 1868.

Karamanski, Theodore J. *Rally 'Round the Flag: Chicago and the Civil War.* Lanham, MD: Rowman & Littlefield Publishers, Inc., 2006.

Katcher, Philip. *American Civil War Artillery 1861–1865.* Oxford: Osprey Publishing, 2002.

Kendall, Henry M. *The Battle of Stones River.* District of Columbia: Military Order of the Loyal Legion United States, 1903.

Kirk, Stephen S. *Sul Ross' Sixth Texas Cavalry: Six Shooters & Bowie Knives.* Independence, MO: Two Trails, 2008.

Lamers, William. *The Edge of Glory: A Biography of General William S. Rosecrans, U.S.A.* New York: Harcourt, Brace & World, Inc., 1961.

Larson, James. *Sergeant Larson, 4th Cavalry.* San Antonio: Southern Literary Institute, 1935.

Legg, Chester Arthur. "The Board of Trade in the City of Chicago in the Civil War," Chicago Board of Trade Collection, Chicago History Museum.

Leonard, John W., ed. *The Book of Chicagoans.* Chicago: A.N. Marquis & Company,1905.

Lindsley, John Berrien, ed. *The Military Annals of Tennessee: Confederate.* Nashville: J.M. Lindsley & Co., Publishers, 1886.

Livermore, Thomas L. *Numbers and Losses in the Civil War in America, 1861-1865.* Boston and New York: Houghton, Mifflin and Co., 1901.

Logsdon, David R. *Eyewitnesses at the Battle of Nashville.* Nashville: Kettle Mill Press, 2004.

Longacre, Edward. *A Soldier to the Last: Maj. Gen. Joseph Wheeler in Blue and Gray.* Washington, D.C.: Potomac Books, Inc., 2007.

Magid, Paul. *George Crook: From the Redwoods to Appomattox.* Norman: University of Oklahoma Press, 2011.

Martin, Samuel J. *General Braxton Bragg, C.S.A.* Jefferson, NC: McFarland, 2011.

Mathes, J. Harvey. *Great Commanders: General Forrest.* New York; D. Appleton and Company, 1902.

McGee, Benjamin F. *History of the 72d Indiana Volunteer Infantry of the Mounted Lightning Brigade,* William Ray Jewell, ed. La Fayette, IN: S. Vater & Co., 1882.

McKenney, Janice E. *The Organizational History of Field Artillery 1775–2003.* Washington, D.C.: Center of Military History United States Army, 2007.

McMurry, Richard M. *Atlanta 1864: The Last Chance for the Confederacy.* Lincoln and London: University of Nebraska Press, 2000.

McMurry Richard. *John Bell Hood and the War for Southern Independence.* Lexington: The University Press of Kentucky, 1982.

McVey, Henry Kratzer. *Two Years and Two Days: A Writ of My Civil War Experiences.* Jefferson County, Iowa: n.p. 2001.

McWhiney, Grady. *Braxton Bragg and the Confederate Defeat,* Volume I. New York and London: Columbia University Press, 1969.

Mead, Homer. *The Eighth Iowa Cavalry in the Civil War.* Carthage, IL: S.C. Davidson, Publisher, 1927.

Memorial and Biographical Record of Butler, Polk, Seward, York and Filmore Counties, Nebraska. Chicago: Geo. A. Ogle & Co., 1899.

Mims, Wilbur F. *War History of the Prattville Dragoons.* Prattville, Alabama: n.p., n.d.

Minty, Robert. "The Fourth Michigan Cavalry," In *History of the Michigan Organizations at Chickamauga, Chattanooga, and Missionary Ridge,* Charles Eugene Belknap, ed. Lansing: Robert Smith Printing Co., 1899.

Minty, Robert. *Minty's Sabre Brigade: The Part They*

Took in the Chattanooga Campaign. Wyandotte, MI: The Herald Steam Presses, 1892.

Morton, John Watson. *The Artillery of Nathan Bedford Forrest's Cavalry.* Nashville, Tennessee and Dallas, Texas: Publishing House of the M.E. Church, 1909.

Moses, John, and Joseph Kirkland. *The History of Chicago,* Vol. I. Chicago and New York: Munsell & Co., Publishers, 1895.

Mosman, Chesley. *The Rough Side of War: The Civil War Journal of Chesley A. Mosman,* Arnold Gates, ed. Garden City, NY: The Basin Publishing Co., 1987.

Obituary Record of the Graduates of Yale University, Deceased from June 1910, to July 1915. New Haven: Yale University Press, 1915.

Official Register of the Officers and Cadets of the U.S. Military Academy. West Point, NY: U.S. Military Academy, 1852.

Onofrey, Joe, and Jim Roubal. *"The Life of a Civil War Soldier 'Traveling Trunk.'"* Gettysburg: National Park Service, 2008.

Otis, Ephraim. "The Murfreesboro Campaign," In *Campaigns in Kentucky and Tennessee include the Battle of Chickamauga, 1862–1864, Papers of the Military Historical Society of Massachusetts* Vol. VII. Boston: Military Historical Society of Massachusetts, 1908.

Pape-Findley, Nancy. *The Invincibles: The Story of Fourth Ohio Veteran Volunteer Cavalry.* Tecumseh, Michigan; Blood Road Publishing: 2002.

Payne, Edwin W. *History of the Thirty-Fourth Regiment of Illinois Infantry, September 7, 1861–July 12, 1865.* Clinton, IA: Allen Printing Company, 1902.

Perry, Henry Fales. *History of the Thirty-eighth Regiment Indiana Volunteers Infantry.* Palo Alto, Cal., F.A. Stuart Printer, 1906.

Peskin, Allan. *Garfield: A Biography.* Kent, Ohio: Kent State University Press, 1999.

Pickerill, W.N. *History of the Third Indiana Cavalry.* Indianapolis, Aetna Printing Co., 1906.

Pond, George E. "Kilpatrick's and Dahlgren's Raid to Richmond," In *Battles & Leaders,* Volume 4. New York: The Century Company, 1888.

Poole, John Randolph. *Cracker Cavaliers: The 2nd Georgia Cavalry Under Wheeler and Forrest.* Macon, Georgia: Mercer University Press, 2000.

Popejoy, Stirling D. "The Second Tennessee Cavalry in the American Civil War," Master's Thesis, 2014, U.S. Army Command and General Staff College, Fort Leavenworth, KS.

Portrait and Biographical Album of Sedgwick County, Kan. Chicago: Chapman Brothers, 1888.

Powell, David. *The Chickamauga Campaign: A Mad Irregular Battle.* El Dorado Hills, CA: Savas Beatie, 2014.

Powell, David A. *The Chickamauga Campaign: Barren Victory.* New York and California: Savas Beatie, 2016.

Powell, David A. *The Chickamauga Campaign: Glory or the Grave: The Breakthrough, the Union Retreat to Chattanooga.* Eldorado Hills, CA: Savas Beatie, 2015.

Powell, David A. *Failure in the Saddle.* New York and California: Savas Beatie, 2010.

Powell, William Henry, editor. *Officers of the Army and Navy (volunteer) Who Served in the Civil War.* Philadelphia: L.R. Hamersly, 1893.

Rabb, James W. *Confederate General Lloyd Tilghman.* Jefferson, NC: McFarland, 2006.

Rafuse, Ethan. "In the Shadow of the Rock: Thomas L. Crittenden, Alexander M. McCook, and the 1863 Campaigns for Middle and East Tennessee," In *The Chickamauga Campaign,* Steven E. Woodworth, ed. Carbondale and Edwardsville: Southern Illinois University Press, 2010.

Reese, J.N. *Report of the Adjutant General to the State of Illinois,* Vol. VIII. Springfield: Journal Company, Printers and Binders, 1901.

Reid, Whitelaw. *Ohio in the War: Her Statesmen, Her Generals, and Soldiers,* Volume I. New York: Moore, Wilstach & Baldwin: 1868.

Richardson, Robert D. "Rosecrans' Staff at Chickamauga: The Significance of Major General William S. Rosecrans' Staff on the Outcome of the Chickamauga Campaign." Master's Thesis, Command and General Staff College, Fort Leavenworth, Kansas, 1989.

Robertson, William G., et. al. *The Staff Ride Handbook for the Battle of Chickamauga: 18–20 September 1863.* U.S. Army Command and General Staff College, Command Studies Institute, Fort Leavenworth, KS, 1992.

Robinson, George I. "With Kilpatrick Around Atlanta," *War Papers, Commandery of Wisconsin MOLLUS,* Volume 1. New York: Nostrand Van Allen, 1891.

Ross, Lawrence Sullivan. "Personal Civil War Letters of General Lawrence Sullivan Ross: with other letters," transcribed and compiled by Perry Wayne Shelton, Master's Thesis, Baylor University, 1938.

Roster and Record of Iowa Soldiers in the War of the Rebellion, Volume IV. Des Moines: Emory H. English, State Printer, E.D. Chassell, State Binder, 1910.

Rowell, John W. *Yankee Cavalrymen.* Knoxville: University of Tennessee Press, 1971.

Rubenstein, David. "A Study of the Medical Support to the Union and Confederate Armies During the Battle of Chickamauga: Lessons and Implications for Today's U.S. Army Medical Department Leaders." Master's Thesis, U.S. Army Command and General Staff College, Fort Leavenworth, KS.

Schaefer, James Arthur. "The Tactical and Strategic Evolution of Cavalry During the American Civil War." Ph.D. Dissertation, The University of Toledo, 1982.

Shaw, William C., compiler. *Illustrated Roster of the Department of Illinois Grand Army of the Republic.* n.p.: n.p. 1914.

Sherman, William. *Personal Memoirs of Gen. W.T. Sherman,* Vol. 2. New York: Charles L. Webster & Co., 1890.

Sherwood, Isaac R. *Memoirs of the War.* Toledo: The H.J. Crittenden, Co., 1923.

Smith, Benjamin T. *Private Smith's Journal:*

Recollections of the Late War, Clyde C. Walton ed. Chicago: R.R. Donnelley & Sons Company, 1963.

Smith, Derek. *In the Lion's Mouth: Hood's Tragic Retreat from Nashville, 1864.* Mechanicsburg, PA: Stackpole Books, 2011.

Smith, Lanny. *The Stone's River Campaign: 26 December 1862–5 January 1863, Army of Tennessee.* (Jasper, TX), Lanny Smith, 2010.

Speed, Thomas. "Cavalry Operations in the West Under Rosecrans and Sherman," In *Battle and Leaders of the Civil War,* Vol. 4. New York: The Century Company, 1884, 1888.

Speed, Thomas. *Union Regiments of Kentucky,* Volume I. Louisville: The Courier Journal Job Printing, Co., 1897.

Stanley, David. *An American General—The Memoirs of David Sloan Stanley,* Samuel W. Fordyce IV, ed. Santa Barbara, California: The Narrative Press, 2004.

Starr, Stephen Z. *The Union Cavalry in the Civil War: The War in the West, Volume III.* Baton Rouge: Louisiana State University, 2007.

Steahlin, George F. "Address and Historical Sketch," In *Pennsylvania at Chickamauga and Chattanooga,* George W. Skinner, editor. Harrisburg, Pennsylvania: William Stanley Ray, State Printer of Pennsylvania, 1897.

Stevens, John Grier. *The Descendants of Samuel Stevens with Histories of Allied Families.* Baltimore: Edward Brothers, Inc., 1968.

Stevens, Walter B. *Centennial History of Missouri (The Center State) One Hundred Years in the Union 1820–1921,* Vol 6. St. Louis-Chicago: The S.J. Clarke Publishing Company, 1921.

Stevenson, Alexander. *Battle of Stones River near Murfreesboro, Tennessee.* Boston: J.R. Osgood and Company, 1884.

Stevenson, Alexander, William Eliot Furness, and Joseph Stockton. *Memorials of Deceased Companions of the Commandery of the State of Illinois Military Order of the Loyal Legion of the United States.* Chicago: MOLLUS, 1912.

Sunderland, Glenn W. *Lightning at Hoover's Gap.* New York, South Brunswick, London: Thomas Yoseloff, 1969.

Taylor Charles H., ed. *The History of the Board of Trade of the City of Chicago,* Vol. III. Chicago: Robert O. Law Company, 1917.

Thatcher, Marshall. *A Hundred Battles in the West: The Second Michigan Cavalry.* Detroit: Marshall Thatcher, 1884.

Thomas, Dean S. *Cannons: Introduction to Civil War Artillery.* Arendtsville, PA: Thomas Publications, 1985.

Tucker, Glenn. *Chickamauga: Bloody Battle in the West.* Dayton, OH: Press of Morningside Bookshop, 1984.

Twenty-Second Annual Reunion of the Association of the Graduates of the United States Military Academy, June 12th, 1891. Saginaw: Seaman & Peters, Printers and Binders, 1898.

United States Army, Ohio Infantry Regiment, 94th. *Record of the Ninety-fourth Regiment, Ohio Volunteer Infantry, in the War of the Rebellion.* Cincinnati: The Ohio Valley press, n.d.

Usher, Ellis Baker. *Wisconsin: Its Story and Biography, 1848–1913,* Volume 8. Chicago and New York: The Lewis Publishing Co., 1914.

Vale, Joseph. "Address of Captain Joseph Vale," In *Pennsylvania at Chickamauga and Chattanooga,* George W. Skinner, editor. Harrisburg, Pennsylvania: William Stanley Ray, State Printer of Pennsylvania, 1897.

Vale, Joseph. *Minty and the Cavalry: A History of Cavalry Campaigns in the Western Armies.* Harrisburg, Pennsylvania: Edwin K. Myers, Printer and Binder, 1886.

Walker, Scott. *Hell's Broke Loose in Georgia.* Athens & London: University of Georgia Press, 2005.

Walsh, George. *Those Damn Horse Soldiers.* New York: A Tom Doherty Associates Book, 2006.

Warvelle, George W., ed. *Historical Compendium of Freemasonry in Illinois,* Vol II. Chicago: The Lewis Publishing Company, 1897.

Welsh, Jack. *Medical Histories of Confederate Generals.* Kent, Ohio: Kent State University Press, 1995.

Welsh, Jack. *Medical Histories of Union Generals.* Kent, Ohio: Kent State University Press, 2005.

Williams, L.B. *A Revised History of the 33rd Alabama Volunteer Infantry Regiment: In Cleburne's Elite Division, Army of Tennessee, 1862–1865.* Auburn, AL: Auburn University Printing Service, 1998.

Willis, William L. "O.H. Miller," in *History of Sacramento County California.* Los Angeles: Historic Record Co., 1913.

Wilson, James H. *Under the Old Flag,* Volumes I & II. New York and London: D. Appleton and Company, 1912.

Wilson, Thomas B. "Reminiscences," 1904, Collection Number: 01736-z, The Southern Historical Collection at the Louis Round Wilson Special Collections Library, University of North Carolina.

Woodworth, Steven E. *Six Armies in Tennessee: The Chickamauga and Chattanooga Campaigns.* Lincoln and London: University of Nebraska Press, 1998.

Worsham, William Johnson. *The Old 19th Tennessee Regiment, C.S.A. June 1861-April 1865.* Knoxville, TN: Press of Paragon Printing company, 1902.

Wulsin, Lucien. *The Fourth Regiment Ohio Veteran Volunteer Cavalry.* Cincinnati: Fourth Ohio Volunteer Cavalry Association, 1912.

Wyeth, John Allan. *The Life General Nathan Bedford Forrest.* New York and London: Harper and Brothers Publisher, 1899.

Wyeth, John Allan. *With Sabre and Scalpel: The Autobiography of a Soldier and Surgeon.* New York and London: Harper Brothers Publishers, 1914.

Yeary, Mamie. *Reminiscences of the Boys in Gray.* Smith and Lamar Publishing House: Dallas, 1912.

Index

Numbers in ***bold italics*** indicate pages with illustrations